Wirtschaft + Gesellschaft

Wirtschaft und Gesellschaft ist ein wichtiges Themenfeld der Sozialwissenschaften. Daher diese Buchreihe: Sie will zentrale Institutionen des Wirtschaftslebens wie Märkte, Geld und Unternehmen sowie deren Entwicklungsdynamiken sozial- und gesellschaftstheoretisch in den Blick nehmen. Damit soll ein sichtbarer Raum für Arbeiten geschaffen werden, die die Wirtschaft in ihrer gesellschaftlichen Einbettung betrachten oder aber soziale Effekte des Wirtschaftsgeschehens und wirtschaftlichen Denkens analysieren. Die Reihe steht für einen disziplinären wie theoretischen Pluralismus und pflegt ein offenes Themenspektrum.

More information about this series at http://www.springer.com/series/12587

Florian Brugger

Ideas, Interests and the Development of the European Banking Systems

Springer VS

Florian Brugger
Institut für Soziologie
Karl-Franzens-Universität Graz
Graz, Steiermark, Austria

ISSN 2626-6156 ISSN 2626-6164 (electronic)
Wirtschaft + Gesellschaft
ISBN 978-3-658-30596-3 ISBN 978-3-658-30597-0 (eBook)
https://doi.org/10.1007/978-3-658-30597-0

Responsible Editor: Cori Antonia Mackrodt
This Springer VS imprint is published by the registered company Springer Fachmedien Wiesbaden GmbH part of Springer Nature.
The registered company address is: Abraham-Lincoln-Str. 46, 65189 Wiesbaden, Germany

Contents

Introduction 1

The central importance of banks for capitalist economies is seldom doubted: producing different arguments, sociologists and economists of most schools of thought usually agree on the pivotal impotence of the banking sector for capitalist economy. However, despite the wide agreement on the central importance of banks, economic and sociological contributions on banking were rare for decades: only the recent banking crisis renewed the interest of social sciences in financial markets in general and banking in particular.

This book analyzes the historical development of the European banking sector between the foundation of the first modern banks in the Italian City-States and World War I. The contribution focuses on the banking revolution that significantly shaped the path along which the leading European banking sectors of France, Germany and Britain developed. In particular, the economic, political and cultural circumstances that caused, fostered and accompanied the banking revolutions are studied. The book focuses on the specific constellation of ideas, interests and institutions that facilitated, caused and hampered the banking revolutions which significantly shaped the historical development of Europe's leading banking sectors.

1.1 Why Banks are so Important: The Economic and Sociological View

Economists and sociologists do not doubt that banks are among the most central organizations of capitalism. Agreeing on the central importance of banks for capitalism, economists develop various, often mutually exclusive, arguments why banks are at the center of capitalism. Werner (2016) distinguishes three main economic banking theories:

F. Brugger, *Ideas, Interests and the Development of the European Banking Systems*, Wirtschaft + Gesellschaft, https://doi.org/10.1007/978-3-658-30597-0_1

"financial intermediation theory of banking", "fractional reserve theory of banking" and the "credit creation theory of banking."

The fist dominates classical and neo-classical economics. According to the financial intermediation theory of banking, banks are mere capital intermediaries: banks absorb savings to lend to the economy. Hence, banks intermediate loanable funds, but are unable to augment capital. Banks foster economic growth and progress by facilitating the investment of idle savings into the most promising projects. For most neo-classical economists banks are only the maturity transformer who borrows short, hence they deposit money of short maturity, to lend long (see ibid.). Business economists usually add that banks also transform risk and scale: banks convert relatively safe small deposits into risky huge investments.

The fractional reserve theory of banking was advocated by several prominent Keynesians like Paul Samuelson (1948b) and Joseph Stiglitz (1997). According to them, banks are just fund intermediaries individually. However, collectively, banks augment money. Their main argument is that banks are unable to unilaterally extend both sides of the balance sheet. But because the same value may be booked simultaneously in different balance sheets, collectively the banking sector creates money by extending banking sectors' total balance sheet.

Advocates of the credit creation theory of banking, like Schumpeter ([1911] 1934), consider that every bank creates money out of nothing. They argue that banks are not intermediaries, but create money by credit granting. Because deposits function as money in advanced capitalist economies, banks create money by booking loans. A loan given to a bank customer is booked on both sides of the balance sheet of the bank: on the active side as a claim of the bank against the customer and on the passive side as a customer deposit. Each theory developed different arguments why banks are so important for the economy, however they widely agree on the central importance of banks for economic progress and growth.

Widely agreeing on the importance of private banks for the economy, most famous economists turned briefly to the topic of private banks and focused instead on money theory and central banking. Most contributors to the history of money economics consider that money economic theories of the last centuries may be ultimately divided into two main strands (Kindleberger 1985; Humphrey 1993, 1999): monetarism and Keynesianism. For monetarists money is neutral—at least in the longer run; hence, augmenting money just raises prices. Convinced by the principle advantages of paper money, for monetarists both private banks and governments have strong vested interests to over-issue notes. To prevent over-issuing, monetarists suggested to found central banks equipped with note-issuing monopolies, which are obliged to follow clear binding issuing rules and target price stability. In contrast, Keynesians argue that money is non-neutral, endogenous and governments lack the ability to determine the money stock. Believing in central banks' ability to actively promote economic progress and to mitigate or even prevent crises by leaning against the wind, Keynesians demand a much more active role of central banks.

For Karl Marx and Max Weber, the capitalist production process is characterized by the use of capital to exploit formally or double free workers to produce more capital; hence, the accumulation of capital is the ultimate goal of all capitalist production. The formation of capital is the precondition and ultimate goal of capitalism. Weber ([1920] 1930) draws a close connection between Puritanical asceticism, the Calvinist predestination doctrine and the accumulation of capital: the puritanical doctrine of asceticism and the interpretation of economic success as a divine sign for predestination facilitated the accumulation of capital and hence the rise of capitalism. For Weber (ibid., p. 53) the "summum bonum of this [puritanical] ethic [is] the earning of more and more money, combined with the strict avoidance of all spontaneous enjoyment of life." Unlike in pre-capitalist times, economic

> acquisition is no longer subordinated to man as the means for the satisfaction of his material needs. This reversal of what we should call the natural relationship, [...] is evidently as definitely a leading principle of capitalism as it is foreign to all peoples not under capitalistic influence (ibid.).

Also, for Marx the earning of more and more money or in other words the accumulation of capital is the ultimate goal of capitalist production. From the Marxist perspective, capitalism is characterized by the dominance of the depersonalized, anonymized mass of capital following its own logics and interests. Capital owners function as carriers of capital interest, but are itself subordinated to the dominance of capital. From the macro perspective, the anonymized and depersonalized capital is driven by the forces of capitalist competition that forces capital into the most lucrative investments. Absorbing huge amounts of money, bankers are the representatives of the concentration, anonymized and depersonalization mass of capital:

> the development of large scale industry money-capital, so far as it appears on the market, is not represented by some individual capitalist, not by the owner of this or that fraction of the capital on the market, but assumes more and more the character of an organized mass, which is far more directly subject to the control of the representatives of social capital, the bankers, than actual production is (Marx [1894] 1984, p. 381).

In addition, according to Marx (ibid., p. 671), it is the "development of the credit and banking business, which tends on the one hand to press all money-capital into the service of production", and hence which absorbs the idle hoards to invest them into promising capitalist projects.

1.2 The Sociology of Banking and the Historical Development of the Banking Sector

For Swedberg (2003, p. 152), money and capital "markets are of special importance to the sociologist because of the enormous amount of money that circulate within them." According to Stearns and Mizruchi (2005, p. 284) "banks are the key institutions through which money is stored, created and distributed." Max Weber was one of the first sociologists interested in banking. In the *General Economic History* ([1923] 1927) he briefly discussed the foundation of the Casa di San Giorgio, Law's Banque Royale and the Bank of England. In just several lines dedicated to each bank, Weber addressed the economic, political and social circumstances and the constellation of interests that accompanied and fostered the foundation of the banks. In much more detail, Weber ([1908] 1998) analyzed in an article on the socalled Landschaften the foundation and impact of the Prussian state owned mortgage banks. The article has two focuses: the political, economic and social circumstances that caused and accompanied the foundation of the Landschaften and its intended and unintended economic and social consequences. Weber's contribution on the Landschaften might have served as a sociological blueprint to analyze banks and their social and economic effects. Unfortunately, Weber's contribution was hardly taken into consideration, also because for decades banking was seldom discussed among sociologists.

Despite the wide agreement on the importance of banks and the pioneering sociological and economic works of the 19th and early 20th century, for decades neither mainstream economists (Werner 2016) nor sociologists (Stearns and Mizruchi 2005, p. 284) gave banking much attention. Just recently, in particular since the banking crises of 2007 and 2008, banking is experiencing a renaissance in economics and sociology (on the sociology of banking and financial markets see Keister 2002; Stearns and Mizruchi 2005; Carruthers and Kim 2011).

While most sociological contributions discus general issues of financial markets, several studies explicitly focus on banks. Sociological studies discus various issues on banking; since the financial crises of 2007 and 2008, central banking in particular receives much attention. Carlo Tognato (2014) analyzed the cultural embeddedness of central banks, how central banks are legitimized by their connection to stability cultures and how central banks constitute and maintain stability cultures. Using the concepts of world culture (Meyer 1977; Meyer et al. 1997) and isomorphism (DiMaggio and Powell 1983), Polillo and Guillén (2005) found a close connection between countries' inclusion into world markets through foreign trade, investments and lending and their adoption of central bank Independence. Abolafia (2010) studied how American elites constructed the FED narrative. Looking at the communication practices of central banks, Holmes (2014) analyzed the communication strategies, channels and practices of several central banks. Focusing on the ECB, Velthuis (2015) discussed the interaction and struggle between the ECB and the mass media on the interpretation and diffusion of money policy relevant information. Lebaron and Dogan (2016) analyzed the biographical, professional and educational background of central bankers.

Even before the recent financial crises caused a banking renaissance, interlocks between firms and banks were intensively studied in sociology (see Keister 2002, p. 44). Contributions on the interlocks between banks and firms have studies specific relations between them. Early historical studies (Gerschenkron 1962; Zysman 1983) distinguished between the capital market dominance in America and Britain and the banking based system in continental Europe: according to them, in continental European and Japan in partite relation between firms and banks was close. In addition, it seems that in America the relation between firms and banks was also close, at least during certain times (Stearns and Mizruchi 2005, p. 284). Others stressed that the continental European model of financing and cooperation significantly changed during the last decades (Streeck and Höpner 2003; Zugehör 2003). However, in America the interlock between firms and banks also shifted (Mintz and Schwartz 1981; Davis and Mizruchi 1999).

Closely related to the interlock of companies and banks is the question of the power distribution between firms and banks and the, often assumed, predominance of capital over production. For Ingham (2004, p. 150) "the most structurally fundamental struggle in capitalism is [...] between debtor (producers and consumers of goods) and creditor (producers and controllers of money)." Traditionally, Marxists highlighted the increasing predominance of banks or organized capital over the economy. For Lenin ([1917] 1999) and Hilferding ([1910] 1955) the deepening of capitalism is characterized by the concentration of capital in the hands of banks. Lenin ([1917] 1999, p. 45) considers: "As banking develops and becomes concentrated in a small number of establishments, the banks grow from modest middlemen into powerful monopolies having at their command almost the whole of the money capital of all the capitalists and small businessmen." Concentrated in the hands of a few bankers, the capital became the most powerful institution dominating economy and policy. The discussion on the financialization of western economies brought fresh impetus to the debate on the power distribution. According to the contributors of the financialization discussion, the new financial capitalism is characterized by the fast increasing importance of financial markets on the total economic output, the increasing importance of financial profits for companies and the economy and the implementation of the logic of shareholder value maximization (Epstein 2005; Krippner 2005; Windolf 2005a; Davis and Kim 2015). Interpreting the rise of financial capitalism from the perspective of the distribution of power between the real economy and the financial economy, Windolf (2005b) considered that the financialization of the economy significantly increased the power and influence of financial markets over real economy. According to him, the increasing influence of financial actors caused the implementation of a new management logic orientated towards the demands of financial institutes.

Despite the increasing interest in financial markets and banking, sociological contributions on the historical development of the banking sector are rare. Notable exceptions are Carruthers (1996) study on the British financial revolution and the foundation of the Bank of England in the late 17th and early 18th century; in the tradition of the World System Theory, Arrighi (2010) analyzed the development of capitalism as a sequence of overlapping cycles of accumulation and capital hegemonies; Ingham (2004) studied the historical development of money by analyzing the central question of what money is, how it is produced and what the value of money is for several crucial historical epochs.

Studying the British financial revolution of the late 17th and early 18th century, Carruthers (1996) stressed the political embeddedness of financial markets. He highlighted the pivotal importance of public debt for the British financial revolution. The state's inability to finance wars and other expenses necessitated a fundamental restructuring of the financial system. The monarchs' unreliability as debtor kept the wealthy from lending more heavily to the sovereign. Facing significant financial problems, the monarch followed the empowered Parliament's suggestion and permitted the foundation of joint-stock companies like the Bank of England. Hence, the monarch's financial hardship was a precondition of the British financial revolution. At the same time, the financial revolution had significant effects on the political landscape. Joint-stock companies reshaped the distribution of power between the monarch and his creditors; they facilitated public lending. Supported by the newly founded joint-stock companies, the balance of power between the European empires shifted in favor of Britain. In addition, according to Carruthers, big investments in public debts were particularly important for the state building process: fearing public debt defaults, elites had a strong vested interests in protecting the political status quo to safeguard their investment.

Arrighi's (2010) primary objective was not to study the history of the European banking sector, but the development of capitalism. He argued that capitalist development was marked by four big cycles of accumulation and hegemonies: the Italian City-State-, the Dutch, the British and the American hegemony. Cycles of accumulation have two phases: in the first, capital accumulation accelerates by the fast extension of production, trade and profits. Falling profits due to rising competition and the inability to develop new markets shift the cycle of accumulation into the second, the financial phase: in the financial phase financial activities increasingly dominate the economy. Using Marx's MCM metaphor Arrighi considers that the first phase of accumulation is characterized by MC and the second by CM:

> In phase of material expansion money capital 'sets in motion' and increasing mass of commodities […] and in phase of financial expansion an increasing mass of money capital 'sets itself free' from its commodity form, and accumulation proceeds through financial deals (ibid., p. 6).

Rejecting economists' view that economic development is the unintended consequence of autonomous individuals' decentralized actions, Arrighi (ibid., p. 10) considers that "the recurrent expansions and restructurings of the capitalists world economy have occurred under the leadership of particular communities and blocs of governmental and business agencies." In particular, he highlights the interconnection between the state and capital; between state and capital expansion that "links the formation and enlarged reproduction of historical capitalism as world system to processes of state formation on the one side, and of market formation on the other" (ibid.). For Arrighi, the foundation and rise of banks plays a central role in the second phase of the cycles of accumulation: bundling huge capital and the bargaining power of the capital in their hands, bankers strengthen the influence of capital on politics.

Rejecting the standard economic view, Ingham (2004) reinterpretiates the history of money by highlighting the importance of the state and conflicts between lenders, debtors and the state. He argues that what money is, who is allowed to produce money and the value of money are the outcomes of negotiations and battles between the three main financial market actors; creditors, debtors and the state: dependent on the specific historical constellation, different answers are given to the three central question. However, Ingham (ibid., p. 116 ff.) argued that in the 17th and 18th century, money radically changed: private money, currency issued by banks, detached from the former metal base. In addition, private money became part of the public currency. As private banks were enabled to produce public currency, the state lost the monopoly on money production. For long, public coin money and private paper money existed side by side; however, with the foundation of the Bank of England, according to Ingham, both moneys were integrated into the public currency.

However, of all the contributions touching on the development of banks at certain historical times, none explicitly analyzed the historical development of banking sectors. In addition, the contributions predominately focused on the influence of groups of interests on the development of financial markets and money, but mostly ignored the influence of ideas. In particular, the influence of economic theory on the historical development of financial markets and banking is hardly taken into consideration. Hence, neither the historical development of the European banking sector nor the influence of ideas and interests on the emerging of modern banking was addressed so far from a sociological perspective.

1.3 The Selection of Case and Time

Most national European banking sectors are oriented to the French, German or British banking system. Still, French, German and British banks dominate the European banking sector: nine of Europe's ten biggest banks are French, German or British banks[1]—the Spanish Banco Santander is the only exception. Historically, almost all banking innovations that significantly shaped the European banking system originated in one of the three countries. In addition, historically the most important money and banking discussions occurred in France, Germany and Britain.

Comparing the fundamental structure of the banking sector at the time of World War I with the recent situation, the heritage is clearly visible. Doubtlessly, the deep crises of the 20th century, the liberalization of banking since the 1970s and the unification of Europe significantly shaped banking. However, much like nowadays, around World War I the leading European banking sectors were dominated by a handful of international

[1]Banks Around the World Data: Total Assets;.

active megabanks. After decades of concentration, the leading European banking sectors are recently as concentrated as around World War I. Almost all leading German, French and British megabanks were founded before World War I and already dominated the national banking sectors at the beginning of the 20th century. Not all pre-World War I megabanks survived the big banking crises of the 20th century, but there are hardly newcomers either.

The transnationalization of central banking by the foundation of the European central bank was doubtlessly one of the most pivotal turning points in the history of central banks. Nevertheless, until the beginning of the 20th century, the cornerstones of central banking were laid: before World War I note issuing was monopolized in France, Germany and Britain. Not necessarily fully state owned, central banks were state dependent and obliged to follow prescribed issuing rules. After heavy debates on money policy, the necessity of central banks was hardly questioned by the leading economists at the beginning of the 19th century: as the British monetarist hegemony spread to the Continent, most leading economists agreed that private profit oriented banks tend to over-issue notes which is why issuing should be monopolized by the central bank. Mistrusting governments, most money economists demanded to restrict issuing by clear binding rules.

In particular in the 19th century non-profit banking spread fast through Europe. Elsewhere, non-profit banks opened. Reaching classes and groups that were still mostly excluded from banking and due to their huge collective scale, non-profit banks became the third main pillar of the French, German and British banking system. Some of the former non-profit banks were privatized or changed their legal status, others are still non-profit orientated. However, banks which were founded as non-profit banks before World War I are still important pillars of the leading European banking sector. In several European countries, predominately in the German speaking world, non-profit banks still dominate ordinary commercial banking.

While the fundamental structure of the leading European banking systems had largely developed until World War I, the first modern banks were founded in the Italian City-States. Money lending against interest payments is old: Visser and McIntosh (1998) consider that lending against interest payments may be found at least in the last 4000 years. However, money lending remain predominately pre-modern until first modern banks were founded in the Italian City-States. Pre-modern means here that lending occurred within personal relations: rich people lent out their own, and maybe their relatives' and friends', idle hoards within their personal networks. In contrast, modern banking means that financial institutions absorb money from a huge crowd of shareholders and depositors to lend to the economy, the general public and the state. With the emerging of modern banks, money lending lost its personal character, capital concentrated and depersonalized in the hands of modern banks and banks became a powerful and important economic and political player. Hence, modern banking emerged in the 15th century in Italian City-States and mostly developed its fundamental structure until World War I.

1.4 General Trends

Before the rise of modern banks, money lending was considered immoral and exploitative. Religious usury restrictions principally prohibited money lending against interest payments. In addition, the general public was quite hostile to all kinds of banking. Heated by widespread xenophobia, anti-Semitism and anti-Protestantism, hostility to moneylenders frequently turned into violent riots and general anti-Semitic and anti-Protestant pogroms. Occasionally, the over-indebted elites incited pogroms to clear debts.

From the foundation of the first modern banks to World War I, banking steadily developed. At the beginning limited to merchants lending to one another, the wealthy lending to the monarch and maybe to the nobility, banking steadily spread to additional classes and groups. At the time of World War I hardly any group or class was completely excluded from banking: even the poorest classes were increasingly involved in banking through the rise and spread of non-profit banks. Due to its deepening and spread, banking and money lending lost its sinful connotation. Banking always caused heated discussions among experts and the general public, however from the medieval times to World War I debates steadily secularized: theological and moral issues on banking were replaced by questions about banks' goals, functions, regulations, ownership, note issuing, the relation between banks, the economy and the state, and about central banking.

The foundation of the first modern banks was accompanied by intensive theological debates on money lending, which fundamental shaped the theological position from 'all interest payments are sinful' to 'money lending is permitted under certain circumstances.' Elites' medieval opposition to banking and money lending was replaced by money-mercantilists' banking enthusiasm. Convinced that money scarcity was the most urgent problem of the time, money-mercantilists argued that big national banks issuing notes and lending to the state would overcome the shortage of money, foster economic prosperity and solve governments' financial problems.

Several deep financial crises highlighted the risk of banking and caused many influential economists, politicians and parts of the general public to demand stricter regulations; in particular of note issuing. Nevertheless, leading economists and politicians of the 19th century remained enthusiastic on banking. For example, several leading banking theorists were convinced that permitting joint-stock banking would foster economic growth and industrialization, democratize capitalism enable also poorer classes to enjoy the fruits of capitalism—and overcome the antagonistic relation between capital and labor. French Saint-Simonians expected that new-style industrial banks would accelerate industrialization, help overcome capitalism and function as the leading planning institutions in a harmonic, socialist, classless industrial society. Hence, the view on banking shifted from moral and theological opposition to banking enthusiasm and realism: those who recognized the central importance of banks for capitalist economies, but also indicated the weaknesses and risks of banking are considered realists.

Overall, the long period between the rise of the first modern banks in Italian City-States and World War I was characterized by the concentration and centralization of banking and the depersonalization and anonymization of capital. For Marxists, the concentration and monopolization, depersonalization and anonymization of capital is the main characteristic of capitalism. Following Marx, Lenin and Hilferding highlight the central role of banks for the concentration and monopolization of capital. Bundling the small savings into a huge crowed of capital banks became the main carrier of capital interests. It is outlined below that from Italian City-States to World War I the development of the modern banking system was pivotal for the concentration, depersonalization, anonymization and emancipation of capital.

As maintained, before the first modern banks were founded, money lending predominately occurred within personal relations: money was mostly lent directly from wealthy lenders to merchants, craftsman, the nobility and in particular to monarchs. In pre-modern banking times, capital was not concentrated and depersonalized. No doubt, even before the rise of modern banks, very rich people, equipped with their own and relatives' and friends' money, lent to various craftsman, merchants, noblemen and monarchs. However, the savings of the wealthy were not bundled into huge anonymous capital. Absorbing money from relatives, friends and colleagues, lending to craftsmen, merchants, noblemen and monarchs, capital hardly ever left personal networks and relations.

The foundation of modern banks caused a qualitative leap. Bundling idle hoards from a great number of the domestic wealthy and even foreigners' capital was concentrated in the hands of state lender associations: Europe's first modern banks. Absorbing money from a huge number of customers, capital depersonalized and anonymized as lending and borrowing left personal relations and networks. Capital emancipated from its owners as savings entered the huge crowd of state lender association managed capital. Founded to bundle savings for public debt investments and to enforce state lenders' bargaining power against the sovereign, state lender associations were soon blamed for being selfish and following their own interests. Using the power of the huge concentrated capital, state lender associations' policy was often directed against borrowers' and lenders' interests. Hence, in the hands of state lender associations, much of Italian City-States' capital concentrated, depersonalized, anonymized and emancipated from its owners by following its own interest, frequently conflicted with borrowers' and capital owners' vested interests.

Similarly, in Central and Northern Europe before the rise of modern banks money lending occurred in the legal grey area of the usury restrictions and hardly left personal relations and networks. Early banking in France, Germany and Britain predominantly developed in the rising trading hubs. Not more than a by-business of merchants, goldsmiths and court agents, early banking was predominately pre-modern as bankers lent out their own, relatives' and friends' capital to colleagues and other acquaintances. From the by-business bankers, in particular in Britain, a group of professional modern bankers emerged who accepted deposits from a wider public and exclusively focused on the banking business.

However, early non-Italian modern banks usually remained regional and relatively small scale. Foremost, the foundation of the big national banks, the Bank of England and the Banque Royale, accelerated and deepened the concentration, centralization, depersonalization and anonymization of capital. Never before was as much capital concentrated and centralized in the hands of two banks: the Bank of England and the Banque Royale. Absorbing capital from a great number of lenders, both banks were heavily criticized by their customers for following their own interests and logics. Using the power of their huge capital, like Genoa's Casa di San Giorgio, the Bank of England and the Banque Royale became states within the state enforcing their own interests, frequently against the interests of their borrowers and lenders.

The Bank of England and the Banque Royale were early modern banking lighthouses in the still mostly pre-modern banking environment. At the beginning of the 20th century, the French, German and British banking sectors were dominated by a handful of megabanks. Absorbing most deposited money, from a great number of smaller and bigger lenders, investing in hundreds of domestic and foreign projects and governments, capital concentrated in the hands of megabanks and centralized in the few European banking centers. Megabanks were the main representative and carrier of the interests of the huge concentrated, depersonalized and anonymized crowd of capital which accumulated until World War I. Depositors or the crowd of shareholders and borrowers were hardly able to influence megabank policy, which often conflicted with both lenders' and borrowers' interests. Hence, from the foundation of the first modern banks in the Italian City-States to World War I capital strongly concentrated, centralized, depersonalized and anonymized in the hands of the rising megabanks. Thus in the hands of the French, British and German megabanks capital became a huge anonymous crowd which emancipated from their owners' wished and followed its own logic and interests.

The development of modern banks significantly changed the structure of interests in the banking sector. Pre-modern money lending was characterized by two main antagonistic interests: the interest of the borrower and the interest of the lender. Generally, lenders are interested in lending money for the shortest possible time, at the highest interest rates, with the greatest possibility to see the money again; it is in the interests of borrowers to pay the lowest possible interests, transfer risk to the lender and not be in a hurry to pay off loans.

By the rise of modern banks, the twofoldness of old-style lending—of lenders and borrowers—changed to the modern banking interest trinity—lenders, borrowers and the bank. Modern banks represent neither the interests of the lenders nor of the borrowers, but follow their own interests, which are principally directed against borrowers and lenders. Generally, it is in the banks' interest to pay the lowest interest possible to depositors and their shareholders and receive the highest possible interest from borrowers. To minimize maturity risk, banks are interested in borrowing long-time from depositors and shareholders and lend for the shortest time possible to borrowers. In addition, banks are interested in transferring risk to lenders and borrowers. Hence, banks' interests are directed against borrowers and lenders. Using the power of the concentrated capital to enforce their interests, in the hands of modern banks capital turned against its owners by undermining the owners' interests.

For most influential economists, banks are pivotal institutions of capitalist economies. However, several deep crises also highlighted financial sector's proneness to crises. Blaming the abundance of money for many deep crises, most liberal economists were convinced that private banks are notoriously prone to over-issuing notes. Unlike the father of liberal economics Adam Smith, many economists doubted that private banks are kept from over-issuing by market forces. For many liberals, note issuing was one of the rare cases where private and public interest are mutually exclusive. In particular in the 19th century when paper money started to spread fast, many liberal economists demanded note-issuing restrictions. To avoid over-issuing of private banks, monetarists suggested to monopolize issuing through central banks. Convinced that governments also tend to over-issue notes, monetarists proposed to follow clear issuing rules to restrict governments' direct influence on central banks. Following the monetarist advice in France, Germany and Britain, during the 19th century note issuing was monopolized by central banks.

The deepening of banking in Italian City-States divided the anti-banking camp into two main groups: those generally opposing all kind of banking and those suggesting that only alternative banking institutes would protect people from usurers. Non-profit oriented Monte di Pietàs, founded by Franciscans, was the Christian answer to fast spreading banking activities. Soon, Monte di Pietàs were also founded outside Italy. In the 19th century, non-profit banking accelerated. Unlike the Catholic Monte di Pietàs, most 19th century non-profit banks were founded by puritanical, liberal, state critical, philanthropic institutions. It was expected that non-profit banks would foster poorer classes' economic rise and participation, educate the poor to become ascetic, puritan capitalists and therefore repel the 'red ghost'. Reaching formerly excluded poorer classes, the spread of non-profit banking accelerated the deepening of banking.

1.5 Three Pivotal Periods

It is not the aim of the book to give a detailed description of the development of the European banking sector between the 15th century and World War I. Indeed, the study focuses on events and periods which were pivotal for the development of the French, German and British banking sector. It is assumed that several historical events and periods fundamentally shaped the path along which leading European banking sectors developed. I suggest that three main events or periods were pivotal for the development of the banking systems: first, the foundation of state lender associations in Italian City-States that caused the first comprehensive concentration, centralization and depersonalization of capital and the formation of the specific banking interest trinity of lenders, borrowers and bank interests. The rise of first modern banks was accompanied by the foundation of first non-profit banks and intensive theological discussions on money lending and banking which fundamentally shifted the theological view.

Second, in the 17th and 18th century the first national banks were founded in Britain, France and Germany. Inspired by Italian state lender associations and the rising money-mercantilism, national banks like the Bank of England and the Banque Royale were founded to promote economic growth and in particular to overcome governments' financial difficulties and facilitate war financing. Like state lender associations, national banks centralized, concentrated and depersonalized capital by absorbing savings on a new scale. National banks were the first central organized experiments of money augmentation by paper money issuing. National banks were not the first banks issuing notes, but the first banks which systematically used note issuing to facilitate war financing and foster economic growth. National banks are the predecessors of modern central banks and their success and collapse strongly influenced later discussion on the relation of money augmentation, financial stability, growth, employment and prices. Around the same time, other modern banks and non-profit banks were founded.

Third, several banking innovation of the 19th century fundamentally shaped the structure of the leading banking sectors. In Britain the permission of joint-stock banks in the first half of the 19th century caused the foundation of several leading banking institutes. Permitting limited liability shares to joint-stock banks enabled and facilitated the rise of megabanks and the fast concentration of the British banking sector. The rise of the Haute Banque marked the first significant change of the French banking system in the 19th century. Financing France's ambitious railway projects and government's deficits, the Haute Banque became one of the most powerful and influential economic and political groups. Napoleon III permitting to several Saint-Simonians the foundation of a joint-stock industrial bank to foster industrialization and facilitate public debt financing significantly shaped the European banking sector. Propelled by the escalating conflict between the Haute Banque and Saint-Simonians, both groups founded and supported new joint-stock banks in France and abroad. In Germany, regional banking aristocracies emerged relatively late in the rising industrial hubs. Inspired by French Saint-Simonians, members of the Rhinish banking aristocracy founded, against the strong opposition of several influential bankers and the land aristocracy, the first German joint-stock banks. Later, but similar to Britain and France, joint-stock banks were founded in Germany and dominated the banking sector at the time of World War I. What makes the German case notable was the rise of the German cooperative capitalism in the late 19th century. Inspired by the rising state- or kathedersocialism in the late 19th century, many German politicians and economists agreed on the necessity of economic cooperation and the central planning of industrialization. To foster fast industrialization and overcome economic cycles, a close cooperation between industrial megaconglomerates, workers, megabanks and the state was suggested. Promoting and fostering economic centralization and cartelization, megabanks had a leading role in the German cooperative capitalism as planers and coordinators. Considered to ensure a smooth industrialization by directing economic progress and avoiding conflicts between conglomerates, megabanks were present on most supervisory boards.

The monetarist hegemony of the late 19th century caused the foundation of modern central banks. In France, Britain and Germany note issuing was monopolized and central banks' note issuing was restricted by stricter of more open issuing rules. In addition, a system of non-profit banks emerged in the 19th century in each of the three countries.

1.6 The Plan of the Book

The book is divided into four main parts. In the first part I developed the heuristic method used to analyze the historical development of the European banking sector. At the beginning, various views from sociology, economics and political science on ideas and interests are discussed. Then different concepts about the relation between ideas and interests and between ideas, interests and institutions are outlined. The first part closes with the description of what is considered the economic, political and cultural order and the interconnection of the three fundamental orders. In addition, a heuristic of stability and change of the three fundamental orders is developed.

In the second part, the foundation and rise of the first modern banks in Italian City-States is analyzed. It is argued that the political dominion of the time was built on a strong coalition between the ruling political oligarchy and merchants. Pre-modern banking developed in the wake of rising trade, but was strongly restricted by scholastics—the leading economic idea of the time—usury restrictions. However, falling trade profits, the abundance of capital, internal political disturbances and increasing foreign pressure caused Europe's first modern banking revolution. Under enormous pressure from domestic uprisings, other City-States' expansive foreign policy and the expansion of the Ottoman empire, wining recurrent wars to repel attacks and conquer new trade routes became a matter of survival for the weak governments. In need of huge sums to finance wars, covering fast rising war costs became the main challenge of City-States governments.

General fears from Ottoman takeover, rising patriotism, domestic problems of covering war costs and the Church's increasing involvement in financial businesses caused intensive theological discussions on money lending. In the debates, the scholastic position on interest payments and public debt significantly changed. The scholastic's permission of *Lucrum Cessans* (the missed profit) fundamentally shaped the Christian position on interest payments: from 'all interest is sinful' to 'interest above a certain benchmark should be banned.' Permitting *Lucrum Cessans* opened the door for modern banks. Still skeptical about lending to private persons, for later scholastic contributors lending to the state became a patriotic duty.

Governments' escalating financial difficulties caused the foundation of state lender associations, Europe's first modern banks. The foundation of state lender associations was in the interest of governments and the wealthy parts of the society: state lender associations bundled wealthy state lenders' bargaining power for negotiations with the government. It also provided a relatively safe investment opportunity for the idle hoards of the wealthy population. Despite the empowerment of state lenders, state lender associations were also in the interest of governments: bundling huge capital available in a short time facilitated war financing which is why state lender associations became pivotal for Italian City-States' military success. Hence, the foundation of state lender associations was fostered by changing merchant and government interests and changing ideas. As a reaction to the deepening of banking and the changing scholastic position on interest payments, Christian organizations founded non-profit banks to save the poor from usurers.

Part three discusses the foundation and rise of the first national banks in France, Britain and Germany and the development of the first modern and non-profit banks in the three countries. The time of socalled absolutism was dominated by the coalition between monarchs, the aristocracy and merchants and mercantilism replacing scholastic economics as the leading economic idea. Mercantilism satisfied the main demands of the new dominance: it was constructed as an economic theory of nation building, national economic autarky, economic progress and military force. Particularly important for the development of the banking was mercantilism's money fetish. Defining the scarcity of money as the most urgent problem, money-mercantilists proposed to found note-issuing national banks to overcome money scarcity, reduce interest rates and facilitate state financing.

Stagnant economic progress, sluggish trade and escalating state and war financing problems made money-mercantilists' proposals for national banks quite popular. However, national bank proposals also had quite powerful and influential opponents. Public debt financing was the biggest and most profitable business of the rising banks and of the aristocracy. Bankers and the aristocracy feared that the foundation of national banks would withdraw their most profitable business; the aristocracy also expected that the foundation of national banks would further accelerate the rise of the bourgeoisie, their main political and economic opponent. Fearing to lose the support of the aristocracy, monarchs shied away from permitting national banks until their financial difficulties left them no alternative.

In both countries, France and Britain, the coincidence of monarchs' near-bankruptcy and deep crises of the aristocracy paved the way for the foundation of national banks. Monarchs' inability to solve their financial problems other than following money-mercantilist advice and permitting the foundation of national banks, and the aristocracies' inability to overcome their own crises and combat the incipient banking revolution opened the historical door for the foundation of the two most money-mercantilist national banks; the Bank of England and the Banque Royale. While the former became one of the most successful banking institutions, the latter soon caused one of the deepest banking crises; nevertheless, both strongly influenced the development of the banking sector. The Bank of England and the Banque Royale became the main predecessors of modern central banks. In addition, their successes and failures caused intensive discussion on the relation between money issuing, employment, economic progress, and prices. Furthermore, the success of the Bank of England significantly shaped the international distribution of power in favor of Britain. While the foundation of the big national banks was the most significant banking innovation between the decline of Italian City-States and the French Revolution, the time was also characterized by the rise of other modern banks and non-profit banks in France, Britain and Germany.

Part four discusses the main banking innovations of the 19th century. The formation of note-issuing central banks was one banking revolution of the 19th century. In Britain the suspension of convertibility at the beginning of the 19th century caused intensive discussions on money theory and money policy. Both mercantilism and (money-) Keynesianism developed in the money debates which lasted for the entire 19th century. Debating various money and banking related issues, monetarists blamed Bank of England's issuing policy for the rampant inflation. More generally, monetarists were convinced that private banks and governments notoriously tend to over-issue notes. In order to prevent over-issuing, monetarists suggested to monopolize note issuing in the hands of central banks and to follow clear and binding issuing rules. Rejected by alternative money theories, monetarism steadily gained ground; first in Britain and later on the Continent. Following the monetarist advice, the Bank of England became the first monetarist central bank holding a note-issuing monopoly and being bounded to strong issuing rules. As the monetarist hegemony spread to continental Europe, elsewhere note-issuing central banks holding note-issuing monopolies were founded in the late 19th and early 20th century.

While monetarists dominated the discussions on money policy, other banking related questions were particularly addressed by money economists not clearly assignable to monetarism. Unsatisfied with the existing banking structure and the dominance of the old elites over banking, several British liberals suggested to permit the foundation of joint-stock banks. It was expected that joint-stock banks would break up the dominance of the old oligarchy, foster economic growth and democratic banking and capitalism by enabling poorer classes to participate in capitalism. Like former national bank ideas, joint-stock banking proposals attracted enthusiastic supporters—liberals, industrialists, middle- and working-class spokesman, even socialists—and strong enemies—banks and the old elites. Again, only a deep crises paved the way for the permission of joint-stock banks. Deep financial crises and banking runs weakened the position of the banking establishment and caused great hostility against banks: to stabilize financial markets and calm the people, the Parliament followed banking experts and permitted the foundation of joint-stock banking. Obliged to issue unlimited liability shares, the permission of limited liability shares opened the door for the massive concentration of the British banking sector in the late 19th and early 20th century.

Fearing to fall further behind, parts of the French and German elites were convinced that a fast industrialization was needed to economically, politically and militarily catchup with Britain. In particular, railway building was widely considered as being of pivotal economic, political and military importance. Lacking the financial means to finance the ambitious railway projects, French and German governments heavily relied on private bankers to finance their infrastructural projects. Due to their central importance for countries' ambitious infrastructure projects and close ties to the government, the rising railway financing banking aristocracy became economically and politically one of the most influential groups.

Despite the rise of the Haute Banque, the French banking aristocracy, railway building was in France closely connected with the rise of Saint-Simonians; the main railway engineers. Unsatisfied with the slow progress of railway building, Saint-Simonians suggested to found joint-stock industrial banks to overcome financing difficulties. Strongly opposed by the Haute Banque, fearing to lose their most profitable businesses and predominance, the Revolution of 1848 and Napoleon III's takeover paved the way for the Saint-Simonian banking proposals. Convinced by the necessity of a fast industrialization and Saint-Simonian economic theory, Napoleon III permitted the foundation of a Saint-Simonian joint-stock industrial banks against the outcry of the Haute Banque. Propelled by their hostility against each other, Saint-Simonians and the Haute Banque founded joint-stock banks elsewhere in Europe to oust the rival. The Saint-Simonian's sense of mission and Haute Banque's fear of falling behind significantly changed Europe's banking sector by spreading joint-stock banking through the continent. Banks founded during the French joint-stock banking boom still dominate the banking sector.

In Germany, banking innovations faced the hostility and opposition of the strong and influential landed classes. Germany's economic backwardness and particularly political fragmentation further complicated banking. Inspired by French colleagues, however, parts of the Rhinish banking aristocracy planned to found joint-stock banks in Germany. Facing the strong opposition of the landed elites and other bankers the Rhinish bankers had to move to the Hessian province to found Germany's first joint-stock banks. Compared with France, the development of joint-stock banking was much slower in Germany. However, the unification of Germany, the facilitation of joint-stock banks' foundation and the rise of state- or kathedersocialism to the leading economic idea accelerated the development of Germany's banking sector. Unification opened new markets and the rise of state- or kathedersocialism promoted the concentration and cartelization of the economy and the close connection between industrial conglomerates, megabanks and the state. In the decades before World War I, the German industrial progress was organized and operated within the trinity of industrial conglomerates, megabanks and the government. Banks were present on almost all supervisory boards, avoided conflicts between companies of the same sector in which they were invested and, due to their better market overview, guided industrial conglomerates and entire sectors. Due to Germany's fast industrialization and the support of state- or kathedersocialism, Germany's leading joint-stock banks became the world's biggest banks until World War I.

Opposing welfare states, particularly for liberals the foundation of non-profit banks was an appropriate measurements for help to self-help to the poor and for overcoming the escalating social problems. It was expected that non-profit banks would increase poorer classes' economic participation, overcome their bad habits and therefore undermine the rising socialist movement. Furthermore, it was expected that non-profit banking would foster economic growth by deepening banking and introducing even small savings to the economy. Throughout the 19th century, private and public saving banks, cooperative banks and joint-stock mortgage banks were founded to support the poor, workers, peasants and craftsmen. Until World War I, in France, Britain and particularly Germany a system of non-profit banks emerged which became the third main pillar, beside megabanks and central banks, of the leading banking sectors.

Ideas, Interests, Institutions and Banking Revolutions

2

The main aim of the book is to analyze pivotal banking revolutions or what Hall (1993) considers "Third Order Changes" of the banking sector from a wider social perspective; in other words, the embeddedness of banking revolutions into wider fundamental economic, political and cultural changes. In particular, I focused on how ideas, interests and institutions determined the historical development of the banking sector; or how changing ideas, interests and institutions facilitated and caused banking revolutions.

Following Kraemer (2017) and Wehler (1989), it is assumed that societies are characterized by three fundamental orders: the economic, political and cultural order. The cultural order consist of ideas. Simultaneously, various ideas form the cultural order. Different ideas are either harmonic or conflicting: ideas are not harmonic or conflicting by nature, but are defined as complementary or mutually exclusive. However harmonic the cultural order seems, there are always alternative ideas challenging dominant ideas. The economic order is the place of production and distribution. Who gets what and how much of it (distribution), who makes what, where, how, with whom and how much of it (production) are the principal questions of the economic order. To each question of the economic order, different groups favor different answers: a group's favored answer is considered its interests. The distribution of products and services among different groups unequally empowers interests. The political order is the place where groups with different interests compete over institutions, permissions, appointments, organizations and distributions. Groups from different fields transfer their interests into political demands or political interests. Carriers of different interests unequally equipped with resources and power use their force to institutionalize their interests. In need of support, groups of interests usually form coalitions to enforce their demands.

The three fundamental orders have a certain degree of independency, but are at the same time strongly interwoven. On the one hand, each order follows its own independent logic. On the other hand, each order inevitable influences the other two orders.

F. Brugger, *Ideas, Interests and the Development of the European Banking Systems*, Wirtschaft + Gesellschaft, https://doi.org/10.1007/978-3-658-30597-0_2

Ideas shape interests and institutions which is why the cultural order influences the economic and political order. Ideas constitute a space of legitimate and illegitimate, of desired and undesired action, interests and institutions. Hence, ideas justify certain economic and political interests, actions and institutions and delegitimize others: ideas are frames and constraints. Following Hay (2011), ideas transfer natural interests into perceived interests. From a materialist perspective, natural interests are persons' and groups' material interests determined by their position in the production and distribution process. However, what persons and groups consider their interests largely depends on their beliefs in ideas. In addition, ideas function as road maps and weapons and facilitate and hamper coalition building. Actors of the political and economic order use ideas to make predictions about the future and to understand the world. Also, ideas frequently serve as the fundament of stable coalitions, but at the same time hamper other cooperation that may seem acceptable from the perspective of interests. The economic order produces groups of shared interests and unequally distributes resources among them, which they use to influence the political and cultural order. Strong groups of economic interest use their means to influence the content of ideas. In addition, economic groups use their power and influence to promote, institutionalize and protect their favored ideas. Similar groups of economic interests use their means to shape political outcomes: groups of economic interests formalize and empower political demands and form coalitions to institutionalize their interests and favored ideas. In the political order, the institutional setting of the economic and cultural order is determined. As ideas and interests institutionalize in the political order they become efficacious, stabilize and binding even to non-believers. Political decisions influence the content and diffusion of ideas, the distribution of resources and means to diffuse ideas to the actors of the cultural order. Also, political decisions highly influence production and distribution, the main dimensions of the economic order.

Following Kuhn (1970) I distinguish between normal and revolutionary times. Normal times are considered as characterized by a harmonic relation between ideas, interests and institutions; or a harmonic relation between the economic, political, and cultural order. Hence, interests of the most powerful economic and political groups are in harmony with the ideas dominating the cultural order and both leading ideas and interests institutionalized in the political order. Normal times shift into revolutionary times as fundamental changes of at least one dimension—ideas, interests or institutions—or one order breaks up the harmonic relation. However, fundamental changes of ideas and interests in the cultural, economic and political order are usually closely connected. The rise of new powerful economic and political groups with new economic and political interests or changing interests of established groups usually also shape the ideal landscape: changing interests shift the content of ideas or empower old ideas. The other way around, shaping ideas shift interests as they redefine the boundaries of legitimate interest and shape the transformation of normal interests into perceived interests. Changed interest and ideas stabilize and become efficacious as they shape the institutional environment. Institutions are usually relatively sluggish. However, once ideas and interests become institutionalized, they stabilize and become efficacious even to non-carriers. Revolutionary times again shift to normal times as a new harmonic relation between ideas, interests and institutions is reached. The main aim of the book is to show how revolutionary times, hence a significant change in ideas, interests and institutions or in the economic, political and cultural order, caused, facilitated and influenced banking revolutions which considerably shaped the path along which the banking sector developed.

2.1 Ideas, Interests and Institutions

At the end of the 19th and early 20th century there were popular theories focusing on how interests, personal or collective, influence behavior, politics and finally the institutional setting. The marginal revolution in economics pushed the heterogeneous approaches of the 19th century toward one vanishing point: applying a radical form of methodological individualism, institutions, politics, prices and action are considered as exclusively determined by the action of utility maximizing atomized individuals. Taking the new reduced methodological individualism seriously, the social order was considered to be determined by people behaving strictly in accordance to their situative, autonomous preferences. Against the rising marginal approach, neo-Marxist contributions highlighted the collective and structural nature of interests: interests are not individual, but class interests determined by the social structure and the conditions of production. Neo-Marxists and marginalists disagree on what are and what determines interests, but agree on the importance of interests for action, politics and institutions. Ideas were mostly ignored by the marginalist- and neo-Marxist approach.

Rejecting both marginalism and Neo-Marxism for their hard materialism, Max Weber, Émile Durkheim and other early sociologists, emphasized the importance of ideas. Max Weber's *The Protestant Ethic and the Spirit of Capitalism* ([1920] 1930) and Émile Durkheim's *The Elementary Forms of Religious Life* ([1912] 1995) are two early sociological studies on how ideas influence actions, institutions and societies. Later contributions in the sociology of religion were often criticized for exaggerating the importance of religious ideas; Max Weber avoided both, a strict restricted materialism and idealism. Unprominentely in the introduction to the "The Social Psychology of the World Religions" (1946, p. 280) Max Weber stated:

> Not ideas, but material and ideal interests, directly govern men's conduct. Yet very frequently the world images that have been created by ideas have, like switchmen, determined the tracks along which action has been pushed by the dynamic of interest.

Two implications of Weber's statement are of particular importance: first, he clearly rejects simplistic materialism and idealism by clarifying that both matter, ideas and interests. Second, particularly directed against Marxist approaches, Weber emphasizes that interests may be both material and ideal.

With the sharpening differentiation between social disciplines, the division between ideal based and interest based approaches intensified. Overall, political science and in particular economics steadily went toward a stricter materialism and sociology increasingly became a science of culture and ideologies. However, in the last decades, institutional approaches are on the rise again taking both ideas an interests seriously. Only several of the most widely recognized contributions are discussed here. In a widely recognized book, Hall (1989) and others discussed the rise and spread of Keynesianism and how it influenced institutions and policies. Analyzing different Keynesian responses to the Great Depression in Britain, Sweden and the USA, Weir and Skocpol (1985) argued that different power constellations, institutional settings and uneven coalitions caused rather different Keynesian politics. McNamara (1999) showed the importance of ideas for the creation of the European monetary union. Sikkink (1991) analyzed the influence of ideas on developmentalism in Brazil and Argentina and why policy based on rather similar ideas caused quite different outcomes. Berman (1998) showed how the rise of social democratic ideas and movements influenced the institutional setting in the interwar period and how it shaped the historical institutional path. Goldstein and Keohane (1993) and other contributors discussed how ideas and interests influenced America's foreign policy. Dobbin (1997) analyzed how different ideas on the relation of the state and private enterprises and on the best general economic policy caused rather different railway policies in France, Britain and America. Studying national security policies, Katzenstein (1996) and his colleagues showed how different cultures, ideas, norms and institutional settings influenced countries' security policies.

After three decades of intensifying discussions on the importance, influence and codependency of ideas and interests, that both ideas and interest matter is not doubted. Sociologic institutionalists, political scientists, and even neoclassical economists recognize that ideas and interests should be taken seriously. Despite the wide agreement on the importance of ideas and interests, much disagreement still persists on the relation between ideas, interests and institutions, the mechanism of how ideas and interests influence action, policies, institutions and entire societies, and more fundamentally what we mean by ideas and interests.

2.1.1 Ideas: In Sociology, Economics and Political Science

For almost a century, most political scientists and in particular economists considered ideas of little importance for politics, economics and human behavior. Mainstream economics steadily went toward the very reduced and closed methodological individualism highly focusing on formal models build on atomized, super rational preferences driven utility maximizers. Political science was long dominated by two main approaches: historical and rational choice institutionalists. The former considers political processes to be dominated by struggles between groups with shared interests. Adopting the economists' methodological individualism, the latter traces politics back to choices of rational self-interested individuals. In sharp contrast, sociology traditionally highlighted the central importance of ideas, beliefs, norms and values for human behavior, cohesion of societies, politics and the economic system.

In the last three decades an "ideational turn" (Blyth 1997) was visible in political science and later economics. Kingdon (1984), Hall (1989), Sikkink (1991), Goldstein and Keohane (1993) are the early pioneers of the ideational turn in political science: Mehta (2011) considered that in political science the question shifted from whether ideas matter to how they matter. Most ideal contributions in political science focused on how ideas influenced and shaped politics and institutions. Others (Hall 1989; McNamara 1999; Blyth 2002) studied ideal revolutions, hence the change of dominant ideas and its effects. Focusing on how changing ideas influence politics and institutions, the production and diffusion of new ideas was usually not studied much (Brugger and Pantelic 2018).

In the last 25 years, research on ideas is among the most dynamic fields of political science: a huge number of empirical and theoretical contributions advanced the understanding of how ideas influence politics. The importance of epistemic communities or thought collectives and carriers and how they influence the implementation of ideas was emphasized (Haas 1992; Yee 1996; Campbell 2002), models clarifying the mechanism of ideas influence were built (Yee 1996; Hay 2011; Rodrik 2014; Mukand and Rodrik 2015), different ways of how ideas influence politics were outlined (Goldstein and Keohane 1993; Blyth 1997; Campbell 1998; Lieberman 2002; Béland 2009; Marsh 2009), distinctions between different forms of ideas were undertaken (Hayek 1949; Sabatier 1988; Goldstein and Keohane 1993; Sabatier and Weible 2009; Sabatier 2011; Leighton and López 2014; Pierce et al. 2017; Brugger and Pantelic 2018) the steady modification of ideas in ongoing discourses was highlighted (Schmidt 2002; Bevir and Rhodes 2003; Schmidt and Radaelli 2004; Schmidt 2008; Carstensen 2011, 2015) and, out of the criticism of the traditional historical institutional approach new schools of thought emerged.

Criticizing other neo-institutionalisms for their focus on path dependency, on static equilibria and for the sharp distinction between ideas and interests, the emerging constructivist institutionalism (Blyth 1997; Hay 2008) considers ideas and interests as interwoven social constructs and focuses on times of uncertainty, disequilibria and path shaping processes (c.f. Hay 2008). Due to their methodological focus on institutional equilibria, constructivist institutionalists argue that historical, rational choice and sociological institutionalists lack the instruments to adequately analyze and understand disequilibria and institutional change. Constructivist institutionalists criticize the outlined standard story of ideal revolutions and argue that interests, crises, political challenges and political programs, hence all ingredients of ideal revolutions, are themselves social constructs highly influenced by actors' beliefs in ideas. Instead of considering how new ideas shape politics, constructivist institutionalists analyze how rising uncertainty questions the social constructions and paves the way for reinterpretations of the social constructs and changes in the ideals, interests and institutional landscape. Discursive institutionalism (Schmidt 2008) has much in common with constructivist institutionalism: the focus on change and ideas and the understanding of ideas, interests, institutions as social constructions. However, discursive institutionalism focuses on discourses and interactions, which develop, shape, legitimize or delegitimize ideas, interests and institutions (c.f. ibid.). Unlike most other approaches, discursive institutionalism highlights that ideas are not exogenously given and static concepts, but steadily change and convey in discourses (Schmidt 2002; Bevir and Rhodes 2003; Schmidt and Radaelli 2004; Schmidt 2008; Carstensen 2011, 2015).

In economics, the case of ideas is curious: many notable economists like Mill ([1845] 1967), Keynes (1935) and Hayek (1949) stressed the pivotal importance of ideas for politics and economics, but ideas are hardly important for their economic theory and models; just recently a smooth ideational zurn also reached mainstream economics. Already classical economics strongly focused on material interests and therefore mostly ignored the importance of ideas. John Stewart Mill, a co-founder of classical economics, was an exception: studying the rise of labor pressure groups in "The Claims of Labour" ([1845] 1967), he rudimentary discussed the influence of ideas on politics. Like many recent contributors Mill (ibid., p. 370) considered that ideas are relatively unimportant during calm times, but become strong weapons and highly influential in uneven times, like in the case of deep crises: "ideas, unless outward circumstances conspire with them, have in general no very rapid or immediate efficacy in human affairs." However, "when the right circumstances and the right ideas meet, the effect is seldom slow in manifesting itself."

Similarly, John Maynard Keynes (1935, p. 383) also stressed, in one of the most quoted passage of his *General Theory*, the importance of ideas:

> The ideas of economists and political philosophers, both when they are right and when they are wrong, are more powerful than is commonly understood. Indeed the world is ruled by little else. Practical men, who believe themselves to be quite exempt from any intellectual influence, are usually the slaves of some defunct economist. Madmen in authority, who hear voices in the air, are distilling their frenzy from some academic scribbler of a few years back. I am sure that the power of vested interests is vastly exaggerated compared with the gradual encroachment of ideas.

However, regardless of the importance he attached to ideas, Keynes never developed a theory of ideas or just further developed his argument.

It was Keyne's main academic opponent Hayek who discussed the issue of ideas in more details. In several contributions, Hayek (1944) left no doubt that the idea of socialism—which to him meant predominately the favor for state interventionism—is the most dangerous idea around, spreads fast and infiltrates parties, groups and individuals from the right to the left, from conservatives to liberals. Apart from stressing why socialism is so dangerous, Hayek analyzed in *The Intellectuals and Socialism* (1949) how and why the idea of socialism spread so fast among quite different people and groups. Like Keynes, Hayek (ibid., p. 417) started his contribution by considering that politicians and economists largely undervalue the influence of ideas:

> In all democratic countries, [...] a strong belief prevails that the influence of the intellectuals on politics is negligible. This is no doubt true of the power of intellectuals to make their peculiar opinions of the moment influence decisions [...] Yet over somewhat longer periods they have probably never exercised so great an influence as they do today in those countries.

Hayek was deeply convinced that socialist ideas are quite influential and on the rise. What accelerated and facilitated the rise and spread of socialist ideas was, according to Hayek (ibid.), not so much the visibility of "original [socialist] thinkers", but the huge bulk of "second hand dealers": people with some intellectual authority, who interpret grand ideas in the light of their daily life and spread it among their, smaller or bigger, audience. Second hand dealers frequently misunderstand and misinterpret the true meaning of grand ideas, they are middleman who spread ideas among ordinary people and facilitate the institutionalization of ideas. Hence, according to Hayek, not the veracity of ideas, but their attractiveness to second hand dealers makes them powerful.

Further marginalized by the mathematization of mainstream economics, just quite recently, particularly among historical and institutional economists, a rising interest on culture, norms and ideas is visible. North (2005, p. 2), usually a strong advocate of rational choice, stated:

> The 'reality' of a political-economic system is never known to anyone, but humans do construct elaborate beliefs about the nature of that 'reality'—beliefs that are both a positive model of the way the system works and a normative model of how it should work. [...] The dominant beliefs—those of political and economic entrepreneurs in a position to make policies—over time result in the accretion of an elaborate structure of institutions that determine economic and political performance.

Besides notable hints on the importance of ideas for economics and politics, several contributors introduced ideas into standard economic models and estimations: Bisin and Verdier (1998) modeled the influence of culture on preferences. Others modeled and empirically tested the relation between culture and institutions (Greif 1994; Tabellini 2008, 2010), the persistence of morals (Greif and Tadelis 2010) and the relation between culture and economic development (Guiso et al. 2006). Widely recognized are in particular the contributions of Rodrik (2014) and Mukand and Rodrik (2015) who attempt to introduce ideas into mainstream neoclassical institutional models. Studies in historical economics also highlighted the central role of culture for economic development (McCloskey 2016; Mokyr 2017).

Unlike in most other social sciences, world views, ideas, norms and values traditionally played a central role in sociology. The sociological research on ideas may be divided into two main strands: the first is located in the sociology of knowledge and focuses on the social determination of the development and distribution of knowledge, ideas and ideologies. The second strand investigates how ideas, beliefs, norms, ideologies influence the social world.

Fundamentally criticizing the Hegelian philosophy of the time, Marx and Engels emphasized in *The German Ideology* ([1846] 1970) the dependency of ideas on the prevailing social circumstances. Rejecting idealists' ideal of the free mind, Marx and Engels (ibid., p. 47) emphasized the dependency of consciousness on human beings.

> The phantoms formed in the human brain are also, necessarily, sublimates of their material life-process, which is empirically verifiable and bound to material premises. Morality, religion, metaphysics, all the rest of ideology and their corresponding forms of consciousness, thus no longer retain the semblance of independence. [...] Life is not determined by consciousness, but consciousness by life.

For Marx and Engels the fundamental economic structure, the conditions of production, determine the shape of ideas and the classes' favor of certain ideologies: slaves prefer other ideologies than slavers, workers other than the bourgeoisie and so on. Hence, the content of the ideas and their popularity is only understood if the class position of its developers and carriers is taken into consideration. Every class has its favored idea and attempts to impose it on the entire society. However, the "ideas of the ruling class are in every epoch the ruling ideas" (ibid., p. 64). Thus, the dominance of ideas only represents the classes' dominance over capital, means of production and political power: "The ruling ideas are nothing more than the ideal expression of the dominant material relationships, the dominant material relationships grasped as ideas" (ibid.). The ruling class "rule also as thinkers, as producers of ideas, and regulate the production and distribution of the ideas of their age" (ibid.).

Following Marx and Engels, Gramsci (1999, pp. 524–535) outlined how the ruling class succeed to spread their ideas among lower classes. According to Gramsci, the ruling classe's stable dominion heavily builds on its ability to spread favored ideas among lower classes and establish a cultural hegemony. In particular the education system is considered a powerful tool in the hands of the ruling class to build a cultural hegemony. Indoctrinated by the educational system and the mass media, the ruled classes are convinced that the dominant ideas are in everybody's best interest or are at least immutable. For Gramsci, the capitalist cultural hegemonies facilitate the dominion of the capitalist state over the governed masses. The Marxist critique of ideology was later renewed by the Critical Theory. According to the Critical Theory, (see Horkheimer and Adorno [1947] 2002; Marcuse 1964; Adorno [1964] 1973), ideology becomes omnipresent in industrialized societies and functions not just as an instrument of oppression, but as gratification, pacification and deflection of the masses (c.f. Knoblauch 2014, p. 121).

Marx's and Engel's critic of ideology is part of their general analyses of capitalism and bourgeois society. Karl Mannheim, usually considered a co-founder of the sociology of knowledge, developed the issue of ideology as a specific research field of sociology. Mannheim followed Marx and Engels in that knowledge and ideas are socially determined, but rejected their (exclusive) focus on material class interests: according to Mannheim ([1925] 1952, p. 183), Marxism recognizes only one social determination of ideas, namely that "intellectual attitude is dictated by a material interest [...] because the initial phase of ideological research was solely motivated by 'unmasking' that being 'dictated by an interest' was the only form of social conditioning of ideas that was recognized." Mediating in the escalating ideological conflict of his time, Mannheim considered that all kinds of knowledge and ideology are socially determined. Unlike most Marxists, Mannheim considers that knowledge is determined by a wide range of social factors, for example class, profession, religion, generation, nation; hence, the economic structure is not the only influence which counts. Nevertheless, Mannheim considers that knowledge and ideologies are often interest based (Knoblauch 2014, p. 105) which is why battles over ideologies are usually also battles between interests. Following Mannheim, Merton (1968, p. 514 f.) developed a useful heuristic theory of social determination where he distinguished various "social" and "cultural" influences and relations between the "existential base" and the "mental productions." Subdivided into various subfields, the social determination of knowledge is however still a core issue for the sociology of knowledge: if there is any consensus among researchers, it is that the "meaning of ideas is not transparent: that meanings are always embedded in socio-intellectual contexts which must be opened up to in-depth investigations before the ideas themselves can be understood" (Camic and Gross 2004, p. 245).

Max Scheler highlighted the importance of carriers for the diffusion and implementation of ideas. Scheler's sociology of knowledge is directed against Marx and Hegel, but at the same time combines the materialism of Marx with the idealism of Hegel: he rejects the vulgar Marxist materialist view that ideas are (just) intellectualizations of vested material class interests. At the same time, he rejects pure idealism which traces the rise and diffusion of culture back to mental, ideal processes. Scheler ([1926] 1960, pp. 17–51) distinguished between the development of new ideas and their diffusion and implementation: the development of ideas is determined by ideal-factors and the diffusion and implementation by real-factors. New ideas emerge in the world of ideal-factors; hence, in the world of the objective mind, culture, language, script, religion, law and rituals. However, unless new ideas coalesce with real-factors (the distribution of power, economic and social structure, interests, geographic and geopolitical situations etc.) they remain powerless and invalid: ideas become powerful and valid, diffuse and institutionalize and maybe replace former dominant ideas if they are carried by strong real-factors. According to Scheler ([1923] 1963, p. 23 ff.), sociology, ethnology and psychology lack the tools to explain the contents of ideas which is why they should instead focus on empowering, diffusion and institutionalization of ideas: hence, not the content of Protestantism, Marxism, Humanism, but why the bourgeoisie, working class, middle class became carriers of the ideas should be the central questions of sociology.

The influence of ideas on the social order, social and economic structure, institutions and organizations was considered the second strand of sociological research on ideas. Contributions about the influence of ideas, knowledge and culture on action, the social order, institutions and the social structure may be found in every sociological subfield. Hence, sociological research on the influence of ideas is too extensive to be discussed here in detail. I give a brief overview of studies which are of particular importance for this study. Max Weber's *The Protestant Ethic and the Spirit of Capitalism* ([1920] 1930) is important for this study because it turns the Marxist causality upside down and shows that ideas also influence the economic structure: for Marxists, the causality runs from economic structure to ideas; Weber showed that the opposite causality also exists. Arguing that the Calvinist asceticism and work ethics were the moral precondition of the occidental rationality and the rise of capitalism, Weber showed how new ideas may fundamentally change the economic and social structure. Suggesting the same causality as Weber, Dobbin (1994) showed how different ideas on political economy and on the relation between the state and private enterprises have caused different implementations of railway technology in France, USA and Britain.

Sociological neo-institutionalism (Meyer and Rowan 1977; Zucker 1977; DiMaggio and Powell 1983; Meyer and Scott 1985; Scott and Meyer 1994) highlights how widely recognized ideas shape organizations' actions and structures. Ideas legitimize actions and structures, but also exert strong pressure on people, organizations and institutions to adopt dominant ideas and accept its advice. Sociological neo-institutionalists show how various coercive processes force organizations to orientate their action and structure towards collective ideas, norms, values, myths. Due to legal pressure, their need for legitimization, to receive resources and to reduce uncertainty, organizations orientate themselves towards widely recognized ideas and beliefs. The sociology of social movements considers movements as carriers and promoters of ideas (see for example Kornhauser 1959; Beer 1980; Gelb 1989; Rohrschneider 1993; Dalton 1994; Benford and Snow 2000; Oliver and Johnston 2000). Movements inspired by ideas actively promote and spread their favored ideas. Apart from carrying and promoting ideas, movements are actively involved in the framing process (in the production) of ideas. Hence, social movements are carriers of ideas, but also actively produce, transform and shape ideas. Market sociologists showed how ideas, values and norms influence interactions and outcomes on markets (see for example Beckert 2005; Zelizer 2009). Zelizer (2009), for example, showed how ideas about the "financial evolution of death" constrained the American market for life insurances in the 19th century. Insurance companies' strong interest to develop the new business of life insurances, was accompanied by people's desire to financially support the family beyond their own death. However, the development of life insurances was much hampered by the widespread belief in the immorality of the financial evolution of death. Contributions studying the performativity of economic theory outlined how economic theory influences economic actions, institutions and economies. They argue that economic models considered as adequate description of the economic reality shape actions of market participants, influence markets' institutional setting, determine research on economics and alter economies (see Callon 1998; Bourdieu 2005; MacKenzie 2006; Garcia-Parpet 2007; MacKenzie et al. 2007).

2.1.1.1 Different Forms of Ideas

Many contributions analyzing how ideas influence politics and economies are not very certain about what they actually mean by ideas. Definitions of ideas are frequently quite abstract and open: ideas are considered as norms, beliefs with transpersonal validity and ideologies, in which the principal aspects of human relations to the world are articulated

(Sigmund 2014, p. 66 f.): “ideas, after all, are a medium by which people can imagine a state of affairs other than the status quo” (Lieberman 2002, p. 698). Following the abstract definition, ideas are world views: world views are, based on formal logics and political programs (Schmidt and Thatcher 2013, pp. 1–50), ideologies and imaginations of a better world and future, systems of assumptions about good and bad, desired and undesired, compasses and roadmaps to build a better future. Theoretically following the abstract definition of ideas, most empirical studies analyze how academic theories influence political processes, institutions, the politics and economics. Elias (2009, p. 194) criticized the focus on scientific ideas: he considered that “book ideas” are just the tip of the iceberg.

Avoiding the over focus on abstract academic ideas, several sounder definitions of ideas were developed which take the diversity of ideas into account. Those alternative approaches may be divided into two main groups: hierarchical and functional views. Hierarchical approaches consider that ideas or world views consist of more and less abstract forms of ideas. Keynes (1935) and Hayek (1949) distinguish between ideas of academics and the derived ideas of the general public (Leighton and López 2014, p. 108 ff.). While Keynes says little about the development of public beliefs, Hayek, as maintained, argues that second-hand dealers transform ideas into vivid simplifications and spread it among their audiences. Hayek subdivides the epistemic community into scholars and intellectuals: the former are the producers of the academic theory, the latter are “journalists, teachers, ministers, lecturers, publicists, radio commentators, writers of fiction, cartoonists” (Hayek 1949, p. 372) who transform and spread ideas. For Hayek (ibid.), scholars are academic experts, intellectuals “may be masters of the technique of conveying ideas but are usually amateurs so far as the substance of what they convey is concerned.” Implicitly dividing the society into three main groups—scholars, intellectuals and the audience—it seems Hayek had three different forms of ideas in mind: academic theories, applied theories—intellectuals’ daily life interpretation of what they have understood from academic theories—and public beliefs—ordinary people’s understanding and interpretation of applied theories.

Focusing on political processes, the Advocacy Coalition Framework (ACF) makes an explicit distinction between three types of ideas: “deep core-”, “policy core-”, and “secondary beliefs” (Pierce et al; Sabatier 1988; Sabatier and Weible 2009; Sabatier 2011; Pierce et al. 2017). The ACF assumes that, at least, political elites are guided by consistent systems of ideas; belief systems (Bandelow 2015) which consist of deep core, policy core, and secondary belief. Deep core beliefs are general norms and assumptions about “human nature the relative priority of fundamental values such as liberty and equality” (Sabatier and Weible 2009, p. 194 f.), policy core beliefs are “applications of deep core beliefs” and secondary beliefs “policy preferences related to specific instruments or proposals dealing with only a territorial or substantive subcomponent of a policy subsystem” (ibid.). Similarly, Goldstein and Keohane (1993, p. 8 ff.) distinguish between “world views”, “principled beliefs” and “causal beliefs”. World views are principle understandings of the world; principle beliefs and causal beliefs usually refer to world views: the first consist of norms of right and wrong and the second are beliefs of causal relations that guide the world.

Criticizing the ACF for its obscurity on the origin of different types of ideas and why they exist, Brugger and Pantelic (2018) focus on the production condition of ideas. Distinguishing four forms of world views—pure theory, applied theory, implementations and popular beliefs—they expose the different production conditions of each type. Applying Bourdieu's field theory, Brugger and Pantelic (ibid.) argue that ideas are produced in various fields under field specific conditions. Pure theories are produced in the scientific field as intellectually consistent constructs of little practical meaning; observers of the scientific field who belong to other fields like politics, education and the media, produce applied theories to address the most urgent problems of their fields in the light of the favored pure theory. Orientated towards pure theory, applied theories follow the logic and needs of the specific field in which they are produced. Implementations are institutionalizations of applied theories in different fields: implementations are even more strongly determined by the structure and actors of the fields than applied theories. Ideas in various forms trickle down by different mechanism to public beliefs, where they merge with other, often contradicting, ideas.

Functional ideas are frequently divided into "cognitive frames" and "normative evaluation" (Campbell 1998b; Braun and Busch 2000, p. 12 f; Surel 2000; Münnich 2010, p. 51 f.). Ideas as "cognitive frameworks" function as "schemata of ordering information" which facilitate the "ordering, retaining and understanding about the world" (Braun and Busch 2000, p. 12). Normative evaluations enable actors to "judge on the basis of values and norms whether a choice […] is good or bad" (ibid., p. 13). Hence, ideas either help to explain the world as it is and to understand the reasons and causalities behind phenomena—cognitive frames—or they are normative statements about how the world should be—normative evaluation. To get institutionalized and be considered legitimate, ideas need to function as cognitive frames and normative evaluation. Cognitive frames are orientated towards and legitimized by a shared understanding of a better world. Normative evaluation needs to translate into cognitive frames to become politically applicable and institutionalizable and lose the image of being merely naïve beliefs. Campbell (1998b, p. 384 f.) extends the division of "cognitive-" and "normative level" by adding the distinction between ideas in the "foreground-" and the "background of the political debate:" ideas on the foreground are "programs" if they are communicated road maps underlying and guiding the daily policy and "frames" if ideas are used to legitimize policies. Background ideas are "paradigms" if they constitute elitist assumption on relations and causalities, and "public sentiments" if background ideas restrict the range of legitimate policies.

In the main part of the book the influence of big epochal philosophical and in particular economic ideas on the development of the European banking sector, like liberalism, absolutism, mercantilism, classical theory, is studied here. It turns out that most big ideas take the form of pure and applied theories, deep core, policy core, and secondary beliefs, implementations, cognitive frames and normative evolutions, programs, frames, paradigms and enter popular beliefs or public sentiments. Ideas are constructed by the leading intellectuals of the time as pure theory or deep core beliefs. Pure theories transfer into core beliefs or applied theories as carriers interpret ideas in the light of their field's reality, define specific applications, and design concrete measurements. Ideas become secondary beliefs as concrete banking policy demands are outlined and become implementations as they institutionalize in the political process. World views usually dominate the academic field as paradigms, are road maps for political measurements (programs), legitimate political demands (frames) and shape and influence public opinions (public sentiments/public beliefs).

2.1.1.2 The Diffusion of Ideas

The diffusion and empowering of new ideas is according to Berman (2001, p. 233) a main issue concerning ideas and politics. Because "new ideas do not enter an ideological vacuum. They are inserted into a political space already occupied by historically formed ideologies" (Sikkink 1991, p. 2), which is why new ideas usually face tough resistance from the advocates and profiteers of the established dominant ideas. Quoting Victor Huge who said that "Greater than the tread of mighty armies is an idea whose time has come" Kingdon (1984, p. 1) asked: "But what makes an idea's time come?" Obviously, ideas need believers, hence ideas need to diffuse.

Gabriel Tarde, a French sociologist of the 19th century, proposed that sociology should focus on innovation and imitation. According to Tarde ([1890] 1903, p. 3), "Socially, everything is either invention or imitation"; repeating innovations and imitations are the cohesive force of societies. All kind of "resemblances of social origin in society are the direct or indirect fruit of the various forms of imitation" (ibid.). For him (ibid., p. 11) humans are imitators by nature; "social being, in the degree that he is social, is essentially imitative." Tarde (ibid., p. 14) highlights that imitation takes various different forms: "custom-imitation or fashion-imitation, sympathy—imitation or obedience-imitation, precept-imitation or education imitation; naive imitation, deliberate imitation, etc." which follow different logic. Discussing an example of what Tarde would consider fashion imitation, Simmel ([1905] 1957) developed a sociological theory of imitation and distinction. Because lower classes imitate the fashion of the higher ones, higher classes are under steady pressure for fashion innovation to distinguish themselves from lower classes. Hence, the desire of the lower classes to imitate higher classes and the higher classes' desire for distinction causes a steady dynamic of innovation and imitation.

Simmel's contribution was pioneering for many studies on the diffusion of opinions. Opinion Dynamic Models (ODM) are recently quite popular among economists, social physicists and mathematic strong sociologists (for sociological diffusion models see Palloni 2001). Applying high-end mathematics, contributors model the diffusion of opinions by using network, contact and convincing based approaches. Inspired by contributions of various disciplines, according to Xia et al. (2011), the ODM literature is dominated by four main approaches: Voter Models describe how the public choose one of two or more candidates (see Galam 2008; Castellano et al. 2009). Sznadj Models are quite popular, but technically just a variation of Voter Models (see Sznajd-Weron 2005). Culture Dissemination Models are usually agent based models describing the diffusion of culture: culture is considered a pool of relatively stable opinions which spread among similar people (see Axelrod 2016). Bounded Confidence Models take into account that, most likely, persons are just influenced by opinions not too far from their own thoughts. Formally, this means that opinions are just influenced by other opinions if the difference between those opinion is not greater than a certain benchmark (see Hegselmann and Krause 2002, 2005).

ODM has many origins, however, almost all refer to Lazarsfeld et al. (1944) *The People's Choice*. Lazarsfeld, Berelson and Goudet analyzed how information from different sources influenced voters' decisions in the presidential election of 1940. Their main finding was that information received from direct personal contacts are more important than those from the mass media. Using their empirical findings, they develop a theoretical two step model, which considers that information trickles down from mass media via opinion leaders to normal voters. Opinion leaders select and analyze information from the mass media and distribute the formed opinion to followers. In a similar study on the diffusion of new drugs among physicians, Coleman et al. (1957, 1966) emphasized the importance of social networks for the adaption of innovations: they found that physicians most strongly integrated into local networks are the earliest adopters and those most isolated from networks are the last. Dividing the diffusion into five main steps, they show that the earliest spread occurs "through dense professional ties", the second "through dense friendship ties", as information enters the non-physicians population the drug spreads to "relatively isolated doctors", while in the last two stages physicians adopt the innovations which are "unaffected by ties to colleagues" (Coleman et al. 1966, p. 131). Methodologically, the main innovation of the study was that it replaced the traditional leader-follower relation with network relations (Friemel 2010, p. 826). Following Coleman and his colleagues several network based diffusion models were developed. Using a Threshold Model Approach, Granovetter (1978) studied the imitation of behavior. Threshold models assume that beyond and above a certain threshold, value results are quite different: for example, below a certain amount of intoxication one has a good chance of surviving, while above the benchmark one's death is almost certain. Granovetter argues that if the proportion of actors performing a certain behavior is smaller than the threshold value, behavior will not imitated, and if it is beyond the value, behavior will be imitated: threshold values are individual factors, hence each person has an individual threshold value, however the threshold value is socially determined by culture, norms, interactions etc. Most contributions assume that personal contacts cause imitation; Burt (1987) showed that imitation also occurs due to mediators without direct contacts.[1]

[1]Valente (2005) surveyed the recent network research on diffusion.

Focusing on how the structure of interaction affects the diffusion of opinions network, approaches of diffusion give little attention to the content of ideas. Rogers (1983, p. 210–240) outlined characteristics of ideas which influence the diffusion of innovation: among them "Relative Advantage", "Compatibility", "Complexity", and "Trialability". The relative advantage of new ideas over existent ones is hardly detectable: ideas differ on goals and measurements, on whose interests should be most taken into consideration and the concept of a good society; hence how they should be compared. Frequently, it is argued that new ideas which are more compatible with the dominant ones are more likely to succeed; "Whether or not consolidation [of new ideas] occurs often depends on the degree to which the new model fits with existing ideologies" (Sikkink 1991, p. 2). Rogers (1983, p. 233 ff.) makes a meaningful distinction between different forms of compatibility; with "Previous Introduced Ideas", "Values and Beliefs" and "Needs". New ideas spread due to dissatisfaction with the previous ideas (Berman 2001, p. 234), but need to be compatible with principal values and beliefs. Hence, new ideas need to be sufficiently different from previous ideas to purport being a real alternative, but at the same time need to be compatible with general values and beliefs. Ideas compatible with the needs and wants of influential persons and groups have a much higher chance of survival. Usually, pure theories are quite complex. Pure theories need to transfer into applied theories to attract followers outside the academic field. Carrier groups are the main transmitter of pure theories into more applicable forms (Brugger and Pantelic 2018). Rogers (1983, p. 230 f.) considers that over-complexity hinders the diffusion of ideas: I would argue that ideas need both to be successful, a complex pure theory which withstands the academic criteria and applied theories understandable for non-academics. Doubtlessly, relative advantage, compatibility, complexity, and trialability are important for the diffusion of ideas, however Rogers pays (too) little attention to actors and conflicts.

Focusing on how the social structure influences the diffusion of opinions, network based approaches usually ignore conflicts. Developing an alternative heuristic to analyze the diffusion of new ideas, Brugger and Pantelic (2018) highlight the conflictual character of ideal revolutions. According to them, dominant ideas constitute and underpin the field specific distribution of power, influence and capital. Challenging the dominant ideas means to challenge the established distribution system. New ideas challenging the privileged position of field leaders usually face the hostility from the establishment using all their means and power to protect their privileged position.

Accumulating most resources, influence and power, the defenders of the status quo are usually in a much stronger position than the challengers, which is why ideal revolutions rarely occur. According to Brugger and Pantelic, two things are necessary for ideal revolutions: crises and strong carriers. Carriers adopt, defend, promote and spread ideas because they are deeply convinced of the superiority of ideas and/or expect that ideas would strengthen their interests. Frequently, it is argued that carriers adopt ideas to legitimize their vested interests (Berman 2001, p. 235); carriers "active promote and embellish a specific value to justify the actions proposed in its name" (Béland 2009, p. 706). In particular, Marxists argue that ideas first and foremost function as legitimizations of ruling classes' vested material interests. Gramsci (1999, p. 378) considered that "the search for direct self-interest should apply to all aspects of history, to those who represent the 'thesis' as well as to those who represent the 'antithesis'" because "ideas are themselves material forces." Equating ideas with vested interests also appears in non-Marxists rational choice approaches (Lieberman 2002, p. 699). However, in addition to legitimizing vested interests, carriers have other reasons to adopt ideas: ideas functioning as road maps for politics, advisers use ideas which seem best suited to solving the most urgent problems; adopting new ideas may facilitate coalition building with new groups etc. For whatever reason they follow ideas, according to Brugger and Pantelic (2018) carriers use their symbolic, cultural, social, and economic capital (for different forms of capital see Bourdieu 1986) to defend, promote and spread new ideas: they argue that in particular those ideas have a good chance of survival and spread, which attracts carriers endowed with different forms of capital.

Almost all contributions studying ideal revolutions emphasize the importance of crises for ideal change. Implicitly, most contributions interdigitate Kuhnian and Marxian arguments to explain ideal revolutions. Following Kuhn (1970) they usually distinguish between normal and revolutionary times. Kuhn (ibid., pp. 23–42) considers that normal science is characterized by a wide consensus in the scientific community around the superiority of one scientific paradigm. During times of normal science, research is much like puzzle solving: the dominant paradigm specifies the narrow corset of science by defining problems, the way of dealing with it and the solution. According to Kuhn (ibid., pp. 66–74), crises visualize the shortcomings of dominant scientific paradigms which is why researchers increasingly search for better alternatives. Developing new paradigms with higher explanation power, the scientific community switches to the new paradigm. In Kuhn's model, scientific revolutions are quite unbloody and harmonic which is why Bourdieu (1975, p. 22) labels him an idealist philosopher: understanding the advantages of the new paradigm, scientists switch to the new idea without resistance. However, most studies on ideal revolutions contain some Marxist elements of power and conflicts. Rooted in the tradition of historical institutionalism, accustomed to study conflicts and negotiation processes of more or less powerful interest groups, many contributors implement the Marxist argument in their principally Kuhnian framework that ideas also need strong carriers to become dominant.

It seems quite reasonable that only deep crises burst the fundamental structure that supports dominant ideas, shake the status quo and open the window for deep change (Surel 2000, p. 504). However, most contributors are not very clear about the meaning of crises and how crises influence the rise of new ideas. Traditionally (Hay 2008; Sabatier and Weible 2009, p. 204), crises were considered to be exogenous shocks like recessions, financial crises, natural disasters, wars etc., which discredit the dominant idea and open a window for new ideas to enter the vacuum. From a constructivist perspective, the traditional story has several shortcomings: the explanation power of crises and ideas is a social construct itself influenced by ideas. What is considered a good or a bad theory, as crises or part of the normal as an adequate explanation of crises, heavily depends on actors' beliefs. Hence, crucial events like deep crises are situations where ideas compete over alternative interpretations. Central to the constructivist approach is that perceived interests are considered social constructions depending on the ideas carriers of interests believe in (Hay 2011). Perceived interests are usually derived from dominant ideas. However, in the case of deep crises, perceived interests and their reference to dominant ideas are under consideration (Hay 2008, p 69 f.). As Blyth (2002) puts it, deep crises question the taken for granted relation between ideas and interests: are dominant ideas actually carriers' best choice or would alternative ideas better suit their vested interests? Hence, crises discredit dominant ideas, cause actors to search for alternatives and questions the relation between ideas and interests; therefore, crises open the window for ideal revolutions. Following Bourdieu (1984), Brugger and Pantelic (2018) argue that crises and the accelerating diffusion of new ideas may lead to what Bourdieu considers a critical moment. The critical moment is a general crises in which the future seems open; where it seems open whether the dominant or the challenging idea prevails. Critical moments are decisive: critical moments force every actor to clearly take sides; all kinds of silent acceptance of the status quo or middle position become illegitimate and the entire complexity of the situation is reduced two one question: are you with us or against us? (Bourdieu 1988, p. 284 f.). Critical moments bring about the decision over which idea will prevail.

According to Brugger and Pantelic (2018), the intensity of hostility and rejection or of support for new ideas depends on the distributions of actors and resources between supporters of the dominant and the challenging idea. Rogers (1983, pp. 247–251) distinguishes between five stages of diffusion: "Innovators", "Early Adopters", "Early Majority", "Late Majority" and "Laggards" (see also Robertson 1967). Brugger and Pantelic (2018) consider that in particular innovators and early adopters face rejection and hostility from the establishment. Similarly, Schumpeter stressed that the diffusion of innovations[2] is not a harmonic, but a contested process (Ebner 2005, p. 267).

Schumpeter asked why entrepreneurs innovate or adopt new ideas if they face the concentrated hostility of the establishment? According to Schumpeter, some people are born as innovative entrepreneurs. Schumpeter distinguishes two ideal types of actors: the first is "hedonic", "static" a person trying to fit into the established order; the second is "dynamic", "energetic" (Kurz and Sturn 2012, p. 106) permanently seeking innovations to attack and alter the established order; the first follows a "hedonic-" the second an "energetic-rationality" (ibid., p. 107). Similarly, for Rogers (1983) innovators are notorious risk taking outlaws who cannot live without the fascination of risk taking. Brugger and Pantelic (2018) adopt Max Weber's concept of charismatic leaders to give reason to early adoptions. Weber develops in *The Sociology of Religion* ([1922] 1964) and *Economy and Society* ([1956] 1979) concept of charismatic leaders: according to Weber

[2]Schumpeter (1934, p. 66) applied a wider definition of innovation which also includes more ideas and organization forms than most of his colleagues' work.

(ibid., pp. 241–245), disciples ascribe to the charismatic leader extraordinary attributes which is why they follow him despite all hostility and disadvantageous. For Kraemer (2010), the attractiveness of charismatic leaders is the main reason to breach isomorphism and break new grounds. Roth (1987) and Kraemer (2002) extended Weber's concept of charismatic leader to ideas: charismatic aspirations are also attributed to charismatic ideas (Kraemer 2010, p. 192 f.). According to Brugger and Pantelic (2018), early adopters follow ideas because they are attracted by the charisma of leaders and ideas.

As maintained, early adopters face the hostility and rejection of the establishment. However, after the diffusion of ideas passes a critical point—or what Bourdieu (1988) considered the critical moment—the social pressure turns over and supports rather than opposes the new idea. Understanding capitalism as an immanent dynamic process, for Marx the individual is condemned by the structural pressure of capitalism to Keep up with the Joneses: pushed forward by capitalist competition, adapting innovations, technical or ideal, is a matter of survival; the bourgeoisie pays with its economic life for resistance against spreading innovations. Overcoming Marxist materialism, sociological neo-institutionalists outlined various social pressures which cause individuals, groups and organizations to adopt ideas, techniques, processes, forms and norms. Meyer and Rowan (1977) argue that organizations adopt rationality myths (ideas, rules, norms, processes) to legitimize the organization and absorb resources. Embedded in a wider institutional context, organizations adopt the specific notion of rationality, efficiency of favorable norms, values and ideas established by the institutional environment to enhance their legitimacy and attract resources essential for survival. Hence, the institutional pressure from the environment causes organizations, groups or persons to adopt ideas, norms, values and processes independent from whether they are convinced by rationality myths. DiMaggio and Powell (1983) further specify different forms of social pressures for imitation. Asking why organizations and institutions are so similar and become even more similar, their answer is that this is due to different forms of "Isomorphism". DiMaggio and Powell distinguish three main mechanism of isomorphism: "Coercive Isomorphism", "Mimetic Isomorphism", and "Normative Isomorphism". Coercive isomorphism means enforced adaption; organizations, institutions or persons are forced by other organization, institutions or person, often the government, to adopt ideas, norms, values processes and innovations. Assuming that uncertainty complicates action and interaction, organizations, institutions or persons reduce uncertainty by copying others; mimetic isomorphism. Well-known and respected academics and professionals exert strong normative pressure on others to adapt their beliefs and ideas: normative isomorphism. Brugger and Pantelic (2018) suggest that after the diffusion of new ideas passed a critical point, the forces of isomorphism accelerate the further spread.

2.1.1.3 The 'Functions' of Ideas

As maintained, the influence of ideas on policies is a core issue of political science and related sciences. Various hypotheses and theories about the mechanism and forms of the influence of ideas on politics have been outlined. Traditionally, historical institutionalism considers ideas as constraints (Campbell 1998b, p. 379 ff.). Ideas are frames which determine the boundaries of legitimate and illegitimate arguments, discussions, measurements, institutions and policies. Ideas as frames facilitate choices by reducing the wide range of possible actions, the over-complexity of the world and give the apparent randomness of phenomena a meaning and fit it into a general coherent explanation of the world (Campbell 1998b; Béland 2009; Münnich 2010, p. 48 ff.). Ideas are cognitive and normative restrictions (Campbell 1998b, p. 378): ideas define normative boundaries between legitimate and illegitimate rhetoric, demands, measurements, institutions and politics. Defining a system of causal relations which guides the society's and the world's development, ideas are cognitive guides creating a shared understanding about the functioning of the world. Ideas as cognitive frames are systems of causal relations which explain phenomena and define the measurements needed to build a better future. In addition to normative and cognitive frames, ideas are "Rhetoric Frames" (Béland 2009, p. 706) defining a set of arguments, symbols and stories usable to strengthen their own position. Shared ideas facilitate communication and coordination between people by constructing a shared understanding of the world and phenomena.

In many recent contributions, the concept of ideas as frames is closely connected with the problem of uncertainty. Knight (1921) and Keynes (1921) drew a meaningful distinction between risk and uncertainty. Risk is defined as likelihood of events to occur, assignable as a statistical probability. In contrast, uncertainty is not statistically quantifiable. Recently, the concept of uncertainty receives much attention in economic sociology and political economy. Assuming that uncertainty is the main problem of coordination and interaction on markets, Beckert (2009) suggested that social order is only possible if the uncertainty problem is solved. Extending Beckert's argument to politics, it was suggested that, in particular at times of crises when institutions fail to coordinate actors, shared ideas reduce uncertainty and maintain the political order (Blyth 2002, p. 35 ff.). Ideas are a "Taken for granted assumption" (Campbell 1998b, p. 384) which often survives deep crises and stabilizes the political order even if other stabilization and coordination mechanism like institutions fail. Hence, as "cognitive filters" (Münnich 2010, p. 48) which reduce uncertainty by restricting over-complexity, ideas facilitate a shared interpretation of difficult situations, and define practicable measurements.

Apart from the rather passive influence as frameworks, ideas are used as active political "programs" (Campbell 1998b, p. 386 f.). Programs are concrete sets of political measurements, blueprints of distinguished institutional settings (Blyth 2002, p. 40 f.), which political actors aim to implement. Ideas as programs are usually openly communicated by political actors (Campbell 1998b, p. 386 ff.) to distinguish themselves from competitors and attract followers and voters. As programs, ideas define the most urgent problems and the political agenda to solve them (Béland 2009, p. 704 f.). As road maps (Berman 2001, p. 235), ideas "'enable' and 'empower' actors to generate solutions to their problems by providing cues and scripts that 'constitute' legitimate forms of action" (Campbell 1998b, p. 382). Hence, ideas affect the choice of political measurements, but also the definition of problems (Béland 2016, p. 233): what is considered normal or a problem much depends on underlying ideas.

In political negotiations and conflicts, ideas are fundaments of coalitions and weapons against the political enemy. Ideas facilitate and stabilize political coalitions. According to Münnich (2010, p. 73), shared ideas constitute a unique view of the world, an agreement on the central causal relations and the most urgent problems within coalitions. Shared ideas may function as a cohesive base for coalitions of quite different actors, even with opposing interests. Ideas "make collective action and coalition building possible" (Blyth 2002, p. 41) by redefining the relation between groups and classes, defining collective goals and facilitating agreements on favorable mechanisms and measurements. Establishing a collective understanding of mechanisms, measurements, outcomes and alternatives, ideas are occasionally the fundament of quite unusual coalitions and cooperation. The quite unusual coalition between workers and the bourgeoisie was held together by the shared expectation that liberal *laissez-faire* policy would be beneficial for both classes.

Ideas are not just instruments of unification and coalition building, but also weapons in the political struggle between parties, movements, unions and actors. Political disputes are generally about whose ideas are better suited to establish a stable, legitimate social order (Münnich 2010, p. 77 f.). Traditionally, it was argued that political groups use their power to implement favored ideas. This view ignores the fact that ideas are themselves resources which strengthen and legitimize positions and groups' interests. For example, in principle a quite weak political group carrying the ideas of civil rights and anti-racist greatly empowered black women in America (Béland 2009, p. 708). Some ideas are considered more legitimate and stronger than others; arguments building on stronger ideas are strengthened over those following weaker ideas. Actors being aware of the power of ideas, groups follow ideas not just because of conviction, but also "adopt new ideas if they promise an edge in the battles of the day" (Berman 2001, p. 235). Marxists in particular emphasize the role of ideas as weapons in the class struggle. As maintained, for Marx, Engels Gramsci and other Marxists, ideas are the veiling material of class interests: from the Marxist perspective, conflicts over ideas are just prolongations of the class conflict. However, as maintained, in particular Gramsci (1999, pp. 524–535) stressed how cultural hegemonies strengthen and facilitate the dominion of the capitalist state. According to Gramsci, the ruling classes' ability to use public institutions to indoctrinate other classes with their favored ideas is a strong weapon used to strengthen their dominance. Emphasizing how ideas fortify the status quo, Gramsci ignores ideas' contribution to change. According to Blyth (2002, p. 39 f.), ideas are important instruments for the attack on the institutional status quo: ideas are used to contest the legitimacy and accuracy of the ideas which underlie the institutional orders and to develop alternative institutional settings.

2.1.2 Interests: In Sociology, Economics and Political Science

Traditionally, interests receive much attention in social science. Among economists, political scientists and even sociologists, hardly anybody doubts that interests matter. However, there is much dispute about the definition of interests. While standard neoclassical economics follow a quite narrow form of methodological individualism, Marxists and most political scientists stress the collective character of interests. Many sociological contributions focused on the definition and description of different forms of interests. Historically,[3] standard economics steadily went toward methodological individualism; like mainstream economics, interests are at the core of political science, but political science much criticized economists' individualistic understanding of interests; sociology rather turned away from interests.

Here, following Swedberg (2005a), contributions on interests are subgrouped into two main strands: first, contributors considering interests the only or main factor that matters, and second, authors assuming that interests are the one important force among others. The first dominates economics, the second is quite present among sociologists, however, both approaches are found in economics, political science and sociology.

2.1.2.1 Interests: The Force of Action

Among those considering interests the main or only force of action are many economists, but also notable sociologists. According to Edgeworth (1881, p. 16), a Co-founder of neoclassics, "The first principle of economics is that every agent is actuated only by self-interest." For Pareto, economics is "a general science of interests" (citied in Swedberg 2005b, p. 28). Like most economists, a group around the Austrian sociologists Gustav Ratzenhofer considered "Interests as the driving force in social life" (Swedberg 2005a). Albion Small (1905, p. 426) leaves no doubt about the importance of interests for behavior: "the notion of interests accordingly serves the same purpose in sociology which the notion of atoms has served in physical science. Interests are the stuff that men are made of [...] the last elements to which we can reduce the actions of human beings." Assuming that human behavior is ultimately traceable back to interests, for Small (ibid., p. 442) "sociology might be said to be the science of human interests and their workings under all conditions."

Thomas Hobbes (1651) and Jean Bodin ([1576] 1955), the two outstanding philosophers of absolutism and early Mercantilists, considered that human behavior is driven by interests. Assuming that group and nation interests are frequently antagonistic, they suggest that only an absolute ruler safeguards politics following the national rather than groups interests. Hobbes and Bodin argue that political systems other than absolutism

[3]The concept of interests has a long history which started long before the 19th century (Swedberg 2005a). For more details in the history of interests see Holmes (1990), Hirschman (1992), Force (2003), Swedberg (2005a).

are notoriously prone to be ruled by small groups following their vested interests: they suggested that if the ruler is the state, like in pure absolutism, no difference between the monarch's and the nation's interests seems to exist.

Early liberals criticized mercantilist thinkers like Hobbes and Boldin for assuming that personal self-interests and societyor nation interests are antagonistic. In contrast, early liberals argue that the best guides to enhance social wellbeing are individual self-interests (c.f. Rothbard 1995a, b). Adam Smith is often considered to have initiated the interest turn in economics and philosophy: according to the usual interpretation, Smith (1776) assumed that the persons' orientation (free from all state intervention) on self-interests, guided by an invisible hand, would best serve the general wellbeing. As evidence, Smith's example is quoted where he argues that only thanks to the bakers' and butchers' self-interests, rather than to altruism, are we supplied with bread and pork. That Smith is considered the philosophic founder of naïve individualism is curious, given that Smith outlined in many examples that self-interests and general interests are not necessarily harmonic and stressed that self-interests are not the only force which drives behavior. However, the view that self-interests are the force behind behavior prevailed in classical economics. Assuming that economies are characterized by the interplay of economic structure and actors' self-interested behavior, David Ricardo ([1817] 2005), the founder of classical economics, developed the general laws of distribution: between wage, rent and profits. Ricardo, like many other classical economists, seemed to switch imprudently between individual and group interests. Classical economists' carelessness concerning the concept of interests allowed two quite opposing interpretations: neo-classical standard economics trace their methodological individualism of atomized actors following individual self-interests back to classical economics. On the other side, Ricardian socialists—like Thomas Hodgsk, William Thompson, John Gray—used Ricardo's theory to emphasize class interests.

2.1.2.1.1 Group and Individual Interests

Many post-classical contributors follow the classical assumption that interests are the main force which guides behavior, but make a big effort to clarify the concept of interests. Post-classical contributions may be divided into two main groups: approaches following the concept of individualized, atomized self-interests and approaches considering that interests are collective artefacts. British utilitarists of the early and mid-19th century were clearer about the meaning of interests than most classical economists of the time: they defined interests as atomized, egoistic self-interest and the actors' aim for pleasure (Swedberg 2005b, p. 20 f.). Roused by the Marxist turn and the growing hostility of conservative circles toward liberal classical economics, several contributors like Hermann H. Gossen, Carl Menger, William S. Jevons, Leon Walras rebuilt liberal economics on the basis of the utilitarian understanding of interests. In the socalled marginal revolution, the objectivist labor theory of value was rejected and replaced by the subjectivist concept of marginal utility. Marginalists suggest that goods values are determined by self-interested, rational choices of the homo economicus guided by his individual, atomized preferences using his resources to maximize personal utility. According to Gossen (1854, p. 1 f.), human behavior follows one central rule, the maximization of the pleasure of life: "Out of this purpose life follows the one and therefore main rule with regards to (human) behavior: man should choose his actions in such a way so as to maximize the sum of his enjoyment of life."[4] Hence, the marginal revolution caused an individual turn in the view on interests: while in classical economics individual, group, and nation interests were often used simultaneously, marginalists are quite clear that interests mean atomized individual self-interests.

The early marginalist contributions on interests are still the fundament of the recent economic mainstream approach. However, later contributions altered the standard economic concept of interests. Paul Samuelson (1938, 1948a) with the concept of "Revealed Preference" turned the former causality upside down: former marginalists derived consumer decisions from budget constraints and latent preference. Samuelson suggested that microeconomics should start with observable consumer choices and budget constraints and extrapolate from consumers' choices, latent preferences.

In sharp contrast to the individual turn of the marginal revolution, Marx initiated a "structural turn" in the view on interest (Münnich 2010, p. 39). Like Smith, Ricardo and the early marginalists, Marx considered that interests are the main force behind human action. However, unlike the subjective, individualistic interest concept of the marginalists, Marx focused on objective, structural class interest. Class interests have a "distinct existence well beyond that of its individual members; and it is thoroughly social in this sense" (Swedberg 2005b, p. 20 f.). For Marx the principle interests of workers and capitalists and the antagonism between them are constituted by the principle structure of capitalist economies—by the conditions of production—independent from individual desires. Marx developed the concept of class interest by answering two main questions: first, is capitalism characterized by an inherent structural conflict between classes? and second, are workers able to develop a shared class interest? In *Wage, Labor and Capital* ([1891] 1902) Marx discussed the view of many liberal economists of his time, that capitalist societies are principally harmonic, because workers and capitalists depend on each other. Marx (ibid., p. 40 f.) agrees: "The worker perishes if capital does not keep him busy. Capital perishes if it does not exploit labor-power." However, still, according to Marx, the relation between labor and capital is antagonistic because capital's ultimate goal is to accumulate as fast as possible, which means first and foremost to reduce wages and release workers: Marx (ibid., p. 49) concludes that "the interests of capital and the interests of wage-labor are diametrically opposed to each other." In *The Poverty of Philosophy* ([1847] 1892, p. 172) Marx analyzed inner working-class interest conflicts and workers' ability to overcome infights and bundle their power to target capitalists.

[4]„Für die Handlungsweise des Menschen folgt aus diesem Lebenszweck die eine und darum Hauptregel: Der Mensch richte seine Handlungen so ein, daß die Summe seines Lebensgenusses ein Größtes werde.“

He stressed that the economic conditions, the massive concentration of capital and workers in capitalist mega factories and the immanent conflict with the capitalists creates a common class interest of workers. At the same time, for Marx (ibid.) "competition divides their interests." However, recurrently defeated in the struggle against the capitalist, workers "mass becomes united, and constitutes itself as a class for itself." Hence, uniting in the unequal struggle against the capital, workers shift from a class by itself to a class for itself which develops unique class interests.

Usually, political scientists also consider that human behavior is guided by interests. Two main approaches concerning interests are often distinguished: interest group based and rational choice approaches (see Swedberg 2005b, pp. 87–94). Like Marx, interest group approaches consider interests structural, relatively stable, collective, fundamental orientations (Münnich 2010, p. 39 f.): Marxist contributions were criticized for over-simplifying political negotiations by focusing only on the two main classes—workers and the bourgeoisie. Except orthodox Marxists, hardly anybody doubts that politics is characterized by a wide range of different interest groups negotiating over practical measurements. Interests group based approaches focus on conflicts and in particular on the coalition building processes between different interest groups.

According to Swedberg (2005b, p. 87), Arthur Bentley broke with the tradition of institutionalism in political science and affirmed the importance of group interests for political processes and decisions. In *Governmental Process* Trumann (1966, p. 33) developed the principles of the interest group approach. He defined interests groups as "any group that, on the base of one or more shared attitudes, makes certain claims upon other groups in the society for the establishment, maintenance, or enhancements of forms of behavior that are implied by the shared attitudes." An interest group trying to influence governments is considered a "political interest-group" (ibid.). According to the narrow interpretation of the interest based approach, individuals with shared interests form interest groups to bundle their power and influence: this interpretation ignores that interest are usually reshaped and redefined in the process of interest group formation. In *The Poverty of Philosophy* ([1847] 1892, p. 172), Marx stressed the importance of worker associations for overcoming conflicts within the working class, for forming unique class interests and for becoming "a class for itself." Worker associations enabled workers to construct working-class interests as contrasts to capitalist interests. In the same vein, Trumann (1966, p. 17 ff.) considers that individual interests are determined by the groups the person joins: he argues that in every sphere of life we join groups which influence our interests. While individuals influence groups' interests, group interests determine individual's interests as well, hence the relation between individual and group interests is mutually dependent.

Interest group based approaches have several advantages: in particular, they take power relations in politics to the center. However, at the same time, group based approaches often failed to explain the foundation and stability of interest groups. Olson (1965) highlighted a fundamental weakness of the group interest approach by asking a rather simple question: what causes individuals to join interest groups? He (ibid., p. 17) derived two main answers from the literature: the "traditional-" and "formal-view." The former assumes a "fundamental human propensity to form and join associations" (ibid.). According to Mosca (1939, p. 163), humans have a "natural inclination toward struggle," but at the same time they are "social animal" which they have the natural tendency of "forming into groups." "This instinct of herding together [...] underlies the formation of all the divisions and subdivisions all the factions." In the same vein, Trumann (1966, p. 14) argues that "man is a social animal" which means that "with rare exceptions man is always found in associations with other men." The formal view distinguishes between small groups of underdeveloped societies and big groups of socially differentiated developed societies: the former are joint because of personal affiliation, the latter due to functional reasons like economic benefits (Olson 1965, p. 17 ff.). Similarly, Durkheim ([1893] 1984) distinguished between mechanic solidarity in premodern and organic solidarity in modern societies. Mechanic solidarity is the solidarity between equals. In societies characterized by little division of labor, solidarity stems from people's equality: everybody being a hunter-gatherer, farmer etc. Organic solidarity is the solidarity between unequals. In modern societies, characterized by a high division of labor, people are solidary due to their functional dependency. Like Durkheim, Trumann (1966, p. 15) argues that "the division of labor or specialization [...] almost by definition involves the mutual dependency of men." From the Durkheimian perspective, it seems reasonable that people join groups in highly differentiated and functionally dependent societies to enforce their positions. However, both the traditional and formal view share empirical and theoretical shortcomings: if it is a natural instinct or functionally reasonable to form groups, Connolly (1983, p. 49 f.) asks why so many people with obviously shared interests fail to form strong interest groups? Applying the usual instruments of economic analyses—self-interests, cost-benefit calculation and free-riding—Olson (1965) argued that individuals have no reason to join big interest groups, even if the existence of interest groups is preferable to many individuals or whole societies. According to Olson, groups negotiate over public goods, which are by definition non-exclusive and non-rival. Because individuals benefit from group negotiation independently from their fellowship, why should they not freeride? Olson (ibid., p. 21) concludes: "Though all of the members of the group therefore have a common interest in obtaining this collective benefit, they have no common interest in paying the cost of providing that collective good."

Meanwhile, famous advocates of the rising neoclassical economics like Kenneth Arrow (1951) and Duncan Black (1958) developed approaches—the so-called public choice, electoral or rational choice approach—to incorporate politics into standard economic models. Public choice uses the neoclassical standard assumption and instruments like methodological individualism, utility maximization and later game theory to model and explain political decisions and choices. Their main assumption is that political decisions are finally reducible to decisions and interactions of super rational individuals with given preferences using their endowments and political influence to manipulate political decisions in order to maximize utility. Occupied and further developed by neoliberal economists like James M. Buchanan, Gordon Tullock and Gary Becker, the public choice theory increasingly also became a political ideology of less state intervention and welfare state reduction. Standard neoclassical economics was and is the epicenter of the rational choice revolution, however the rational choice logic also found a wide resonance in other social sciences, like political science and sociology: James Coleman (1990), Jon Elster (2007), Hartmut Esser (1996) and Mancur Olson (1965) were the main sociological rational choice advocates; as maintained further, inspired by neoclassical neo-institutionalism the so-called rational choice institutionalism emerged in political science.

Compared to the group interest approach, the rational choice approach has the advantage of making quite clear the underlying assumption and theories of human action. It also better allows for misinterpretation of own interests by misinformation or miscalculation (Connolly 1983, p. 53). Using the economic concept of self-interested, atomized, utility-maximizing individuals, it fails to take into consideration reasons for political choice different from self-interests (Swedberg 2005b, p. 91) and ignores that interests are hardly given exogenously to the political process, but are rather formed and shaped within discussions and confrontations (Connolly 1983, p. 54). In particular, it ignores the importance of power and coalition building, by tracing back political choices to voter majorities: the political power is equally distributed among all voters in the sense of one vote one power; which seems quite unrealistic given the huge influence of pressure groups.

2.1.2.1.2 The Meaning of Interests

Marx's and marginalists' interest concept seems to also differ concerning the temporal stability: interests derived from individual preferences seem predominantly short-term. Individual preferences seem quite unstable and open for frequent changes. In contrast, for Marx class interests are usually quite stable over longer time periods. Hence, for Marx interests are "general long-term stable basic orders" and for marginalists interests are "situative, concrete preferences" (Münnich 2010, p. 37). Tocqueville made a similar distinction between long- and short-term interests (Swedberg 2005b, p. 5).

The group of sociologists around Ratzenhofer focused on the distinction of different groups of interests. Ratzenhofer (1898, pp. 56–66) distinguished five main groups of interests: "species interests", "physiological interests", "individual interests", "social interests" and "transcendental interest". Species interests are the most primitive instincts which ensure a specie's survival and reproduction. Similarly, physiological interests are lower instincts, which ensure the physical preservation of the body. According to Ratzenhofer, due to the emancipation from the mother's care, people's awareness for the own interests develops. In the higher stages of social and individual development, peoples' interests exceed the fundamental instincts of species and physiological interests: interests which exceed species and physiological interests are considered individual interests. Ratzenhofer's individual interests are similar to the neoclassical concept of preferences: individual interests cover in principle all kind of individual wants. Important to note that Ratzenhofer traces individual interests back to widened primal instincts. Love for others makes, for Ratzenhofer, the fundament of social interests; in its primitive form, social interests arise from species' interests in survival and the physiological interests in sexual satisfaction. However, lower instincts steadily disappear behind people's awareness of their own dependency on and embeddedness in the wider social environment: once the social environment becomes an "integrated part" of the self (ibid., p. 62), the social interest loses its instinctive fundament and builds on "higher interests" (ibid.); like the interest for the nation's or the world's prosperity. The transcendental interest means the individuals' effort to act in accordance to religious guidelines.

Ratzenhofer's followers continued to distinguish different forms of interests. Discriminating between low and high interests, for Small (1905, p. 426) "human beings contain one group of interests which are generically identical with the factors that compose plants and animals": all the lowest interest which secure the survival of the body Small calls "health interest". In addition to low health interests, Small (ibid., pp. 425–442) defines a wide range of less basic high interests: for him, the "most general classes of interests which we find serviceable in sociology" are "health, wealth, sociability, knowledge, beauty, and rightness" (ibid., p. 434 f.). However, depending on the situation, many other forms of interests may exist. Edward A. Ross (1905, p. 164 f.) distinguishes between two core categories: desires and interests. Desires are "primary forces as they well up in consciousness." He further distinguishes between "natural" and "cultural" desires; the first are "Appetitive", "Hedonic", "Egotic", "Affective", "Recreative" and the second "Religious", "Ethical", "Esthetic", "Intellectual" desires. Interests are "the great complexes, woven of multicolored strands of desire, which shape society and make history." Ross (ibid., p. 170 ff.) distinguishes four main groups of interests: "Economic-", "Political-", "Religious-" and "Intellectual-Interests". Ross's categorization of desires and interests may be criticized, but the principal distinction between desires and Interests seems quite reasonable. Economic models usually analyze how desires shape markets; for example, how a representative actor's priority of apples over oranges determines market prices. Political science and sociology usually focus on interests; for example, how changing interests of workers shift the institutional setting. Of course, desires and interests are interconnected, but it makes a huge analytical difference to analyze the impact of persons' desire to quench thirst and workers' political interest of a strong middle-class society. Like Marx, Arthur Bentley (1908) emphasizes the collective character of interests, but adds that apart from classes, many other collectives like cities, nations, and diverse pressure groups form collective or group interests.

2.1.2.2 Interests: One Force of Action Among Others

Many notable economists, sociologists and political scientists considered that interests are one important force behind human behavior, among others. To act rationally and self-interested—in the sense of the economic theory—the individual has to be fully informed about all possible alternatives and consequences. The pivotal assumption of full information was targeted by various contributors as unrealistic and pure theoretical (for example Akerlof 1970). Relaxing the assumption about individuals' information, many economic publications studied different forms of imperfect and asymmetric information and its consequences, like adverse selection and moral hazard. Hence, following information economics, human behavior is also determined by actors' information and the distribution of information between actors. The most significant alteration of the concept of interests in mainstream economics was caused by the rise of game theory. Unlike the atomized homo economicus of the standard neoclassical model, game theory suggests that the outcome of human behavior, and hence the self-interest of actors, also depends on others' behavior and strategies. Hence, an individual's self-interest is only determinable against the background of others' preferences and responses to possible actions.

Game theory has, in principle, much in common with Georg Simmel's action theory. For Simmel, interests are the main driving force behind human actions (Swedberg 2005a, p. 368 ff.). Simmel ([1908] 2009, p. 22) suggests that "drives and purposes [...] indeed a 'society'." Propelled by impulses or interests, individuals need to interact with others to satisfy their wants: a "society exists where several individuals enter into interaction" (ibid.). Interests become social as "separate forms, in which individuals for these reasons—sentient or ideal, momentary or lasting, conscious or unconscious, causally driven or propelled teleologically—come together as a unity in which these interests are realized" (ibid.). Hence, according to Simmel, egoistic self-interests drive action. However, only if actions are altruistically orientated on others, self-interests and individuals desires may be satisfied (Abels 2007, p. 103).

Several economists also criticized the mainstream economic assumption that humans act like animals, purely self-interested, egoistically without concern for others, unrealistically and ignorant to the fact that humans are social beings. Adam Smith develops in *The Theory of Moral Sentiments* ([1759] 1853) the concept of sympathy, which accounts for humans' empathy and the dependency of well-being on the happiness of others. He starts the book by suggesting: "How selfish so ever man may be supposed, there are evidently some principles in his nature, which interest him in the fortune of others, and render their happiness necessary to him, though he derives nothing from it except the pleasure of seeing it." Solidarity and the sense of unity in particular augments happiness: "nothing pleases us more than to observe in other men a fellow feeling with all the emotions of our own breast" (ibid., p. 9). Hence, according to Smith, sympathy is a natural human feeling which makes one's own happiness or utility dependent on others.

Like Smith, Amartya Sen (1973, p. 252 f.) criticized the view on humans as asocial, egotistic, self-interest orientated animals: "I would argue that the philosophy of the revealed preference approach essentially underestimates the fact that man is a social animal and his choices are not rigidly bound to his own preferences only." However, Sen rejects Smith's concept of sympathy as unable to account for the wide range of individual actions which seem irrational from the perspective of self-interests. Sympathy is not irrational from the perspective of standard economic models and may be threatened as a normal preference in utility functions (Sen 1977, p. 326 f.): sympathy is still an egoistic force because people care for others to enhance their own utility. According to Sen, Smith's concept of sympathy fails to account for all those actions which violate superficial self-interests. Quoting various studies from behavioral economics where individuals fail to act in accordance to their self-interest, for Sen (ibid., p. 341) the "puzzle from the point of view of rational behavior lies in the fact that in actual situations people often do not follow the selfish strategy." Unlike most behavioral economists who explain irrationality behavior with actors' limited cognitive capacities, Sen suggests that commitments cause individuals to violate self-interests: "choice may reflect a compromise among a variety of considerations of which personal welfare may be just one" (ibid., p. 324). Sen (ibid., p. 327) considers behavior to be based on commitments if it is "non-egoistic" and causes "person choosing an act that he believes will yield a lower level of personal welfare to him than an alternative that is also available to him." The central point is that Sen criticized the standard economic approach for ignoring the wide range of beliefs, norms, values, social pressure, tradition, which all highly influence choices and behavior, but are difficult to include in ordinary preferences and utility functions.

Sen is not quite clear about the practical meaning of commitments: it seems that commitment is an umbrella term for influences on choice and behavior other that self-interests. Sen did not deny the influence of self-interests on action, but suggested that other forces also shape actions. Similarly, several famous sociologists, like Weber and Bourdieu, consider "Interest as one major force in social life" (Swedberg 2005a) among others. As quoted above "material and ideal interests, directly govern men's conduct," which shows that Weber considers interests themain force of behavior, but interests may be ideal and material. In the same vein, Simmel criticized the simplistic historical materialism in social science: in *Die Probleme der Geschichtsphilosophie* (1905) Simmel stressed that since Enlightenment, social science tends to ignore metaphysical factors and focus instead on empirical measurable facts, like economic structures. Religious ideas may seem unenlightened from a scientific perspective and still they influence believers behavior: "God's Kingdom" as a "final goal of history" may seem abstruse, but as a religious idea it guides and influences actions (ibid., p. 166). Despite interests—material or ideal—Weber highlights the influence of ideas on behavior which "like switchmen, determined the tracks along which action has been pushed." In *Economy and Society* ([1922] 1978, p. 24 ff.) Weber develops four types of social action: "instrumental rational" (zweckrational), "value-rational" (wertrational), "affectual" and "traditional". He further distinguishes between types of social action and types of action orientation. According to Weber (ibid., p. 29 ff.), actions are orientated towards "usage" (Brauch), "custom" (Sitte) and "self-interest": they are orientated towards usage if it is "based on nothing but actual practice", towards custom if the "practice is based upon long standing" and towards self-interest if "actors' conduct is instrumentally (zweckrational) orientated." Hence, actions are guided by interests and ideas and orientated towards self-interests or other logic, like usages and customs.

Like Weber, Bourdieu stressed the importance of interests for actions. According to Bourdieu, a sound sociological analysis should be build on four central concepts:

habitus, field, capital and interests (Swedberg 2005b, p. 2). Bourdieu's concept of interest is closely linked to habitus, field and capital. In his later work, Bourdieu clarifies his understanding of interests by developing the concept of illusio (Böning 2009, p. 129). Bourdieu starts his main work on interests, *Is a Disinterested Act Possible?* (1998), by identifying the central assumption of sociology that people "have reasons to act and that reasons are what direct, guide, or orient their actions" (ibid., p. 76); fields are, in Bourdieu's sociology, pitches on which players compete with the usual passion and dedication of athletes (Müller 2016, p. 146). But if people have reason to act, why do players play? "Illusio [interest] is the fact of being caught up in and by the game, of believing the game is 'worth the candle' or, more simply, that playing is worth the effort" (Bourdieu 1998, p. 76f.). Interest means, therefore, that it is worth to participate, to compete, to play. Because interests mean the belief that it pays off to play in a specific field, there are as many different interests or illusios as there are fields (Swedberg 2005a, p. 381).

2.1.3 The Relation Between Ideas and Interests

As many agree nowadays that ideas and interests matter, the question about the relation between ideas and interests receives more attention. Marsh (2009) distinguishes between five main views on the relation between what he calls the "Material and the Ideational": "Materialism", "Idealism", "Post-Structuralist-", "Additive-" and "Dialectical-Position". The materialist view is particularly widespread among Marxist and rational choice contributors (Lieberman 2002, p. 699). The materialist view is characterized by the superiority of interests—"interests are given and logically prior to any beliefs held by the actors" (Goldstein & Keohane 1993, p. 4). However, materialist approaches may be divided into two subgroups: for the first, the more radical, ideas are just the idealization of vested individual or class interests. The second considers ideas and interests as substantially independent, but assumes the choice of ideas to be determined by vested interests. As maintained, for Marxists, ideas are just the veiling of vested class interests. Considering ideas as weapons in the class conflict, Gramsci outlined how institutions are used to create ideal hegemonies which facilitate and confirm the dominion of the ruling class.

Unlike Marxists, most rational choice approaches consider ideas exogenously given—which means that ideas are not the outcome of individuals' utility maximization. However, individuals chose ideas from the wide range of alternative beliefs which seem most suitable to enhance utility. Rational choice approaches distinguish between the production of ideas and the choice for ideas and this has, in principle, much in common with Max Scheler's sociology of knowledge: as maintained, Scheler distinguished between the development of new ideas determined by ideal-factors and the adoption and institutionalization of ideas influenced by real-factors. However, while Scheler outlined various real-factors and mechanisms for how ideas become powerful and institutionalize, the usual rational choice approaches focus on the functionality of ideas and the choices of atomized individuals: "ideas are reduced to functional devices employed by agents to facilitate Pareto-superior outcomes" (Blyth 1997, p. 241). In most formal rational choice approaches, the decision for ideas, like whether to follow socialism or capitalism, Christianity or Islam, is not different from choosing apples over oranges.

In contrast, idealism gives "little, if any, causative powers to the material world, rather ideas, or discourses, shape outcomes" (Marsh 2009, p. 680). From the idealistic perspective, interests are either highly restricted by ideas or little more than an expression of ideas. Idealistic perspectives are common among sociologists: for example, in Parson's structural functionalism and Luhmann's systems theory (Swedberg 2005b, p. 73; Münnich 2010, p. 42 f.), interests are considered of little primary importance. For Parsons, norms and values rather than self-interests are the fundament of social order. Discussing Durkheim's theory of social control, Parsons (1949, p. 402 ff.) argues that a social contract between the sovereign and self-interested individuals, as suggested by Hobbes, seems unrealistic for building a stable order: according to Parsons, shared norms and values are the bases of stable orders and of formal and informal rules. Hence, "the ultimate source of the power behind sanctions is the common sense of moral attachment to norms" (ibid., p. 404).

Under additive position, Marsh (2009, p. 680) subsumes the wide range of contributions which consider that ideas and interests matter, but rejects a one fits all theory of the relation between ideas and interests. Many contributions consider the relation of ideas and interests to be an empirical rather than a theoretical question. They argue that the relation between ideas and interests significantly varies from case to case which is why it can only by addressed empirically.

According to Marsh (ibid.), the dialectic position considers that the "relationship between the material and the ideational is interactive and iterative." Using Weber's switchmen metaphor, Lepsius (2009, p. 42) considered that interests and ideas are densely interwoven as ideas are interest based and interests are ideas based. In particular, constructivists highlight the interdependency of ideas and interests (Hay 2002, p. 206): ideas influence interests and interests influence ideas. Constructivists consider that true interests or pure interests only appears under the unrealistic assumption of full information and equal processing abilities of all actors (Blyth 2002, p. 28 ff.). Hence, if the future is uncertain, then "specifying interests becomes less about structural determination and more about the construction of 'wants' as mediated by beliefs and desires" (ibid., p. 29). According to Hay (2011), naturalism—which applies to most rational choice approaches—makes a systematic failure to assume a direct causal relation between context, interests and behavior. The point is that behavior is not determined by natural material self-interests, but by perceived interests: the former are considered as being determined by the economic structure, the latter are social constructions which are determined by ideas, values, norms and experiences. Naturalist interests are "objective", action guiding perceived interests are "subjective" (Schmidt 2008) constructions determined and developed by discourses, ideas and experiences. Hay (2002, p. 206) distinguish between "Thin-" and "Thick-Constructivism": the distinction is not very sharp, but the former gives a priority to ideas (for example Schmidt 2002; Schmidt and Radaelli 2004), the latter to material interests (for example Marsh 2009). Ideas determining the notion of interests—desires, wants and demands—they also indirectly determine the economic structure and therefore natural interests: shifting desires, wants and demands change the economic structure, which alters natural interests. The other way around, interests influences ideas. Mannheim (1952), Merton (1968), Bourdieu (1975) and many others highlighted the influence of interests on the production of ideas. However, they agreed that interests are one among other social forces which influence knowledge. According to Hay (2002, p. 214), the "material-ideational dialectic" is cyclic: "Cognitions" influence "Strategic Action" which shapes the "Context" and the context influences the "Discursive Selection" which influences "Cognitions".

Several contributors argued that the distinction between ideas and interests is by itself ill-founded. Post structuralists argue that there are no true interests independent from ideas, beliefs and discourses (Marsh 2009, p. 680). According to Münnich (2011), interests are determined by the interaction of "Material Interests", "Available Ideas" and "Situative Context". He considers Material interests to be the answer to the question 'what do I need?', the available ideas determine the answer to 'how should the world be?' and the assessment on the situative context frames the answer to 'given the current situation, what should I do to best satisfy my interests?'. Rather than sharply distinguishing between ideas and interests, Münnich suggests to understand interests as a three step process: at the beginning there is the social position; then people have knowledge about and beliefs in ideas; together, the two steps form the material and ideal interests, which turns into practical goal when it matches in the third step with the person's assessments about the current and future situation.

2.1.4 The Relation Between Ideas, Interests and Institutions

Due to the ideal turn in social science, the relation between ideas, interests and institutions receive more attention. Neo-institutionalism in political science and economics, which arose from the synthesis of the behavioral revolution and institutional counter-revolution, suggested that behavior is principally driven by self- and group interests, but restricted, framed and guided by the institutional setting. Considering that institutions and interests are the two factors which constitute the social order, neo-institutionalists focused on the relation between institutions and interests. More recently, due to the rising interests in ideas, it was suggested to extend the duality of institutions and interests by ideas. The difficulties of the mainstream neo-institutionalist approaches to include ideas caused contributors to develop new approaches which take ideas more serious.

Institutions have long been a central issue of social science, but in the 1960s and 1970s the treatment of institutions changed significantly; it is common to speak of a neo-institutionalism. Steadily, new neo-institutional approaches emerged. It is an open question how many different neo-institutionalisms already exist. Peters (1999) distinguishes between seven different approaches; others added further neo-institutionalism. Frequently, three main neo-institutionalisms are distinguished: historical institutionalism (HI), rational choice institutionalism (RCI) and sociological institutionalism (SI) (Hall and Taylor 1996; Blyth 2002, p. 17 ff.). According to Thelen and Steinmo (1992, p. 4 ff.), the starting point of neo-institutionalism in political science was the "behavioral revolution" of the 1950s and 1960s. Behaviorists broke up the structuralist prison of old-institutionalism by suggesting to look beyond structures and focus instead on "observable beliefs and behaviors of groups and individuals". Behaviorism closed the door for institutions. However, behavioral approaches' inability to account for differences in strategies, goals and actions among groups with rather similar preferences, reopened the door for institutions: for example, behavioral approaches failed to explain the national differences between groups with obviously similar interests. Neo-institutionalist argued that behaviorists' difficulties stem from their ignorance of institutions: both HI and RCI arose from institutional criticism on behaviorism, but maintained the principles of the behavioral revolution.

HI (Thelen and Steinmo 1992; Hall and Taylor 1996; Sanders 2008) considers politics an interaction, struggle and cooperation between individuals and in particular between unequal powerful interest groups; the interaction is framed, shaped and influenced by the institutional setting. According to Hall and Taylor (1996, p. 937), HI is strongly inspired by "group theories of politics and structural-functionalism": from the former it "accepted the contention that conflict among rival groups for scarce resources lies at the heart of politics" and from the latter the understanding of "policy as an overall system of interacting parts;" however, HI considers the "institutional organization of the policy or political economy as the principal factor structuring collective behaviour and generating distinctive outcomes." The main issue of HI, like RCI, is to study how given institutions influence political behavior. While RCI focus on how institutions influence the behavior of rational actors with given preferences, for HI the development of preferences, interests, strategies and goals are themselves the research subjects, considered to depend on the institutional setting (Thelen and Steinmo 1992, p. 8 f.). For the HI, different preferences, interests, strategies and goals of rather similar interest groups may be traced back to different institutional environments. Interests shape political interaction, and at the same time HI considers that institutions are themselves the outcome of past struggles between unequal powerful groups with certain preferences, interests, strategies and goals. Representing a long history of past political interactions, HI considers institutions path dependent formations. To explain institutions and actions within the institutional setting, it is necessary to understand the path dependent "historical development of the institution" and the "original, distinct culture and problems in which it arose" (Sanders 2008, p. 39).

RCI (see Hall and Taylor 1996; Weingast 2002; Shepsle 2008) is strongly orientated towards the standard neoclassical approach and assumes that guided by their exogenously given preferences individuals form strategies to maximize utility. Politics are considered collective action dilemmas in which institutions are formed and supported because of their functional value (Hall and Taylor 1996, p. 944 f.). According to Weingast (2002, p. 661), the RCI targets several main questions: "The effects of institutions" and "why institutions take particular forms, why they are needed, and why they survive." However, RCI may be divided into two main approaches (Shepsle 2008): the first treats institutions as exogenously given frames and the second as endogenously negotiated and formed by rational behaving actors. The first focus on how institutions affect rational individuals: generally, it is considered that "institutions constrain individual choices, how individuals interact, their information and beliefs, and their payoffs" (Weingast 2002, p. 662). Institutions are the "strategic context" (Thelen and Steinmo 1992, p. 7) in which rational self-interests actors behave. The second approach understands institutions as rules of the game on which players agree (Shepsle 2008, p. 25). Hence, the second strand analyses why institutions exist, why they take certain forms and why they survive. The answer of the RCI is: institutions exist because they are functional; they reduce costs or increase gains, facilitate coordination and solve collective action dilemmas. The forms of institutions are determined by actors' specific incentives and survive if self-enforcing mechanisms support their existence (c.f. Weingast 2002).

As maintained, SI (see Hall and Taylor 1996; Brinton 1998; Peters 1999; Hasse and Krücken 2009) focus on how ideas, culture, norms, values and taken for granted assumptions influence organizations and actors. SI may be divided into two main groups: the world policy approach and the neo-institutionalism of organization sociology (Hasse and Krücken 2009). Based on the works of Max Weber, the neo-institutionalism of organization sociology analyzes forms, structures and processes of organizations. As Meyer and Rowan (1977) maintained and DiMaggio and Powell (1983) argued, organizations are forced by different social mechanism to adopt widely shared general ideas and beliefs to gain legitimacy, resources and stability. Dobbin (1997) extended the concept of the SI to politics.

Focusing on organizations and their interaction, neo-institutionalism of organization sociology misses a macro-sociological perspective. The world policy approach fills the gap and develops a macro-sociological, institutional perspective (Hasse and Krücken 2009). Collective value systems like "culture theories, ideologies, and prescriptions about how society works or should work" (Meyer et al. 1994, p. 9) given to people by their socialization determine, guide and frame individuals' actions. According to the contributors of the world policy approach, global culture steadily converges. The heterogeneous premodern cultures are steadily replaced by a unique western culture of rationality, fairness and cosmopolitism (Hasse and Krücken 2009, p. 243). Due to the diffusion of the unique modern culture, the world's societies are increasingly dominated by three entities: individuals, organizations and states.

As maintained, HI and RCI are traditionally focused on institutions and interests. Challenged by theoretical and practical problems, both HI and RCI took an "ideational turn" (Blyth 1997). According to Blyth (ibid., p. 230), HI made its ideational turn due to "problems in conceptualizing change by agents" and the RCI due to the "inability of game theory to identify a priori specific Nash equilibrium." However, he (ibid., p. 229) criticizes that both approaches "treat ideas instrumentally and functionally, rather than as progressive extension of their research programs." Campbell (1998: p. 377 f.) criticized that HI over focus on how ideas frame and constrain actions, but mostly ignore the empowering and facilitating character of ideas. In the last decade, ideas gained ground in HI studies, but much still has to be done to overcome the divide between ideal approaches and HI (Blyth et al. 2016).

In rational choice approaches, ideas, like institutions, are functional; ideas are applied if they reduce costs, increase benefits and facilitate coordination. Goldstein and Keohane (1993: 12) outlined three main mechanism of how ideas influence politics compatible with the rational choice approach: first "ideas serve as road maps", second "ideas contribute to outcomes in the absence of a unique equilibria" and third "ideas embedded in institutions specify policy in the absence of innovations." Uncertain about the future, the consequences of actions and the best choice from the wide range of possible alternatives, according to Goldstein and Keohane (ibid., p. 13 ff.), actors use ideas as road maps. Ideas help actors transfer preferences into favored goals and policies, to form expectation about the future and the consequences of actions, and to reduce the costs of searching for the best action and means to reach their goals. Game theory studies have shown that many games are characterized by multiple equilibria. In multiple equilibria games, shared ideas help coordinate actors to reach and maintain the Pareto optimal solution. According to Goldstein and Keohane (ibid., p. 20 ff.), ideas also influence political outcome as they enter various institutions. Because institutions usually change slowly, institutionalized ideas still influence politics even if ideas as widely shared beliefs vanish. Several contributions in the book of Goldstein and Keohane studied the three outlined mechanisms empirically: John Ikenberry, for example, showed how Keynesianism became America's post-World War II political road map. Geoffrey Garrett and Barry Weingeits argued, in a widely recognized chapter, that shared ideas enabled European countries to reach an agreement on the implementation and the design of free trade. Katzenstein argued that the response to terrorism in Germany and Japan was quite different because their institutions were built on different ideas. However, rational choice approaches have several major shortcomings: Blyth (1997, p. 239) considers that in the rational choice approaches "ideas merely supplement other forms of explanation." In the RCI, ideas account for the residual: ideas explain what cannot be explained by atomized individual self-interested actions. Overall, ideas are considered functional: ideas help reduce uncertainty and costs, and help find solutions in difficult situations; hence, ideas are not dysfunctional in the sense that they increase uncertainty or make coordination more difficult.

Because the SI traditionally focused on ideas, norms and values, unlike HI and RCI, the SI was not in need for an ideal turn: many sociological contributions analyzed how norms, culture templates, internalized practices, taken for granted assumptions, hidden ideas, influence organizations, relations, interactions, actions and the collective memory. Acting in accordance to norms, taken for granted assumptions and values that represent hidden ideas, actors institutionalize and therefore reinforce hidden ideas. The main strength of the SI is that it also takes into account hidden, unknown ideas which are somehow institutionalized as norms, values and taken for granted assumption. At the same time, the SI was, rightly, criticized for over focusing on ideas and hidden cultures and therefore overlooking political power, political agency and vested interests (Campbell 1998; Finnemore 1996). In addition, SI intensively discussed the influence of a given culture, but had little to say about why and how ideas or cultures change.

As maintained, each of the three approaches were fiercely criticized: SI pays little attention to interests and hardly addresses the relation between ideas and other institutions. In addition, SI usually treats ideas as a given which is why the rise and implementation of new ideas are hardly analyzed. For RCI, ideas matter if ideas are needed and ideas are always functional and never dysfunctional. HI understands ideas first and foremost as constraints and ignores the empowering character of ideas. In particular, HI and RCI were criticized for threatening, at last implicitly, ideas and interests as independent factors, what Pojani and Stead (2014, p. 2405) consider the "Competing Variables" approach. Inspired by the critic on HI and RCI competing variables, the developing constructivist institutionalism (CI) and discursive institutionalism (DI) treat ideas, interests and institutions as highly interwoven and mutual dependent: the "Mutually Determining Variables" approach (ibid.).

Possible cross-influences between ideas, interests and institutions are manifold. As maintained, various sociological studies, like Mannheim and Merton, argued that interests shape ideas and knowledge. Ideas need strong carriers to diffuse and institutionalize. Often, carriers support ideas which underpin their vested interests: doubtlessly, ideas carried by the most influential and powerful groups are most likely to become dominant and institutionalize. However, as maintained, carriers shape ideas by transferring pure into applied theories. Transformations are hardly neutral as carriers usually develop applied theories particularly supportive of their vested interests: "carriers are never neutral modes of transmission, but affect the nature of the message and the ways it is received" (Scott 2014b, p. 96). Supported and carried by widely recognized experts, the mass media, policy advisers and other second-hand dealers (Brugger and Pantelic 2018), ideas institutionalize as formal and informal rules, curricular, road maps, taken for granted assumption, myths etc. Once institutionalize ideas become efficacious, stabilize and force even non-believers to act accordingly, they "become embedded in organizations, patterns of discourse, and collective identities" (Berman 2001, p. 238); in particular as they enter formal rules, ideas influence emancipates from its initial carriers (Yee 1996, p. 89). Berman (2001, p. 238) distinguishes between two approaches of institutionalization of ideas: the first "focuses on how ideational variables become embedded in organizations like bureaucracies and political parties, tangible institutions […] the other focuses on how ideas become embedded in social norms, patterns of discourse, and collective identities, intangible institutions." The former approach is widely used by political scientists; the latter dominates sociological contributions.

Interests are influenced by institutions and ideas. As maintained, according to the HI interests are developed within and shaped by the institutional setting. Contributors of the

HI argue that similar groups develop different interests because they are influenced by different institutional settings (Thelen and Steinmo 1992). At the same time, as highlighted by the HI and the RCI, vested interests institutionalize and therefore shape the institutional environment. Despite institutions, ideas shape interests: the CI considers that actors are orientated towards perceived interests rather than towards natural interests. Perceived interests are determined by actors' beliefs. In addition, ideas legitimize and empower vested interests and shape the institutionalization of interests: according to Lepsius (2009, p. 42), interests are ideas based because ideas constitute a set of legitimate means. Ideas strengthen vested interests as they attract supporters, function as weapons in the political process and facilitate coalition building. Ideas shape the institutionalization of interests as they transfer general interest into political demands.

According to the HI, institutions restrict ideas and interests. Institutions frame ideas and interests as they specify the boundaries within ideas and interests may operate: institutions determine legitimate and illegitimate interest, ideas and demands. As maintained, institutions are often previously institutionalized interests and ideas that survived in resistant institutions. Goldstein and Keohane (1993, p. 20 f.) considered that institutions reflect the "power of some idea" and the "interests of the powerful," but that institutions shape policies even if "interests that promoted some statute may fade over time" and no one still "genuinely believes in them [ideas]." Hence, present ideas and interests are framed and empowered by institutions which are build on former interests and ideas. In addition, the institutional setting accelerates or hinders the diffusion of new ideas (Rogers 1983; Strang and Meyer 1993; Navaretti 1998).

Hence, like maintained by Pojani and Stead (2014, p. 2406), the relation between ideas, interests and institutions is cyclic, highly interdependent and interwoven: ideas shape perceived interests and influence the institutional setting as they institutionalize. Interests shape ideas as groups of interests influence the content of ideas and which ideas diffuse and institutionalize by using their means to promote, spread and protect favored ideas and fight the unwelcome ones. Interests also influence institutions more directly by shaping the process of institution building. Institutions specify the frame within which ideas and interests operate. The given institutional setting facilitates or hinders the spread of ideas and interests. Thus, the relation between ideas, interests and institutions is highly interdependent, interwoven and cross-stimulating.

2.2 Three Main Orders: Political, Economic and Cultural

The theory of social differentiation is a core concept of sociology. Advocates consider that modernity is characterized by the differentiation of society into relatively autonomous subsystems. From contributors to the early beginnings of sociology like Durkheim ([1893] 1984), Simmel ([1908] 2009), Marx ([1867] 1977), to more recent authors like Parsons (1951), Luhmann and many others (Schimank 1996), famous sociologists developed theories of social differentiation. Identifying subsystems and describing the relation between them, theories of social differentiation are far from any consensus about the number and type of subsystems. According to Schimank (2010, p. 261), at least dozen subsystems are frequently distinguished: economy, politics, law, military, religion, art, science, journalism, education, health, sports and sexuality.

Following the principles of the theories of social differentiation, several contributors argued that societies may be divided into more fundamental subsystems. Michael Mann (2012, pp. 1–33), for example, distinguished four main sources and organizations of power: "Ideological", "Economic", "Military" and "Political". Kraemer (2017) and Wehler (1989, pp. 6–12) argue that Max Weber distinguishes three fundamental types of order: the cultural, economic, and political order. According to Wehler (ibid., p. 7 ff.), every society is characterized by a unique cultural, economic, and political order. He considers that economy, culture and dominion or the cultural, economic, and political order are the three basic or fundamental dimensions which constitute societies. Wehler argues that the three fundamental dimensions are principally, at least theoretically, equally important, relatively autonomous, but at the same time interwoven and interdependent.

2.2.1 The Political, Economic and Cultural Order

Principally following Wehler and Kraemer that societies consist of the three fundamental orders, the meaning of economic, political and cultural order needs clarification. The cultural order consists of ideas. As maintained, it is relatively common to distinguish between different forms of ideas, along the continuum of abstract theories on the one end and practical application and popular beliefs on the other: Keynes and Hayek distinguish between ideas of academics and the derived ideas of the general public; the Advocacy coalition Framework approach differentiates between deep core, policy core, and secondary beliefs; for Goldstein and Koehane, there are world views, principled beliefs and causal beliefs; and Brugger and Pantelic (2018) distinguish between pure theory, applied theory, implementations and popular beliefs. Empirically, in particular when looking at historical events, a clear-cut distinction between different forms of ideas is difficult which is why they are subsumed under the umbrella term of ideas.

No doubt that the cultural order of societies is characterized by a wide range of, more or less harmonic, ideas. As maintained, Schimank found at leasta dozen subsystems—economy, politics, law, military, religion, art, science, journalism, education, health, sports and sexuality—which are considered relatively autonomous by the theories of social differentiation. Of course, different ideas influence different subsystems. Because subsystems are relatively autonomous, ideas influencing different subsystems are also relatively autonomous: for example, ideas highly influencing religion are not necessarily present in sports. However, world views are naturally imperialistic and have the aspirations to influence all subsystems: looking at the great theories of liberalism or socialism, for example, both theories have the aspiration to determine each and every subsystem.

Hence, various ideas simultaneously influence different subsystems: certain ideas are in relative harmony, while others are more conflicting.

As outlined, according to Kuhn (1970), science is during normal times characterized by dominating paradigms or ideas that are hardly contested. Deep crises question the adequacy of the dominant paradigm or idea and often cause ideal revolutions in which the old idea is replaced by a new and better idea. Empirically, it seems that there are times in which certain ideas dominate subsystems or even various subsystems, however there are always challenging ideas carried by more or less powerful groups. Analyzing the field of science, Bourdieu (1975) argued that carriers of ideas compete over the monopolization of scientific authority: however, "monopoly" and "full competition" of scientific authority (ibid., p. 29) are ideal types that are never reached practically. Normal times are usually close to monopolies, but there are nevertheless always what Fligstein and McAdam (2015) consider "Challengers"; people who follow alternative ideas and challenge "Incumbents" positions. Within subsystems, big ideas like liberalism, socialism and nationalism compete against each other. However, disputes between applied theories orientated towards the same big theory are often not less intensive than between big theories.

Analyzing the historical development of the European banking sector, I here focus on ideas which seemed to have had most influence on the development of banking. The historical study of the development of the banking sector yielded three main findings on the relation between ideas and the development of the banking sector: first, the development of the banking sector was largely determined by ideas. Second, great breaks and most fundamental innovations of the banking sector were induced or accompanied by fundamental changes in the cultural order. Third, subfields of the banking sector were dominated by different, often conflicting, ideas.

The economic order is characterized by what Marx calls production conditions, institutions,—markets, formal and informal rules, ideas, traditions, taken for granted assumption etc. –, framing, constraining and enabling organizations and actors whose actions are "concerned with the satisfaction of a desire, for 'utilities' (Nutzleistungen). 'Economic action' (Wirtschaften) is any peaceful exercise of an actor's control over resources which is in its main impulse oriented towards economic ends" (Weber [1922] 1978, p. 63). Inspired by Karl Marx, Wehler (1989, p. 10) defined the economic order as characterized by actions in which actors' metabolization with the nature aims to satisfy their material wants.

The economic order is dominated by two main dimensions: distribution and production. Who gets what and how much of it (distribution), and who makes what, where, how, with whom and how much of it (production) are the principle questions of the economic order. The economic order is the place where goods and services are produced. Answering the main question: what is produced, where, how, by whom and how much of it is contested and conflictual. However, despite all conflicts, there exists a need that production of goods and services reach a certain degree of cooperation. Hence, each major production question opens much space for conflicts between different groups and persons; however, to every production question a certain degree of cooperation, a compromise, is needed to ensure the production of goods and services. Who gets what and how much of it, hence the distribution questions, are closely related with the production question. Answering the question of who gets which goods and services and how much of it is as conflictual as answering the production question. Like in the case of the production questions, despite all deep conflicts, the production of goods and services can only succeed if a minimum consensus on the distribution questions exists.

To each fundamental production and distribution questions, groups of the economic order favor different answers. The different (theoretical) position of groups, determined by the economic structure, on the central questions of the economic order we consider as natural interests. Hence, despite the traditional conflictual question of who gets how much of the produced services and goods, the fundamental questions of the economic order create various additional natural interests; some of them may be harmonic, others conflicting. Historical answers to the fundamental production and distribution questions always distribute the economic means to enforce the specific natural interests. The answers to who gets what and how much of it, who makes what, where, how, with whom and how much of it, always distributes the power to enforce carried natural interests among the actors of the economic order: for example, the answer of what is to be produced where and with which technique makes certain groups more pivotal and others more superfluous. The distribution of the produced goods equips certain groups with better means to enforce their interests than others. Hence, the economic order determines natural interests and the ability to enforce them.

Their is little doubt that the banking sector is at the core of the economic order. The structure of the banking sector highly determines the central production and distribution questions and the distribution of power and influence between groups of natural interests: who has access to credit, on which conditions and of what scale, who is permitted to open banks under which conditions, and what are the goals of banks, strongly determines the answers to the central production and distribution questions and the distribution of power and influence. Analyzing the historical development of the European banking sector has shown that: the development of the economic order and the banking sector are highly interdependent and interacting; fundamental changes of the banking sector deeply influenced the structure of the economic order; natural interests were strengthened, others weakened and new ones emerged. Hence, the banking innovations fundamentally changed the structure of natural interests and the distribution of power and influence between economic groups. At the same time, fundamental changes of the economic order, hence in the structure of natural interests and the distribution of power and influence between economic groups, usually caused deep changes in the banking sector.

The political order is the place where groups with different political interests compete over the implementation of their interests. Following the HI political processes are conflicts between interests groups striving to realize outcomes best suitable to their interests. According to Bourdieu (2001), in the political field actors compete over the monopolization of the political interpretation and separation principle, and hence for legitimate political influence. Different groups use their resources of "legal authority", "public opinion", "information", "mobilizable troops", "financial resources", "skillful leadership" (Sabatier and Weible 2009, p. 201 ff.) and their ability to form stable coalitions to enforce their demands. Actors compete over institutions, permissions, appointments, organizations and distributions. Political actors are groups which represent interests of actors of other subsystems—like economy, politics, law, military, religion, art, science, journalism, education, health, sports and sexuality—and transfer their specific interests into political demands. Considered representatives of non-political interests, like other subsystems, the political order still has a certain degree of autonomy and follows its own logic. As maintained, groups' ability to enforce their demands depends on their resources and means and their ability to form coalitions, but is also highly determined by the institutional setting and the specific political structure. Politics is not a free play of forces, but actors are rather constrained, framed and empowered by various political institutions, like formal and informal rules, ideas, political traditions, voting systems, political regimes and so on. Hence, constrained, framed and empowered by political institutions, political groups of interests use their resources, means and abilities to form coalitions that will influence institutions, permissions, appointments, organizations and distributions.

Studying the historical development of the European banking sector shows that hardly any other market was more contested politically. Several reasons made the banking sector in particular a hot topic: first, political groups were usually aware that deep changes in the banking sector fundamentally alter the economic order and the political distribution. Hardly any important group of the political order was unaffected by the structure of the banking sector. Second, facing recurrent financial crises, politicians were aware of the danger of unwise banking innovations. Third, the banking sector was considered pivotal for the economic, political and military development of the country. Most fundamental banking innovations were caused, accompanied by or entailed far-reaching political decisions. Indirectly by changing the institutional setting, but also directly by founding, shaping or prohibiting banks, the political influence on the development of the European banking sectors was huge. Various political groups, many of them not very predestined for deeply changing financial markets at first sight, strongly influenced the development of the banking sector. Far-reaching banking innovations usually significantly changed the political order: they empowered certain groups and weakened others and considerably altered the states' financial situation. In addition, there was hardly any other economic group with a more direct and strong political influence than bankers. Financing governments' deficits, economic and political projects and in particular their military adventures, bankers were often hated but needed partners: aware of their pivotal importance, bankers frequently used their political power to influence decisions and blackmail the government.

2.2.2 The Interdependence of the Three Orders

As maintained, the three orders are to a certain extent autonomous, but at the same time highly interwoven and mutually dependent. Each order influences and is influenced by the other two orders. The mechanism of orders' mutual influences are different; several main ways of how orders influence each other will be outlined here.

The economic order is influenced by the cultural order in various ways: directly and indirectly. Several economic and sociological studies showed how ideas, norms and values influence economic behavior and interests. Three main mechanism for how ideas directly influence the economic order may be distinguished. First, ideas as moral constraints and social expectations: above, several studies of the sociology of markets were outlined, which studied how moral boundaries influenced markets. Contributors of the SI described how economic actors are forced by isomorphism to meet social expectations derived from widely recognized ideas. Second, as outlined, the CI considers that interests are social constructions determined by ideas. Natural interests are defined here as groups' and persons' objectively favored answers—in the sense of being determined by the economic structure—to the main production and distribution questions. However, the CI considers that actions are guided by perceived rather than by natural interests. Following what Hay considers thin constructivism, it is assumed that perceived interests emerge from the interaction of natural interests and actors beliefs: perceived interests are interpretations and specifications of natural interests using specific ideas. Third, ideas function as road maps: as road maps, ideas are imaginations of the function of the world which translate perceived interests into concrete desires and demands and guide actors' behaviors. In addition, ideas indirectly influence the economic order as they shape the political process and therefore institutions.

Usually, direct influences of ideas on markets are rather difficult to detect: sociological studies on the direct influence of ideas on markets use some of the relatively rare examples were the influence is particularly pronounced. The banking sector seems to be one of these rare examples where ideas directly influence development. Until the beginning of the 19th century, widespread religious and moral reservations on money lending against interest payments highly influenced and hampered the development of the banking sector. Religious prohibition of money lending also entered laws, and kept many from participating in the banking market within the legal boundaries. In addition, many banks, several of them of the utmost importance, were founded and operated by people propelled by their beliefs: non-profit banks, but also many of the big joint-stock banks were founded by men who followed their convictions, without vested material interests in banking.

The political order's influence on economic is a central topic of political science and in particular of economic neo-institutionalism. Various economic neo-institutional contributions (see for example Williamson 1985; Ostrom 2011; North 2005; Greif 2006) highlight how institutions formed in political processes shape and influence economics.

Institutions are usually considered as political agreements that restrict self-interest behavior, overcome market failures and therefore maintain the economic order. Practically, politics' influence on the economic order oversteps the relatively passive intervention of just keeping things going: widely recognized politics heavily intervenes in every dimension of the economic order. Political interventions significantly shape distributions and influence productions even in countries which are considered particularly market-friendly: elsewhere, politics heavily intervenes into macroeconomic goals, legitimized mechanism, actors' status and resources, relations between economic actors, forms of economic organizations, action alternatives and the fundamental economic structure.

However, in addition to the intended consequences, political interventions usually cause unintended effects. Hence, politics are the place of intended effects; the true practical and perhaps unintended effects of political measurements turn up in institutions' implementation in the economic order; broadly speaking, the economic order decides on the practical consequences of political interventions. As maintained, interventions in the banking sector were politically particularly controversial: hardly any other economic sector caused more long-lasting and controversial political discussions. Historically, the political influence on the banking sectors was quite pronounced. The issue of central banking and money was frequently discussed and heavily regulated: what is money, who is allowed to produce money and how much money should be distributed, was usually determined by governments. In addition to central banking, ordinary private banks and even non-profit banks were heavily regulated and most of the time guided by government. Changing institutional settings causing several of the most pivotal banking innovations, the development of the banking sector was strongly marked by unintended effects of political decisions.

As maintained, the political order is characterized by the struggle between unequally powerful political interest groups. The economic order produces groups with different natural and perceived interests which enter, in one way or another, the political order and pursue their demands. Groups' ability to enforce their demands depends on the resources they receive in the economic order. Hence, the answer to the fundamental questions of the economic order strongly influences political processes. More generally, as the place of production, the economic order produces the resources to maintain the political apparatus and to implement political measurements. Frequently, bankers were among the politically most influential groups of the economic order. Several reasons made bankers particularly powerful: due to their strong ties to all economic sectors and their good overviews and economies' needs for bankers, they often became the mouthpiece of the bourgeoisie. Considered particularly important for the smooth economic development, politicians maintained close ties to bankers; economies' main financers. Most importantly, bankers were governments' main lenders: highly indebted and in need of bankers' support to implement their ambitious projects, politicians heavily depended on bankers.

Above, various mechanisms of how ideas influence politics were outlined: as maintained, ideas are constraints and frames, they legitimize and prescribe demands and behavior, empower groups, function as road maps, programs and weapons, reduce uncertainty, facilitate coalition building and so on. More generally, the political order is the arena where ideas meet interests. To become institutionalized, ideas need strong carriers, political groups which use their means to support and spread ideas and defend them against attacks. At the same time, political groups use ideas to legitimize their interests, as weapons against other groups, as road maps to constructing their political demands. In the political order, ideas and interests become efficacious as they institutionalize or remain ineffective if they fail to enter institutions. Once institutionalized, ideas and interests often remain efficacious if groups stop carrying them. Ideas on banking frequently strongly influenced political decisions. Usually, the influence of economic ideas and political decisions is, at best, indirect: frequently, economists complain that politicians are not listening. In the case of banking, this was often quite different: banking economists dominated political discussions and regulations and closely followed economists' advice. Left-wing and liberal banking theorists quite directly influenced political decisions.

As maintained, the sociology of knowledge highlighted how political and economic interests influence the production and distribution of ideas. Mannheim considered that all knowledge and ideas are determined by a wide range of social factors; like the economic and political structure, the distribution of power, interests and so on. Scheler ([1926] 1960) argued: to diffuse, institutionalize and become powerful, ideas need to attract Real Factors like political and economic power, networks and intellectual authority. Hence, there can be little doubt that economics and politics highly influence the content and the diffusion of ideas. Once again, the influence of economics and politics on banking theories was more open than for many other ideas. Many of the outstanding banking theorists were also notable bankers and/or politicians.

2.2.3 Stability and Change of the Three Orders

Explicitly or implicitly, mainstream sociology, political science and economics share the assumption that fundamental social orders are in principle relatively stable. Introductions to sociology often start with the allegory that societies are like oceans: the waves on the top are the visible recurrent change, but the more interesting fundament, the deep structure, the ocean layers, change very slowly or are almost stable. Focusing on equilibria stages, rather than on changes, at least implicitly, the neoclassical standard model suggests that economics is static. In sharp contrast, Karl Marx and the Austrian School of economics (see Schumpeter [1911] 1934, [1939] 1989; Hayek 1945) regard capitalist economies as a restless dynamic process of innovation and imitation. Contributors of the HI, RCI and SI usually assume that institutions are sticky which is why they predominately focus on the description of the institutional status quo rather than on change. Developed to analyze static systems, each of the three neo-institutionalist approaches leaves little room for change. Focusing on the path dependent development of institutions and institutional lock-in effects, the HI lacks the instruments to account for major institutional changes; considering that institutions are functional agreements between rational utility maximizing actors, the RCI perspective leaves little space for endogenous institutional change; arguing that organizations and actors are forced by the social pressure of isomorphism to adopt cultural norms, it seems that the SI approach also lacks an endogenous explanation of change.

More recently, the interest in deep changes seems to increase in social sciences. However, the notion of social change is by no means clear: returning to the allegory that societies are like oceans, it seems reasonable to distinguish between minor changes—the small waves—and major changes—shifts in the deep structure, in oceans' layers. For Hall (1993, p. 278), policymaking is a process of "three central variables: the overarching goals that guide policy in a particular field, the techniques or policy instruments used to attain those goals, and the precise settings of these instruments." He considers frequent changes in the precise settings of instruments: "First-Order Changes"; less frequent shifts in techniques and instruments: "Second-Order Changes"; and very rare changes in overreaching goals: "Third order Changes." Similarly, Thelen and Steinmo (1992) distinguish between minor "policy change within stable institutions" and major changes with "Institutions as objects of change." Using the developed heuristic, minor changes in the economic order are for example new products, technical adjustments and new firms; new laws and political players, changing instruments and measurements in the political order; and in the cultural order new applied theories and implications and smaller changes in the popular beliefs and pure theory. The important point is that minor changes leave the fundamental structures of orders unchanged. However, because the three types of orders are interdependent, minor changes in one order usually induce minor changes in other orders. Major changes fundamentally shape the deep structure of the economic, political and cultural order; a major change in one order usually entails major changes in the other two orders.

In social science, two principal approaches on social change may be distinguished: evolutionary and punctual equilibrium approaches. Both are found among sociological, political science and economic studies. Evolutionary approaches consider societies, politics and economies as immanently dynamic, which is why they focus on the processes of change rather than on short times of stability. Recently, evolutionary approaches enjoy a renaissance in economics (Nelson and Winter 2004) and political science (Kerr 2002; Steinmo 2010; Blyth 2011).

However, punctual equilibrium approaches still dominate social science. According to the punctual equilibrium approaches (see Krasner 1984; Pierson 2004; Baumgartner and Jones 2009; Thelen and Conran 2016), long-term stable equilibria are disrupted by rare breakdowns. Deep crises, uncertainty and the rise of promising alternatives cause the shift from one stable equilibria to another. Sociologists like Comte, Marx and Durkheim suggesting a stepwise development of societies and neoclassical mainstream dynamic models understanding economic change as a gradual shift from one to another equilibria are in principle punctual equilibrium approaches. Recently giving more attention to institutional change, neo-institutionalists predominately use punctual equilibrium approaches (Thelen and Conran 2016): punctual equilibrium approaches have the advantage to be compatible with the assumption of principally stable institutions. Principally following the punctual equilibrium approaches, it is assumed that the deep structure of the economic, political and cultural order hardly changes. According to the outlined heuristic, stability means that dominant ideas, most powerful interests and important institutions are in harmony; dominant ideas are carried, or at least not opposed, by the most powerful and influential groups of the political and economic order, and dominant ideas and interests institutionalized in central institutions. Hence, if ideas, interests and institutions build a closed harmonic set, the social order is principally stable. Major changes are caused by, out of whatever reason, fundamental changes in the economic, political and cultural order, which disturbs the harmonic relation between ideas, interests and institutions.

As maintained, for the punctual equilibrium approach crises are the main force of change. Deep crises shake the fundamental structure, the status quo and open the window for deep change (Surel 2000, p. 504). Usually, it is assumed that exogenous disturbances, like economic crises, wars and the rise of new ideas make visible institutions' inability to deal with challenges, causing elites' critic of the status quo. Many contributions followed Kuhn's (1970) idea that crises and the critic of the status quo causes scientific, institutional, political and social revolutions. Unsatisfied with the cursory treatment of crises and change, several institutional contributions outlined endogenous mechanisms of change. Thelen and Conran (2016, p. 46 ff.) surveyed new HI, RCI and SI approaches on institutional change. RCI considers that change may stem from exogenous disturbances or endogenous reasons like "amendment rules", "suspensions of rules" and "broken rules". SI focuses on the diffusion of new ideas and how institutions hamper and facilitate change. Institutional gaps are considered by HI contributions as the main force of change: Thelen and Conran (ibid., p. 57) categorize the gaps as "Limits of Institutional Design", "Compromises", "Time" and "Power". Limits of institutional design means the gap between the planned and the real functioning of institutions. Compromises between groups of interests bring institutions far from the blueprint. Gaps in time mean the unequal durability of institutions and the political conditions from which institutions arise: as maintained, institutions originate from specific historical combinations of ideas and interests. However, because institutions are usually stable, new ideas and interests are inconsistent with old institutions. Power takes account of the fact that institutions always create winners and losers; or incumbents and challengers. Each gap is a potential source of fundamental critic and institutional change.

Using the outlined heuristic, crises are deep changes in the cultural, political, and economic order which corrode the harmonic relation between ideas, interests and institutions. Crises may stem from each order, but deep change in one order usually causes fundamental changes in the other orders. Technological change, institutional change, the rise of new ideas, shifts in the power distribution and economic crises are major changes in the economic order, which fundamentally questions the agreements on the distribution and production question. Various mechanisms transfer major changes of the economic order into disturbances of the other orders: creating and empowering groups with specific natural interests and redistributing goods, services, power and influence, usually shifts the power balance in the political order. Likewise, changing forces behind natural interest alter the cultural order as carriers of specific ideas are empowered and other weakened, new groups demand and support the development of new ideas.

Breakdowns of strong and stable collations, the rise of new political powers, regime changes, the infiltration of new interest groups and the rise of new ideas are potential sources of major changes within the political order. The redistribution of political power among groups carrying different ideas and interests questions the established harmonic system between ideas, interests and institutions. New or strengthened groups strong enough to change the institutional setting by institutionalizing their own ideas and interests alter the institutional environment of the economic order. In addition, the shifting balance of power affects the cultural order as strengthened groups demand new ideas and develop new applied theories.

The rise of new ideas which attracts many supporters or a significant shift in the balance of power between supporters of different ideas, dominant ideas failing to explain new phenomena (Kuhn 1970; Hall 1993; Surel 2000; Blyth 2002) and their being considered inadequate road maps in changing environments, may cause deep crises of the established cultural order. Ideal revolutions, and hence the change of dominant ideas, usually significantly changes the economic and political order. New dominant ideas carried by powerful groups change the political order as they bring about new road maps, explanations of the world, political weapons and fundaments for new coalitions. As new ideas institutionalize in the political process, they indirectly change the economic order by altering the institutional environment. More directly, as maintained, ideas influence the behavior of participants of the economic order as road maps or moral boundaries.

As maintained, stability means that dominant ideas, interests of the most powerful groups and the institution setting are in a harmonic relation. Harmonic does not mean the absence of alternatives and critics; harmonic means that most powerful groups and coalitions support the institutional setting because their vested interests and carried ideas institutionalize and dominate the institutional setting. Harmonic systems are relatively stable because of the support from the most powerful actors; dominant ideas have the predominance over interpretation, guidance and legitimization; institutionalized ideas and interests also affect non-carriers and non-believers; and stable harmonic systems are functional in the sense that they reduce uncertainty and facilitate the formation of stable expectations. Minor changes of the economic, cultural and political order do not affect the harmonic relation.

In contrast, major changes usually bring the established relation between ideas, interests and institutions out of harmony. Disturbances of the harmonic relation may arise from changes in each of the three dimensions: ideas, interests and institutions. Various studies showed how new ideas influence and shape politics and economies (Kingdon 1984; Hall 1989; Inglehart 1997; McNamara 1999; Blyth 2002; Leighton and López

2014). It was already outlined how new ideas emerge, spread, become powerful or fail. New ideas which diffuse and become powerful question perceived interests and the adequacy and legitimacy of institutions. Perceived interests and institutions are legitimized due to their orientation towards dominant ideas. Ideal revolutions force perceived interests and institutions to adapt to the new dominant ideas in order to regain legitimization. Propelling interests and institutions to adjust, the new dominant idea "creates its own backers" (Mehta 2011, p. 29). By institutionalizing and entering perceived interests, new ideas become efficacious.

As maintained, economists and political scientists in particular assume that interests are the main driver of behavior and consider that changing interests are the main reason of change (see Schickler 2001; Swenson 2002). Using the outlined heuristic, major changes in the political and economic order break up the harmonic relation by shifting naturalist and perceived interests. Changing interests or shifts in the balance of power of interests make carriers question the adequacy of dominant ideas and institutions. As outlined, according to the sociology of knowledge, interests influence the content and the diffusion and power of ideas which is why fundamental changes in the structure of interests often cause ideal revolutions. Institutions representing old interests and ideas, politicians face the demand from carriers of new interests and ideas to adapt the institutional setting to the rising interests and ideas. Losing the endorsement of powerful carriers of new interests and ideas, in order to regain support institutions need to adjust to the rising interests and ideas. Institutionalizing and shaping the cultural order, new interests stabilize and become efficacious.

Institutions dissolve the harmonic relation in two ways: as brakes or as boosters. Because institutions tend to adapt more slowly than interests and ideas, the harmonic relation breaks up as institutions fail to change simultaneously with ideas and interests. At the same time, institutions are also drivers of change: institutions as boosters. For example, if institutions are initiated from outside, like in the case of international laws implemented in national institutional settings, institutional change breaks up the harmonic relation and propels change. Unable to ward off institutional change, ideas and interests need to adjust to the changing institutional setting to re-institutionalize in the changed institutional frame.

Hence, major change and the breakup of the harmonic relation may arise from all three dimensions: ideas, interests and institutions. Wherever change originates, the adaption to disturbances is often a long-lasting, conflictual process. No matter how long it takes and how bloody it is, a new punctual equilibrium is reached if ideas, interests and institutions adjust and arrive at a new harmonic relation. Because ideas, interests and institutions are highly interconnected and often change simultaneously, it is not always clear where major change had initially originated.

3 Italian Financial Capitalism: The Birth of Modern Banking

Despite all moral reservations and hostility against the idle usurer, money lending against interest payments and other banking activities are thousands of years old. The rise of merchant capitalism in the Italian City-States accelerated the spread and deepened banking activities, but the fundamental banking structure and activities hardly changed: banking still mostly occurred within personal relations between lenders and borrowers, highly limited by interest restrictions and usury laws. Just as governments faced serious problems to finance rampant war costs and profitable investment opportunities became quite scarce, a historical window opened for a far-reaching banking innovation: the foundation of the first modern banks.

Impelled by governments' need for fast money to finance wars and elites' desire for banking innovations, intensive debates on interest payments and usury restrictions significantly changed scholastics' position on banking and money lending. Relaxing restrictions on money lending opened and facilitated the foundation of first big modern banks. In addition to the altering ideal landscape, changing governmental and wealthy citizens' interests fostered banking innovations. Around the same time when first modern private banks emerged, first public and non-profit banks were founded. Hence the basic trinity of private, public and non-profit banks which dominates the European banking sector since it emerged in the medieval Italian City-States and in Catalonia. In addition, political and economic elites' and leading economists' view on banking changed significantly. Quite hostile toward all forms of banking and money lending at the beginning, changing economic and political conditions altered the elites' view: political, economic, and even religious elites recognized the necessity of big-scale banking for economic progress and military success.

F. Brugger, *Ideas, Interests and the Development of the European Banking Systems*, Wirtschaft + Gesellschaft, https://doi.org/10.1007/978-3-658-30597-0_3

3.1 Ideal Constrains: Usury Laws

As maintained above, ideas may function as constraints, restricting political and economic behavior. Scholastic usury restrictions are an ideal example of moral boundaries constraining economic behavior: despite all circumventions, medieval usury laws restricted financial activities in general and money lending for interests in particular. Never fully stopping financial activities however, dominant economic ideas of medieval Europe much hampered and slowed the development of financial markets and the banking sector.

Every world religion (Hinduism, Buddhism, Islam, Judaism, and Christianity) at some point in time permitted some sort of interest payments (usury) for lent money (Visser and McIntosh 1998). From the oldest written laws of China, India, Greece, to the religious laws of Christianity, Islam, and Judaism, usury was prohibited (Westen 1967). Apart from the Church's rejection of usury, interest payments on lent money were refused by most philosophers, from Plato, Aristotle, Catos, Cicero, Seneca, Plutarch (Visser and McIntosh 1998) to Thomas Aquinas (Burke 2008).[1] Christian usury prohibition was quite complex, a law with many grey areas and exemptions which frequently changed; however, overall, the "prohibition of usury was a prohibition against any interest charge on a loan" (Rothbard 1995a, p. 43).

Usury restrictions were an integrative component of scholastic theory—the leading economic theory of the time. Langholm (2008, p. 305) describes the economics of scholastics as

> part of the system of scholastic moral theology and philosophy taught [...]. Its purpose was the construction of viable norms of commercial behavior in a Christian world. The literary authorities on which it was based include the Bible and the writings of the Church fathers.

Almost all scholastic contributors were Christian theologians: the scholastic approach was highly determined by the contributors' Christian and Aristotelian approaches. In general accordance with the scholastic view, all usury, which broadly speaking meant all kind of interest payments on lent money, was robbery, and hence sinful. Agreeing that interest payments on lent money are prohibited, contributors put great effort into demonstrating why interest is sinful. Several arguments are found in many contributions: first, interests force borrowers to act against their own will. From a liberal perspective, this argument seems unsound because loans are, usually, voluntary agreements. Scholastics considered that interest payments are forced and not free will, because interest payments are against borrowers' self-interest, therefore undermining borrowers' free will. Secondly, the usurer (the lender) sells time that only belongs to God. Thirdly, money is a consumption good which is consumed through its use, and has no additional value.

---

[1]For more details on usury restrictions see Grice-Hutchinson (2015), Maloney (1973) and Rothbard (1995a, p. 43 ff.).

Fourthly, an Aristotelian argument, bullion ca not breed, hence interest payments are a multiplication of money out of nothing (c.f. Langholm 1998, pp. 59–74). Overall, the scholastic position meant: "Any charge that was not attributable to cost or risk [or work] or some other extrinsic title to interest was inherently unjust" (ibid., p. 76). Usually considered as very closely connected to Christian moral philosophy, Sombart (1913, p. 320) somehow secularizes the scholastic rejection of interest payments. According to him, the scholastic position on interests reflects its love for innovative, diligent, risk-taking entrepreneurs and its hostility toward idleness. Interest payments are permitted, or even desired, where lenders get part of the profit if a project is successful, but bear loses if the enterprise fails; hence, if investors also take risk, and/or if investors promote the enterprise with their work and ideas, interest payments are permitted. For scholastics it is permitted or even desired that investors receive parts of profits if they actively support the enterprise and bear parts of the losses. What they adamantly refuse are fixed annual payments irrespective of the businesses' success, because such interests are the "deadly enemy of all capitalist entrepreneurial spirit"[2] (ibid., p. 322). Sombart (ibid., p. 314) summarized the scholastic position: "interest on money is always prohibited and interest on capital is always permitted".[3]

In line with the scholastic position, the public opinion leaned toward the anti-usury movement; "outside business and finance, widespread support existed for usury laws" (Kindleberger 1993, p. 44). According to popular opinion, interest payments are the instrument which enables the rich economic elite to exploit and destroy destitute farmers, craftsmen, and other people in financial distress by lending them money at horrendous rates of interest (Newman 1851; Marx 1984). More distinctive contributions—for example Heers (1974) and Goldthwaite (2009)—showed that money lending in medieval Italy did not just occur between the rich and the poor, but that money was lent within classes and professions (Heers 1974). For example, merchant credits among merchants and between merchants and their customers, were quite common in medieval times (Postan 1928). However, popular stories about the exploitation of the ordinary man by usurers, enriched by strong antisemitism, whipped up hostility against all kinds of lending.

The effect of usury prohibition on real economy is still controversial. According to Kindleberger (1993), the prohibition of usury encouraged the lenders' inventiveness rather than affected lending for interest: "the usury laws of the Church did not so much cut down the amount of lending and borrowing as complicated them by the necessity to disguise the state of affairs" (ibid., p. 43). Weber ([1920] 1930) considered, in response to Sombart, that "the treatment of usury on the part of the canonists was generally purely legal and formal," and "the prohibition of usury and its fate can have at most a symptomatic significance for us, and that only to a limited degree." What, according to Weber (ibid.), the discussion on usury really shows, is the synchrony of "on the one hand, a

[2] „Der Todfeind alles kapitalistischen Unternehmertums".

[3] "Einfacher Leihzins in jeder Gestalt ist verboten; Kapitalprofit in jeder Gestalt ist erlaubt."

traditional, mostly inarticulate hostility towards the growing power of capital" and "on the other hand, the necessity of accommodation to practical needs." Others, like Abulafia (1997) and Munro (2003), consider that interest restriction had a significant impact on money lending and banking. Contributors denying a significant effect on the economy usually argue that financial business was too big and too developed already to have suffered much from usury restrictions. No doubt money was lent against interest payments for thousands of years (Visser and McIntosh 1998) and financial markets developed fast in the medieval trading hubs (Mueller 1997; Goldthwaite 2009). However, restrictive usury laws much complicated the development of the banking sector.

3.2 From Merchant to Financial Capitalism

Between the periods of the Crusades and the rise of Spain and Portugal, Italian City-States were Europe's main trading hubs. "Italy was still only a poor 'peripheral' region [...]. All this was before the Crusades and the confrontation between Christendom and Islam" (Braudel 1984, p. 107). Lopez (1998) considered the fast economic rise of the Italian City-States a "Commercial Revolution". Several contributors (Abu-Lughod 1989; Lopez 1998) argued that Italy's Commercial Revolution started before the Crusades; however, there is little doubt that the Crusades paved the way for the hegemony of Italian City-States in Mediterranean trade. Disguised as religious fanaticism, Venice and Genoa were particularly quite successful in using the Crusades to develop and conquer new markets (Abu-Lughod 1989, p. 105 ff.). After the Crusades, Venice dominated the entire East Mediterranean sea trade and had a quasi-monopoly on Byzantine land trade (Pirenne 1937, p. 18 ff.). Shortly after Venice, Genoa took off and became Italy's second sea trade hub (ibid., p. 29 ff.). Through economic imperialism, Italian City-States quickly extended their trade dominance (Abu-Lughod 1989, p. 108 f.). At the beginning of the 14th century, the Mediterranean sea and land trade was dominated by Venice, Genoa, Florence, and Milan. According to Arrighi (2010, p. 89), the cooperative trading policy of the four great Italian trading hubs facilitated and fostered the rise and dominance of Italian City-States: each city occupying a trading niche—Florence the textile and Milan the metal land trade with Central and Northern Europe; Venice the sea trade with South Asia and Genoa with Central Asia—the Commercial Revolution of the Italian City-States was rather cooperative than conflicting. Closely linked to their geographic proximity, each equipped with a quasi-trade monopoly, the Italian trade quadrangle –Venice, Genoa, Florence, and Milan –was a fertile ground for trade dominance. The economic order being dominated by trade and merchants as the most powerful group, the economic system of the Italian City-States was considered the first example of merchant capitalism or at least a pre-form of it (Mielants 2000).

The accelerating Commercial Revolution fostered the development of financial markets and early forms of banking: "Commerce and banking went hand and hand" (Goldthwaite 2009, p. 205). Trade, in particular over long distances, was risky, but also quite profitable. Since it was them who dominated the most profitable trade routes, capital quickly accumulated in the Italian City-States. Simultaneous production and extension of trade fostered the demand for investments. Due to the quickly rising demand for financial services, financial markets emerged within the (shifting) boundaries of the prevailing usury restrictions. Attracting merchants from near and far, money exchange was a fast extending and profitable business (Mueller 1997). Extending (long-distance) trade was accompanied by the rise of trade-based financial business, which was predominately performed by merchants: pre-financing resources and materials, accepting prepayment deposits, transferring money and credit between ports, exchanging coins, allowing overdrafts, requesting interest for long delays, and so on were the usual financial services of the merchant bankers (Goldthwaite 2009, p. 205). Steadily, financial markets grew and became more complex. Insurances for oversea traders (ibid., pp. 98-103), bills of exchanges (ibid., p. 210), and many other trade-facilitating financial services were developed. Despite trade-based financial services, early forms of ordinary banking like depositing money and longer time lending emerged. Long-distance trade was quite profitable which is why capital accumulated fast. Well-endowed with investable capital, merchants diversified risk by investing elsewhere (Kohn 1999a). Accepting deposits from relatives and colleagues, lending larger scale and for longer times, a group of professional bankers arose from byproduct bankers who lived on banking and operated their merchant business just to veil their true occupation. Due to the developing financial market, Italian trading centers also became financial hubs.

Initially focused on trade-based financial services and private investments, bankers' main business steadily shifted toward public debt financing. Using the wide networks inherited from their merchant origins, merchant bankers pooled much available capital and lent it to Europe's rulers (Goldthwaite 2009, pp. 230–235). In particular, bankers invested in their own governments: due to the wastefulness of the political oligarchy and in particular due to recurrent wars, governments were notoriously hard up. For merchants and bankers, a fast extending public debt was a welcome opportunity to overcome the saving glut and invest their idle hoards.

According to Arrighi (2010, p. 91 ff.), sometime in the late 13th and 14th century, lucrative trade places were mostly occupied by the trading hubs. Trading routes being divided among Italian City-States, peaceful trade extension became quite unprofitable. The difficulties in extending trade and the general economic slowdown made profitable investment opportunities quite scarce and caused a huge oversupply of investable capital. According to the World-Systems Theory (Wallerstein [1974] 2011) the Commercial Revolution, which lasted from the Crusades to the beginning of the 14th century, was characterized by fast extending trade and increasing agrarian productivity. Falling agrarian production, shortage of food, the Black Death, escalating conflicts between countries for the best trading routes, between the ruling elites and the peasants and between the 'popolo' and the 'nobility', initiated and characterized the disastrous Long Fourteenth Century (see Braudel 1981, 1982, 1984). Fighting recurrent wars against each other, against the Turks and elsewhere in Europe, the Italian City-States' hunger for public debt sharply increased during the Long Fourteenth Century. According to Arrighi (2010, p. 94), due to decreasing trade profits and the oversupply of investable capital, the governments' hunger for capital was very much in the interest of merchants and bankers, for whom it provided a profitable investment opportunity.

Increasingly replacing trade with financial services, the economic system of Italian City-States steadily transferred from merchant to financial capitalism. The rise of financial capitalism and the governments' increasing indebtedness strengthened financial interests to a great extent. Closely connected to familial and business relations, merchant and financial interests merged and strongly dominated the economic order of the Long Fourteenth Century. Suffering from falling profits, wars for new trade routes were in the interest of merchants. Lacking profitable investment opportunities for surplus savings, costly wars were also in the interests of the financial elites. Hence, recurrent wars served the interests of the strongest economic groups: financers and merchants.

However, financial elites faced two main challenges: first, interest restrictions still complicated banking and other financial businesses. With the rise of banking and the financial sector, many new ways to circumvent usury restrictions were found. Nevertheless, usury laws much hindered the development of the banking sector. Secondly, lending to the sovereign seemed particularly risky because of the asymmetric distribution of power. One that would lend to the sovereign faced a huge crowed of atomized lenders: the borrower holding the monopoly of violence and having the ability to change laws if necessary distributed bargaining power in favor of the borrower. Being in the weaker bargaining position, state lenders had a strong interest in increasing their position against the sovereign. Hence, the most powerful economic groups had four main interests: the conquest of new trading routes, the creation of profitable investment opportunities, relaxing or abolish usury laws, and strengthening the lenders' bargaining position.

3.2.1 Shifting Politics and the Rise of Public Debt Capitalism

The politics of the Italian City-States was dominated by a small ruling oligarchy. Initially dominated by nobility, merchants, their political influence steadily increased: many noblemen themselves were involved in long-distance trade, marriage between successful merchants and the nobility was not unusual and merchants got involved in many state affairs (Martines 1988, pp. 29–33). Fast extending trade steadily strengthened the political power of merchants, which is why Arrighi (2010) considers that, with the exception of Genoa, Italian City-States politics was dominated by merchants. During the Commercial Revolution, the political order of the Italian City-States was dominated by the silent coalition between the merchants' and the oligarchies' interests: merchants tolerated and supported the governing nobility, while the oligarchy safeguarded merchants' interests by securing and extending profitable trade routes. Safeguarding the most powerful economic interests, being relatively independent from the Church—Mattingly (1955,

p. 48) considers City-States the first and for a long time the "only secular states"—the dominion of the small "oligarchy" (Martines 1988, pp. 22–29) was for a certain time relatively stable and peaceful.

The political situation fundamentally changed in the Long Fourteenth Century. It is widely agreed that the Long Fourteenth Century was a time of deep recurrent crises (Wallerstein [1974] 2011, pp. 14–66). All three orders faced serious crises: the economic order was shattered by falling productivity, decrease in population (due to the Black Death), and a decrease in trade profits. Recurrent political instability and wars shook the political order. Wars between Christian nations and the rising pressure from Muslim Ottomans disturbed the cultural order. Italian City-States were hard hit by the Black Death, they were unable to develop new profitable trade routes, and faced strong domestic and foreign policy challenges. Unable to peacefully extend profitable trade, the powerful coalition between mercantile and oligarchy interests started falling apart at the seams. Under pressure from economic slowdown and increasingly dissatisfied with the ruling oligarchy, power struggles between the ruling old nobility or 'magnati' and the upstart 'popolo' or 'nobiltà' shook the political order (Rothbard 1995a, p. 180). Studying the social composition of the oligarchy and the 'popolo', Martines (1968) showed that the lines of conflicts run between, but also within classes: parts of the new rich merchants and bankers supported the oligopoly, others the 'popolo'; the sidelined nobleman often became the spokesman of the 'popolo'. Bloody uprisings and takeovers caused the nobility to nestle closer to the new rich merchants and bankers. Facing domestic political pressure, foreign policy successes were often considered the only possibility to maintain power.

According to Mattingly (1955, p. 49), since it was surrounded and threatened by enemies, the governments' power heavily dependent on its military force. Wars expanding the nation's borders were welcome means of enhancing the collective self-consciousness and of calming opposition; wars were welcome red herrings, which incited the rising of "Communal Patriotism", "Civic Nationalism" and "City-State Chauvinism" (Karataşlı 2016) and averted the look from inner political instability. In addition to the rising hostility between regional powers, the quick conquest of the Balkans by the Ottoman empire took the City-States by surprise. There is no doubt that the ruling elites predominately feared losing trading routes, rather than a religious takeover (Goffman 2006), however, instigated by the Church, the general hysteria about the possible fall of Christianity in face of the Muslim enemy pervaded the folk (Meserve 2008). Glorifying the battle against the Turks to the level of a religious self-defense legitimized wars against the expanding Ottoman empire. Despite all religious and national rhetoric, wars were predominately fought for economic reasons: all lucrative trade routes being occupied by trading hubs and many threatened by the Ottoman extension, the old trade routes could only be saved and new once developed through wars against the neighboring City-States and the Ottoman empire. According to Arrighi (2010) during the Long Fourteenth Century the former cooperative relation between Italian City-States turned competitive and caused cities to battle over profitable trade routes. Hence, wars were usually legitimized by relying on regional patriotic sentiments, but were thought to satisfy the merchants' interests for new profitable trade routes. Due to the rising hostility between European entities and inner political problems, war became "endemic all over northern and central Italy" (Mattingly 1955, p. 49). According to Braudel (1995, p. 388), in the Hundred Years' war between Italian City-States "City fought City, State tackled State."

Considered essential for survival, wars seriously tightened the financial difficulties of the City-States. Wars fought by paid soldiers, who got adequate payments on time ensured the fighters' loyalty (Stasavage 2011, p. 25–29). In addition, technological change significantly complicated war financing. The development of fire arms necessitated capital-intensive war industries and the construction of costly fortifications (Ehrenberg [1896] 1928, p. 27). The constant readiness of various enemy states to finance costly wars made war a matter of survival (Molho 1995, p. 99): "One principle became prominent at this time which expressed a new view of the essence and significance of money capital. The principle runs 'Pecunianervus belli' (money is the sinews of war)" (Ehrenberg [1896] 1928, p. 22). How to cover rampant war costs became the most challenging and essential question for Italian City-States.

In principle, governments have two possibilities at their disposal for covering war costs: taxes and public debt. Tax financing was disadvantageous and unpopular. The governments' ability to immediately raise a large amount of money was pivotal to the fortunes of war. The long time it took to collect taxes and the resistance it caused made tax financing quite disadvantageous. The greater elasticity of public debt—the idle hoards of rich citizens are much faster and more easily absorbed by borrowing than by taxing—made credit war financing quite popular among rulers (Stasavage 2011, p. 27). In addition to the disadvantages for war financing, the abolition of many taxes was a core demand of the bourgeoisie and the 'popolo' (Martines 1988, p. 176 f.).

In the interests of rich citizens in need of profitable investment opportunities, and the sovereign in need of fast money, tax financing of wars was widely replaced by government credit. Recognizing the danger of relying on voluntary lending in times of war, the sovereign and the bourgeoisie agreed on forced lending: rich citizens could be forced by the sovereign to lend to the government, but governments were, in principle, obligated to pay loans and interests on lent money. Doubtless, citizens were not always happy about being forced to lend huge amounts to an unreliable borrower. Nevertheless forced lending was much in the interests of wealthy citizens because the government, or at least that is what it promised, paid interests and returned the money they would have lost anyway through taxation: "Despite these disadvantages [defaults and suspend interest payments], the Florentine elite considered public debt preferable to the alternative of direct taxes on private property" (Armstrong 2004, p. 177). Forced lending was a welcome opportunity for rich merchants and bankers to get rid of the oversupply of investable capital and to bypass usury restrictions; because citizens were forced to lend, interest payments were permitted. Due to the quickly rising financial needs of the government, and the availability of huge idle hoards, public debt increased fast (Martines 1988, p. 176 f; Arrighi 2010;

Stasavage 2011). In addition to the state, the Church also became increasingly indebted (Caselli 2013).

Recurrent wars and the wastefulness of the political class spun public debt out of control. Steadily investable capital shifted from private business toward public lending. With big parts of the capital being invested in government lending, a kind of public debt capitalism emerged. The rise of public debt capitalism had far-reaching political, social, and economic consequences and shifted the wealthy citizens' main interests: initially dominated by merchant interests, state lenders' interests were on the rise. Governments' dependency on private capital steadily increased the political influence of the financial elites (Martines 1988, p. 176 ff; Arrighi 2010, p. 93).

Paradoxically, mounting public debt stabilized the political order. Steadily extended to less wealthy groups, forced lending made all citizens but the very poor government lenders as well (Pezzolo 2007): "The institutionalization of the state debt brought about an important process of socialization of debt. [...] Almost all the social groups in the main central-northern cities [of Italy] held or dealt with government bonds" (Pezzolo 2008, p. 24). Lenders' fears of credit defaults and governments' fears of revolutions and takeovers converged citizens' and governments' interests. Because major political disturbances usually cause public debt defaults, government lenders had a strong vested economic interest to safeguard their investment and maintain the public order: radical opposition, revolutions, and bloody takeovers were strongly opposed by elites because they endangered public debt investments. Hence, forced lending and the popularization of public debt reconciled governments' and economic elites' interests and therefore renewed the alliance between political and economic elites.

At the same time, mounting public debt caused much unrest. Providing a welcome investment opportunity for wealthier citizens, lower classes payed with their taxes for the fast rising interest burden. Eating up 20% to 40% of governments' total revenues (Molho 1995: 109), public debt extension caused much unrest among the heavily taxed lower classes. Traditionally hostile towards money lenders, heavily taxed to cover governments' interests burden, and critical of the rising influence of money lenders, the anger against public debt rose fast among the lower classes.

> Despite the blessing of the Florentine political and economic elite, deficit financing was highly controversial. The creation of the monte commune was associated with challenges to the traditional distribution of power in the commune and the debt remained a central factor in political and class struggles for well over a century (Armstrong 2004, p. 178).

The opposition of the lower classes to public debt turned violent in the 14th and early 15th century, when records of creditors and banks were burned and rebels requested the relaunch of direct taxes (Pezzolo 2007). Due to protests and the aggravating financial problems, most City-States had, against the angry protest of the wealthy, temporarily reintroduced personal taxes (Martines 1988, p. 179). However, the temporal relaunch of direct taxes changed little of the general tendency of rising public debt and the "steady upward circulation of wealth" (Molho 1995, p. 107).

Threatened from the inside and outside, winning recurrent wars became pivotal for the ruling political elites to hold on to power. As previously outlined, a high elasticity of government lending—and hence the availability of huge capital in a short time—was considered to be of central political importance; governments therefore had a strong interest in increasing the elasticity of government credit. Lenders, one of the most powerful groups of the time, had a strong interest in undisturbed financial businesses and a 'safe heaven' for their idle hoards. Forced loans were, compared to taxes, an advantageous war-financing instrument. However, forced loans' involved several problems: first of all, the citizens' inability or unwillingness to lend the prescribed sums, and also high exploitation costs (Martines 1988, p. 179). Second of all, the compatibility of interest payments on public debts with the usury prohibition was questionable. Thirdly, deep financial crises demonstrated that public debts are not a 'safe heaven', but actually quite risky and frequently default investments. Public debt defaults and interest suspensions emphasized that, ultimately, lenders have no means of forcing governments to pay off loans. Historically lenders were often in the much stronger position than borrowers (Ingham 2004); this is obviously not the case if the borrower is the sovereign who holds the monopoly on violence and has the ability to change laws if necessary. According to (Ehrenberg [1896] 1928, p. 32), there are "three condition for any credit—the belief that the debtor can, will and must pay." No condition was satisfied with the government as main borrower. Hence, lenders had a strong interest in rebalancing the power distribution between lenders and the borrowing sovereign.

Situations like the ones above, in which important ideas, interests, and institutions are not conflicting, are considered to be relatively stable and harmonious relations. It seems that during the Long Fourteenth Century the relation between scholastic ideas and main groups interests became increasingly conflicting. Scholastic interest restrictions, to a certain extent, opposed the interests of governments and wealthy citizens in easy and uncomplicated money lending. Scholastic ideas of institutionalization of various usury laws and restrictions much complicated the development of banking and the institutionalization of lending. Institutions like forced loans were unable to fully serve governments' interests of elastic credit granting and lenders' interests of a 'safe heaven' for their idle hoards: forced loans were often inadequate for covering quickly rising war costs and too slow to immediately provide the capital for big battles. The governments' interests as lenders were not satisfied because they still lacked the 'safe heaven' for their idle hoards and were unable to safeguard their investments against recurrent public debt defaults.

3.2.2 Changing Ideas: New Perspectives on Interests

Scholastics' usury restrictions and widespread aversion against all kind of money landing stood in sharp contrast with the behavior and interests of governments and rich citizens. As maintained above, the argumentation was that usury laws could hardly influence economies because they were easily circumvented: no doubt that much lending occurred also under the strictest usury restrictions, but in its strict form it was a major concern for the development of modern banks. As demonstrated, the strict scholastic rejection of money lending conflicted with the common practice and with governments' and investors' interest for facilitated lending.

Like outlined above the sociology of knowledge, most notably Robert K. Merton and Karl Mannheim, stressed how the environment, meaning interests of scientists and import groups, politico-economic circumstances influence the emerging, diffusion, and content of knowledge. Scholastics faced strong pressure from powerful economic and political groups to reconsider and change usury laws, which, like the sword of Damocles, hung over private and public financing. In particular, the fact that public debt was also used to ward off Ottoman attacks and to save Christianity from Muslim conquest, underpinned the anti-usury coalition. "The necessity of raising ready money for war first set the stone rolling, which—if we may adapt the saying of a modern Pope—shattered the Colossus of the Scholastic teaching as to usury" (Ehrenberg [1896] 1928, p. 25). Despite all philosophical, theological arguments for and against the permission of interest payments. The Church was in a practical dilemma: many rich clergy and church organization themselves lent heavily to the government (Kirshner 1977, p. 113). Most destructive for a clear and strong anti-credit position was the Church's own indebtedness. Church indebtedness (Caselli 2013) undermined its theological position, but in particular increased bankers' power inside the Church, which the bankers used to influence the Church's position on public debt and interest (Kirshner 1977, p. 123); bankers held important positions in the Curia and in the papal Depositeria Generale (Caselli 2013, p. 211).

Fostered by the changing environment, new ideas emerged and others were rediscovered, fundamentally altering the scholastic position on interests. Already in the 13th century, Pierre de Jean Olive developed the concept of capital by defining capital as the money which is invested in order to improve productivity; his writings, at first, were put on the papacy's banned list (Munro 2003). One of the most influential scholastic economists, the Franciscan San Bernardino of Siena, was a strict ascetic and an objective of usury; however, his capital theory marked a turning point in scholastic position on interest payments. Building on Pierre de Jean Olive's utility and capital theory, San Bernardino's capital theory admitting *Lucrum Cessans* (the ceased profits) opened the door for a deep reform of the usury ban. According to his capital theory money has two faces: first, money is a means of payment—money is the equivalent of wealth—and second, money is an investment in future profits—money as capital. A businessman who lends money gives up capital which would have most likely generated profit if invested in one's own business. Restricting the legitimacy of interest payments to charitable loans, San Bernardino considered that a person who gives up their capital and therefore misses profits should be compensated through interest payments (c.f. Rothbard 1995a, pp. 59–85). San Bernardino's argument that lending money causes opportunity costs shares similarities with the neoclassical theory of interest: Neoclassics argue that lenders must be compensated for omitting to use all money for current consumption. Already in

San Bernardino's time most authors permit *Damnum Emergens*: *Damnum Emergens*—meaning that lenders should be compensated for costs and inconveniences, as in a delayed repayment. *Lucrum Cessans* is an extension of *Damnum Emergens* because it considers that lending by itself is costly and needs compensation: arguing that lending always means being entitled to a legitimate compensation, *Lucrum Cessans* legitimizes interests payments far beyond *Damnum Emergens*, because even if investors run no risk and payments are not delayed, lenders need to be compensated for missed profits. It seems that San Bernardino's capital theory always legitimizes interests, because it is quite unlikely that investors would not have the possibility to invest the capital profitably elsewhere. Hence, San Bernardino of Siena, a strict ascetic monk and a clear advocate of interest prohibitions, unintentionally became a strong advocate of banking and the gradual permission of lending for interest.

In the long and intensive scholastic discussions on public debt, according to Kirshner (1970) most contributors agreed that private lending differs from public debt in three main respects. First, most scholastic theologians agreed that public debt is of general interest because governments raise debts to defend the homeland and to develop the country. "Lending to the commune was considered a duty as much as servicing the urban militia" (Pezzolo 2007, p. 9). Assuming that public debts increase the general utility, it seems appropriate to consider public debt as charity loans, on which, according to San Bernardino, interests may be charged: "The chasm between rule and practice was bridged by 'utilitas' 'publica' and 'necessitas'" (Kirshner 1977, p. 156). Second, interests on forced lending are not immoral because lending is not voluntary, which is why lenders could not be blamed for lending against interest. Disagreements prevailed over volunteer lending: some influential contributors argued that even volunteer lending for interest is ethical, because there is no force which may oblige the government to actually pay interests even if there is a written contract. Like outlined above scholastics opposes interests because lenders force borrowers to pay interests against their will. In the case of public debt, it seems unlikely that the numerous groups of autonomous lenders are able to force the state to pay off debts. Because governments are free to choose whether they pay interest or not, several scholastics argued that repayments above the lent money should be treated as a gift from the government to its patriotic citizens, and not as interest (c.f. Kirshner 1970). Third, by lending to the government, a businessman misses to make profit. The fact that big parts of the society had become government lenders, or had in one way or another something to do with government bonds, altered the general view on money lending, in particular on public credit.

It would be over-simplified to argue that shifts in the economic and political order necessitated a specific change in the cultural order; it was rather what Max Weber calls an elective affinity (Wahlverwandtschaften) between the changes of the three types of order. Implicitly in Max Weber's *The Protestant Ethic and the Spirit of capitalism* ([1920] 1930) the causality runs from new ideas to changing economic order; in the case of Italian City-States, the causality runs in the opposite direction: from the changing economic order via alterations of the political order to shifting cultural order. However, the discussion on usury and public debt overall significantly altered the Church's position on interests: the scholastic view on interests shifted from "all interest is usury" to "excessive interest is sinful" (Visser and McIntosh 1998, p. 179). Those changes in the Church's position on interests were the first important step in a process lasting hundreds of years that steadily relaxed the position on interest payments. As already said, usury restrictions never completely stopped money lending against interest payments, but the relatively restrictive usury laws hampered the development of the banking system. The scholastics' altered view on interests did not abolish the usury ban, but much extended the boundaries within which the banking sector could develop. In particular, the changed treatment of public debts opened the door for the development of first modern banks. Broadly speaking, the shift in the scholastic view on interests reconciled the dominant economic idea and the rich citizens' and governments' interests.

3.3 The Rise of Modern Banks

As maintained, recurrent wars and the popularization of public debt by forced lending created two main interests regarding governmental financing: the governments' interest in the highest possible elasticity of credit, and the lenders' interest in rebalancing the asymmetric distribution of power between lenders and the sovereign as borrower.

3.3.1 The Foundation of the State Lender Associations

Startled by public debt defaults and the suspension of interest payments, rebalancing the distribution of power between creditors and the sovereign became the main demand of government lenders. One borrower, empowered by his own monopoly on violence and the ability to change laws, versus thousands of atomized small and big lenders; this, distributed the bargaining power much in favor of the former. Pooling the bargaining power of the creditors was hoped to rebalance the bargaining power in favor of the lenders. State lender associations were founded to strengthen the position of lenders by speaking in one voice. Founded in 1407 by the biggest public debt investors, Genoa's Casa di San Giorgio was the kind of state lender associations which concentrated the creditors' power and therefore enhanced the lenders' bargaining position. Founded in the worsening conflict between lenders and the government over Genoa's financial policy (Scott 2014a), Casa di San Giorgio's support became essential for the government's survival. The Casa used its power to actively influence Genoa's financial policy: "Beginning from 1407 the foundation of the Casa di San Giorgio—that is a consortium of creditors of the government—allowed a close control over state finance and debt management" (Pezzolo 2007, p. 15). Casa di San Giorgio's influence became so powerful that the Doge of Genoa had to swear at his inauguration that the freedom of the bank is unassailable. In 1463, the pope awarded the right to excommunicate defaulting debtors to the bank

(Obst 1930, p. 14). For Machiavelli, Casa di San Giorgio was a "state within the state" (cited in Scott 2014a, p. 78). In mid-15th century the Casa managed almost the entire public debt financing and was heavily involved in politics. Pooling public debt investments in the hands of one institution like the Casa di San Giorgio or a family like the Medici's in Florence, was not a guarantee against defaults, but the lenders' augmented ability to influence fiscal politics made defaults quite expensive for governments because of the inability to take a position toward other lenders. In addition, it enabled lenders to directly or indirectly influence the government's financial policy. Founded as state lender association, their business steadily expanded toward the private sector. As the state lender association extended their business, they became the favored investment vehicles of the wealthy population. Founded by the economic elites, stockholding soon became a mass phenomenon: for example, in mid-15th century more than 10% of Genoa's population owned shares in the Casa di San Giorgio (Heers 1974).

The foundation of big capital pooling public debt investment institutions was also in the interest of the government (Marsilio 2013). For example the Banco di San Giorgio was founded

> in order to extinguish the public debt and to eradicate certain bad practices of bankers, who are so devoted to their own interest that they barely blush as they ruin the public good, and have become accustomed to spend out and hold money not at the required price, but at an unusual and irrational price (Marengo et al. cited in Roberds and Velde 2014, p. 8).

No doubt that rebalancing the distribution of power between lenders and the sovereign was disadvantageous to governments. However, notoriously in financial difficulties (Usher 1943, p. 155) and obliged to immediately raise huge amounts of capital to win wars, a high elasticity of credit became the government's primary interest. Pooling big capital, state lender associations were able to raise huge amounts in short time. The support of financially strong lender organizations became pivotal for military success: "In the case of Venice, the readiness of Rialto banks to lend money in times of war was a crucial factor in maintaining its military strength" (Mueller 1997, p. 426). Steadily fighting wars against each other and other European powers and the Ottomans "the credit of the cities was [...] their most powerful weapon in the struggle for their freedom" (Ehrenberg [1896] 1928, p. 45). Because "states found that access to public was a critical ingredient for survival" (Stasavage 2011, p. 27), overall the governments welcomed the foundation of the state lender association because it increased the elasticity of government credit and therefore made the rulers' political survival much more likely. In addition to facilitating war financing, many governments were convinced that a well-functioning bunking sector fosters economic development (Kindleberger 1993, p. 45). The Church's position on the foundation of state lender associations like the Casa di San Giorgio was dominated by the developing utilitarianism and the confession that wars, and therefore war financing, were inevitable in order to protect the motherland against enemies, in particular against the Muslim Ottomans:

> Cardinal Lodovico Mezzarata Scrampi dell'Arena, papal chamberlain, was charged with investigating the merits of San Giorgio's petition. After receiving the advice of experts, he reported that such contracts should and can be permitted for reasons of necessity and utility (Kirshner 1977, p. 125).

Hence, the Casa di San Giorgio and other state lender associations were built on a strong coalition between governments and the financial elites, tolerated by the Church.

I consider the Casa di San Giorgio the oldest European modern bank. But what makes it the oldest modern bank? As maintained above, money lending against interest payments has existed for at least several thousand years. However, lending was usually relatively personalized: a rich man lent to a monarch, a craftsman to a college, a merchant to his customers, a landlord to a farmer and so on. Even forced lending is somehow personal, because of the direct relation between the lender and the sovereign. Although banking professionalization and rudimentary deposit banking emerged during the Commercial Revolution (Goldthwaite 2009, pp. 437–442), banking was still built on personal relations between the depositor and the banker, between borrowers and lenders. The foundation of the Casa di San Giorgio was a quantum leap into depersonalization and anonymization. State lender associations became the intermediary which absorbed capital from a huge anonymous crowd of people to invest it in a profitable way. Founded to enhance the lenders' bargaining power, the state lender associations increasingly developed and followed its own interests, which were relatively independent from both lenders and borrowers. Hence, the foundation of the Casa di San Giorgio promoted what is most characteristic for the modern banking system: the depersonalization and anonymization of capital and lender-borrower relations and the development of the usual interest trinity of lender, borrower, and intermediary interests.

3.3.2 Early Public Banks

Around the same time, the first public banks were founded. The close connection between medieval banks and the government makes a clear cut between private and public banks difficult. In Italy and Catalonia the oldest public banks were established in the 15th century. The Taula de Canvi (1401) and Banch de la Ciutat (1609) in Barcelona, Banco di Rialto (1584) and Banco del Giro (1619) in Venice, Monte dei Paschi di Siena (1472) are the oldest European public banks.

In the 14th century, at least a dozen public bank proposals were written. Looking at the medieval debates on public banking shows that the main arguments for and against the foundation of public banks have not changed much in the last six hundred years. Like in many recent discussions about state interventions and state role in the economy, those who argue that governments are the better entrepreneurs and bankers because governments are oriented towards society's well-being are opposed by those who belief that governmental intervention or state enterprises make things even worse, because in them corruption and cronyism are more present and as such more prone to crises than in private entrepreneurships. Opponents of public banks argued that public banks are vulnerable to corruption and that banking is not the business of governments (Roberds and Velde 2014). Back then, like nowadays, public bank advocates argued that private bankers due to their selfishness and short-term profit orientation hinder rather than support economic development. According to them, private banks are quite prone to crises, unreliable, and act against public interest. It was hoped that public banks may ensure a good and secure society, overcome the private banks' shortcomings, and bring about progressive development. In particular, two arguments were brought forward which also dominated Mercantilist proposals on public banking: first, public banks facilitate public debt financing, and second, public banks may overcome tight money (Mueller 1997, p. 110).

The senate of Venice had an intensive discussion about the advantages and disadvantages of public banks. Senator Tommaso Contarini held a long speech on the advantages of public banks (see Lattes 1869): he argued that Venice needs a reliable and well-functioning payment system to defend its position as a trading center. Private banks, he stated, have proved to be unreliable, steadily over-issued credit, and must be blamed for volatile exchange rates. According to him, public banks may overcome all these problems. Advocacy of and opposition to public banks also reflected the actors' vested interest: governments advocated for public banks in hope to facilitate public Financing; fearing the loss of a profitable business, private bankers usually opposed public banks. However, the public bank debate highlights that sometimes in the late Middle Ages and early Renaissance the question shifted from whether big banks are needed, toward who should operate big banks and what their goals are.

The advocates of public banks had the historical momentum on their side, as several bankruptcies of private banks shattered trust and further regulations failed to stabilize the banking system (Kohn 1999b). Legitimized by possible societal benefits, the governments' vested interests became the facilitator of public banks. Notoriously, in financial difficulties governments hoped that public banks would act as an uncritical, unlimited lender. Governments' interests for public banks coincided with merchants' and craftsmen's interests in having a trustworthy money store. Due to the powerful coalition between the government and business, the idea of public banks spread fast. "By mid-century [17th] there was widespread belief that some public bank was needed" (Roberds and Velde 2014, p. 13).

In hindsight, early public banks did not live up to the expectations. Shortly after their opening, many public banks ran into trouble and failed. In many cases, the fear of the opponents were confirmed. Public banks often became the government's main lending institution that was at the same time in the government's own hands. "The city [Barcelona] proved unable to resist the temptation of easy credit. It borrowed copiously from the Taula both to finance emergency purchases of grain and to cover military expenses" (Kohn 1999b, p. 24). Public banks being increasingly unable to satisfy the government's financial needs, laws were often changed. In the case of Catalonia, since several measures like state guarantees for Taula de Canvi deposits and the limitation of private banking failed to satisfy the government's financial hunger, private banking was prohibited (Roberds and Velde 2014, p. 28). Several public banks collapsed because of lending too heavily to the government and private business (for example the Taula of Valencia in 1613 and the Bank of Amsterdam a hundred and fifty years later (Kindleberger 1993)) and were eroded by corruption and cronyism.

3.3.3 Early Cooperative Banks

As usury restrictions were 'softened' and banking extended, voices were raised within the Church that usury restrictions are insufficient to overcome usury practices. It was argued that the poor who got into dire financial troubles need an alternative place where they can borrow money. The advocates of Christian banking argued: non-profit orientated Christian banks lending for zero or very low interest to the poor and storing the small savings of the hardworking people would break up the usurers' power by providing a Christian banking alternative for the poor (Tawney 1948, p. 65).

In 1462 in Perugia the first Monte di Pietàs opened its doors. Until 1515, Monte di Pietàs were founded in most Italian cities. Following the Italian example, religious cooperative banks were open elsewhere in Europe (Holzapfel 1903). In order to protect the poor from usurers and undermine what the Church considered the evil Jewish money lenders, the Monte di Pietàs deposited money and lent small amounts for short times to the poor (Caselli 2013, p. 212). Monte di Pietàs were the Catholic answer to spreading money lending. Mostly formed and promoted by Franciscans, the Monte di Pietàs were inspired by the Catholic moral code. However, at least at the beginning, resistance against Monte di Pietàs within the Church was strong: many argued that Monte di Pietàs are also sinful because they lend money (Holzapfel 1903, p. 9). Despite the theological discussion on the lawfulness of Monte di Pietàs (see Tawney 1948, p. 55), the general public was very pleased by the foundation of them (Holzapfel 1903, p. 24) and started to borrow heavily from the new Christian credit institutions. Refusing interest payments on lent money brought Monte di Pietàs close to early bankruptcy and caused the pope to allow them to demand low interests to cover their costs and to built up capital reserves (Caselli 2013, p. 212). Unable to cover the fast rising credit demands with the deposited money, Monte di Pietàs started to borrow capital from the inter-banking market: obliged to pay interests on borrowed capital, Monte di Pietàs themselves had to demand interest payments for lent money to cover their own interests costs (Holzapfel 1903, p. 17). Soon, almost all Monte di Pietàs demanded low interest payments for lent money. Monte di Pietàs were quite successful in the sense that the idea of Christian non-profit banking spread fast, the number of customers increased quickly, and private money lenders faced a decreasing demand for their money. In mid-16th century, the Monte di Pietàs were closely linked to the government and served a wide public (Caselli 2013, p. 213).

Marx ([1894] 1984, p. 601) was quite cynical about the Monte di Pietàs and stated that they "are noteworthy mainly because they reveal the irony of history, which turns pious wishes into their very opposition during the process of realization." Founded to provide a non-profit alternative to the poor, Monte di Pietàs were quite successful, attracted many depositors and small borrowers and therefore somehow tamed the private money market. Successful in Italy, Monte di Pietàs spread quickly across Europe, inspired later cooperative banking, and never fully disappeared since then. At the same time, Marx had a point in that the Monte di Pietàs often undermined the noble wishes of its founders. Founded to break the power of usurers Monte di Pietàs strongly undermined the Church's usury restrictions: by demanding small interest payments to cover their own costs, the Monte di Pietàs provided the strong argument for the pro-interest coalition that even Christian institutions receive interests for lent money. More fundamentally, the foundation of Monte di Pietàs highlighted that even the Church, for a long time the most outspoken opponent to all kind of banking and financial services, accepted the necessity of banks.

3.4 The Regulation of Medieval Italian Banks

Banking and banking crises emerged simultaneously. The time between the development of the first modern banks and their first bankruptcies was short. In medieval times, financial disturbances and banking crises were not less frequent than nowadays (see Mueller 1997, pp. 121–251). Governments were aware of the vulnerability of the banking sector to crises and took much effort to reduce risk by regulating the banking sector. Two main reasons caused governments to regulate banking more heavily than other businesses: first, the banks' involvement in money exchange made them quite important to the mercantile-based economy. Second, economies became heavily dependent on banks' credit; the fall of big banks often dragged down entire economies (Kohn 1999b).

Several financial market regulations, like laws regulating coin exchange and banking hours, are owed to the special historical situation. However, other regulations targeted problems which are still at the core of financial market regulation: for example, minimal reserve requirements to avoid bank runs and bank failures and private bankers' exclusion from distinct public affairs to prevent conflicts of interest.

Lending out their own and deposited capital, the banks' investments were not fully covered by reserves. Not different from the situation in the present, early banks bore liquidity risks as deposits were typically of shorter maturity than investments. Soon several banks ran out of liquidity and went bankrupt or had to be saved by the government. Recurrent bank runs and failures illustrated the risk stemming from unregulated banking sectors. In 1499 a huge bank crisis brought the whole financial system close to the brink of collapse. After several banks had failed, regulations were tightened to calm down protesters after revolts broke out. A senator made clear how serious the situation was: "If banks are not trusted, the state has no credit"[4] (Malipiero 1844, p. 716). To reduce the risk of bank failures, safeguard depositors, and increase the banks' trustworthiness, minimum reserves and guarantees were required from banks (c.f. Mueller 1997, pp. 121–251

Entry into banking was restricted in most medieval financial centers (Kohn 1999b), and regulation measures were taken to prevent conflicts of interests and exclude bankers from holding multiple offices. The private bankers' influence on financial policy was considered a conflict of interest, which is why most states banned private bankers from holding office at the mint. Nevertheless, the private banks' influence on the government steadily grew as governments became increasingly dependent on the banks' financial support (c.f. Mueller 1997, pp. 121–251)

3.5 Conclusion

During the Commercial Revolution, merchant capitalism emerged in the Italian City-States. The cultural order relevant to banking was dominated by the scholastic interest restrictions which complicated financial market developments, but left enough room for the professionalization of trade-orientated banking. Ruled by a small oligarchy that satisfied merchants' interests, getting rich by exploiting distinct quasi trade monopolies, the relation between Italian City-States was, at the beginning, relatively peaceful. Overall the relation between the main interests, ideas and repetitive was relatively harmonious, or at least not conflictual. Shrinking trade profits and the resulting oversupply of capital, domestic and foreign political challenges, and the rising financial capitalism strongly undermined this harmonious relation. The fast availability of capital in the case of recurrent wars became the governments' main interest and interest-bearing safe investment opportunities for idle hoards became the central interest of the wealthy population.

The foundation of big state lender associations, which became the first modern European banks, was in the interest of public debt investors and the government: associations enhanced the lenders' bargaining power and strongly increased the elasticity of available capital. Being the only institution able to lend huge sums immediately, state lender associations became the cities' most powerful organizations. In addition to the redistribution of bargaining power, modern banks developed new and stabilized investment markets. Providing investment opportunities for the idle hoards, big modern banks became the favored investment vehicles of the well-off. Unlike pre-modern banks, big state lender associations deposited huge amounts of capital from a wide range of customers and were typically owned by a bigger or smaller group of shareholders.

While common people still opposed banking and lending against interest, the position of the Church and the most influential economists changed considerably. The rising public debt capitalism was a turning point in the Church's usury position. The scholastics'

---

[4]"E quando i banchi no ha fede, la Terra no ha credito."

position on usury had already changed, but several key points remained untouched: first of all, taking profit on loans was universally considered usury. Secondly, interest payments were only permitted to charity loans. Thirdly, lending to the government was allowed, but heavily restricted. With the increasing importance of financial markets and in particular with the quick rise of public debts and Church's own indebtedness "the business of the moralist and the morals of the businessman [was] one of binary opposition" (Kirshner 1977, p. 110). The widening gap between the scholastic theory and the business praxis created the environment which facilitated fundamental change in economic thought: built on the emerging utility and capital theory, credit granting against interest payments was legitimized by the argument that credit, in particular to the government, increases general utility and that lenders need to be compensated for the forgone profits *Lucrum Cessans*. Practically, the Church's position steadily changed from interest as sinful to interest as acceptable above a certain limit: 5%, 8%, 10%, would still be usury.

Markets having been disrupted by several deep banking crises, financial market regulation was tightened. Spreading fears about bank safety relatively frequently caused panic and bank runs. Saving banks from bankruptcy was costly, and bankruptcies and financial market crises had quite a negative effects on public and private financing. As a reaction to escalating financial market disturbances, new regulations like minimum reserve requirements and banning bankers from holding office at the mint were introduced. Unfortunately, stricter regulations failed to prevent further deep financial market crises.

Hence, changing interests, the lifting of the ideal restriction, the suggestion of the Church that the poor need protection from usurers, enabled and fostered the emerging of the first private, public and non-profit modern banks in Italian City-States and Catalonia. Exclusively invested in public debt at the beginning, modern banks soon extended their business into all private lending and other kinds of financial services. Early modern banks became the main investment vehicle of the wealthy population and governments' and private businesses' main lender. Italy's first modern banks market represents a turning point in the history of banking: pre-modern banking was characterized by a personal lender-borrower relation. Italian modern banking broke up the personal relation and absorbed huge, domestic and foreign, loanable funds from a wide range of depositors and shareholders, in orded to lend it to the government and many smaller private businesses. Early modern public banks were founded to fulfill the same functions as their private counterpart: facilitating government financing. However, it was expected that public banks would improve borrowers' and in particular governments' credit conditions and bypass private, profit-oriented bankers. Early non-profit-oriented banks were founded by Christian organizations to enhance the credit conditions for the poor, save them from usurers and break the power of banks.

3.6 The Heritage from Medieval Banking

The emerging of modern banking in the Italian City-States shaped the path along which the European banking sector' developed: first of all, modern banks emerged and became blueprints for newly founded banks elsewhere. Secondly, the first modern banking regulations were developed. Thirdly, ideas on interest payments and usury and the duties of banks changed.

The modern Italian banking sector was the model for banking development in other European areas. Italian bankers greatly contributed to the development of the European banking sector by founding banks elsewhere in Europe. Marx ([1894] 1984, pp. 593–613) emphasizes the structural break caused by the rise of first modern banks. According to him, the foundation of Italian capital associations freed governments and merchants from the clutches of usurers' tyranny. Breaking the lending monopoly of usurers accelerated the rise of capitalism by facilitating credit granting to the first capitalist class: the merchants. In addition to facilitating credit, according to Marx (ibid.) modern banks increased early capitalists' power over the government: "getting tighter and more secure control over the state." No doubt the foundation of modern banks induced and accelerated the long and slow death of old-style banking and significantly increased bankers' influence on fiscal politics. However, most importantly, and unmarked by Marx, the foundation of modern banks depersonalized and anonymized banking and added to the traditional twofoldedness of banking—lenders and borrowers—a third dimension: the bank. Founded as lender associations, modern banks soon became an independent force standing between borrowers and lenders, following their own interests and logic. Hence, the twofoldedness of old-style banking changed to the modern banking trinity—lenders, borrowers, and the bank. Considering modern banks as lender institutions, Marx misunderstands modern banking; modern banks are neither the extended arm of lenders, nor of borrowers. Modern banks borrow from depositors and lend to borrowers; paying interests to depositors and receiving interests from borrowers, banks have their own vested interests directed against lenders and borrowers; it is in the banks' interest to minimize interest payments to depositors and maximize interest payments from borrowers. Early modern banks became very powerful and influential. However, increasingly, the power of the bank was not the power of a wide range of bigger and smaller lenders; the power of the bank was increasingly the power of an independent organization using its power to put pressure on depositors and borrowers equally. Hence, in Italian City-States a new, one of the most influential and distinguished political and economic player emerged: the big modern banks.

Almost always and everywhere financial markets were restricted by laws. However, banking regulations of the Italian City-States followed a new logic. Before the rise of the first modern banking systems, financial market restrictions predominately expressed moral scruples against financial services. In contrast, Medieval Italian City-States' financial market regulations aimed to create a well-functioning and stable banking sector.

Medieval Italian City-States' banking regulations were built on similar assumptions as more recent regulations: banking is a politically and economically necessary business which accelerates economic progress and stabilizes political domination, but is, at the same time, prone to crises and if unregulated may become dysfunctional. Meaningful regulations overcome or at least diminish risks and the banks' dysfunctions and therefore enhance economic progress and stabilize politics. Hence, the main orientation of the banking law shifted from prohibiting sinful activities to a juridical embeddedness which creates a well-functioning effective banking system. Since then, the ultimate goals of banking regulation have not changed much.

Before the rise of Italian modern banks, interest payments on lent money were sinful, during the rise of modern banking they remained sinful and continued to be sinful afterwards. However, San Bernardino's contributions were the starting point of a century-long process in which money lending became steadily 'less sinful'. San Bernardino's capital theory permitting interests payments due to *Lucrum Cessans* was the turning point in Christian usury legislation: before the scholastic position significantly changed, the Church's, most philosophers', and the scholastic view was that all interest is usury. Since then, many agree that excessive interest is immoral and should be forbidden (Visser and McIntosh 1998). Hence, the former opposition of the Church, the general public, and most intellectuals against credit, interest, and banking as such has changed to the view that banking is needed, but requires stronger and clearer regulations.

Throughout the history of financial markets, bankers were criticized and faced much hostility. Pre-modern bankers were seen as devils that profit from others' financial difficulties, infidel Jewish usurers that use hard working Christians. Money lending and all forms of banking were usually entirely rejected as sinful. Early modern banks were thought to be selfish, use their power to extort higher interest, and are very prone to crises. However, step by step the view on banking fundamentally changed: banishing bankers was long considered the 'right way' to deal with sinful usurers. Still facing much popular hostility, the economic and political elites' view on banking steadily changed: from hostility toward recognizing the importance of strong banks for wining wars, financing governments and developing the economy. Proposals for public banks and non-profit banks heavily criticized private banks, but acknowledged the necessity of big modern banks. Hence, discussions on banking shifted from whether there should be any kind of banking, to who the banker should be, what the duty of banks is and with whom banks should take side.

Since then, the central issues and lines of conflicts have not changed much: private banking advocates argued that bankers' profit orientation, like an invisible hand, directs bankers' actions toward the general interest. For them, public banks only mean corruption and inefficiency. Public banking advocates argue that with only governments overlooking entire societies and economies, they are able to direct investments to the general interest. In particular, public banking advocates demanded that banks should take side with the government and make an effort to finance public needs at the lowest possible interest rate. Advocates of non-profit banks acknowledged the necessity of banking to help the poor during financial difficulties, but suggest that non-profit banks should strictly take side with the poor. Hence, the European banking sector inherited several things from medieval Italian City-States: early big modern banks, the depersonalization of capital and lender-borrower relations, and the trinity of banking, which became quite significant for the European banking sector of public, private, and non-profit banks. Quite important for the development of the European banking sector was the change in ideal: in the medieval Italian City-States, the intellectuals' view on banks changed from rejection and hostility to the recognition that 'right' banking is necessary, that it fosters economic development and the country's military successes.

4 Absolutism, Mercantilism and Banking Revolutions

From the Italian City-States banking spread to other parts of Europe. Italian bankers brought banking to many European cities, where they founded banks as branches of their Italian banks (Kohn 1999b; Bogaert et al. 1994). The first non-Italian banks emerged in autonomous cities and Hanseatic centers: banks were founded in Bruges, London, Lübeck, and several other Hanseatic cities (see Kohn 1999b; North 2013). However, it was South-German cities that became Europe's new banking hotspot (Kindleberger 1993, p. 46 f.). Located between the Mediterranean South and the Hanseatic North-, South-German cities were ideal trading places. In South-German trading hubs, like in Nuremberg, Augsburg, and Regensburg, trade-based banks were founded. Most private banks were founded and owned by merchants, haulers, shippers, goldsmiths, and jewelers: those crafts were highly profitable and included wide networks and good market overviews. However, the foundation of the big national banks, like the Bank of England, the Banque Royale in France and later the Giro- and Lehnbanco in Prussia, were banking revolutions which significantly shifted the historical development of the European banking sector.

4.1 The Rise of Hanseatic Banks

First and foremost, entrepreneurs founded banks in order to invest their profits (Born 1977, p. 48); "the need to find employment for accumulated wealth" was the main motive to found banks" (Kohn 1999a, p. 3). Again, the main borrowers were monarchs in need of financing costly wars. Private banks offered a wide range of financial services; from coin exchange to small-scale money depositing; however, their main business was investing bank owners' idle money reserves. Hence, founded in the rising European trading hubs, early private banks were predominately pre-modern, as they focused on the

F. Brugger, *Ideas, Interests and the Development of the European Banking Systems*, Wirtschaft + Gesellschaft, https://doi.org/10.1007/978-3-658-30597-0_4

profitable investment of the owners' idle reserves. Banking was still mostly operated as a by-business and capital was hardly depersonalized as bank owners invested their own, their relatives' and their colleagues' reserves.

The decline of Italian City-States was accompanied by the rise of Holland as Europe's new economic superpower. After its de facto independency from the Spanish Crown, Holland dominated the European and in particular the oversea trade; Holland was almost an ideal type of merchant capitalism. The Dutch Republic had a lot in common with Italian City-States: being a republic, being threatened by neighboring forces, and having a trade-dominated economy. Recurring wars with, regarding its size and population, superior neighbors, forced the Dutch Republic to invest heavily in its armed forces. In financing wars through public debt, unlike in the case of Italian City-States, banks played a minor role in public debt financing (Vries and van der Woude 1997, pp. 113–116). Overflowed with investable capital, interest rates on safe investments like public debt were very low compared to other countries. Searching for higher profits, Dutch banks predominately invested in trade and foreign public debts (ibid., p. 139–147).

Private banks were being founded to invest the rich traders' idle capitals, and the rising Dutch banking system was particularly dominated by money exchange. As already maintained, Italian City-States faced the problem, which became even more serious in the Dutch trading centers, of an unmanageable diversity of coins. Dutch trading hubs cities were overflowing with different foreign coins of unclear value. The rampant exchange risk and merchants losing track of the diversity of foreign coins caused serious difficulties for the trade-based Dutch economy. Antwerp with its big fairs became Netherlands' forerunner of exchange banking in the early 16th century (Bogaert et al. 1994). To overcome the exchange problem, other cities also founded state-owned exchange banks, so-called Wisselbanken. Alongside the state-owned Wisselbanken, private exchange banks existed as well (van Borght der 1896, p. 202). Founded to facilitate trading by reducing the coin exchange risk, Wisselbanken increasingly lent out money and in times of wars they also lent out to the state.

The emerging Dutch banking was too trade based to become the blueprint for the banking systems of Europe's rising empires. However, more indirectly, the Dutch banking system strongly influenced banking in bigger countries. First, the question was raised of how Holland, a small, decentralized country, was able to win wars against Europe's huge empires like Britain, France, or Spain. The answer lay in the superior war financing system; its highly developed financial markets and banks enabled Holland's governments to borrow huge amounts for long-term at low interest rates. Financially well-equipped Holland was able to set up competitive armies. Second, the development of Holland's financial markets supported the republic-thesis: since the very beginning of modern banking it was argued that only republics are able to develop well-functioning financial markets. The argument was that modern banks deposit plenty of money, which in monarchies lacks the protection against a monarch's excessive spending. According to the republic-thesis a strong parliament, which also represents depositors' interests, would protect banks from the governments' access to its capital. Taking together the two arguments was good news for republicans and bad news for monarchists: it seemed that states needed the support of strong banks to win wars. However, strong banks only emerged in republics. Hence, the main thesis was that to win wars, property or, better said, deposits and banks, needed strong protection.

4.2 The Rise of Modern Banking

As outlined above, several European trading centers came to symbolize the economic and banking development of North and Central Europe. However, in contrast to the Italian City-States' autonomous trade centers and the decentralized character of Holland, the period between the Religious Wars and the French Revolution was dominated by the rise of great, centralist monarchies in North and Central Europe. While banking in merchant cities remained exchange- and trade-dominated, in the rising financial centers of the developing empires banks of a very new kind emerged. Particularly important for the European banking system were the developments in England, France, and to a lower extend in Prussia. It was the emerging of absolutism and its twin the economic idea of mercantilism which changed the European banking system significantly and made it much of what it is today.

4.2.1 Mercantilism: The New Leading Economic Idea

In terms of the development of ideas, innovations with far-reaching impact were taking place. As outlined above, the medieval discussion about lending, banking, and usury was dominated by contributors of a theological background and by religious ideas of morality. Still, in particular in the earlier times of absolutism, the influence of the Churches and religious morals strongly affected the discussions around credit, banks, and financial markets. However, the great battles on religious usury restrictions had been fought out earlier in Italy. Hence, the ambivalent Christian attitudes to credit and interest had some influence on the development of the early North- and Central-European banking system, but were much less important than for the earlier Italian banking system and relatively soon lost their practical relevance altogether (Tawney 1948). Cunningham (1892) stated about England:

> During the sixteenth century public opinion [according to usury] underwent a change; (a) the law was modified [...], (b) the changed circumstances of trade affected the attitude taken by practical men, while (c) the phalanx of theological authority was broken, and (d) the argument from expediency were no longer convincing.

Doubtlessly, England was a pioneer of secularism, but the situation was not very different in other European countries. The continuous reduction of religious influence was accompanied by the replacement of scholasticism by mercantilism as the leading economic ideology: "mercantilism was the guiding principle of economic policy (and the related theory) in the age of absolute rulers in Europe" (Braudel 1982, p. 542).

The rise of absolutism as the leading political idea and mercantilism as the most influential economic theory was closely connected. How close this connection was has caused much dispute. Discussing the theory of mercantilism is difficult, because authors have not regard themselves as part of an economic school of thought. Contributions who were later considered mercantilists outlined heterogeneous ideas and several strong theoretical breaks significantly shaped the theory. The notion of mercantilism, whose contributions are part of the mercantilist school of thought, and the core elements of mercantilism were defined by mercantilism's liberal opponents like Adam Smith, David Hume, Francois Quesnay, and Victor Riquetti Marquis de Mirabeau. Classical economics and physiocracy emerged from the opposition to mercantilism. The liberal economists' illustration of mercantilism is full of cynicism and focuses strongly on its anti-liberal tendencies. More recent studies on mercantilism, like the monumental work of Eli F. Heckscher (1935a, b), Jacob Viner (1975), and Murray N. Rothbard (1995a), as well as the classical authors analyze mercantilism from the perspective of liberal economic thought. Yet mercantilism has its modern defenders (see Allen 1970); the most famous ones are Keynes, who discusses in one chapter of his *General Theory* (1935) what may be learned from mercantilism and Sombart (1928a) who showed what liberal economist may have got wrong.

4.2.1.1 The Social Environment of Mercantilism

The different position of advocates and opponents of mercantilism was particularly visible in the understanding of how the economic, political, and intellectual environment influenced the theory, and how certain interest groups, like merchants and new rulers, shaped mercantilism. To my knowledge not yet analyzed by the sociology of knowledge, the discussion about the social influence on mercantilism is a prime example of different assessments of the influence of the social environment on ideas. It shows that the assessment of the influence of the social environment is by itself not free from ideology.

For liberal opponents, mercantilism was little more than the ideologization of the interests of monarchs, generals, and rich merchants. Advocates of mercantilism claimed that mercantilism is a quite complex and innovative dynamic view on economies, which addresses the questions of nation building, employment, economic prosperity, and trade, all in one theory. Induced by different views on powerful groups' influence, more fundamental questions raised, like what mercantilism ultimately is about.

Like other schools of economic thought, mercantilism's main goal was to maximize nations' wealth and glory. Opponents of it criticize mercantilist economists for not distinguishing between the wealth of the nation and the wealth of the monarch—"Louis XIV [...] totally identified his own private interest as monarch with the interests of the state and with the public good" (Rothbard 1995a, p. 249). Criticizing that mercantilists were unable or unwilling to distinguish between the interests of a small group or one person and the interest of an entire empire is too superficial, but also rings true, as mercantilists were often quite unclear about whose wealth they are addressing. Highlighting the fact that most mercantilist contributors were merchants and bureaucrats (ibid.), liberal critics often considered that contributors had a strong vested interest in equating their own interests with the general well-being. According to Smith (1776, p. IV 7), the mercantile system was a series of "arguments […] addressed by merchants to parliaments and the counsels of princes, to nobles and country gentlemen; by those who were supposed to understand trade." He continues: mercantilists "knew perfectly in what manner it [their theory] enriches themselves. […] But to know in what manner it enriched the country, was not part of their business." For Viner (1975), mercantilists supposed that concerns about societies prosperity are just empty phrases used to conceal their real attempts:

> The laws and proclamations were not all […] the outcome of a noble zeal for a strong and glorious nation […] but were the product of conflicting interests of varying degrees of respectability. Each group, economic, social, or religious, pressed constantly for legislation in conformity with its special interest.

Following the liberal view that mercantilism steamed from an 'unholy alliance' between monarchs, bureaucrats, and rich merchants, one easily comes to Rothbard's (1995a) conclusion that mercantilism was just a complex system of lobbyism and cronyism. According to him, absolutistic monarchs unable to rule the country alone built coalitions with the nobility and large-scale merchants. In return for their loyalty, Kings assigned "patents of monopoly" to their allice, which were legitimized by mercantilist "propaganda arguments" (ibid., p. 213 f.).

Challenging the simplistic liberal view that mercantilism was just the scientification of merchants' vested interests, Viner (1948) stressed that mercantilists principally assumed that the interests of kings, merchants, and whole populations are principally in harmony with one another. He quotes Lord Bolingbroke (1749, p. 184) who stated in his description of a "Patriot King": "By trade and commerce we grow a rich and powerful nation, and by their decay we are growing poor and impotent". Central to Hobbe's absolutistic state theory is the assumption that: "In monarchy the private interest is the same with the public" (Hobbes 1651, p. 115). According to Hobbes, democracy and aristocracy are in inherent danger of being destroyed by rulers who follow their own instead of the nations' interests. In contrast, absolutistic monarchs have no reason to be corrupt or act in any other way against the general interests, because they are the state, the states' interests are their interests. Jean Bodin, Hobbes' French counterpart, stressed why absolutism is the state system which leads to harmony and justice. He considers that "geometric proportion" is the principle of democratic, and "arithmetic proportion" the principle of aristocratic justice. Only absolutism harmonizes both principles: "Harmonic is a fusion of the two [geometric and arithmetic justice]" (Bodin [1576] 1955, p. 213). "The monarchical state is necessarily founded upon the principles of harmonic justice, and if it is governed royally, that is to say harmoniously, it is the best, the most happy, and the most perfect type of state there is" (ibid.). For Bodin (ibid., p. 220), the absolutistic monarch "represents the principle of unity", but bellow him the three "estates" of "ministering to religion", "military estate" and "scholars, merchants, craftsmen, and peasants" all "should have a share in public offices, benefices, jurisdictions, and honourable charges." Hence, the absolutistic state theory, and following it mercantilism, assumes that the interests of monarchs, merchants, and the entire population are, under certain conditions, in harmony. Interest are not harmonic per se, quite the contrary: people freely following their interest often harms the general well-being, but interests may be harmonized by rulers holding the absolute power.

The liberal view on mercantilism was fundamentally criticized by the two Germans: Werner Sombart and Gustav von Schmoller. They argued that liberals got it all wrong. In his monumental work on *Der moderne Kapitalismus* Sombart (1928a, pp. 912–942) argued that classical economists were misguided by their understanding of economies and mythology. For classical and neoclassical economists, markets are principally static entities which notoriously tend toward equilibria. In contrast, for mercantilists economies are restless, steadily changing organisms. Unlike the partial equilibrium approach of neoclassical economics, mercantilists consider that partial markets are only understandable in the context of the entire organic entity. According to Sombart, classical- and neo-classical economics are the sciences of exchange, mercantilism is the science of production. For classical economists, the free man, guided by an invisible hand following its vested interests, overall best serves the general well-being. In contrast, mercantilists assume that economies need guidance: only a strong sovereign intervening in the economic process, harmonizing opposing interests, overseeing the entire development may guide economies in the right direction. Liberal economic theories favor individuals. Contrary to this, mercantilism strongly favors the interest of the community, which is the interest of the strong, imperialist, powerful state, over individuals: "The interest of the community is in principle state's interest: power and independency of the state are its prime goal" (ibid., p. 926).[1]

For Schmoller (1944), mercantilism is first and foremost a nation building theory. According to Schmoller, nations are build on national sentiments. He further claims that absolutistic monarchs faced the problem of inheriting a segmented, differentiated entity, inhabited by people without national sentiments. Economic unification of the fragmented nation was hoped to foster the political integration of the segmented regions. Intensifying domestic trade was expected to glue together the segmented economy and to build the national economic organism. Intensifying national trade, protectionism against the enemies and the foundation of national economic champions was hoped to foster national sentiments, patriotism, and national solidarity. Hence, according to Schmoller, the main goal of mercantilism was economic state or nation building: integrating the segregated parts of the national economy into one autarkic organism that fosters national sentiments and facilitates political integration. "Mercantilism's core is nothing else than

[1]"Das Gemeininteresse ist im wesentlichen das Staatsinteresse: Macht und Selbständigkeit des Staates ist ihr oberstes Ideal".

state-building, but not only state-building: it is state-building and economy-building" (ibid., p. 36).[2] In a summation of Schmoller's view, we can note that monarchs followed four main goals: first, to develop the economy, in particular domestic trans-regional trade and the industry. Second, develop national markets and national economic champions in order to foster national sentiments and the economic integration of the nation. Third, economic autarky, economic independency from the potential enemy was considered a military necessity. Fourth, to collect as much bullion as possible; armies were paid in hard coins, which is why nations' bullion treasury was pivotal for their military force. Mercantilism provided the economic theory for the monarchs' main goals: nation building, the glory of the monarchy, and military force.

4.2.1.2 Two Main Mercantilism

The banking- and money-relevant mercantilist contributions may be divided into two main strands: bullion-mercantilism and money-mercantilism. Liberal opponents of mercantilism predominately focused on the first. For the development of the European modern banking system and the foundation of the predecessors of central banks (in particular the later), money-mercantilism was pivotal. In the following section a short introduction to both is given.

4.2.1.2.1 Bullion-Mercantilism

No other issue is more closely connected with mercantilism in the general perception than its love for bullion. Early mercantilists' favor of bullion is most visible in their theory of wealth: "gold bullion and treasure of every kind as the essence of wealth" (Blaug 1992, p. 10). Bullion was seen as the nature of countries' wealth. It was considered that a nation's wealth decreases as bullion flows out and increases as bullion flows in. However, classical economists' presentation of mercantilists' favor of bullion is usually very superficial and interspersed with their aversion towards mercantilism. Criticizing the classical tenor of mercantilism's love for bullion, Dühring (1879, p. 32) stated: "They (classical Authors) often treated mercantilism as if businessmen and statesmen believed that bullion may be used to feed a human body."[3] Sombart (1928a, pp. 912–942) considers the classical economists view that mercantilists equalized wealth and bullion "naïve" and "absurd". According to him, the strong favor of bullion does not originate in an inexplicable favor of hard currency, but from mercantilism's focus on trade and production. For Sombart the mercantilist favor of bullion stems from the belief that bullion is "the very life of trade" and that it "keeps the wheels of the machine in motion." For him, it

[2] "Er [Merkantilismus] ist in seinem innersten Kern nichts anderes als Staatsbildung—aber nicht Staatsbildung schlechtweg, sondern Staats- und Volkswirtschaftsbildung".

[3] "Sie haben oft genug so geredet, als wenn die Geschäftsleute und Staatsmänner beinahe geglaubt hätten, dass sich die edlen Metalle zur Nahrung des menschlichen Körpers gebrauchen liessen".

originates in the assumption that the abundancy of money fosters trade, production, and economic prosperity.

Bullion was particularly important for absolutism because armies were paid in coins. Heckscher (1935b, pp. 13–49) outlined that mercantilism was also a system of power. Monarchs' power heavily dependent on the ability to pay soldiers and hence, on their bullion treasury. When the French King Louis XII asked his advisor Gian Giacomo de Trivulzio what would be necessary to take over Milan, his answer was; three things must be ready: money, money, and once again money (Ehrenberg [1896] 1928, p. 29). Times were violent (Wilson 1967, p. 573) and economists were well aware of the pivotal importance of bullion for military success; "there was a widespread opinion that treasure was the only type of wealth worth accumulating, an opinion which had more than a grain of truth from the point of view of the state, in an area in which wars were won with gold" (Screpanti and Zamagni 2005, p. 32). Bullion was considered the life insurance for nations in case of war and the life juice of trade and therefore of economic development. "The length of the national pursue determines the strength of the national defensive forces. With some limitation Hobbes' maxim 'Wealth is power and power is wealth' is true" (Barker 1906, p. 194). According to Hobbes (1651), an absolute monarchs legitimacy stems from their ability to protect the people from foreign aggression and bring peace to the nation. A monarch who fails to bring peace to his people loses legitimacy. Given that bullion was pivotal to forming armed forces and therefore for self-protection the accumulation of bullion legitimated a monarch's dominion.

Recapitulating the logic of mercantilism, Adam Smith (1776, p. 5) stated that a nation has "two great engines" to increase its wealth if it has no domestic natural resources: promoting exports and/or hindering imports. Both measures were part of the trade policy of most absolutist states. "The [mercantilist] theory of economic policy […] was simple. Commercial policy had to be protectionist. Export duties had to be abolished and import duties raised" (Screpanti and Zamagni 2005, p. 35). Therefore, mercantilist protectionism was propelled by the view that bullion is the engine of trade and production and in particular that gold wins wars and therefore legitimizes the absolutistic dominion.

Hence, the mercantilist bullionism—"Bullionism had dominated the opinions circulating in the European courts up to the end of the sixteenth century" (ibid., p. 32), following several main logics: first, bullion is the engine of economic prosperity, military force, national glory, and ultimately political dominion. Second, everything that decreases the bullion treasury, like imports, needs to be avoided, and everything that increases the treasury, like exports, should be supported. Third, trade is the most important business because it facilitates state building and enhances the bullion treasury by exporting domestic goods. Fourth, in sharp contrast to liberal thought, trade was considered a cold war because everyone tries to beggar thy neighbor.

4.2.1.2.2 Money-Mercantilism

Spreading utilitarianism in the 18th century shifted political goals toward economic development and public welfare (Kunisch 1999, p. 27). Encouraged by the new goals, mercantilism changed from bullion-mercantilism to money-mercantilism—or paper money-mercantilism as Heckscher (1935a, b) calls it. Money-mercantilism was one of the first consistent theories of industrialization, employment, money, and interest. It is money-mercantilism which bred the most famous mercantilist writers, which inspired Keynes, but which also caused some of the most serious financial crises.

Developing a, for the time, quite sophisticated macroeconomic theory of employment and prosperity, mercantilism remained loyal to the view that economic development needs guidance; hence, the transfer to state intervenionism. Money-mercantilists were convinced by the usefulness of state inventions, which guide private interests and increase general welfare (Heckscher 1935b, pp. 316–324). Stemming from the organic understanding of economies. For mercantilists the regulating, overlooking, and guiding government is an integrative part of well-functioning economies (Sombart 1928a, p. 928). In contrast to the invisible hand of classical economics, mercantilists favored the protectionist guiding strong hand of the state which develops the economy for a higher purpose; Heckscher (1935a, p. 26) calls mercantilism a "protectionist system." According to Cunningham (1892, p. 157), "the regulation of industry was universally regarded as right and necessary" and desirable: firstly, because of "political purposes", secondly "to maintain the quality of goods," and thirdly "to reward those who introduced some new trade or improved process." Particularly keen was François du Noyer, who proposed to form just one big company with a monopoly of the whole economy. Hence, mercantilism was characterized by the belief in heavy regulation and protection, state granted monopolies, and the promotion of export and import restrictions.

From bullionism to the later money-mercantilism, the ultimate aim of economics shifted; the shift was particularly important for the banking system. Bullionism strongly focused on the bullion treasury, money-mercantilism followed two (interrelated) aims: the bullion treasury and full employment (Wilson 1967, p. 569). "The mercantilist 'fear of good' was nourished, among other things, by the idea of creating work at home and of taking measures against unemployment" (Heckscher 1935b, p. 121). The focus on employment impressed many leftist economists. Rothbard (1995a, p. 235) warns against a common misunderstanding: he considers that the mercantilists' favor of employment was "scarcely humanitarian," but rather more a theory for "forced labour" to eradicate the suggested idleness of the poor. However, it was the mercantilist theory of employment, money, investment, and interest that strongly inspired Keynes. In Chapter 23 of his, *General Theory of Employment Interest and Money* (1935) Keynes discuses, by his standards relatively extensively, mercantilist ideas about trade balance, employment, interest, and money. According to Keynes, four central points constitute the (money) mercantilist theory: first of all, there is no mechanism which automatically adjusts interests rates toward a rate which ensures full employment. Secondly, mercantilists lined out that cheapness may worsen the terms of trade, because the country sells cheap abroad and buys expensive from abroad. Thirdly, the scarcity of money causes unemployment. Fourthly, economic nationalism and mercantilism have a "tendency to promote war."

Keynes stressed a very important point: money-mercantilists suggest a positive relation between the abundance of money and employment; the more money, the less unemployment. Mercantilist view on the relation between these two stemmed from their newly developed concept of capital and the price of money: "money was identified with capital" (Heckscher 1935b, p. 199). John Locke, maybe the most profound money economist of his times, lined out in a letter to the Parliament from 1691 entitled *Considerations of the Consequences of the Lowering of Interest, and Raising the Value of Money* ([1691] 1824) that the value of money depends solely on demand and supply. As a general law of prices for money, land, and any other commodity, he notes: "[what] makes land, as well as other things dear: plenty of buyers, and but few sellers: and so by the rule of contraries, plenty of sellers and few buyers makes land cheap" (ibid., p. 40). However, Locke (ibid., p. 33) considers that money has a "double value." First, money as a means of exchange has an exchange value: "money has a value, as it is capable, by exchange, to procure us the necessaries or conveniencies of life, and in this it has the nature of a commodity; only with this difference, that it serves us commonly by its exchange, never almost by its consumption" (ibid., p. 34). Secondly, money as a means of production has a capital value. In its form as a means of production "it is capable, by its interest, to yield us such a yearly income: and in this it has the nature of land (the income of one being called rent, of the other use)" (ibid., p. 33). Adopting Locke's view that money is a means of production, money-mercantilists conclude that, like land or labor, the extension of money enhances production (Heckscher 1935a, p. 200). Money and labor being considered as the two main means of production, mercantilists assume that capital is usually scarce and labor abundant: hence, to increase production and employment more money would be needed. Picking up Locke's concept that interests are money's price as a means of production, money-mercantilists developed a production theory of money with shares many similarities with Keynes (1935) theory of interest, investment, and employment and Wicksell's ([1898] 1936) money theory. Like Keynes and Wicksell, in a much more rudimentary form, mercantilists argued that businessmen invest if the expected profits on the investments exceed the interest to be paid to the money owner. From this it follows: with high interest rates fewer investments seem to pay off, less will be invested, and therefore employment is low. Contrary, in the case of low interests rates much will be invested and hopefully full employment will be reached. Using Locke's argument that supply and demand determine the value of money (the interest rate), several English and French mercantilists stressed that the abundance and scarcity of money decreases, respectively increases, interest rates (Heckscher 1935a, p. 200). An extension of the supply of money reduces interest rates and therefore increases production, employment, exports, and therefore the bullion treasury; the contrary holds if money becomes scarcer. According to Keynes (1935, p. 340), three means seemed available to keep down interest rates: "usury laws", "maintaining the domestic stock of money" and "discouraging rises in the wage-unit."

Assuming that an increase in the available money would foster production, trade, employment, the bullion treasury, and therefore the pride of the nation, money-mercantilist thought "was dominated by the idea that money was inadequate" (Heckscher 1935b, p. 218). That the "scarcity of money was a strong theme" (Murphy 1997a, p. 2) also stemmed from the specific historical situation: "the mines could not produce enough precious metals, bad money drove out good over the years, and the evils of hoarding were always lurking" (Braudel 1982, p. 112). Considering the scarcity of money the most urgent economic problem, economists took much effort to develop strategies for overcoming the money shortage. The obvious solution to the money scarcity problem was paper money not fully covered by bullion. Many famous mercantilists knew the Italian financial markets from journeys or trough reports and were quite impressed that Italian banks over lent coins and bullion reserves. They were impressed that Italian, like Dutch, banks augment the money stock by credit granting. The most recognized mercantilist authors of the time, Mun, Potter, Robinson, Child, and Petty praised the advantages of uncovered paper money and many suggested to establish a similar banking system (Heckscher 1935b, p. 232). Those contribution "sented a challenge to the established orthodoxy that specie was the only type of money that could be used" by moving "from metallism to cartelism"; hence by questioning the full coverage of paper money by bullion (Murphy 1997a, p. 21 f.). With the decoupling of paper money from bullion, the scarcity of money seemed surmountable. Humphrey (1999, p. 58) summarizes the mercantilist money theory: "(1) money stimulates trade, (2) real cost-push forces determine the price level and the inflation rate, (3) the interest rate is a purely monetary variable whose level, high or low, is proof of the scarcity or abundance of money."

4.2.1.3 Mercantilism on Banking

It is not too bold to say that overall the time of absolutism and mercantilism was pivotal for banking in Europe. With the formation of various protestant Churches and the Church of England, Europe became much more diverse in terms of religion. However, on the question of usury, Protestant Churches (Lutheranism, Calvinism), the Church of England, and the Catholic Church somehow inherited from the medieval Church the ambivalent relation to credit, interest, and banking (Tawney 1948; Riemersma 1952). Still, long battles were fought between the Churches, conservative parts of the society, and moralists on one side and the economic elites, in particular bankers, on the other side. However, generally speaking, the bankers were on the rise and the clergy and moralists in the retreat. Ashley (1888) and Cunningham (1892) provide a detailed description of how the Churches and moralists gradually lost influence. Many heated debates about banking and interest took place, but those discussions became increasingly secular; debates on the opportunities and risks of banking and about the social dimension of interest were still around, but the arguments became increasingly economic and utilitarian and much less theological. Utilitarianism on the rise and Christian morality on the retreat, arguments shifted from whether developments are compatible with religious moral to whether they increase the general utility. Tawney (1925, p. 170) stated that in England a "growth of a body of opinion which argued that economics were one thing and ethics another" used their influence to push back the Church's influence in economic questions. Of course, England was a pioneer, but similar trends could be found in most European countries.

As maintained above, the scholastic view was replaced by the mercantilist view as the leading economic Idea. However, in particular the transformation from bullionism to money-mercantilism was of importance for the development of the European banking system. Still ambivalent toward banking, the scholastics reached the position that credit and banking are necessary. Contrary to this, money-mercantilists were enthusiastic about banking and the banks' ability to create money. For money-mercantilists, far-reaching banking innovations foster production, trade, employment, a favorable trade balance, and the military force. Expecting that credit facilitation would enhance production, trade, and therefore the pride of the nation, it is not surprise that mercantilists advocated strongly for banking innovations.

In the late 17th and 18th century, at the time of money-mercantilism, according to Heckscher (1935b, p. 232): "On the continent [Europe], there was a general move towards banking." In his *political Arithmetick*, Petty ([1676] 1899, p. 265) argues that Holland's banks were an important factor in its trade preeminence as they "encrease Mony". Somehow reluctant towards big private banks due to their proneness to hazard and crises and the fact that "thousands are in danger of ruin at once" if big banks fail, Potter (1650, pp. 71–72) explicitly suggested the use of bills of credit as money and considered that the "degree of credit" (amount of paper money) may be extended to "any degree needfull." Thomas Mun, one of the most notable mercantilist authors, postulates in his *England's Treasure by Forraign Trade* ([1664] 1895) 24 "admirable feats supposed to be done by Bankers, and the Merchants." Needless to say, he was quite certain of the advantages of banking. The most influential Austrian mercantilist, Wilhelm von Schröder ([1686] 1737, pp. 355–356), lamented in his book *Fürstliche Schatz- und Rent-Cammer* that rich men waste and hoard money while trade increasingly suffers from money shortage. To overcome the money shortage he suggested to found banks like those of Italian City-States to give out credit bills which may be used as paper money.

Enthusiastic about banking innovations, many money-mercantilists were quite dissatisfied with the existing banking system. Charging banks for taking sides with the idles, for money-mercantilists the ideal banks create paper money, help to overcome the money shortage and supply capital to merchants, industry, and in particular to the government, and at the lowest interest rate possible. In the late 17th century many contributors of the interest rate debate lamented that too high interest raters harm economic development and trade. Recommending a wide range of possible measures from interest rate regulation to more competition at the financial sector (Murphy 1997a), many contributions recognized the extension of banking and paper money as an effective measure against high interest rates. Given mercantilists' favor for state interventionism and state monopolies, it is not surprising that many proposed the foundation of public banks with paper money issuing monopolies. It was assumed that, because public banks aim for the wealth and glory of the nation rather than being focused on profit maximization, they lend out more money at lower interest rates. However, practically the strongest argument for the foundation of public banks was that monarchs were convinced that public banks would be able to lend to them without limits at very convenient interest rates. This was particularly important as public finance elsewhere in Europe was out of control: "The sixteenth century was a period of great stress on government budgets everywhere" (Miskimin 1977, p. 159). Most contributors agreed that even state-owned banks with paper money issuing monopolies should not freely choose the amount of issued paper money freely: widespread was the idea that paper money should be collateralized by land.

Hence, the rise of mercantilism and in particular money-mercantilism significantly shaped the dominant ideas on money and banking. Usually, mercantilists suggested heavy state intervention and state guidance. Mercantilists were deeply convinced that the scarcity of money was a central economic problem, which caused unemployment and backwardness and hampered economic progress. Measurements augmenting the money stock were considered the best because they foster trade and production by reducing interests rates and facilitate war financing. Paper money issued by credit granting banks captivated mercantilists. It seemed that uncovered high issuing elasticity of paper money would overcome the suggested shortage of money, stimulate production and trade, and facilitate full employment. Quite unsatisfied with the status quo, money-mercantilists expected that an improved banking system, augmenting the money stock by issuing notes, would become the driving force of the fast developing economy. Believing in the advantages of heavy state interventions and state guidance, many money-mercantilists proposed that note-issuing public banks pursuing to facilitate prosperity and employment rather than maximizing profits would best support economic development and employment. Hence, mercantilism replacing scholastics as the leading economic idea turned the mainstream view on banking upside down: while scholastic contributors were at best ambivalent on banking, money-mercantilism was euphoric on banking and banks' ability to augment the money stock by issuing uncovered paper money.

4.2.2 The Rise of Merchants and Bankers

In the rising European empires, the economic situation was quite diverse: more details about the specific national economic circumstances are given below in the chapters on the developments of the national banking systems. However, there are several main trends which may be found, more or less pronounced, in most states.

Generally, a monarch's power and glory was considered to be closely connected to economic prosperity. As maintained above, mercantilism considered that heavy state intervention and guidance fosters economic prosperity and progress. According to the political elites of the time, the state's and therefore the monarch's power and glory depended on two main issues: first, the economic and political cohesion of the homeland, and second, its military force. Both issues were considered to depend strongly on the economic order. As outlined, according to mercantilism, intensifying national trade and the creation of economic national champions fosters the integration of the segregated state and the spread of national sentiments. In addition, economic development was considered of central importance for military strength: economic autarky was the main goal of mercantilism because economic dependency was considered to undermine military power. Soldiers paid in coins everything that increased the state's bullion treasury, like exports. Heavily depending on credit for war financing, the wealthy bourgeoisie became an important state lender.

Trade was the engine of growth. Between the Religious Wars and the French Revolution, the trade of the leading European empires extended fast and became the main driver of economic progress (O'Rourke et al. 2010, pp. 96–121). "Everywhere along the western seaboard of Europe and along the coastline of the Mediterranean […] in the centuries that stretched from the Renascence to the enlightenment the merchants were the dynamic element in society" (Wilson 1967, p. 487). The dominance of merchant capitalism was especially visible in the booming trade centers. Due to wide networks, fast accumulation of trade profits, and traders' role as hinges between regions and classes, merchants were among the most influential economic groups. The merchants' power and influence was further strengthened by their central role in the bullion treasury and in the state-building process: as maintained, mercantilists considered trade the driver of economic progress, one that facilitates state building by integrating the segregated economy and that develops the military force by enhancing the bullion treasury of the state. Granting state monopolies to loyal traders and taking protectionist measures to ward off annoying foreign competition were the usual political measurements to support traders. Notorious partners of the monarchs (Rothbard 1995a, p. 213), provided with state monopolies, shielded by protectionism and supported by the leading economic theory, merchants were one of the most influential groups of the economic order. Together with successful craftsmen and the rising small-scale industry, merchants built the rising early bourgeoisie.

Accumulating much lendable capital, in need of credit and other financial services and hardly restricted by moral reservations against money lending, the rising bourgeoisie became the main pillar and supporter of banking. Two groups were particularly predestined for banking: merchants and craftsmen in contact with the wealthy, like goldsmiths. Extending (long distance) trade induced financial market deepening: money exchange, short-term (and also, increasingly, long-term) lending and money depositing were typical financial services augmented by the extension of trade. In particular, on the continent merchant banks were founded in fair cities and trading hubs operating coin exchange, short-term lending, and depositing. In addition to trade-based financial services, merchants demanded broader banking activities. Long-distance trade was risky, but quite profitable and successful and necessitated huge investments in advance. The merchants inability to fully cover investments through their own reserves made long-term credit essential for overseas trade: "The entire commodity trade of Europe was governed, remote-controlled so to speak, by the rapid movement of credit and discounting" (Braudel 1982, p. 395). Operating a profitable but risky business, merchants were in need of alternative investment opportunities to diversify risk. Hence, merchants had several reasons to support the deepening of banking: their need of credit and investment opportunities and the suggested positive effects of money augmentation on trade.

Still, relatively small and weak small-scale industry was on the rise. The credit needs of the early industry were often highly overestimated: early industries were less capital intensive than widely believed and the investments were predominately covered by owners' or owners' relatives' savings. "The industrialization of England had proceeded without any substantial utilization of banking for long-term investment purposes" (Gerschenkron 1962). However, Tawney (1925, pp. 43–60) showed that the early English textile and mining industries were relatively dependent on credit. They often complained bitterly about high interest rate and the power of creditors who dictated their business. However, the former victims of high interest rates—the early industrialists—did not demand the restriction of credit, but quite on the contrary emphatically called for the foundation of (state-owned) industrial banks.

Hence, merchants and industrialists had a strong vested interests in the deepening of banking. Inspired by money-mercantilism, merchants were convinced that the abundance of money fosters and the scarcity of money harms trade: therefore, banks issuing notes foster trade. In need of credit and vehicles to invest their accumulated capital, merchants needed banks as borrowers and depositors. Supporting the financial market deepening, merchants requested a more lax credit regulation and demanded the extension of money (Heckscher 1935b, p. 201) and credit. Money-mercantilists considered that augmenting the money stock would foster production due to cheaper capital. It comes as no surprise that blaming money lenders for usurious practices, money-mercantilists' promise of low interest and easy lending convinced productive businesses. Broadly speaking: merchants and small-scale industrialists had a natural interests in economic policies fostering their business and borrowing at the lowest possible interests rates. Money-mercantilism suggested that, despite other measurements, the augmentation of the money stock by paper money issuing fosters trade and production and lowers interest rates. Hence, money-mercantilism transferred merchants' and small-scale industrialists' natural interests into the perceived interests of money stock augmentation and the foundation of paper money issued by big banks able to lend at lower rates.

Merchant and goldsmith bankers, in particular the former, invested in trade and the rising small-scale industry. Apart from investing into the growing economy, a second banking strand emerged: bankers with close ties to the wealthy and needy absorbed huge amounts of capital, from the nouveau riche bourgeoisie and the old money of the nobility, to invest in predominately non-economic activities; consumer loans to the nobility and predominantly war loans to the monarchs. Traditionally, the old land aristocracy was the bulwark against banking. The aristocracy was traditionally skeptical about banking: partly due to theological objections, but mostly because banking was the business of the rising bourgeoisie. Competing with the bourgeoisie for political influence, modern banking was considered the epitome of the rising bourgeoisie. However, the aristocracy's increasing involvement in banking and lending much defied its rejection of banking and money landing. For Marx ([1894] 1984, pp. 593–613) the aristocracy's rampant indebtedness became the nail in its coffin. Tawney (1925, pp. 31–42) analyzes in "The Needy Gentleman" British aristocracy's growing dependency on credit: to cover daily-life expenses, British noblemen increasingly relied on bourgeois money. At the same time, the nobility became the state's main creditor: Zmora (2001) showed that the nobles here the monarch's main lenders: traditionally land based, the high nobility steadily shifted toward state lending.

Initially, banking was mostly a side business of merchants and goldsmiths. From amateur bankers, a group of professional bankers emerged: by-business bankers predominately carrying interests of their core business, professional bankers developed and enforced pure banking interests. Depositing money from the rising bourgeoisie and even the nobility, lending to merchants, craftsman, the nobility and the state, professional bankers became the hinge between different classes, professions, and orders. The outcry of Christian moralists like Wilson ([1572] 1925) against the emerging and professionalization of banking was loud and hysterical, but failed to push back banking. It was easy and relatively effective to denounce banking as long as lending for interest was predominately in the hands of outsiders like Jews, Italians, and Protestants. That financial activities entered the mainstream of society—the moralists' own class, the guild, maybe even the family—much shattered the anti-banking coalition: slowly, due to the popularization of money, lending credit lost its sinful connotation. Often, the only institutions were idle reserves could be stored profitably, the only big lender to the increasingly indebted nobility, industry and trade and the monarchs, and the glue between classes, professionals, guilds, and the monarch, were private bankers, who had wide networks and whose political influence increased fast. Pooling capital to lend to the crown, private bankers became the voice and negotiator of state lenders. Public debt banking was a double-edged sword for bankers: on the one hand becoming a pivotal lender to the crown much increased bankers' power; on the other, bankers were blamed for being unpatriotic and blackmailing and draining the state dry.

Like in Italian City-States, lending to monarchs steadily extended and became the main financial business. Bankers and the nobility were the main state creditors: in Britain predominantly the former, and on the continent the latter. Lending to the sovereign was a lucrative, but quite risky business. Italian City-State lenders complained about the asymmetric power distribution between them and the sovereign as borrower: the asymmetry of power was even more pronounced with the absolutistic monarch as borrower. Frequent defaults and monarchs' access to bank deposits emphasized the unequal power distribution. Rebalancing the power between the borrowing monarchs and their lenders again became a central demand of bankers and depositors.

4.2.3 Political Coalitions

The political order of the rising empires, France, Britain, and Prussia was diverse and took rather different developments. More country-specific details are given below, in the discussions on the developments of the national banking sectors. However, general trends are found in most empires and several national political events had significant impacts on the political order of all empires.

Previously the entire historical period between the Religious Wars of the 16th century and the French Revolution was regarded as a period of absolutism. Due to the political diversity of the time, the notion of absolutism for the entire period became more uneven. However, absolutism as a political idea spread widely (Sommerville 1991) and influenced the rising empires of the time: the French political system of the 17th and 18th century is often considered an ideal-typical example of an absolute state; in Britain absolutism tightened in the 17th century until absolutistic tendencies were swept away by the Glorious Revolution; and Prussia developed the so-called enlightened absolutism in the 18th century.

The period between the Religious Wars and the French Revolution is usually regarded as a time of state building. State building means the political, but also economic integration of the former highly segregated empires. Traditionally, a close connection between absolutistic ideas, political centralization, and state building was suggested. According to Sommerville (2012, p. 117 f.) and Wilson (2000, p. 1) for centuries absolutism was considered: a political and military centralization, a formation of centralized states and the shift of power from the local nobility toward the absolute ruler who builds their power on bureaucracy, and newly founded standing armies; "absolutism was once a certainty" (ibid.). Sommerville (2012, p. 117) summarizes the "old view" on absolutism: the "power of the state expanded" and "centralized," "military institutions were transformed and the standing army became 'both the type and the instrument of the new order'" and the "powers of nobles were eroded." Tocqueville (1856), an advocate of the old view, considered in *The Old Regime and the Revolution* that governmental activities increasingly shifted from the regional aristocracy to the Royal Council. The crown with its Royal Council was we, the aristocracy and the folk were they. Hence, according to Tocqueville, from the perspective of the small political elite, the ruled people become a relatively uniform mass: the unification was reflected in the harmonizing taxation of all citizens. In the old view the centralization of political power was an important step towards a "modern state" and towards the crushing of feudal nobility: absolutism paved the way for the "transition from feudalism to capitalism" (Wilson 2000, p. 1).

More recently, the new view strongly questioned the central propositions of the old view. In particular the absolute power of the monarch and the centralization of power are strongly doubted. According to the new view (see Sommerville 2012) absolute monarchs were relatively weak rulers whose direct power hardly exceeded the frontiers of the capital. To maintain power, monarchs formed coalitions. Noblemen, armed forces, and the economic elites (Kunisch 1999) were the notorious coalition partners of monarchs. "The rule of absolutism was created through a series of alliances between the king, his nobles [...] and various segments of large-scale merchants or traders" (Rothbard 1995a, p. 213). To expand and exercise its domination in rural areas, monarchs heavily relied on the local aristocracy to collect taxes and break local resistance. Hence, rather than breaking the power of the aristocracy, the absolute ruler depended and therefore maintained the power of local aristocratic elites (Sommerville 2012, p. 118).

Armed forces shifted from mercenary armies to huge standing armies: the standing army of Louis XIV, for example, was many times greater than any other army before (Rowlands 129). Standing armies always ready to protect the empire from domestic and foreign enemies became an important pillar of the absolute monarch's power. At the same time, standing armies posed a grave threat to the monarch's dominion: concentrated and always ready military coups were much easier to organize for standing armies. Always fearing the power of the army, monarchs took care to safeguard the army's interests.

Three main reasons made merchants one of the most influential groups of the time: trade was considered the driver of economic growth. Secondly, trade integrated the segregated economy and therefore was considered important for state building. Thirdly, traders exported goods which brought new bullion to the state. Merchants being the traditional economic coalition partner of the crown, the rising bankers also became important partners: steadily in need for credit, monarchs heavily depended on bankers' support.

Relying on the three coalitions—with the nobility, the army, and the rising merchant bourgeoisie—tensions between the three groups, in particular between the nobility and the rising bourgeoisie, jeopardized monarchs' power. Initially, the nobility was the uncontested ruling class (*Herrschaftsstand*) (Kunisch 1999, p. 42) in the absolutistic state: "all the forms of absolutism in Europe served the interests of the nobility or proprietors and expressed the political rule upon the other classes" (Kimmel 1988, p. 10). However, the rise of the bourgeoisie increasingly questioned the nobility's predominance. In addition, the nobility's refusal and inability to accept many, more technical, positions, opened the gate for bourgeois experts. Due to their increasing proximity to the crown, the bourgeoisie influence increased steadily (Kunisch 1999, p. 50). The rise of the bourgeoisie caused increasing tensions with the nobility, but the absolute state still "preserved feudal relations by incorporating the bourgeoisie" but "it was never an arbiter between the aristocracy and the bourgeoisie [...] it was the political carapace of the threatened nobility" (Kimmel 1988, p. 10).

The times between the Religious Wars and the French Revolution were violent: Britain, France, and to a lesser extend Prussia competed over political, military, and economic dominance. Military success, the ability to conquer new lands and protect the homeland from enemies was considered the most important expression of the glory and power of the state' and the ruler, and the main legitimization of the monarchs' dominion. For Hobbes (1651) the absolutist regime is build on a specific social contract between the people and the absolute ruler: people lend their freedom to the king and receive security and prosperity in return. According to Hobbes, the monarchy is legitimized by the monarchs' ability to protect its subjects from foreign and domestic enemies. Recurrent wars between Europe's rising empires necessitated the formation of huge standing armies and other expensive military investments.

Fast extending military costs brought monarchs close to financial ruin. Legitimized by military success, the monarchs' dominion was built on their readiness to finance costly armies and military expeditions: their ability to collect taxes and, in particular, to raise loans. Lacking direct access to rural areas, monarchs heavily depended on the local aristocracy to collect taxes: for example, in France taxes were collected by the rural aristocracy and lent to the monarch (Murphy 1997b, p. 130 ff.). Cooperating with local elites to collect taxes had advantages and major disadvantages: collecting taxes was quite profitable to local elites, which strengthened the coalition between the crown and the rural aristocracy. On the other hand, any adjustment of a government's financing system was strongly rejected by the aristocracy and shattered the coalition between the crown and the nobility carrying the danger of an aristocratic uprising. Monarchs had various financial resources, like taxes and selling favorable administrative and political positions, but the importance of public debt steadily increased: it is to be noted that there was not always a clear-cut distinction between taxation and public debt. Two main reasons caused monarchs to increasingly cover fast rising expenses with public debt: tax rises caused a lot of resistance, in particular from rulers' allies, and secondly, debts were much faster available and therefore advantageous for war financing.

The nobility (Zmora 2001) and, particularly in Britain, the emerging private bankers, (Richards 1965; Andreadēs 1966) were the main state lenders. Mounting public debt had far-reaching political and social consequences. Highly dependent on the nobility's and to a lower extent the bankers' support, rulers granted extensive privileges to the lending members of the nouveau riche, like entrance to court or the right to collect taxes, and to bankers, like new licenses or the extension of their businesses. Both the nobility and the bankers extensively used their crucial importance for the monarchs' political survival in order to shape politics according to their interests. Depending on each other, the monarchs on the creditors' readiness to lend and the creditors on the monarchs' readiness to pay off loans, heavy state lending synchronized the interests of the lenders (the nobility and the bourgeoisie) and the borrower (the monarchs) (Zmora 2001). In his sociological book on the development of the British banking sector, Carruthers (1996) focuses on the state-building process and the political implications of public financing. He (ibid.) states that "post-feudal English monarchs were weak" and had to form coalitions to maintain power. Public debts were the main instrument to form coalitions with economic elites: "trough the growth of the national debt, the state also managed to create alliances with Britain's mercantile and commercial classes" (ibid., p. 22). Borrowing heavily to the crown, economic elites had a strong self-interests to maintain the political order and avoid bloody revolutions and unorganized takeovers. Hence, economic elites became attached to the regime by lending to it: "creditors of the sovereign acquired an interest in the political health of the regime to whom they had loaned money, for they were among the biggest losers if the regime 'died'" (ibid., p. 9 f.). In addition, the nobility's heavy lending against interest payments gravely weakened the anti-banking coalition.

European monarchs depending on nobility's and bankers' credit to cover the fast rising expenses (Zmora 2001) was an inefficient but stable system. It was inefficient because rising money was still difficult and took time: lacking institutions like the Italian City-State state lender associations, rising credit necessitated convincing or forcing a great number of smaller or bigger lenders. Despite the profitability of state lending, frequent defaults kept the wealthy from heavier voluntary lending. All big among empires facing similar difficulties of raising funds for military ventures balanced the power between themselves: as long as no ruler was supported by a superior war-financing system, the distribution of power between Europe's big empires remained relatively stable.

The relatively stable power distribution between the empires was shaken significantly by the British Glorious Revolution and the induced financial revolution. Discussed in more details below, the Glorious Revolution empowered the Parliament over state financing and paved the way for the foundation of the Bank of England and the making of the big British trading companies public. Absorbing most idle hoards to lend exclusively to the state, the Bank of England considerably changed the balance of power in Europe. Other empires still struggling to raise money, Britain's elasticity of public credit significantly increased with the foundation of the Bank of England. Its ability to raise money on an entirely new scale, in very short time, significantly shifted the fortunes of war toward Britain. The advantage of Britain's centralized public debt financing (North and Weingast 1989) compared with the still decentralized continental system (Epstein 2001) startled continental empires, in particular France, the traditional rival of Britain.

Recognizing the disadvantage of lacking an institution like the Bank of England, France failed to reform its state finance system due to the heavy resistance from the nobility. The French monarch was in a bind: under strong pressure due to military failures, he was too dependent on the support of the nobility to touch the public financing system. Only the deepest financial crisis of French absolutism opened the historical window for change: with their back to the wall financially, the monarch found no other way to plug the financial holes than prosecuting the aristocracy through the Chambre de Justice. The Chambre de Justice broke the long-lasting coalition between the monarch and the aristocracy. On trial and busy with hiding its wealth, the French aristocracy was too weak to combat profound innovations in the French banking and state financing system. The deep crisis of the aristocracy was accompanied by the appearance of John Law, one of the most innovative paper money contributors. The French monarch being, again, close to bankruptcy, Law's proposal for a note-issuing public bank seemed like the last chance to prevent the financial crash. The monarch trapped and the aristocratic opposition being on the ropes, the way was open for Law and the greatest money-mercantilist project in history: the foundation of the Banque Royale.

Therefore, the rulers' dominion was usually much less absolute than believed: it was built on complex, difficult, and often quite fragile coalitions between the court, economic and military elites, and the old aristocracy. In particular, state financing was a core problem. The military demanded huge financial resources and the monarchs' legitimization highly depended on their ability to win wars against enemies. Raising huge amounts of money in a short time being pivotal for military success, the military and the monarchs had a strong vested interests in a well-functioning state financing systems. Unable to cover quickly rising government costs by taxes, European empires increasingly relied on public debt. State lending fulfilled two main functions: it helped the ruler cover war and other expenses. It also bound economic elites and the old aristocracy, the main lenders, closer to the government: heavily invested in the political system, both had a strong interest in promoting and protecting the monarchy. Thankful for the boundless profitable investment opportunities, economic elites and in particular the old aristocracy, had an interest in maintaining the state financing status quo. However, major weaknesses of the established state financing system became increasingly apparent. The long time it took to raise the money for wars complicated military escapades. High interest rates and monarchs' financial imprudence caused governments to frequently default on loans.

4.2.4 The Rise of Private, Public, and Non-profit Banks

The cultural, political, and economic order changed significantly in the 17th and 18th century. The rise of money-mercantilism, absolutism, and the bourgeoisie considerably changed the environment of the banking sector. New ideas on banking, the accumulation of capital, the deepening of credit, and in particular the monarchs' financial problems, caused discussions and negotiations about appropriate institutional change in the banking sector. The institutionalization of money-mercantilist banking ideas in the form of national public banks and of modern private banks was a conflictual process: different interests and ideas about the banking system came into conflict. The usual lines of conflict ran between, on the one side, the rising bourgeoisie and the bureaucracy who promoted money-mercantilist ideas on banking and advocated for modern banking and the foundation of big national banks, and on the other side the established small private bankers and the old aristocracy who feared that profound changes of the banking sector would thwart their money-lending business. Rarely the conflict would be solved by a compromise between the two sides; transformations usually occurred when the coalition in favor of profound change took advantage of the other side's weakness and created precedents by founding banks or changing laws. In the following chapters, changes in the private, public, and non-profit banking sector in Britain, France, and Mosaic-Germany are outlined.

4.2.4.1 Private Banking in Britain, France, and Germany

Between the Religious Wars of the 16th century and the French Revolution, private banking developed in the rising European empires of France, Britain, and Germany. Significant changes occurred in all three countries; however, the development was rather different. In Britain a distinctive and strong private banking system emerged. In France and Germany the development was much more difficult and slow: French banking in particular suffered from the opposition of the strong aristocracy and the rejection of the people; in Germany the political segregation hindered the emerging of modern private banks. However, in all three rising empires the foundation for future development of the banking sector was laid.

4.2.4.1.1 Private Banking in Britain

Politically, Britain faced difficult times during the 17th century. Escalating religious conflicts, between Catholics and the Church of England on the one side and Protestants on the other, and between the absolutistic King and the predominant puritan republicans, brought to the civil war of the mid-century. The Glorious Revolution of the late 17th century ended British absolutism. Weakening the position of the Crown, the Glorious Revolution paradoxically opened the door for Britain's dominance in the world. Politically unstable, Britain's economic rise began to take shape in the 17th century. Britain took the spot of Holland as the biggest overseas trader: the rise of overseas trade was closely connected to Britain's early colonialism. In addition to fast extending overseas trade, industrialization started to take off. After the Glorious Revolution, Britain became the protector of Protestants and France their notorious opponent. Despite the much bigger population of France, the fortune of war leaned toward Britain thanks to its stronger financial system.

Britain was the first of the three later dominant European empires, Britain, France, and Germany, to see a modern banking system emerge. It has also been maintained that religious objections against money lending influenced the development of banking much less than in the Italian City-States: this is true as a general trend, but it should not obscure the fact that, in particular at the beginning, heated moral debates on banking were not unusual. Throughout the entire period, usury laws restricted interest rates: during the emerging of British banking "the question at issue was not whether the usurer should be punished—a point as to which there was only one opinion—but who should have the lucrative business of punishing him" (Tawney 1948, p. 63). Thomas Wilson's ([1572] 1925) *A Discourse Upon Usury* is a detailed description of moral reservations against the lending of money and banking. He warns (ibid., p. 177) against the "ouglie, detestable and hurtefull synne of usurie, whiche, [...] being nowe so rancke througout Englande." Tawney (1925) considers in his historical introduction to Wilson's contribution that anti-interest and anti-credit sentiments were still widespread. Moralists complained bitterly about the involvement of people from different classes, professions, and religions in banking and financial services. That so many were involved in "a thinge directlye against all lawe, against nature, and against god" caused Wilson ([1572] 1925, p. 177) to believe that "the end of thys worlde is nyghe at hande." Certainly that Wilson's position "is typical of one side in the discussion of credit and money-lending" (Tawney 1925, p. vii), however, it emphasized that moral resentment against banking still existed and did not lose much of its medieval radicality: the conflict between the economic necessity and moralists' reservation caused a long-lasting "struggle between the new economic movement of the age and the scheme of economic ethics expounded by churchmen" over "credit, money-lending and prices" (Tawney 1948, p. 155). Nevertheless, looking at the entire period, there can be little doubt that moralists and theological banking opponents were on the retreat and banking advocates on the rise (Ashley 1888; Cunningham 1892, p. 153–159).

With the moralists' opposition against banking on the retreat, the spread of money-mercantilism further fostered the rise of banking. Ito (2011) surveyed the British economic contribution to banking between the years 1600 and 1688: he found that at least two dozen contributions supported the extension of banking and proposed several banking innovations. Various money-mercantilist arguments were used to legitimize and promote banking. Fully in line with money-mercantilism, banking-friendly contributors assumed that Britain's economy suffers from money shortage. They suggested that imaginary paper money and bank credit would foster trade and economic prosperity. Competing with Holland for overseas trade dominance, contributors lined out that Holland's trade force stems predominately from its strong banking sector. In order to foster their own overseas trade and to outstrip Holland, a strong banking sector was needed, it was emphasized. In addition, it was suggested that (as a very money-mercantilist argument) deepening banking is the most effective measure against usury: extending banking activities and the supply of (paper) money would reduce interest rates and therefore foster employment, trade, and production; hence the wealth and glory of the nation. Perhaps inspired by the remains of scholastic thought, early proposal often demanded the foundation of charity banks. Later, the clear cut division between profit-oriented and charity banks vanished behind the general view that banking is a good thing, in particular for the poor. According to Richards (1965, p. 92) the debate on banking formed "an important field of economic literature from which it is evident that a large number of Tudor and Stuart writers fully realised the need of a well-organised credit system."

During the 17th century, the Crown, the aristocrats, the merchants, and the developing industry became increasingly indebted. Changes in the economic structure necessitated credit on a new scale: overseas trade was very expensive and required big capital in advance. Similarly, the credit needs of the prospering industry increased fast (Braudel 1984, p. 605). Merchants and industrialists usually still covered their financial needs through their own, or their relatives' savings. However, the developing economy increasingly also depended on anonymous bank credit. For Marx, the aristocracy's increasing indebtedness became the nail in its own coffin. It is beyond the scope of this study to analyze in what way debt ruined Britain's aristocracy; however, like Tawney (1925, pp. 31–42), the aristocracy's indebtedness extended quickly. Despite the growth of private debt, the sovereign was still the main borrower, just like in Medieval times: Carruthers (1996) and Dickson (1967) analyzed Britain's fast increasing indebtedness and its social and political consequences. Increasing demands for credits were accompanied by the rising supply of investable capital. Loanable funds increased elsewhere in Europe (Braudel 1982, p. 386), but in particular in Britain. Overseas merchants and industrialists quickly accumulated capital; in addition, as the wealthy nobility increasingly got attached to banking, a great amount of idle money was invested rather than hoard. As money lending lost much of its sinful connotations, even conservative aristocracy started to invest its hoards via newly founded banks. Hence, on the borrower side of the credit, table merchants, industrialists, the aristocracy, and in particular the Crown demanded much credit; on the lender side, "merchantmen, citizens, noblemen, courtiers, gentlemen, grasiers, farmers, plowmen, artificers and even the clergy lend money at interest" (Tawney 1925, p. 87).

In the late Tudor period, brokers, scriveners, merchants, and goldsmiths discovered the business of banking; in particular the latter two lent heavily to the Crown. According to Richards (1965, pp. 1–22) banking was still a by-business. Banking as a profession had not yet developed, which is why Tawney (1925) considers the time "semi-capitalism"; financial markets were in an intermediate stage between the pawnbroking business of the medieval times and the professionalization of banking in the later 17th century. Banking became visible as banks opened elsewhere, but they still remained pre-modern, as early bankers still predominantly invested their own idle and their relatives' savings. Soon, parts of the by-business bankers widened the depositor spectrum. Steadily, British private banking professionalized as banking became the bankers' core business. Well-known, and often told as an introduction to banking courses, is the story that says British banking emerged from goldsmith business; "It is hitherto been generally assumed that the English goldsmith bankers [...] were very rudimentary exponents of banking technique" (Richards 1965, p. 23). Tawney (1925, p. 101 f.) doubts that goldsmiths were the (core) founders of British banking: he considers the story that goldsmiths are "the heroes of the drab history of financial capitalism" a myth, because goldsmiths were only one group of money lenders among many. However, as banking professionalized, lending depersonalized and anonymized, and hence became steadily more modern; professional private British bankers absorbing deposits from "thousands of provincial and metropolitan customers" (Richards 1965, p. 24) and lending it to merchants, industrialists, aristocrats, and the Crown, bankers became, in addition to depositors and borrowers, the third main group of the banking market. Predominately intermediating loanable funds, banks developed independent vested interests: as maintained above, it is in the modern banks' interest to minimize interest payments to depositors and maximize those received from borrowers and to pass on as much risk as possible to either the borrowers or the depositors.

Public debt intermediation became the core business of the early professional bankers. Even as industrial production and credit-intensive overseas trade increased, steadily mounting public debt absorbed the biggest parts of the investable funds. In the early 17th century, most money was still lent directly to the exchequer. However, bankers' importance as intermediates between savers and the exchequer steadily increased: "Those with money refused to lend directly to the Crown, still preferring to deposit it with Lombard Street goldsmith-bankers, who would then loan it to the Crown. Hence, the treasury orders [...] innovations of 1665 were mostly bought by goldsmith-bankers" (Carruthers 1996, p. 61). Several factors fostered the private bankers' public credit business: the high profitability of banking enabled bankers to pay relatively high interest on deposited money. Even more importantly, the unreliability of the mint helped bankers recruit new depositors. The mint was traditionally the bankers' public competitor for idle reserves.

As the mint was used by the monarchs as a private financial repository, it lost its reputation as a safe place: mistrusting the mint, the wealthy increasingly deposited money with private banks (Richards 1965, p. 35). Charles I using the merchants' bullion in the Tower for his own expenses caused merchants to turn toward private bankers. The savers' mistrust of public institutions greatly increased private bank deposits. Flooded with new deposits, bankers were in a comfortable position to borrow at low rates from the wealthy and lent at horrendous interest rates to the Crown (Andreadēs 1966, p. 19). Thanks to high profitability, new banks sprung up like mushrooms. Outside London, so-called country banks and merchant banks were founded (Kindleberger 1993, pp. 81–84). The breakup of the dominance of private banks' public debt in the late 17th century through the foundation of new institutions like the Bank of England caused private banks to search for new investment opportunities: however, private banks were traditionally involved in a wide range of private and public banking activities (ibid., pp. 77–84).

Modern banking in Britain was built on a strong coalition. According to Tawney (1925), modern bankers use their power to influence the government, the king and the parliament. Depositors from various classes, professions, and guilds had a strong interest in supporting banks and refusing heavy banking regulation or the nationalization of banks. London bankers may be divided into city- and west-end bankers. The former were predominately involved in government debt banking and the Bank of England, the East India Company, and the South Sea Company stock trading, the latter were the favored investment vehicle of the gentry and aristocracy (Kindleberger 1993, p. 79). The former ensured the goodwill of the big financial and trade institutions and the government, and the latter the goodwill of the wealthy parts of society. Hence, much of the wealthy population had a vested interest in the survival and prosperity of private banks. For many borrowers, private banks were the only creditors. In particular, their dominance in public debt financing made private bankers, for a certain period, political untouchable: investing huge sums into public debt, the ties between the state and the private bankers intensified and the banks' influence on politics significantly increased (Richards 1965, p. 207 f.): "soon the Crown could not do without the bankers, and entered into the closest relations with them" (Andreadēs 1966, p. 33). Private enterprises and monarchs frequently complained bitterly about the unreliability of private bankers and the horrendous interest rates. However, as long as no alternative existed, private entrepreneurs and monarchs were heavily dependent on banks: without the "powerful group of bankers [...] the second Dutch war (1665–1667) could not have been waged" (Richards 1965, p. 26). Although often complaining about the behavior of bankers, merchants, industrialists, the aristocracy, and monarchs heavily depended on banks as depositors or borrowers.

British modern private banks were not just money intermediaries, but augmented the money by issuing bank notes against deposits and as credit instruments. Augmenting money was a core demand of money-mercantilists who blamed the scarcity of money for hampering trade and economic progress. To the Crown it seemed that paper money issuing provided their main creditors with an instrument for endless credit. The bankers' readiness to issue new (paper) loans and the Crown's recurring costly wars against

Holland became a dangerous combination. That "orders were no longer tied to revenue already voted, there was no automatic limit to the number issued" (Horsefield 1982, p. 511) and recurrent costly wars made public debt into an epidemic during the 1660s. Overstretching indebtedness caused Charles II to stop payments on public debts; which is considered in the literature as the Stop of the Exchequer. The effect of Stop of the Exchequer on the states' major creditors—the banks'—causes dispute: Horsefield (ibid.) argued that goldsmith bankers were the biggest loser of Stop of the Exchequer; Richards (1965: 23) considers that goldsmith bankers' loses were largely overestimated. However, Stop of the Exchequer made it very clear that public debts are by no means a safe investment haven and creditors have few means to enforce their interests against the powerful rulers.

In conclusion: in the 17th and early 18th century private banking in Britain fell on fruitful soil. Money-mercantilists ideas were widespread among British economists. It was generally believed that the British economy suffers from money shortage and that an extension of credit would lower interest rates, increase trade, employment and national wealth. At the same time, religiously motivated reservations against banking were in retreat. The cultural order changed in favor of banking. Politicians' aim to become Europe's leading nation was costly: costly wars against continental opponents brought public debt out of control. Governments being highly dependant on private banks' lending steadily increased the bankers' political influence. In addition to the leading political class, economic elites also heavily depended on banks: costly trade and industrial investment necessitated credits of new scale and banks functioned as the preferred investment vehicle for the fast accumulating capital. Overall, the times for private banking were good, which is why the number of private banks increased quickly and steadily throughout the 17th and 18th century (Cottrell 1994). However, Stop of the Exchequer was a turning point in the British financial history and for the emerging modern private banks. Stop of the Exchequer made political and economic elites aware that the public debt system needs a fundamental restructuring.

4.2.4.1.2 Private Banking in France

In France the takeoff of banking was bumpier than in Italy, Britain, and the Netherlands. Unlike in Britain and the Netherlands, in France money lending was dominated at the beginning by Italian bankers and Jews, both considered foreigners (Plessis 1994). Jewish money lending was predominately pre-modern; rich Jews directly lent to the Crown or private debtors. Around 1530 Giulio and Lorenzo Strozzi from a well-known Florentine family founded a banking house in Lyon. In the following 50 years many Florentine exiles came to the fair city of Lyon and founded banks or became involved in financing and banking in one way or the other; they predominately lent to the Crown (Ehrenberg [1896] 1928, pp. 216–218). French fair cities of the champagne region and Lyon were a fertile soil for Italian bankers. A wide range of banking activities were brought by the so-called Lombards (Italian bankers) to French trading centers (Plessis 1994): like elsewhere, the main business of early French bankers was "supplying funds for business enterprises, in opening credit accounts, and in discounting paper; but the chief business appears to have been that of making loans directly to the government" (Essars Des 1896, p. 8). The ineptness of King Henry II caused the financial crash of 1557. Losing great capital in the crisis, the Lombards moved to Paris (Ehrenberg [1896] 1928, p. 217), which became France's main banking center. Despite the banking developments in the French trading hubs, the overall French banking system remained hugely underdeveloped until the early 18th century.

Like elsewhere in Europe, early banking in France was focused on trade-related activities and state financing. Unlike in Britain, the development of the banking sector came to a halt in the 17th century. Banks emerged in Paris, along the South-French trading routes connecting France with Italy, Spain, and the East and in particular in the fair centers (Bussière 1997). However, banking predominately remained pre-modern: usually, banking was a by-business and bankers normally lent out their own or their relatives' money. Of course, banks also deposited and lent, but compared with Britain and Holland, banking in France remained rudimentary.

Xenophobia directed against bankers hindered the development of the French banking system. Resentments against both Italians and Jews were widespread. Jews lent money to ordinary people and monarchs. Using the widespread anti-Semitic atmosphere, monarchs and upper classes initiated pogroms against the Jewish minority. Pogroms, banishment, and the persecution of Jews were a part of the monarchs' and the upper classes' debt-relief strategy. Ironically, usually soon after the Jewish community was expelled losing their main creditors, monarchs encouraged Jews to return (Essars Des 1896, pp. 1–10). Italian and Jewish money lenders' space was steadily taken up by, mostly Protestant, Frenchmen. In the late 17th century, French Protestants shared the fate of Jews and Italians as they were expelled and persecuted. Modern banking requires a certain minimum level of legal certainty: hardly anybody deposits money at a bank that frequently gets burnt down by an anti-Jewish, anti-Italian, or anti-Protestant mob. The legal uncertainty greatly harmed the development of modern banking in France.

In addition to the hostility against foreign bankers, and even more destructive for the development of banking, was France's disadvantageous, but stable system of state financing. Elsewhere, modern banking was in particular fostered by public debt financing; in France, bankers lent to the sovereign, but, unlike in Britain, they were unable to overtake the business. According to Carruthers (1996, pp. 106–114), French absolute monarchs had a credit record so bad that anybody would have lent to them on very big scale. Monarchs, at least theoretically chosen by god and accountable to nobody, unable to raise enough capital to finance costly wars, heavily relight on rural aristocracy to solve their financial hardships. Murphy (1997b, p. 132) considered that French rulers used four instruments to cover their mounting expenses: direct taxes, indirect taxes, venality, and borrowing. Practically, taxation and lending were hardly distinguishable. State financing in France had two goals: to cover court expenses and to satisfy the interest of local elites. "Merging the financial interests of elites with those of the state gave them a stake in the success of the absolutist regime" (Carruthers 1996, p. 111). In return for their loyalty, local elites were enabled to participate in the very profitable tax-collecting business. Local tax farms were granted the right to collect taxes in return for a fix payment to the Crown (Murphy 1997b, p. 134 ff.). Others, like merchants and aristocrats, contributed to state financing by purchasing political positions (Carruthers 1996, p. 111). Doubtlessly, the French state financing system was pivotal for the state-building process: granting the right to collect taxes to local elites and enabling elites to enhance their status by paying political positions safeguarded the elites' loyalty to the Crown. Profiting from the status quo, the political and economic elites had a strong interest in the stability of the political system. At the same time, the state financing system also showed the courts' main weakness: "French monarchy was delivered, until the very end of its existence, into the hands of private interests" (Braudel 1982, p. 537 f.).

Local elites collected taxes and used their own money to lend to the Crown (Murphy 1997b, p. 133 ff.). That the nobility became the Crown's main creditor did not distinguish France from Britain. However, the system of collecting and lending loanable funds was quite different. British modern banks emerged from pooling capital and lending it predominately to the Crown. In France, money lending, in particular to the Crown, was still considered immoral and sinful. Money lending for interest was seen as ignoble. Unwilling to leave the profitable business of lending to the Crown to someone else, aristocrats installed stooges to cover their involvement in public debt financing. Officially, the French public debt was financed by the so-called, financiers. Usually, financiers were Jews, Italians, Protestants, people who principally faced hostility and therefore had 'no reputation to lose'. However, financiers were just intermediaries who masked the true origin of the invested money (ibid.). Braudel (1982, pp. 537–542) estimated that among the 200 to 300 public debt financers, more than 70% were noblemen. Murphy (1997b, p. 132) concluded that "monarchy was not financially independent. It needed money, money that was lent by the rich nobility via the mediation of the financiers."

For the nobility, the established state financing system was quite beneficial: it allowed the nobility to have a "hand in the most profitable of all [business sector], the king's finances" (Braudel 1982, p. 540) without being morally condemned for lending against interest payments. Hence, it was the "aristocratic grouping that was the principal beneficiary of France's cumbersome financial system" (Murphy 1997b, p. 130) which had a strong interest in maintaining the status quo. Connected by marriage and family relations, clandestine state lenders and tax collectors built quite a powerful clique (Dickson 1967, p. 11) that dominated state financing. Challenging the established state financing system was much too risky even for absolutist monarchs, which is why they avoided altering the system for centuries. Fearing to lose its privileges, the powerful state financing clique thwarted all kind of financial market innovations (Murphy 1997b); the opposition caused a financial market standstill for almost a century.

The French financial system was inferior to the British in various respects: money collected by stooges was cumbersome, slow, untransparent, susceptible to corruption, and denied the Crown's access to taxes. Vested interests in the maintenance of the status quo prevented intensive discussions on the financial system and the emerging of modern banks. Hence, the influence of the profiteers of the status quo prevented far-reaching financial innovations which would have significantly changed state financing. However, Braudel (1982, p. 540) asked: who could alter a system which constitutes "the very heart of privileged society" and ensure the loyalty of the rural elites?

There was little change until a deep public financing crises in the early 18th century unhinged the financial system. Described in more details below, the monarch financially with his back to the wall had no other choice than to dismiss the coalition with the nobility and place its financial destiny in the hands of John Law. The rise and fall of Law's Banque Royale had far-reaching consequences for the French political and economic development. Important for the development of the French banking sector, the rise and failure of Law's experiment broke the power of the old public debt clique which had hampered the development of a modern banking system. At the same time, Law's failure made the general public even more hostile toward banking. In particular, paper money was discredited, which delayed its wide use for centuries. After Law's system failed in 1720, several, mostly Protestant, banks were founded throughout the country, but in particular in Paris (Plessis 1994). The number of Parisian banks increased fast in the second half of the 18th century: mostly involved in public debt banking, banks lent little to industry and commerce (Sée [1928] 2004, p. 103). However, compared to Britain, the French private banking sector remained largely underdeveloped until the French Revolution.

During the time of French absolutism, the private banking sector remained underdeveloped:

> There was nothing comparable [to the 'highly developed' credit markets of Holland and England] in mid-eighteenth century France, which had not yet begun to catch up with Holland and England in business matters. Credit seems to have been poorly and almost clandestinely organized there (Braudel 1982, p. 389).

Several factors prevented the development of modern private banks: xenophobia against bankers, the sustained rejection of money lending against interests payments, and the slower accumulation of capital. However, most importantly, the old nobility, the powerbase of the monarchy, strongly combated changes in public financing and the banking system. Hence, "the social climate [for credit and private banking] was not particularly encouraging" (ibid.).

4.2.4.1.3 Private Banking in Mosaic-Germany

Before the unification in the 19th century, Germany was fragmented. The economic and politic situation was quite diverse and so was the development of the banking system. Banking in the North- and the South-German trading hubs was dominated by trading-based activities, and in most other small German states by public debt financing. Overall, private banking was underdeveloped in the 17th and 18th century in most German states; unlike in France, where the development was hampered by political coalitions, Germany's economic underdevelopment, and in particular its fragmentation, hindered the emerging of a modern banking system.

German banking took off at the beginning of the 19th century, but most of the successful private banks were founded in the 18th century. Most German banks emerged from one of two strands: first, rich businessmen, mostly merchants, who lent out their idle hoards, predominately to monarchs. Many of the big and famous German banking houses were founded as merchant banks in the 18th century (Born 1977, p. 54 ff.). Secondly, banks founded by Hoffaktoren (court agents) or their children. Hoffaktoren are in a way the German counterparts to the French financiers: Hoffaktoren organized the Crown's financial affairs and acted as intermediary between the King and its creditors. Like modern banks, Hoffaktoren raised loanable funds to finance the monarch's deficit: but unlike modern banks who deposit and lend money, Hoffaktoren just organized potential lenders. Several Hoffaktoren-Families, like the Oppenheimers, the Wertheimers, and the Rothschilds, founded some of the most successful private banking houses (Kunisch 1999, p. 116). What made Hoffaktoren predestined for banking was not their wealth, but their financial market experience and wide networks among the wealthy and the Court. Especially curious is the story of the founder of Europe's most influential banking dynasty, Meyer Amschel Rothschild. Hessen-Kassel's Kürfürst (Prince-Eslector) became extremely rich by selling soldiers to Britain. As part of the old aristocracy, he was unable to invest his reserves profitably because profit-seeking was deemed ignoble. To circumvent the cultural boundaries, he lent the idle money to his Hoffaktor Meyer Amschel Rothschild, who invested the money elsewhere. Both men profited; the Kürfürst was not blamed for profit-seeking and Rothschild became very rich and was able to enlarge his bank (c.f. Born 1977, p. 48 f.). However, overall, banking in Mosaic-Germany remained underdeveloped and predominately pre-modern.

Mosaic-German private banking was largely underdeveloped until the 19th century. The German modern banking system emerged from two strands: rich merchants and craftsmen formed banks, as a by-business, to lend out idle money. Secondly, Hoffaktoren used their financial market experiences and networks to found private banks. Mosaic-Germany also had its financial crises: for example in the 1760s many banking houses failed (Kindleberger 1993, p. 119). However, crises did not cause a financial revolution like in France. What makes this time important to Germany's banking development, however, is that many private banks which became later the core institutions of Germany's private banking sector, were founded during this time by rich merchants and in particular by Hoffaktoren.

4.2.4.2 The Foundation of Public Banks

In the 17th, 18th, and early 19th century, many public banks were founded in Europe. Gradually, public banking shifted from exchange banking to central banking. In the 17th century, many merchant centers saw their main business trade being threatened by a confusing variety of different coins overflowing the cities. To overcome the problem, cities founded public exchange banks whose claim was to exchange different coins to one city currency. In the 17th century, the first countries started to found central banks. Most countries followed in the 18th and 19th century. Unlike public exchange banks, the newly founded central banks issued banknotes, managed public debt etc.: more or less doing what central banks usually do.

4.2.4.2.1 Public Exchange Banks

Founded at the beginning of the 17th century, public exchange banks are the oldest Central European public banks. The Bank of Amsterdam (1609) was the blueprint for other Dutch and German public exchange banks founded right afterwards: Middelburg (1616), Hamburg (1619), Delft (1621), Nuremberg (1621), Rotterdam (1635). Like Mediterranean public banks, public exchange banks were usually founded and operated by municipalities. However, Mediterranean public banks and central European public exchange banks followed quite different ideas: Mediterranean public banks were predominately founded to facilitate public lending. On the other hand, public exchange banks were founded to facilitate trade by reducing money exchange risk: in principle, public debt banking was not their business, but many public exchange banks were used to pay the sovereigns.

International trade was the main source the huge wealth of trading centers like Amsterdam, Rotterdam, Hamburg, and Nuremberg. Increasingly, trade was complicated by exchange risks. Traders from near and far brought their domestic coins to the cities. Due to the political fragmentation of Central Europe, trading hubs were overflowing with a vast number of different coins. Trader faced two main problems: in contact with a wide range of different coins from bigger and smaller political entities, even professional traders lost track of exchanges rates between different coins. Secondly, the true value of coins was often unclear. The widespread practice of Kippen and Wippen often considerably reduced the true (bullion) value of coins. Escalating war costs and the decline in mining production caused a bullion shortage in Central Europe: monarchs close to bankruptcy secretly reduced the bullion content of their coins by adding less valuable metals. Many coins containing less bullion than suggested, traders were becoming increasingly uncertain about the true value of coins.

Public exchange banks had two main functions: first, to define the true value of money, and second, to reduce the unmanageable variety of different coins in the city (Schnabel and Shin 2006). Like big public exchange banks, older small German municipal banks (Stadtwechsel) were founded to reduce the uncertainty about the value of coins: "The stated reason for the founding of a municipal bank was always to maintain the quality of coinage within the city" (Roberds and Velde 2014, p. 40). Hence, public exchange banks were predominantly "giro banks" (Riemersma 1952, p. 23). The Bank of Amsterdam deposited foreign and domestic coins and exchanged foreign coins and bullion into bank money, which became the only money in Amsterdam. Very skeptical about public banking and the Bank of England, Adam Smith welcomed the foundation of public exchange banks. According to Smith (1776, p. IV, III), public exchange banks are advantageous because they reduce exchange risks by establishing one paper currency convertible to a wide range of domestic and foreign coins. According to Smith, unlike most paper currencies of the time, public exchange banks' paper money was good money because it was not used to augment money. Hence, merchants could count on its value and exchangeability. He concludes that Amsterdam profited from its Bank of Amsterdam, whose main "object was to relieve the merchants from the inconvenience of disadvantageous exchange" (ibid.). Founded as a trade bank that exclusively deposits and exchanges money, soon the Bank of Amsterdam started to grant loans, in particular to the state, similarly to how the Bank of Hamburg and the Banco publico of Nuremberg granted loans (Schnabel and Shin 2006).

Public exchange banks did much of what current central banks do: exchanged currency, deposited money, lent money, and issued banknotes. However, the Bank of England and the Banque Générale are usually considered the predecessors of more recent central banks: the business model of the Bank of England and the Banque Générale and public exchange banks were quite different. The former were founded to overcome the shortage of money, reduce interest rates, and facilitate state lending. Public exchange banks had, at least theoretically, no intention of augmenting money or facilitating public debt financing. Hence, public exchange banks are institutions which were founded to overcome typical market failures; to reduce uncertainty and asymmetric information. National banks like the Bank of England and the Banque Générale were legitimized by solving money-mercantilist or Keynesian market failures: overcoming money shortage and high interests and facilitating lending.

4.2.4.2.2 National Banks

As maintained above, money-mercantilism considered that economic prosperity was hampered by the general shortage of money and too high interest rates. According to money-mercantilists, trade and production would be extensible, full employment reachable, trade balance improvable, and the general welfare increasable, if the shortage of money would be overcome and interests rates significantly lowered. Overall, like many later Keynesian approaches, money and banking takes center stage in money-mercantilism: the shortage or abundance of money determines the rate of interests, employment, trade, and production and therefore the military force and the glory or weakness of the nation.

For money-mercantilism, the interest rate is a key variable: high interests rates hamper economic progress, cause unemployment, and reduce trade; low interests rates foster growth, trade, employment, and the nation's successes and military force. Hence, like scholastics, money-mercantilism emphasized the harm of high interest rates, but proposed quite different measurements against high interest rates: while scholastic contributors demanded legal restrictions, mercantilists proposed the augmenting of the money supply.

That high interest rates harm economic prosperity is a key idea of money-mercantilism. However, the interest rate debate changed the understanding of what may be done against high interest rates. Former contributors proposed to restrict interest rates by (usury) laws. Later economists were quite critical about the positive effects of interest rate restrictions: for example, John Locke and William Petty stressed the impossibility and harmfulness of restricting interest rates by laws (Murphy 1997a, pp. 16–21). Locke's critic of interest rate restrictions was built on his belief in the natural laws of economics. He considered that fundamental economic variables, like interest rates, are driven by market forces which are, at least in the long run, not restrictable by law. Most money-mercantilists followed Locke in the sense that economic variables, like interest rates, are just alterable by changes in the guiding economic variables. Hence, according to money-mercantilists, radical economic measurements are needed to overcome the shortage of money and to decrease interest rates.

As maintained, for money-mercantilists banks play a key role in economic prosperity. Despite money-mercantilists favoring banking, their relation to the existing private banks was at the least ambivalent: they often recognized that private banking fosters economic development by granting credit to merchants and the industry. On the other hand, private bankers were blamed for being selfish, demanding too high interest rates, and taking too many risks. Principally convinced by the importance of banking, money-mercantilists widely agreed that the established banking sector was insufficient to incorporate the great project of mercantilist economic prosperity, industrialization, and full employment. Open to state interventions, many money-mercantilists suggested governments to heavily intervene in the banking sector; others were more reserved about state interventions.

Agreeing that the shortage of money and high interest rates are the evils of the time caused most money-mercantilists to call for radical innovations in the banking sector: the foundation of national banks became the idea of the time. Dozens of proposals suggesting the foundation of paper money issuing national banks were published by distinguished money-mercantilists. National bank proposals were quite diverse: there was no consensus about the duties of national banks, the amount of paper money which should be issued, what should be used as collateral against the issue of paper money, and who should own the banks. Despite all differences, several core ideas may be found in almost all proposals: it was suggested that national banks should be the 'bank of the banks'; owned by the state or by many shareholders; that they should issue paper money and lend to the state; and that they should be orientated towards general well-being rather than towards profit maximization.

Despite the support of the most notable money-mercantilists and the promise to overcome the shortage of money, reduce interest rates, and facilitate state financing, the opposition to national banks was strong and their implementation difficult. Merchants and economists being the main supporters of national banks, fearing to lose their economic privileges, other influential groups used their position to strongly oppose the foundation of national banks. As maintained above, the nobility and private bankers were the main public debt financers. Highly profiting from state financing, both groups feared losing the public debt market to national banks. Although various contributions stressed the advantages of national banks, it seems that opposition would have been too strong, had not the significant economic and political crises and changes paved the way for national banks. Almost everywhere, the foundation of national banks was made possible by the deep crisis of the old (financial) elites, in particular by serious problems to finance governments' expenditures, predominately wars.

4.2.4.2.2.1 Sveriges Riksbank

The nationalization in 1668 of the failed Stockholms Banco, which was renamed to Riksens Ständers Bank and later to Sveriges Riksbank, makes it the world's oldest central bank. After receiving the right from the Swedish King Charles Gustavus, Johan Palmstruch established the Stockholms Banco in 1656. The bank was, at least formally, divided into a bank of exchange, operating much of the business of Wisselbanks, and a regular lending bank. Issuing notes predominately as credit rather than against deposits was different from the usual business of the Wisselbanks, which is why Heckscher (1964, p. 169) stated that the bank "was the first issue of actual bank notes in Europe." Most loans were issued to the private sector and collateralized by land (Roberds and Velde 2014, p. 52). Inflationary pressure and problems to reconvert paper money into copper, Sweden followed a copper standard, causing the government to close the bank in 1664. Nationalized after its closing, the bank was reopened four years later as Riksens Ständers Bank. Retaining the division between the bank of exchange and the lending bank, the banks stopped issuing notes and instead concentrated on lending. As the Hats, a "nationalistic and ultra-mercantilistic" Party (Heckscher 1964, p. 177), took over the bank, they restarted issuing notes, which soon became the dominant tender. Governed by their mercantilist worldview, the Hats used the banks for easy credit to the industry and to finance wars against Russia. Overlending caused a serious depreciation of money, disturbances, and the suspension of convertibility (c.f. ibid., pp. 161–200).

4.2.4.2.2.2 Bank of England

The profound changes in the structure of the British financial markets which followed the Glorious Revolution are usually considered a financial revolution (see Dickson 1967; Wennerlind 2011). According to several contributors, the Glorious Revolution and the following financial revolution lay the foundation of Britain's, and in particular London's, financial predominance (Dickson 1967; Carruthers 1996). According to North and Weingast (1989), before the Glorious Revolution the power distribution between the King and the Parliament leaned heavily toward the former: the institutional setting offered various possibilities to the King to circumvent the Parliament. Importantly, the King had quasi-dominance over financial issues: to collect taxes, extent public expenses, raise state credits, default and credits, and suspend interests payments. "Prior to the Glorious Revolution, payments on loans were subject to manipulation by the Crown; rescheduling and delays in payments were common" (ibid., p. 819). Uncertainty about public debt repayments caused the wealthy to shy away from lending voluntarily to the state or to lend only at horrendous interest rates. The Glorious Revolution "initiated the era of parliamentary 'supremacy'" (ibid., p. 816). Particularly important for the financial revolution was the "Parliamentary veto over expenditures, combined with the right to monitor how the funds they had voted were spent, placed important constraints over the Crown" (ibid.), which gave the wealthy state creditor a parliamentary veto right over financial affairs. The story told by North and Weingast was much the reprint of the old republican theses: according to Ehrenberg ([1896] 1928, p. 33), the republicanism of Italian City-States was pivotal for the development of the modern financial system because the Parliament's power enabled state lenders to influence the government's financial affairs. Following the same thesis, Marx ([1894] 1984, p. 602) quoted the English Tories in saying: "Banks are republican institutions. Flourishing banks existed in Venice, Genoa, Amsterdam, and Hamburg. But who ever heard of a Bank of France or Spain?"

There can be little doubt that the Glorious Revolution was the pivotal event which facilitated the financial revolution. Many contributors assume a direct relation between the empowering of the Parliament, the rule of law, and the development of institutions of the financial revolution like the Bank of England. A closer look at the developments emphasizes that particular historical circumstances like specific distributions of power between groups and widespread ideas were important for the birth of institutions such as the Bank of England.

In 1694, the Bank of England was founded after a proposal by William Paterson. The adapted proposal suggested that 1,2 million pounds would be lend to the government in return for a 100.000 lb interest payments a year and the right to issue notes equal to the value of the bank's total capital—the claim to make notes legal tender was refused (Andreadēs 1966, p. 65). No person was allowed to invest more than 20.000 lb (ibid., p. 73) and all capital had to be lent to the government. The foundation of the Bank of England was a banking revolution according to the scale of banking and its organization form as a join-stock company. No other single bank influenced the development of the European banking system more strongly than the Bank of England. However, the foundation had important economic, political, and cultural preconditions.

Wennerlind (2011) in his book on the financial revolution does not doubt the usual story that the institutional change of the Glorious Revolution facilitated the financial revolution. However, he considers that the financial revolution had important cultural preconditions that are usually ignored. According to Wennerlind, the British financial revolution was preceded by a scientific revolution which lasted for the entire century: at the beginning of the 17th century a group around Malynes, Misseldon, and Mun, and in the time around the Civil war the Hartlib Circle, argued for a restructuring of the monetary system—both groups may be considered money-mercantilists. According to the former group, the money supply directly influences trade, production, military power, and employment or more abstract categories such as "justice", "balance" and "harmony" (ibid., p. 20): for them, the scarcity of money was Britain's main problem. Similarly, the Hartlib Circle blamed the shortage of money for Britain's economic problems, suggesting that the steady growth of money supply would release hidden resources and enable the endless growth of nature and society; they proposed to give out a credit currency (ibid., pp. 44–79). Hence, the rise of money-mercantilist ideas paved the cultural way for the British financial revolution.

However, money-mercantilist ideas needed strong carriers to overcome resistance and to get implemented. After the Glorious Revolution the foundation of a big state-lending, note-issuing joint-stock bank had enthusiastic supporters, but also diehard opponents. William Paterson (1694), one of the later founders of the Bank of England, outlined how the Bank of England would be beneficial to almost everyone. Heckscher (1935a, p. 335) and Rothbard (1995a, p. 229) highly doubt the philanthropic nature of the Bank of England and considered vested economic interests the main reason behind the foundation. Merchants and industrialists and their political representatives, the Whigs, were the main supporters of a new-style bank; on the other side, landed aristocracy represented by the Tories and private bankers were the main opponents. Merchants and industrialists hoped that augmenting money by issuing notes would facilitate their business; a huge national bank absorbing great capital and polling shareholders' bargaining power would provide the 'safe haven' for their idle hoards. Landed aristocracy feared that the deepening of banking would further increase the power of the bourgeoisie and private bankers were afraid of losing their most profitable business, public debt banking.

The Bank of England was founded after a long and intensive political controversy. The rising bourgeoisie and its political representatives, the Whigs, were the main supporters of the Bank of England. In the late 17th century, money-mercantilist banking ideas were widespread among the bourgeoisie and the Whigs. Two main advantages were expected from the foundation of a national bank: the reduction of interest rates and the easier extension of the money supply by facilitating paper money issuing (Andreadēs 1966, p. 68). Outlining the advantages of national banks for trade and economic prosperity and the disadvantages of small private bankers, Barbon (1690) wondered why "the Merchant and Traders of London have not long before this time Addressed themselves, to the Government, for the Establishing of a publick [national] Bank." However, for Pincus (2009, p. 390 f.) "the main proponents of the bank were ideologically predictable [and] the proponents schemes and the defenders of the Bank of England clarified the ideological assumption that undergirded their enthusiasm." Representing the interests of the rising bourgeoisie, the Whigs supported politics which seemed to foster trade and industrialization. Using money-mercantilism to translate abstract interests into concrete demands, the Whigs supported projects which were deemed to increase the supply of money, which in turn was supposed to foster trade, industrialization, employment, and Britain's military force.

Opponents of the Bank of England were numerous and influential. As outlined by Carruthers (1996) and Pincus (2009, p. 388), following its conservative voter base, the Tories were principally skeptical of banking: banking was considered a Jewish, foreign, liberal, merchant business, hence everything that the Tories and their conservative voters found suspicious. Apart from ideological reservations, the opposition to the Bank of England had powerful political reasons: the Bank of England was considered "the most Whiggish" (Carruthers 1996, p. 139) join-stock company, and its failure would have weakened the political opponent. Facing strong opposition, Paterson (1694, p. 6), a co-founder of the bank, frustrated by a parliamentary discussion, reported: some criticized that the Bank of England would make the King absolute, others feared the corrosion of the monarchy. Fearing to lose their most profitable business, public debts, private banks went to great lengths to criticize and prevent national banks. Andreadēs (1966, p. 68) summarized the critic of the Bank of England: (1) The bank would absorb all the money and compel all others to borrow at usurious interest rates; (2) No investable money would be left for trade and industry; (3) The bank would become too powerful; (4) It is just to the advantage of a small group of rich people; (5) The bank would undermine the monarchy; (6) Supported by the bank, the King would again become an absolutist ruler.

Under different circumstances, the opposition to a joint-stock bank would have been, most likely, too strong. What made the time specific and opened the historical window for the foundation of the Bank of England was the war with France which seemed to be getting out of English hands due to financial difficulties. According to Pincus (2009, p. 388 f.), who intensively studied the political debates of the time, war financing was the major topic of the time. A widely recognized letter considered that "war is changed from fighting into eating, drinking and campaigning. To carry on which new sort of military art, I am sure money is the one thing necessary" (cited in Pincus 2009, p. 389). When William III ascended to the throne, public finance was in serious difficulties: his predecessor had left him mounting public debts, the strong dependency on private bankers and a financial market shattered by the Stop of the Exchequer made public debt financing quite difficult. Having no other choice than to borrow from private bankers, the King had to accept interest rates of 20 to 30 per cent: according to the general public, the King was a victim of usurers (Andreadēs 1966, p. 68). Hence, "war-related expenses necessitated financial innovation" (Carruthers 1996, p. 158). Under enormous financial pressure, William III had only two options: "scale back the war against Louis XIV as the Tories wished or adapt the full radical implication of the Whig understanding of political economy [which implied to permission of a 'national bank]" (Pincus 2009, p. 388). The King chose the second alternative: Whigs' empowering paved the way for the Bank of England. Consolidating Whig dominance of the newly-founded national bank, the Whig-related Bank of England shareholders outnumbered Tory-affiliated ones by more than two to one (Carruthers 1996, p. 158).

In particular at the beginning, the Bank of England was quite successful: it easily absorbed great capital for public debt financing. Dickson (1967) argued that the most important thing for England's fortune in recurring wars against its more powerful enemy France was "the system of public borrowing developed in the first half of the period, which enabled England to spend on war out of all proportion to its tax revenue." Compared with other countries and the pre-Bank of England situation, interest rates were quite moderate (North and Weingast 1989). Supported by the Bank of England, William was ready for a successful offensive in Flanders. According to Dickson and Carruthers, the fast increase in English public debt was the kick-off for the development of the

English and in particular the London financial market and laid the bases for London's financial predominance. Carruthers (1996, p. 11 f.) stressed that without public debt securities "City's complex structure of services could not have been built up by the mid-eighteen century, for there was no industrial sector whose bonds could be used for the same purpose." Dickson (1967, pp. 3–14) argued that the development of "the new partnership banks", "the new insurance offices", "the trading companies", "brokers and jobbers of the City of London" was caused by war finance; hence the diverse financial system of England which later became pivotal for England's industrialization and the "origins of the system of public borrowing."

Focusing in his sociological work on the state-building effect of the financial revolution, Carruthers (1996) considered that the financial revolution in general and the foundation of the Bank of England in particular fostered state building: heavily borrowing from the Bank of England, William increasingly depended on bank's credit. However, in order to safeguard their investment, shareholders had a vested interests in political stability and the regime's survival. Hence, unintendedly, the financial revolution forged a strong "alliance" between the King and "those who invested in the national debt acquired a financial stake in the political viability of the regime" (ibid., p. 22). The close ties between the King and the Bank of England stood symbolically for the new alliance between the state and the bourgeoisie.

The success of the Bank of England's significantly changed the Tories' position. Strongly opposing national banking at the beginning, the Tories changed their mind as they ran into danger of entirely losing the successful story of national banks to the Whigs. The Tories' position shifted from 'Britain needs no national bank' to 'Britain also needs a Tory-Bank'.

> Some of the Bank's opponents recognized that given the size of its loan to the government, the Bank was not going to disappear anytime soon. This suggested that rather than try to eliminate the Bank, the best strategy might be to create a rival to check its power and influence (ibid., p. 141).

Many national bank proposals were published in the late 17th and early 18th century: most suggested to found land banks rather than Bank of England-style banks. Proposals for land banks were written long before the Bank of England was founded. William Potter (1650) published a land bank proposal in 1650: deeply rooted in money-mercantilism, he argued that note issuing would overcome the money shortage, foster trade and the economic development. Unlike most former national bank contributors, he considered collateralizing notes by land rather than issuing against coins. Despite Potter's innovative idea, the land bank debate just took off after Bank of England's foundation; much encouraged by the Tories' search for an alternative. Opposing the Bank of England idea, famous authors, like Hugh Chamberlen (1700), John Briscoe (1694), and John Asgill ([1696] 1906), published land bank proposals. Differing in detail, the main argument was always the same: issued notes, meaning credit, should be collateralized by land. With John Law's *Money and Trade* ([1705] 1750), the debate reached its peak:

implemented in France, Law's proposal was rejected in England and Scotland (Murphy 1997a: pp. 21–29).

The Tories' support for land banks was ideological and interest based. Bank of England-style banks were considered to serve merchants' and industrialists' interests; land banks seemed favorable to land owners: investing in land and mortgages, it was suggested that land banks would increase land prices and decrease land loan interest rates (Carruthers 1996, p. 141). Despite serving landowners' interests, support and opposition for land bank was also ideological. The land bank proposal mirrored the nobility's and the Tories' economic thinking: according to conservative economics, land is the ultimate base of wealth, which is why economic policy should first and foremost target the agrarian production. In contrast, the Whigs and related groups considered that manufactural production predominately fosters economic development (Pincus 2009, p. 460).

Hence, the land bank proposal became the blueprint for the nobility's and the Tories' financial counter-revolution: John Briscoe (1695 or 1696) considered that "The national land bank is properly so-called, the fund being land, the society landed men, who appoint landed men to be to be trustees, governors, treasurers" (cited in Pincus 2009, p. 460). According to Murphy (1997a, p. 25), one main reason to support land banks was "a perception on the part of the landed interests that, due to financial innovation, they were losing out at the expense of the merchant and moneyed men." Hence, demanding the foundation of land banks was driven by the fear of landed classes' of falling further behind the rising bourgeoisie. Rubini (1970, p. 697) summarized many land bank advocates' position:

> some form of long-term borrowing was necessary, but the Bank of England seemed to them inherently anti-agrarian, too much allied with commercial interests and with the growing bourgeoisie. It appeared to be the spearhead of a financial revolution which was furthering the change from a landed to a commercial economy.

The land bank was an attempt to regain lost economic ground: "The national land bank, as opposed to the Bank of England, explicitly sought a clientele of landowners" (ibid., p. 394).

Chamberlen, the most influential land bank supporter, promised the King that a land bank would be able to lend twice the amount that the Bank of England lends (Andreadēs 1966, p. 104). Tempted by the attractive offer, the Parliament and the Crown permitted the foundation of a land bank: it was suggested to gather two million pounds and lend it to the government. Due to massive problems to absorb capital, the persistent opposition of the Whigs and the Bank of England, the plan failed completely. The foundation of the land bank was expected to reduce the influence of the Bank of England. Just the opposite occurred: to digest the failure of the land bank, the government had to ask the Bank of England for a new loan. Taking advantage of land bank's failure, the Bank of England demanded what it had always desired: note-issuing monopoly. Immediately receiving a smaller concession, in 1707 it was decided that no other bank with more than six shareholders was allowed to issue bank notes (c.f. ibid.).

The failed land bank experiment had two important indirect effects: first, the effort to build a land bank emphasized that the view of the most influential banking opponents—landed aristocracy—has changed. Traditionally, landed aristocracy opposed banking as liberal, bourgeois, Jewish; demanding the foundation of a more landed joint-stock bank was a clear signal that they considered banking a fact. Secondly, the failure of the land bank put attempts to found a Bank of England competitor into the background. Empowered by its monopoly position, the Bank of England more openly demanded the legal enforcement of its position, like asking for the note-issuing monopoly.

From the fast death of its main rival the land bank to the French Revolution, the Bank of England faced difficult times as parliaments changed, opponents united, and bank runs occurred. However, overall, the 18th century was a big success for the Bank of England. Increasingly, the Bank of England became the pivotal lender to the state: it was the bank's readiness to raise huge funds in a short time that made the Bank of England pivotal for Britain's war fortune. Bank of England's managers had a good instinct for giving the bank an edge from its unique position. In particular at times when the government faced serious financial difficulties, credit was granted against further privileges.

With its highly developed stock market and the Bank of England, London became the financial center of the world. The rise of London strengthened the financial highway Amsterdam-London: capital accumulated very fast in the Netherlands due to its prospering overseas trade, but it increasingly lacked profitable domestic investment opportunities. Trading the stocks of the big British joint-stock companies, the London stock market became a fruitful investment place for Dutch capital: "English 'funds afforded them [Dutch Investors] not only a convenient investment, but higher interest rates. [...] It was to England then that the surplus capital of Dutch businessmen now began to flow" (Braudel 1984, p. 261). The Bank of England, the Bank of Amsterdam, and the Bank of Hamburg were the central institutions of the international financial market. However, the Bank of England had an important advantage over the others: Bank of England's possibilities to extend the money supply were much bigger. Due to its elastic credit supply, the Bank of England became the international lender of last resort (Schubert 1988).

In the history of European banking, several turning points sustainably changed the paths along which the banking system developed: the foundation of the Bank of England was, doubtlessly, one of them. No other institution was more important for London to became the world's financial center and to connect Europe's financial hubs. As predicted in money-mercantilist proposals, the foundation of the Bank of England significantly decreased interest rates, which fostered trade and industrialization, but in particular enhanced states' financial situation: around 1690, the interest rate for public debt was 14%; in the 1730s the government borrowed for 3% (North and Weingast 1989, p. 823). The Bank of England's readiness to lend huge sums at low rates in a short time was a pivotal military advantage which shifted the fortune of war toward Britain and facilitated the foundation of new colonies. Most importantly for the development of the European banking sector, the Bank of England became the blueprint for joint-stock and central banks.

4.2.4.2.2.3 Banque Royale

In the late 17th and early 18th century parts of the French political elite realized that France's military inferiority—compared with its great enemy Britain—steamed from its less developed financial sector. "In theory, the French Crown wielded more domestic power than the British Crown but the latter proved much better at rising money" (Carruthers 1996, p. 141). Rising money for wars was difficult, lengthy, and financiers usually demanded horrendous interest rates. Profiting most from the state credit system, the landed aristocracy used all its power to prevent any financial innovation and the development of a modern banking system. Frequent defaults on public debts, military misfortune due to its inferior war financing system and public debts out of control, revealed that France was in urgent need of a financial revolution. As maintained before, the Glorious Revolution there was a certain power balance between France and Britain. However, the foundation of the Bank of England and the caused increase in the elasticity of war credit strongly shifted military power toward Britain.

After decades of financial mismanagement, permanent warfare and his own luxurious life, Louis XIV was completely bankrupt. Public debt interest rates of 50% were not unusual: around 1715 the government had to give out government bonds for 32 million Livre just to receive 8 million in coins (Murphy 1997b, p. 128 f.). Raising new money and repaying old loans was almost impossible; the state was bankrupt, although this was undeclared. Three measures were discussed in order to get rid of the public debt crisis: first, a default on the entire public debt; second, defaulting parts of the public debt *(Visa)*; third, prosecuting financers *(Chambre de Justice)* who financially exploited the King. A total default was too risky, which is why the second *(Visa)* and third *(Chambre de Justice)* measurement were implemented; with far-reaching economic and political consequences (ibid., p. 135 f.). Debt defaults and the suspension of interest payments bankrupted many private businesses, which stopped paying suppliers and workers. Paranoid by the Chambre de Justice financiers hid their wealth to escape persecution (ibid.). Both measures heavily deteriorated the French economy: public debt defaults caused a deep recession. Due to high unemployment and slack economy, the demand from ordinary people was weak. Rich public debt financers who feared judicial prosecution hid their wealth in order not to call attention. Hence, people had no money and the financiers no courage to demand; commerce almost came to a halt. At the beginning of the 18th century, the treasury was empty, the King covertly bankrupt, the economy facing a deep recession and the financiers getting increasingly paranoid.

The King being unable to raise new money and the nobility frightened by the Chambre de Justice, a historical window was opened for a financial revolution: the time had come for John Law, the Scottish gambler. Law, the main opponent of Hugh Chamberlen's land bank ideas, walked the world to find a government willing to implement his land bank proposal. John Law was a firmly convinced money-mercantilist: he argued that the abundance of money and low interest rates would fosters production and trade, cause full employment and provide an advantageous trade balance (Kerschagl 1968, pp. 47–53). Law strongly believed that France's main problem "was a shortage of money" (Murphy 1997a, p. 2). When Law returned to France in 1708, Marquis of Torcy noted: "his intentions are not good" (Hamilton 1967, p. 275). Whatever Law's intention may have been, he was fully convinced that a land bank like he proposed would foster economic prosperity and solve the King's financial difficulties.

Law's failure is often considered an ideal example of what happens if inapt speculators turn into powerful bankers. Taking the historical context into consideration, John Law was, for sure, an important money-mercantilist and his land bank proposal differed little from other authors' suggestions; his failure had less to do with his personality than with the shortcomings of the usual national bank proposals. In *Money and Trade* Law ([1705] 1750) lined out his principal economic ideas; the book is among the outstanding money-mercantilist contributions. Discussing fundamental topics of macro- and international economics the central issue is money and credit. Following the usual money-mercantilist argumentation, Law suggests that economic prosperity, foreign trade and employment are highly dependent on the abundance of money. He considers that most economic problems originate in the shortage of coin money—a country like Scotland without its own natural resources relies on bullion imports, so it puts the money supply, and therefore its destiny, into the hands of potential enemies. According to Law, in contrast to coins paper money has, in principle, an infinite elasticity—the supply is infinitely extensible—and allows governments to make their own independent money policy without relying on foreign bullion. Rather than covering paper money by bullion, he suggested to collateralize money with land: a widespread idea among mercantilists. Law also discussed possible effects of the extension of money on prices: he considered that augmenting money increases prices in the case of full employment; unless full employment is reached, the extension does not cause inflation.

Law's later proposals and writings focused on two issues: first, how coins could be replaced by paper money. Second, how to connect the public debt policy with the monetary policy (Murphy 1997b, p. 105). Law was fascinated by the Bank of England. He considered that the British big join stock companies, the Bank of England and the East India Company, enabled the Crown to borrow huge sums at relatively low interest rates. What he had in mind for France was a public bank which combines a note-issuing join-stock bank, like the Bank of England, with a trade join-stock company, like the East India Company or the South Sea Company. The Banque Générale, which later became the Banque Royale, was founded as the French counterpart of the Bank of England. The East India Company was the blueprint for the French Compagnie d'Occident (Mississippi Company), which held the monopoly for trading with the overseas territories around the American Mississippi and the antilles. The Banque Royale and the Mississippi Company were merged into one huge company. On the asset side, the new conglomerate merged bullion, working capital, colonial trade monopolies, and in particular public debt, and on the liability side the equity of the Banque Royale and Compagnie d'Occident, bank notes, and deposits (ibid., p. 111).

In France, Law had influential promoters and enemies (ibid., p. 123–149): the public opinion was quite hostile toward financial innovation and the Scotsman with his 'weird' ideas (Kaiser 1991). Ordinary people and even experts doubted the health of Law's experiment: still many thought that paper money not fully covered by bullion is worthless. Saint-Simon adapted the old republican argument: he stated that"as good as this establishment [Law's bank] could be in itself, it could not exist except in a republic or in a monarchy like England, whose finances are governed only by those who provide them and who provide them only as much as it pleases them" (cited in Kaiser 1991). For Saint-Simon, national banks in absolutistic regimes are too easily overthrown and exploited by the monarch. Maybe the King was not very convinced by Law's ideas, but with public debts completely out of control he had no other choice than to take the last solution offered to him and permit Law the foundation of the Banque Générale. Planning to manage the entire public debt, financiers and the nobility had most to lose through Law's land bank. Under different circumstances, financiers and the nobility would have most likely been easily able to bring down the Scottish money-mercantilist and ward off the foundation of national bank. But the prosecution by the *Chambre de Justice* destroyed and hushed financiers and nobility's resistance; never before were times more convenient for a financial revolution in France than in the early 18th century.

Law suggested that the Banque Générale would solve the two, according to Law, most serious problems of France: the money shortage and the public debt problem and high interest rates on state lending. Convincing the political elite that he, John Law, is the man who can solve France's financial problems (Murphy 1997b, p. 138 ff.), John Law was allowed to found the Banque Générale in 1716. As demanded by Law, a note-issuing monopoly was granted to the bank. However, in one important point the government did not follow Law's suggestion: it rejected to own the bank. Law's Banque Générale was a success (Kindleberger 1993, p. 99); interest rates decreased, the money shortage relaxed, the bank made high profits (Murphy 1997b, p. 188 ff.) and stimulated trade and industrialization (Kindleberger 1993, p. 99). Difficult to distinguish between the real success and Law's propaganda, he convinced the government to take the last step and nationalize the Banque Générale: in 1719 the Banque Générale was converted into the state-owned Banque Royale. In addition to the note-issuing monopoly, the government supported the notes' legal tender character by forcing provinces to pay taxes in banknotes. Several laws restricting the use and possession of coins slowly removed coins from circulation. Notes became the full legal tender and the bank being owned by the state public, credit seemed endless: now the King had his own public credit machine. Critics of national banks often warned that a bank able to infinitely extend lending by printing money would be used by the government to over-print credit unless clear and binding rules or strong institutions restrict money issuing. The Banque Royale lacked a clear banknote-issuing limit.

Fast rising stock prices (Murphy 1997b, p. 213–230) made the Mississippi Company shares a favorable investment vehicle and Law's system worked. The booming Mississippi Company stock attracted a lot of foreign capital: the European financial market on the relation London-Amsterdam became a triangle: London-Amsterdam-Paris (Schubert 1988). Stimulating the weak economy and feeling the empty state treasury, Law was at the peak of his power in 1720: "In 1720 he dominated the Royal Bank, or first Bank of France, as no other man has ever dominated a national bank" (Hamilton 1967, p. 273). In addition, he controlled the Company of the Indies, owned various hotels and real estates, and became Minister of Finance.

The rise of the Mississippi Company's was fast, its decline even faster. Just a year after its completion, Law's system started to fail. Overheated stock markets, the money supply out of control, Law's opponents regained ground –the brothers Paris were particularly unpleasant enemies—Law was fighting on several fronts. In the same year of Law's meteoric rise, his system broke down (Murphy 1997b, pp. 231–292). Massive capital outflow toward Amsterdam (Schubert 1988, p. 303), Law's escape and the return to coins, marked not just the end of Law's ideas, but the end of paper money and big banks in France for a long time. For a certain time, France suffered politically and economically from Law's heritage. However, much more importantly for the development of the French banking system, Banque Royale's failure became a collective memory for the coming decades, which made financial innovations almost impossible: "French experience with John Law was such that there was hesitation in even pronouncing the word bank for 150 years thereafter—a classic case of collective financial memory" (Kindleberger 1993, p. 100). Law's failure encouraged the old financial elite, the notorious opponents of Law, and all kinds of financial innovations opposition, with a frequently used argument: that it will end up like Law's project. Necker complained bitterly that "his own financial program suffered above all from the memory of the troubles caused by the bank of Law" (Kaiser 1991, p. 25).

4.2.4.2.2.4 Caisse D'Escompte

At the end of the 18th century, a new attempt for public banking was made in France. The Seven Years' war caused major financial difficulties. Inspired by his liberal economic thinking, Jacques Turgot, as financial minister, prescribed drastic treatments to balance the French budget. Still, public debt remained horrendous. Turgot was convinced that a new note-issuing bank would foster the Parisian capital market and facilitate public debt financing by bringing down interest rates. Demanding the foundation of an issuing bank, Turgot supported Isaac Panchauds bank proposal (Roberds and Velde 2014, p. 66). In 1776, two foreigners, the Swiss Panchaud and the Scott Clouard founded the Caisse d'Escompte. Operated by the most powerful private bankers (Plessis 1994), "the bank became a bankers' bank" (Roberds and Velde 2014, p. 67): the Caisse d'Escompte was engaged in a wide range of banking activities and note issuing (Liesse 1909, p. 9). The bank's opponents recalled the collective memory of Law's failure and fueled xenophobia against the foreign Protestants to thwart the new bank: "The example is still in our sight [and] the wound is still too bloody for one to forget all the extravagances of the Rue Quincampoix" (Kaiser 1991, p. 24), the opponents stressed to connect the Caisse d'Escompte with Law's project and to attack the new financial minister Jacques Necker.

Relatively successful at the beginning, Panchaud encouraged the bank to become more active in public lending: in 1787, public lending reached its peak when a 100 million Livres loan was granted to the King (Kindleberger 1993, p. 100). Due to heavy public lending, the ties between the bank and the government intensified: "the Caisse d'Escompte, as a result of closer and closer relations with the State, became nothing more than a branch of the public administration of finance" (Liesse 1909, p. 9).

Caisse d'Escompte lending heavily to the state worried its customers. After the revolution, the bank was the only remaining lender to the state. The revolutionary government was in a dilemma: facing serious financial difficulties, the government was in need of much more money. On the other hand, binding the Caisse d'Escompte even closer to the government would have fueled worries about its sustainability and bankers' fears to follow Banque Royale's example. Convinced that paper money needs a solid base, the nationalized Church land was used as collateral for Caisse d'Escompte notes (Roberds and Velde 2014, p. 68). However, strongly affected by the war in 1792, the Caisse d'Escompte was liquidated in 1793.

4.2.4.2.2.5 Giro- and Lehnbanco

Prussia's Frederick II was convinced by the successful story of the Bank of England that a public bank is compatible with a monarchy, fosters economic development, stabilizes the currency, and provides profits to the government (ibid., p. 74). In 1765, two public banks were founded in what was later to become Germany; the Prussian Giro- and Lehnbanco (1765) and the Braunschweigian Leyhaus (1765). Both were founded to financially support the country's reconstruction after the Seven Years' war (Born 1977), to overcome the financial crisis and the deflationary tendencies (Kindleberger 1993, p. 119). Like the Bank Royal, the Giro- and Lehnbanco held a note-issuing monopoly (Born 1977), fully owned by the state, but managed relatively independently (Roberds and Velde 2014, p. 75).

In many respects, the Prussian Giro- and Lehnbanco was history's most money-mercantilist bank: expected to foster economic development and to overcome deflation (the shortage of money), equipped with a note-issuing monopoly, the Giro- and Lehnbanco was founded to ease credit, overcome the money shortage, and foster growth. However, Prussia turned back half way toward money-mercantilist banking: the outlined mercantilism was widespread in Britain and France. In Germany, mercantilism had a different spin: the so-called cameralism was a special German-Austrian form of mercantilism that suggested heavy state interventionism and treasury hoarding. Inspired by the widespread cameralism, Prussia hoard a huge treasury. At the same time, Giro- and Lehnbanco's assets were too small for considerable banknote issuing. Driven by his cameralistic view, Frederick II refused to deposit his idle treasury at the Giro- and Lehnbanco, which would have enabled the bank to augment paper money issuing and credit granting (Born 1977). Hence, the German cameralism undermined Giro- and Lehnbanco's function of easing credit and fighting the shortage of money. In the late 1770 s, the bank's funding difficulties relaxed gradually as more private and public institution deposited money (Roberds and Velde 2014, p. 75). Rising lending to the state and against land indicated a developing prosperity; however, the Napoleonic wars (1806–1813) again caused serious difficulties.

4.2.4.3 Cooperative Banking

As maintained above, Italian bankers spread banking throughout Europe. Simultaneously, the idea of cooperative Mont de Piétés reached the rest of Europe. In the early 16th century Monts de Piétés were established in France, Germany and Holland (Tawney 1948, p. 65). At the end of the 16th century, several Monts de Piété-style banks "banks of relief of common necessity" were founded in England (Richards 1965, p. 93). With the foundations of Monts de Piétés the theological discussion on interest and usury also intensified in Central and Northern Europe. Elsewhere advocates of Monts de Piétés argued that credit is an immutable fact which does not disappear by restricting money lending. Advocates suggested to found Monts de Piétés to overcome usurer practices and save the poor from exploitation by lending out at low rates (Tawney 1948, p. 65). Founded elsewhere in Europe, even in Catholic countries like France, Monts de Piété still played a minor role compared with medieval Italy.

It was only in the 19th and 20th century that non-profit banking became the third pillar of European banking: in countries like Germany and Austria it was, and is, a pillar of economy. Inspired by Monts de Piété, later non-profit banks were mostly not part of the Catholic banking empire. Usually founded in the 19th century as a reaction to industrialization, harbingers of the non-profit banking boom are to be found earlier. Non-profit banking was especially popular in Britain: several non-profit banking proposals were published in the 18th century (c.f. Ito 2011, p. 494 ff.). Inspired by the proposals, several cooperative saving banks were founded in Germany, Britain, and elsewhere in the late 18th century (Born 1977, p. 199 ff.). Having its beginnings in the late 18th century, non-profit banking was a child of the industrialization and 19th century, which is why the emerging of the non-profit banking will be discussed in more details in the next part.

4.3 Conclusion

The cultural, political, and economic order significantly changed between the Religious Wars of the 16th century and the French Revolution: mercantilism replaced the scholastic theory as the leading economic idea. Fast extending trade and the emerging of the early industry strengthened the rising bourgeoisie. Politics were dominated by the state building process, by coalitions between the monarchs and various powerful groups, and by the rising empires' battles for predominance. The changes in the three orders had far-reaching consequences for the development of the banking sector. However, the development of professional private banks, big national banks, and paper money was by no means a gradual process, but interlaced by deep conflicts, setbacks, and financial disasters.

As outlined, the scholastic was the leading economic theory in the medieval Italian City-States. Scholastic discussion on banking and credit was dominated by theological reservations against money lending. Christian and conservative anti-banking sentiments did not disappear: moralists complained bitterly that more and more ordinary people of all classes, professions and guilds, were engaged, as landers or borrowers, in money lending against interest payments. Despite all adjustments and differences between different theological approaches, the principle Christian interest persisted until the French Revolution (for a detailed discussion see Tawney 1948).

However, from the Religious Wars to the French Revolution moralist (theological) arguments against banking steadily lost ground in the great discussions on banking: the discussions on interest and banking secularist. The position on interests rates of the scholastic and money-mercantilism were rather similar, that interest rates should be as low as possible, but the arguments were quite different: scholastic authors emphasized the sinfulness of (high) interest, money-mercantilists focused on how high interest rates harm growth and economic prosperity. Scholastics remained rather dismissive of banking, money-mercantilism were overall enthusiastic about banking. The different views on banking stemmed from different convictions about effective measurements against high interest rates: scholastics favored usury laws, money-mercantilists rejected legal restrictions as ineffective and proposed instead a fundamental change of the banking system and the augmentation of money.

Mercantilism, the leading economic theory of the time, was a comprehensive theory about economic development, economic nationalism, state building, social harmony and the nation's military potential. In principle, mercantilism followed several distinctive goals: economic development and industrialization; state building; social harmony; economic autarky; and the strengthening of military forces.

For money-mercantilists, the shortage of money and high interest rates were the most serious and destructive problems of the time: the shortage of money and high interest rates harmed trade and industrialization, disturbed social harmony through high unemployment rates, and withdrew financial means from the military. Central to money-mercantilism was the question of how the shortage of money could be overcome and interest rates reduced. The main answer of the money-mercantilists was that paper money issuing national banks would augment the money supply, reduce interests rates, make the nation less dependent on foreign bullion, and strengthen the military force with public credit. At least a dozen national bank proposals were written at the time of money-mercantilism; technically different, the basic postulate idea was that big note-issuing national banks would overcome money shortage, lower interest rates, facilitate public lending, foster economic progress and strengthen the military forces.

From public lending, other state financial affairs and trade banking professional private bankers emerged. Meeting rising demands for different kinds of financial services, private bankers were frequently scathed, in particular by money-mercantilists and their supporters, for being selfish, unpatriotic and acting like extortionists. National banks, as proposed by money-mercantilists, had their supporters and their enemies; usually, the rising bourgeoisie, merchants and industrialists, hoped that national banks would foster growth, reduce interest rates, and break the private bankers' lending monopoly. Governments, at least clandestinely, supported national banks in order to facilitate public credit. All the groups that most profited from the status que strongly opposed national banks: private bankers feared losing the most profitable businesses; the nobility feared the strengthening of the rising bourgeoisie and losing their dominance over profitable public lending. What made the foundation of national banks particularly difficult was the monarchs' dependency on coalitions with bankers and with the nobility.

Despite the support for national banks of the money-mercantilists' and the support from the bourgeoisie and the governments, the opposition of the nobility and of private bankers remained strong enough to delay the foundation of national banks. Only a serious political and economic crisis shattered the anti-banking coalitions and paved the way for the national banking revolution: the Stop of the Exchequer shook the British public financing system, the Glorious Revolution strengthened the bourgeoisie and gave the parliament the power over financial affairs. However, the King's difficulties to finance the war against France caused him to turn away from the nobility and allow the Whigs to found the Bank of England. French monarchs were even more dependent on the support of the rural aristocracy to rule the big fragmented country than their British counterparts. The French system of taxation and lending was at quite a disadvantage to finance the courts' fast growing expenses and even less to finance recurrent wars, but it bound the nobility to the Crown and therefore stabilized the political system. Despite all problems, only the deep political and economic crises which shattered the coalition between the King and the nobility paved the way for Law to found a national bank. In the early 17th century, the French monarch saw no alternative for avoiding bankruptcy and maintaining his military force other than to dare a financial revolution. Hence, once again the military necessity to finance costly, recurrent wars shattered the opposition against financial innovations and paved the way for the national banking revolution.

4.4 The Heritage of Early European Banking

The time between the Religious Wars and the French Revolution provided four main relevant heritages in banking: the development of modern private banks outside Italy, money-mercantilism, national banks, and a much wider acceptance of banking activities. Around the time of the Religious Wars, Italian bankers founded branches in several European trading hubs (North 2013). Until the time of the French Revolution, the first modern private banks emerged in most European countries (Pohl 1994). In addition to private banks, several European countries made their first experiences with big national banks, which became the predecessors of later central banks.

In the 16th century in Prussia, France, and Britain private banking was predominantly pre-modern: the wealthy lent predominately their own or maybe their relatives' and colleagues' idle reserves directly to merchants, craftsman, or the monarch. Out of the rising by-business bankers, a class of professional bankers emerged step by step. Professional bankers were predominately modern private bankers, who lived on managing the wealth of other: professional bankers' main business was capital intermediation, hence the absorption of idle reserves from a wide range of depositors and investing the absorbed loanable funds in private businesses and public debts. The emerging of modern private banks had far-reaching consequences: first, loanable funds were concentrated in private banks; hence capital depersonalized. Second, by-business bankers were first and foremost carriers of their core-business interests: merchant interests, goldsmith interests, etc. professional bankers developed and carried out particular banking interests. Hence, the typical modern banking interest trinity of depositors, borrowers, and bankers interests emerged: bankers interests are directed against depositors' and borrowers' interests because the banks seek to maximize interest rates for borrowers and minimize those on deposits and transfer risk to depositors and borrowers. Bankers were often a despised, but economically and politically influential group: as the main or even the only lender to the economy and the state, bankers carried most of the capital's concentrated power. Third, size, maturity, and risk transformation became the bankers' core businesses: banks absorb smaller savings, of short-term maturity, to lend bigger capitals for longer term, hence transforming size, maturity, and risk.

Among contributions on the history of economic thought, the scholastic is usually considered the curious beginning of economic thought without much influence on more recent theories. Contrary to this, the influence of mercantilism on more recent theories and political economics is undeniable. In particular, the mercantilist theory of money and Interest inspired famous economic theories. Despite all theoretical innovations, the history of monetary theory is characterized by two competing, conflicting, recurrent strands of thought: one covers money-mercantilism, the Banking School, Keynesian and post-Keynesian theories. The other includes classical theories, the Currency School, and monetarism (for a detailed discussion see Humphrey 1993, 1999; Brugger 2015): "the history of monetary theory reduces to a struggle between opposing mercantilist and classical camps" (Humphrey 1999, p. 56). Many central concepts of money-mercantilism, like the relation between money supply, interests rates, economic prosperity, industrialization and employment, in one way or another, are echoed in the Banking-School and Keynesian money theories. Apart from its influence on later money theories, mercantilism inspired the 19th century economic nationalism. Similar to the later theory of economic nationalism, mercantilism follows the goal of state building and national economic autarky. The money-mercantilist banking theory has similarities with the later Saint-Simonianism and state- or kathedersocialism: all three considered that big national banks would foster economic progress and employment.

The starting point of money-mercantilism was the deep conviction that money is too scarce for economic prosperity and full employment. Recently, the idea that the quantity of available money influences economic activity has been deemed outdated. However, the money-mercantilist assumption of a positive relation between the growth of money supply and employments, is, in one form or another, still part of most macroeconomic theories. Despite different starting points and arguments, money-mercantilists and more recent economic theories frequently come to rather similar conclusions: money-mercantilism was the first consistent economic theory which suggested a positive relation between banking and economic prosperity. Hardly any economic theory since then denies a principally positive effect of well-functioning banking sectors on economic growth. However, the arguments are rather different: money-mercantilists argued that banks foster growth by augmenting the money supply, more recent (neo-)classical approaches consider that banks reduce transaction costs by facilitating the exchange of savings. Money-mercantilists argued for national or central banks: besides a few remaining free-banking advocates, the necessity of central banks is hardly questioned. Also, the money-mercantilists claim that national banks should act as lenders of last resort and hold a note-issuing monopoly would be supported by most economists. However, other ideas would cause more dispute: the money-mercantilists demand that national banks play an active role and facilitate trade and growth by augmenting the money supply, shares similarities with the later Keynesian theory, but is strongly rejected by monetarism, which considers that the central banks' main duty is to ensure price stability.

As maintained above, first modern private banks emerged in European empires, but national banks are the most important banking heritage from the discussed time. Usually the Sveriges Riksbank is considered to be Europe's oldest central bank. However, the foundation of the Bank of England was the starting point of a new age. Drawing a close connection between the foundation of the Bank of England and Britain's financial and military supremacy, other empires were convinced that empires need to be supported by national or central bank in order to reach their ambitious goals and remain economically, politically, and militarily competitive. Failed attempts like the Banque Royale and the Giro- and Lehnbanco did not stop the triumph of national or central banks. Even disasters like the fall of the Banque Royale could not bring down the money-mercantilist idea, strongly fostered by the success of the Bank of England, that a nation, to be successful, needs a national bank that acts differently from the usual modern private banks. Hence, the idea that industrialization and economic prosperity needs a national bank that overcomes money shortage by issuing notes and that war fortune largely depends on the support from an institution ready to lend huge amounts in a short time was widespread. At the end of the 17th century, less than a handful countries had a bank that may be considered a central bank: a hundred years later just a handful of countries had no central bank.

In many respects, the Bank of England was quite different from recent central banks: it was long owned by private stockholders and its core business was government lending. Recent central banks are usually state-owned and government lending is not their core business or even prohibited for central banks. In addition, unlike most central banks nowadays, early national banks like the Bank of England or Banque Royale were quite Keynesian: expected to facilitate public debt financing, reduce interest rates, augment the amount of money, promote the economic development, and reduce private bankers' bargaining power. Nevertheless, despite all notable differences, the Bank of England became the central bank blueprint due to its function as a lender of last resort and its note-issuing monopoly. The lender of last resort function of central banks is often considered the central issue of central banks: "The hallmark in the development of the 'Art' of central banking over the last two hundred years has been the evolution of the concept of a lender of last resort" (Kindleberger 2005, p. 225).

Most important for the development of the European banking system was the national bank's note-issuing mandate. Paper money was not an invention of money-mercantilism, but is very old and emerged several thousand years ago in China. National banks were also not the first European institutions which issued notes: even before, private banks issued banknotes (Born 1977, p. 17) not fully covered by coins (Richards 1965, p. 40). What changed significantly was the governments' involvement in note issuing and the legal status of paper money. According to the state theory of money (Knapp [1905] 1973), money is what the state declares to be money. States define money by accepting it as legal tender for payments, in particular tax payments. Advocates of the state theory argue that modern paper money did not emerge from exchanges between private persons, but from the state's declarations that something will, exclusively or not, be accepted for tax payments (Ingham 2004, p. 47). Early notes (pre-modern paper moneys) were issued by private institutions, not necessarily banks, as credit notes for deposited coins or goods etc. Principally, people were free to accept notes. Gradually, the status of paper money changed: money-mercantilists demanded and the Bank of England and the Banque Royale received limited note-issuing monopolies.

In addition, private banks issued notes which functioned as paper money. However, thinks changed significantly with the foundation of national banks which held in one way or another a note-issuing monopoly. Previous notes were issued by private banks or other institutions, without much involvement of the central authority. With the foundation of state-owned or state-reliant national or central banks, governments became much more involved in paper money issuing. Hence, the state granted the exclusive right to issue notes to one bank by excluding all others from issuing. Demanded by many money-mercantilists, step by step, notes became legal tender: accepting paper money was increasingly not an act of goodwill, but people and institutions were obliged to use notes in certain transactions. Hence, the main difference between pre-modern and modern paper money was not its function or spread, but its legal status. Citizens and institutions were free to issue and accept pre-modern paper money. In the case of modern paper money, one institution had the right and the obligation to issue notes, while the others were excluded from issuing and all citizens and institutions were obliged to use it in certain transactions. The legal tender status of money and note-issuing monopolies are inherited from that time: currently, hardly any country lacks a note-issuing monopoly and a legal tender currency.

There should be no confusion: the 18th century paper money praxis was quite diverse and different from the current praxis. In the case of France and Germany, national banks had a note-issuing monopoly and the currency was made legal tender: France strongly restricted the use and holding of coins in 1720 (Murphy 1997b, pp. 244–264). On the other hand, the Bank of England for centuries only held an issuing monopoly for London and the government refused, time and again, to make its notes legal tender (Andreadēs 1966); this is why a wide range of coins and non-London banknotes circulated beside the Bank of England notes. However, money-mercantilism and the praxis of national banks started a steady trend toward issuing monopolies and legal tender currencies.

The Development of the European Banking Sector as We Know It 5

The political order altered significantly in the 18th and 19th century. French absolutism crashed and burned in 1789. The British Parliament' political power further strengthened since the Glorious Revolution. Doubtlessly, the step-by-step unification of Mosaic-Germany was the most fundamental change in the European political landscape of the 19th century. By the unification of Germany, Western Europe's great power trinity of France, Germany and Britain—the big three—was established, and has dominated the European political order since then. The entire 19th century was characterized by struggles between republicans, rising socialists and the conservative parts over political dominance and political systems. Overall, in Britain parliamentarianism steadily deepened in the 19th century, in France the entire century was characterized by revolutions and sharp political breaks until the Third Republic was established at the end of the century, Germany's 19th century was marked by its unification. Political orders of the big three were quite diverse, but also shared important similarities: everywhere the bourgeoisie first and later the middle and working class was on the rise and the old aristocracy on the retreat. Liberal and socialist ideas spread; they were not equally successful everywhere, but influenced politics, and in particular the economic policy. Still, at the end of the 19th and beginning of the 20th century Europe was marked by authoritarianism, but, overall, political participation was more pronounced than a century before. Economically, Europe was not uniform either: Britain started its industrialization at the end of the 18th century. In France and Germany industrialization did not really take off before mid-19th century. While the government remained relatively passive in Britain, the state's role in the industrialization of Germany and France was much more active. However, several issues characterized the 19th and the early 20th century: the dispute of the aristocracy and bourgeoisie over political influence; the battle of Britain, France and Germany over world hegemony; the nation's commitment to imperialism and industrialism; the rise of

F. Brugger, *Ideas, Interests and the Development of the European Banking Systems*, Wirtschaft + Gesellschaft, https://doi.org/10.1007/978-3-658-30597-0_5

new leading economic theories; new forms of banking and the concentration of the banking sector.

Political disputes of the 19th century were dominated by the ongoing struggle between the bourgeoisie and the old aristocracy over political power. Absolutism was built on the loyalty of the landed aristocracy. Even back then the rising bourgeoisie entered many offices and governments, but absolutism subordinated the bourgeoisie to the aristocracy. Europe's industrialization steadily increased the bourgeoisie's political power to the detriment of the aristocracy's dominance. Despite the first steps toward industrialization, continental European economies remained heavily dominated by agriculture in the first half of the 18th century. However, the bourgeoisie's influence rose fast due to countries' agreement on industrialization, its higher education, pivotal position in the economy and its ability to form coalitions with the lower middle class and workers; increasingly, the bourgeoisie was able to prevail against the old aristocracy. Overall, the 19th century was the century of the bourgeoisie. The bourgeoisie's dominance was visible in many areas, in particular in the economic politics which became increasingly industry-, banking- and generally market-friendly. However, governments, in particular liberal ones, dominated by the bourgeoisie, were even more nationalistic and imperialistic than their absolute predecessor: bourgeois governments were enthusiastic advocates of national industrialization, building world hegemonies and imperialism.

European empires' aversion to each other did not shrink as governments became less noble. Quite the contrary: the battle over a European hegemony intensified in the 19th century. Empires' geographic extension and international influence was still the strongest symbol of political power and military development. Increasingly, the struggle over European hegemony extended throughout the world as countries intensified their colonial ambitions. The big three rarely attacked each other directly: the battle over world hegemony was fought by building coalitions with smaller countries and colonies the world. As direct military confrontation became less frequent, the rivalry between the big three turned economic. Coalitions with smaller countries were usually built on military pressure, but also close economic relations. In particular, credit played a central role: coalitions were often built by credit for loyalty. Big empires granted public debts for smaller countries political and military loyalty. The success of the empires' colonial ambitions depended first and foremost on their economic and financial ability: developing and binding new colonies was costly and necessitated a financially potent partner.

Several wars and their colonial advantages drastically highlighted Britain's superiority. It was widely agreed that Britain's political and economic power stems from its economic superiority. Much more industrialized than its continental European challenger, Britain's ability to equip armies, its huge military and trade fleet and its economic ability to exploit newly conquered lands was a pivotal advantage for its ambitions to form a world hegemony. French and German elites got convinced that the battle against Britain for world hegemony will be lost if they are not able to catch up economically. Hence, a nation's glory and an empires' greatness became dependent on the question of an empire's readiness for fast industrialization. Elites being aware of homeland's economic backwardness industrialization became the major goal of European countries' economic policy. France and Germany built a kind of industrialization fetish: the enlightened industrial society became the highest ideal, negative effects of industrialization were ignored. In the golden age of teleological thought, industrial society was considered the final stage of societies' historical development. The intellectual environment of the early 19th century France produced the most notorious advocates of the industrial society: Auguste Comte and Henri de Saint-Simon. However, fears of falling further behind, rather than utopias of good industrial societies convinced French and German elites' that industrialization is they only way out of nations' inferiority. From protectionism, easy credit, railway construction, industry-friendly laws to state monopolism and cartelism, many measures for industrialization were taken in France and Germany. Britain was the model of industrialization, but German and French economic policy was usually quite contrary to the British. The British Industrial Revolution was accompanied by laissez-fairism, while in contrast the state played a quite active role in France and Germany and politics were strongly focused on promoting industrialization.

Absolutism and mercantilism as leading economic ideas disappeared together. The decline of mercantilism was marked by the rise of the economic liberalism. Mercantilist ideas were heavily criticized by the emerging classical economic liberalism in England and France. Due to the liberal critics, theoretic inconsistencies and the collapse of absolutism, mercantilism in its traditional form lost ground. At the end of the 18th century it seemed that classical economic liberalism may replace mercantilism as the new leading economic idea in Europe. In France and England classical economic liberalism emerged simultaneously. German economists of the late 18th and early 19th century were quite impressed by the rise of classical economists, but German contributors are usually not considered a key player of early classical economics. However, with the exception of Britain where classical economic liberalism was, at least until the late 19th century, the relatively uncontested leading idea, on the Continent less liberal economic theories emerged, and often became more influential than classical economic liberalism.

Traditionally, liberalism had strong advocates in Britain. The fast rise of the bourgeoisie in the late 18th and early 19th century was a strong push toward liberalism. Unlike in most other countries, liberalism was not just the ideology of the British bourgeoisie, but attracted many from the middle and even the working class. Liberalism and laissez-fairism in Britain was used for a frontal attack on the old aristocracy and other privileged groups: hence, liberalism was first and foremost anti-cronyism. Central to British liberalism was the view that contracts between freeman provides the best outcome for the society as a whole. Monopolies and privileges—in particular the politically granted ones—are expressions of old elites' power and prevent faster progress and the equal participation of all. British liberals' demand for equal right for equal men facilitated the relatively stable coalition with the rising social movement: liberals became aware that they need the rising worker organizations to form a powerful coalition, but it was also expected that liberalism overcome the antagonistic relation between capital and labor.

Directed against mercantilism, the classical economic theory became the best known economic theory of the 19th century. Classical economics target citizens' wealth rather than bullion; the best advocate of nations' wealth is the decentralized agreement of free-men rather than state interventions, and free trade is beneficial to everybody, while protectionism destroys wealth. The classical economic theory was primarily British, but it was the most influential economic idea of the 19th century as it strongly affected other theories. Its money, interest and banking theory strongly influenced the development of the European banking sector. Liberalism, in particular economic liberalism, had a strong fascination for academics throughout Europe, but on the Continent its political influence was often relatively small and of short length.

In Germany and France the time between the breakdown of absolutism and World War I was marked by a back-and-forth of liberalism. Most German economists of the early 19th century were highly impressed by Adam Smith. However, the first half of the 19th century was characterized by the superimposing idea of unification. Still divided into many small entities, the unification of Germany was the goal which subordinated everything else. Unification also became the main economic goal. Due to its unificationism, at first glance the early 19th century German economic thought shared many similarities with mercantilism: nation-building was the main goal of early 19th century German economic thought. Like mercantilism, the early German economic thought assumed that national sentiments—Germany in the mid-19th century was often still a country without a people, as people still felt as Brandenburgians, Prussians etc. rather than Germans—would be fostered by heavy trade within the newly formed nation, by protection against foreign trade and by national champion enterprises. It was assumed that unification requires inward free trade—between the German countries—and outward protectionism. Later, Hegelianism and conservativism of the Bismarck era was marked by a half-hearted economic liberalism: markets were little regulated, but the influence of politics on economics was huge. The time of German conservativism was characterized by colonialism, industrialism and the subjection of economics to politics. While British liberalism was built on a relatively strong coalition of confirmed liberals, liberal politics in Germany was usually opportunistic; liberalism and restrictive interventionism alternated and were applied depending on what seemed more helpful to achieve the higher goals of industrialization and unification. Overall, it may be said that Germany's 19th century political economy was orientated towards the ideas of unification and industrialization. German economic thought of the 19th century was characterized by different theoretical approaches to unification and industrialization. In the Bismarckian unified Germany, unificationism, Hegelianism, conservatism and influences of the classical economic liberalism merged into relatively wired German economic theories.

France in the late 18th century was, together with Britain, the starting point of the liberal classical economic thought. This tradition of liberal economic theory continued throughout the 19th century, but unlike in Britain liberal economic ideas had little direct influence on French economic policy. Like in Germany, economic nationalism and the strong commitment to industrialization strongly influenced French economic thought. France was politically unified, but economically as segregated as Germany. Building one economy, one market for one nation, was the main goal of French economic policy: hence it was still expected that the economy builds the nation and national sentiments. France was the motherland of 19th century industrialism. Germany's industrialism was rather opportunistic: it was suggested that a fast industrialization would unite the country, create national sentiments or at least calm German opponents and foster Germany's world power aspirations. In France, industrialization was often associated with the hope of a new better society. Popular French economic theories of the early 19th century were in particular protectionist. Protectionist theories in France were often little more than developed mercantilism. It was argued that the still underdeveloped French economy needs protection against foreign competitors for a fast industrialization. However, like in Germany and Britain, rising groups like the new bourgeoisie were increasingly unsatisfied with the dominant theory. Apart from the classical economic thought and protectionist theories, several utopian socialists ideas emerged: most notably the theory of Saint-Simon. Ironically, in the native land of laissez-faireism, the socialist Saint-Simonianism deeply changed the French and the continental European banking landscape.

Saint-Simonianism was successful for integrating the main issues of the time without frightening too many: Saint-Simonians were enthusiastic advocates of industrialism, the theory was interpretable in a nationalist way and unlike many other socialist ideas, Saint-Simonianism rejected any class struggle between the bourgeoisie and the proletariat, and instead suggested that both classes should work in a fair way, together, to build the dream of a just industrial society. The time of Saint-Simonian hegemony in France was relatively short, but it changed the European banking landscape like no other theory. Hence, industrialization and to a smaller extent nationalism built the core of French economic theories.

In all three countries industrialization was a core issue of the 19th century. Three things seemed to be pivotal for industrialization: a mobile working class, the availability of capital and a well-functioning transportation. A wide range of social, economic and legal changes caused the formation of an industrial proletariat in most European countries. Capital was the main issue of the time: it was widely agreed that what hinders faster industrialization is the scarcity of capital. Most contributors complained about the scarcity of money and its negative effects on growth: more recent economic historians doubt that there was a scarcity, but economies lacked the financial institutions and cultural factors hampered investment. As maintained, industry financing was difficult and underdeveloped in the early 19th century. The industrial take-off in Britain was predominately financed by factory owners and their relatives. Britain's step-by-step industrialization assured that even bigger investments were covered by saved profits. Hence, bank credit played a minor role in Britain's industrialization. The problem of capital was much more serious in continental Europe. Germany and France started hasty industrialization without a financially strong bourgeoisie; industrialists usually lacked their British competitors' financial possibilities. At the beginning of industrialization banks predominately lent short-time: it seemed too risky to lend deposited money with immediate maturity for longer-term projects such as factories and mines. Longer-term credit almost exclusively consisted of public debt investments. According to more recent contributions, capital was not scarce in principle and accumulated fast due to relatively high interest rates, but was not invested into the rising industry. Idle reserves were hoarded, invested in property or wars.

As maintained, in France, Germany and Britain rather different economic theories emerged, but they banking theories had much in common. Financial markets and in particular the banking sector were usually considered the heart of capitalist economies. As maintained above, for money-mercantilism, banks' ability to create paper money 'out of nothing' was the core banking function which legitimized the existence and prosperity of the first European megabanks. Money-mercantilists expected that banks would overcome the scarcity of money by printing new paper money, which would foster trade and growth. Liberals in particular criticized money-mercantilist money theory and policy. The central point of liberals' critic is that mercantilists misunderstand the difference between money and capital. Money is just a means of exchange: its scarcity or abundancy does not augment economic activity, but only changes prices. In contrast, capital is a means of investment and is always considered to be scarce by classical economics. Capital may take the visual form of money, but capital actually represents the goods or, better said, the means of production purchasable by the money. Visibly, a lender lends money to the borrower, but what he truly lends is the right to own and use certain goods. Hence, according to classical economics, more money does not inspire trade or investment, because it makes paper money abundant, which increases prices, but means of production remain scarce: what is needed for economic prosperity and growth—is capital.

The classical economic distinction between money and capital has far-reaching consequences for banking theory. From money-mercantilism to classical economics, banks' main aim shifts from note issuing toward loanable fund intermediation. According to the classical economic banking theory, banks foster growth by absorbing idle reserves and transfering them into investable capital. People deposit money and banks transform deposits into capital by investing the money. Hence, through banks idle reserves are fed into the capitalist allocation process.

> It [the banking system] places all the available and even potential capital of society [...] at the disposal of the industrial and commercial capitalists so that neither the lenders nor users of this capital are its real owners or producers. [...] At the same time, banking and credit thus become the most potent means of driving capitalist production beyond its own limits (Marx [1894] 1984, p. 607).

From money-mercantilism to classical economics, the major reason or legitimization of the existence of banks shifted from the scarcity of money to the scarcity of capital. Banks are unable to create capital out of nothing: banks are able to create paper money, but they are unable to create the means of production which lie behind the money. What still makes banks pivotal to capitalist economies is their ability to transform maturities, size and locations: small size short-term London deposits are transformed by banks into huge long-term investment in a North-England industry. For classical economics, banks' ability to transfer size, maturity and location—what is usually called loanable funds intermediation—is their main legitimization. According to classical economic theory, economic growth is restricted by the scarcity of capital: by transferring idle reserves into capital, banks reduce the scarcity of capital. In addition, classical economists argue that banks are important for capitalism because of the invalidation of class and status by the distribution of capital. At the beginning of industrialization, investments were financed by former profits and owners' and their relatives' savings. Because financial markets were too shy to lend to long-term industrial projects, the success of an industrial enterprise dependent on the owner's and his family's financial means: this was a contradiction to liberalism. According to the liberal view, economic success should be independent of one's own financial means, family background and class, but should only depend on a person's innovativeness, effort, economic instinct. It was hoped that by the depersonalization of capital—lender and borrowers are not in direct contact—banking would facilitate credit being granted to those with the best ideas and economic instincts rather than those with the best heritage.

5.1 The Cultural Order of the 19th Century

Europe's cultural orders of the 19th century were quite diverse. Once again it must be emphasized that it is not my aim to present the wide range of ideas of 19th century Europe, but those which influenced the development of the European banking system. Mercantilism crashed and burned in the late 18th and early 19th century and was replaced by the liberal classical economics as the leading economic idea. Although simultaneously developing in France and Britain, Britain became the center of liberal classical economics. However, elsewhere in Europe economists and other intellectuals were quite impressed by liberal economics. The development of liberal economics was accompanied by the rise of liberalism as the leading political idea. Elsewhere in Europe, the question of economic and political participation, the relation between the sovereign and the people and civil rights were discussed from a liberal perspective. Closely connected to spreading liberalism was the rise of nationalism. Nationalism became liberalism's most visible twin. Nowhere was the question of nation and nationalism more pivotal than in Germany: politically and economically highly segregated at the beginning of the 19th century, unification became the central issue in Germany.

Meanwhile, the competition between France, Germany and Britain intensified. Two developments disrupted the power balance in Europe: first, the rise of Germany as a new superpower and, second, British imperialism. Traditionally, Europe's politics were characterized by France and Britain's battle over European hegemony. With its unification, Germany also joined the battle over hegemony. While before this battle was predominately fought militarily and within Europe. After the Napoleonic wars, direct military attacks between the big three became more rare. However, the big three's conflict over hegemony became more economical and was taken out to the world. Imperialism was a central element of European empires' battle over hegemony. Imperialism had two main forms: the empires used their political, economic and military means too bind smaller European countries closer to the empire. The second was colonialism: conquer overseas territories and incorporate them into the growing empire. Imperialism was underpinned by an ideological consensus for the necessity of imperialism. Economists argued that colonies are new markets for idle industrial products and capital and for the supply of cheaper row materials to the home country. Economic arguments were underpinned by social Darwinist reasons for imperialism. In accordance with spreading social Darwinism, empires able to conquer overseas territories were considered global powers with a legitimate ambition to form a world hegemony. Big countries unable to subject new territories and bind smaller countries to the empire were considered weak and underdeveloped. In addition, several other arguments for imperialism fostered the ideological consensus for imperialism.

Hardly were ever economic ideas more present and discussed than in the 19th century. Economic theory was not just an issue between economists, but was heavily discussed in parliaments and in daily newspapers. In most textbooks on the history of economic thought, the 19th century is considered the time of classical economics. Classical economics was the leading economic idea as it influenced many notable economists elsewhere in Europe, however, in particular on the European continent, anti-liberal economic theories emerged which were, at least for a certain time, highly influential and became pivotal for the development of the European banking sector. According to a widely shared agreement, Britain's political and military superiority stemmed from its much faster industrialization. Leading economists in France and Germany agreed that liberal *laissez faire* was unsuitable for fast industrialization and catching up with Britain economically. It was argued that protection from the superior British industry and heavy state intervention and guidance would be the right measures to develop the domestic industry. In Germany more aggressive nationalism, the need for economic unification and the agreement on industrialization was the cultural environment in which economic nationalism emerged. Unlike liberal utilitarianism, for the German economic nationalism economic progress not only enhances citizens' utility, but fosters the nation's military and political force and the unification of the still segregated country. France was the second homeland of liberal economics in the late 18th century; however, in the 19th century anti-liberal theories emerged which heavily influenced its economic policy and in particular the development of the European banking system. Saint-Simon and the Saint-Simonians rejected *laissez faire* and instead proposed a highly planned and guided industrialization.

The 19th century was characterized by fundamental discussions on money and banking between different schools of economic thought. In the heated debates, liberal economic liberals faced early Keynesians, economic nationalists and Saint-Simonians, advocates of the emerging quantity theory of money faced the rising Keynesian money theories, supporters of central banks competed with advocates of free banking. The discussions deeply changed money and banking theory. More recent debates on money and banking usually address few new topics not discussed at least rudimentarily in the great debates of the 19th century. The great money and banking debates fundamentally shaped the European banking sector. However, various liberal and anti-liberal theories had a strong influence on the development of the banking sector.

5.1.1 The End of Mercantilism as the Leading Idea

Even at its zenith in the 17th and early 18th century, mercantilism was still heavily criticized. 17th century liberal criticism of mercantilism arose in England and in particular in France—the motherland of absolutism and mercantilism. The opposition to mercantilism and high taxation was sustained mainly by two groups: merchants and noblemen. It seems surprising that criticism came from those two groups: as maintained, the nobility was the monarch's power base, which is why they enjoyed many economic and political privileges. Mercantilist economic policy privileged merchants: trade monopolies were granted to merchants, foreign competition was restricted, cheap credit was granted and much else was done to promote merchants. However, suffering from high taxation and fearing the rising power of the bourgeoisie, noblemen increasingly turned against the crown, absolutism and mercantilism. While some merchants enjoyed many privileges, others, in particular newcomers, were excluded from profitable sectors. Therefore, the mercantilist economic policy produced merchants who were in and those who were on the out of the profitable economic sector: those who enjoyed many privileges and those whose business was complicated by the policy (c.f. Rothbard 1995a, pp. 253–305). Hence, absolutism and mercantilism were unable to satisfy their own powerbase and increasingly faced the criticism of the ones on the out.

The emerging classical economic liberalism became the coffin nail of mercantilism as the leading economic idea. Early classical contributions were a frontal attack on mercantilism as it was a new economic theory. Many weak points of mercantilism were not new, but the criticism of mercantilism of the French physiocrats and British classical economists was more fundamental and well-founded. The liberal criticism was built on three main ideas: utilitarianism, economic natural laws, and the rejection of state interventionism.

As maintained, mercantilists' unit of analysis was the society or the nation rather than the individual. Classical economists using methodological individualism criticized mercantilism for its anti-individualist perspective. Mercantilists' favor for production and protectionism stemmed from their views on nations as segmented, militarily threatened entities: economic policies' main goal was therefore to unite the nation and enhance its military power. Liberals criticized mercantilism for equating the nation's or king's wealth with the wealth of the people. For liberals, the wealth of the nation was equal to the sum of wealth of its citizens. Focusing on the individual's rather than on the nation's power, for liberals consumption rather than production enhances individuals' utility.

Classical economic liberalism made a strong point by asking mercantilist why the focus on production rather than on consumption, on employment rather than on what workers can consume and on what a country may export rather than what people can enjoy. According to classical economic liberalism, there is no reason to foster exports in order to enhance the nation's bullion reserves: why should a good government intentionally restrict domestic consumption in order to support foreign utility. Elsewhere, free trade became a core demand of liberal economists: from Quesnay and Smith to Turgot, Mill and Ricardo, free trade was a central part of liberal economics, which reached its classical peak with Ricardo's trade theory. Liberals' sound free trade arguments were a major setback for mercantilist protectionism, as mercantilists mainly failed to rebut free trade arguments.

Following the philosophical trend of the time, the belief in natural laws of the social order heavily influenced state and economic theories of the 19th century. According to Plato's *Euthyphro Dilemma* the essentialists gained ground against the voluntarist. Plato raised the question of whether something is good or just because God wants it so, or if God wants it because it is good in and of itself and therefore God permits it.

> If the former, then justice is arbitrary, having no essential nature; it subsists contingently, by divine fiat, and can be humanly known only as empirical knowledge of the facts of God's utterance. This is called the voluntarist, or nominalist, doctrine. But if the later answer is correct […], the justice does have an essence distinct from its being willed, and it can be intuited by rational agents (Goldie 1994, p. 589).

Liberals of the 18th and 19th century defined their essentialist position against the more voluntarist position of Hobbes and the absolutistic state theory. Hence, philosophers, state theorists and economists increasingly advocated for the view that justice and social order follow natural laws. *Laissez faire* economists used the natural law concept to argue that:

> In the economy, free trade and free markets, through the harmony of reciprocal benefits, advanced the interest and happiness of all by each seeking his own personal utility and self-interest […] was the natural law that uncovered the key to social harmony and economic prosperity (Rothbard 1995a, p. 272).

Considering that economies follow unchangeable natural laws had far-reaching consequences for reasonable economic policies. Altering the trade balance was a core goal of mercantilism. A major blow to mercantilist trade policy was classical economists' prominent theory of the self-regulating mechanism of international specie distribution: according to Hume's price-specie-flow-mechanism, in the long run the balance of payments between countries and international prices tends toward equilibrium (for a more detailed discussion see Menton 1947; Viner 1975). Therefore, regardless of governments' trade policy, in the long run the foreign trade is balanced; if Hume's theory is true, mercantilists' foreign trade theory crashes and burns, because governments lack the mechanism to sustainably alter the trade balance. Hence, it was argued by classical economists that economies, at least in the long run, follow unchangeable natural laws which determine fundamental economic relations between demand and supply, production and consumption, money and prices, saving and interest and so on. If those natural laws exist, of course, much of the mercantilist economic policy is pointless.

Both mercantilists and classical economists considered that the individual's and societies' interests are usually in harmony, but occasionally collide. The belief in the harmony between individuals' and societies' interests, well-being and utility was more pronounced in classic economic liberalism. Adam Smith's invisible hand harmonizing selfish economic actions with the general well-being became one of the most fundamental principle of liberal economics. Like mercantilists, almost all classical contributors recognized that individuals' and societies' interests are not always in harmony. However, while mercantilists called for a strong state and state interventionism to guide personal interests toward the general well-being, classical economists were opposed to strong states and state interventionism. What made classical economists particularly dismissive of state intervention was their strong belief in natural laws. If economies follow unchangeable natural laws, state interventions are at best useless: usually, classical economists argued that interventions make things even worse because they cause long adjustments with high costs. This does not mean that classical economists rejected all kind of state intervention, for example Adam Smith (1776) demanded interventions into financial markets, education etc., but overall the mercantilist idea of a strong leading state disappeared in the classical theory: according to the mercantilists, it is a ruler's duty to guide the economy so as to maximize the power of the nation. In contrast, classical economists agreed that state interference usually does more harm than good (Heckscher 1935b, p. 318).

Hence, several factors caused a quick end of mercantilism. The mercantilist system increasingly lost its ability to form coalitions. For more and more bourgeois newcomers, mercantilist economic policy restricted their development. Mercantilism's shrinking integrative power caused much criticism from its traditional supporters, the rising bourgeoisie, merchants and the nobility. As immanent cronyism produced more losers than winners and land taxes sharply raised, the bourgeoisie and nobility increasingly turned against mercantilism. Inner contradiction and the creeping collapse of absolutism made it easy for alternative theories to attack the swaying building of mercantilism. Attacked from many sides, after 200 years of dominance mercantilism disappeared as the leading economic idea: "After Hume and Smith had written, mercantilism was definitely on the defensive and was wholly or largely rejected by the leading English economists" (Viner 1975, p. 74).

5.1.2 The Rise of (Economic) Liberalism and Nationalism

It is not my aim to give a rough summary of European liberalisms of the 19th century. Only several main figures, which became important for the development of the European banking system will be outlined. The 19th century was the century of liberalism. Geographically, liberalism originated in Britain with the contributions of John Locke, David Hume, Adam Smith, Jeremy Bentham, David Ricardo, Steward Mill and in France with Montesquieu, Voltaire, Nicolas de Condorcet, Jacques Turgot, Frédéric Bastiat, Jean-Baptiste Say, Alexis de Tocqueville. However, in Germany liberalism also emerged and became influential (Henning 1966). The main pillars of liberalism were the rising bourgeoisie (Pilbeam 1990, p. 235 ff.), the middle class (Langewiesche 1988; Pilbeam 1990) and to a lower extent the working class (Breuilly 1994).

However, liberalism was always quite diverse. Not even the fundamental principles of the wide range of theories and policies considered as liberal are easy to define. I agree with Schapiro (1976) that the most fundamental theorem of liberalism is that: in principle, humans are good. Considering that individuals' rationality is the best guide of peoples' happiness and nation's development, liberals emphasized the need of protecting individuals from governments' interference. Defining all people as equal in their rights, liberals principally rejected all kind of economic and political privilege. However, the equality of people was defined as a passive equality, which meant equal in rights, rather than an active equality like equality in material property. Hence, individual freedom and the equality of people were the most fundamental issues of liberalism.

Jeremy Bentham defined the greatest happiness of the greatest mass as the ultimate goal of liberalism: "the greatest happiness of the greatest number that is the measure of right and wrong" (Bentham 1823, p. vi). Quite skeptical about Smith's and Turgot's concept of natural laws, Bentham attacked the natural law concept on various grounds—for example for being untestable, rather metaphoric, a bad guide for politics etc. –, utilitarianism became the central concept of Bentham's philosophy (Paul 1979, pp. 47–57): for Bentham the pursue of happiness and the avoidance of pain are the only two important anthropologic constants. Bentham stated: "My notion of man is, that, successfully or unsuccessfully, he aims at happiness, and so will continue to aim as long as he continuous to be a man, in everything he does" (Bentham 2004, p. 293). Maximizing individuals' and societies' utility is, according to Bentham, the ultimate moral goal of persons and political actions.

> Nature has placed mankind under the governance of two sovereign masters, 'pain' and 'pleasure'. It is for them alone to point out what we ought to do, as well as to determine what we shall do. On the one hand the standard of right and wrong, on the other the chain of cause and effects, are fastened to their throne (Bentham 1907, p. 1).

In contrast to Bentham, most post-revolutionary French liberals rejected the concept of utilitarianism; often, rather the wording than the meaning of the concept. Both absolutistic suppression and revolutionary terror were legitimized by utilitarian arguments.

Because of the bad experiences with utilitarianism, French liberals favored a more radical version of individual rights (Welch 1989). However, even French liberals did not reject that individual happiness is the ultimate goal, their reluctance targeted more the collective aim of Bentham's utilitarianism.

Defining the greatest happiness of the greatest mass as the ultimate goal, two opposing political approaches seemed to exist for reaching the goal: *Laissez faire* and state interventionism. In principle, liberals favored the first over the second. Liberals' main argument for *laissez faire* was: individuals are always better informed about their needs and desires than governments, which is why state interventions lack important information and intervention restricts individual liberty; hence, state interventions usually do more harm than good (Paul 1979, pp. 57–66). "As a general rule, the greatest possible latitude should be left to individuals, in all cases in which they can injure none but themselves, for they are the best judges of their own interests" (Bentham 1894, p. 63). While Benthaminian utilitarianism is interpretable in a more state-affine way, other liberals focused on defining rights of the individual against the sovereign. John Locke declared in 1689 that citizens' life, liberty and property needs to be protected against government's access. Later contributors extended citizens' rights over the sovereign. However, liberals principle demand for citizens' protection frequently conflicted with other goals and challenges of the time. For example, according to Bussmann (1958) the main challenge of the early 19th century German liberals was to follow two opposing ideals: freedom and unification.

On the social issue, in particular early British, liberals' panacea was participation. According to early liberals, the mercantilist system of economic and political privileges was the main (or only) reason for social injustice, slow growth and poverty. Politically, the one man one vote became the main claim of liberals. It reflected liberals' conviction that all male citizens are born equal in rights and dignity and should therefore have political equal weight: "every Man to count for one and no Man for more than one" (Dicey 1905, p. 157). It was expected that politically empowering poorer classes would foster their case and give them the ability to help themselves. According to Bentham, "Every man follows his own interest as he understands it, and the part of the community which has political power will use it for its own objects. The remedy is to transfer political power to the entire community" (Maine 1886, p. 83). Mill stressed three reasons why the working class needs better parliamentary representation and participation: first, to force the government to pay more attention to workers' concerns. Second, it would motivate workers for higher education, and third, every important interest group should be represented in the parliament (Reeves 2008). In addition, liberals blamed economic privileges for poverty and economic exclusion. For them economic privileges and entry barriers prevent that most capable, most entrepreneurial and smartest persons start businesses, that economies grow faster and that the poor classes rise economically. However, theoretically most liberals supported the demand for more democracy. Practically, in particular in France and Germany, liberals often rejected one man one vote for fear of strengthening socialist parties.

In the mid-19th century the social issue became the leading topic of the time. Everywhere in Europe the social issue caused groups of various backgrounds to call for reforms or socialist revolutions. As maintained, early 19th century liberals were convinced that the same rights to participate and the liquidation of all economic and political privileges would be enough to ensure the economic participation and rise of lower classes. "The ordinary liberal seems to have thought [… that] in a truly just society, the individual should be free to develop his good qualities. Labor should be transformed efficiently into comfort, health and happiness" (Herrick 1944, p. 69). As the social issue aggravated, liberalism was increasingly in danger to lose workers' and lower middle class' support. Their political influence being built on the coalition of bourgeoisie and workers, British liberals were particularly sensitive to the social issue. "The social problem of the future we considered to be, how to unite the greatest individual liberty of action with an equal ownership of all in the raw material of the globe and an equal participation of all in the benefits of combined labour" (Mill [1873] 1981, p. 232). The social issue caused Mill ([1848] 1965a, p. 796) to reject the classical minimal state theory:

> In attempting to enumerate the necessary functions of government, we find them to be considerably more multifarious than most people are at first aware of, and not capable of being circumscribed by those very definite lines of demarcation, which, in the inconsiderateness of popular discussion, it is often attempted to draw round them.

Mill (ibid.) asks "why should people be protected by their government, that is, by their own collective strength, against violence and fraud, and not against other evils" and demands that liberal states should do much more than protecting citizens from "force and fraud". However, Mill (ibid., 945) remains a principal advocate of laissez-fairism: "Laisser-faire, in short, should be the general practice: every departure from it, unrequired by some great good is a certain evil". To solve the social issue, Mill divined various political measurements as acceptable and unacceptable from a liberal perspective: unacceptable are protectionism, usury laws, political cheapening or rise in price of goods, grants of monopolies, laws declaring maximal wages, controlling opinions; acceptable are unemployment benefits, inheritance restrictions, care, income tax, regulation of joint-stock companies, nationalization of monopolized industries, provision of education, housing etc. (Paul 1979, p. 190 ff.). Becoming more open for state intervention and giving more attention to social harmony were the first steps toward social liberalism (Seaman 1978, p. 780). Unlike in Britain, the escalating social issue did not cause a rapprochement of liberals and workers in France and Germany: in France the relation between liberals and laborers remain difficult, in Germany liberals' rejection of any softening of laissez-fairism further divided liberals and workers.

Economic liberalism replaced mercantilism as the leading economic idea in the late 18th and early 19th century. Britain was the hotspot of classical economics, but the new liberal theory also strongly impressed German (Brandt 1992, p. 160 ff.) and French (Béraud 2016) economists. Classical economics are quite diverse; however, several fundamental theorems and methods are shared by most contributions: most liberal economists apply utilitarism in one form or another, the belief that economies follow natural or economic laws and have a principally liberal worldview. Despite the huge differences, classical economics usually favored free trade, strong property rights, free entrepreneurship, little state intervention and strongly believed that individuals' actions according to their self-interest is the best that can be done for a nation's wealth. However, in the late 19th century, economic liberalism lost ground against more interventionist economic theories.

The rising liberal classical economy was the economic theory of the third estate. Classical economics' labor theory of value that all wealth originates in human work was a frontal attack on the aristocracy: the landed aristocracy was degraded to a social ulcer that consumes without producing anything. Smith's invisible hand parable made it unambiguously clear that, according to the liberals, a freed bourgeois is the best advocate of a nations' wealth and economic development. That uncoordinated selfish actions of freemen are more beneficial for nations' wealth than any state intervention: this was a strong attack on the mercantilist favoring of state interventionism. *Laissez faire* as the new political principle disempowered liberals' main enemies: the absolute monarch and the bureaucracy. Assuming that free trade is superior to any trade restriction was a major assault on mercantilist trade theory and its favor for protectionism. Worldwide division of labor opposed mercantilism's national self-sufficiency. Demanding that political office should be held by experts rather than by uneducated noblemen legitimized the higher educated third estate's political ambitions. Hence, the liberal classical economics puts the third estate at the center of society.

> The emerging social classes created by capitalist development, and excluded from government by the absolutist States, strived to obtain what they considered to be their rights, if it is true that money is power. On the one hand, therefore, was the need for a political philosophy by which the civil society could justify itself independently of the State. On the other hand, it was necessary that such a justification take into account the real processes of wealth formation. If Hobbes' 'Leviathan' assumed the natural egoism of individuals in order to justify the State, then it was necessary to demonstrate that a free social life is possible even in the presence of selfish individuals (Screpanti and Zamagni 2005, p. 66 f.).

The rise of liberalism was part of the rise of the third estate.

Nationalism is often considered liberalism's 19th century twin. Elsewhere in Europe, nationalism was on the rise in the 19th century. According to a popular thesis, the French Revolution caused the rise of nationalism in France, but also elsewhere, against French military aggression. Others doubt that interpretation: British nationalism is considered to have emerged with the English Civil War and the Glorious Revolution (Guizot [1640] 1854; Pincus 1996). According to Bell (2003), French nationalism was widespread even before the French Revolution. In his book about the history of European nationalism Lemberg (1950) draws a close connection between liberalism and nationalism. According to him, absolutism was already a major push toward nationalism, but not until the democratization of Europe did nationalism become a popular ideology. In medieval times, the peoples' identities consisted of many belonging to different groups: the religious, the professional, their landlord or count etc. During the time of absolutism, the state steadily deepened and took over separated identity building fields: absolutism was accompanied by a nationalization of religion, personal rights, occupations etc. Although nationalism deepened at the time of absolutism, Lemberg argued that nationalist sentiments were still not widespread. Political liberalism deepened nationalist sentiments: universal suffrage made politics and the state an issue for everyone: the state no longer exclusively belonged to the crown, or a religious leader, but became the case of the people. According to Lemberg, peoples' ability for political participation awoke nationalist feelings, because people increasingly considered the state their political affair. Many liberal contributors like Rousseau (Vossler 1937, p. 21 ff.), Mill (Woolf 1996) and others had strong national attitudes.

5.1.3 The Anti-liberal Turn on the European Continent

Nowhere was the question of nationalism and state building more present than in 19th century Germany: still highly fragmented at the beginning of the 19th century, Germany's unification and nation building was the central political and economic issue of the 19th century. German nationalism had to prevail over other rising nationalisms, like Prussian, Brandenburgian and Bavarian nationalism. Pursued by the governments, facing the hostility of the powerful nobility, German nationalism soon became more aggressive and violent than the more liberal British one. France was officially unified, but practically, economically and politically, still quite segregated.

On the continent, two main interwoven issues highly influenced economic discussions and the economic policy. The first was state building. In particular in Germany many economists and politicians were convinced that economic integration was the key to national unification. Like former mercantilist contributors, it was suggested that increasing trade between the highly segregated areas and the development of economic national champions would bring people together and foster national sentiments. Second, the 19th century was marked by the battle over world hegemony. After the reign of Napoleon Bonaparte, France fell into a deep depression; French military force and ability to subjugate other nations crashed and burned at Waterloo. In French perception, the defeat of Waterloo was much more than a lost battle, it was a clear and strong sign of Britain's new superiority. The social, political and economic elites agreed that Britain's superiority ultimately stemmed from its strong industry. According to them, Britain's high productivity was a pivotal military advantage; Britain was able to equip huge armies in a relatively short time. French social, political and economic elites were convinced that France, first and foremost, needs a fast industrialization to catch up with Britain.

The unified Germany became the third superpower of western Europe. Three reasons made a fast industrialization quite important for Germany: first, the newly found nation lacked national cohesion. People still felt as Prussians, Brandenburgians etc., rather than as Germans. It was hoped that a German industrialization with German national champion enterprises would foster national sentiments and identity, or that at least economic success would weaken centrifugal forces. Second, Germany needed to demonstrate the world that it is a leading European empire. Industrial power was a strong symbol of a nations' power and force. Third, taking part in the colonial run and fearing French attacks necessitated a strong and very costly military. It was expected that fast industrialization would cover the costs.

Hence, industrialization was considered an economic, political and military question of survival and the fundament of an empire's power, extension and ability to be a global leader. In the first half of the 19th century, a kind of industrialization-fetish emerged in continental Europe. France and Germany of the 19th century became the epicenter of the golden age of teleological thought. Henri de Saint-Simon and Auguste Comte were among the leading French intellectuals of the time, both were fervent supporters of industrialization: for Saint-Simon the industry is the only "Guarantee of Mankind's Existents", the "Source of all Wealth and Happiness" and "Industrial Ideas" are the "Cohesive Force of the Society" (Muckle 1906, p. 7): according to Saint-Simon: "The whole of society rests upon industry. Industry is the sole guarantee of its existence, the single source of all its wealth and all its prosperity. The state of things most favorable to industry is by that very reason the most favorable to society" (cited in Mason 1931, p. 652). Both Comte and Saint-Simon considered industrial society as the ultimate and best stage of societies' historical development. For Saint-Simon, the industrial society is a classless, socialist society with the following principle: from each according to their ability, to each according to their need. Saint-Simonians' influence was steadily on the rise, at least until the Third Republic. Also, non-Saint-Simonian elites were mostly convinced by the necessity of a fast industrialization. In Germany, advocates of industrialism, like Friedrich List, were usually less utopian, but not less convinced of the necessary fast industrialization. However, although the principal need for industrialization was accepted by most groups and classes, much disagreement existed about the form of industrialization and its implementation. Industrialization was the main economic goal of the 19th century.

From the widespread conviction that continental European empires are in need of a fast industrialization in order to catch up with Britain, anti-liberal economic ideas emerged and spread fast. Although liberal classical economics received much attention and spread among continental European economists, anti-liberal economic theories were, at least for a certain time, quite influential. Most influential anti-liberal theories, like economic nationalism in Germany and Saint-Simonianism in France, were an intellectual mixture of nationalism, industrialism, socialism, state interventionism enriched by utopias of a better industrial world, which were more compatible, at least practically, with authoritarian regimes. However, both theories rejected *laissez faire* and proposed the clear and strong economic lead of the state.

5.1.3.1 German Economic Nationalism

In Germany, aggressive nationalism, industrialism and the all-dominating question of unification fostered the rise of theories of economic nationalism. Although liberal classical economics attracted many well-known German economists, economic nationalism became quite influential. In Germany, economic nationalism was, in particular, advanced by a group of economists around Friedrich List and by Johann Gottlieb Fichte. While List's theory must be taken seriously, Fichte's approach is a striking example of the aberrations that happen if a philosopher starts with economics in old age. However, economic nationalism was usually built on three main fundaments: industrialization was defined as the ultimate goal of economic policy, the nation was considered the central economic entity and state interventions were considered needed in order to foster economic progress.

As maintained, for liberal economists the greatest happiness of the biggest mass was the ultimate goal. In contrast, for economic nationalists the ultimate goal was the industrialization and productivity of the nation. Friedrich List suggested that economic policy should target the productive power of the nation (Levi-Faur 1997b). Germany's industrialization was the main topic and goal of List's economic writing. While liberal economists considered that the invisible hand is the best guide for economic prosperity, economic nationalists suggested that industrialization needs the guidance of strong states.

Economic nationalists criticize economic liberalism for ignoring and misunderstanding the importance of national states. Loosely speaking, economic liberalism recognizes individuals and mankind, but nothing in between. For economic nationalists, the nation is the most important and central economic entity. Unlike liberal economists, economic nationalists consider that nations develop autonomous interests and logic: national interests are not just the aggregate individual interests, but nations develop and follow distinctive interests and logic. Economic nationalists assume that states have the power to shape the direction of economic development; they expect governments to foster industrialization and guide economic progress in directions favorable for the nation. Hence, economic nationalists reject the idea of unchangeable national laws, which characterized the development of economies and in contrast to liberal economists, economic nationalists believed in the necessity of state interventions for fast industrialization.

Before and at the time of Friedrich List, several German economists may be considered as nationalists (Brandt 1992, p. 33 ff). However, there is little doubt that List was "the most important and prominent economic nationalist of the 19th century" (Helleiner 2002, p. 311). As maintained, for List the primary goal of economic policy was to foster the nation's productive power. Productive power was considered the economic contribution to a nation's power (Levi-Faur 1997a, p. 361). In the preface to his famous work *The National System of Political Economy* ([1841] 1909), List defines his method against the "bottomless cosmopolitanism" (ibid., xlii) of the classical economics, but also against the "(so-called) 'mercantile' system [mercantilism]" (ibid., p. 218) In contrast to classical economists' methodological individualism, economic nationalism was built on methodological nationalism. National interests and national logics are the starting and endpoint of List's political economics: "I would indicate, as the distinguishing characteristic of my system, NATIONALITY. On the nature of nationality, as the intermediate interest between those of individualism and of entire humanity, my whole structure is based" (ibid., p. xliii). According to List (ibid., p. 141), classical economics has three main errors: first, "boundless cosmopolitanism" which ignores nations and their interests; second, "dead materialism" which causes classical economics to focus solely on values and prices rather than on the "mental and political, the present and the future interests, and the productive powers of the nation"; third, "disorganising particularism and individualism" which ignores the social character of economies, groups and labor. What List aims to develop is the economies of the nation. For List (ibid.), the nation is in between the individual and the mankind, but follows its own interest and logic:

> Between each individual and entire humanity, however, stands THE NATION, with its special language and literature, with its peculiar origin and history, with its special manners and customs, laws and institutions, with the claims of all these for existence, independence, perfection, and continuance for the future, and with its separate territory; a society which, united by a thousand ties of mind and of interests, combines itself into one independent whole, which recognises the law of right for and within itself, and in its united character is still opposed to other societies of a similar kind in their national liberty, and consequently can only under the existing conditions of the world maintain self-existence and independence by its own power and resources.

Unlike classical economists who considered that all individuals' interests are principally in harmony, for List the world is divided into nations with different material, political and cultural interests (Helleiner 2002, p. 312). The interests of nations are not, usually, in harmony, but nations compete over influence, power, glory, markets and resources: the relation between nations is conflictual (Levi-Faur 1997a, p. 367). Despite List's rampant nationalism, for him nationalism was a transitory stage toward the last stage of history: the industrial society. In particular in *The Natural System of Political Economy* ([1841] 1909) List outlined the close connection between economics, politics and culture: for List the industrial society is the highest stage of economic, political and cultural development. According to him, in the last stage of social development, the industrial society, national economies are replaced by cosmopolitan economies. Hence the conflictual nationalism of industrialization turns into a peaceful, cooperative, universal, industrial society (Helleiner 2002, p. 313 f.).

Hence, according to List the economy should be orientated towards a nation's reputation and military power. At the same time, much like former mercantilist economists, List considers that economies foster the state building process (ibid., 312). He argued that increasing national trade and the foundation of economic national champions would foster nationalist sentiments. Having just started its political unification in the mid-19th century and having struggled with the integration of the segregated entities, Germany was particularly open for economic theories highlighting the integrative power of national economies.

List was deeply convinced that the state has the possibility and the mission to guide industrialization and economic development. Levi-Faur (1997b) lists four main characteristics of economic development which make state interventions, according to economic nationalism, necessary: "The collective nature of economic activity in a developed economy"; highly differentiated processes necessitate the coordination of the state. "Social conflicts in a developed economy"; the fragmentation of group interest necessitates the state as mediator and referee. "Time preferences in a developed economy"; states needs to smooth time preferences of people. "Culture and the productive powers in a developed economy"; the productive power is highly determined by the institutional setting in which the economy is embedded. List was by no means an aloof theorist, but intensively studied the German economy and developed a plan for Germany's industrialization.

List starts the proposals for Germany's industrialization with the observation that Germany is an economically backward country. He proposed several measurements to foster Germany's industrialization; most famous was his call for protectionism. List was not the principal opponent of free trade. However he argued that free trade is advantageous if trading economies are economically roughly equally strong (Harlen 1999, p. 739 ff.). However, he considers that if countries, like Britain and Germany, are unequal, the economically weaker state, Germany, needs protection from the highly industrialized competitor, Britain. According to List, to industrialize their economies, weaker countries need protection from the superior competitors until they reach the same level of industrialization.

Johann Gottlieb Fichte proposed a much more radical form of economic nationalism in his *Der geschlossne Handelsstaat* ([1800] 1920). Fichte's proposal was odd and radical even for 19th century standards. Fichte's proposal had little direct political influence until ultra nationalist theories became acceptable in World War I and the Third Reich (Heilperin 1960, p. 83). However, it gives insights into the economic ideas of German radical nationalists. Refusing *laissez faire* (Roll 1974, p. 219 f.) and all kinds of liberal economics, Fichte acknowledged private property in principle, but proposed in his utopian economy that states have the full command over production. Privately owned, the highly authoritarian state decides how property is used to produce a certain quantity of a prescribed goods (Saage 1996, p. 48). Fichte's proposal is a weird combination of ultra nationalism, primitive socialism, and radical protectionism, all interpreted in the most authoritarian way. Fichte's economics were interpreted as a manifest of national autarky. I agree with Heilperin (1960, p. 86) and Roll (1974, p. 220) that Fichte's ideas are even more radical.

What Fichte proposes is a fully planned national economy. National autarky is necessary because it ensures that no external influences disturb the economic plan: he argues ([1800] 1920, p. 26 f.) that international trade thwarts a nation's ability to fully control the economy. Hence, Fichte was aware of the "perennial conflict between national planning and foreign trade. The state can control economic life within the country but not beyond its boundaries" (Heilperin 1960, p. 86). Beside enhancing a nation's power, fostering state building and strengthening military capacities, Fichte had two more fundamental arguments for national autarky and planed economies: first, turning the liberal argument upside down, Fichte beliefs that economic dependency caused by international trade is the main reason for wars, while economic autarky is the fundament of a peaceful world (Saage 1996, p. 53). Second, independence from foreign influences and economic planning makes a fully rational economic development possible. According to Fichte ([1800] 1920, p. 8 ff.), it is the state's duty to ensure that citizens' essential needs are satisfied. To cover essential needs of citizens and to guide economic progress, for Fichte governments need to control production, distribution and prizes (ibid., p. 14 ff.).

Later Kardorff (1875) in his critic of liberal free-tradeism revitalized the nationalist rhetoric of List and Fichte. According to him, maximizing a nation's wealth should be the ultimate goal of economics. Like other nationalist economists, Kardorff draws a close connection between economic, political and military power: according to Kardorff (ibid., p. 4) "National Wealth" is a "precondition for National Power". Following List and Fichte, he (ibid.) argues that the classical trade theory is built on the naïve cosmopolitan view that all men are brothers and all (liberal) nations have the same interest of peaceful trade. In contrast, he assumes that nations have opposing interests, which is why their economic and political relations are conflictual.

5.1.3.2 French Saint-Simonianism

The rise of the industrial proletariat and the July Revolution encouraged the issue of distribution. In the 19th century a wide range of non-Marxist socialist ideas emerged in France (Bellet 2016). Socialists ideas of the 19th century were quite heterogeneous and ranged from moderate social democratic ideas to radical anarchist views. Among the wide range of socialist ideas, one became more important for the development of the continental European banking system than any other idea: Saint-Simonianism.

Henri de Saint-Simon's and his followers' contributions, usually subsumed as Saint-Simonianism was for a certain period the most influential theory in France. Saint-Simon's success much stemmed from his ability to slip the most influential ideas of his time in his own theory and to give a positive vision of the future at a time of much disturbance and unrest. He denounced the unequal distribution of wealth, without attacking private property in principle; demanded a strong organization at the top of the state and concurrently rejected every form of harsh dominion; was an enthusiastic advocate of industrialization without exploitation of the worker; widely followed the classical economic theory, but rejected their favor for *laissez faire* and criticized the blind eye turned on the distribution of wealth; demanded a clear and fair order at a time of chaos and unrest and, like the French revolutionists, he was a clear advocate of the third estate.

Henri de Saint-Simon was probably France's most influential intellectual of the 19th century. Few economist ever had more direct influence on economics and politics than Saint-Simon and the Saint-Simonians: after Saint-Simon's death, his followers had a dense network in politics, banking, engineering, bureaucracy and education (Eckalbar 1979) and used the influence to shape the country in accordance to their ideas. However, Saint-Simon's work is full of deep breaks and contradictions. In addition, what is considered as Saint-Simonianism is usually a synopsis of Saint-Simon's and his followers' works. Much of what is considered Saint-Simonianism is relatively far away from Saint-Simon's own writings (Booth 1871; Gide and Rist 1923, pp. 216–250). Differences between Saint-Simon's work and his followers' contributions are not of greater relevance here as the focus lies on beliefs in ideas of a better world and their influence on the development of the European banking sector, rather than on breaks and differences within Saint-Simon's writings and between his and his followers' contributions.

Saint-Simon's thought was highly influenced by the economic, political and social situation of his time: he was quite impressed by the potential of the rising industry, in France and Britain, and the progress of science. At the same time, Saint-Simon was shocked by the misery and inequality the *laissez faire* industrialization had created and was disappointed by the French Revolution which caused, according to him, much chaos without fundamentally attacking the old feudal distribution of wealth and means of production.

The 19th century, in France and elsewhere, was dominated by a teleological theory of history, an, in particular in the first half of the 19th century, strong progress-orientated optimism, and the increasing abolishment of the misery of workers; Saint-Simon was a child of his time. Like his follower Auguste Comte, Saint-Simon's theory of history is teleological; history and the development of societies is considered a targeted process of consecutive stages of history: from feudalisms, over absolutism to the final stage of industrialism (Salomon-Delatour [1919] 2011, p. 28). The driving force of the history is the development of production or industry, but history and social change is characterized by class struggles between the idle aristocracy and the industrious bourgeoisie (Muckle 1906). Although Saint-Simon focused production, techniques and the industrial development, his historical theory is not "economic materialistic", but "sociological-intellectualistic" because he considers economic development dependent on intellectual development: every technical industrial stage is dependent on the corresponding philosophical Intellectual stage (Salomon-Delatour [1919] 2011, p. 28 f.). According to Saint-Simon, the ultimate stage of history is technical industrialism with the corresponding intellectual positivism and political socialism—what what he considers industrial society.

Saint-Simon's main issue throughout his life is how industrialization and industrial society is possible; understanding industrialization in the wider social context means to bear in mind economic and social policy, dominion, distribution of wealth and distribution of means of production, competition and the class question. For Saint-Simon, much like British liberals, citizens' happiness and satisfaction is the ultimate goal of economics and politics. Production and productivity is the path toward happiness and satisfaction, but not the goal in itself. The social order in Saint-Simon's industrialisms is dominated by the obligation to work of all members (Petermann 1979, p. 100 ff.), and also the right to work of everybody (Muckle 1908, p. 221).

The question of which social organization fosters and enables industrialism was central to Saint-Simon's work. At the beginning of his academic career, Saint-Simon was quite impressed by Adam Smith and other members of the classical school. Soon he and his followers started to criticize the classical thought for turning a blind eye on distribution and refused laissez-fairism as the appropriate system of resource and income distribution for industrialization (c.f. Mason 1931). According to them, *laissez faire* causes chaos and an unfair distribution of wealth, hence the quite opposite of what Saint-Simonians expected from industrialization. In contrast to the liberal *laissez faire*, Saint-Simon promoted the elaborate organization and planning of industrialization and industrial societies. He argues that feudalism and absolutism cause militarism and an unfair and inefficient distribution of wealth and means of production, *laissez faire* causes chaos, disorder and inefficiency. Rejecting those three types of order, he proposed that the accurate order of industrial societies is positivism. According to Saint-Simonians, industrial economies need to be carefully planned. However, the plan should strictly follow scientific knowledge rather than the ideas of the monarch, or the interest of small groups.

Saint-Simon's historic theory suggests that society undergoes three stages with the corresponding philosophic system; feudalism with the Catholic theology, absolutism and the revolution with the Protestant metaphysic and the ultimate stage—industrialism and its positivism (c.f. Salomon-Delatour [1919] 2011, p. 27–33). The science of production should be the only guide and underlying principle of the positive political economy (Muckle 1906, p. 8), which distributes all means of production according to scientific knowledge of production. However, for Saint-Simonians, as Petermann (1979, p. 115)) outlines, the science of production is a comprehensive science of society; society as an interwoven organism only understandable as such. Petermann (ibid., pp. 100–194) describes Saint-Simon's "Industrial Society" as a "Society as Factory"—a metaphor also used by Saint-Simon: according to Petermann, for Saint-Simon, industrial societies are legitimized by their superiority in producing goods and accumulating, while pre-industrial societies were characterized by domination, war, blind faith, the interests of small groups. In contrast, industrial societies are characterized by rationality and scientific organization and the optimal use of all people and means of production: only the cooperation of industry, politics and science, with the lead of the latter, enables the optimal organization of production. Hence, for Saint-Simonians, societies are interdependent organisms: social development, politics, production, consumption and distribution must be understood as interdependent.

Whether Saint-Simon was a socialist caused much dispute: Mason (1931) denies he was one, Gide and Rist (1923, pp. 216–245) stress that his followers were much more socialist than he was and for Salomon-Delatour ([1919] 2011, pp. 33–36) he was a socialist according to a wider definition of socialism. On the question of private property Saint-Simon unmistakable did not demand its abolition; he was critical regarding inheritance without demanding its full prohibition (Petermann 1979, pp. 122–126). However, for Saint-Simon property right is not an unchangeable natural law, but needs to be adjusted to the historical situation and should never place private interests over general interests (Muckle 1908, p. 216). His followers were more critical of private property and rejected every form of private inheritance (Gide and Rist 1923, p. 240). Hence, Saint-Simon and the Saint-Simonians did not reject private property, but promoted a strict meritocracy ownership structure without any private inheritance and remunerations according to persons' merit.

According to Saint-Simon, inheritance excludes big parts of the society from private property, creates a class of idle capital owners, concentrates capital and the power of capital and sustains the feudal ownership system. In contrast, private property in the industrial ownership system is legitimized by the industrial necessity of private ownership: hence, private property in industrial society exists because it is advantageous to industrial production (Salomon-Delatour [1919] 2011, p. 30). Hence, private property is distributed strictly according to merit and productive necessities,—"according to ability" and "according to performance" (Bellet 2016, p. 189).

The recognition of immanent recurring class struggles is usually threatened as a central element of socialist ideas. Class struggles are in particular central for Marxists and other proletarian socialist ideas, but the French political left was at the beginning of the 19th century much less proletarian than in other countries. Like Marx and the Marxists, Saint-Simon considers history a recurring class struggle. However, unlike Marxists, who focus on the struggle between the proletariat and the bourgeoisie in capitalist societies, for Saint-Simon history is determined by a recurrent struggle between the bourgeoisie and the aristocracy or better said between the hardworking and the idle (ibid., p. 189). Saint-Simon and the Saint-Simonians divide societies into two classes: the working population and the idle population. Both the bourgeoisie—as long as it participates actively in the production process—and the proletariat are considered working populations. For Saint-Simon, a classless society is reached if all citizens are obligated to work.

According to Saint-Simon, the French Revolution marked the ultimate political victory of the bourgeoisie over aristocracy. However, the old aristocratic ownership structure survived and was solidified by inheritances (Gide and Rist 1923, p. 230 ff.). The main obstacle for a classless society is the persistence of the old aristocratic ownership structure. For Saint-Simon, replacing the old aristocratic ownership structure by a meritocracy ownership structure would be the final step toward a classless society. According to Saint-Simon and the Saint-Simonians, in an industrial society, the bourgeoisie and the proletariat understands their cooperative relation: all citizens realize the advantages of scientific organization and the cooperative nature of industrial production. As all citizens and classes understand the cooperative nature of industrial societies, according to Saint-Simon and the Saint-Simonians, governing changes from oppressing people—rule over people—to organizing the distribution of means of production—rule over goods (Salomon-Delatour [1919] 2011, p. 31).

For the highest possible output, resources must be distributed to regions, industries and persons where they are used most efficiently (Eckalbar 1979, p. 84). Refusing *laissez faire* as the optimal system to distribute resources, Saint-Simonians stated that an optimal distribution of resources is only possible if the distribution follows a higher plan made by the most successful industrialists, bankers and entrepreneurs. Economic rationalization in the sense of using resources in the most productive way, is, according to Saint-Simonians, only possible if resources are distributed according to a central planning organization: overall organization and rationalization are central concepts of Saint-Simon's economic policy (Mason 1931, p. 641 f.). In an industrial society where everything else is subordinated to economic progress, politics is reduced to the scientific organization of production. Planning organizations (governments) of industrial societies possess significant competence as they have the ability to distribute the nation's means of production, however, they are considered highly restricted by their obligation to strictly follow scientific findings. Hence, like economic nationalists, Saint-Simon proposed the strict political guidance of economic progress.

However, there is an important theoretical difference between Saint-Simonianism and economic nationalism regarding the government's role in the economy. Saint-Simonianism was erroneously interpreted as state interventionism: actually, Saint-Simon was quite skeptical about state interventions (Muckle 1908, p. 211). Treating Saint-Simonianism as state interventionism misses the difference between governing in a pre-industrial society and in an industrial society. Usually, state interventions are considers acts of state power to intervene in markets in order to reduce negative collective outcomes of personal interests. Hence, state interventions are actions against individuals' or a group of individuals' vested interests for a higher social goal. In contrast, according to Saint-Simon, governments in an industrial society are not acting against, but in accordance with the interests of all societies' members. He believes that if the most capable economic professionals rule the country strictly in accordance with scientific means, the outcome would be in favor of all members of the productive class (Mason 1931, p. 663 f.).

As the people realize that the positive governance of the economic professions is the best of all alternatives, politics shifts from domination to organization. Pre-industrial forms of governance are the rule of a small group, a person, a class over the rest of the society, hence the assertion of the interest of a small group over those of the whole society. In contrast, the scientific policy in industrialism pursues the interest of the whole productive class, hence the entire society (Muckle 1906). Unlike in pre-industrial societies, in industrial societies the relation between the bourgeoisie and the proletariat is cooperative as both classes have an vested interest in expanding the nation's wealth (Salomon-Delatour [1919] 2011, p. 31 f.). According to Saint-Simonians, the harmonic industrial society necessitates the lead and scientific organization of the production by the bourgeoisie, because the rule of the uneducated proletariat only caused famines and chaos. Saint-Simon aspired not to a proletarian revolution, but to a fair wage for hard work (Muckle 1906, p. 33 f., 1908, p. 220). Hence, industrial society is organized or governed by a small group of economic experts, able to distribute all means of production and consumption goods. However, because the industrial policy safeguards the interest of the entire productive class, the rule of the experts must not be enforced because it is voluntary accepted by everyone (Mason 1931, p. 660 ff.); governors bloody rulers are replaced by bureaucrats. Due to the cooperative nature of industrial societies, for Saint-Simon neither regulations nor state interventions seemed necessary, because entrepreneurs and workers accept the wise policy of the governing experts and no further intervention or legal restriction is needed. Hence, for Saint-Simon and the Saint-Simonians, an industrial society with an industrial policy is a cooperative society without major class antagonism and with no need for strict ruling or a government in the common sense.

5.1.4 Intensifying Imperialism

Despite the rise of liberalism, imperialism and colonialism intensified in the 19th century. In the 19th century the economic, political and military competition between the big three (Britain, France, Germany) expanded throughout the world. Analyzing German imperialism, Wehler (1976a) considered that in the third half of the 19th century Germany was characterizes by an ideological consensus over the necessity of imperialism. Besides Germany, French and British elites were also mostly convinced that imperialism was militarily, politically and economically necessary. Several main arguments for imperialism could be found in Germany, France and Britain: economists and many politicians were convinced that their domestic economies suffer from overproduction, oversupply of capital and high prices for natural resources. They argued that colonies would be new markets for products and capital and would provide the home country with cheaper raw materials. From the social Darwinist perspective it was argued that empires' and races' ability to subordinate 'the savages' is a sign of their power and superiority: or that only nations able to subordinate the savages may raise the claim to being an empire. Hence, those empires most able to conquer new territories were considered as most ready to instate world hegemony. Britain, France and Germany competing over hegemony, falling behind in colonial conquests was interpreted as weakness. In addition, governments feared turmoil and revolutions. Deporting the insurgent parts of the society to new colonies was expected to stabilize the political order.

Early contributors on imperialism usually suggest that imperialism had predominantly economic reasons. Marxists and non-Marxists may be found among the advocates of the economic theses; famous are the Marxist contributions of Hilferding ([1910] 1955), Lenin ([1917] 1999) and Rosa Luxemburg ([1913] 2003) and the non-Marxist ones of Hobson (1902). Coming to different conclusions, Marxist and non-Marxist economic imperialism theses follow the same line of argumentation. The starting point of Hobson's, Lenin's and Luxemburg's analyses is the assumption that 19th century economies were characterized by oligopolization and overproduction. Industrialization in general and oligopolization and monopolization in particular accelerated the accumulation of capital. Accelerating capital accumulation and production accompanied by diminishing demand caused the oversupply of investable capital and goods. According to them, steadily falling interests rates threatened the survival of capitalism. Imperialism was considered the only possibility to save capitalism from destroying itself: investing capital abroad and sending industrial goods to the colonies was seen as the only way to break through falling interest rates and overproduction. Hobson (ibid., p. 76) traced the capitalists' argumentation for imperialism:

> We must have markets for our growing manufactures, we must have new outlets for the investment of our surplus capital and for the energies of the adventurous surplus of our population: such expansion is a necessity of life to a nation with our great and growing powers of production.

Despite many non-economic arguments outlined by colonial advocates, according to Hobson the patronage of capitalist interests, in particular financial interests, paved the way for colonialism. Hobson (ibid., p. 200) concludes that "imperialism, as we see, implies the use of the machinery of government by private interests, mainly capitalist, to secure for them economic gains outside the country"; in particular financial interests advocated for imperialism (ibid., p. 60 ff.).

For Lenin ([1917] 1999), imperialism is the highest stage of capitalism. Lenin's main thesis is rather similar to Hobson's argument. He considers that capitalism is characterized by the tendency toward monopolization. Capital concentrates in the hands of a few megabanks. Fast accumulation and concentration of capital causes interests to fall. Threatened by falling interests rates, the financial oligopoly searches elsewhere for better investment opportunities and impels governments to develop new investment markets. For Lenin, the financial oligopoly is the main driving force behind imperialism; "finance capital has led to the 'actual' division of the world" (ibid., p. 74). Rosa Luxemburg ([1913] 2003) argues in *The Accumulation of Capital* that imperialism is the last stage of capitalist colonialization. According to Luxemburg, to survive, capitalism must colonialize non-capitalist fields: the colonialization of the non-capitalist environment takes place in "three phases: the struggle of capital against natural economy, the struggle against commodity economy, and the competitive struggle of capital on the international stage for the remaining conditions of accumulation" (ibid., p. 348). Imperialism is the last form of capitalist colonialization of non-capitalist areas. Imperialism secures capitalists' survival by occupying new non-capitalist areas, which ensures the accumulation of capital, but at the same time destroys capital's future accumulation possibilities:

> With the high development of the capitalist countries and their increasingly severe competition in acquiring non-capitalist areas, imperialism grows in lawlessness and violence, both in aggression against the non-capitalist world and in ever more serious conflicts among the competing capitalist countries. But the more violently, ruthlessly and thoroughly imperialism brings about the decline of non-capitalist civilisations, the more rapidly it cuts the very ground from under the feet of capitalist accumulation (ibid., p. 426).

Quite critical of the economic imperialism theses, Sulzbach (1959, p. 211 f.) outlines several weak points: he asks if bankers are really fully aware of their vested interests, and if they have the courage to express their view and how they are able to bring the government to declare war and attack other countries. Sulzbach has a good point: frequently, Marxist theories are close to conspiracy theories as they fail to explain how the bourgeoisie is able to enforce its vested material interests other than thanks to corrupt governments.

Looking at the 19th century discussions on colonialism shows us that many economists and politicians highlighted the economic importance and necessity of conquering new lands. Liberal and anti-liberal economists likewise promoted imperialism. Economically, colonies were considered advantageous as new markets, production places, raw material suppliers and investment places. According to the French premier Jules Ferry, "colonial politics is the daughter of industrial politics" (cited in Daughton 2006, p. 10). Fearing the superior British competition, France and Germany implemented various trade barriers. Principally convinced of the advantages of trade, for liberal and anti-liberal economists imperialism entailed the possibility to trade with selected partners: Saint-Simon and many Saint-Simonians, for example, stressed the positive effect of colonialism on trade and economy prosperity (Pilbeam 2014, p. 108 ff.). Continental European countries aggravating trade barriers, British liberals saw imperialism as the only possibility to maintain free trade with the colonialist countries. Mill ([1861] 1977, p. 565) argues that great empires "at least keeps the markets of the different countries open to one another, and prevents that mutual exclusion by hostile tariffs, which none of the great communities of mankind, except England, have yet completely outgrown." Pierre Paul Leroy-Beaulieu, the famous French economist, argued that colonialism is a byproduct of industrialization (Daughton 2006, p. 10). He argued that colonialism fosters the economy by first providing cheaper raw materials and then opening new sales markets for domestic products (Murphy 1948, p. 125 f.).

In addition to the trade argument for imperialism, many, even liberal, economists of the time argued that new investment opportunities are needed to overcome the capital oversupply. According to Leroy-Beaulieu the "lowering of profit [...] is, in our opinion, a real evil" which may be overcame by transferring the excess capital abroad: "It is therefore, useful that in a country where capitalization is more rapid than elsewhere, a part of the annual savings should be transported to the new lands where they return more intense services" (cited in Murphy 1948, p. 123).

Traditionally, liberal classical economics consider that capital is always scarce in capitalist economies. Classical economists were usually convinced that the shortage of capital slows economic development and by Say's Law any capital supply creates its own demand, which is why it cannot be too abundant. Edward Gibbon Wakefield (1834, p. 12 f.) was one of the first who openly argued that Britain faces the problem of capital oversupply: "Abundance of capital invested, and ready to be invested, is the most marked, nay the peculiar, characteristic of England." Sending the capital abroad was the obvious solution to Wakefield. Also, John Stuart Mill ([1848] 1965a, p. 733 ff.) argued that Britain's capital accumulation is too fast and pushes the profit rate toward its ultimate lows and the economy toward a stationary state. Sending the excess capital to colonies is one of Mill's preferred options to deal with the oversupply, because it counters the downward trend of the profit rate without wasting the capital, as it may be used to increase agricultural production.

Liberal economists' new favor of imperialism was part of a more general trend in the liberal position. Old liberals, like Adam Smith, Jeremy Bentham and James Mill, the French Diderot and Voltaire were overall anti-imperialistic. On economic, political and moral grounds, old liberals refused imperialism. Economically, old liberals consider that colonialism harms trade when compared with a free trade regime because it monopolizes it. In addition, colonialism tightens the scarcity of domestic means of production by exporting capital and labor. Politically, old liberals saw no advantage in imperialism because it increases military costs and the frequency of conflicts without enhancing political power. Morally, old liberals rejected imperialism because of the submission of people and the increasing frequency of wars (Sullivan 1983).

The position of the new liberals on imperialism in the second half of the 19th century was quite different: as maintained, classical economists of the second half of the 19th century considered imperialism an economic necessity; to foster trade and overcome the abundance of capital. To legitimize the new position on imperialism, new liberals had to refute old liberals' moral arguments against imperialism. The position of the old liberals seemed to be a logical consequence of liberal universalism:

> liberal theoretical claims typically tend to be transhistorical, transcultural, and most certain transracial. [...] The political rights that it articulates and defends, the institutions such as laws, representation, contract all have their justification in a characterization of human beings that eschews names, social status, ethnic background; gender, and race (Mehta 1999, p. 51).

The unequal treatment of colonized people, which contradicted liberal universalism, was legitimized by downgrading colonized people to underdeveloped barbarians. Locke ([1689] 1824, p. 372) states that "Lunatics", "Idiots" and "Children" are "never capable of being a free man, he is never let loose to the disposure of his own will." In his considerations on representative government, John Stuart Mill discussed the colonies' demand for freedom and political participation: principally refusing the colonies' demand for representation in the British Parliament, Mill distinguishes between developed and underdeveloped colonies. He proposed ([1861] 1977, p. 564 ff.) to give developed colonies, like Canada, Australia and New Zealand, so those with a big white population, a wider autonomy including a domestic parliament with great authority. However, Mill suggests to maintain the empire as an assemblage of equals, for its economic and political advantages. Underdeveloped "barbarous or semibarbarous" (ibid., p. 567) peoples of the colonies in Africa and Asia, lack, according to Mill, the mental development to be freemen. Only an autocratic foreign developed power like Britain may help those areas to reach a stage of development which makes them ready for liberalism. Those areas

> which have not attained that [developed] state, and which, if held at all, must be governed by the dominant country, or by persons delegated for that purpose by it. This mode of government is as legitimate as any other, if it is the one which in the existing state of civilization of the subject people, most facilitates their transition to a higher stage of improvement (ibid.).

Hence Mill, like most other new liberals, divides countries into developed ones ready for liberalism and underdeveloped ones still in their childhood and therefore not ready for liberalism. "The sacred duties which civilized nations owe to the independence and nationality of each other, are not binding towards those to whom nationality and independence are either a certain evil, or at best a questionable good" (Mill [1859] 1984, p. 119). According to many new liberals, being colonized is a blessing rather than an oppression because it fosters the development of underdeveloped areas. Like their British counterparts, for many French (liberal) intellectuals and politicians, civilizing 'the savages' was a moral obligation. Overall, French old liberals like Diderot and Voltaire were quite skeptical of imperialism. Liberals' position changed with and after the French Revolution. Proud of their revolution French republicans started to believe in the superiority of the French race and France's mission to civilize 'the savages' (Daughton 2006, p. 10 f.): "Spreading republican ideals, culture, know-how, and technology was inseparable from colonialism itself; putting 'uncivilized' regions of the world on the road to progress was, according to colonialists, France's chief goal" (ibid., p. 11). In the 19th century many influential French liberals became strong advocates of imperialism (Pitts 2005, pp. 163–259). In particular Tocqueville's arguments for imperialism received much attention (Richter 1963; Pitts 2000, 2005; Welch 2003; Duan 2010). Like other liberals, Tocqueville associated imperialism with the enlightenment of 'the savages'. However, he did not shy away from legitimizing extreme violence against the native population and imperialism without development if it enhances the power of France itself (Pitts 2000). Practical politicians like the republican Prime Minister Jules Ferry were convinced that France fulfills its republican mission by civilizing 'the savages' (Aldrich 1996, p. 98). The influential Jean Dupuis wrote that "it seemed beautiful to me to admit to the advantages of civilization half-barbarous [...] to walk in the light of modern ideas" (Murphy 1948, p. 68).

The 19th century was also the time of social Darwinism: on an individual, but also collective, national level. Only nations able to extend their borders to overseas territories and their influence in Europe were considered a first-class world power nations (Baumgart 1975, p. 48 ff.). Only first-class world power nations were considered to legitimately aspire to establishing world hegemony, the ultimate goal of the big European empires. With the industrialization of Britain and the defeat of Napoleon, Europe's balance of power fell out of joint. Britain's rampant imperialism of the 19th century put a lot of pressure on France and Germany not to lag behind. The rivalry of the big three and the French, and later German, fear of falling behind spurred on all three empires to steadily extend their influence; in Europe and elsewhere. Germany, starting its imperialist ambitions relatively late, after full unification, was also driven by the fact that the world would soon be divided between the big colonial empires and nothing will be left for Germany. Fearing a British world hegemony and further falling behind the fast extending British empire, France and Germany also started colonial projects. The rivalry between the European empires caused each of them to push colonial extension far beyond any economically, politically or military reasonable means.

In particular in France and Germany imperialism also had social and psychological reasons (ibid.). Falling into a deep collective depression after Napoleon's defeat and the lost war with Germany, French imperialism enhanced its dented self-confidence. It functioned as a compensation for the destruction of the French hegemony on the European continent. Unified Germany's imperialism showed the world and its own people its first-class world power nation ambitions. Still threatened by sectarian tendencies, the newly unified Germany demonstrated with its colonial projects its force, power and viability.

In addition, Baumgart (ibid.) subsumes a wide range of other imperialism explanations under political-historical-theses: from ending slavery, the Christian mission, eldorado prospects, technical change, to fighting overpopulation. Technical change, in particular in transportation, accelerated imperialism. In particular, in the second half of the 19th century, railway imperialism accelerated. Connecting extensive territories to the empire by railways was considered politically, economically and military advantageous. Politically, it was expected that connecting foreign territories to the empire would increase their dependency. Economically, railways widened markets: raw materials, machinery, workers and consumption goods became transportable over great distances. Militarily, railways facilitated transporting troops into remote regions of the empire and its allied territories. Hence, railway building became the main form of peaceful 19th century imperialism.

Malthus's (1798) theses in *An Essay on the Principle of Population* that the material improvement of the poor would cause an explosive population growth frightened many intellectual and politicians. Fast population growth was considered politically quite dangerous: it was expected that explosive population growth would increase the likelihood of turmoil and revolutions in countries unable to employ and accommodate the fast rising masses. Sending the surplus population to colonies was often considered the best solution for an impending over population.

5.1.5 Quantity Theory of Money and New Keynesian Money Theories

Hardly anywhere the difference between mercantilism and classical economic theory is more visible and fundamental than in money theory. As previously mentioned, the history of monetary thought is characterized by two opposing lines of thought: Kindleberger (1985) calls one Keynesian and the other monetarist. His wording is somewhat misleading, as Keynesian and monetarist theories emerged in the 20th century, but demonstrates that the two main rival money theories are continuations of a much older debate. Money-mercantilism was in many respects a forerunner of the Keynesian money theory. In contrast, the quantitative theory of money developed by classical economists builds the fundament of later monetarist approaches. Classical monetarist economists' views on interest rates, money, prices, the relation between money, interests rates, employment and prices, central banks and banking in general highly influenced later monetarist approaches. The great 19th century debates on money and banking were quite fertile for both monetarist and Keynesian theories, however, overall, monetarism was on the rise and became dominant at the end of the 19th and early 20th century. Nevertheless, theories which may be considered as rather Keynesian highly influenced the development of the European banking sector.

5.1.5.1 The Quantity Theory of Money

It has been previously mentioned that the Keynesian money theory had its highs when unemployment was seen as a bigger problem than inflation, and that monetarism was more widespread if the opposite was true. In the late 18th and early 19th century, inflation was 'out of control' in many countries. Mercantilists' expansive money policy and the severe inflation caused a lot of economic and political disturbance; for example, a rampant war inflation fostered the French Revolution. Liberal economists blamed first and foremost mercantilist expansive money policy for high inflation and the turmoil: classical money economics assumes a close connection between the price level and the quantity of money. To the question: what happens if a country increases the circulating money?, the answer given by mercantilists and classical economists differed significantly. Usually, mercantilists argue that the abundance of money increases trade and production. Classical economists were convinced that, at least in the long run, an increase in the amount of money first and foremost raises prices. Assuming that printing money increases prices, classical economists blamed the mercantilists' money policy for inflation and suggested that only a 'sounder' money policy could stop prices from rising. Hence, the inflation "shifted the story concerning monetary shortages to one of excessive monetary expansion" (Murphy 1997a, p. 3), and therefore the "debate swung from concern over a shortage of money to fear of excessive monetary expansion" (ibid., p. 2).

The theories of the two most notable early monetarists, David Hume and Jacques Turgot were a frontal attack on money-mercantilism. All fundamental assumptions of money-mercantilism were rejected by the rising quantitative theory of money. Money-mercantilism was built around the fundamental theorem that the scarcity of money harms trade and prosperity: augmenting money fosters trade because people start to buy more and decreases interest as money becomes more abundant. On reasonable grounds, the fundamental theorems' of money-mercantilism were rejected by Hume and Turgot. Does the amount of money make any differences for trade? The answer given by classical economists was a loud *no*. Hume (1752, p. 27) states that

> money is not, properly speaking, one of the subjects of commerce, but only the instrument which men have agreed upon to facilitate the exchange of one commodity for another. [...] If we consider any one kingdom by itself, it is evident that the greater or less plenty of money is of no consequence, since the prices of commodities are always proportioned to the plenty of money.

In the same manner, Turgot argues: if money "circulates freely, [it] is always sufficient to meet the needs of the State, and that it matters little whether there are 100 million marks or one million" (Turgot [1749] 2011, p. 73). According to classical economics, money is nothing else than an instrument of commerce, a means of exchange that overcomes the difficulties and inefficiencies of barter economies. Money is the general accepted symbol of wealth, the general equivalent of all wealth. As a means of exchange, the amount of money in circulation is irrelevant: the same trade activity may be done with one, ten, or a hundred billion money units; according to early monetarists, money is a veil which mercantilists failed to remove. The point seems obvious: if an increased amount of money in circulation faces a constant supply of goods, only prices increase, but no additional commerce must take place. Hence, according to liberal economists, any amount of trade may be carried out with any amount of money: what they really mean by scarcity of money remains unclear throughout the mercantilists' contributions (Heckscher 1935b, pp. 221–231).

> Hume argues that the role played by the quantity of money in the economy, particularly in the process of wealth creation, had been misunderstood by the mercantilists. An increase in money in a society will only change the prices of commodities [...] the level of prices, thought, is of no significance to the wealth of nation (Arnon 2011, p. 13).

Hence, according to the quantitative theory of money, the amount of money in circulation, as a means of exchange, only determines prices, but an increase in money adds no additional wealth nor does it increase trade or production; money is neutral. Usually, classical economists considered that money is neutral in the long run, it was only more recently that neo-classical economists of the 1960s and 1970s tried to prove that under certain circumstances money neutrality holds also in the short run.

However, the mercantilist view that the amount of money is important for the development of economies was rejected. Many mercantilist contributors had already discussed the relation between the abundancy of money and prices (Heckscher 1935b, pp. 224–231), but had not achieved the classical conclusion that money is neutral. That the amount of money makes no difference in the trade of a given amount of goods between a given amount of people seems obvious, but the mercantilist argument is more complex: the price of money in the form of capital is the interest rate. Using supply and demand theory, mercantilists argued if the supply of money increases, the price for it, the interest rate, must fall: it is the reduced price for capital which fosters investments and therefore production and employment. That the abundance of money reduces interest rates and augments investment seems right at first glance, but it builds on the weakness of mercantilists failing to clearly distinguish between money and capital. If the additional money is used to buy goods or is hoarded in cellars, if it does not became capital—if it is not invested—why should interest rates fall? Turgot ([1766] 2011, p. 49) stated that interest rates, "the price of money is regulated like that of all other commodities, by the balance of offer and demand: thus, when there are many borrowers who need money, the interest of money becomes higher; when there are many owners who are ready to lend, it falls." According to Turgot, the interest rate is not determined by the abundance of money, but by the demand and supply of loanable funds; of capital. Hence, the rate of interest depends on the relation of savings and desired investments: if people save a little money, but would like to invest big capital, the supply of capital is low and the demand high, and therefore interest rates are high. On the other side, if much is saved and little invested, interest rates are low. Using the quantitative theory of money, Turgot analyzes the effect a doubling of the available money would have on interest rates. He states that if a country with one million ounces of silver gets another million which it distributes among people like the first ounce, prices of commodities would rise. If, for example, prices double, consumers need two times the money to consume the same amount of commodities. Assuming that people do not change their saving desires nominal savings double, but because prices for investment goods also double, at the end the relation between the supply and demand for capital, and the real interest rate, remains the same. Turgot (ibid., p. 51) concludes that

> it does not by any means follow from this [the doubling of the available money] that the interest of money falls, if all this money is carried to the market and employed in the current expenses of those who possess it, as by supposition the first million ounces were; for the interest of money falls only when there is more money to be lent, in proportion to the wants of the borrowers, than there was before.

Like Turgot, Hume (1752, p. 64) states that interest rates depend on the supply and demand for capital and on profits "High interest arises from 'three' circumstances: a great demand for borrowing; little riches to supply that demand; and great profits arising from commerce," but not on the amount of money in circulation.

Hence, early classical economists money theory attacked money-mercantilism on two central issues: first, the relation between the abundance of money, growth, and prices. Second, they rejected mercantilists' interest rate theory. Those two issues, the relation between the abundance of money, growth, and prices, and the determination of interest rate are the central topics of most monetarist theories since the 19th century. Having crashed money-mercantilism, it became the main aim of the 19th century monetarists to develop an alternative interest and price theory.

5.1.5.2 The Classical Theory of Interest

The classical interest theory builds on four fundamental theorems of classical economics: first of all, industrialization, economic development and growth, and therefore capitalist economic progress, is a good thing. Second, credit—in the sense of lending and borrowing money—is a fundamental necessity for capitalist economic progress. Third, the supply of saving and the demand for investment determines interest rates. Fourth, capital is always scarse in capitalist societies and its scarcity restricts economic growth.

In the late 18th and early 19th century, the social issue of industrialization received more attention as socialist, social movements, and several religious groups denounced the rising social injustice. Still, for the political and the economic elites, the merits of industrialization were numerous. A few were as convinced by the Industrial Revolution and capitalism as classical economists. Not entirely oblivious to the negative sides of capitalist economies, classical economists strongly believed that at the end of capitalism there will be good for all social classes and groups.

Credit was a central issue of classical economics, as the most promising capitalist projects usually faced to the problem of financing. Turgot ([1769] 2011, p. 209) expressed a widely spread view among classical economists when he spoke of the "absolute necessity of lending for the prosperity and the maintenance of commerce." Why is credit so pivotal for capitalist economies: Mill ([1848] 1965b, p. 63) in his *Principles of Political Economy* developed two main doctrines of the classical capital and Production theory: first, the "industry is limited by capital". Assuming that capital is scarse in principle, every enterprise's, project's, factory's extension is limited by the scarcity of capital. Capitalism receives much of its own legitimization from the promise of fast economic progress. Fast growth is only possible if those with the most desirable projects have credit. According to the classical view, lending ensures that the ones with the best ideas, the brightest minds, the best entrepreneurs, the most promising projects receive the scarse idle money reserves of the country: money lending assures that capital is used in the most efficient way, in projects which foster prosperity the most, so that economies grow as fast as possible. Lending was also desirable from an ideological point of view: absolutism's cronyism and the system of inherited privileges were a red flag for the rising liberal economists. Credit was seen as the liberal and capitalist instrument to redistributing economic opportunities: due to money borrowing, economic success becomes independent from class and a person's or a family's history. According to the liberal view, the instrument of credit ensures that capital flows into the most promising hands regardless of whether those hands belong to a workingman or an aristocrat. Hence, for classical economists the readiness of loanable funds is a condition for industrialization, economic prosperity, and a dynamic capitalist development.

Mill's (ibid., p. 68) second main doctrine is that "it [capital] is the result of saving;" credit presupposes savings. According to classical economics, only capital which has first been saved can be lend to potential investors. The claim that capital originates from saving has wide reaching consequences for the classical interest theory. The classical economic theory recognizes that high interest rates are harmful for economic progress, since little will be invested, which in turn hinders the expansion of production. Three things decrease interest rates: less risk, less investment, and more saving. Little risk on financial markets is always desirable and many classical authors elaborated a wide range of measurements to reduce risk and market disturbances. Less investment is undesirable because it slows economic progress. In particular necessary for economic development are therefore higher savings, capital building. The firm recognition of the importance of money saving for economic progress was accompanied by a new view on savers and money lenders. Over centuries, earning interest from money lending was considered unjust and immoral or at least a doubtful business. Overall, for scholastic contributors, lending for interest was sinful, mercantilists recognized the necessity of money lending, but had an ambivalent and often hostile relation to the lazy class of money lenders. For classical economists, the saver who lends his money waives present consume for future consumption: the saver resists present consume seduction in order to be prepared for future hardships.

Classical economics oppose the negative picture of the scholastic usurer who lends money to exploit the poor borrower, by painting one of the saver and money lender who takes care of his own and his family's future. Turgot and Hume introduce their own interest theory by a discussion of the scholastic position on the sinfulness of money lending: they develop their interests theory in sharp contrast to the scholastic position. Turgot ([1769] 2011, p. 215) argues that a person who saves money in order to lend it to someone else must be compensated for delate consume and for forgoing liquidity. His parable that "a bird in the hand is better than two in the bush" should demonstrate that people usually have what we nowadays call a positive time preference: people naturally prefer present consume over future consumption. In addition, Turgot (2011, p. xxii) follows the later scholastic by recognizing *Lucrum Cessans* when he states that a lender misses the "profit or the revenue he would have been able to procure by it [the capital]" Recognizing the classical economist position that people have a positive time preference and miss profit opportunities by lending money, it seems quite reasonable and fair that lenders get back more than they have lent: following the classical view, if a lender gets back the same piece of metal in the future, as proposed by the scholastics, the person loses wealth by lending money.

> Now if a sum actually owned is worth more, is more useful, is preferable to the assurance of receiving a similar sum in one or several years' time, it is not true that the lender receives as much as he gives when he does not stipulate interest, for he gives the money and receives only an assurance (Turgot [1769] 2011, p. 215).

The classical and neo-classical approach, implicitly, states that the scholastic contributors misunderstand the difference between wealth and money. Scholastics argue that it is fair if one gets back the same piece of metal which was lent out. Classical economists counter by asking why one should be glad to get back the same piece of metal if it makes the person less happy than it would have made him at the time of lending? According to classical economics, interest payments equalize present and future wealth, happiness, utility. Hence, the lender gets back the same that he or she lent; not the same piece of metal, but the same wealth, happiness, and utility.

The classical interest rate theory is much more complex then often considered, if interdependency of risk, wage rate, rent rate, profit rate etc. are all taken into consideration. Here the very basics of classical interest rate theory are enough to understand the general idea. Interest rates are determined, according to the classical theory, by demand for and supply of savings: or, more technically, the rate of interest is given by the intersection of the investment demand schedule and the saving schedule. Not the abundancy of money, but people's will to save money for future consumption, compared with the demand for loanable funds, gives the interest rates. Classical interest theory was a clear rejection of the money-mercantilist interest theory: the classical interest theory insists that printing money, as advocated by money-mercantilists, has no effect, at least in the long run, on real interest rates. Augmenting paper money raises prices and nominal interest rates, but has no effect on real values. What lowers interest rates is an increase in saving and a reduction of transaction costs. Increasing savings seems to be hardly achievable by a certain economic policy.

Still, at the time of early classical economics most European countries had, in one form or another, interest rate restricting laws. Given the classical economists' reluctance towards state intervention and their belief that interest rates are determined by a self-adjusting mechanism, it seems reasonable that classical economists collectively reject usury laws: surprisingly, this was not exactly the case. Among the early liberal economists, we find opponents and advocates of usury laws. Already in 1691, John Locke ([1691] 1824) criticized the restriction of interest rates in his article "Some Considerations of the Consequences of the Lowering of Interest and the Raising the Value of money." Assuming that interest rates can ultimately not be reduced by law, Locke states that usury laws may have various negatives effects. Principally complicating lending, usury laws decrease the amount of money in circulation as more will be hoarded and flow abroad. Although his arguments remain unclear and inconsistent, Locke believes that usury laws improve the position of bankers and other money lenders as they will find ways to circumvent the law, while it will harm the people who are worst off. With one foot in mercantilism and with the other in classical economy, Locke's arguments are somehow ill-founded, as he fails to distinguish between money and capital. Building on many arguments of Locke, Turgot was the first who developed a comprehensive liberal opposition on usury laws by anticipating the main monetarist arguments against interest rates restrictions. Turgot ([1769] 2011, p. 207) believed that a very rigid enforcement of interest prohibition would "mean the destruction of all commerce," but because laws were not rigidly enforced, money was lend and borrowed on black markets at market rates. The legal restriction caused the natural law of demand and supply to work behind closed doors on the black market: "this will always happen when the law prohibits what the nature of things requires" (ibid., p. 208). Throughout liberal economic writing we find the argument that state interventions do not change the natural laws of economy, but cause them to work behind closed doors or find other ways. Even more important for the liberal position on usury law was Turgot's fundamental attack of the scholastic's position on moral grounds. The two main arguments were developed by Turgot on why interest payments are not sinful: first, lenders lend their property; free citizens should not be restricted in their use of their property. "The legitimacy of lending at interest arises from the inviolable right of private property. The owner of an object can do with it what he likes: he can sell it or let it" (ibid., p. 211). Secondly, lending money is a contract between two free citizens; because the contract represents their free will, it must be in both of their interests. Lending money, Turgot (ibid., p. 207) argued

> is a reciprocal contract, free between the two parties, which they make only because it is advantageous to them. [...] Now on what principle can a crime be discovered in a contract advantageous to two parties, with which both parties are satisfied, and which certainly does no injury to anyone else?

Equalizing loans with all other market transaction, he concludes that condemning a lender for exploiting the borrower "is as absurd an argument as saying that a baker who demands money for the bread he sells, takes advantage of the buyer's need for bread" (ibid.).

Ironically the 'Holy Master' of liberalism Adam Smith was an advocate of usury laws. Not only on the issue of usury laws, Adam Smith's money theory often opposed the canonic classical view. His dissenting opinion caused Kindleberger (1984) to ask "Was Adam Smith a monetarist or a Keynesian?": he gives no clear answer to this question. Liberal economists are quite astonished that Smith did not follow the quantity theory of money, but developed such "nonsense," as Rothbard (1995a, p. 462) calls his Real Bill Doctrine. According to Viner (1975, p. 87), it is "one of the mysteries of the history of economic thought" why Smith did not follow Hume closer. However, Smith and other economists of the time supported usury laws. But, unlike scholastic contributors' overall reluctant toward money lending, Smith recognized the pivotal importance of money lending for economic prosperity. Smith argued that usury laws ensure that entrepreneurs have credit.

Smith feared that without any restrictions on interest rates, money will be lent almost entirely to speculators and little will remain for productive investments. Smith divides borrowers into two groups: ordinary capitalist who borrow to invest in real economy production and speculators who borrow to invest in highly risky ventures. Because the second group is willing to pay much higher interest, much more money will end up in their hands. But according to Smith, if the government sets an interest rate celling slightly above the market rate for low-risk investors, few would be willing to lend to high-risk speculators as they get just a little higher interest for much more risk (c.f. Jadlow 1977). Classical economists recognized that Smith's usury law position was hardly consistent with their interest theory: according to the classical interest theory interest rates are determined by the natural law of demand and supply, which is why they do not change through state interventions in the long run.

Ten years after Smith argued for interest rate restrictions in his *Wealth of Nations* (1776), Jeremy Bentham responded with *Defence of Usury* (1787), where he developed the main liberal arguments against interest restrictions. Bentham's view extended by several arguments became the canonical anti-usury law view of classical economists. According to Hollander (1999), Bentham rejected Smith's arguments on five grounds: first, Smith puts innovators among speculators. Innovations are usually risky, but very profitable if successful. Restricting interest rates too slightly above low risk rates bounds investments to existing techniques, and therefore riskier innovative approaches would be excluded from credit markets. Second, usury restrictions do not separate good from bad projects, but good and bad projects would be restricted. Third, in the usual liberal way, Bentham argued that state-restricted solutions are always worse than individualistic free-market solutions. Fourth, a dynamic development of capitalism needs to allow failures. Fifth, no law can really reduce the market rate of interest, but it can produce evasion and black markets. Bentham (1787) lined out that prodigals (speculators) would hardly be prevented by usury: as long as prodigals have securities to offer, loans will be granted even if laws restrict interest rates. Bentham's strongest argument against usury laws is that innovations are always risky, but innovations are the fundament of an economy's dynamic development: restricting interest rates complicates financing innovations and harms the economic progress.

For Schumpeter ([1911] 1934) credit is a core institution for innovations, as innovative projects need financing. As maintained, for liberals money lending is crucial for capitalism, as it ensures that those with the best ideas, the most innovative people, are not lacking the financial means to implement the projects. Forbidding risky speculation is usually popular, but where to put the line between speculation and desired investment? In addition, Bentham argues that usury laws are disadvantageous to borrowers, in particular those borrowers who have to borrow above the legal interest rate maximum, due to illegality premiums on the black market.

Scholastic contributors, like more recent supporters of interest rate restriction, consider that interest rate restrictions protect the very poor from exploitation through horrendous interest rates and excessive ineptness. Liberal economists turn the argument upside down by stating that interest rate restrictions are particularly disadvantageous to the poor because they get excluded from legal credit markets: John Stuart Mill was the author of the Golden Age of English classical economics, which relatively extensively discussed the case of usury laws. In his monumental contribution, *Principles of Political Economy* ([1848] 1965a, pp. 922–926), he follows Bentham's criticism of usury laws when Mill (ibid., p. 924) stated that

> though the [usury] law intends favour to the borrower, it is to him above all that injustice is, in this case, done by it. [...] What can be more unjust than that a person who cannot give perfectly good security should be prevented from borrowing of persons who are willing to lend money, to him, by their not being permitted to receive the rate of interest which would be a just equivalent for their risk?

Hence, both usury law advocates and opponents argued that their view would help improve the situation of the very poor.

> Advocates of usury laws typically claim they protect poor and naive borrowers. Critics argue that the presumption is that borrowers know what they are doing when they take high-interest loans, so by curtailing such lending, a usury law harms those most in need of funds (Coco and Meza 2009, p. 1701).

As maintained, Turgot argued that credit contracts are agreements between two free citizens, which is why they are always to the best interest of both. Bentham (1787, p. 10) took the same line; as well as Ricardo ([1823] 2005b) who stated "that money ought to be placed on the same footing as any other commodity. The lender and borrower ought to be allowed to bargain together, as freely as the buyer and seller did when goods were to be disposed of." Mill develops a further issue against usury laws which is closely connected to the classical capital theory and which became the most fundamental argument against interest restriction for classical and neo-classical contributors. As outlined, classical capital theories' first fundamental theorem is that capital is scarce. Interest payments provide that idle money reserves be activated for production and trade. Mill ([1848] 1965a, p. 922) fears that interest rate restrictions may cause savers to dismiss lending reserves: "Where law or conscientious scruples prevent leading at interest, the capital which belongs to persona not in business is lost to productive purposes." He argues that if natural laws of demand and supply create a market clearing interest rate of e.g. 6%, to restrict the interest rate to 4% causes that demand for credit increases while supply shrinks. The same savers who supply their reserves at 6% also lend at 4%, but others rather hoard money or switch to black markets, where interest rates are higher than 6%. Hence, according to Mill, usury laws decrease loanable funds and force poor people to pay higher interest. In addition, Mill states that borrowers may be exploited by lenders only if the latter have the market power that the former lack. But under perfect competition neither of the two sides has any market power, hence there is no reason to believe that with perfect competition any borrower gets exploited.

For centuries, economists had ambivalent attitudes to lending against interest payments. For scholastic contributors, all interest payments are sinful. Money-mercantilists recognized the necessity of interest, but were hostile toward the 'lazy money lenders' who live on interest payments. Classical economists' view was the clear contraposition to the scholastic position: industrialization, economic growth, innovation; the nature of capitalism needs people with idle money reserves lending to brilliant minds with innovative ideas and entrepreneurial abilities. According to the classical interest theory, interest payments are the compensation for saving rather than immediate consumption, for lending rather than hoarding and for the risk to never see the money again. For classical economists, lending for interest payments is not different from any other business; if money lending is sinful, selling bread, food, or wood is equally unjust. Adam Smith (1776, p. 434) expressed the general view of classical economics by stating: "as something can everywhere be made by the use of money, something ought everywhere to be paid for the use of it." For classical economics, lending for interest payments is not sinful or immoral, quite the contrary: credit is one of the most fundamental institutions of capitalism, interest payments are the just compensation for keeping the wheels of capitalism running. "The initiators of the modern credit system take as their point of departure not an anathema against interest-bearing capital in general, but on the contrary, its explicit recognition" (Marx 1984, p. 601).

5.1.5.3 Monetarists vs. Keynesians: The Bullion Controversy

In the late 18th century, the British banking system changed significantly. Increasing credit from country banks caused two financial crises, in 1783 and 1793 (Hawtrey 1919, p. 255). However, not the banking crisis, but the declaration of war against France and its financial consequences caused a long-lasting money theory discussion in Britain, which significantly changed the canonical money theory and the European banking system. The fast increasing war-financing burden caused the government to sharply raise state credit bills exchangeable into Bank of England notes. Political changes in France and Britain caused a massive gold outflow from Britain and a drop of Bank of England's bullion reserves from almost 7,000 lb to slightly more than 1,000 lb (Arnon 2011, p. 65 f.). When the French army landing in Britain caused a bank run, the British government saw no other alternative for taking pressure from Bank of England's bullion reserves than prohibiting the convertibility of Bank of England's notes into species in 1797: the Bank Restriction Act. The suspension of convertibility was not a new measure; in times of great distress in particular France frequently abolished convertibility. However, in 1799 a year-long inflationary phase begun: exchange rates fell, gold was traded with a 9% premium in London (Hawtrey 1919, p. 266), Bank of England's bullion reserves dropped (Arnon 2011, p. 70), bank notes in circulation and prices rose sharply (Silberling 1923; Arnon 2011, p. 68 ff.).

From a pure historical perspective, the suspension of convertibility, which lasted no more than two decades and was accompanied by medium-size financial disturbances, is not much more than a small note in the long British financial history. What made the time so important for the history of economic thought was the induced bullion controversy. The bullion controversy yielded the most fundamental ideas and theorems of both the monetarist and Keynesian money theory. Three central questions dominated the controversy: first, was there high inflation from 1799 to 1802 and 1809 to 1813 and if yes, what caused it? Second, has inconvertibility caused an over-issuing of notes and is the abundance of money the reason for rising prices? Third, if paper money was over-issued who should be blamed for it: the Bank of England, country banks, or both?

On all three core questions bullionists and anti-bullionists developed opposing answers; bullionists further developed the monetarist position. In contrast, anti-bullionists, in the tradition of Keynesian money theory, outlined many weaknesses of the quantity theory of money. After 10 years of recurrent high inflation, the most famous economists supported the bullionist position. Horner, Thornton, and Huskisson presented the so-called Bullion Report to the English Parliament in 1810. Treated as the main bullionist manifesto, the Bullion Report outlines the main bullionist positions and claims to return to convertibility within two years. Although the Bullion Report failed to find a majority in parliament, in the mid-1810s it was widely recognized that the reintroduction of convertibility was near. Two main reasons shifted opinions inside and outside the parliament toward the bullionist position: first, the war with France, the main argument to suspend convertibility ended and second, Ricardo—the extreme bullionist—became more and more the economic authority of Britian. From the mid-1810s onwards, the resumption of the gold standard was prepared. In 1819, the time had come for Ricardo and the bullionists, when the government resumed the exchangeability of notes into gold bullion. The parliament followed Ricardo's Ingot plan, which suggested notes being convertible into gold bullion, but not into coins; Ricardo hoped that this would keep people from really converting paper money into gold, while preventing the over-issuing of paper money.

Around the same time, a 30 years long period of deflation started. Ricardo estimated that the resumption would cause a slight deflation; the true deflation in the years after the resumption was far above Ricardo's estimations (Viner 1975, pp. 171–185). Already in 1821, the government decided to move away from Ricardo's Ingot plan when it allowed the Bank of England to give out coins.

Serious deflation and the economic slowdown caused much criticism of Ricardo and an intensive discussion about the relation between prices and economic prosperity. Apart from the debates on the effects of inflation and deflation on the economy, a much more fundamental question was raised: what are and should be the ultimate goals of monetary policy. Again, in the discussion two main opponent theoretical lines emerged: the Currency School and the Banking School. Critical of many bullionist positions, the Currency School theories were notable developments of the monetarist position. Banking School theories are still present in many recent money theories; in particular in the Keynesians ones. Quite different in many respects, the Banking School was the continuation of earlier Keynesian theories. Since then, no entirely new ideas emerged either on the monetarist or the Keynesian side.

5.1.5.4 What Determines Prices

What caused British prices to rise was the main question of the first round in the bullion controversy. Bullionists' criticisms of inconvertibility was in principle a repetition of Hume's quantity theory: the suspension of convertibility removed the limits to paper money issuing, which caused banks to excessively give out new notes. In particular the Bank of England was blamed for using inconvertibility to sharply increase their outstanding notes.

It was widely agreed that the price of bullion is governed by the exchange rate; regardless of convertibility or inconvertibility. Assuming that exchange rates are predominantly determined by the amount of bank notes, bullionists argued that the rise in paper money depreciated the pound, which caused the rise in gold prices. Countering the bullionist argument, anti-bullionists stated that under inconvertibility the exchange rates are not governed by the same mechanism as under convertibility: under convertibility the price for bullion may not fall under a certain limit, while under inconvertibility this limit does not exist. According to them, the war and bad harvests lowered the exchange rate and raised gold price rather than any over-issuing of notes. Critics of bullionists divided them into two groups: moderate bullionists acknowledged that money transfers influence the price of bullion, but insisted that the over-issuing of paper money was the predominant reason for high bullion prices, and extreme bullionists—Ricardo and Wheatley—who denied that money transfers have any effect on the price for bullion (c.f. ibid., p. 138 f.).

The anti-bullionists' main argument is that bullionists theory is ill-founded because the causality runs from prices to notes and not, like bullionists believed, from notes to prices. Using Smith's Real Bill Doctrine, anti-bullionists argued that no over-issuing occurred, because the Bank of England just issues paper money against sound bills. Anti-bullionist hardly took into consideration the fact that Smith's Real Bills Doctrine necessitates convertibility and the competition between note-issuing banks. However, anti-bullionist stated that it was not note issuing that caused high prices, but bad harvests, which increased the amount of money needed for commerce and the financial support of their alliance in the war against France. Hence, according to anti-bullionists, the rising amount of money was the consequence and not the cause of high prices. Although paper money over-issuing was the central issue of the bullion controversy, both sides had few convincing arguments about the right amount of paper money. For bullionists, the amount that circulated under convertibility is the right amount; however, they had little to offer as to why this is the case. Building on the shoulders of Smith, anti-bullionists argued that the right amount is given by the demand of commerce for money.

Henry Thornton, the cleverest money theorist of the time, developed a fundamental critic of Smith's Real Bills Doctrine and the bullionist position. In his *Enquiry into the Nature and Effects of the Paper Credit of Great Britain* (1802), Thornton criticized Smith's money and banking theory on many grounds. Smith (1776, p. 300) stated that:

> The whole paper money of every kind which can easily circulate in any country never can exceed the value of the gold and silver, of which it supplies the place, or which (the commerce being supposed the same) would circulate there, if there was no paper money.

Thornton (1802, p. 95) asked what Smith really means by: "The whole paper money of every kind?" Against Smith's Real Bills Doctrine, Thornton argued that there is a wide range of possible fictitious bills. Malthus (1811, p. 457) states that merchants' favor of liquidity—for buying abroad or speculation—was misinterpreted by the Bank of England as a sign for paper money scarcity. Anticipating a heavily discussed issue of the later Currency- Banking School debate, Thornton (1802, p. 44 f) accuses Smith of lacking a clear definition and idea about what money actually is:

> Does Dr. Smith mean to include, in his idea of 'the whole paper money of every kind which can easily circulate,' all the bills of exchange of a country, or does he not? And does he also include interest notes, exchequer bills, and India bonds, and those other articles which very much resemble bills of exchange?

In addition, Smith ignores the velocity of money: assuming that paper money circulates faster than coins, Thornton asks, would that not mean that less paper money than coins is needed to carry out the same commerce? Criticizing Smith for his unclear money definition, Hume and the bullionists had an even more reduced money conception. Strongly focused on regulating paper money, bullionists turned a blind eye on other forms of money. Both bullionists and anti-bullionists ignored that in principle a wide range of commodities and financial assets may function as money. Strongly regulating one form of money, for example paper money as suggested by bullionist, may cause people do use alternative forms of money; "if bills and bank notes were extinguished, other substitutes than gold would unquestionably be found" (ibid., p. 54). Hence, the real amount of all money depends on what functions as money and how fast different moneys circulate. Focusing strongly on paper money ignores the fact that much more is used as money or may have been used in principle if situations were different.

Hence, bullionists further developed the main argument of the quantity theory of money or monetarists: an increase in the stock of money raises prices. Because banks are notoriously prone to over-issuing, the amount of money should be bounded to a good—gold—which is given by God and therefore not enlargeable by humans' hand. Opposing the bullionist position, anti-bullionists used the usual Keynesian argument that the causality runs from prices to money; the amount of money is high because prices are high and not the other way around. They argued that, because banks follow Smith's Real Bill Doctrine, no paper money over-issuing occurred; something else like bad harvests and war increase prices. According to Thornton, both theories are too reduced and ill-founded: he argues that money has many more forms, like different forms of credit, than coins or notes. Controlling coins or notes does not imply controlling the stock of money. Using monetarist and Keynesian arguments simultaneously, Thornton developed one of the first inflation cycle theories. Building on quantity theory, he argues that an extension of money raises prices. Now becoming a Keynesian, Thornton states that because money is an endogenous variable, the demand for money increase as prices raise; this may lead to a self-sustaining inflationary cycle (for more details of his argument see Hetzel 1987).

5.1.5.5 The Non-neutrality of Money and the Goals of Money Policy

As previously maintained, around the year 1820 a 30 year long period of deflation started. The persistent deflation and the accompanying economic slowdown caused an intensive discussion about the relation between prices and growth. Discussions on the connection of inflation, growth and employment were a forerunner of the mid-20th century Philips-curve debate. Most economists of the time—notable classical economists like Malthus, Bentham and Mill, former bullionist like Wheatley, the free spirit Thomas Joplin, Thomas Attwood and his followers from the Birmingham School—agreed on the positive short-run effects of money augmentation. Applying a wide range of different arguments, they reached the same conclusion; money is not neutral, at least in the short-run (Viner 1975, pp. 185–200). Humphrey (1993, pp. 251–270) found nine main arguments for how money effects output and employment. Most notable are those of Sticky Prices, Sticky Wages, Fixed Charges, and Forced Savings: usually it was argued that effects are short-term, but long-term effects were also found. Bad news for Ricardo, most of his colleagues agreed on the (short-run) negative effects of deflation.

Unimpressed, Ricardo remained quite cautious on the effect of the quantity of money on real economy. His reluctance stemmed from the strong favor for long-run analysis, the conviction of metallic currencies, and the strong belief in Say's idea that production always creates its own demand (Viner 1975, pp. 195–197).

Apart from the debates on the effects of inflation and deflation on the economy, a much more fundamental question was raised: what are and should be the ultimate goals of monetary policy? Since Hume, at least implicitly, monetarists favor price stability as the main goal. Following the monetarist tradition, bullionists were convinced that a metallic standard would be the best way to achieve the goal of price stability. Rampant deflation caused a lot of criticism of bullionist money policy and raised the question: is price stability the right goal and, if yes, is the metallic standard the right instrument to achieve it? Most classical economists maintained their favor for metallic standards and proposed how a further fall in prices may be limited. According to them, a more flexible approach may smooth short-term price disturbances without fully falling away from the gold standard. Others maintained the principle goal of price stability, but suggested to replace the metallic standard by a paper money standard; however, they were unable to convince most influential economists (ibid., pp. 203–217). Overall, most prominent classical economists did not abandon price stability as the main goal of monetary policy and the gold standard as its principle instrument.

Opposing the classical money theory, Thomas Attwood and the so-called Birmingham School demanded the change of the main money policy goal and the abandoning of the money standard. Rejecting Ricardo's Manchester School theory of an automatic full employment mechanism, the Birmingham-scholars suggested that under-consumption caused unemployment and political measurements have to be taken in order to achieve full employment (Checkland 1948). The Birmingham School left no doubt that it favored full employment over price stability as the ultimate goal of money policy. Attwood (1819, p. 44) suggest to renew the Bank Restriction Act in the way that "the Bank shall [...] be obligated or otherwise be induced, to encrease the circulation of their notes as far as the national interests may require, that is to say, until all the labourers in the kingdom are againin full employment at ample wages." While "the bullionists were preoccupied with the stability of the exchange" (Checkland 1948, p. 4) Attwood's monetary theory was built on five main fundaments: "(1) full employment as the political goal, (2) primacy of monetary policy, (3) feasibility of monetary fine-tuning, (4) benefits of price inflation, and (5) costs of price deflation" (Humphrey 1993, p. 272). Unlike many other economists, Attwood was convinced that deflation is no temporal phenomenon, but inherent to metallic standards; he argued that the economy tends to grow faster than the available bullion, which causes a deflationary tendency (Checkland 1948, p. 6). Advocating a non-metallic standard, for the Birmingham School the right amount of money is given by the amount needed to satisfy full employment. Strongly focused, maybe over focused, on money, Attwood (1816, p. 48) stated that "nothing can feed the labourers, nothing can serve the country, unless it has the effect of creating, or bringing into action, an additional quantity of the currency, or circulating medium, of the country." The Birmingham School completely rejected classical money theories' theorem of money neutrality. Mill was Attwood's main classical opponent: he strongly questioned the possibility of pegging employment via inflation. Mill believed that negative effects of inflation exceed possible positive effects and suggested to follow clear rules of money policy. He argues that positive effects of an increasing quantity of money are at the best temporary and inflation only has a positive effect on output if people are not expecting inflation (Humphrey 1993, p. 272 ff.). Hence, classical economists responded to the Birmingham School Keynesians with the usual monetarist arguments: positive effects of inflation on employment are at best temporary, exist only if people are surprised by inflation, and in the end the harm of inflation is much bigger than the good.

Since the very beginning of the division between Keynesians and monetarists there is one central question: is the division between Keynesians and monetarists just a normative issue of different opinions on what are the most serious social problems or is there a reason to believe that one side is right from a positive perspective. If there exists, as has often been alleged, a strict trade-off between the two goals of monetary policy, full employment and price stability, and both goals are equally reachable through money policies, the disagreement between the Birmingham School and the Manchester School is purely on normative grounds: the Birmingham School favors the former, the quantity theory or monetarists the latter. However, the Birmingham School and the quantity theory heavily debated whether inflation and employment are variables determinable by money policy, for how long they may be influenced and what are the side effects of a policy targeting one or both variables.

For a short while, the Birmingham School was quite influential, but soon lost its attraction for new economists. However, the dispute between the Birmingham School and the Manchester School was the forerunner of the deep division between Keynesians and monetarists around the question whether there is a natural tendency toward full employment, if money policy may influence real variables and in general about the role of the state and its money policy.

5.1.5.6 The Golden Age of the Quantity Theory

After the Currency School, the Banking School debate ended with the institutional victory of the Currency School marked by the Bank Charter Act of 1844; money theory was less discussed during the second half of the 19th century. Heated debates on money and banking continued throughout the second half of the 19th century, but no fundamental money theory controversies like the bullion-anti-bullion and Banking School-Currency School, occurred. The years between the Bank Charter Act and the 1880s were characterized by the deepening of what Fetter (1978) calls the British monetary orthodoxy. In the early 1870s, the classical monetary theory or monetarism was at its peak (Laidler 1991, p. 7); its theories and advice were general accepted (Fetter 1978, pp. 225–256). The principal ingredients of the classical monetary orthodoxy are well-known; Humphrey (1993, p. 77 f.) sums it up: as prices rise proportionally to the rise of the quantity of money, the causality runs from the quantity of money to prices;

besides transitional periods, money is neutral in the sense that real economic variables are not affected by monetary variables and the nominal stock of money is given exogenously, and is hence independent from the demand for money. Laidler (1991, p. 8 ff.) has a point in saying that much of the classical monetary position stems from its strong focus on the exchange function of money. For many economists—like Menger (1900)—the main utilitarian advantage of a well-functioning money system is that it facilitates exchange. As maintained, early classical authors were convinced that extending money has positive short-run effects, while later contributors increasingly highlighted the negative effects of transitory price fluctuations. Hence, according to classical economists, the best monetary system facilitates exchanges and preserves the price level; it was widely agreed that bullion-based money would best satisfy both goals.

Several crises of the 1850s strengthened the Banking School position. In particular, it was recognized that the Currency School's strong focus on base money seemed to be outdated as banking activities and the importance of credit instruments steadily increased. From that perspective, the widely shared opinion that the British monetary orthodoxy is the continuation of the Currency School and inherited little from the Banking School (Diatkine and Boyer 2008) seems surprising: to me, this view seems too hasty and general. Doubtless that the British monetary orthodoxy was the logical continuation of Hume, the bullionists and the Currency School. However, at the same time the monetary orthodoxy recognized Banking School's main points of criticism and adapted the money theory accordingly. For example, to the central questions of what money is and how interest rates influence prices, the monetary orthodoxy was strongly influenced by Banking School's criticism of Currency Schools' latent bullionism: Banking School's influence is particularly visible in Mill's money theory. According to Diatkine and Boyer (2008) overall, the 1870s were good times for the quantity theory of money, as the general opinion strongly leaned toward the Bank Charter Act and the Gold Standard (Fetter 1978, p. 232) and the classical monetary theory spread through Europe. New developments in the monetary theory and

> the then ruling idea that it was the principal business of monetary economics to explain the behaviour of the general price level, combined to give the quantity theory a more central position in monetary economics [between the 1870s and World War I] than it has enjoyed at any other time, whether before or since (Laidler 1991, p. 1).

The late 19th and early 20th century marked a turning point in economics: with the marginal revolution, the classical school of economic thought was replaced by the neoclassical as the leading economic theory. The quantity theory of money was also reformulated and brought into line with the emerging neoclassics. Three senior economists and a young talent became the leading money economists of the late 19th and early 20th century: Arthur Cecil Pigou, Alfred Marshal, the American Irving Fisher, and the young John Maynard Keynes.

The early neoclassical money theory consists of two main strands: the Cambridge School, which focuses on the demand for money, and Fisher's approach, which focuses on the supply of money. Marshall, maybe the first neoclassical money theorist, agreed with the traditional quantity theory that if everything else remains equal, a rise in the quantity of money rises prices. However, due to the restrictive in *ceteris paribus* assumption, for Marshall the central statement of the traditional quantity theory is of little practical importance. He considers that changes in other things, which are assumed to be equal, are practically of bigger importance for changes in prices and the money system than the increases and decreases of the base money (Laidler 1991, p. 57). According to Humphrey (2004, p. 2), Marshall "gave the quantity theory [...] its distinctive Cambridge cash-balance formulation" by rigorously applying its microeconomic demand and supply framework and accepting the usual fundamental proposals of the quantity theory like exogenous money stock supply, the proportionality of money and prices, the causality from money to prices and the long run neutrality and short run non-neutrality of money. However even if the Cambridge School accepted much of the classical quantity theory it's novelty lies in the strong focus on the influence of money demand on prices: "the most important influences on the price level as far as the Cambridge economists were concerned lay on the demand side of [...] the market for currency" (Laidler 1991, p. 58). Marshall argued that the relation of prices and the quantity of money is given by the following equation: $P = \frac{M}{D}$; P being prices, M the quantity of currency (notes and coins) and D the demand for currency. D, the important variable for the Cambridge School, is given by $D = KY$. Y represents the GDP, K is usually called the cash-balance ratio and gives the share of the whole GDP held in cash. Marshall lines out a wide range of possible influences of the cash-balance ratio: for example, the opportunity costs of holding cash, the availability of investment alternatives strongly determined by the development of financial markets, expectations of future profits and prices, confidence in the financial markets etc. The important point is that according to Marshall and the Cambridge School all those factors influencing K, determine people's willingness to hold cash, the demand for currency and therefore prices (c.f. Humphrey 2004). Marshall and the Cambridge School accept the classical quantity theory's main conclusion that *in ceteris paribus* the rise in the supply of money increases prices—$P = \frac{M}{D}$ holding D fix an increase in M, increases P. However, more important, but much more difficult is to identify what influences D. Pigou and Keynes, the other two well-known Cambridge-scholars further developed Marshal's ideas. Pigou developed the influence of opportunity costs and expectations and Keynes the expectations of interest rates and confidence in the demand of money; but the main idea remained the same (Laidler 1991, pp. 53–68).

Fisher's (1911) *The Purchasing Power of Money* is one of the most quoted monetary contributions. It is an ongoing discussion about to what extend the Cambridge School stands in the tradition of the quantity theory of money; Fisher's money theory is the clear logical continuation of the classical quantity theory. While the Cambridge School is mostly focused on the demand for money, Fisher puts the supply of money and its effects on prices in the center of his analysis. Fisher's Equation of Exchange is still present in most neoclassical contributions. It describes a causal relation between the quantity of base money (M), its velocity (V), the quantity of deposits and other credit products (M′), their velocity (V′) on the one side and prices (P) and the total amount of trade (T) on the other side; $MV + M'V' = PT$. The equation of exchange was in particular modelled to answer the main classical monetary question: how does an increase in the quantity of money (M) influence prices? Fisher's answer is equal to the one given by the classical quantity theory: *in ceteris paribus* an increase in the quantity of money increases prices. According to Fisher, the purchasing power of money and hence prices depends on "five definite factors (1) the volume of money in circulation; (2) its velocity of circulation; (3) the volume of bank deposits subject to check; (4) its velocity; and (5) the volume of trade" (ibid., vii). According to Fisher, the volume of money is given exogenously by states policy. Fisher (ibid., p. 79) describes a wide range of variables which may influence the velocity of money: among them, the "habits of the individual" and the "system of payments." The Cambridge School and Fisher follow the Banking School view that base money, deposits, and other banking instruments influence prices. However, like Torrens and most monetarists since then, they assume that deposits are a constant multiple of the base money: if this assumption holds, the central bank's control over base money enables it to control the whole money supply. Unfortunately, this assumption too often seems highly unrealistic.

5.1.5.7 The Discussion on Central Banking

Already David Hume suggested the foundation of a central bank; he proposed the abolition of private banking and the foundation of one big note-issuing public bank. Hume assumes that if the bank is obliged to cover paper money by a 100% reserve in coins and if credit granting is prohibited to the bank, the country would be able to enjoy the advantages of paper money, but must not fear over-issuing. Hume ([1777] 1987, p. 284 f.) stated:

> No bank could be more advantageous, than such a one as locked up all the money it received [for Hume the Bank of Amsterdam is the blueprint for such a bank], and never augmented the circulating coin, as is usual, by returning part of its treasure into commerce. A public bank, by this expedient, might cut off much of the dealings of private bankers and money-jobbers.

Fearing paper money over-issuing, the Old Bard of liberalism David Hume demands the harsh restriction of private banking and the foundation of a huge public bank (central bank). In line with later monetarist approaches and against money-mercantilist national bank proposals, Hume suggests the foundation of a public bank in order to restrict paper money rather than augment it.

In the same vein, bullionists demand the restriction of note issuing. For bullionists, excessive paper money-issuing caused two periods of high inflation. Following the monetarist tradition, bullionists argued that high prices are always, and at least according to the extremist bullionists, solely a monetary problem. Country banks alongside the Bank of England issued notes, but bullionists blamed the Bank of England exclusively for over-issuing and rising prices. Bullionists argued that country banks issue notes, but are unable to augment the amount of notes. Assuming that country banks always hold a fixed percentage of their own liabilities as reserves at the Bank of England, bullionists absolved country banks from over-issuing. Thornton (1802, pp. 215–222) argues that over-issuing—country banks would automatically balance by rising regional and therefore falling money value. According to Thornton, because buying back outflowed notes is costly for country banks, they have a strong interest in avoiding over-issuing. King (1804, p. 103) argues in the same way that converting notes may be quite costly for country banks. Ricardo ([1810] 2005, pp. 86–88) stated that country banks will issue notes proportionally to Bank of England, because over-issuing by the country bank would be self-clearing, as Thornton described. Hence, for bullionists, at least indirectly, the Bank of England determines the amount of paper money in England. Boyd (1801, p. 20 f.) stresses that the fact that "the operations of country banks tend to facilitate speculation and enterprize, and to augment the general circulation of the whole country, is unquestionably true," but it was the rise of Bank of England notes which enabled them to augment their own issuing (ibid., p. 23). All bullionists, except Wheatley, agreed that high prices were Bank of England's fault (Viner 1975, p. 154). Most anti-bullionist contributors did not take part in the discussion about who is to be blamed for excessive paper money issuing, because they denied that there was over-issuing in the first place: however, several anti-bullionists argued that if paper money was issued in excess at all, it was predominately the failure of country banks (ibid., p. 156). For bullionists, the main problem of the English financial markets was the inconvertibility of Bank of England notes, which is why they first and foremost demanded the reintroduction of convertibility. Other measurements like note-issuing monopoly of further restrictions were usually not demanded by bullionists.

5.1.5.7.1 National Bank: Ricardo's Plan

As the reintroduction of convertibility did not stabilize markets, currency-scholars asked what else must be done to stabilize financial markets. Ricardo, the extreme bullionist, shortly after the failure of his Ingot Plan started to work on an alternative concept. Ricardo ([1823] 2005a) anticipated much of the Currency School position in one of his last contributions, named *Plan for the Establishment of a National Bank*. For Ricardo (ibid., p. 276) the amalgamation of the two main banking businesses within the Bank of England, "it issues a paper currency as a substitute for a metallic one; and it advances money in the way of loan, to merchants and others", is the main reason for instability. Ricardo proposed to strictly divide the Bank of England into a note-issuing and a banking department. For most of his life, Ricardo followed Smith in the conviction that under convertibility private banks just have to be compelled to hold the same securities against issued notes (Arnon 1987, p. 274), so that the forces of competition would prevent over-issuing. In his national bank article, Ricardo broke away from Smith's view of regulation by competition: Ricardo ([1823] 2005a, p. 282) proposed a national bank with a note-issuing monopoly independent from government influence, "in the hands of Commissioners, not removable from their official situation but by a vote of one or both

Houses of Parliament." With the proposal Ricardo "was moving toward a consistent integration of views on both the rejection of the application of the invisible hand mechanism to money and credit and the adoption of a basically central banking theory" (Arnon 1987, p. 279). That David Ricardo, the most recognized monetarist authority of the time, proposed to found a national bank with a note-issuing monopoly signalled that a new monetarist time was ahead.

5.1.5.7.2 National Bank: Currency School's Plan and Banking School's Critic

The Currency School was inspired by Ricardo's plan for national banks, but went far beyond. Two main convictions guided the Currency School: first, convertibility is not enough to ensure financial market stability. Second, a further currency reform is needed in order to bring the mixed currency closer to a metallic one (Daugherty 1942, p. 142 f.). The Currency School gave two main reasons, present in various money theories ever since, which is why over-issuing and market disturbances continued under the regime of convertibility: confidence cycles and time lags. Convertibility does not prevent over-issuing: if banks over-issue simultaneously, they are not hindered by a metallic standard because the clearing balances against each other remain constant. McCulloch shows that even one bank may over-issue for a certain time (Viner 1975, p. 240 f.). Periods of general optimism and pessimism cause trade activity cycles and over- and under-issuing. Overstone (1837, p. 44) describes the trade or business cycle as: "a state of quiescence,—next improvement,—growing confidence,—prosperity,—excitement,—overtrading, convulsion,—pressure,—stagnation,—distress,—ending again in quiescence." At times of general optimism and prosperity, bankers are forced by their customers to support the extension of their business by issuing notes: "A Banker cannot contract his accommodation at a period when the whole trading and mercantile world are acting under one common impetus of expansion" (ibid., p. 45). Ultimately, the banker would usually use their "power to issue" to "to give a further stimulus to the existing tendencies of the trading world, and ultimately to aggravate the convulsion to which they must lead" (ibid., p. 46). According to Overstone, a system in which private profit-seeking banks perform all usual banking activities and issue notes is immanently prone to over-issuing at times of economic prosperity: optimism causes customers to demand more paper money credit. Through the excessive issuing, the economy gets further overheated and the unavoidable crash gets deeper. Hence, private banks' over-issuing in times of prosperity and under-issuing during slowdowns, is from the perspective of the Currency School not the fault of misbehaving bankers, but a systemic error.

The other main problem are time lags. It was suggested that a pure metallic currency would react immediately to inflows and outflows of species. Mixed currencies do not react immediately and automatically to bullion flows, but the quantity of money reacts with a delay (Viner 1975, p. 221). Long time lags delay Bank of England's reaction to gold drains which may cause that a bank's policy fails to counteract the reduction of bullion reserves. Or the slow reaction of the exchange rate—Bank of England's target variable—on bank note extension may be wrongly interpreted by the bank as a signal for their sound policy (Humphrey 1993, p. 83 f.).

Most currency-scholars suggested establishing a national bank with a note-issuing monopoly; usually, it was proposed that the Bank of England should function as the national bank. Note issuing should be taken out from private profit-maximizing hands: as maintained, it was argued that private banks over-issue at times of optimism and under-issue at times of pessimism, which causes deep crises and recessions. According to currency-scholars, there is no mechanism which ensures, not even temporarily, that private banks' note issuing is in harmony with the public interest. The Currency School's cycle theory was a clear rejection of Smith's Real Bill Doctrine which assumes that private and public interests are in harmony if private banks just issue notes against sound short-term exchange bills. Unlike Ricardo, the Currency School was convinced that the note-issuing policy should not be determined by a commission, but by clear and bounding rules. If a non-profit orientated national bank holds a note-issuing monopoly and issues in accordance with clear and meaningful rules, the Currency School was convinced that the mixed currency—of paper money and coins—would act like a pure metallic. The Currency School position may be summarized in the following way: (1) the currency should vary precisely like pure metal money; (2) the currency should be convertible; (3) the exchanges are the proper guide in the control of a paper currency; (4) the rate of interest is a significant factor in determining the volume of bank issue; and (5) the Real Bills Doctrine is completely invalid (Mints 1945, p. 75).

The so-called Banking School was the main opponent of the Currency School: a group of bankers and economists loosely kept together by their opposition against the Currency School. The Banking School's main point was that the Currency School ignores that much more than just coins and paper money functions as money and influences prices. If a wide range of contracts, promises, and goods function as money only at least may function as it, why should financial markets become much more stable if just one form of money coins and paper money is regulated? According to the Banking School, in order to achieve the goals of the Currency School, all kinds of money and possible money—deposits, bills of exchange, the wide range of credit instruments and what else may function as money—would have to be regulated heavily. However, the Banking School did not demand the heavy regulation of all moneys and near-moneys, but suggested that competition between small private note-issuing banks would best solve the problem of paper money.

The Currency School proposal which suggests to gives the Bank of England a note-issuing monopoly and to divide the bank into a note-issuing and a banking department was heavily criticized by the Banking School: they argued that even if the note-issuing department has a note-issuing monopoly, other private banks and the banking department of the Bank of England still determine prices by other forms of money. Most Currency School contributors recognized the existence of near-moneys (other forms of money), but assumed that all other forms of money are unimportant for prices or a constant multiplying of the base money (notes and coins). The Banking School rejects both assumptions: according to them, other forms of money are important and are not just a stable multiplier of base money. Thomas Tooke (1844) the outstanding contributor of the Banking School, asks in *An Inquiry into the Currency Principle*: what would happen if the Bank of England withdraws all its notes? His answer is that people would use other forms of money such as "cheques and bills of exchange and settlements" (ibid., p. 21) instead. He argues that all functions of Bank of England notes may also be fulfilled by other forms of money. Unlike most other contributors of the time, Took analyzed the different forms of money by asking what function financial instruments such as notes, coins, deposits, bills of exchange, and any form of credit fulfill in the economy. He distinguished between three fundamental groups of money: "considerations of money, convenience and security" (Smith 2011, p. 163). The first group includes financial instruments "such as the coin of the realm, and Bank of England notes and country bank notes (although not a legal tender)," (Tooke 1840, p. 297); Tooke calls this group currency. The second category includes "only the bank notes in the hands of the public" (ibid.)—"notes of the Bank of England, and of country banks, payable on demand" (ibid., p. 298). The third group includes "all instruments of interchange by which the productions and the revenues of the country are distributed; every thing which serves and is received as a mode of payment, or which constitutes the nominal money price which appears in price currents" (ibid.).

Tooke distinguished between transactions among dealers and those between dealers and consumers. The second was predominately undertaken with notes and coins, while for the first base money played a minor role and was facilitated mostly by any form of credit (Smith 2011, p. 164 f.). Overall, Tooke found that checks on deposits are increasingly used for exchange. He (1844, p. 23) concludes: "They [deposits] perform the functions of money not only as perfectly as bank notes, but in the description of transactions to which they are applicable, they are more convenient than bank notes." Tooke's definition of money is not very different from the usual Currency School one. However, the important difference is that, unlike currency-scholars, Tooke did not believe that there is, at least in the short run, a functional relation between the amount of notes and coins (base-money) and the quantity of what he calls considerations of money. According to Tooke, while the quantity of base money is usually relatively stable, the consideration of money varies significantly (Smith 2011, p. 166). Took stressed a very weak point of the Currency School proposal: first, what people use as money depends on what is offered to them as money: a shortage of one form of money—for example notes—cause people to increasingly use other forms; the textbook case is usually that inmates use cigarettes as money because the legal tender is scarse in prisons. Second, given that a wide range of money and near-money functions or may function as money, why should regulating notes and coins stabilize financial markets. Hence, according to Took, restricting paper money does not restrict prices, in the way expected by the Currency School.

Thomas Tooke formulated another fundamental critique of the Currency Principle: he argued that not even under a pure metallic currency regime does the bullion flows necessarily affect the quantity of money. Bullion is hoarded by private persons and banks, hangs as a clock on someone's hand, is the raw material of jewelers, hence not all bullion circulate as coins. If bullion is exported or imported out of idle hoards, for jewelry or other non-monetary reasons it does not affect neither the quantity of money in circulation nor prices. Hence, bullion flows do not necessarily correspond to a proportional change in the quantity of money (Viner 1975, p. 222). Tooke (1844, p. 102) states:

> the whole of the ground on which the theory of the Currency Principle proceeds is unsound. The error of supposing that, if the currency were purely metallic, every export or import of bullion would be so much taken from or added to the quantity of money in circulation, is so obvious, so palpable, as to make it a matter of surprise that such a notion should ever have been entertained.

The main problem lies in the proposed division of the Bank of England in a note-issuing and a banking department. According to Tooke, the export of bullion may fall to the note-issuing department or to the banking department; he declares (ibid., p. 107) that "In all probability, this demand [for export] would almost exclusively fall upon the deposit department [banking department]." But if it falls on the banking department, the effect on notes is less clear and most likely not one to one. Currency School advocates hoped that the separation of the Bank of England would give the English financial market much more stability. Tooke (1840, p. 253) attacks Currency School's proposal for separating the Bank of England into a note-issuing and banking department; if the bank would be separated "fluctuations as great, if not greater, might, and most probably would, occur, in the rate of interest, and in the state of credit, and in the markets for produce." In a well-known example, Tooke (1844, p. 106 ff.) demonstrates that a separated Bank of England may cause huge financial market disturbances from a moderate bullion outflow. It is beyond this study to give a detailed description of Tooke's example (for good summaries see Arnon 2011, p. 220 ff.; Smith 2011, p. 192 ff.). However, he showed that if the Bank of England is separated according to Currency School's plan, a moderate outflow of bullion may cause a huge narrowing of credit and a sharp increase of interest rates and under certain circumstances the suspension of cash payments against demand from the Bank of England (the Super-GAU). In opposition to the Currency School plan, Tooke proposed that the Bank of England should be freed from government's influence, orientate its policy towards concrete situations, but should be obliged to hold higher reserves in order to be armed for leaning against the wind if necessary (c.f. Smith 2011, pp. 180–188).

Increasingly, economists assigned to the Bank of England the role of Britain's central bank. Many stressed the bank's role as lender of last resort, its unique position in the government's debt financing, its pivotal role in leaning against financial crises, its status as the main reserve institution and its demand to give the bank a note-issuing monopoly. Also, it was being discussed whether Bank of England's notes should be legal tender (Fetter 1978, p. 158 f.). As maintained, even before the 19th century national bank proposals circulated and Hume was the first monetarist who suggested to found one big national bank, the Currency School developed the first monetarist central banking theory:

like more recent monetarist central bank theories, the Currency School suggested a on goal—the compliance of the Currency Principle—on instrument—issuing notes against a 100% cover of bullion reserve—approach. Hence, the Currency School favored clear and bounding money policy rules over flexible policies, and price stability over full employment as the main goal of monetary policy. The Currency School approach was also a clear political statement: the central bank's mission is to follow the Currency Principle, and hence to target price stability, but not to go against the wind when markets are in trouble or to promote growth and employment as demanded by the Birmingham School. Bounded to restricting rules, the note-issuing department does not even have the ability to play an active role to prevent financial crises or foster employment.

The advantage of a one goal one instrument approach is that the bank's job and how it will be done is quite clear; the general public has an idea about how the bank will behave and may build expectations of future actions. In addition, it reduces government's direct influence on central banks. The Currency School's theories and proposals appear quite clear and straightforward: like most monetarist theories, Currency School's clarity was enabled by a complexity reducing harsh assumptions. For example, the high complexity of different forms of money and near-monies was reduced by assuming that only base money influences prices because all other monies are constant multipliers of the money base. As the complexity is highly reduced, it is relatively easy to find rules that satisfy the theory's goals; however, the theories were often ill-founded due to the harsh assumptions. In contrast to the Currency School, like many other Keynesian theories, the Banking School foregoes unshakable rules, goals, and instruments, but favors a more flexible approach: goals and instruments depend on the situation. Intuitively, the Keynesian approach seems favorable: financial market disturbances may have rather different causes, look quite different and have quite different consequences, which is why it appears doubtful that the rule of one fits all exists. If central banks may be used for a wide range of political measurement—to foster and stabilize growth, enhance employment, lean against financial market disturbances etc.—why just focus on price stability? However, the problems arising from the Keynesian approach are also obvious: the goals and possible actions of central banks remain unclear. Monetarists' critic that Keynesians dream the dream of an all-potent super money, is plausible: Keynesian hopes of money policy power frequently widely overstep the mark. In addition, monetarists have a good point in claiming that Keynesian money policies often look quite reasonable from a present perspective, but may have long run consequences that are hard to predict.

5.1.5.7.3 Bagehot's Central Banking Theory

As maintained, the Bank Charter Act of 1844 was the ultimate victory of the Currency School and marked the starting point of the monetarist hegemony that lasted until World War I. After the Charter Act, no important money theory controversy like the bullion debate took place. Calm times for money theory, but for central banking theory, the time was quite fertile. On the continent, the discussion of free banking vs. monopolist central banking reached its peak in the second half of the century, in Britain most contributions focused on what kind of policy central banks should follow rather than whether central banks should exist (Smith 1936, p. 116). In particular Walter Bagehot advanced a monetarist central banking theory. His *Lombard Street: A Description of the money Market* ([1873] 1962) is usually considered the pioneering central banking contribution of the 19th century. According to Morgan (2013, p. 238) Bagehot developed a few really innovative ideas; however, *Lombard Street* was a genial synthesization of the most advanced money theories and discussed them against the background of the existing English banking system. Bagehot combined much of the Currency and the Banking School (Arnon 2011, p. 284 f.). He was not much of an advocate of monopolist central banking, but considered Bank of England's status as a quasi-central bank a historical fact. According to Bagehot, the British banking system was characterized by a one-reserve system (ibid., pp. 287–295): all banks held reserves in one bank, the Bank of England. Bagehot had much sympathy for free banking approaches which considered free bank note issuing and decentralized reserve holding. However, he argued:

> We are so accustomed to a system of banking, dependent for its cardinal function on a single bank, that we can hardly conceive of any other. But the natural system—that which would have sprung up if Government had let banking alone—is that of many banks of equal or not altogether unequal size. In all other trades competition brings the traders to a rough approximate equality (Bagehot [1873] 1962, p. 32).

Despite the disadvantages of central bank systems against free banking, Bagehot rejected the revolutionary change from a central banking to a free banking system as unrealistic and too radical (Smith 1936, p. 124). Accustomed with a one-reserve system, changing it to free banking would take too long and would have unforeseeable consequences. After Bagehot described the importance of a well-functioning banking system, he demonstrated why banking systems are imminently prone to crises and the danger arising from a one-reserve system (Arnon 2011, p. 285 ff.). The central question of Bagehot's *Lombard Street* is how central banks should act to stabilize markets in case of disturbances? His answer is: lending to those institutions which most need it, hence becoming the lender of last resort. He suggested that central banks should hoard enough reserves to be liquid at times of market turmoil.

Armed with enough reserves, it is the central bank's duty to lend at times of market disturbances at quite high interest rates to banks in need of credit: Bagehot ([1873] 1962, p. 96 f.) states that "in time of panic it [central bank] must advance freely and vigorously to the public out of the reserve." Two rules should be followed: "First. That these loans should only be made at a very high rate of interest" and "Secondly. That at this rate these advances should be made on all good banking securities, and as largely as the public ask for them." Bagehot intended with his two rules that the central bank lends enough money to overcome credit crunch caused by crises. However, just lending at very high rates ensures that only those banks that have no credit elsewhere borrow from the central bank. For Bagehot, the central bank's function as lender of last resort was the central issue of central bank policy.

5.1.5.7.4 German and French Cantral Banking Discussions

In the second half of the 19th century, the question of central banking was also intensively discussed in Germany and in particular in France. Smith (1936) gave an excellent overview of the German and French discussion. According to Smith (ibid., pp. 100–115) the German discussion was dominated by four economists: Otto Hübner, Johann Ludwig Tellkampf, Adolf Wagner, and Otto Michaels. She labels (ibid., p. 127) Wagner as a free-banking banking-scholar, Hübner and Michaels as free-banking currency-scholars, and Tellkampf as central banking currency-scholars.

Adolf Wagner was among the most prominent German economists of the late 19th century. Highly convinced by the Banking School and free banking theories, Wagner (1857, pp. 228–287) intensively discussed the disadvantage of big national banks (central banks): following the usual free banking arguments he states that central banks have too much power and are quite vulnerable to crises and cronyism. Among other arguments against central banks, Wagner stated that central banks fuel speculation by lending at too low interest rates. He argues that governments use their influence on the central bank to pressure discount rates below the market rate because of high public debt, to foster growth, or satisfy people. According to Wagner, even without the government's influence interest rates frequently fall fast because of the abundancy of capital. Rampant speculation soon returns discount rates to healthier rates. Fearing rising rates, governments often intervene with central banks to artificially hinder interest rates to rise: consequently, speculations further spreads rather than to decrease due to rising interest rates. The artificially low interest rates usually end in bursting bubbles. In contrast, small note-issuing banks lack the ability to artificially lower rates, which is why interest rates fast adapt to changing market circumstances. Wagner uses the two main arguments to show why no issuing regulation is necessary: first, the demand for money determines the amount of money. Second, applying Smith's law of reflux Wagner argues that over-issued money will immediately return to the bank. Hence, Wagner suggests that a system of competitive small note-issuing banks would be much less prone to crises and do much better than a central banking system. In the same vein, the German congress of the 'Deutsche Volkswirte' and its most famous member Otto Michaels proposed a free banking system. Much discussion took place on the question of currencies coverage; the majority and Michaels favored no bounding coverage obligation (Smith 1936, p. 104 ff.).

Like Wagner, Hübner (1854, p. 32) favored banking competition over-issuing monopolization: that USA banks became least often insolvent during banking crises than English banks showed for Hübner that less regulated banking sectors are less prone to crises. He argued: Scotland, where banking is least regulated has seen no big banking crisis, while on the continent with its privileged monopolized banks and heavy governmental involvement all big banks failed at least once. Government's influence is, for Hübner (ibid., p. 33), the main reason for the failure of national banks: governments usually demand huge public debt investments at low interest rates from privileged monopolized national banks. While private banks' business decisions are made by entrepreneurial considerations, government's logic influences national banks' investment decisions, which is why national banks are much more prone to crises. Unlike Wagner, Hübner demanded paper money's convertibility into species. Like Hübner, for Tellkampf (1867, p. 208 ff.) the convertibility of notes into species is essential for stability. According to Tellkampf, the full benefits of paper money will only be gained if the whole nation uses unique notes: different notes would complicate and regionalize trade. On the question of note issuing, Tellkampf favored the Scottish system where unlimited liable joint-stock banks issue notes over monopolization. Hence, much dispute prevailed between the leading German money economists about the best banking system, but free banking advocates outnumbered central banking advocates.

The British financial crisis of 1857 and the Bank of England's reaction shaped the opinion in Germany toward central banking: several proposals in favor of English central banks got published (Smith 1936, p. 108 ff). In his main book Lasker (1871) asked the central question of the time 'Bankfreiheit oder nicht?' [free banking or not?]. Sympathetic towards free banking, he argued that it was not shown why all business should be free, except private banks. According to Lasker (ibid., p. 67) people's fear of change rather than good arguments delayed free banking. Advocating free banking, Lasker was the exception rather than the rule in the second half of the 19th century, when most German economists became advocates of central banking and the strict restriction of note issuing. Nasse (1866) was one of the influential late-19th century central bank advocates. According to him (ibid., pp. 20–32), the advantage of central banks are: they are under permanent control of the public, overlook the whole market, and have bigger liquid assets for credit granting in times of market disturbances. According to Nasse, central banks should not be restricted by general rules as advocated by the Currency School, because rules cannot cover the wide range of useful policies at times of crisis. He suggests instead that central banks should hold enough liquidity to lean against the wind in times of great financial market disturbances: free banking systems lack a central institutions which overlooks the whole market and has the means to lean against the wind and provide the market with liquidity if necessary. Nasse argues that because private banks have a strong vested interest to reduce liquidity as much as possible in times of disturbances, central banks should be owned or be under advice of the state. Tellkampf's (1867, pp. 210–219) central bank proposal is a translation of Currency School ideas: he suggests to give a private bank a note-issuing monopoly. Advocating private banks over public banks to reduce state influence, he proposes to divide the private banks into a note-issuing and banking department: the former should act without any profit interest and must fully cover notes by bullion. Hence, Tellkampf's central bank ideas are congruent with the Currency School proposal. Even Adolph Wagner became more open to banking regulations and took side with those who favored a 'Dritteldeckung' [one-third species cover] (Smith 1936, p. 114); so, Wagner also left the free banking champ.

In France, the discussion about the banking systems, central banking, and note issuing was hardly less intensive than in Britain. Three main issues dominated the discussion: free banking versus central banking, note issuing, and the goals of money policy. While the first two issues dominated the discussion in Britain, the last was the main topic in France. Like in Germany, free bankers who advocate the unlimited right of note issuing to all private banks dominated around mid-19th century. At early times in France, note issuing was identified with coining, which should only belong to the king or the sovereign. Around the mid-19th century, a group of relatively influential free banking advocates emerged (ibid., p. 81 ff.). The free banking movement demanded a general liberalization of banking and most of them also the right to issue notes for private banks. Opposing free note issuing, French monetarists, for example Louis Wolowski, suggested giving Banque de France the note-issuing monopoly (Kindleberger 1985, p. 55). The discussion between free banking and central banking advocates continued throughout the 19th century: the arguments of both sides were those already outlined by their English predecessors. Advocates of free note issuing argued that notes cannot be over-issued as long as they are convertible into species; unlike in the case of central banks, the failure of note-issuing banks is not of systemic relevance and banking needs competition. Supporters of central banking stated that only a national currency fosters trade on a national scale, free banking cause over-issuing and only a central bank is able to oversee and clear bullion flows (c.f. Smith 1936, pp. 84–99). However, the issue of note issuing was also discussed in France and was overshadowed by more fundamental debates between Keynesians and monetarists.

In Britain, most Keynesians were free-banking advocates. French Keynesians cared little about note issuing: usually, French Keynesians demanded that the Banque de France should open branches elsewhere in the country to also equip the provinces with notes, others sympathized with free note issuing and almost all agreed in the necessity of issuing limits (Kindleberger 1985, pp. 41–62). However, the main topic of French Keynesians was how the Banque de France may and should foster growth, industrialization, employment, economic growth and prosperity. French Keynesians were convinced that central banks are able to foster economic development by keeping interest rates low; French monetarists responded in the usual liberal manner that interest rates are fixable as temperatures (ibid., p. 53 ff.).

French Saint-Simonians, the biggest group among French banking Keynesians, proposed the foundation of national industrial banks. At first glance, industrial banks seem to have a lot in common with monetarist central banks. However, as maintained below, Saint-Simonian's industrial banks' tasks far exceed monetarist central banks' tasks. Industrial banks are the central economic planning and organization institute in industrial societies. Hence, industrial banks are the main governing institution that determines production and distribution.

Saint-Simonians did not reject Banque de France's central bank entitlement, but were highly unsatisfied with its practical policy. Péreire (2010, p. 134) blamed the Banque de France of taking sides with the idle capital owners against the productive parts of the society. Frequently, the Banque de France was criticized by Saint-Simonians because of its conservative policy. The relation between the Banque de France and the Saint-Simonians steadily worsened as Saint-Simonians' criticism of the bank's policy got louder. It escalated when Saint-Simonians attacked Banque de France's quasi note-issuing monopoly. Highly disappointed by Banque de France's policy, Laffitte, Chevalier, and the Péreires started to openly oppose the note-issuing monopoly and to call for competitive banking institutions (Kindleberger 1985, p. 55 ff.).

5.1.5.8 Discussions on Banking

In the Early classical British writings of Hume and Smith, the issue of banking was closely related to paper money and inflation. Law's failure in France and the resulting hyperinflation, recurrent financial crises and high inflation in Britain, and the fast increase in the amount of paper money made early classical contributors aware of financial markets', and in particular banking sectors', proneness to crises. How paper money credit influences financial markets and prices became the central question for the early classical contributors.

David Hume was by no means a great advocate of private banking: admitting the practical advantages of paper money—it is "the oil which renders the motion of the wheel more smooth and easy" (Hume 1752, p. 27)—in principle, he warns that private banks are prone to over-issue paper money. According to Hume, the positive short-term effect of money extensions like an increase in the demand for labor and investment, the stimulation of output and forced saving (Humphrey 1993, p. 80) causes banks to notoriously overextend paper money credit. Hume fears that rising money destabilizes financial markets (Wennerlind 2008, p. 109), but in particular raises domestic prices. In an open economy, raising domestic prices deteriorates the international competitiveness: imports increase and exports decrease. Worsening trade balance causes bullion outflows which deteriorates a nation's military capacity (Viner 1975, p. 84). Hume ([1777] 1987, p. 284) concludes that "to endeavour artificially to encrease such a credit, can never be the interest of any trading nation; but must lay them under disadvantages, by encreasing money beyond its natural proportion to labour and commodities, and thereby." Blaming private banks for over-issuing and worsening the trade balance "made me entertain a doubt concerning the benefit of 'bank's and 'paper-credit', which are so generally esteemed advantageous to every nation." (ibid.) Hume suggested two measures to prevent over-issuing: first, a 100% cover of paper money by coins. Second, highly regulating private banking and the foundation of one big note-issuing public bank. Hence, through fear of over-issuing paper money, David Hume demands the harsh restriction of private banking.

Like Hume, Smith is quite convinced by the advantages of paper money: he considers (Smith 1776, p. 388) paper money to be "the great wheel of circulation [...,] a sort of waggon-way through the air." According to Smith (ibid., p. 350), "the substitution of paper in the room of gold and silver money, replaces a very expensive instrument of commerce with one much less costly, and sometimes equally convenient." For Smith (ibid., p. 345 f.), every money "require a certain expence, first to collect it, and afterwards to support it, both which expences." Because gold and silver monies are particularly costly, the introduction of paper money was considered an innovation by Smith

(Kurz and Sturn 2013, p. 186 f.). However, Smith's banking theory is a sharp contrast to Hume's view that private banks notoriously over-issue notes. According to Smith, only irrational banks issue more notes than needed by commerce. For Smith, the banking system is a self-regulating organism which needs no further regulation to avoid over-issuing if two rules are followed: first, paper money must be convertible into species. Second, banks should only be allowed to issue notes against Real Bills. Smith's Real Bill Doctrine is among the most heavily discussed issues of classical economics. Smith states that if customers fully trust banks, bank notes have the "same currency as gold and silver money, from the confidence that such money can at any time be had for them" (Smith 1776, p. 351). As notes fully function as money, borrowers are willing to pay the same interest on notes and coin credit. Because paper money is convertible into species, banks need to store bullion reserves to meet customers' demand for bullion to maintain people's confidence: according to Smith, a 25% coverage of paper money by bullion is sufficient to maintain confidence. If a bank issues more notes than needed for commerce, notes will lay idle in the coffers of bank's costumers. Idle money is expensive as holders pay interest on credit, which is why excessive money "must immediately return upon the banks to be exchanged for gold and silver" (ibid., p. 362). Providing bullion to meet customer demand is quite expensive for banks, and that is why banks avoid any over-issuing. Smith (ibid., p. 364) concludes: "Had every particular banking company always understood and attended to its own particular interest, the circulation never could have been overstocked with paper money." Hence, according to Smith, if banks are just allowed to issue against Real Bills and notes are convertible, the banking sector will be self-regulating in the sense that bankers' profit maximizing behavior ensures that, at least in the long run, paper money in circulation tends to be the right amount.

Heavily criticized by many later contributors (see Mints 1945, p. 29; Laidler 1981, p. 196; Humphrey 1993, p. 29), the Real Bills Doctrine inspired many money theorists (Humphrey 1993, pp. 21–31) and was adapted by the Federal Reserve System (Fed) in the late 1920s and early 1930s (Timberlake 2005, p. 215). According to Smith, competition between banks ensures that those who follow the Real Bills Doctrine survive and the irrational over-issuers disappear: hence a well-functioning banking sector needs competition rather than big national banks holding a note-issuing monopoly. He was an outspoken opponent of Hume-style national banks or a bankers' bank; Smith was in "clear opposition to what we now know as central banking" (Arnon 2011, p. 43). Believing in the self-regulating of private banks' note issuing, Smith was quite aware of financial markets' proneness to crises, which is why he proposed a wide range of financial market regulations. In addition to the regulations necessitated by the Real Bills Doctrine, Smith claims to build firewalls to reduce the infectiousness in times of financial market disturbances (Smith 1776, p. 392 f.), restrict notes to a value of at least five pounds because small notes would "many mean people are both enabled and encouraged to become bankers" (ibid., p. 391), and supported the prohibition of option clause (Carlson 1999).

5.1.5.8.1 Classical Economists' View on Banking

Classical economists' principle view on banking hardly changed from the 18th to the 19th century: they believed that paper money and banking fosters economic progress if applied correctly, but feared banks' proneness to over-issue notes. Many classical economists agreed that paper money replacing bullion as the circulating medium fosters economic prosperity by replacing a quite unwieldy and expensive form of money by a cheaper and handsomer one. Despite the heavy criticism of the Bank of England, and later of country banks, classical economists mostly agreed on the positive function of (private) banks for economic prosperity. Classical economists belief in banks' positive function for the economic development is deeply rooted in their capital and production theory. As already maintained, Mill developed two main doctrines of the classical capital and Production theory in *Principles of Political Economy* ([1848] 1965a): first the "industry is limited by capital" (ibid., p. 63) and second "it [capital] is the result of saving" (ibid., p. 68). According to the first, the creation or accumulation of capital fosters economic progress, wealth creation, and employment. The second means that only the wave of immediate consumption in favor of future consumption creates capital. Capital usual takes the form of paper money, but Mill warns us not to get confused by the form of capital and to misunderstand what capital actually is. Capital in the form of paper money will be used as a means of exchange: however, it is not used by the owner, but by machinery or labourers. Capital is consumed, in classical economists' ideal world, in the production of new goods. Unveiling mercantilists 'money veil', for classical economists it is irrelevant that savings usually take the form of notes and coins, the important point is that savers abandon immediate consumption and lend the right to consume to someone else: it is irrelevant which form savings take—like notes and coins, deposits at banks, consumable goods; the owner of capital gives up its right to eat and lends the right to a capitalist who uses the right to feed his worker in order to produce new goods.

As maintained, classical theory makes a clear cut between currency and capital: money as currency fulfills money's exchange function—money as currency facilitates the exchange of goods; money as capital fulfills money's function as a store of value (a store of consumption) and its function as a means of investment. Money as capital is usually invested in production and increases output. According to the classical and later neoclassical view, printing money augments money as means of exchange, but does not augment saving and therefore capital building. Following the quantity theory of money, printing money—at least in the long run—increases the nominal price of bread, because more money meets the same amount of available bread, but makes no worker full because paper money is not nutritious. Only an augmentation of capital through increasing savings—this goes without any increase in the quantity of money—fosters production, growth, and the wealth of the nation.

The division between currency and capital marks a clear break with the money-mercantilist approach: for money-mercantilists the increase in the quantity of money fosters industrial production because more money is available, which reduces interest rates. According to the classical school, it is just the formation of capital, hence additional saving which spurs growth: an increase in the quantity of money makes no difference other than rising prices, as long as it does not augment further saving.[1] Money-mercantilists feared the shortage of money, classical economists feared its abundance: several financial market disturbances which caused rampant inflation "shifted the story concerning monetary shortages to one of excessive monetary expansion" (Murphy 1997a, p. 3), therefore the "debate swung from concern over a shortage of money to fear of excessive monetary expansion" (ibid., p. 2). But what is always scarce in the view of classical economists is capital.

For money-mercantilists, the banks' ability to issue notes legitimized their existence. Building on the classical capital theory for the classical banking theory, capital intermediation legitimized the business of banking. As maintained, from the liberal perspective it is pivotal for a capitalist society that a capable entrepreneur, a crafty innovator gets the capital needed to promote his business independently of his own social background or financial abilities. Armed with the classical capital theory and the principle liberal affection on banking, in the liberal view the banks' main function is to bring together those with the idle money and those with the good ideas. A rich London merchant saves much of his profits while a Lancashire industrialist is short of capital: now the bank comes into play. The bank's main function is, according to classical economics, to ensure that the merchant's savings find their way up to Lancashire, where it is used by the industrialist to be invested into a new Spinning Jenny. Hence, the bank's main function became the intermediation of capital or loanable funds.

Following recent banking theory, loanable fund intermediation may be divided into four sub-functions: pure intermediation; it is less costly if the Lancashire industrialist asks for a loan at the bank branch in Liverpool and the bank transfers the merchant's deposits from the London headquarter to Liverpool, than the industrialist travelling all the way to London knocking on every rich man's door and asking for a loan. The other three sub-functions are size, maturity, and risk transformation. Size transformation: an industrialist asks for a loan bigger than every single saving. No individual saver may grant a loan big enough for the industrialists, but the bank has the ability to pool many savings into one big loan. Maturity transformation: savers usually prefer to be able to immediately withdraw deposits if they need it; savings are usually of immediate maturity. Unfortunately, entrepreneurs usually make long-term investments. Banks transfer maturity by granting a loan to the saver if the deposited money gets withdrawn against the asset of the loan granted to the industrialist. Risk transformation: Savers are often risk averse while investments are risky by nature. Banks transfer the different risk aversion of the saver into risky investments by underwriting some of the risk, for which

---

[1]In many classical money contributions, we find the concept of forced saving, hence the idea that an increase in the available currency may force people to save more and therefore to build more capital (for an overview of forced saving in classical economics; see Hayek 1932).

they are compensated by the interest differential between the deposit and the loan rate. Thornton (1802, p. 164 f.) states that:

> Country banks are also useful by furnishing to many persons the means of laying out at interest, and in a safe manner, such money as they may have to spare. […] All who have money to spare know where they can place it, without expence or loss of time, not only in security, but often with pecuniary advantage: and all commercial persons of credit understand in what quarter they can obtain such sums, in the way of loan, as their circumstances will fairly warrant them in borrowing.

Despite most classical economists' favor of banking, Ricardo remained quite reluctant toward banking (Satō and Takenaga 2013). However, loanable fund intermediation overall became the main legitimization for private banks in the classical economic theory. For Joplin (1827, p. 10), capital intermediation is the core business of private banks: "The original and proper business of a Banker is to trade in capital. He ought to be that medium between the borrower and lender in the money market, which a merchant is in other commodities." According to Tooke (1844, p. 36), an important part of "banker's business is to collect capital from those who have not immediate employment for it, and to distribute or transfer it to those who have." The central issue of capital intermediation for banks was also stressed by the early neoclassical contributors: Fisher (1911, p. 37) states that

In the ultimate analysis, and outside of its function of insuring credit, a bank is really an intermediary between borrowers and lenders. It is by virtue of bringing borrowers and ultimate lenders together and providing the former with a supply of loans which would not otherwise exist.

In the same manner, Pigou (1920) stresses several times in his monumental work *The Economics of Welfare* the importance of banks for loanable funds intermediation. Marx was quite an expert in the classical school of economics, which he heavily criticized. According to him, financial markets in general and banking in particular build the core sectors of capitalist economies. The indispensability of banks for the capitalist society lies, according to Marx ([1894] 1984, p. 607), in its ability to absorb all unemployed capital and supply it to capitalists in need of it:

> It [banking system] places all the available and even potential capital of society […] at the disposal of the industrial and commercial capitalists so that neither the lenders nor users of this capital are its real owners or producers. […] At the same time, banking and credit thus become the most potent means of driving capitalist production beyond its own limits.

Marx makes a clear-cut distinction between destructive pre-capitalist lending, outlined above, and modern banking which he considers capitalism's most central institutions. Newman (1851, p. 44 f.) distinguishes between usurers and early modern bankers on moral grounds:

> The primitive Banker is a lender of his own money; but differs from the old Usurer in this respect, that he lends to the rich and seldom or never to the poor. Hence he lends with less risk, and can afford to do it on cheaper terms; and for both reasons, he avoids the popular odium which attended the Usurer. Thus wealthy and honourable men publicly professed the Banker's trade, and their competition gave to the borrower the best terms which the state of the market made possible.

The quotes from Marx and Newman emphasize how the views on banking have changed: early forms of money lending were considered exploitative and ruinous; in contrast, modern banking was seen as pivotal for capitalism.

Hence, for most classical economists, like for money-mercantilists, banks foster economic development and are central institutions of capitalism. However, money-mercantilists argue that banks foster industrialization by augmenting the quantity of money. In contrast, classical economists worried about banks' ability to issue notes, which is why they suggested a wide range of note-issuing regulations. For classical economists, banks' loanable fund intermediation fosters growth and economic development and is pivotal for a well-functioning capitalism. Thus, money-mercantilists implicitly assumed that banks are able to create capital out of nothing, while classical economists strictly reject that banks create capital: of course banks create money, but not capital.

5.1.5.8.2 French Banking Enthusiasm

Apart from the outlined classical theory of banking, in France in particular an alternative Keynesian approach to banking developed (Kindleberger 1985, pp. 41–62). 19th century Keynesian banking was influenced by important money-mercantilist like John Law, but at the same time the theories were significantly different: for example, most Keynesians rejected a crude money expansionism like the one suggested by money-mercantilist. Like classical economists, Keynesians believed that a well-functioning banking sector fosters growth and economic development. While for classical economists the role of the banks is passive, they intermediate loanable funds and therefore, unintendedly, foster growth, but are not active promoters of economic progress. In contrast, French Keynesians stated that the "society needs active banks to push the expansion of commerce, agriculture, and industry, to keep busy, and to achieve growth" (ibid., p. 46). It was widely agreed among classical economists and Keynesians that low interest rates foster economic growth. However, while for classical economists free market mechanism are the best guides to promoting economic prosperity, for Keynesians the selfishness of free bankers did a lot of harm and needs to be overcome. In line with classical economists, for most Keynesians of the 19th century, banks are capital intermediaries. However, in contrast to more liberal theories Keynesians were convinced that capitalist forces of free markets are not always the best guides for capital distribution, which is why they usually called for state guidance and intervention.

19th French Keynesians already lined out a rudimentary central point of Keynesian money theory: according to them, investment augments saving (ibid.) rather than the other way around. This became the central Keynesian argument against the classical economic theory: Keynesian take the classical relation between saving and investment upside down. Frequently, in particular after World War II, the argument that investment augments saving was used to legitimize money expansions. Impressed by Law's failure, French Keynesians remained quite reluctant to printing money; instead they often proposed financial institutions better able to absorb idle hoards for investments, which augment future savings.

Saint-Simonians were the most powerful and influential French banking Keynesians of the 19th century. Highly unsatisfied with the banking system of the time and accusing the banks of assisting the idle capital owner in exploiting the productive class (Enfantin 1905, p. 101), Saint-Simonians demanded a significant change of the banking sector. Enfantin (ibid., p. 100 ff.) outlined that according to Saint-Simonianism banks should be mediators between the idle capital owner and the diligent producers, who always take side with the latter. He demands the foundation of industrial banks, which clearly take side with the diligent producers against the idle capital owners and follow the goal of liberating the diligent from the eploitation and slavery of the idle capital owners. Saint-Simonian industrial banks should be founded and governed by selfless Saint-Simonians whose only goal is the foundation of classless industrial society. Building on Saint-Simon's general theories, Prosper Enfantin, Jacques Laffitte, Michel Chevalier, and the brothers Emile and Isaac Péreire were the main developers and supporters of the Saint Simonian banking proposals: in particular Enfantin and Chevalier developed most of the Saint Simonian banking theory. The Saint-Simonian banking theory was strongly inspired by both Keynesians and monetarists: the Keynesians John Law and Adam Smith and the monetarists David Ricardo and Jean-Baptiste Say were its main sources (c.f. Bellet 2011, p. 11). However, the Saint Simonian banking theory should be considered as a Keynesian theory.

As maintained, almost all 19th economic theories argued that a well-functioning banking system facilitates the economic progress: however, no other economic theory was more focused on banking than Saint-Simonianism. Credit is the most central institution in the Saint-Simonian theory: "The Saint-Simonian school understood that credit was both 'stimulator and regulator', with the function of 'impelling and directing', 'exciting and coordinating', acting as 'motor and brake'" (Kindleberger 1985, p. 43). For Saint-Simonians, by granting loans, banks stimulate and regulate the economy, guide resources toward the most necessary sectors, coordinate different parts of the economy by transferring resources from one part to another and if necessary slow down progress. Due to their possibilities to guide the economy and society, for Saint-Simonians banks are the central institutions of an industrialized economy. Saint-Simon suggested the governance of the economic professional, but according to him no other group is more predestined for the organization of industrial society than bankers. Saint-Simon saw the

> producers organized in a natural hierarchy with the banks at the top, governing, through there dissemination of credit, the activity of all. The bankers, then, are the obvious representatives of the interests of the whole producing class. 'This being the situation, the most important banking houses of Paris find themselves called upon to direct the political activity of the producers (Mason 1931, p. 675).

Hence, for Saint-Simonians bankers should form the inner circle of the Industrial policy governance as they have the best view on the whole economy and distributing resources is their core business.

Much of the Saint-Simonian banking theory was inspired by Law's contributions. Similarly to Law, for Saint-Simonians the adequate supply of capital and the reduction of the interest rate are the central tasks of a banking system. According to Saint-Simonians, active banking fosters growth and industrialization and reduced unemployment. However, Saint-Simonians, like other French Keynesians, were quite reluctant to printing money to foster growth. Like the classical economic theory, Saint-Simonians blame Law for overlooking the difference between money and capital. Saint-Simonians, predominately, followed the classical economic theory that capital exclusively arises from savings, so banks have no possibility to create capital by printing money or any other banking activity; "The banks have nothing to do with the creation of capital; their loans to the producing class are strictly limited by their borrowings from the possessing class." (ibid., p. 677). The central role of banks is not to print money, but to excavate the idle hoards of the people. Banks absorb idle funds from savers and lend it to the diligent: industrial banks' capital intermediation is a "peaceful way of insuring the progressive transfer of property to producers" or "the instrument to bring together, peacefully and progressively, property and workers" (Bellet 2011, p. 14). Unlike classical economists who expect that private banks' vested interest are the best advocate of progress, Saint-Simonians blame French private banks for their selfishness: according to Saint-Simonians, selfish capitalist banks take side with the money lender and force up interest rates as high as possible. In contrast, industrial banks take side with the borrower and lower interest rates as much as possible. Believing in the possibility to persistently reduce interest rates (Kindleberger 1985, p. 45), Saint-Simonians were convinced that industrial banks would be able to significantly lower interest rates. Central to the persisting reduction of the rate of interest was the industrial bank. The mobilization of idle savings gave the bank the ability to decrease interest rates: if industrial banks, as Enfantin (1905, p. 102 f) proposed, act strictly in accordance with workers' interests, the augmentation of capital translates into lower interest rates. In addition, industrial banks should use their good reputation to lower interest rates on deposits and transmits lower rates to the industry by reducing the risk premium for industrial credit (Mason 1931, p. 676 ff.): industrial banks create "confidence" (Bellet 2011, p. 14), which is why idle capital owners are more willing to lend to well-organized industrial banks than directly to most other industries (Mason 1931, p. 676 ff.).

As maintained, for Saint-Simonians industrial policy means to organize the most efficient use of all means of production. According to their policy understanding, industrial banking absorbs idle hoards and distributes the capital to industrial sectors where they are used most efficiently. According to Saint-Simonians' idea, the industrial bank is a huge bank, present in all regions, and it absorbs loanable funds all over the country and invests the capital according to the general interest of the nation. In addition to the absorbed loanable funds, it was suggested that the bank should manage and invest states' inheritances (Enfantin 1905: 103 ff.). Given that many Saint-Simonians suggested the state to be the only inheritor and all inheritance to be managed by the industrial bank, Gide and Rist (1923, p. 237 f.) are right in claiming that Saint-Simonian imagine the government as a huge central bank: "In the Final State industry is organized by the banks; 'everything is interlocked and all is planned' in the 'interest of all'" (Eckalbar 1979, p. 84).

5.2 The Rise of the English Banking System

At the beginning of the 19th century the British banking sector was dominated by a large number of small goldsmith, merchant and country bankers and the Bank of England: the former operated a wide range of small scale private banking businesses, the latter was predominately active in public debt banking. At the beginning of the 20th century the British banking sector looked much like nowadays: a handful of megabanks dominated the financial market, operated branches in almost every small British town and was highly active across the globe. Megabanks were the most visible institutions of the economic strength of the British Empire and its economic superpower ambitions. In addition, the Bank of England shifted toward the world's first modern central bank.

The significant change of the British banking sector in the 19th century was facilitated, enabled, and induced by profound economic, political, cultural, and legal changes. Hardly any money controversies received more attention than the British bullionists and Banking vs. Currency School debates. However, most contributions strongly focus on professional economists' thoughts, like the outstanding contributions of Viner (1975), Arnon (2011), Humphrey (1993), while most ignorethe economic, political, and cultural circumstances: notable exceptions are Fetter (1959, 1975, 1980) who published several outstanding works on the political aspects of the debates, and Liepmann (1933) who analyzed the formation of the British financial market regulation in *Der Kampf um die Gestaltung der englischen Währungsverfassung*. In addition, the money debates received much more attention than the banking discussion although the latter were at least as important for the development of the British and the European banking system.

According to Dicey (1905), the early 19th century was dominated by Old Toryism, until it was replaced by Benthamism or liberalism at the end of the war with France, which then turned into collectivism at the end of the century. Particularly during Old Toryism and Benthamism/liberalism the British money and banking system deeply and fundamentally changed. The shift from Old Toryism to liberalism was based on a deep change of the social structure caused by industrialization. Due to the increasing importance of the industry, the bourgeoisie, the middle class, and the working-class aristocracy was on the rise and the old landed aristocracy in retreat. It was a British peculiarity that the progeny of the downgraded old aristocracy entered the rising service sector and dominated the financial sector. "Gentlemen investors" (Veblen 1917, p. 250 ff.) used their strong ties to the government to influence banking-relevant politics.

However, the rising bourgeoisie, the middle class, and the working-class aristocracy became the main carriers of liberalism. Supported by the three-class coalition –the bourgeoisie, the middle class, and the working-class aristocracy—liberalism became the hegemonic political idea of mid-19th century: liberalism not only influenced the liberal parties, but also the conservative Tories. Traditionally favoring *laissez-faire*, around mid-19th century British liberals became more open to state interventions as the social issue got worse and became one of the main topics of the time, as the rise of the socialist movement threatened the Lib-Lab coalition—of liberals (Lib) and workers (Lab)—and as it turned out that, due to monopolization, unequal starting conditions etc., pure *laissez-faire* may harm liberalism.

Despite the increasing openness to state interventions, *laissez-faire* was the guiding principle of the British political liberalism. What caused the bourgeoisie, the middle class, and the working-class aristocracy to principally support *laissez-faire* was their joint battle against old corruption: old corruption refers to a system of economic and political privileges which secured the influence and dominion of the old elites. The three rising classes blamed the system of old corruption for their economic and political underrepresentation. Their attack on old privileges mirrors the view of the leading liberals of the time: particularly early 19th century liberals, but also later contributors, were deeply convinced that Britain's social problems originate in the economic and political exclusion of poorer classes. The British liberals' panacea was participation, meaning the revokation of old privileges and the creation of an institutional frame which fosters the participation of highly excluded groups of the society.

For liberals, the banking system was an ideal typical example of old corruption, of old-style cronyism, elitism and inefficiency. Ruled by a small closed old elite, holding a quasi-monopoly for treasury bill banking and reserve storing, the Bank of England was part of the powerful clandestine organizations which dominated the economy. Heavily depended on the credit from the Bank of England, it was not always clear whether the government or the bank was the true sovereign of Britain. The structure of the banking sector was highly determined by privileges granted to the Bank of England when governments were particularly hard up,: the Bank of England's privilege to be the only (note-issuing) bank allowed for more than six shareholders and ensured Bank of England's unique position as the only big English bank. Most of the small private London and country banks were also dominated by the old elites. Many country banks held quasi-monopolies for banking in their geographical area. Close (secret) ties to regional authorities and the government ensured banks' political influence. Hence, at the beginning of the 19th century the English banking sector looked much like an old mercantilist system: dominated by a small closed old elite with close ties to the sovereign, sustained by privileges and quasi-monopolists.

Properly serviced with its quasi-monopoly for profitable state banking, the Bank of England was not interested in credit granting to the more risky private sector. Protecting their geographic quasi-monopolies, country banks often rejected notes from and business with other country banks. Due to conservative credit granting and the policy of geographical isolation, country banks hampered industrialization, interregional trade, the interregional exchange of loanable funds and the economic integration of the country. Entrepreneurs and economists frequently complained about country banks' unwillingness to accept collateral other than land, Bank of England's focus on public debt, and banks' inability and unwillingness to foster industrialization.

Given the dominance of the old elites and the exclusion of the rising classes, status quo-preserving privileges and the sluggish lending to private enterprises, it is not surprising that liberals demanded the comprehensive restructuring of the banking sector. As maintained, for classical economists the banking system is at the core of capitalism: it transfers idle hoards into productive investments and ensures that the creative minds, independent from class and status, receive the financial means to implement their ideas. At the beginning of the 19th century, the English banking system hardly fulfilled the functions intended by classical theory: rather than dissolving social and financial barriers, banks strengthened the old division by lending against land, but mostly refusing to lend to the industry and to innovative descendants of the middle and working class. Hence, rather than supporting the rising industry and increase the social mobility, the banking sector of the early 19th century was the cash cow of the old elites and sustained the economic exclusion of the rising classes.

Banking laws and regulations became a central battlefield between the old elites and the newcomers. Hidden behind money and banking theories and political arguments, the great debates on the money and banking system were always also battles between old elites protecting their privileges and newcomers demanding participation. Removing legal and informal entry barriers, fostering middle- and working-class participation, abolishing privileges, and creating a free banking sector which effectively supports economic development were the main claims of the rising liberal newcomers. On the other side, the old elites, in particular the Bank of England and country bankers defended the status quo and their privileges. Debates and legal changes modifying the money system kindled by the great debates on money theory were also monetarist attacks on Bank of England's privileges: monetarist proposals also aimed to revoke Bank of England's privileges and restricting its scope of action. The great legal changes of private banking regulation aimed to revoke Bank of England's and country banks' banking privileges, to increase the participation of excluded classes, to foster capital building, and facilitate credit to private business.

Several legal changes permitted the foundation of joint-stock banks and allowed them to issue limited liability shares. Banks enabled to attract an unlimited amount of limited liable shareholders caused the unprecedented concentration of the banking sector in the second half of the 19th and early 20th century. Accelerating capital formation and the oligopolisation of capital in the hands of a few megabanks steadily reduced profits on new investments. Convinced that only fast growing institutions survive the increasing domestic and foreign competition, megabanks faced a dilemma: fast growth was only possible if banks were able to offer relatively high interests to depositors and shareholders, while high interest rates were hard to offer in an environment of falling profits on investments. Searching for new profitable investment opportunities caused banks to increasingly look abroad. Facing more competition from continental European competitors, British banks escaped to less developed overseas territories. Lacking the domestic legal protection, British banks highly relied on the government and military force to protect their foreign investments. Dependent on new investment markets to maintain interest payments to their depositors and shareholders, banks became notorious supporters and profiteers of British colonialism. Bankers needed the support of the government to protect their investments in the overseas territories and develop new markets for investments, while at the same time governments relied heavily on the financial support of the bankers to develop the conquered colonies.

Overall, the entire British economy faced tough times in the second half of the 19th century. Fast rising industrial production and sluggish demand, accompanied by deep crises, caused the long-lasting economic slowdown in the second half of the 19th century. High unemployment, low wages and the oversupply of industrial products put much pressure on governments to fix the economy and accelerate growth.

It was widely agreed that Britain needs new markets to overcome the oversupply slowdown. Developing new markets was complicated by the rise of new industrial competitors like France, Germany and the USA and the new protectionism of the European continent. Conquering and developing colonies was often considered the only possibility to develop new markets for British industrial goods and capital. Hence, imperialism was regarded as a measurement to overcome the oversupply of industrial goods and capital, reduce unemployment, and increases wages. Apart from the notorious supporters of imperialism like conservative groups fearing to lose ground against France and Germany and fortify Britain's status as world's greatest empire, the economic slowdown caused many groups, like industrialists and workers, traditionally reluctant towards imperialism, to support the colonial policy. Hence, in the second half of the 19th century many supported and demanded colonialism due to economic reasons; searching for profitable investment opportunities, bankers were in the forefront of the colonialism discourse.

5.2.1 The Time of Old Toryism

Old Toryism was characterized by the glorification of the constitution and the past, anti-Jacobin rhetoric and increasing authoritarianism. According to Dicey (1905, p. 62 f.) Old Toryism was a time of "legislative quiescence". In addition to the traditional Tory conservativism, several reasons made the early 19th century particularly unfavorable for change. Old Toryism was strongly inspired by, as Dicey calls it, Blackstonian Optimism—Blackstone's constitution theory of balanced powers clearly favors the status quo over deep change (Kraus 2006, p. 178). Revolutionary terror in France and the recurrent wars against the Revolutionary Army and Napoleon boosted anti-Jacobin sentiments. Britain was accustomed to fight wars elsewhere in Europe and outside. However, the wars against Revolutionary France and Napoleon's France were different because the British sovereignty was under threat: the landing of the French Revolutionary army in Britain in 1797 was a dramatic collective experience which legitimized all measurements taken to win the war against the archenemy. Reform proposals and criticism of the Tory government were usually threatened as Jacobin assaults and friendly fire. Open political disputes were stifled by the necessity for unity. Criticism of the government was usually considered an attack on the homeland. In addition, increasing authoritarianism augmented Tory government's ability to pursue their enemies. Hence, Blackstonian Optimism and in particular recurrent wars against France made the early 19th century unfavorable for deeper reforms and a period of relative political deadlock.

5.2.1.1 Suspension of Convertibility

Costly recurrent wars against the revolutionary France quickly raised Bank of England's lending to the government and its allies after 1794. In 1795 the exchange rate turned against England: bullion started to flow out heavily and signs of crisis became frightening (Hawtrey 1919, p. 255 ff). Bank of England's difficulties to maintain heavy lending to the government and deepening financial market disturbances forced the British government to take radical measurements: suspending convertibility of Bank of England notes into species in 1797 was expected to stabilize financial markets, stop the bullion outflow and in particular to ease Bank of England's public lending. Britain's government hoped that increasing Bank of England's public credit elasticity would turn around the fortune of war.

Several studies investigated the suspension of convertibility and its effects on the war fortune: many agreed (Chadha and Newby 2013; Friedman 1990; Bordo and White 1991) that the suspension of convertibility was pivotal for Britain's military success. It was argued that the suspension of convertibility facilitated British war financing compared to the sluggish French war-financing system. The collective memory of Law's failure and the hyperinflation during the revolution caused Napoleon to rejected the suspension of convertibility in France (Friedman 1990, p. 90). Because the metallic standard prevented extensive lending, France heavily relied on taxes to finance rampant war costs. Bank of England's lending flexibility was Britain's main advantage: in contrast to the cumbersome French war-financing system, the suspension of convertibility strongly increased Britain's public credit elasticity and enabled the government to raise huge funds for military operations in a short time: "Britain was able to adopt a set of flexible policies to finance the war, but Napoleon's inability to rise large amounts of income in a short period of time was one of the factors that led to his disastrous Russian Campaign" (Chadha and Newby 2013, p. 4).

After centuries of convertibility, its suspension was a profound legal change. However, at the beginning, the suspension of convertibility was not widely criticized. Considering the measurement a war time necessity prevented opponents from openly criticizing the Act. In addition to the legitimization by the war, the suspension was in the interest of influential groups: according to Liepmann (1933, pp. 49–63), the industrial bourgeoisie welcomed the suspension because it facilitated industrial credit. Enabled to invest much bigger sums into profitable public debts, the Bank of England appreciated the deregulation. However, the suspension was in particular in the interest of the government because it stretched its budget constrains.

5.2.1.2 The Failed Bullionist Attack

Apart from notorious war opponents (Silberling 1924, p. 402 f.), it took some time until the inconvertibility opposition raised. As maintained, accelerating inflation caused the first round of the bullion controversy, which systematized and sharpened the monetarist and anti-monetarist position. Boyd (1801), Wheatley (1803), and King (1804) were the first bullionists who blamed the Bank of England for rising inflation. On the other side, Baring (1797), the first anti-bullionist, defended the suspension as a wartime necessity, the policy of the Bank of England as prudent, and rejected that rising prices were caused by extensive note issuing. As the bullion controversy intensified, Francis Horner, a leading bullionist, was assigned to form a committee, later called the bullion committee, to investigate "high price of gold, the exchanges, and inflation" (Arnon 2011, p. 133). The released Bullion Report focus on three main questions:

> (1) What is the cause of the present price of bullion and Hamburg exchange; (2) To what extent should the Bank, while the Restriction continues, pay attention, in its credit policy, to the exchange and bullion market; and (3) When should specie payments be resumed? (Fetter 1942: 660)

The report suggested a clear causality between note issuing and prices, blamed the Bank of England for high prices and unfavorable exchange rates and proposed to restore convertibility within two years at the 1797 parity (Laidler 2000, pp. 14–17). Intended or not, the Bullion Report was a frontal attack on the Tory government and its main financer the Bank of England. The anti-bullionist defenders of the status quo developed two main arguments against the Bullion Report and its propositions: first, money was considered an endogenous variable, which means that the quantity of money is determined by the demand for money; hence, much money is the result of, not the reason for, high prices. Second, defending the Bank of England it was argued that the bank strictly followed Smith's Real Bill Doctrine, which is why it cannot be blamed for high prices because it has not over-issued.

Overemphasizing personal interests, Silberling (1924) argued that bullionist predominately followed economic self-interests and were incited by the Whigs who hoped to harm the Tory government. Fetter (1959, 1980) strongly doubts Silberling's view: he shows that the bullion committee consisted almost equally of Whigs, Tories, and Independents; no Whig leader openly supported the Bullion Report in the Parliament, and both the Whig- and Tory-affiliated press supported and rejected the investigations. Nevertheless, Whigs were overall more open to the report than Tories: as shown by Fetter, the Whig fraction in the bullion committee mainly supported and the Tory fraction mainly rejected the end version of the report. While the Whig press mainly supported the report, relatively divided at the beginning, pressure from the government caused the Tory-affiliated press to increasingly take side with the opponents.

Bullionists faced ruthless, and often unfair, criticism: they were blamed for pursuing their vested material interests, being unpatriotic clandestine Jacobins and secret supporters of France. I think vested material interests and political positions less than their deep beliefs in monetarism influenced the authors' arguments: the Bullion Report was the logical consequence of the classical quantity theory. Despite its prominent advocates, the Bullion Report failed to attract enough supporters. Fearing indirectly destructing the military force and being considered anti-patriotic and Jacobin prevented supporters from openly taking side with the report. D'Ivernois wrote that the report "committed a most grievous and deplorable fault in putting such a Weapon into the hands of the Enemies of their country" (cited in Fetter 1959, p. 110).

After a long Parliamentary debate, the report was clearly defeated: both the theory and the practical suggestions were rejected (Arnon 2011, p. 133). The rejection was a victory of the anti-bullionists, but the Parliamentary defeat had little to do with money theory: anti-bullionist arguments were often rather counterproductive (Fetter 1942, p. 665). While bullionists failed to organize support, the inconvertibility camp formed a strong coalition to maintain the status quo: the government rejected the motion because of its need for easy credit; the Bank of England and country banks rejected it because they feared to lose profits if lending is higher regulated; and entrepreneurs because they welcomed the credit easing and the possibility to invest their idle capital (Chadha and Newby 2013). For the bullionist camp in particular the widespread view that inconvertibility was "a necessary instrument of war finance" (Fetter 1942, p. 665) much complicated the formation of a strong coalition: easily being blamed for anti-patriotic friendly fire even the Whigs refused to openly support the Bullion Report. Although the first round of the bullion controversy had few direct political effects, it induced the most fundamental money debates in the 19th century which deeply shaped the British money and banking system.

5.2.2 The Time of the Liberal Hegemony

Old Toryism was sustained by the war against France and fears from radical French ideas of Robespierre and Napoleon. When Napoleon was defeated, the main legitimization for old Tory authoritarianism vanished: tensions were covered by the war and anti-French sentiments, but reinvigorated after the war.

Industrialization and the decreasing importance of agriculture significantly shifted economic and political power. Overall, the 19th century was the time of the middle class: for (Dicey 1905, p. 128) the middle class was the "true sovereign" of the time: the middle class is usually loosely defined as people in between smaller industrials at the upper end, small tradesmen, and shopkeepers at the base (Tames 1972, p. 143). Apart from the middle class the influence of the rising bourgeoisie and working class also increased steadily. Associated with exploitation and catastrophical living and working conditions, the factual situation of the working class was quite different. Rather than collectively pauperizing, the industrialization polarized the working class (Brugger and Gehrke 2018): the industrial Lumpenproletariat faced an advancing working aristocracy. While the Lumpenproletariat was highly excluded, the political and economic influence of the working aristocracy increased steadily.

In addition to the rise of the bourgeoisie, the middle class, and the working class the old aristocracy changed significantly. Unlike in many other countries, the British old aristocracy was quite adaptable to the changing economic circumstances: the old aristocracy steadily descended as landed class, but returned as London gentleman capitalists (Cain and Hopkins 1986; 1987; 1993). Agriculture being on the retreat, the old aristocracy was in need of a more contemporary business. Occupations like manufacturing were considered ungentle, others like the service sector as gentle (Cain and Hopkins 1986, p. 505), which is why many descendants of the old aristocracy entered the booming service sector. In particular British financial markets were crowded with gentleman capitalists. Veblen (1917, p. 250 ff.) described the gentlemen investors as routed in the old aristocracy with close ties to the government: "At the top of the gentlemanly order, the barriers between business and government were no more than mobile Chinese walls" (Cain and Hopkins 1993, p. 28), capitalists of the old aristocracy were predestined for the money business: close ties to the aristocracy, the main saver and borrower of the time, and to the political elite facilitated their financial business. Lending heavily to the private sector and in particular to the sovereign, gentleman capitalists became central economic and political players. Maintaining their dominance over land and occupying the financial markets, "The nineteenth-century gentleman was therefore a compromise between the needs of the landed interest whose power was in decline and the aspirations of the expanding service sector" (ibid., p. 33); this saved the aristocracy from economic and political decline.

Overrepresented by the voting system and their say in the Tory Party, aristocracy's political power much exceeded their true economic power and population share. Hence, at the beginning of the 19th century the political balance of power, which still strongly leaned toward the old aristocracy, hardly reflected the fundamental social changes. The underrepresentation of the rising social classes was caused by the British voting system favoring the status quo: the rising industrial bourgeoisie, the middle class, the working class and North-English industrial hubs were strongly underrepresented. Adopting the voting system to the changing circumstances and rebalancing the power was the main political demand of the rising classes. In addition to the demand for more political influence, the rising classes attacked the system of economic privileges, which excluded newcomers from most profitable companies and sectors.

Blaming political and economic privileges for their underrepresentation, the industrial bourgeoisie, the working class, and in particular the middle class became the main carriers of liberalism and *laissez-faire*. The three classes were united in their combat against the old political and economic cronyism and demanded the liquidation of all economic and political privileges. Traditionally, the bourgeoisie was the main carrier of liberalism (Ashcraft 1972) because it ideologically underpinned their struggle with the old aristocracy over economic and political influence and power. As maintained, the British working-class movement was less interested in ideologies and World Revolutions than in immediate improvements. The British working aristocracy was principally open to liberal views (Breuilly 1994). Due to conviction or tactical reasons, the working aristocracy formed a long-lasting coalition with other liberals: the coalition of workers and liberals was institutionalized by the Lib-Lab alliance between the Liberal Party and the most important working-class movements (ibid., p. 115). Well educated, economically on the rise, but politically excluded, the middle class had the most to win through *laissez-faire*, liberalism, and the end of old cronyism. Quickly rising in number and influence, the middle class became the main pillar of liberalism: "Benthamism [liberalism] was fundamentally a middle-class creed" (Dicey 1905, p. 186). The unusual three-class coalition of the bourgeoisie, the middle, and working class behind liberalism was strong enough to establish a liberal hegemony which dominated Britain politics around the mid-19th century. Traditionally, the Whigs were the Parliamentary carriers of liberalism, but the liberal hegemony also fundamentally shaped the position of the Tories toward more liberal approaches.

5.2.2.1 The British Liberalism

For Dicey (ibid.) Jeremy Bentham was the most important intellectual of the British liberalism why he considers the entire period of the liberal hegemony as Benthamism. Doubtlessly, Bentham was quite important for early 19th century British liberals, but due to theoretical and in particular practical problems, liberals steadily turned away from Benthamism and became more open for state intervention and active social policies. While Bentham was the leading head of the early British liberalism around mid-century, John Stuart Mill became quite important for the changing liberal movement.

Bentham suggested a liberal state which protects citizens from pain, attacks from inner and outer enemies, and safeguards their political and economic rights. Overall, Bentham was quite reluctant to state interventions. Not principally opposing all kind of state interventions, for Bentham *laissez-faire*—"faith in *laissez-faire* which was in practice the most potent and vital principle of Benthamite reform" (ibid., p. 144)—was the norm and every deviation from it had to be extensively discussed and carefully considered. Like Jeremy Bentham most British early-19th century liberals had a strong favor for negative rights: denouncing social grievances like the discrimination of women and homosexuals, the exclusionary voting system, opposing death penalties and slavery, early-19th century liberals highly focused on negative rights. Already in the early 19th century the social issue was a core topic for liberals. Most liberals of the time, like Bentham, were strongly convinced that most social tension and unrest arise from the unfair post-absolutistic system of economic and politic privileges and exclusion. They expected that granting participation rights to the excluded and removing privileges from the chosen would automatically bring social justice, more equality, and help the poor help themselves.

Laissez-faire "was a war cry. It sounded the attack upon every restriction, not justifiable by some definite and assignable reason of utility, upon the freedom of human existence and the development of individual character" (ibid., p. 148). Defining the fundamental rights and dignity of individuals as sacrosanct and beyond the access of governments distanced the British liberalism from French revolutionary terror. *Laissez-faire* was in particular directed against the absolutistic heritage of political and economic privileges which liberals blamed for restrained economic growth, inequality, corruption, and poverty. Liberalism and *laissez-faire* was a frontal attack on the old corruption—as 19th century liberals usually called it–(Rubinstein 1983). Old corruption referred to the political, economic and bureaucratic elites who owed their power and influence to the close ties with the Crown and governments, their financial means to support the state in times of financial difficulties, old laws, or simply corruption.

For early 19th century liberals, economic and political participation was the tool to make the lower classes help themselves. Reforming the undemocratic voting system was a key demand of liberals. That "every Man to count for one and no Man for more than one" (Dicey 1905, p. 157) reflected the liberals' conviction that all male citizens are born equal in rights and dignity. Apart from the ideological favor for the one man one vote rule, the demand was a political calculation: lower classes—in particular the middle class—were overwhelmingly followers of liberal parties, hence allowing more ordinary people to vote meant more votes to Whigs, Radicals, and the Liberal Party. The presentation of the People Act of 1832 was a major victory for liberals—in particular the Whigs—because it strengthened the Whig strongholds at the expense of the Tory-affiliated rural arias. The reform Acts of 1867 and 1884 were further steps toward the one man one vote rule. In addition, liberals also denounced the economic underrepresentation of certain classes. Early-19th century liberals were quite convinced that *laissez-faire* was the best policy to advocate the economic participation of the poorer classes': fighting economic privileges was considered the best measurements to fight poverty.

Jeremy Bentham died when liberalism was on the rise. When liberalism became the dominant political idea in the late 1820s and early 1830s, Bentham's intellectual successors had to deal with more practical problems. In particular Bentham's favor for utilitarianism and *laissez-faire* often seemed contradictory. Theoretically, utilitarianism and *laissez-faire* were, from the liberal perspective, two sides of one coin. Soon it turned out that state intervenions may practically outperform *laissez-faire* solutions: for example in the case of poverty, monopolies, inheritances, economic participation, and education state intervenions seemed necessary to foster the liberal society. A few, like Nassau William Senior, entirely discredited *laissez-faire*: most liberals maintained utilitarianism and the favor for *laissez-faire*, but reinterpreted the relation between utilitarianism, *laissez-faire*, and state intervenions. As the issue of poverty, monopolies, inheritances, economic participation of excluded groups, and education took center stage, pure *laissez-faire* seemed unsatisfactory. Increasingly rejecting pure *laissez-faire*, the core questions for the leading liberals became how much state intervention and of which kind are compatible with liberalism. Apart from practical problems with *laissez-faire*, the rise of socialist ideas imposed questions on states' role in economy. Socialist ideas influenced liberalism in two ways: first, many liberals were somehow impressed by socialist ideas. Second, the new liberal hegemony was built on the support from the middle class and the upper working class, both were usually open to socialist ideas which is why liberals feared to lose their power base to the socialist movements.

5.2.2.2 The Rise of Social Liberalism

In the mid-19th century, the social issue became the central topic. The answer of British liberals on the social issue was participation, *laissez-faire*, but also state intervenion were it seemed necessary. Liberal intellectuals like Mill made an effort to emphasize that certain interventions are compatible with liberal ideas; increasingly it was argued that interventions are necessary to form a society which seems readier for liberalism. Liberals' increasing interest in the social issue also had practical reasons: social movements being on the rise, liberals feared losing workers and the middle class to leftist groups. Groups supporting the working man's cause were founded all over Europe. Continental European social movements usually demanded an extensive redistribution of wealth and called for socialist revolutions.

In contrast, British social movements focused on economic participation and were more open for liberalism. Overall, most British social movements accepted the "inevitability of gradualness", were little interested in ideology and favored immediate social improvements over World Revolutions (Herrick 1944, p. 71). Unlike most continental European socialist groups, many British social movements did not suggest a principally antagonistic relation between capital and labour. *Beehive*, a trade union newspaper, considered that "capital formation was essential to working-class prosperity" (Sykes 1997, p. 72), because capital formation increases employment and wages. No doubt that social movements treated the status quo as unfair, antagonistic, and exploitative. However, most social movements were convinced that a fair, synergetic relation between capital and labour is possible. Many British trade unions were relatively open to *laissez-faire* (see for example Dicey 1905, p. 180). Doubtlessly, trade unions' openness for *laissez-faire* was often rather tactical to foster their claims in a *laissez-faire* dominated environment (Webb and Webb [1894] 1920, p. 293 ff.) Most intellectuals, the Parliament and the public opinion leaned toward *laissez-faire* (Dicey 1905; Crouch 1967; Jones and Aiken 1995). However, the British worker movement often had a pronounced puritan touch why they often favored self-help, freedom, and independency (Sykes 1997, p. 72 f.) over redistribution or socialist revolutions. Social movements' and trade unions' openness for coalitions with liberals shaped liberal parties.

Reaching out the hand to workers, the liberal Prime Minister Gladstone stressed that rising wages and better living condition for workers and the prosperity of the economy are good for both workers and capitalists, why there is no immanent conflict between the two classes (Steele 1991, p. 36). Hence, both social movements and liberals were convinced that the workers' situation must be improved and that an adequate economic participation of the working and middle class is possible without a fundamental system change: for Liberal Party leaders, a "union of class to class" or a "unity of classes" was possible because of the compatibility of workers' and bourgeoisie's interests (Sykes 1997, p. 69). However, many liberals of the mid-19th century were convinced that more than *laissez-faire* is needed to overcome social tensions and foster the participation of excluded classes.

5.2.3 Changing Money and Banking Laws

After Napoleon's defeat in 1815 the main legitimization of the suspension of convertibility vanished. Still, inconvertibility had its advocates, but the pressure on Parliament to reintroduce convertibility rose. A rather unusual coalition demanded the resumption: Fetter (1978, pp. 64–73) describes the pro-convertibility coalition as a consortium of the classical economics orthodoxy, banking enemies, radicals, and the general public. The spreading view that while the ordinary man suffers from inflation bankers live on the fat of the land (ibid., p. 67 f.) turned public opinion strongly against banks and credit flexibility. Banks were blamed for using the higher credit flexibility to sharply increase profits, while people suffer from inflation and frequent bank defaults. Tories were strongly criticized for their close ties with the Bank of England (ibid., p. 69 ff). Monetarists always rejecting the suspension of convertibility, political influence sharply raised as Old Toryism was on the retreat. David Ricardo became one of the most respected spokesmen of the convertibility camp. As maintained, he developed a widely recognized proposal for a metallic based paper currency, the Ingot Plan.

5.2.3.1 Reform of the Money System

From 1816 on, measures were taken to return to the gold standard at old par (Viner 1975, p. 172). When prices started to fall, the first critical voices were raised saying that the return to a gold standard at the old par would cause serious deflation, stagnation and unemployment. Attwood (1819, p. 41) and the Birmingham School criticized the Parliamentary committees saying they seem to believe that "farmers, and landlords, and labourers, was not at all affected by this reduction of 'transactions', [by the restoration of convertibility] which seems so harmless a thing." He warned that the return to the gold standard would harm entrepreneurs, farmers and workers. Fears from escalating deflation were dispelled by Ricardo who estimated a moderate deflation for the transitory time. Despite the warnings from the Birmingham Keynesians, in 1819 the Parliament voted with an overwhelming majority for the resumption of convertibility within two years. Hence, just eight years after the resumption of convertibility was rejected by a vast majority, it passed the Parliament with votes from all fractions.

What caused so many parliamentarians to change their mind? First, dissatisfaction with Bank of England's policy spread across party lines. Second, many former supporters of inconvertibility got convinced that note issuing needs clear rules and regulations. Third, Tories favored being united behind convertibility over splitting up the party into a convertibility camp and inconvertibility camp (Fetter 1978, p. 92 ff.). Fourth, inside and outside of the Parliament, the monetarists' influence steadily increased. Fifth, and most important, the war as the main legitimization for inconvertibility ended.

The resumption of convertibility was the first great monetarist victory of the 19th century: the Parliament followed monetarists' advice and inside and outside the Parliament many shared their view that the Bank of England and other financial actors used their privileges in their own vested interests, meanwhile harming the general well-being. Using their rising influence on political decisions and on the public opinion, monetarists were quite successful in spreading their view that high prices stem from note over-issuing.

> The discussions of the Bank Restriction period ended in the triumph of the simplest and crudest form of the quantity theory. There were few people remaining after 1819 [...] who denied that the quantity of money had any influence upon the price of gold or upon the exchange (Feavearyear 1931, p. 216).

Restating convertibility in accordance with Ricardo's Ingot Plan, the plan did not practically live up to its promises. Deflation was much more serious than estimated by Ricardo: Ricardo predicted that the resumption would cause a deflation of around 5%, and in reality Silberling's price index dropped from 136 in 1819 to 93 in 1830. Rampant deflation hushed many of Ricardo's former supporters; others openly joint the anti-Ricardo campaign. Many agreed—the general public, the press, many of his colleagues—that escalating deflation was Ricardo's fault (Viner 1975, pp. 174–185).

Rampant deflation triggered an intensive discussion about the relation between prices, economic prosperity, and employment and about the goals of money policy; economists of various schools agreed on the negative effects of deflation on economic prosperity and employment. Hence, escalating deflation evoked harsh criticism on the Act of 1819. Two groups were particularly hostile to the Act: representatives of industrial hubs and the landed aristocracy (Fetter 1978, pp. 73–79, 99–107). The landed aristocracy complained about rising real taxes and real debts and lamented that deflation further redistributes wealth from borrowers to lenders. Industrialists and workers blamed deflation for slower growth and unemployment. The heated monetary debates of the time were much about social justice and distribution: the opponents of the Ingot Plan considered that escalating deflation entails the unjust redistribution from the diligent to the lazy. Baring argued before the Parliament in 1821: "The effect [of the act of 1819] was, that the industrious were obliged to labour under difficulties, that the drones might live in the great affluence" (cited in Fetter 1978, p. 102). Despite the rising hostility against Ricardo's plan, its opponents failed to organize a Parliamentary majority for a re-examination of the Act from 1819 and were sedated by side payments (ibid., p. 99 ff). However, the deflation discussion was a harbinger of coming disputes within the liberal coalition; while classical economists and most liberal politicians were convinced that the reintroduction of convertibility was necessary and price stability should be the highest goal of money policy, industrialists and workers doubted that convertibility was also in their interests and demanded to shift goals more toward economic progress and employment.

As maintained, the persistent instability of the money system caused the Banking-Currency School debate. Principally following the monetarist tradition, the Currency School recognized that convertibility is insufficient to stabilize the money system. After two deep crises in 1836 and 1839 shook the financial markets again, the Currency School publishes dozens of papers analyzing the crises and clarifying their positions. The Currency School developed two main measurements to stabilize the financial system: first, granting a note-issuing monopoly for England and Wales—and maybe Ireland and Scotland—to the Bank of England. Second, the separation of the Bank of England into a note-issuing and a depositing department. In 1844, the Bank Charter Act passed the Parliament by an overwhelming majority. The Act reads much like a Currency School proposal: it granted the Bank of England a quasi note-issuing monopoly[2] and the bank was divided into a note-issuing and a banking department. The Bank of England was allowed to issue 14 million pounds against government securities and every additional note had to be covered with a 100% bullion reserve.

Given that the Bank Charter Act was among the most fundamental breaks in the history of British money legislation, it seems surprising that it passed so easily. Several reasons much weakened the opposition against the Act: private banking spokesmen protested at the Parliament when Peel presented the plan (ibid., p. 186), but the bankers' position was quite weak as many blamed them for recurrent crises. Revoking several privileges initially it seems surprising that the Bank of England remained relatively silent. Horsefield (1944) found that the Bank of England has strongly changed its mind from a total opposition, to a silent tolerance of the Act. Through a closer look, the Act was not that unfavorable for the Bank of England even if it withdrew important privileges: the bank was allowed to continue its ordinary banking business, the note-issuing monopoly further legitimizes its existence, and the bank was freed from being blamed for wrong money policies as a clear rule pretended its issuing policy. Private bankers lacking social support, the Bank of England remaining relatively silent, the Banking

[2]'Private Banks' were allowed to continue note issuing of the amount of 1844, but no issuing right was given to new banks, if banks went bankrupt, stopped issuing or merged with others, they lost-lost the right.

School was the only serious opposition against the Act: Tooke attacked the Act with all sound arguments against the Currency School and the Currency Principle. His conclusion was that the Act would destabilize financial markets rather than stabilize them (Smith 2011, pp. 188–197). Like Tooke, the second generation of the Birmingham School fully rejected the Act (Fetter 1978, p. 177). However, two main issues weakened the Banking School: first, traditionally much less influence than the Currency School, in the case of the opposition against the Bank Charter Act the Banking School in particular lacked support from other groups. Second, the Banking School was united in their opposition against the Act, but failed to reach an agreement on what else should be done instead to stabilize financial markets. The Bank Charter Act was the most important monetarist victory of the 19th century and strengthened its predominance. The Bank Charter Act institutionalized the central components of the monetarist money and central banking theory. The monopolization of note issuing, the depoliticization of issuing and the implementation of clear and transparent rules which determine the money policy were the central demands of mid-19th century monetarists. The Bank Charter Act was the monetarist central banking blueprint which was carried to other European countries.

5.2.3.2 Reform of the Banking System

Regulative change in the first half of the 19th century fundamentally shaped the British banking system. Two legislative changes were particularly important for the development of the British banking system: the joint-stock legislation and the permission of limited liabilities.

In 1825 and 1826, British financial markets were hit by deep financial crises. The crash of 1825 and 1826 had many reasons (Neal 1990) and it caused the bankruptcy of more than 60 country banks (Pressnell 1956, p. 443), heavy bullion outflows from the Bank of England, a deep recession, and that the public opinion turned strongly against banking. Both the general public and leading economists—in particular the Currency School—blamed country banks for the disturbances; "country bankers emerged as the main scapegoats, being held largely responsible for the crises" (Collins 2012, p. 17). Everywhere, stricter regulations were demanded.

> The events of the years immediately preceding had convinced a large part of the public to the need for such legislation [Act of 1826]. It simply required the event of 1825 to bring action. [...] With the losses from the failures of country banks and the growing resentment against the Bank of England, it was an easy task for a strong Government to put across its program. (Fetter 1978, p. 121)

As maintained, for almost three decades the money system and in particular note issuing dominated monetary discussions. With the crises of 1825 and 1826, the focus shifted towards the banking system: many economists, parliamentarists, and the general public became more interested in banking issues and demanded a regulative change for more stability. The banking system was usually considered as being strongly dominated by old corruption. Many blaming the banking elites for having caused the crises, the time for reformers had come to attack the banking elite and its privileges.

Country banks' defaults in particular affected their less wealthy customers. The ability of unlimited small note issuing was used by country banks to expand credit, also to less wealthy citizens, which caused a considerable credit boom (Feavearyear 1931, p. 217 f.). Country banks' opponents argued that banks' extensive issuing of small notes attract many poorer customers inexperienced in banking issues and therefore particularly affected by bank defaults. Economists liked Tooke (1826, p. 122) demanded the prohibition of small notes to protect poorer classes from banking crises. Already in 1818 a bill was introduced to prohibit the issuing of notes smaller than 5£, but failed due to country banks' opposition (Fetter 1978, p. 69). As the banking run spread, the Parliament had to act. Most parliamentarians held the country banks' extensive small note issuing accountable for the crises: "When Parliament met, opinion was nearly unanimous in condemning the small notes and the country banks" (Feavearyear 1931, p. 224). Country banks being unable to organize support for their case in a rather hostile environment, in 1826 the Parliament followed Took's advise and prohibited the issue of notes smaller than 5£.

The old banking elite being weakened by the crises and the rising criticism from the general public, economists and politicians, times seemed good for profound legal change. Country banks and the Bank of England being dominated by the old elites, the middle- and working-class fraction of the liberals demanded legal changes, which fostered their participation. Permitting joint-stock banks was expected to democratize banking because it would enable less wealthy citizens to also hold shares. Already in 1822 Joplin argued in the first version of his *General Principles of Banking*—which became in its later version the most influential joint-stock bank proposal—that Scottish joint-stock banks are much less prone to crises than English country banks, because they are able to absorb a much bigger equity base (see also the revised version; Joplin 1827, p. 1 ff.). Parnell (1827, p. 121) stated that "in order to establish in a country a sound system of banking, it is indispensably necessary, that care should be taken not to impose any legislative restrictions in the way of large bodies of partners associating together, to form joint-stock banking companies." Tooke as well, as the most famous and influential Banking School contributor, believed that joint-stock banks would stabilize financial markets (Smith 2011, p. 21). After 1826, country banks' low equity rates were in particular held accountable for the failure of banks. Important economists—like John Sinclair (1826, p. 98)—and influential politicians—like Lord Liverpool and Robert Peel (Cottrell and Newton 1998, p. 82)—became the main carriers of Joplin's joint-stock banking proposal. Prime Minister Lord Liverpool stated before the Parliament that Bank of England's joint-stock banking monopoly was outdated and demanded the issuing of joint-stock license also to other banks (Feavearyear 1931, p. 224). Conservatives like Liverpool and Peel openly arguing for joint-stock banks further legitimized the issue. However, the idea of joint-stock banks was mainly carried and promoted by the rising liberal middle class. According to Alborn (1998, pp. 85–115), middle-class representatives expected that joint-stock banking would democratizes the banking sector:

permitting the foundation of joint-stock banks should enabled poorer classes to form their own banks. Forming their own joint-stock banks was expected to free the middle and working class from their dependency on the gentry banking aristocracy: "Unlike gentry opponents of the state, who pinned their hopes for reform on the 'permanent' interests of landownership, middle-class republicans sought an alternative form of permanence by pooling their funds and manpower in self-governing clubs and society" (ibid., p. 93).

However, joint-stock banking was not considered a middle- and working-class project, but was expected to facilitate banking participation of all citizens: when country bankers attacked joint-stock banking proposals its advocate responded in the *Bankers' Magazine* that "joint-stock banks were not formed for the purpose of accommodating those already in affluent circumstances, and totally neglectful of the tradesman and poorer classes. Joint-stock banks are in a position to accommodate all grades of society" (cited in Alborn 1998, p. 85). Hence, it was expected that permitting to found banks with more than six shareholders would stabilize financial markets and democratize the banking sector.

In addition to the stabilization and democratization of financial markets, it was frequently argued that joint-stock banks would augment capital formation. For the classical capital theory, capital is notoriously scarce in capitalist economies. According to the classical banking theory, the absorption of idle capital and its supply to the economy, and hence loanable fund intermediation, is the banks' main function in capitalist economies. It was widely agreed that the banking system of the early 19th century was unsatisfactory: according to its opponents, banks were unable to absorb the huge idle reserves and lend large-scale to the rising industry. In particular banks' small equity capital was considered responsible for inadequate capital intermediation and their proneness to crises. Being restricted to six shareholders kept country banks' equity base small. Joplin (1827, p. 138 ff.) argued that in theory even a bank with a few shareholders and equity is not limited in its capital intermediation: the bank may lend what it attracts as deposits, independent from its equity base. But, he states that in practice banks cover losses from debt defaults by their equity. A bank with little equity compared to its outstanding loans is always in great danger of bankuptcy. Restricting banks to six shareholders much complicates the augmentation of the equity base. Hence, banks limited to six shareholders either lend out heavily and are therefore quite prone to crises or lend little and are therefore not beneficial to economic progress. Practically, frequent defaults and a small equity base prevented many from depositing at country banks why they lacked the means for lending on a big scale. The Bank of England was focused on government debt and little interested in private industry financing. Hence, in the early 19th century, England lacked banks able and willing to facilitate economic progress. "By 1822 the government had come to the conclusion [...] that the Bank of England's monopoly of joint-stock banking constituted a financial constrain to economic development" (Bowen and Cottrell 1997, p. 101).

Joint-stock banks appeared to be the ideal institutions to form and support a liberal capitalist economy: giving out many smaller shares enables poorer classes to participate in the banking sector and activates smaller savings. Theoretically able to attract an unlimited amount of shareholders and equity, capital was expected to enable joint-stock banks to lend on a very big scale to the rising industrial and mercantile enterprises. Parnell (1827, p. 121) argued: "The trade of banking is of such a nature, that it is scarcely possible for any but a very numerous body of partners to furnish a capital sufficiently large for carrying it on advantageously to the public."

Country banks had most to lose from the permission of joint-stock banks: allowing to found much bigger private banks seemed to outdate their business model. Realizing the danger of joint-stock banking, country bankers tried to organize the opposition: country bankers' counterattack was directed toward joint-stock banking proposals and the Bank of England (Liepmann 1933, p. 97 f.). However, the time was quite difficult for country banks why they failed to form a strong coalition against joint-stock banking. Country banks found no argument which would have calmed their opponents other than that "the prosperity of trade, the support of agriculture, the increase of general improvement, and the productiveness of the national revenue, are intimately connected with the existing system of banking" (From a country banker resolution transmitted to the First Lord of the treasury; cited in Gilbart 1837, p. 68). In particular country banks failed to argue why they should be less prone to crises in the future and what makes country banks the right banking institutions to support industrialization and economic progress.

In contrast, joint-stock banking advocates had strong arguments and most liberal economists, middle class and working class friendly politicians, and the public opinion on their side. The Banking Act of 1826 which permitted joint-stock banking easily passed the Parliament, also because its advocates managed to split up the opposition camp. Country banks and the Bank of England had a strong vested interest to defend its privileges and oppose the Act. However, Peel managed to erode Bank of England's opposition: the Act revoked Bank of England's joint-stock banking monopoly, but granted the bank the right to branches in the province which broke Bank of England's opposition (ibid., p. 81 ff.).

Shortly after the first joint-stock banks were founded, tougher regulation regarding the equity base and bank branching was demanded (Cottrell and Newton 1999, p. 88). However, in 1833 it was further deregulated as joint-stock banking was permitted within London. The Banking Act of 1826 permitted the foundation of note-issuing joint-stock banks outside greater London. Hence, the Act did not touch the center of the old financial elite: the Bank of England and the surrounding gentry financial businesses. For middle-class radicals, London was the financial Bastille which had to be stormed in order to overthrow the corrupt financial aristocracy: "By 1832 a new class of radical politicians and reform-minded clerks had set up shop in London and were anxious to support the new system of joint-stock banking" (Alborn 1998, p. 100). Driven by the "middle-class radicalism" (ibid., p. 92) of the time, advocates demanded the foundation of joint-stock banks elsewhere to gain "independence from the aristocratic circle of London financiers who hovered around the Bank of England and whom most new joint-stock banks suspected to be tainted with 'old-corruption'" (ibid., p. 87). Joblin questioned Bank of England's joint-stock banking monopoly by referring to an ambiguity in the banking legislation: holding the note-issuing monopoly for wider London meant that the Bank of England also had the joint-stock banking monopoly for London. Alternatively, Joblin argued that the legislation permits non-issuing joint-stock banking in London (Crick and Wadsworth 1936, p. 18). The Bank of England and the London banking dominating "noblemen, gentlemen, merchants and tradesmen" (Born 1977, p. 125) built a powerful block against the permission of joint-stock banking in London. However, the middle class promoting liberalism being on the rise, the Parliament followed Joblin's advise and permitted joint-stock banking in London: "Joplin's view [on joint-stock banking] had been confirmed by high legal opinion, and the Government, in an access of new-found radicalism, favoured a further curtailment of privilege" (Crick and Wadsworth 1936, p. 18). In addition to permitting joint-stock banking within London, the Banking Act of 1833 withdraw usury restrictions. The law which prohibited the Bank of England from interest rates above 5% was lifted for bills of exchange with a maturity less than three months: this meant the quasi-end of usury restriction.

The Acts of 1826 and 1833 were turning points in the development of the British, but also of the European banking system. Both Acts laid the foundation for banking concentration; the most visible and significant change in the structure of the European banking sectors. Prior to the joint-stock banking legislation, private banks other than the Bank of England were restricted to six shareholders; releasing the amount of shareholders paved the way for banks of a completely new size. At the time of World War I, the British banking sector was dominated by just five joint-stock megabanks. British joint-stock megabanks also became the blueprint for banking conglomerates in other European countries. As a consequence of the joint-stock banking permission, old-style country banks vanished: "the resultant legislation of 1826 marked the close of the era of private [country] banks, although they continued for many years to rival the joint-stock banks in the affections of the public" (Pressnell 1956, p. 507).

From a political perspective, the Acts of 1826 and 1833 were two great victories of the rising liberals: the Acts weakened the old financial corruption—the Bank of England, country banks and the London financial gentry—the foundation of joint-stock banks was expected to foster the economic participation of the middle and working class and facilitate credit to the rising industry. In addition, revoking privileges other than the note-issuing monopoly further pushed the Bank of England toward a classical monetarists central bank. Four issues facilitated the legislative change: first, the need for stabilizing financial markets; second, the crisis of 1825/1826; third, the idea that capital is scarce and investment presupposes saving; fourth, the general liberal hegemony.

Overall, the Acts of 1826 and 1833 strongly reflected liberals' central claims: breaking up economic privileges, reducing entire parries, fostering economic participation of all classes and protecting those in need. Permitting private joint-stock banking targeted the first three goals and the prohibition of small note issuing the last.

The three Acts—the limited liability Act 1855, the joint-stock companies Act (1856) and the companies Act (1862)—permitting limited liabilities to companies with more than seven owners were doubtlessly among those legislative changes with the most far-reaching consequences. Joint-stock banks had to wait for 1858, respectively 1879, until they also received the full right of limited liability shares. Prior to the Acts, shareholders were liable with more than their investment; limited liability reduced its liability to the invested capital. The Acts caused a fast rise in the number end length of joint-stock companies (Ireland 1984) and significantly shaped the British economic structure, in particular the banking sector.

Debates on unlimited and limited liabilities caused fundamental controversies on the nature of capitalism, the relation between capital and labor, justice, and democracy in capitalist societies. Battle lines on limited liabilities run through parties, professions and ideologies; "A close reading of the voluminous discussion of the first half of the 1850's does not suggest any clear-cut division of opinion between easily identifiable groups or economic interests" (Saville 1956, p. 431). According to Bryer (1997), supporters and opponents of limited liabilities may be found in almost all professions and classes: classical economists were divided as well. However, supporters of limited liabilities were particularly recruited from four main groups: wealthy London capitalists, liberal politicians, several socialist groups and parts of the classical economists. On the other side, the opposition stemmed from conservative parts of the Tories, provincial industrialists, bankers, lawyers and parts of the classical economics and socialists.

Supporters of limited liabilities built their arguments on the ideas of the classical capital theory, shareholder democracy, contract freedom, liberalism and social justice. Following the classical capital theory that capital is scarce, advocates of limited liabilities argued that restricted liability would increase people's willingness to invest: Cobden, one of the main supporters, stated: "What we wanted in this country was greater facility for the employment of capital—greater facilities for those possessing capital to employ it" (cited in Bryer 1997, p. 40 f). They argued that only wealthy people without anything to lose—usually persons of bad reputation—hold unlimited liability shares; permitting limited liability shares would attract capital from wealthy people with good reputation, the middle class and even workers with small savings. Left-wings and liberals considered that limited liabilities foster shareholder democracy, social justice and overcome the antagonism between capital and labor. Liberals expected that limited liabilities would enhance middle and working class's economic participation. According to the report of the Select Committee on the Law of Partnership (1851, p. xvii) "it is a great benefit to enable the middle and even the more thriving of the working classes to take shares in such investments, under the sanction and conjointly with their richer neighbours." Left-wing supporters of limited liabilities went even further and hoped that the working and middle class would pool small savings to form their own joint-stock companies; it was expected that permitting limited liability shares would enable the working class, with the guide of the middle class, to build co-operations to improve their communities (Loftus 2002, p. 100).

John Steward Mill doubted that many workers would take part in joint-stock companies. However, according to him, workers would take advantage of limited liabilities due to the formation of capital and the easing of credit:

> I think that the great value of a limitation of responsibility, as relates to the working classes, would be not so much to facilitate the investment of their savings, not so much to enable the poor to lend to those who are rich, as to enable the rich to lend to those who are poor (Mill [1850] 1967, p. 409).

Others went even further and argued that big limited liability companies overcome the antagonism of capital and labor as both shareholders and workers have a strong interest in the best outcome. "Limited liability was used by social reformers to promote a vision of social harmony through consensual market relations based on a free and equal (male) partnership between capital and labor" (Loftus 2002, p. 102).

Debates on fair risk—how much an investor should lose in the worst case—induced a long-lasting discussion on the personalization of capital and the role of the Schumpeterian entrepreneur in the economy. Supporters of limited liabilities demanded what Bryer (1997) calls the "enfranchisement of capital" motivated by their "vision of social capital." They argued that limited liabilities emancipates capital from its personal owner. In the form of limited liability shares, capital develops a anonymized, self-sufficient, independent existence by following capitalist rules independently from its immediate personal owner. The elimination of the Schumpeterian entrepreneur evoked harsh criticism from old-style Smithians and lawyers. Already in the 18th century Adam Smith was critical of joint-stock conglomerates, the division between capital ownership and management and the limitation of entrepreneurs liability (Djelic 2013). In line with Smith, John Ramsay McCulloch and Thomas Took in particular criticized limited liabilities.

For liberals, the freedom of contract was a strong argument for limited liabilities. Liberals argued that if freemen agree on the limitation of liability, the state should not intervene. In a speech before the Parliament, Robert Lowe stated: "My object at present is not to urge the adoption of limited liability. I am arguing in favour of human liberty—that people may be permitted to deal how and with whom they choose, without the officious interference of the State" (House of Commons 1856, p. 131).

As maintained, limited liabilities had many opponents: classical economists fearing for entrepreneurial capitalism; socialists fearing that the economy would become more prone to crises (Djelic 2013); industrialists fearing the competition of new joint-stock companies; traders worrying that limited liabilities may shatter British traders‘ reputation; and bankers opposing limited liabilities because it diminished the collateralization of loans. However, once again it has to be emphasized that support and opposition to limited liabilities runs through professions and classes: analyzing opinions of Parliamentary witnesses Taylor (2006, p. 151) showed that half of the merchants and manufacturers supported and opposed limited liabilities, while the vast majority of bankers opposed it. Despite the strong opposition, after heavy discussions inside and outside the Parliament, the limited liability Act (1855), the joint-stock companies Act (1856) and the companies Act (1862) passed the Parliament.

In the joint-stock company Act (1856), banks and insurance companies were explicitly excluded from the right to issue limited liable shares: concerns about the deposits' safety caused the Parliament to prohibit limited liabilities to banks (Alborn 1998, p. 129). However, several influential economists, like Walter Bagehot and others in the orbit of *The Economist,* requested the extension of limited liabilities to banks and insurance companies. Their main arguments were much the same as the ones outlined for other limited liabilities: unlimited liability banks only attract shareholders with little to lose, hence usually people of poor reputation. Able to attract more capital, limited liability shares make banks more stable and safer for depositors due to their sounder equity base. On the other side, opponents of limited liability banks argued that unlimited liability shareholders are less willing to accept banks' escalating risk-taking (Hickson and Turner 2003). However, in 1858 and later in 1879 the full right of limited liability share issuing was granted to joint-stock banks. In hindsight, the limited liability Acts were as much a turning point for the British banking system as the Act from 1826 and facilitated the concentration of the banking sector.

The Acts of 1819, 1826, 1833, 1844, 1858 and 1879 are landmarks of a more general trend: the revokation of economic privileges, hence the attack on the old corruption. The legal changes were mostly victories of the rising liberals and of classical monetarists. Overall, the legal changes followed three main logics: laissez fair, participation and monetarism. However, rather than general deregulation, regulation was turned upside down: at the beginning of the 19th century the size and business of private banks was heavily restricted by Bank of England's privileges, but note issuing was almost unregulated. At the beginning of the 20th century, the picture looks completely different: note issuing was strongly regulated, but the rest of the banking business was dominated by *laissez-faire*; the size of banks, the number of shareholders, mergers, their activities and capital base was de facto unregulated. Granting a note-issuing monopoly to the Bank of England and dividing the bank into a note-issuing and banking department was a victory of the monetarists over their Keynesian opponents. Permitting joint-stock banking was in particular the victory of the liberal coalitions between the bourgeoisie, middle and upper working class over the old corruption. Revoking banking privileges for the old elites was a significant strike against the economic power base of the old corruption. At the same time, banking *laissez-faire* failed to live up to many promises: neither the antagonism between capital and labor was overcome, nor the participation of poorer classes facilitated.

For the liberal ideal of a competitive economy in which no one has market power, permitting joint-stock banks issuing limited liability shares became a significant boomerang effect. As maintained, at the time of World War I only a handful of joint-stock megabanks dominated the banking sector of the British empire. However, despite the strong concentration, governments shied away from breaking up the trust and introducing further regulations. Several reasons kept the government from curbing the concentration of banking despite all warnings from various directions: for many liberals, megabanks were the outcome of a fair market process in which governments should not intervene. Megabanks were the only financial institutions big enough to finance capitalist megaprojects like railway building or the rising heavy industry. To develop and exploit the colonies, governments needed the megabanks' financial support. America, France and Germany increasing challenging Britain's economic supremacy, governments feared worsening the domestic economy's international competitiveness by regulating the banking sector more heavily. In addition, it was argued that megabanks would enhance Britain's capital formation by attracting foreign capital. Hence, when the concentration of the banking sector seemed to endanger the economy and politics, governments shied away from heavier regulation.

5.2.4 The Intensification of Imperialism

Imperialism was among the few issues which was supported by politicians and groups of all political colour. From conservatives, liberals, to working-class lefties, many feared losing economic competitiveness and political influence. Conservatives fearing the decline of the empire, liberals the anti-liberal continental European takeover and workers unemployment; for many imperialism was part of the solution for Britain's most urgent problems. Intellectual liberal, social Darwinist, missionary and many more arguments in favor of liberalism were produced, but the main reason was economy: the widespread belief that imperialism may help solve Britain's economic problems caused various different groups to support colonialism.

As maintained, in the 19th century, the liberals' position on imperialism significantly changed: old liberals mainly rejected imperialism; mid-19th century new liberals mostly legitimized and supported imperialism as necessary and moral. The shifting position on imperialism was in particular visible in Britain: while Adam Smith, Jeremy Bentham and James Mill clearly rejected imperialism, liberal intellectuals and governments of the later 19th century were quite open, partly euphoric, of imperialism. For new liberal intellectuals, imperialism was an economic and political necessity, but also a moral duty to develop new countries and enlighten the savages. In addition to intellectual arguments, for liberals imperialism was necessary to protect the British liberalism from German and French anti-liberal tendencies. Highly influenced by social Darwinist views, liberals believed that Britain needs to be great and powerful to protect the liberal homeland from authoritarian and anti-liberal continental European forces; for British liberals, Britain was the protecting power of liberalism that spreads the idea of the free man and acts in the "interest of humanity" (Sullivan 1983, p. 612).

Colonialism was considered necessary to keep up with the French and the German; the only empires able to conquer the savages were considered first-class world powers, which may legitimately raise the aspiration to form a world hegemony. Britain was accustomed to be the world's most powerful empire economically, politically and in terms of the military. The rise of Germany, France and in particular America strongly challenged Britain's position. Restoring the greatness of the nation and the military race with Germany (Chamberlain 1989, p. 156) legitimized British imperialism for groups without strong colonial interests. Hobson (1902), who draws a close connection between the interest of capital and colonialism, argues that "non-economic factors of patriotism, adventure, military enterprise, political ambition, and philanthropy" are the "motor-power of imperialism," but "finance manipulates the patriotic forces which politicians, soldiers, philanthropies and traders generate." Hence, European empires' battle for supremacy pushed the British colonialism beyond economic, military and political reasonability.

Frequently it was argued that the ones with the Bible in their hand were the most notorious and fanatic supporter of imperialism. Johnson (2003, p. 99 ff.) shows that the relation between British missionaries and colonialists was rather difficult: pleased with the support and protection, missionaries frequently criticized the colonial administration and the British landlords for their brutality. Porter (1999) showed that colonial administration supported missionaries if it was in their interest, but there was no general close relation between missionaries and the colonial administration. However, parts of the Church openly supported colonialism and demanded a further extension of the empire.

Conservative arguments like that the criminal and rebellious surplus of the population may be deported to colonies, that imperialism sustains Britain's position against the challengers Germany and France, and colonialism fosters militarism (c.f. Hobson 1902, p. 119 ff.) and social Darwinist views that colonialism is part of the survival of the fittest (Johnson 2003, p. 214) were present throughout the 19th century. Like elsewhere, British conservatives were enthusiastic supporters of imperialism, dominated institutions like the Imperial Federation League and yielded important political advocates of imperialism like Benjamin Disraeli (Leach 2015, p. 67 ff; Cain and Hopkins 2016, p. 202 ff.). However, conservative arguments for imperialism were not the dominant reasons for Britain's colonial expansion.

Quite important for Britain's colonial expansion was the widespread belief that imperialism was an economic necessity. Economic arguments caused many from the rising bourgeoisie, the middle class and even the working class to support imperialism. In addition, gentleman capitalists were notorious supporters of colonialism due to economic reasons. It was widely believed that the economic slowdown of the second half of the 19th century was caused by over-supply and restrained demand. Economic difficulties fostered the foundation of a strong coalition supporting and promoting colonialism. Two main issues were the driving force behind the coalition: first, the widespread belief that over-supply caused the long-lasting economic slowdown and second, the abundance of capital and the shortage of sound investment possibilities.

The Fuel Revolution sharply increased industrial production. Unable to sell the fast rising amount of industrial goods on domestic markets, industrializing countries increasingly looked abroad. Trade barriers of many European countries and the rise of new competitors like the USA worsened the over-supply problem. Developing new markets for the fast rising industrial product was considered the way out of the over-supply crisis. Many European countries restricting foreign trade, colonialism seemed the only way to find new markets for domestic products (White et al. 2010, p. 135). Sir Frederick Lugard (1893, p. 585) put the industrial argument for imperialism in a nutshell when he stated:

> As long as our policy is one of free trade, we are compelled to seek new markets; for old ones are being closed to us by hostile tariffs, and our great dependencies, which formerly were the consumers of our goods, are now becoming our commercial rivals. It is inherent in a great colonial and commercial empire like ours that we go forward or go backward. To allow other nations to develop new fields, and to refuse to do so ourselves, is to go backward; […] We owe to the instincts of colonial expansion of our ancestors those vast and noble dependencies which are our pride and the outlets of our trade today; and we are accountable to posterity that opportunities which now present themselves of extending the sphere of our industrial enterprise are not neglected, for the opportunities now offered will never recur again.

Facing raising competition from abroad and increasing difficulties to sell the fast rising industrial products, many industrialists became notorious supporters of imperialism. The prospect to develop new markets for their goods and receive cheaper raw materials was tempting for struggling industrialists.

Britain's long history as trading hub yielded a quite wealthy and influential group of traders. The fast extension of overseas trade was also owed to the colonial extension of the empire. The Empire's support in exploring new and protecting old trade routes became even more important as continental European countries increasingly protected their home markets with trade barriers and competition for profitable trade routes increased. Traditionally, merchants notoriously supported colonialism to maintain their most profitable business, overseas trade (Cain and Hopkins 1993, p. 42 ff.).

As maintained, many Marxists like Hilferding ([1910] 1955) and Lenin ([1917] 1999), but also non-Marxist like Hobson (1902) draw a close connection between the concentration and abundancy of capital and imperialism. According to them, falling interest rates on investments caused the financial aristocracy to demand the conquest of new colonies to develop new markets for the abundant capital. Britain's abundance of capital increasingly challenged financial markets, in particular the banking sector. Like outlined the diplomat, politician and colonist Edward Gibbon Wakefield was one of the first who openly argued that Britain faces the problem of too much capital. Sending the capital abroad to the colonies was the obvious solution to Wakefield. Facing increasing domestic and foreign competition, British megabanks believed that only fast growing banks would survive. To grow, banks had to attract shareholders and depositors with high dividends and interest rates, which became quite difficult in an environment of falling interest rates. Facing falling interest rates, British megabanks were grateful for opportunities to invest the idle money more profitable elsewhere.

Reinterpreting the theses of the close connection between financial capitalism and imperialism Cain and Hopkins (1986, 1987; 1993) argued that gentleman capitalists were the driving force behind British imperialism. As maintained according to them released by the decreasing importance of agriculture, the progenies of the old aristocracy entered the service sector in particular the financial market'. Dominating the financial markets, gentlemen investors were particularly affected by falling domestic interest rates. When domestic private and public investments became scarce and unprofitable "a large proportion of these savings was moved into similar investments abroad" (Cain and Hopkins 1987, p. 3). At home, protected by the domestic laws abroad, investors relied on the goodwill and power of the foreign government to enforce investor rights. Increasingly facing the competition of French and German investors in Europe, British financial institutions escaped the competition by entering far off territories (Feis 1930, p. 4 f.). Extending overseas investments, financial institutions needed the military and political presence of the motherland to enforce their rights. Due to the fast increasing overseas investments, the "City of London, the institutional hub of the southern 'moneyed class' [...] was the outstanding beneficiary of the open economy" (Cain and Hopkins 1987, p. 4). The City's 'financial institutions' and in particular the joint-stock megabanks "spread London's influence across the globe" (ibid.). At the same time, the governments needed the financial institutions, in particular megabanks, to finance the development and exploitation of the colonies: half of the huge British foreign investment flowed into colonies, financing infrastructure, agricultural and industrial projects (Feis 1930, pp. 3–32). Due to the coincidence of vested interests, a strong coalition between gentleman investors and governments promoted colonialism. Hence, the governments' need for financial support and the banks' need for profitable investment opportunities caused a:

> complex and sometimes uneasy partnership between bankers and governments. The banks were inclined, for purely commercial reasons, to strike up cosmopolitan alliances which could embarrass their political patrons [...] Governments occasionally forced their financial backers into international schemes against their will, pushed them further than their commercial instincts would have taken them [...however] financiers and governments needed each other's support. Bankers could not raise funds profitably or use them effectively on these uncertain frontiers without the backing of the state. Governments could not hope to create the infrastructure which would provide the conditions for spontaneous flows of capital and trade, and enhance Britain's power and prestige, without the means provided by the money brokers and their connexions in the City (Cain and Hopkins 1987, p. 12).

Suffering from rampant unemployment, the working class hoped that exports to colonies would bring back jobs and open an exit option if things get worse. For working-class advocates, imperialism was a "bread and butter question" (Chamberlain 1989, p. 148). As maintained, most British working-class advocates were less interested in big revolutions, new political orders, international solidarity than in immediate improvements of workers' living conditions. High unemployment and fears that the situation may get worse dominated the British working-class political position. The Corn Law debates cemented the opinion in the population that protectionism means expensive bread, while free trade preserves economic prosperity, employment and social harmony. The working class shared the view that colonialism ensures free trade, develops new markets for

British products and therefore overcomes unemployment and low wages. Lord Mayor expressed what was widely believed by many working- and middle-class representatives:

> It is the continual growth of our population at the same time that our trade and industry does not grow in proportion, and if we want our trade and industry to grow we must find new markets for it. […] unless we can find new countries which will be free to take our goods you may be quite satisfied that lack of employment will continue to be one of the greatest of social evils (ibid., p. 156).

British workers' openness for imperialism divided them further from continental European socialist movement. Engles wrote to Kautsky:

> You ask me what the English workers think about colonial policy. Well, exactly the same as they think about politics in general: the same as the bourgeois think. There is no workers' party here, you see, there are only conservatives and liberal-radicals, and the workers gaily share the feast of England's monopoly of the world market and the colonies (Marx and Engels [1847–1894] 1972, p. 57).

Hence, overall, in particular in the second half of the 19th century, governments were under enormous pressure to pursue colonialism. For governments, colonialism was a double-edged sword: on the one hand, colonialism gave governments legitimacy by satisfying many groups' economic interests and nationalist sentiments. On the other hand, colonialism was extremely expensive and increasingly caused problems of public financing. Unable to cover all costs, governments were in need of potent private finances to develop and exploit the captured territories.

5.2.5 British Private Banks: From the Late 18th Century to World War I

As outlined, private banking increased steadily in the 17th and early 18th century. However, the period from the late 18th century to World War I was pivotal for the development of the British banking system. As maintained, around mid-18th century banking was still a relatively small business. At the beginning of the 20th century, British banking was a multibillion pound business, dominated by a few international active megabanks and the Bank of England, which became the central bank of Britain. Decades of heavy acquisitions and mergers generated a handful of megabanks. During the 19th and early 20th century, banking activities—the amount of bank offices, deposits and assets—fast increased (Cottrell 1980, p. 196 ff.). Dominating the banking system at the beginning of the 19th century, at the end of it smaller banks still existed, but became relatively unimportant. Rising domestic and foreign competition and falling domestic profit rates caused British megabanks to increasingly look abroad for profitable investment opportunities.

During the British Industrial Revolution, usually dated from mid-18th to around mid-19th century, the demand for banking services increased steadily. Several factors fostered the deepening of banking. As maintained, banking steadily lost its sinfulness: for classical economists lending against interest payments is essential for economic progress and desirable rather than sinful. Morally innocuous, even aristocratic capital entered the banking sector, mostly absorbed by gentleman investors. Industrialization and increasing interregional trade steadily increased the demand for banking services. Urbanization, industrialization and the shift from subsistence to wage labor economy brought banking services to ordinary people; what Crick and Wadsworth (1936, p. 42) considered the "rapid democratization of banking service." Workers were increasingly payed in banknotes and deposited wages and their small savings with banks. Changing agricultural production, industrialization and increasing interregional trade necessitated the extension of many banking services. The industry and agriculture demanded short- and medium-turn loan for raw materials, wages, seeds and tools and banknotes for payments like wages and long-term investments for machinery and land. Extending interregional trade sharply increased the demand for short-term merchant credit against exchange bills and banknotes exchange. Hence, banking was overall popularized in the early 19th century as even ordinary people got in contact with banks and it extended due to industrialization and interregional trade:

> economic development called for more advanced [...] finical arrangements. Here, the commercial banker played a central role: in the provision of credit, media of exchange and remittance facilities; as well as providing the more traditional service as a safe repository for valuables (Collins 2012, p. 12).

The rising demand for banking activities caused a banking boom and a significant increase in the number of banks: in 1750 not more than 50 banks existed in England, until 1825 the number increased to 600 to 900 banks (Cameron 1967b, p. 20; Collins 2012, p. 64 ff.). In mid-18th century banking was dominated by smaller private London banks and the Bank of England: the former offered a wide range of banking services to wealthy customers, the latter was focused on public debt. The extension of banking in the late 18th and early 19th century stemmed from the fast rising number of country banks. Industrialization, changing agricultural production and interregional trade augmented the demand for banking outside London. According to Pressnell (1956), the rising country banks became the bankers of the growing industry, the changing agriculture, regional governments and in particular merchants.

Country banks thrived in the specific situation of rising demand for banking services and the legal boundaries of the time: no other bank than the Bank of England was allowed to have more than six shareholders why just small banks emerged. Because Bank of England notes were hardly used outside London for ordinary transactions, country bank' notes covered the increasing demand for notes. Unlike the Bank of England, country banks also offered small notes that were used in many transactions why even ordinary people got in contact with banknotes. In addition, country banks offered a wide range of banking activities and granted, in particular, short- and medium-term lending. The inconvertibility of Bank of England notes was the fuel of country banks' lending as it indirectly increased banks' credit elastic. Private London banks became country banks' main gatekeeper to the London financial market: London banks used their close ties to provincial banks to connect country banks with the London international market for capital and banking services. Beside its quasi-monopoly for public debt banking, the Bank of England became the main reserve institution for private banks where they stored assets to underpin their note issuing and credit granting.

The banks' importance for England's industrialization was widely discussed. Marx, quoted above, draws a close link between Britain's industrialization and the extension of banking. Others question the banks' importance for the industrialization of England. According to Gerschenkron's (1962) banking was much less important for industrialization of the early developers (England) than for late developers (Germany, France etc.). He (1962, p. 14) stated that "The industrialization of England had proceeded without any substantial utilization of banking for long-term investment purposes." Three main arguments were outlined for why the rising industry was not dependent on banks: first, at the beginning of the industrialization, techniques were not capital intensive. When industries became more fix-capital intensive they had already accumulated the capital necessary for bigger investments (Pollard 1964; Gerschenkron 1962). Second, the British industry was less fix-capital intensive than is usually believed (Pollard 1964; Sokoloff 1984). Third, British financial markets were highly developed; industries found other ways to borrow (Cottrell 1980, p. 244). Looking at banks' balance sheets shows that banks granted a lot of short-term credit to merchants and industries, but few for long-term investment. On the active side of the balance sheets banks held some cash, many short-term assets like exchange bills from merchants and other short time lending, but hardly any long-term investment (Collins 2012, pp. 103–114). On the passive side of the balance sheet deposits increased fast (Cameron 1967b, p. 42; Collins 2012, pp. 92–97).

When the demand for banking services sharply increased in the late 18th and early 19th century, the legal restrictions defined by the Act of 1707 determined the development of the banking system. The Act granted the Bank of England a note-issuing monopoly for wider London and the exclusive right to have more than six shareholders. Hence, banks outside wider London were permitted to issue notes, but all banks other than the Bank of England were restricted to maximum six shareholders. In the early 19th century the banking sector was blamed by liberals for being a stronghold and the cash cow of the old corruption, a system of privileges and quasi-monopolies which strengthened the dominance of the old elites, maintained the exclusion of poorer classes and contributed little to the industrialization of the country. Liberals' assessment was maybe exaggerated, but correct in principle: the development of the entire banking system was largely determined by Bank of England's privileges, most country banks held quasi-monopolies for their region which they protected by their banking policy and close ties with regional governments, and London financial markets were predominantly in the hands of the gentry. In addition, banks were blamed for being prone to crises and not helpful for the industrialization of the country.

The banking Acts of 1826 and 1833 were direct attacks on the banking elites and a major setback for country banks. Reintroducing convertibility in 1821 indirectly reduced private banks' credit elasticity. As maintained, many blamed country banks for their proneness to crises and for having dragged poorer classes into crises by issuing small notes that were also used by less wealthy citizens. Following the suggesting of many liberal economists, the prohibition of notes smaller than 5£ deeply affected country banks' credit business, since much credit was granted by small notes. However, the permission of joint-stock banking by the Acts of 1826 and 1833 had less immediate, but far-reaching consequences for country banks. Country banks' success was based on the legal restrictions which prohibited the foundation of superior competitors: a system of small regional banks unable to lend bigger amounts for a long-term and all issuing their own notes may seem inefficient from an economic perspective, but due to the legal restrictions of the time, little else was possible. Permitting joint-stock banking, the Acts of 1826 and 1833 fundamentally challenged country banks by allowing the foundation of banks that seemed more competitive: many bankers feared that their small banks with a handful of shareholders are not competitive against the new joint-stock banks with unlimited shareholders. Despite small immediate effects, the Acts of 1826 and 1833 were turning points in the history of the British and Europe banking system;

> with hindsight it can be seen that the joint-stock bank Act of 1826 laid the legal foundation for the emergence of the modern form of bank – a bank whose corporate structure and large capital resource enabled it to build up an extensive national, indeed international, business (Collins 2012, p. 10).

The Acts caused the slow but steady destruction of country banks, which were replaced by joint-stock megabanks.

As maintained, it was argued that permitting joint-stock banking and limited liabilities would make the banking sector less prone to crises, democratize banking and breakup the dominance of the old elites over banking and would yield a new banking system more able and willing to support the rising industry. Legitimized by noble arguments, the Acts permitting joint-stock banking and issuing limited liability shares prepared the ground for one of the heaviest banking concentration in history. Not competitive against the newly founded joint-stock banks, most country banks and small London banks merged with rising joint-stock banks. From around 600 to 900 in 1825, the number of banks decreased to around 70 at the beginning of World War I. At the early 20th century several big joint-stock banks merged to five megabanks (the big five) who dominated the entire British banking sector (Collins 2012, p. 78 ff.). The big five founded several thousand branches in the whole country and elsewhere (ibid., p. 74 ff.). Permitted to stabilize the banking sector, it seems that branching joint-stock banks were less prone to crises (Crick and Wadsworth 1936, p. 38; Collins 2012, p. 81 ff.). However, just looking at the frequency of banking crises is misleading. Even if crises became less frequent, the concentration of banking entailed a tremendous potential risk: the big five were too big to fail, but also too big to save. Their advocates expected that joint-stock banks would be more willing and able to support the rising industry. Gerschenkron considered that banks played a minor role for the industrialization of England. Other contributions showed that joint-stock banks' long-term investments were much bigger that often thought (Cameron 1967b, p. 52 ff.; Cottrell 1980, p. 237). Maybe the strongest argument for joint-stock banking was that it would breakup old-corruptions' dominance over the banking sector. Bringing down the old banking system and its profiteers, the new banking system yielded a much more influential and exclusive banking elite than the old system. Once introduced to overcome monopolization and privileges, the rise of joint-stock banks hardly dismounted privileges and market power; quite the contrary. The oligopolization of the banking market, which concentrated much of the financial power in the hands of a few bankers strongly, increased the influence of joint-stock megabanks. Hence, never before was the entire banking power more concentrated than at the beginning of the 20th century.

In most European countries, the banking system was concentrated in the second half of the 19th century. Increasingly, French, German and British megabanks competed over the most lucrative investment opportunities. Falling interest rates on investment and the economic slowdown intensified the international competition between banks. Apart from the foreign, also the domestic competition steadily increased: British megabanks competed over market shares, the remaining smaller banks over further merges and over deposits and equity capital. Megabanks were convinced that only fast growing institutes will survive difficult times. To grow, banks needed to attract equity and deposits. Competing with each other and other joint-stock companies over equity capital and deposits, banks offered relatively high interest rates to absorb enough capital. Under pressure in an environment of falling interest rates on investments, megabanks increasingly went abroad to develop new profitable investment opportunities. Feis (1930, p. 5) estimated that at the beginning of the 20th century around half of British savings were invested abroad; many of them by megabanks. Facing increasing competition in Europe from French and German banks, British capital flowed into empires oversea departments. As maintained, due to their need for lucrative investment opportunities international active banks became silent collaborators of the British imperial ambitions. Britain's megabanks had nothing else in mind than their profit rate when they strongly extend business to smaller European countries and the oversea colonies. It was the coincidence of megabanks' and governments' goals which brought them together. Megabanks were heavily in need for foreign assets. The government needed strong economic partners for their colonial ambitions and to maintain their power within Europe. Megabanks were quite important organizations for the economic exploitation of the colonies and the closer economic connection with the homeland. Bonin (2014, p. 1) calls the extension of banking to colonized areas part of "softer forms of colonialism and imperialism." According to Kawamura (2015, p. 179), "the banks soon became an indispensable part of the British empire" by facilitating trade between the Asian colonies and the British homeland.

When the big five emerged from mega-merges, the general public and parts of the Parliament increasingly worried about the monopolization of the banking business and the power of megabanks. The governmental Colwyn Committee investigating banking concentration found that the concentration reduced competition among banks and concentrated too much power in the hands of a few banks (Newton 2003, p. 146). Despite the warnings from various sides, the Parliament refused to take measurements against banking concentration: "there was no serious attempt at anti-trust legislation in Britain until after the Second World war" (Collins 2012, p. 80). Several reasons may be found for Parliaments reluctance: still adhering to *laissez-faire*, the concentration was considered a side effect of the survival of the fittest. According to their liberal *laissez-faire* ideology, the fittest should not be punished by state interventions: "As in other markets, concentration in banking benefited from the *laissez-faire* attitude adopted by successive British governments to the rise of oligopolies and cartels" (ibid.). Despite ideological reasons, several political and economic arguments were produced for non-interference. Megabanks were considered the only ones fit enough to compete with rising German banks; "The rapid increase in the size of industrial and banking units on the continent, more particularly in Germany, injected a sense of patriotic necessity into the situation" (Crick and Wadsworth 1936, p. 40). However, due to its close relation to America, it was not openly expressed that Britain particularly feared American banks' competition (Born 1977, p. 134). Joint-stock bankers argued that big banks are better capable to lend large sums to big-scale industries and that they are more suited to absorb idle capital in surplus areas to invest it in capital scarce regions (Newton 2003, p. 147) also convinced politicians and economists. In addition, governments needed the financial support of megabanks for their colonial ambitions. Capital exports became pivotal for the development and therefore for the economic exploitation of conquered colonies and for overcoming the domestic capital oversupply: British megabanks played an important role for capital exports and oversea investments (Feis 1930, pp. 3–32). Hence, several arguments were produced to legitimize the size and power of British megabanks and keep the government from regulating the banking sector more heavily.

5.2.5.1 Country Banks: Fast Rise and Slow Fall

Around 1750 there existed between 50 and 70 banks in England; only a handful outside London. In the 1780 s there were around 100 country banks, in the 1800s between 300 and 400 and the number peaked around 600 to 900 in 1825 (Cameron 1967b, p. 24 ff.). Geographically, banking was quite unequally distributed, but reached most English regions around mid-19th century (ibid., p. 26 f.). Usually, country banks were relatively small: on average, country banks had three partners and an average equity of just 10.000£ (Pressnell 1956, p. 226). Their small equity base strongly restricted the size of banking: deposits, note issuing and intermediation. However, the total size of country banking was substantial: in 1825 country banks' equity capital was, at least, around 6 million pounds, much more than the 2,5 million of the London private banks, other than the Bank of England (Cameron 1967b).

For Cameron (ibid., p. 24) early country banking was facilitated by three issues: remittance facilitation; the rising demand for intermediation; the need for currency. According to Pressnell (1956: pp. 45–74) the first, which includes usual trade and production-related transfers, the money business with London and government revenue collection, was by far the most important and mostly in the hands of merchant bankers. The second was dominated by money scriveners: their main business was to raise money in the region and in London for local governments, local joint-stock companies and farm mortgages. Industrial bankers emerged from the need of currency to pay wages and raw materials. Started as a secondary business "only as the scale of the financial side of their business grew did the eighteenth-century industrialist, merchant, or scrivener, move more fully into banking" (Collins 2012, p. 14).

When industrialization took off, no widely accepted means of payment was available to cover industry's needs to pay for raw materials and wages. Coins were scarce and other means of payments like exchange bills were not accepted by workers (Pressnell 1956, pp. 12–74). Lacking alternatives, industrialists started to give out their own notes: "Given the condition of the currency during the Industrial Revolution [...] private individuals endeavoured to fill a gap left by the failure of the Mint and of the Bank of England to supply money of everyday need" (ibid., p. 136). Some industrialists becoming professional bankers and other country banks also starting to issue bigger and smaller notes, country banks' notes became the first banknotes widely used in transactions of almost all classes. However, the note system had several shortcomings: notes were usually just accepted in the region of the country bank. Two main reasons strongly restricted the territory: most country banks had a quasi issuing and banking monopoly for their region. To defend their regional central bank position they rejected all other notes. Second, notes were not secured by any authority—not by the general government nor by the local one—hence holding notes was risky and people did not trust in notes of banks from other regions (c.f. Liepmann 1933, pp. 91–95). Inadequate for interregional trade, notes of country banks lost much of their importance as economic activities became increasingly supra-regional. Economic booms often caused country bank founding boom, but many of the new banks usually went bankrupt in times of crises (Collins 2012, p. 15 f.). Receiving wages and holding savings in notes, in particular poorer classes were often deeply affected by banking failures, which caused much criticism of country banks.

Bank of England's privileges defined in the Act of 1708 prohibited the foundation of bigger banks and therefore paved the way for the country bank system with its hundreds of small autonomous banks all over England and Wales. The Bank of England showing little interests in extending deeper into the private sector—private banking seemed risky and not quite profitable, and the regulative boundaries of branching further complicated bank's private banking outside London—country banks closed the gap. Country banks were also promoted by strong supporters: industrialists in need of notes and short-term credit, merchants to exchange money and for short time trade credits, the landed classes in need of mortgages and regional governments searching for funds principally supported country banks. In the bullion controversy, both sides supported or at least did not oppose country banks: bullionists argued that country banks support economic progress, but are not to be blamed for over-issuing. Anti-bullionists usually followed Smith and argued that an over-issuing is impossible for the Bank of England as well as country banks.

However, when cascades of country bank failures erupted, financial markets (see Pressnell 1956, pp. 470–500), the public opinion and classical economists turned against them: both blamed country banks for the deep crisis of 1825/1826. Country banks used all their political power to combat the Banking Act of 1826, but were too short of good arguments to convince the Parliament. The Banking Act of 1826 gave the country banks two blows, the permission of joint-stock banks and the prohibition of issuing notes smaller than 5£, from which country banks never recovered. Bank of England's attempt to curb regional note issuing and the increasing issuing competition from new joint-stock banks pushed back notes of country banks (Liepmann 1933, pp. 91–95) until the Bank of England received the quasi note-issuing monopoly in 1844.

From the Banking Act onward country banks were on the retreat: the decline of country banks was not abrupt, but lasted for almost a century. Some went bankrupt, or stopped business, most merged with joint-stock banks; by World War I, only a few of the hundreds of country banks were still independent. The crisis of 1825/1826 was the crucial event which brought country banks in the retreat by breaking their power and fostering their opponent. However, even before economists and banking experts argued that a major restructuring of the British banking system was needed to adopt banking to the changing economic circumstances. Even if the period of country banks importance did not last for much longer than 50 years, they were quite important for the development of banking: being paid in notes, stored savings with country banks and raising small consumer credits first, even ordinary people got used to banking by dealing with country banks.

5.2.5.2 The Rise of Joint-Stock Banks

When the Parliament permitted note-issuing joint-stock banking outside wider London in 1826, just a few joint-stock banks were founded: in 1827 only three opened their doors, until 1830 another eleven emerged and by 1833 around 30 existed (Cameron 1967b, p. 29). Several factors caused the slow growth of joint-stock banking: the Banking Act of 1826 was imprecise about the legal status of joint-stock banks. The public remained skeptical about joint-stock banks: Barnes and Newton (2014) lined out how early joint-stock banks tried to convince the general public of their soundness. Most importantly, the opposition against joint-stock banks was still strong and the recession caused by the crisis generally complicated banking. Newcomers always face the resistance of the establishment: in the case of joint-stock banks the opposition was particularly strong because established banks feared that the whole banking sector and their own position would change significantly by the foundation of joint-stock banks. In their opposition to joint-stock banks, country banks, London banks and the Bank of England were united

(Crick and Wadsworth 1936, p. 18). Provincial joint-stock banks faced the opposition of country banks; when a group of entrepreneurs and country families established the first joint-stock bank in the industrial hub of Leicester "the project was met by a storm of opposition, largely inspired […] by the efforts of established private banks to obstruct the creation of a powerful rival" (ibid., p. 249). The Bank of England particularly opposed London joint-stock banks. The Bank of England unsuccessfully used its political influence to prevent the permission of joint-stock banking inside London. After the Act passed the Parliament, the Bank of England's and London private bankers' opposition continued: banks refused to include the newly founded joint-stock banks into the London clearing system and the Bank of England rejected to deposit reserves from London joint-stock banks (Born 1977, p. 126).

Despite the heavy opposition, London joint-stock banks were successful: they were managed by unlimited liable well-known and influential directors, and this enhanced public's confidence and their favorable conditions, in particular high interest on deposits, attracted many customers (Crick and Wadsworth 1936, p. 20). In the 1830s Britain saw its first joint-stock banking boom. Around 80 joint-stock banks were founded between 1834 and 1836. In 1844 around 150 joint-stock banks existed with approximately 600 branches (Cameron 1967b, p. 29). Already in the 1840 s joint-stock banks operated more banking offices than the country banks (ibid., p. 25).

In particular in the industrial centers of North England and the Midlands joint-stock banking increased fast (Crick and Wadsworth 1936, p. 17). Because the "pace of industrial development was outstripping that of financial evolution" (ibid., p. 50) often old-style banks were unable or unwilling to cover industry's demand. Unlike in London and many rural areas, in industrial hubs the foundation of joint-stock banks was welcomed by most entrepreneurs and politicians. Country banks usually strongly opposed joint-stock banking. This was less the case in industrial hubs where old-style banks were often founded by industrialists. More open for the new-style banking in industrial hubs, country banks often founded and merged to joint-stock banks (for more details see ibid.). Booming industrial centers were well equipped with capital; the early joint-stock banks in the industrial centers usually had few difficulties to attract equity capital. With the successes of first joint-stock banks, potential investors and the general public became more open. However, successful in the industrial centers of North-England and the Midlands, joint-stock banking in London in particular developed slowly at the beginning: after joint-stock banking was permitted inside London, not more than five banks were founded in London until 1840 (Born 1977, p. 126). However, joint-stock banking was on the rise, in particular in the second half of the 19th century. Joint-stock banks' readiness to attract deposits contributed to their fast growth: neither the Bank of England nor country banks payed interest on deposited money. When joint-stock banks started to pay moderate rates of interest on deposits, they attract most of the money. Well equipped with deposits, joint-stock banks started to lend heavily.

The fast rise of joint-stock banks not only startled their traditional enemies, but within their own ranks the alarm bell was ringing that the extension was too fast and unsound. In the late 1830s, strong crises erupted Britain's financial market and caused several joint-stock banks to go bankrupt. Rising criticism on joint-stock banking caused the Parliament to tighten regulations in the Peel's Act of 1844. In addition, the quasi-monopolization of note issuing restricted joint-stock banks' issuing, but the effect was rather small, because most refused to issue notes voluntarily. In addition, the foundation of new joint-stock banks was restricted. After the Act the extension of joint-stock banking slowed down as just four new banks were founded until 1857 (Crick and Wadsworth 1936, p. 27).

The Acts of 1858, 1862 and 1879 were turning points in the history of British banking. As maintained, the Acts of 1858, 1862 and 1879 permitted and facilitated limited liability share issuing. Before 1858 banks were unlimited liability conglomerates: hence shareholders of banks, whether country banks or joint-stock banks, bore liable in case of a bankruptcy with more than their invested capital. The permission of limited liabilities shares facilitated the growth and extension of joint-stock banking. Three main reasons made limited liability shares quite attractive to shareholders: first, in the worst case of bank's bankruptcy shareholders just lose the invested capital. Second, shareholders were anonymous. Third, because of the first two reasons, liquid secondary share markets emerged where shareholders could easily sell shares. However, the Acts fostered the massive concentration of the banking sector. It seems quite unlikely that a similar concentration would have been possible in a system of unlimited liabilities. Absorbing new equity capital was pivotal for banks' sound growth; a sound equity base reduces banks' risk and therefore attracts depositors. Banks' ability to attract more equity capital by issuing limited liability shares (Born 1977, p. 129) fostered their growth, but also facilitated mergers as shares were easily transferable.

The time between the 1880 s and World War I was characterized by an almost unique concentration of the British banking system. In 1913 just 70 independent banks, 41 joint-stock banks and 29 other banks, still existed; the 41 joint-stock banks operated around 6500 branches (Collins 2012, p. 74): the whole British banking sector was dominated by just five joint-stock megabanks; the big five.[3] Capie and Rodrik-Bali (1982, p. 287) showed that in 1870 the five biggest banks held 25% of all deposits in England and Wales; in 1920 the big five counted for more than 80%. Several factors fostered the strong concentration of the British banking system: facilitated communication due to the developing railway system was a prerequisite for bank branching (Crick and Wadsworth 1936, p. 4 f.). Fast extending international trade, in particular with the colonies, necessitated banking on a new scale; old-style banks were unable to deal with the new scope of banking necessities (ibid.). Increasing domestic and foreign competition convinced bankers that only fast growing banks survive. To growth fast banks' needed to attract deposits, equity capital and increase profits. Keeping up profits was in particular difficult in the environment of falling average profit rates on investments (Cottrell 1980,

[3]Barclays Bank, Midland Bank, Westminster Bank, Lloyds Bank, National Provincial Bank

p. 258 ff.). Increasing costs due to the overstretching branching system further worsened the situation (Born 1977, p. 132). To maintain and increase profits, banks took more risk by investing in risky projects and extending assets. Banks reacted to falling interest rates with a significant extension of total assets and assets per equity (for the extension of assets see Braggion et al. 2012).

As the British investment sector was grazed, megabanks increasingly invested abroad. Due to the rising competition in Europe (Battilossi 2000) British investors increasingly invested overseas. As maintained, half of British savings were exported. Megabanks played a central role for capital exports and in the development of new investment markets abroad: in same colonies British megabanks became the quasi central bank (Cottrell 1980, p. 241). Hence, in the late 19th and early 20th century the British banking sector was dominated by just five joint-stock megabanks, with close ties to the government, which heavily invested at home and in particular abroad.

5.3 The Rise of French Banking

At the end of the 18th century there was hardly any private banking system in France. Paris became a low scale banking center and in the French trading hubs several small private banks were founded. However, Paris banks and the provincial banks were still mainly disconnected and banking did not reach the wider population. At the beginning of the 20th century, a handful of French megabanks dominated the market and also became quite active abroad. Hardly any continental European railway was built without the support of French megabanks. More than any other institutions megabanks became the assistants of the French imperialism. Nowhere was the rise of banking more closely connected with ideas: in France it was widely believed that megabanks are the organizations most appropriate to lead the economic development and fast industrialization. The first megabanks were founded by men deeply convinced that France economically backwardness stemmed from its lack of megabanks. Managers' missionary enthusiasm, but also competition caused them to spread the idea of industrial megabanks throughout the continent.

5.3.1 Saint-Simonianism and Imperialism: Pivotal Ideas for French Banking

Frequently, the French 19th century is considered to have been characterized by the conflict between the old elites or the aristocracy on the one side and the rising bourgeoisie, supported by the other rising classes, on the other side. Despite recurrent conflicts between the old and the new elites, with the better end on the one or the other side, overall the 19th century is considered as the time of bourgeois takeover. More than anywhere else bankers were often the spearhead of the bourgeoisie.

At first glance, the French 19th century shares some similarities with the British: the victory of the new elites against the old aristocracy, the rise of liberalism and imperialism and the coalition of the rising classes—predominately of the bourgeoisie and the working class—against the old elites. However, a closer look emphasizes that, despite certain similarities, the situation and development was rather different: while Britain was politically relatively stable, the French 19th century was market by revolutions, civil wars and turmoil. In Britain, the distribution of power between the King and the Parliament and between the conservatives and liberals was better able to absorb demands and criticism of the important groups within the political system. What particularly stabilized Britain was a certain consensus over fundamental questions: a few questioned the constitutional monarchy, and the relatively strong Parliament; liberalism, in one or another form, entered most movements and was hardly threatened; fiercely contested reforms of the voting system were usually accepted once they had been implemented. In contrast, profound political change in France were usually brought about by bloody Revolutions. Overall, the coalition of the rising classes gained upper hand in the showdowns, but was too fragile to establish stabile political conditions after their big victories.

As maintained, in Britain the coalition between the bourgeoisie and the middle and working class against the old corruption, which was underpinned by a principal shared belief in liberalism and *laissez-faire*, was relatively stable and successful in pushing back the old corruption. The French coalitions between the bourgeoisie and the working class were destabilized by mutual mistrust and different goals: working-class representatives often blamed the bourgeoisie for following their own vested interests—replacing the old aristocratic elite by a new bourgeois elite—and the bourgeoisie accused the working class for aspiring an anti-bourgeois, proletarian revolution. While the working class complained about the bourgeois overdraw of their joint Revolutions, the bourgeoisie feared that the extension of poorer classes' political power would strengthen Marxist and socialist ideas. In particular, the bourgeoisie and the working class lacked a shared ideal fundament: neither liberalism nor constitutionalism or any kind of socialism united the various splinter groups of the reform camp.

As maintained European political and economic liberalism had two birthplaces: France and Britain. In the 18th century liberalism emerged simultaneously in Britain and France. The French tradition of intellectual liberalism continued throughout the 19th century; for example, Alexis de Tocqueville and Jean-Baptiste Say were among the most notable political and economic liberals. However, quite successful in Britain, liberalism was much less influential in France. Principally, the French bourgeoisie, middle and working class was also attracted by liberalism: in France liberalism's power to attack the old cronyism was realized. However, in France the classes open for liberalism failed to agree on uniting main principles.

French Revolutions of the 19th century had a principally liberal touch: the uprisings were directed against political and economic cronyism, privileges of the old elites and usually demanded the right to work, the redistribution of land and one-man-one-vote rights. However, revolutions were soon occupied by the different fractions following their particular interests and ideas: by left-wing workers and young intellectuals pushing the revolutions towards radical republicanism and left-wing authoritarianism, conservative groups favoring a constitutional monarchy with a strong monarch and the bourgeoisie open to a constitutional monarchy, but with a weak monarch.

Taking control of the July Revolution of 1830 and the February Revolution of 1848, the bourgeoisie enforced their idea and established a constitutional monarchy. Radicalized by, more or less, bloody infights with the left-wing fraction, startled by the rise of radical left ideologies the bourgeoisie, governance soon became more and more authoritarian (Tombs 1999). Hence, French liberalism was jammed between different fraction of the reformer camp following different goals and ideas.

While liberalism steadily lost its appeal, its main opponent, in particular in economics, Saint-Simonianism was on the rise. The spreading view that fast industrialization is pivotal for France catching up with Britain and that *laissez-faire* is inappropriate for fast industrialization accelerated the rise of Saint-Simonianism.

5.3.1.1 The Rise of Industrialism and Saint-Simonianism

For centuries, France was the main power in continental Europe and competed with Britain over European hegemony. At the time of absolutism, France was the dominant force in Europe, at least for certain time. Becoming the first real republic during the French Revolution, defeating half of Europe in the Revolutionary Wars and subjugating more than half of Europe with Napoleon Bonaparte, France was proud of its nation, culture and military ability. However, in the Battle of Waterloo it became visible that France lost much ground against Britain. In addition, with the accelerating industrialization and the rise of the working class carrying new socialist ideas, the social issue became urgent.

After the reign of Napoleon Bonaparte, France fell into a deep depression; French's military force and ability to subjugate other nations crashed and burned in Waterloo. In the perception of the French, the defeat of Waterloo was a clear and strong sign of Britain's superiority. Elsewhere in continental Europe, fears about Britain's superiority and dominance spread: the defeat of Napoleon and the fast extension of the British Empire were impressive demonstrations of Britain's power. On the Continent Britain's superiority was traced to its fast industrialization. According to a wide-spread view Britain's industrial productivity was at a military advantage; Britain was able to equip huge armies in relative short time and send them to the world. Hence, it was widely believed that France and Germany's military backwardness had predominately economic reasons. German and French elites were quite convinced that fast industrialization was necessary to close the gap with Britain and to be able to compete with other rising empires for influence, power and land. From the belief that the nation's competitiveness and glory highly depends on its economic power, a kind of industrial fetish emerged in continental Europe; in particular in France and Germany. It was suggested that countries' ability to conquer territories, subject other nations, hence the legitimate ambition of being world power nations, all depends on their economic power and stage of industrialization. In the environment of the widespread industrial fetish, intellectuals on both sides of the Rhine started to dream of a superior industrial society in which everything else is subject to economic progress and industrialization.

Accelerating industrialization, the formation of the industrial proletariat and the July Revolution brought the social issue and the question of distribution to the fore. Inspired by the escalating class conflicts and the discussions on the social issue various non-Marxist socialist ideas emerged in France (Bellet 2016). French socialists ideas of the 19th century were quite heterogeneous and ranged from moderate social democratic ideas to diehard anarchist views. Overall, French socialists, in particular the more influential of the first half of the 19th century, were less proletarian, more state affine and often closer to the ruling elite than elsewhere (Judt 2011, pp. 1–11). However, escalating class conflicts and turmoil convinced non-socialists liberals, even conservatives, that the social issue needs to be solved; at least to avoid socialists revolutions. Hence, from the political left to the right many were convinced that the social issue was a pivotal topic of the time.

The spreading industrial fetish became a fertile ground for teleological thoughts considering industrial societies the ultimate goal of social development: unsurprisingly, France and Germany became the epicenter of the golden age of teleological thought. Various contributors on both sides of the Rhine considered that industrialization creates a superior nation, society and individuals and is the last, golden stage of society's development. Henri de Saint-Simon and Auguste Comte, two of the leading French intellectuals of the time, were the main French prophets of the industrial society. For Saint-Simon ([1821] 1998: 1823), the positivistic industrialism is the ultimate stage of a society's development. Industrial societies are classless, socialist society in which everything is subordinated to the planned scientific economic progress. For him, in industrial societies all kinds of class antagonism vanish and get replaced by the general cooperation under the leadership of scientists and production managers organizing the industrial economy in the best interest of the entire society.

Saint-Simon attracted influential followers who further developed the theory. Saint-Simonianism was for a certain time the most influential economic theory in France. Saint-Simonianism's success stemmed from the historical circumstances and its compatibility with many other ideas and views; Saint-Simonianism inspired intellectuals and politicians from the political right and left, progressive and rather conservative circles. Perhaps more than any other school of thought Saint-Simon and the Saint-Simonians succeed to integrate the widely accepted parts of other influential ideas into their theory and omitted the more contested parts. In particular, they had the ability to match the reasonable parts of various ideas into a quite positive vision of the future at a time of disturbance and social unrest. Saint-Simonians orientated their theories towards the challenges of the time and gave answers which seemed quite straightforward. As maintained Saint-Simonians the unequal distribution of wealth, but uphold private property in principle. They demanded a strong organization at the top of the state, but rejected every form of oppressive dominion. Saint-Simonians were enthusiastic advocates of industrialization, but condemned the exploitation of workers. In addition, they widely followed the classical economic theory, but rejected their favor for *laissez-faire* and criticized their turning a blind eye on the distribution of wealth. Overall, Saint-Simonians demanded a clear and fair order at a time of chaos und unrest and were clear advocates of the rising third estate.

Like already said a few economic ideas had more direct influence on economics and politics than Saint-Simonianism. After Saint-Simon's death his followers built a dense network into politics, banking, engineering, bureaucracy, education etc. (Eckalbar 1979) and used their influence to shape the country in accordance with their ideas. Propelled by their industrialism Saint-Simonians acquired much knowledge about industrial production, financing and industrial megaprojects like railway building. Putting them on the organizational top of the industrial society Saint-Simonianism was in particular attractive for bankers and engineers. In mid-19th century the École Polytechnique was full of Saint-Simonians (Pilbeam 2014, p. 12), Saint-Simonians dominated French railway projects and formed a close circle among influential bankers. Many capable engineers and financers of industrial project being strongly inspired by Saint-Simonianism French industrialization was carried out by Saint-Simonians.

Promoted by many influential engineers and bankers, the strength of Saint-Simonianism was that it attracted carriers from different classes and groups, and attracted followers and inspired people with various backgrounds. Most likely, their utopian ideas of the future industrial society were bizarre for many politicians of the time, but Saint-Simonians were considered the ones who know how to industrialize France. Saint-Simonians' acquired practical knowledge about industrialization and economic development and developed quite convincing practical proposals about institutional change and new organizations which fosters industrialization. What made Saint-Simonianism particularly attractive for rather strong, authoritarian governments was the rejection of the British *laissez-faire* liberalism and the proposed economic leadership of the state; theoretically rejecting rude dominion, practically Saint-Simonianism was quite compatible with heavy state intervenions of rather authoritarian governments. From all ideas of the 19th century, hardly any influenced the development of the continental European banking sector more directly and sustainable than Saint-Simonianism.

Railways were 19th century's symbol for technical progress, industrialization and nation's economic power. No doubt, economically railways were a pivotal innovation, or a General Purpose Technology, because they revolutionized transportation, of raw materials, people and industrial goods, and communication. However, beyond all economic means, railways became the symbol of nations' engineering skills and progressing industrialization; in the second half of the 19th century a kind of railwayism emerged. Nowhere was railwayism more pronounced than in France.

Railway building was not just an economic question; railways were of great military importance, expected to integrate and unite the still fragmented nation and considered the most important project for industrialization. A nation closely connected with railways was considered a highly industrialized, powerful and glorious nation. Apart from the symbolic character railways were expected to foster patriotic sentiments by bringing people closer together (Mitchell 2000, p. 255). Spreading Saint-Simonianism was a strong push for railwayism in France: "The influential advocates of railroads in France during the decade following the revolution were nearly all followers of the idealist Saint-Simon" (Dunham 1955, p. 58). Working their entire life on industrialization, Saint-Simonians were quite aware of the crucial significance of railroads for industrialization and economic progress. In addition, the same Saint-Simonians were convinced that railways bring peace to Europe: Michel Chevalier argued that railway networks enable ordinary people to travel abroad. He expected that the intensified international exchange would break up old chauvinist, prejudice views and enforce a permanent peace in Europe (Booth 1871, p. 168 f.). Convinced by the advantages of railways, many Saint-Simonians "carried on an active propaganda for railway building" (Clough 1939, p. 144 f.). High-ranking military stressed the importance of railways for the wars of the future. The nation's ability to quickly transport armies and equipment over huge distances was considered pivotal for future military successes: in France, like elsewhere, military considerations played a central role for railway routing (c.f. Mitchell 2000). In particular, railways were important for economic progress, even if the connection between growth and railways is more complex than widely believed (O'Brien 1983). Railways were considered to economically unit big, fragmented countries like France by more closely connecting the relatively autonomous economic hotspots. Railway building was also part of the military, economic and political competition between Britain, France and Germany: as competitors built an extensive railway network, French had to follow (Mitchell 2000). Hence, according to a wide-spread view, extensive railway building was politically, militarily and economically necessary.

In Britain, the 19th century was the time of free trade. The contrary was true of France, at least most of the time. Free trade was a central demand of the 18th century physiocrats (Rothbard 1995a, p. 367) and, of course, of the liberal forerunner Turgot (ibid., p. 386). Despite the long tradition of France in liberal classical economics—Jean-Baptiste Say, Charles Comte, Charles Dunoyer, Pellegrino Rossi and others pursued the classical school in France through the 19th century (Béraud 2016)—advocates of free trade remain relatively unheard in France. The Zeitgeist of the early 19th century France was protectionism (Todd 2015, pp. 20–54). Charlies Ganilh, François-Louis-Auguste Ferrier and Louis Say, the brother of the free trader, developed several, strong and widely accepted, arguments for protectionism: like most other protectionists, their main argument was that underdeveloped economies (like France) need protection from cheaper industry goods of highly developed nations (like Britain). According to the protectionists, to foster industrialization, production and independency, and hence homeland's glory and greatness, trade walls are needed (c.f. Clough 1939, pp. 105–109). Even Jean-Baptiste Say recognized that under certain circumstances, for certain time protectionism seems justified (Todd 2015, p. 31). Free trade had always strong advocates in France, and sometimes they were able to convince governments of their ideas, however overall the 19th century was dominated by protectionists arguing that France higher goal of fast industrialization necessitates the protection from more competitive foreign economies.

5.3.1.2 The Rise of Imperialism

The 19th century was the time of French imperialism. French imperialism had two main forms: direct colonialism and indirect imperialism. The first means the conquest of new territory; the second the use of military, political and economic power to extend the influence on other mostly European countries. Like in Britain and Germany moral, economic, and social arguments for colonialism and imperialism were produced.

For many intellectuals and politicians, civilizing the savages was the moral obligation of France. Mill and other British liberals legitimized their consent to colonialism with Britain's obligation to spread its superior world views. In the same vein, many colonialists demanded from the French government to spread the ideas of the Grande Nation through the globe: "Every people must have a mission. Civilization was that of France" (Murphy 1948, p. 175). Two main groups produced moral arguments for colonialism: liberals or republicans and Catholics. The first generation of British liberals like Adam Smith were quite skeptical on imperialism: the same is true for France were Diderot and Voltaire criticized France's imperialistic ambitions (Pitts 2005, p. 165). Liberals' view on imperialism changed with the French Revolution. Proud of their revolution French republicans' got convinced of the superiority of the French race and the French mission to civilize the savages (Daughton 2006, p. 10 f.): "Spreading republican ideals, culture, know-how, and technology was inseparable from colonialism itself; putting 'uncivilized' regions of the world on the road to progress was, according to colonialists, France's chief goal" (ibid., p. 11). In the 19th century influential French liberals were advocates of imperialism (Pitts 2005, pp. 163–259). In particular Tocqueville's imperialism received much attention (Richter 1963; Pitts 2000, 2005; Welch 2003; Duan 2010). like other liberals Tocqueville supported imperialism to enlighten the savages; but even he legitimized extreme violence against the native population and advocate imperialism as a possibility to enhance France brightness (Pitts 2000). Practical politicians like the republican Prime Minster Jules Ferry were convinced that France fulfills its republican mission by civilizing the savages (Aldrich 1996: 98): Jean Dupuis wrote that "it seemed beautiful to me to admit to the advantages of civilization half-barbarous […] to walk in the light of modern ideas" (Murphy 1948, p. 68).

However, distributing French ideas meant first and foremost spreading Catholicism. The Catholic Church was an enthusiastic supporter of colonialism because the extension of France facilitated Church's mission to spread their faith to the world (see Daughton 2006, p. 11 ff; White and Daughton 2012). Of course there was much opposition against imperialism from Marxists, Christians and liberals (Aldrich 1996, pp. 111–114) but the influence of anti-imperialists was rather weak. As in Britain, even some socialists welcomed imperialism: "On the left, Louis Blanc agreed with other French socialists when he argued that 'to spread out, to overflow, is a duty" (Pitts 2005, p. 167).

Further arguments in favor of imperialism were produced. What Baumgart (1975, p. 39) considers the social-psychological-theses, France imperialism was expected to strengthen the lost collective self-confidence. Collectively depressed after the great defeat of Waterloo, imperialism should have helped to regain national pride. Again, in the late 19th century the French reacted with colonial expansion to the defeat from Germany in order to overcome the collective depression. According to Baumgart (ibid.) France suffered three main humiliations in the 19th century: Waterloo, the defeat against Germany and the expulsion from Egypt; France always reacted with rampant imperialism to overcome the rising inferiority complex. In addition, to regain collective self-confidence, French imperialism was propelled by its fears from following behind its great enemies Germany and Britain: "French expansion occurred in connection with—and often in response to—actions by France's international rivals" (Aldrich 1996, p. 89).

Colonialism was also a response to the perceived aggravating Malthusian crisis. High birth rates and improving medical standards steadily increased the European population. Closely following Malthus (1798) it was argued that the scarcity of land brought the domestic agrarian production to its limits, why the steadily rising population needs to be sent to the sparsely populated colonies. In particular, the delinquent population was deported to colonies. Beside ordinary delinquents, the colonies served as a deposit for revolutionaries (Aldrich 1996, p. 93). However, Murphy (1948, p. 111 ff.) showed that in France the emigration to colonies was welcomed and opposed: those welcoming emigration argued that emigration solves the problem of excess population, exports problems of criminality and political rebellion and develops new allies and markets. Opponents argued that French economy and military strength will be harmed by sending parts of the domestic population abroad.

However, like in Britain and Germany, economic arguments dominated the discussions on imperialism. Supporters argued that colonies would provide new markets for French products and capital and supply the domestic industry with cheaper raw materials. For Jules Ferry "Colonial politics is the daughter of industrial politics" (cited in Daughton 2006, p. 10). Following Mill, Leroy-Beaulieu argued that colonialism is a by-product of industrialization (ibid.). He considered that colonialism is economically important for two reasons: it provides cheaper raw materials and it opens new sales markets for domestic product (Murphy 1948, p. 125 f.). Saint-Simon and many Saint-Simonians were also convinced by the positive effects of colonialism for the French economy (Pilbeam 2014, p. 108 ff.). It was widely considered that Britain's access to its colonies' raw materials was an important industrial advantage: it allowed Britain to produce more cheaply and exclude its competitors from important raw materials. Rising protectionism constricted markets to France industrial products. Conquering new colonies was expected to develop new markets for French products: curiously, in France the same persons who called for protectionism often demanded the colonial extension to exploit new markets for domestic industries' products. Empirically, the economic effect of French colonialism is rather mixed: Aldrich (1996, p. 164 ff.) stressed the importance of raw materials from colonies for industrial production. In contrast,

Andrew and Kanya-Forstner (1976) doubt the positive economic effects of colonialism. However, in particular the new European allies, bounded to the empire by the French carrot and stick tactic, became important trading partners (Cameron 1961).

Colonialism and imperialism had many supporters in 19th century France: liberal intellectuals supported imperialism on moral grounds (Pitts 2005, pp. 163–259); increasing political and military power in particular attracted high high-ranking military and conservative politicians who became important colonial lobbyists (Aldrich 1996, p. 100 ff); expected profits convinced the big business (Abrams and Miller 1976). Abrams and Miller (ibid., p. 702 f.) which considered that big business and megabanks were the main drivers behind imperialist lobbyism:

> Although civil servants, members of the middle-classes and personnel of the armed forces sympathized with the aims of the colonial 'comites' and comprised their audience, it seems highly improbable that they exercised any active control over their direction. It is clear that through the 'comites' officers, members and sources of funds, a group of the most important corporations and banks in France were in a position to control the 'parti colonial' and to employ it as their direct political arm.

In particular, French joint-stock megabanks profited a lot from imperialism, which is why they became strong supporters of the imperialist project. Facing decreasing interest rates in France, French banks were quite grateful for the opportunity to invest heavily abroad.

5.3.2 Bourbon Restoration: The Conservative Backlash

Despite the persecution and land confiscations from the old aristocracy and the Church, during the revolution the conservative forces were back after Napoleon's defeat. Regardless of revolutionaries' aim to break up its dominance, the landed aristocracy again became the silent ruler of the country. Land confiscations from noblemen and the Church during the revolution weakened the traditional landowners. However, much of the confiscated land ended up in the hands of the old aristocracy again. In addition, parts of the rising bourgeoisie were quite land based which is why they bought much of the confiscated land and adopted landed interests (Pilbeam 1990, pp. 55–73). Industrial production and trade grew in size, but the industry remained small scale, big investments were the exception and industrial production was orientated towards the needs of the landed classes (Kemp 1985, pp. 49–77). However, despite the disturbances of the French Revolution and the Napoleon years, the old elites regained ground. However, the mercantile and industrial bourgeoisie was also on the rise. The time of the Bourbon Restoration was characterized by a complex balance and power sharing between the old elites, in particular the landed aristocracy, and the new elites, predominately the rising bourgeoisie. Balancing the interests of the old and the new elites predominately meant developing a system of privilege distribution which sedated both sides with various privileges: the Bourbon Restoration had a lot in common with the old mercantilist systems where privileges to elites ensured the loyalty to the crown.

The constitution of the Bourbon Restoration strongly favored the political power of the rich: politically a quasi-absolut monarch ruled together with the Chambre des Députés elected by not more than 90,000 very rich predominately landowners: something that Clough (1939, p. 94 ff.) considered the "Rule of the Rich" until the July Revolution of 1830. The Chambre des Députés was dominated by three ideologically disparate parties: The Ultra Royalist, the Royalists and the Liberal Party. All three parties were representatives of the rich: ultra royalists of the old aristocracy and the clerics, the liberals of the bourgeoisie. Deeply divided on the favored political system—old-style monarchy or republic — the parties were unified in their opposition to free trade and the demand for protectionism. The time of the Bourbon Restoration was characterized by a relatively stable system of reciprocal privileges: most groups of the landed and mercantile elites, bankers, industrialists were satisfied with privileges. Hence, the old privileges were just extended to new groups.

When Louis XVIII left the Chambre des Députés a free hand in choosing their favored trade policy, it was not surprising that the parties introduced an ultra-protective tariff system. The ultra royalists wanted protection from foreign competitors for their landed clientele and the liberals demanded protection for the mercantile and industrial bourgeoisie; they met at a high protection for agricultural and industrial products, hence for almost everything (ibid., pp. 96–100). The tariff system was just part of the general conservation of the old system: old oligopolies continued to dominate the French economy. According to Todd (2015, pp. 20–55), the protectionism and cronyism of the Bourbon Restoration was part of a wider strategy of the ultra royalists to withdraw all the changes of the revolution and reintroduce the old system.

Around the mid-1820 s the coalition between old aristocracy and the mercantile and industrial bourgeoisie started to break down. Louis XVIII took much care to balance the interests of the old aristocracy and the mercantile and industrial bourgeoisie; his successor Charles X was less diplomatic and upset the liberals by taking sides with the Ultra Royalist Party (Clough 1939, p. 120). Jean-Baptiste de Villèle's takeover as new Prime Minister in 1821 was in itself a provocation against the liberals. Villèle was a clear advocate of the landed interests; granting the families which lost property by the confiscations during the revolution a 650 million franc indemnity was particularly unpopular among liberals. A sharp increase in the import tariffs on sugar, iron and cattle further heightened the conflict between the landed old aristocracy and the mercantile and industrial bourgeoisie: for industrialists, iron became more expensive and merchants feared a sharp reduction of trade (Todd 2015, p. 47 f.). Changes in the inheritance law and the increasingly pro-clerical policy escalated the conflict and caused the uprise of 1830.

5.3.3 July Monarchy: 'Bankers Reign'

The July Revolution was considered the ultimate victory of the (financial) bourgeoisie over the aristocracy (Henderson 1967, p. 108) and sweeped away Charles X and the Ultra Royalist Party. Two blocks dominated the revolution and the negotiation over the new political structure: the bourgeoisie, which gathered behind the famous banker Jacques Laffitte and suggested to give the crown to the Duke of Orleans, and young left-wing intellectuals and the lower classes who favored to see Lafayette as the president of a new republic. Finally, the bourgeoisie prevailed and the Duke of Orleans ascended the throne. This victory revealed the new political era of the latent bourgeois quasi-autocracy. Kindleberger (1964, p. 194) exaggerated that "the government was corrupt in the interest of business under the July Monarchy;" Tocqueville came to the similar conclusion that the government of the July Monarchy "took on the character of private industry [...] posterity will perhaps never know to what degree the government of that time was a capitalist enterprise in which all action is taken for the purpose of profit for its members" (Clough 1939, p. 125).

5.3.3.1 The Domination of the Small Clique

Sée (1936, p. 144) considered that only a small minority of the wealthiest parts of the bourgeoisie replaced the old aristocracy as the leading political class. According to Henderson (1967, pp. 108–126), the July Monarchy was domination by the financial bourgeoisie, which formed, from time to time, coalitions with the iron, steel and coal bourgeoisie; the banking bourgeoisie was the clear leader within the coalition. In 1830 Laffitte declared "From now on the bankers will reign", a year later he resigned from all offices and apologized to the French people for helping Louis-Philippe to ascend the throne. However, bankers remained one of the most powerful groups behind the Crown and the Parliament. In the late 1810s and 1820s a small group of successful Protestant and Jewish merchants started do dominate the segregated French banking sector; the Haute Banque. Taking over state financing from traditional banking houses, the Haute Banque also became the main financer of the rising trade and industry, organized the technological-train from Britain to France and was the main shareholders of the Banque de France (Smith 2006, p. 49 f.): "It was the members of the 'haute banque parisienne', more than anyone else, who orchestrated French economic development and the modernization of French business practices" (ibid., p. 50). Haute Banque's huge political and social influence (Kemp 1985, p. 61) stemmed from its role as state financer and middleman between the state and the economy: the Haute Banque was the main state financer and therefore indispensable; due to its close networks with various economic sectors, the Haute Banque also became the main representative of economic interests.

Politically, the reign of Louis-Philippe was for many who expected a more liberal monarchy a disappointment. Liberal measurements were enforced at the beginning of the July Monarchy: the end of Catholicism as state religion, public education, free press and changes in the voting law which sharply increased the number of voters (Clough 1939,

p. 124). Although the number of entitled voters increased from 90.000 to 170.000, after early liberalism Louis-Philippe soon became more authoritarian and conservative: workers, for example, the spearhead of the July Revolution, remained marginalized, excluded from elections and their organizations were banned.

As maintained, around the same time of the July Revolution in Britain the bourgeoisie, supported by the middle and working class pushed back the old elites. Hence, broadly speaking, in France and Britain the bourgeoisie took over in the 1830s. Nevertheless, the situation was rather different: in Britain the coalition, built on the fundament of liberalism and *laissez-faire* of the bourgeoisie and the middle and working class, was able to initiate a liberal turn which extended the boundaries of traditional liberal parties and groups. In contrast, in France parts of the Parisian bourgeoisie, many of them involved in banking, formed a small powerful clique which acted like the old elites. Following a half-hearted liberalism, during the July Monarchy the France bourgeoisie usually advocated protectionism, frequently opposed equal rights for all men because of their fear of working-class radicalism, and was relatively open to state interventionism. After the July Revolution, an intensive discussion on trade barriers took place. In the first years of the July Monarchy the free traders received much attention: touring the whole country to explain to their audience the benefits of free trade, many got convinced by free trade. However, the system of trade tariffs changed little; people were accustomed to trade tariffs and many industrialists were still too afraid of the superior foreign competitors (c.f. Todd 2015, p. 89 ff.).

According to Dunham (1955, pp. 399–419), at the time of the Bourbon Restoration and the July Monarchy the French economy was under strong government control and leadership. In particular the rising socialist like Saint-Simon and Villeneuve-Bargemont and other contributors like Blanc, Pecquer, Vidal, Sismondi and Dupont-White (Clough 1939, p. 142) demanded state interventions. State intervention was always and everywhere important for the economic development. As maintained, British liberals also demanded the intervention of the state if necessary. However, British liberals remained principally reluctant to state interventions overall. Contrarily, in France broad state interventionism was widely accepted as necessary for fast industrialization. Britain's rising bourgeoisie was a bulwark against heavy state interventions, the rising French bourgeoisie openly demanded state leadership in economic affairs (Landes 1949). Due to the wide agreement on the necessity of state leadership, in particular since the beginning of the July Monarchy state interventionism was a central part of most influential economic ideas (Clough 1939, p. 141 f.). French state interventionism had many forms: regulations and control of companies, importation of new technique, legal protection of workers and the improvement of their living conditions and in particular the promotion of infrastructure projects.

5.3.3.2 The First Railway Boom and the Rise of the Haute Banque

At the beginning of the July Monarchy, French railwayism took off: "In the 1820s and 1830s, France's political and business elite came to realize that, if their country was to industrialize and remain among the world's leading nations, it had to have a modern, multilevel system of transportation" (Smith 2006, p. 62). Railwayism had a strong lobby: Saint-Simonians, enthusiastic supporters of railways, held important offices—the most influential advocates of railwayism were almost all Saint-Simonians (Dunham 1955, p. 58), the army feared that Germany's closer railway network would enable them to dominate the Rhineland, politicians needed new railways as status symbols and most importantly the industrial and financial 'bourgeoisie smelled the most lucrative business of the 19th century (Clough 1939, pp. 143–148). Due to the close ties between rulers and the business, governments of the July Monarchy were much more aware of the needs of the economy (Sée 1936, p. 209), but the railway-enthusiasm of the 19th century France went far beyond economic means.

Railway building at the time of the Bourbon Restoration was a private business without much assistance from the government (Cameron 1961, p. 204). With the Law of 1833 a new era of railway building began (Dunham 1955, p. 57); the Law of 1833 was the starting point of France's state-led railway system. The Law of 1833 defined the necessity of a railway-system and augmented legislators' ability to influence railway projects (Cameron 1961, p. 205). After the Law of 1833, several regulative alignments should have facilitated the building of railways (Clough 1939, p. 146). However, despite the commitment to the necessity of railways expressed in the Law of 1833, railway building remained difficult: the Parliament was trapped in endless debates about the ownership and financing of railways, the King remained relatively unenthusiastic, the general public was skeptical and opponent interest complicated he realization of big railway projects. That French railway building had not come to a halt before it had really begun was owed to the effort of influential Saint-Simonians (Cameron 1961, pp. 204–208). Saint-Simonians' enthusiasm for railways—above all the brothers Péreire—accompanied by James de Rothschild's instinct for big business overcame many resistances, difficulties and reservations against railways. Surprisingly, in hindsight it was the cooperation between the Saint-Simonians and the Haute Banque that facilitated most French railway building during the July Monarchy: "The 'Haute Banque' joined with the young civil engineers and promoters associated with Henri Saint-Simon to found the private companies that, after many false starts, eventually succeeded in giving France a world-class system of rail transportation" (Smith 2006, p. 62).

However, railway building progressed much slower than hoped and expected. Private companies remained relatively uninterested and the government lacked the financial means to accelerate railway building (Clough 1939, p. 147): financing was the main problem (Dunham 1955, p. 68) and railway building still heavily depended on the enthusiasm and conviction of the Saint-Simonians. Private savings were still locked up in idle hoards or real estate because ordinary people shied away from railway investments; unable to attract much capital, interest rates for railway capital remained quite high (Doukas 1945, p. 18).

Dissatisfied with the slow development, the French government started to intervene more heavily in railway building. The year 1838 "marked the beginning of an endless procession of public appropriations and guarantees which for a century plagued the national treasury" (ibid., p. 21). 1838 was the beginning of the close cooperation between the state and private actors to foster railway building. It also marked the beginning of the state's heavy intervention and support for industrialization. A new deal between the public and private business was needed: the railway Law of 1842 reordered the relation between the government, local authorities and private business. Governments provided the land and covered one third of the infrastructure costs; local authorities bore the other two thirds of the infrastructure costs and private companies covered all operating costs (Henderson 1967, p. 111 f.). The Railway Law of 1842 did not work well: the law was an "unwise" compromise between "hostile interests"—mainly between advocates of state-owned railways and those favoring private business—without any sustainable solutions to the main problems (Dunham 1955, p. 73 f.) and caused endless discussed between the partners (Cameron 1967a, p. 207).

The state's massive financial needs opened new political doors for the raising Haute Banque (c.f. Mehrens 1911, pp 9–26). However, railway financing remained quite difficult. The Parisian Haute Banque was accused of hindering faster railway construction (Dunham 1955, p. 69) by restraining capital or lending only at horrendous rates. In particular the relation between the Haute Banque and the Saint-Simonians worsened as railway building developed slowly. For Saint-Simonians, the Haute Banque became an obstacle on the way to the industrial society. Due to the increasing hostility, Laffitte broke off with his former supporters of the Haute Banque and the smoldering conflict between the Péreires and Rothschild over railway financing became deeper (Kindleberger 1985, p. 49). Doubtlessly, some bankers would have been able to invest more, but the true problem was more fundamental and hardly the fault of the Haute Banque: still traumatized by the financial crises of the 18th century, the French people remained unwilling to invest in riskier projects like railways or big industries; rather, they preferred to hoard savings or invest in real estate. Unconnected small regional banks also contributed to the low capital mobility (Dunham 1955, p. 68 ff.). Private bankers who managed their own and their few customers' wealth (Cameron 1967c, p. 105) were usually unable to accumulate loanable funds big enough to finance industrial megaprojects. Doubtlessly, many bankers were quite conservative and invested predominately in their traditional business, public debts. However, at the same time the Haute Banque was much more innovative and open for new investments than their German counterpart: Haute Banque was quite innovative in facilitating industrial banking (Born 1977, p. 97 ff.) and developed early forms of investment banking and the insurance business (Cameron 1967c, p. 105 f.).

Rather than the selfishness of bankers or their despondency, the established banking regulation hampered huge long-run investments needed for railways and the big industry. Principally permitted since 1807, financial institutions were excluded from the right to form limited liability joint-stock companies. Governments of the July Monarchy were convinced that the right to form limited liability joint-stock companies should only be granted to companies using natural means of production such as railway or heavy industries companies. It was considered that the success of companies using natural means of production depends on the nature of things, which is easier to prove for shareholders and the government. In contrast, it was argued that companies' success exclusively depends on the managers' ability whereas means of production are not 'natural'. Because the managers' ability is more arbitrage and harder to prove, those companies should be excluded from the right to found limited liability joint-stock companies (c.f. Mehrens 1911, p. 16). Prohibiting limited liability joint-stock banks prevented banks from becoming big enough to finance huge industrial projects without excessive risk taking.

Hence, the July Monarchy marked a fundamental change: the July Revolution was the ultimate victory of the financial bourgeoisie over the old aristocracy. From the 1830s onwards, the 19th century was the time of the bourgeoisie's latent governance. It was also the time of Haute Banque's political rise: no other bourgeois group was political more influential than the Parisian bankers of the Haute Banque. Financing the Crown and its infrastructure megaprojects, the government largely depended on the Haute Banque. Saint-Simonians were the second group whose influence steadily increased. Saint-Simon's ideas spread fast among engineers and technicians, but also influential bankers. Government infrastructure projects brought many Saint-Simonians into central offices and positions. At the end of the July Monarchy, many educational institutes, ministries and planning organization were in the hands of Saint-Simonians (Pilbeam 2014, pp. 5–25). At the beginning, Saint-Simonians and the Haute Banque formed a strong coalition for industrialization. However, the relation between them soon worsened as Saint-Simonians blamed the Haute Banque for selfishness and for making little effort to support industrial projects; in the late 1840s, the conflict turned into open hostility.

5.3.4 Napoleon III and the Banking Revolution

Louis-Philippe's ignorance of the social issue and his ignorance of the bourgeoisie backfired in the mid-19th century. When rioting workers were politically joined by the bourgeoisie, the Revolution of 1848 broke out and overthrew Louis-Philippe.

The Revolution of 1848 was carried out by a not untypical coalition for France between the bourgeoisie, the middle and the working class against the King they previously brought to power (Henderson 1967, p. 127 f.). It flushed out much of the old elites. The years after the revolution were characterized by the struggle between the bourgeoisie and the working class over power (Clough 1939, p. 163 ff.). In particular, workers' demand for a formal right to work caused a quarrel between socialists and radicals on the one side and conservatives and moderate republicans on the other (Tombs 1999, p. 65). Politically naïve and inexperienced, socialists and radical republicans increasingly lost ground against the liberal middle class and bourgeoisie (Henderson 1967, p. 126 ff.). However, the lower classes' main demand of universal male suffrage was conceded. Tired from revolutions and political conflicts, citizens longed for a compromise candidate. Louis Napoléon, the nephew of Napoléon Bonaparte, was the compromise candidate on whom many agreed: for conservatives, he was the strong man to bring back to France the glory of his uncle's time, for rural workers and peasants he was the provincial person, for socialists and republicans he was the social reformer (Tombs 1999, p. 66). Due to his aristocratic background, he was supported by the Conservative Party, his business friendliness pleased the bourgeoisie and his sensitivity for the social issue calmed the working class. Attracting votes from all classes (Clough 1939, p. 170), Napoléon won the presidential elections with an overwhelming majority of 5.5 million votes out of 7.4 million. Elected president in 1848, he crowned himself king Napoleon III in 1851. After bloody battles against his opponents, in particular against the democrat socialists, Napoleon III submitted to vote a new constitution, which approved the establishment of a Second Empire. Almost 80% voted for the new constitution (Tombs 1999, p. 67), which almost suspended democracy. Napoleon III held reign until 1870. In Napoleon's reign the old aristocracy disappeared from office, the bourgeoisie was still at the lever of power, but their power was restricted by the strong monarch and the "Saint-Simonian Imperialism" (Sée 1936, p. 282).

5.3.4.1 Napoleon's Industrialism and the Rise of the Saint-Simonians

Napoleon III fought many wars, conquered new territories, spurred nationalistic sentiments, but in particular, what distinguishes him from his successors is that he was the king of economics. Already Louis-Philippe tried to foster industrialization, but he was a week monarch and reforms were half-hearted. In contrast, Napoleon III was a strong ruler deeply convinced that France needs a fast industrialization; in particular the first decades of his reign were dominated by economic issues. Napoleon III was quite impressed by Saint-Simon and the Saint-Simonians and their proposals for industrialization: "Louis Napoleon drew heavily on the inspiration of Saint-Simon and had a sweeping vision of planning and state action" (Kindleberger 1964, p. 186). Napoleon III was impressed by the Saint-Simonian plan for industrialization, but uninterested in Saint-Simon's plan of a classless, domination-free socialist society. Professor Michel Chevalier, a moderate Saint-Simonian and free trader, became Napoleon III's main economic advisor. Napoleon III's authoritarian rule heavily depended on economic growth: economic growth and territorial extension for a political free hand was the latent agreement between the king and his people (Tombs 1999, p. 67).

As maintained, during the July Monarchy Saint-Simonians entered the central education and planning institutions. Involved in many infrastructure projects, Saint-Simonians accumulated a lot of practical knowledge about railways, canals and road building. Independently from Napoleon's close relation to the Saint-Simonians, it would have been difficult to pursue industrialization without any support from Saint-Simonians: Émile and Isaac Péreire were the most famous railway pioneers; after studying the American transport system Michel Chevalier became professor of political economy at the Collège de France and senior engineer of mining; Prosper Enfantin was a notable banker and Jacques Laffitte was doubtless the most famous French banker of the first half of the 19th century. Napoleon III being deeply convinced by Saint-Simonians' plan for state-lead industrialization, their political and economic influence vastly increased. Napoleon's huge interest in industrialization stemmed from his nationalism—a highly industrialized France, closely connected with railways would enhance the citizens' national sentiments—from his military ambitions—modern wars are won with modern arms produced in big industries and by mobile armies siting on trains rather than on horses—and in particular that people would accept his authoritarian system as long as the economic progress continues. For Napoleon III the Saint-Simonians were the experts of industrialization who promoted an economic idea which seemed much more compatible with a strong monarch than classical economists' *laissez-faire* policy. The rise of the Saint-Simonians was accompanied by the decline of Haute Banque's political influence.

Napoleon III followed two main economic projects: the building of Great Paris and in particular the extension of the railways system (Henderson 1967, p. 136 ff.). Both projects required big capital. Financing was already the main problem of Louis-Philippe's railway projects. Napoleon III agreed with the Saint-Simonian's that France does not lack the capital needed for industrialization, but the established banking system is enabled to absorb idle capital and prefers to invest elsewhere rather than into industrialization (c.f. Clough 1939, pp. 173–175). After the Revolution of 1848, the conflict between the Haute Banque and the Saint-Simonians escalated. Saint-Simonians openly blamed the Haute Banque for the laggard industrialization. According to Laffitte "the insufficiency of credit institutions in France was responsible for that country's inferiority to England" (cited in Kindleberger 1985, p. 46). As outlined, Enfantin developed a theory in which big banks absorb the nation's idle capital and invest it into the rising industry and industrial megaprojects. According to him and other Saint-Simonians, a good industrial banking system takes side strictly with the diligent against the idle and supports the industrialization of the country with cheap capital. Blaming the established banks of taking side with the idle, the foundation of a Saint-Simonian industrial bank that would lend the highest possible amount at lowest interest rates to the rising industry became a core demand of the Saint-Simonians. Disappointed by the difficulties of railway financing during the July Monarchy, Saint-Simonian's blamed the Haute Banque of being selfish representatives of the old idle aristocracy which hampers industrialization by pushing up interest rates and refusing to lend to the industry except at horrendous interest rates. In addition, Saint-Simonians also attacked the Banque de France for its too conservative credit policy. Against the Saint-Simonian attack, the argument must be made that the Banque of France followed a conservative discount and note-issuing policy, but frequently leaned against crises and promoted the economy in recessions (Kindleberger 1993, p. 106 ff). However, Napoleon III, who opposed the July Monarchy loyal Haute Banque, got convinced by the Saint-Simonians that France needs a totally new form of banking to support his ambitious projects and to foster industrialization.

5.3.4.2 The French Banking Revolution

Joint-stock companies were Saint-Simon's favored instrument of promoting industrialization (Smith 2006, p. 71). Principally permitted since 1807, the deregulation of 1832 should have made the foundation of joint-stock companies more attractive; however, the number of limited liability companies remained relatively limited before the Second Empire (Clapham 1921, p. 131). Société Anonyme are "full-fledged limited-liability joint-stock company" which was permitted since 1808, but strictly licensed by the government and seldom used since 1848 (Smith 2006, p. 71). Limited liabilities joint-stock companies became Napoleon III's preferred instrument of supporting his economic projects. For example, unlike in other countries, French railways were overwhelmingly operated by joint-stock companies (Henderson 1967, p. 140). As outlined, limited liability joint-stock company license were usually not given to banks. Napoleon III broke with the tradition and allowed banks to form limited liability joint-stock companies (Mehrens 1911, p. 89) and "threw the full authority of his government behind the creation of joint-stock banks" (Smith 2006, p. 72). The law of 1867 defined the creation of limited liability joint-stock companies—under certain circumstances—a general right. Hence, unlike his predecessor Napoleon III was quite permissive with limited liability license; in particular at the beginning of his reign, he openly supported the foundation of joint-stock companies (McMillan 1991, p. 139) and changed laws which made the foundation of limited liability joint-stock companies easier (Price 1997, p. 26 f.). Napoleon permitting the foundation of limited liabilities joint-stock banks paved the way for Saint-Simonians to found industrial banks. As maintained, Saint-Simonians proposed limited liabilities joint-stock industrial banks which clearly takes side with the diligent, supports industrialization, lends at the lowest possible interest rate and issues small shares and accepts deposits to absorb bigger and smaller idle savings.

The foundation of the Crédit Mobilier—the first Saint-Simonian-style limited liability joint-stock bank—further escalated the conflict between the Haute Banque, the Banque de France on the one side and the Saint-Simonians on the other. When the die-hard Saint-Simonians Émile and Isaac Péreire asked Napoleon III to permit the foundation of a limited liability joint-stock bank, the Haute Banque, in particular James de Rothschild, unsuccessfully used all their influence to keep Napoleon III from approving the Péreire Bank (Smith 2006, p. 72 f.). Rothschild's intervention failed because of Péreires' ability to organize a strong coalition against Rothschild (Cameron 1961, p. 134 ff.) and Napoleon's conviction that a Saint-Simonian bank further pushes back the Haute Banque, the economic power base of the old royal house.

The hostility between the Péreires and James de Rothschild continued and fundamentally changed the continental European banking system far beyond the French borders. Propelled by their Saint-Simonian sense of mission, the Péreires spread Saint-Simonian industrial banking through the continent by founding branches elsewhere in Europe. Roused by Crédit Mobilier's fast extension, James de Rothschild used his influence and founded rival joint-stock banks, which looked a lot like the Crédit Mobilier in Europe.

Driven by their mutual hostility, joint-stock banks opened in most European countries either founded by Rothschild or the Péreires and their allies (c.f. ibid., pp. 148–171). Due to the fast spread of French-style banking, Paris became, together with London, Europe's most important financial center (Henderson 1967, p. 148).

In France the financial support from joint-stock banks enabled the government to extend the railway system. Napoleon III was an enthusiastic supporter of railway building and the Transport Revolution. He resumed the plan to build six main rail roads; from Paris to the South, West, East, North and to Orléans and from Bordeaux to Toulouse (Doukas 1945, p. 29 f.). Well aware of the main railway building problems before his reign, Napoleon took over Émile Péreire's proposal to merge the existing private companies into six joint-stock mega-railway conglomerates, granting each a concession for 99 years to operate one of the six new lines and support them with state guarantees for low interest rates (Smith 2006, p. 82). After successful years, the government made further concessions to private conglomerates in 1859 to overcome the railway crisis (Doukas 1945, p. 33 ff.). However, thanks to the financial support of joint-stock banks and Napoleon's enthusiasm, French railway kilometers increased from around 1,850 in 1848 to 11,500 in 1865 (Smith 2006, p. 87).

Overall, for Napoleon III the permission of joint-stock banks was a great success: the Crédit Mobilier, managing at its height one third of all Parisian securities, became the government's main financial supporter, financed the government's huge Parisian construction projects, railways, public companies, private industries, overseas trade and public debt (Henderson 1967, p. 146). Newly founded joint-stock banks activated much of the idle capital—in particular before the crisis of 1857 when the middle class was enthusiastic to support the industrialization of the homeland (Kemp 1985, p. 63). Crédit Mobilier received a lot of sympathy from the general public (Henderson 1967, p. 152), lowered interests rates and facilitated the lending of the industrial bourgeoisie. Soon, further limited liability joint-stock banks were founded. According to Smith (2006, p. 68), the Second Empire was marked by two "revolutions in banking and transportation" and "both revolutions were the work of the same group of men, mainly the Saint-Simonian promoters and Paris financers." The rise of limited liability joint-stock banks destroyed the Haute Banque; the clandestine rulers of the July Monarchy.

As maintained, Napoleon's rule was built on two main promises: economic progress and imperialist extension (Tombs 1999, p. 67). Considering that he is "as much the emperor of the Arabs as emperor of the French" (Aldrich 1996, p. 93), Napoleon III significantly extended the French influence and the empire. New colonies were conquered and others developed, but French influence in Europe was particularly strengthened: during his reign, France once again became the most powerful empire in continental Europe. Wars against Russia and Austria and diplomacy were part of Napoleon's strategy to regain influence; in addition, economic expansion, in particular investments of the joint-stock banks, were used to increase the influence of the nation.

Napoleon extensively used the "industrial expansion" and "capital accumulation" to increase the French influence in Europe and the Levant (Henderson 1967, p. 136). In the first half of the 19th century, Britain was Europe's railway pioneer. As Britain increasingly invested elsewhere, France took over its place at the continent. French railway engineers fanned out to Europe and beyond to connect Europe with France by a close railway network. Railway financing facilitated railway building: James de Rothschild and the Péreires competing over lucrative investment opportunities and the King's grace were quite willing to finance the ambitious French railway projects elsewhere in Europe. At the beginning of the 20th century, from Portugal to Sicily, Turkey, Russia a close network of railways owned by French companies, built by French engineers, or at least financed by French capital covered the whole continent (c.f. Cameron 1961, p. 204–283). Building and operating railways was profitable for French banks and companies, demonstrated French engineering skills and technological abilities and in particular increased French political power and allies' dependency. Hence, Napoleon's foreign policy was underpinned by its railway imperialism financed by the newly founded joint-stock banks.

Supported, protected and directed by the government, French joint-stock banks invested big capital abroad: into railways, industries and public debt. As maintained, the government directed French capital by supporting and protecting investments where it liked to see them. The government followed the logic of credit for loyalty (Feis 1930, p. 132). Allied countries profited from French joint-stock banks' investments; renegaded allies were threatened with capital drain, which was usually enough to restore the cohesion. French capital imperialism was a vested interest in two regards: foreign investments supported Napoleon's imperialist ambitions, government's support facilitate banks foreign investment and fostered the rise of France as continental Europe's main banking hub.

5.3.5 The Third Republic: The Rise of Megabanks

The French defeat in the French-German war in 1870/1871 marked the end of Napoleon III's reign and the end of monarchy in France. Royalists calling for a strong monarchy, socialists trying to take over, workers rioting on the street; times were politically quite instable after Napoleon III stepped down. The foundation of the Paris Commune escalated the conflict between socialists and the conservative government. After troops loyal to the government stormed Paris and ended the Paris Commune, political conflicts cooled down, but remained latent.

When the Comte de Chambord rejected the royalist government's offer to ascend the throne, the path was open for the Third Republic. The Parliament's decision to establish a presidential republic was a compromise between non-republican forces. The royalist majority was deeply divided between Legitimists striving to a totalitarian, Catholic absolutistic monarchy and Orleanists favoring a constitutional monarchy; a conservative republic was, as the Orleanist Adolphe Thiers considered, the "government that divides us least" (Tombs 1999, p. 69). Not always quite stable, the Third Republic lasted until 1940. Despite the rise of left-wing parties, the political power remained in the hands of the bourgeoisie: "During the entire period of the Third Republic capitalist interests, whether industrial, commercial, or agricultural, have practically dominated the political arena" (Clough 1939, p. 210). Holding the balance between right-wing royalists and left-wing socialists fostered the political center occupied by the bourgeoisie and the upper middle class. While the Third Republic turned more republican before World War I, the right-wing (royalist, nationalists, fascists) and left-wing (socialists, communists, anarchists) opposition was increasingly excluded (Tombs 1999, p. 69 f.).

Apart from political instability, the Third Republic had to deal with several major challenges. With the defeat against Germany, France was pushed into a deep collective depression and sense of inferiority. As in Britain and Germany, the economy slowed down. The economic slowdown had several main reasons: in particular at the beginning of the Third Republic, the political situation was unstable. Secondly, former growth was also driven by high fertility; slower population growth reduced economic progress. Thirdly, the new protectionism shrank markets for French goods (c.f. Clough 1939, pp. 212–250). The economic slowdown raised the danger of further escalating class conflicts. Several measures were taken to boost the economy: protectionism should have protected the domestic economy from foreign competition, ambitious railway projects were expected to facilitate transportation and boost demand and imperialism should have developed new markets for industrial products and investments.

In the late 19th century, capital became increasingly abundant. After decades of fast economic progress in which capital was scarce, growth slowed down and profitable investment opportunities became scarce; periods of high profits and the foundation of joint-stock banks quickly increased the capital stock (Hoselitz 1955), which became too big at times of economic slowdown. Hence, several decades after the Crédit Mobilier was founded to overcome the scarcity of capital, capital owners increasingly lacked profitable investment opportunities. In particular after the crisis of 1882, banks' investable capital became abundant.

Increasing competition between joint-stock megabanks for profitable investment opportunities steadily decreased interest rates. Henri Germain, the head of the Crédit Lyonnais, was convinced that the only possibility to survive in the difficult market environment was to grow even more; a view which was widely accepted among joint-stock bankers (Mehrens 1911, p. 210 ff.). Hence, bankers believed that they are in a grow or die situation; only banks which grow fast have a chance to survive. Like in Britain, French megabanks were in the difficult situation of increasing competition, the need to grow and lower interests rates. In order to maintain high dividends and attract new capital, banks steadily took more risk by extending the asset per equity rate and investing in riskier assets.

As maintained, railway building was the main business of the rising joint-stock banks during the reign of Napoleon III. Governments of the Third Republic were not less railway enthusiastic, but the relation between private financers and the state was quite difficult. Two main groups of arguments in favor of railways were produced in the late 19th century: military necessity and economic reasonability. It was widely agreed that

France's inferior railway system contributed to the defeat against Germany (Doukas 1945, p. 52) and further railway building was necessary to stimulate trade (Clough 1939, p. 234) and overcome economic slowdown. After Napoleon's resignation, the state's role in the railway market was heavily discussed. Voices for railway nationalization were raised. Unprofitable railway routes and military and commercial complaints about the underdevelopment of the railway system caused many to demand the total or partial nationalization of railways. Merchants and the military complained that railway conglomerates are only oriented towards profit and ignore the needs of commerce and national defense. The Freycinet Plan proposed to stimulate the economy and employment by huge national railway projects (Doukas 1945, pp. 39–55). Agreeing on the Freycinet Plan, the government faced serious financing problems: railway projects turned out to be much more expensive than expected, the liquidation of the L'Union Générale further charged the state budget and railway nationalization being a constant liability, scared away private investors. Soon the government got convinced that a new agreement was needed to foster railway building (Clough 1939, p. 236). In 1883, the state and railway companies agreed on a redistribution of costs. In addition, treasury guarantees from the government to private railway companies were reformed (Doukas 1945, p. 45 f.). The new agreement turned out to be quite fertile ground for railway building. Encouraged by the new agreement, joint-stock megabanks—grateful for every relatively safe domestic investment opportunity—again invested heavily in new railway projects. Hence, after the difficult initial period, railway financing again became a core business of rising joint-stock megabanks.

Despite the economic stimuli from railway building, the economic slowdown continued. Due to the economic slowdown, protectionism again strengthened. The land-based aristocracy and the industrial bourgeoisie loudly demanded more protection from foreign competitors (Chapman 1963, p. 364 f; Mayeur and Rebérioux 1984, p 93 f.): falling food prices due to increasing supply pressured French agriculture. The fragmented French industry increasingly feared the concentrated German competition. Both the land-based aristocracy and the industrial bourgeoisie blamed free trade for falling prices and the economic slowdown. Neo-protectionism was also supported by left-wing politicians who were convinced that foreign competition increased unemployment (Clough 1939, p. 220). Two waves of increasing trade tariff in 1881 and in particular the Méline Tariffs of 1892 brought back heavy protectionism.

European protectionism deepened the economic problems of industrialized countries like France, which increasingly lacked markets for their industrial products. Imperialism was expected to develop new markets for domestic products. As maintained, French imperialism was promoted by a strong coalition of military, political and economic interests, underpinned by the belief in the obligation of the French nation to develop underdeveloped territories and bring enlightenment to the savages. As already outlined, France usually reacted with rampant imperialism and great military defeats; this was in particular the case after the lost war against Germany in the early 1870s. To conceal domestic political disturbances and the loss of Alsace-Lorraine, regain self-confidence and foster nationalistic sentiments, the Third Republic conquered a great deal of territory in Africa, Asia and elsewhere. The French imperialism of the late 19th century was also the reaction to Britain's new conquests, but in particular Germany's entry into the colonial race.

Several influential politicians of the Third Republic were convinced of the necessity of imperialism: Minister and Prime Minster Jules Ferry, for example, was an enthusiastic supporter of imperialism who took much effort to convince the Parliament and the public of the necessity of colonialism. Underpinned by rising nationalism and the pride in the empire, late 19th century French imperialism was particularly supported by economic interests. Protected from foreign competition by rising trade tariffs, the French industry lost much of its foreign markets by deepening European protectionism. In need of new markets (ibid., p. 245), often the same groups calling for protectionism supported colonialism to develop new markets for the French industrial oversupply. Facing economic slowdown and fearing its political consequences, like the rise of socialist groups, imperialism was considered a possible way out in France. Developing new markets were expected to take pressure off domestic economy.

Colonies and in particular the European allies provided new investment opportunities for French excess capital. The increasing abundancy of capital (ibid., p. 253 ff.) steadily decreased interest rates and increased the competition for profitable investment opportunities. Increasingly the abundant French capital searched for new investment markets abroad (Feis 1930, p. 33 ff). According to Pierre Paul Leroy-Beaulieu the "lowering of profit [...] is, in our opinion, a real evil" (cited in Murphy 1948, p. 123), which may be overcome by transferring the excess capital abroad: "It is therefore, useful that in a country where capitalization is more rapid than elsewhere, a part of the annual savings should be transported to the new lands where they return more intense services" (ibid.). It was widely agreed: "France needed colonies [...] for the investment of surplus capital" (Clough 1939, p. 254). Jules Ferry spoke explicitly of the abundance of capital which needs to be exported (Majumdar 2007, p. 84).

However, foreign investments were quite risky as banks lacked measurement to enforce their rights. In particular abroad the support of the French government protecting megabanks' investments with their political and even military means was important. At the same time, foreign private investments became one of the strongest imperialist instruments of the French government and it bound allies and colonies closer to the empire. At the end of the 19th century the relation between governments foreign policy and the banking system was close in Britain and in Germany, but nowhere as close as in France. The deal between the government and big finance was protection for direction; the government protects foreign investments if investors follow political directions. Occasionally, governments used their legal means to direct capital; usually, the influence was rather indirect as governments just protected French investments where it was intended: in the selected investment countries the government "stepped into aid and protect them [French Banks] in the event of default by a foreign government, or action injurious to an established French financial interest abroad" (Feis 1930, p. 146). In the French colonies, private banks became quasi public institutions as the colonial government granted them note-issuing monopolies and a wide range of further privileges. Using their bundled capital power, megabanks became important collaborators of French imperialism. Rather than sending the military, it was usually enough to threaten with the capital drain to convince renegade allies. The Prime Minister told the Chamber that "combine with French military and naval power, as converging and connecting forces, the financial power which is so great an aid to France" (ibid., p. 123), as "financial pressure or forceful menaces were applied to prevent these regions from escaping French hegemony" (ibid., p. 144). Hence, the coincidence of interests between joint-stock banks searching for profitable investments to invest the abundant capital and governments' attempt to increase their influence abroad underpinned the stable coalition between big finance and big politics for imperialism.

Again the coincidence of political and financial interests was the fertile ground for French imperialism: the nation's glory, national sentiments and pride, and hence government's legitimacy and political stability dependent on its ability to extend the empire. Facing difficult times due to rising European competition and falling interest rates, big finance became the notorious supporters of government imperialist ambitions. Due to the close connection between big finance and the governments' foreign policy, France net capital exports rose from 525 million francs between 1816 and 1830 to 45.825 million francs between 1898 and 1913 (Cameron 1961, p. 79): around one third to one half of French savings were invested abroad (Clough 1939: 254). The scope of French capital invested abroad made it a powerful instrument to penalize and remunerate foreign alliance and develop colonies. Joint-stock megabanks were the main investors abroad, which intensified their partnership with the governments.

Hence, low interests rates and the need for fast growth, accelerating railway building and intensifying foreign investment facilitated by government imperialism was the fertile ground for banking concentration and the emerging of joint-stock megabanks.

5.3.6 The Development of the French Banking System

After Napoleon's defeat, the government was under pressure to close the economic and military gap with Britain. However, France was hardly prepared for a fast catch-up industrialization: still, the landed aristocracy was highly influential politically, governments appeased the economic and landed elites by clientelism and the state economic role was by no means clear. In particular France lacked a developed financial market which would have been able and willing to support a fast industrialization. In early 19th century the French banking sector "was no doubt the most highly developed on the continent; even so, it was far from adequate for the tremendous task of industrial expansion which lay ahead" (Cameron 1961, p. 112). Like in Britain before the legal Acts of the 1820s, the French banking system was highly fragmented and dominated by small disconnected regional banks (Dunham 1955, p. 68 f.). The Parisian financial market was dominated by the wealthy bourgeoisie investing its idle hoards into domestic and foreign public debt.

Usually, regional banks were hardly connected to the Parisian financial market; regional banks absorbed the funds of their region to invest into the region. Small private regional and Parisian banks absorbed the owners', their relatives' and friends' wealth to lend it to the old aristocracy and the established small industry. Borrowing and lending usually occurred within personal relations; hence, small private banks borrowed and lent within an "intimate circle" (Landes 1949, p. 47) usually including members of the old aristocracy and the established industrial bourgeoisie: newcomers were excluded.

Capital was hoarded or mainly invested in land. Even the rising bourgeoisie was still land orientated: land was considered a safe investment and allowed the entry to the noble landed class (Landes 1949, p. 56 ff; Dunham 1955, p. 240; Pilbeam 1990, p. 55 ff.). The rising industry was still mainly small-scale, most companies having less than ten employees, financed by owners' or relatives' savings or small loans from regional banks (Kemp 1985, p. 59 ff.). Despite increasing lending to small industries, public debt and mortgages was the core business of regional banks (Cameron 1961, p. 107 ff.).

The emerging of the Haute Banque was the first deep change in the French private banking system in the 19th century. At the beginning predominant merchants and small bankers, the Haute Banque was formed in the early 19th century and was dominated by Protestants, but also consisted of Jewish and Catholic bankers (Smith 2006, pp. 49–56). Attracted by the liberal religious laws of the Revolutionary and Napoleon area, members of the Haute Banque were not, at the beginning, wealthier or more influential than other bankers and merchants, but bolder than other bankers to invest into risky public debt when other bankers shied away from lending to the unstable state: "what distinguished members of the 'haute banque' was not so much the quantity of their assets as how they employed them" (ibid., p. 49). At the beginning of the Bourbon Restoration, French public debt was almost exclusively underwritten by British and Dutch bankers; however, the Haute Banque steadily took over public debt financing at a large scale (Cameron 1961, p. 109). Building a close network of banking families (Smith 2006, p. 49), heavily involved in public debt financing, the government's dependency on the Haute Banque steadily increased its political influence.

Banking at the time of the Bourbon Restoration much reflected the general political and economic situation: France was dominated by small privileged groups. Regional banks were the fragmented, disintegrated banking vehicle of the old elites. However, the rise of the Haute Banque that became the government's main bankers, was the harbinger of more profound change. Despite the rise of the new banking elite, economic newcomers remained excluded from access to credit and banking (Landes 1949, p. 47).

Already during the time of Bourbon Restoration, progressive bankers around Jacques Laffitte argued that the existing banking sector is inadequate for the desired industrialization of the country. In 1821 Laffitte proposed to the government to found an industrial bank with a fantastic capital of 240 million francs; in 1825 he submitted a revised version suggesting a bank with a capital of 100 million francs. Liberals were enthusiastic about his project, the who's who of the Haute Banque were ready to invest, but the government refused both proposals fearing the concentration of capital and the rising power of liberals (c.f. Cameron 1961, p. 113).

5.3.6.1 The Dominance of the Haute Banque

As maintained, the July Revolution marked the victory of the rising bourgeoisie, in particular the financial bourgeoisie, over the old aristocracy. During the July Monarchy, the Haute Banque became one of the most influential groups in France. Soon, the Haute Banque became Europe's main public debt financer (Born 1977, p. 77).

Founded by Napoleon Bonaparte, the Banque de France was the bank of banks. It held a note-issuing monopoly for wider Paris, operated tranches in Lyons, Rouen and Lille; independent note-issuing banks were founded in Rouen, Nantes and Bordeaux (Kindleberger 1993, p. 105), however the Banque de France remained the leading institution. Formally, the Banque de France stood above private banks; practically the Banque de France was dominated by the Haute Banque that monopolized the chairs on the board (Smith 2006, p. 49). Overall, the early 19th century financial sector was characterized by small regional banks; the Haute Banque in Paris, above the Banque de France and a wide range of the regional fiscal administrations (Comptables du Trésor public), notaries and other groups were somehow involved in the financial business (c.f. Mehrens 1911, pp. 9–41). Effectively, the entire French financial market was dominated by the Haute Banque, ensuring that the Banque de France safeguards its interests and heavily influencing politics by its quasi public debt banking monopoly. Hence, during the July Monarchy, French banking was dominated by a close, exclusive network between the Haute Banque, the Banque de France and the government.

The Haute Banque was often criticized for not supporting the rising industrialization. It is usually ignored that the Haute Banque financed the rising industry sooner than private banks of other countries and on a larger scale (Born 1977, p. 97 ff.). Investing in trade and the rising industry and in particular public debt, no other project changed the French and the Europe banking system more fundamentally than railway building. Various influential groups—industrialists, military forces, politicians—demanded the expansion of the railway system. While government infrastructure projects were quite ambiguous, the finance planning was usually slow. Governments and the economic and military elites being enthusiastic about July Monarchy's grant railway projects, little attention was given do the fact that France lacked the financial institutions able to cover the costs of the fantastic projects. Unable to finance railways by its own revenues, the government heavily depended on the financial support of private financial institutions. Throughout the time of the July Monarchy, railway financing remained a major problem. France just lacked financial institutions able to raise huge funds in short time for long-term investment. Unable to finance railways by itself, the governments' claim to lead railway projects (Sée 1936, p. 212) and refusal to hand over controlling rights to private investors (Dunham 1955, p. 70) further complicated railway financing.

Despite all difficulties and the tense relation with many engineers and the government, the Haute Banque became the main railway financer. For bankers, railway financing was a double-edged sword: on the one hand, the business was risky and full of serious challenges. On the other hand, railway projects offered almost unlimited, profitable if successful, investment opportunities and close ties to the needy government. Entering the railway financing business, the Haute Banque increasingly differentiated its investment away from public debt banking (Cameron 1961, p. 111). Closely cooperating with Saint-Simonian engineers, railway miles increased from 38 in 1831 to 1912 km in 1848 (Clough 1939, p. 148) during Haute Banque's railway financing dominance. Holding a quasi-monopoly for railway banking (Mehrens 1911, p. 13), the French railway boom changed the Haute Banque. Investment opportunities on a new scale yielded a small clique of successful railway bankers which outgrew the former scale of banking. James de Rothschild's rise to France's most powerful and richest banker was emblematic for Haute Banque's benefit from the railway boom: bolder than most of his colleagues, James de Rothschild became the main financer of French railways. Due to French companies' and banks' involvement in foreign railway building, French capital exports accelerated (Cameron 1961, p. 76 ff.), which increased its economic and political influence.

During the July Monarchy, the governments' dependency on the Haute Banque and therefore its influence was huge. Notoriously hard up, the Haute Banque was the governments' main financer. Hardly any war or palace could have been fought or built without the financial support from the Haute Banque. Railways were considered pivotal for economic, political and military progress and success, for national glory and France's legitimate claim to being a first-class nation. Under huge pressure to intensify its railway building to catch up with Germany and Britain, or at least keep up pace with them, governments lacked the financial means to implement their ambitious projects. No group had the financial means and the boldness to finance the huge railway projects other than the Haute Banque. Financing the monarch's foreign allies and his military ventures (Born 1977, pp. 64–83) the Haute Banque became important collaborators of the French foreign policy. Already during the time of the July Monarchy, Haute Banque's foreign investment was used to underpin French foreign policy. Due to governments' mutual and huge dependency on Haute Banque's financial support, the Haute Banque became one of the most influential, maybe the most influential, group in Paris.

Hence, the time of the July Monarchy was characterized by the rise of the Haute Banque and its close and stable coalition with the Banque de France. For thirty years the French banking system was a stable, malfunctioning system, dominated by the coalition of the Banque de France and the Haute Banque and government dependency on bankers' support: it was malfunctioning and heavily criticized because it failed to absorb more idle capital, reduce interest rates and provide enough capital for fast industrialization. The dominance of the Haute Banque was heavily criticized throughout the July Monarchy, but stable due to close connections to and the dependency of the Crown. Overall, during the July Monarchy the French banking system remained predominately pre-modern in the sense that it was still dominated by banks which first and foremost invested the owners', their relatives' and friends' capital; hence, capital and lender-borrower relations remained predominately personalized.

5.3.6.2 Intensifying Critique of the Status Quo

Increasingly, the Haute Banque was criticized for selfishness, too little support of the industrialization and hampering rather than fostering economic progress. The comprehensive critique of Haute Banque's business was fueled by popular anti-banking, anti-Protestant and anti-Semitic resentments. In particular Saint-Simonians openly demanded a banking revolution to overcome the power of the Haute Banque.

Already at the time of the Bourbon Restoration and in particular during the July Monarchy, several banking experts, most notable Jacques Laffitte and other Saint-Simonians, considered that France lacks the financial institutions needed to implement its ambitious industrial projects. Many contributors of the time blamed the scarcity of French capital for the slow development. In contrast, Saint-Simonians argued that not the scarcity of capital, but the lack of ability in financial institutions in France to absorb the idle hoards and invest large scale into industrial projects was the problem. In hindsight, it seems that Saint-Simonians were right: France was overcrowded with investable capital, but lacked financial institutions to absorb the huge funds and lend it to the industry and railway companies (Dunham 1955, p. 213 ff.).

As maintained, at the beginning of the French railway boom, the cooperation between Saint-Simonian railway engineers and the Haute Banque was quite fertile. However, Saint-Simonians increasingly criticized the Haute Banque for making too little of an effort and providing too little capital for the country's industrialization. The deepening conflict between the Saint-Simonians and the Haute Banque caused the break between Laffitte and his former supporters of the Haute Banque, Enfantin, to directly attack bankers and the escalation of the latent conflict between the Péreires and Rothschild over railway financing (Kindleberger 1985, p. 49). As maintained, around the time leading Saint-Simonians like Prosper Enfantin, Jacques Laffitte, Michel Chevalier and the brothers Emile and Isaac Péreire heavily criticized the Haute Banque for taking sides with idle capital owners and exploiting the diligent with high interest rates. According to them, the established banking system puts the vested interest of a small group over the general interest and this is quite insufficient to absorb the needed capital for industrialization. Saint-Simonians proposed to found big industrial banks able to absorb all idle hoards, which clearly takes side with the industry and the diligent and whose ultimate goal is the industrialization of the country rather than maximizing profits. In particular Laffitte, after his career as Banque de France governor, became a famous and widely heard advocate of industrial banks. However, during the July Monarchy proposals failed due to Haute Banque's and Banque de France resistance (Cameron 1961, pp. 115–118).

Saint-Simonian critics, supported by public anti-banking attitude, anti-Semitic and anti-Protestant sentiments were fueled by the governments' increasing dissatisfaction with the railway building progress. There is little doubt that interest rates were high and many industrial projects lacked the needed credit (c.f. Dunham 1955, pp. 213–242). But who is to be blamed? As maintained, credit was not scarce due to small loanable funds, but because of underdeveloped financial institutions. Besides, banks' underdevelopment, Banque's de France conservative discount policy and private banks' cautious lending policy raised interest rates (Mehrens 1911, pp. 19–25). However, governments' rejection to permit joint-stock banks locked in the dissatisfactory banking system.

Rather than for their banking policy, the Haute Banque and the Banque de France must be blamed for forming a strong and influential coalition to repel all kind of banking innovation and reinforce the status quo. Protecting their favorable position, the Haute Banque and the Banque de France used all their political and economic power to prevent any banking innovation which would have questioned their privileges. Infiltrated by and in particular highly dependent on the Haute Banque and its extended arm the Banque de France, governments usually shied away from supporting any change which would upset the Haute Banque. Apart from the institutional barriers and the rejection of the Haute Banque and the Banque de France, collective banking traumas hampered banking innovations and the extension of banking. The big banking crises of the 18th century became collective national traumas which survived the involved generation: in the 19th century France was still traumatized by John Law's failure. Peoples' mistrust and hostility toward banking prevented the extension of banking and the absorption of idle capital. Afraid of bank defaults, many preferred to hoard the idle reserves or invest them elsewhere over lending them to banks. In particular, people were cautious with big banks were they lacked personal relations to the management: "French people were suspicious of banks even if many of their writers urged the government to charter more to them, and the larger the bank and the further from their homes, the greater was their suspicion" (Dunham 1955, p. 223).

5.3.6.3 The Rise of Joint-Stock Banks

Increasingly facing difficulties to finance railways, the government responded with two main measures: the Railway-Act of 1842 was the last attempt of the July Monarchy to overcome the railway problems. To facilitate financing, the government permitted Laffitte to open a joint-stock bank. In 1837 Laffitte won a late victory when he was allowed, now 70 years old, to found a Caisse Générale du Commerce et de L'Industrie as a Limited Partnership with a nominal capital of 35 million francs (Redlich 1948, p. 154). Enthusiastic about his first proposals in 1821, the Haute Banque turned against Laffitte (Kindleberger 1993, p. 106). Frequently facing problems to raise enough funds, the Banque Laffitte nevertheless became an important financer of the big industrial projects (Redlich 1948, p. 153 ff.). However, Laffitte's bank was particularly important because it became the first Saint-Simonian bank.

The financial crisis of 1847 had negative political and economic consequences for the dominant financial elites: economically many banks of the Haute Banque went bankrupt, politically the Revolution of 1848 overturned the July Monarchy and the latent rule of the financial bourgeoisie. The rulers of the July Monarchy were quite dependent on the Haute Banque and safeguarded their interests; Napoleon III, the new ruler, was convinced by Saint-Simonians' banking proposals and left no doubt that he would end the latent dominion of the Haute Banque.

As maintained, Napoleon's political and economic program was quite ambitious: he intended to extend the French influence, rebuild the French hegemony on the Continent and economically catch-up with Britain. Ambitious projects are typical for monarchs, in particular if they are French, but Napoleon III was quite aware of the relations of economic progress and political and military success. Wars were fought by mobile armies transported by fast railways across the country and equipped with weapons made in the heavy industry. All kind of imperialism increasingly depended on economic means: on a country's ability to economically develop newly conquered territories, connect allies to the empire with improved transportation and make them increasingly economically dependent. For railway building, accelerating industrialization and binding foreign allies closer to the empire, Napoleon III needed the support of big finance: predominately banks able to finance ambitious railway projects and fast industrialization and bind foreign allies closer to the empire by huge foreign investments.

Quite impressed by Saint-Simonians' political economy, Napoleon III was convinced that France lacks financial organizations able and willing to finance his megaprojects and support his foreign policy. Even before Napoleon's reign, Saint-Simonians dominated many technical education institutions and were famous engineers and bankers. With Napoleon's takeover, Saint-Simonians' power increased: they became the most influential advisors, occupied new professions and started to dominate the financial sectors: "A large proportion of the men who reached positions of economic and financial influence upon Napoleon's advent to power were not isolated individuals. They belonged to a rather well-defined group. They were not Bonapartists but Saint-Simonian socialists" (Gerschenkron 1962, p. 23). As Saint-Simonians' influence steadily increased, the Haute Banque was on the retreat. Still, the Haute Banque and the Banque de France combatted every banking innovation. However, strongly influenced by his Saint-Simonian advisors and convinced that France needs a banking revolution, Napoleon III was much less willing to succumb to old banking elite's pressure.

Railways and universal banks are the two legacies of Napoleon's ambitious economic policy, which sustainably shaped Europe's economic landscape long beyond Napoleon's death. As maintained, Napoleon III was quite aware that railways are of pivotal military, economical and political importance. To finance his ambitious railway projects, Napoleon was convinced that a banking revolution was needed. Highly influenced by his Saint-Simonian advisors, Napoleon III permitted the foundation of limited liability joint-stock industrial banks; against the angry protests of the banking establishment. Overall closely following Saint-Simonians' advice, Napoleon III refused to permit note-issuing rights to the new joint-stock banks: permitting note-issuing license would have been a frontal attack on the Banque de France and would have reminded people of John Law's failure.

According to Kindleberger (1993, p. 115 ff.), in terms of the development of the financial system, Britain was a hundred years ahead of France. The French financial backwardness also stemmed from banking elites' power and willingness to fight every profound innovation and maintain the status quo. The weakness of the Haute Banque paved the way for the French banking revolution during Napoleon's reign. Blamed for being selfish and following their money interests (Plenge 1903, p. 62), of having delayed the Industrial Revolution and of supporting the old rulers (ibid., p. 65), Haute Banque's position and resistance was particularly weakened by the financial crisis of 1847. The coincidence of the weakness of the Haute Banque and Saint-Simonians opened the historical window for continental Europeans' most far-reaching banking innovation of the 19th century.

Convinced by the necessity to facilitate credit granting (Mehrens 1911, p. 89), Napoleon granted the first joint-stock banks license to the brothers Péreire, which permitted the foundation of France's first industrial bank. Already in 1830 the brothers Péreire proposed the foundation of an industrial bank, but failed to convince the government; with Napoleon III holding power and the Haute Banque being marginalized, the circumstances for their project were much better. In 1852 Napoleon permitted the foundation of Péreires' Crédit Mobilier, against the angry protests of the Banque de France and the Haute Banque (Henderson 1967, p. 148): for many contributors in economic history, the foundation of the Crédit Mobilier was the most important innovation in the history of continental European banking (Kindleberger 1993, p. 111). Enthusiastic about Saint-Simonian projects, Gerschenkron (1962, p. 12) wrote about the development of industrial banking during Napoleon's reign:

> the industrial development of France under Napoleon III must be attributed to that determined effort to untie the strait jacket in which weak governments and strong vested interests had inclosed the French economy. [...] French industry received a powerful positive impetus from a different quarter. The reference is to the development of industrial banking under Napoleon III.

Founded with a capital of 60 million francs, the Crédit Mobilier closely followed the accompanying theory: according to its directors, the Crédit Mobilier was founded to overcome the insufficient credit for business and the big industry, to boost capital, supply credit in better conditions, use the available capital to the advantage of all citizens and supply a new currency (Henderson 1967, p. 145 f.). As the fist limited liability joint-stock bank in France, the Crédit Mobilier was an overwhelming success: the Crédit Mobilier fast extended its business and became Napoleon's main financer and took "a leading part in fostering the industrialization of France" (ibid., p. 148).

The Crédit Mobilier was the blueprint for the foundation of further French joint-stock and deposit banks like the Crédit Industriel (1859), Crédit Lyonnais (1863), Société Générale (1864), Banque de Paris et des Pays-Bas (1872), Banque de lIndochine (1875), the Société de l'Union Générale (1874) and the Banque Française pour le Commerce et l'Industrie (1901), Banque de l'Union Parisienne (1904)—the last was a merger of smaller joint-stock banks. As maintained, the foundation of the Crédit Mobilier was strongly inspired by Saint-Simonianism; the founders of later joint-stock banks cared little about Saint-Simonianism, but just copied the successful business model of the Crédit Mobilier. The Crédit Industriel was France's first big private Depositbank, the Crédit Lyonnais (1863) the first Universal-Bank; just a year later, the old Haute Banque founded the Universal-Bank Société Générale (1864) as a counterweight to the Crédit Mobilier. The investment bank Banque de Paris et des Pays-Bas was the bank of big business which absorbed huge capital by giving out a few shares to very rich businessman. The Catholic investment bank Société de l'Union Générale was founded as a Catholic counterweight to the Protestant and Jewish banking dominance (c.f. Born 1977, pp. 146–151). Already in 1848 the government founded the joint-stock bank the Comptoir national D'Escompte de Paris to mitigate the negative effects of the economic crisis (c.f. Mehrens 1911, p. 42 f.). Indented as a temporal institution, the Comptoir D'Escompte was transformed into an ordinary joint-stock bank in 1853.

For the Péreires it was their Saint-Simonian mission to diffuse industrial banking through Europe. Welcomed by many –ordinary people, merchants, industrialists, engineers, politicians—the foundation of the Crédit Mobilier was the most profound attack on the Haute Banque since its rise in the early 19th century. Failing to prevent the foundation of the Crédit Mobilier, James de Rothschild used all his influence to dam the extension of the Crédit Mobilier. Ironically, the hostility between the Péreires and Rothschild became the main driving force which diffused Crédit Mobilier-style joint-stock banks throughout Europe.

> The Crédit Mobilier was from the beginning engaged in a most violent conflict with the representatives of 'old wealth' in French banking, most notably with the Rothschilds. It was this conflict that had sapped the force of the institution and was primarily responsible for its eventual collapse in 1867. But what is so seldom relized is that in the course of this conflict the 'new wealth' succeeded in forcing the old wealth to adopt the policies of its opponents (Gerschenkron 1962, p. 12 f.).

Together with Oppenheimer and other German bankers, the Crédit Mobilier founded the Darmstädter Bank using the Crédit Mobilier as blueprint. Afraid of falling behind, Rothschild used his influence to found the Creditanstalt, Austria's first joint-stock banks, likewise using the Crédit Mobilier as blueprint. Directly supported by the Crédit Mobilier and Rothschild or just copying the blueprints, Crédit Mobilier-style joint-stock banks were founded in Italy, Spain, Belgium, the Netherlands, Sweden, Prussia and several more countries (Cameron 1961). Most European megabanks which still dominate the banking sector were founded in the race between the Péreires and Rothschild. Maybe it is exaggerated that "a new form of banking [Crédit Mobilier] was evolved; this, more than any other event, cut the gordian knot binding the forces of industrial progress" (Hoselitz 1955, p. 306), but undeniably "the banking system of every nation in continental Europe bore the imprint of French influence" (Cameron 1961, p. 203). However, the continental European banking system is still characterized by "creative adaptation of the basic idea of the Péreires and its incorporation in the new type of bank, the universal bank" (Gerschenkron 1962, p. 13): most French, German and other leading continental European banks have its origin in Crédit Mobilier-style joint-stock banks.

Rothschild and the Péreires competed over Europe's best places to found joint-stock banks and over Europe's best investment opportunities. The continental Europe railway boom necessitated huge amounts of capital, but was also quite profitable if successful. The decades after the foundation of the Crédit Mobilier were marked by an unprecedented race between the Crédit Mobilier and Rothschild and his allies for railway financing in Europe. From Portugal over Spain, Swiss, the Benelux, Italy, Austria, Germany, Russia and Turkey either Crédit Mobilier, Rothschild or both financed railways (c.f. Cameron 1961, pp. 204–283). Propelled by the competition between Crédit Mobilier and Rothschild, France replaced Britain as the main railway engineer of the continent (Cameron 1961); other infrastructure and industrial projects were also financed by them elsewhere in Europe.

Economically and politically the race between the Crédit Mobilier and Rothschild had far-reaching consequences. Politically, France's heavy involvement in railway building elsewhere in Europe and beyond strongly increased its political influence. Connecting Europe to the homeland augmented France military access to the Continent. After the great defeats at the beginning of the century and ongoing inside turmoil, France showed the world its engineering skills and its economic power: lamenting France's economic backwardness for decades, in mid-19th century France was back as the leading industrial nation of continental Europe. Economically, French international activities accelerated its capital exports; started by the Crédit Mobilier and Rothschild, other French joint-stock banks soon also exported capital heavily. Between 1852, the foundation of the Crédit Mobilier, and 1870, the end of Napoleon's reign, in 1870 France's capital net export rose to almost 13,000 million francs; between 1816 and 1847 the net export was just around 2,500 million (Cameron 1961, p. 79).

For banks and their customers, French international economic activities had the positive effect of providing new profitable assets to capital owners and reducing the competition for domestic investment opportunities. Politically, huge capital exports augmented the government's foreign influence: Napoleon III frequently used foreign investments to form alliances and put pressure on possible renegades (Feis 1930, p. 133 ff.). Due to their close relation, Napoleon particularly directed Crédit Mobilier's foreign investments. Directed by political rather than economic reasons, Napoleon's strong hand increasingly became a problem for the Crédit Mobilier, which was forced to invest into unprofitable foreign assets to underpin the Crown's foreign policy (Plenge 1903, p. 85 ff.).

Hence, what started as a Saint-Simonian project to foster French industrialization became one of the most pivotal innovations of the continental European banking system. Soon, joint-stock banking emancipated itself from its Saint-Simonian origins. Banks founded during the joint-stock banking boom—Crédit Industriel, Crédit Lyonnais, Société Générale, Banque de Paris et des Pays-Bas, Banque de l'Indochine, Société de l'Union Générale—were hardly based on Saint-Simonian ideas, the Société Générale was even founded as an anti-Saint-Simonian counterweighed. Nevertheless,

Saint-Simonianism was pivotal for the takeoff of continental universal, deposit and investment joint-stock banking: Saint-Simonians were the main developers of joint-stock industrial bank proposals. Propelled by their deep conviction in the superiority of industrial societies and the need for fast industrialization, Saint-Simonians remained steadfast and promoted and advanced their banking ideas against all resistance. Saint-Simonians' engineering expertise made them indispensable even to governments reluctant to Saint-Simonianism.

However, Napoleon III's ascension to the throne opened the historical window for the Saint-Simonians. Reluctant towards the Haute Banque, but in need of a reliable and potent financer, Napoleon III turned toward the Saint-Simonians. Deeply convinced of the need of a banking revolution and accompanying proposals caused Napoleon to permit joint-stock industrial banks against all resistance and warnings. However, the rise of Saint-Simonian-style joint-stock industrial banks elsewhere in Europe is an ideal example of how successful projects shake off the ideal fundament on which they were once built and often go into reverse. Nevertheless, Saint-Simonian ideas were the initiators of modern banks in France and elsewhere in continental Europe. Before the joint-stock banking revolution, banking was predominately pre-modern: bankers invested, predominately, their own or their relatives' capital into friends' projects; hence, borrowing and lending was predominately characterized by personal relations. In contrast, the rising joint-stock banks usually absorbed capital from hundreds and thousands of stockholders and depositors and invested it into hundreds of smaller and bigger domestic and foreign projects. Hence, with the rise of joint-stock banks, capital de-personalized and the interest trinity of modern banking emerged: despite the interests of the borrowers and lenders, joint-stock banks followed their own interests.

5.3.6.4 French Banking Concentration

As maintained, Saint-Simonian expected that joint-stock industrial banks would augment investable capital by absorbing most idle hoards and therefore reducing interest rates. From the perspective of early founders, the intentions of joint-stock banks was an outstanding success: absorbing much more funds than former fragmented, small scale banks interest rates fell steadily (Mehrens 1911, p. 210 f.). Founded to overcome the scarcity of investment funds, capital increasingly became abundant due to the deepening of joint-stock banking. The newly founded joint-stock banks played a "truly momentous role of investment banking of the period for the economic history of France and of large portions of the continent [… to] build thousands of miles of railroads, drill mines, erect factories, pierce canals, construct ports, and modernize cities" (Gerschenkron 1962, p. 12).

After the founding phase between the early 1850s and early 1870s, no new joint-stock banks were founded, which played a major role for the French banking system. Ironically, overstretching its business, Europe's joint-stock banking blueprint, the Crédit Mobilier, was almost liquated in 1867; the Catholic Société de l'Union Générale had the same destiny and collapsed in 1882. Like in Britain in the late 19th century, the French banking sector was characterized by fast concentration (Sée 1936, p. 349), strong competition and falling interest rates. The deepening economic slowdown and the fall of the Société de l'Union Générale accelerated the general late-19th century tendency of falling interest rates, abundance of capital and increasing competition for profitable investment opportunities between rising megabanks. The worsening situation for French banks was interpreted by the leading megabanks as a grow or die situation. As maintained, Henri Germain, the head of the Crédit Lyonnais, openly insisted that only the fast growing banks will survive the growing domestic and foreign competition. In order to extend its business, the Crédit Lyonnais was the first bank pursuing a rampant extension of all kind of banking business, throughout France and to all social classes; other joint-stock banks followed suit (Mehrens 1911, p. 212 f.).

As maintained, governments of the Third Republic were as enthusiastic about railway building as their predecessors. Hungry for all kind of investment opportunities, joint-stock banks again became the main railway financers. After the Freycinet Plan was withdrawn, due to the government's problem to finance new railways, France returned to the old system; with the endless financial help from the joint-stock megabanks railway building became faster than ever before: from 1879 to 1909 3,300 km of waterways were improved and 650 new ones constructed (Henderson 1967, p. 174), the railway network increased between 1890 and 1912 from 37,000 to 52,000 km; the longest railway network in Europe by total kilometer and kilometer per capita (Sée 1936, p. 369 ff.).

To realize their ambitious imperialist projects, governments of the Third Republic depended on the support from big finance. The imperialist coalition between the government—legitimizing their rule, overcoming collective depressions and expecting to stimulate the economy by extending the empire and its foreign influence—and big finance—glad about every new profitable investment opportunity—successfully extended France's influence abroad. French foreign influence was extended by colonial conquests and increasing economic and political dependency of smaller and less developed European countries: for both, megabanks played an important role. Megabanks were quite important for the development of new and old colonies and extended French influence by investing heavily into allied countries.

Underpinned by governments' support, franc was continental Europe's biggest capital exporter at the beginning of the 20th century (Born 1977, p. 239). Heavily investing in its traditional investment strongholds, railways and public debt (Cameron 1961), French foreign investments rose from an already huge 12 billion in 1870 to an enormous 45 billion francs in 1914 (Feis 1930, p. 47). Due to close ties with the governments and foreign elites, joint-stock megabanks—like the Comptoir D'Escompte, Crédit Lyonnais, Société Générale, Banque de Paris et des Pays-Bas—became the main capital exporters (Born 1977, p. 241). Absorbing French capital to invest it profitably abroad, joint-stock megabanks depended on governments safeguarding their investments and therefore reducing risk. In addition, several regulations enabled governments to direct foreign investments. Hence, private megabanks' foreign investment and governments foreign policy were often two sides of one coin: "To retrace the history of French foreign lending would be, as a French writer had said, almost equivalent to writing the history of French political sympathies, rapprochements, vague dreams of influence, alliances in arms" (Feis 1930, p. 50).

Like in Britain, falling interest rates, the abundancy of capital and bankers' belief that they are in a situation of grow or die caused the strong and fast concentration of the French banking sector in the later 19th and early 20th century. On a par with its British competitors in size and market concentration, the vehicle of concentration differed: British banks grew by merges, French banks by branching (Born 1977, p. 318 f.). French joint-stock megabanks opened branches even in small towns to absorb new deposits and reach all people and classes with their banking services. British country banks almost disappeared in the process of market concentration; in France during World War I many small regional banks still existed side by side with joint-stock megabanks. The Haute Banque almost disappeared as independent bankers, but survived as the main shareholders and mangers of the big investment banks. After decades of fast concentration in the early 20th century, the French banking sector was dominated by the big three plus three: the big three are the Comptoir D'Escompte, Crédit Lyonnais, Société Générale and the plus three the investment banks Banque de Paris et des Pays-Bas, the Banque Française pour le Commerce et l'Industrie and the Banque de l'Union Parisienne. The equity capital of the big three was twice as big as the equity of its 17 nearest competitors. Even more impressive the big three managed deposits of around 4400 million francs, their 17 nearest competitors just 860 million together (ibid., p. 317). Hence, the biggest three deposit banks were times bigger than the 17 banks next in size together and strongly dominated the banking sector.

5.4 The Rise of German Banking

North- and South-Mosaic-Germany cities were among the first places in North- and Central-Europe where banks were founded. Predominately involved in trade related banking, short time lending and coin exchange, the first private banks did not emerge until the late 18th and early 19th century, and they were focused on the ordinary capitalist banking business, like loanable fund intermediation and long-term lending. It was not until the takeoff of German industrialization and unification that megabanks emerged; closely linked with the rising German industry and the governments, at the time of World War I German megabanks were among Europe's biggest financial institutions. Saint-Simonians demanded the close connection and cooperation between the industry and banks, with the lead of the latter; in the late 19th and early 20th century, Germany came close to the Saint-Simonian suggestion. The relation between German megabanks and the big industry was often so close that they were hardly distinguishable.

No other European country changed more fundamentally—economically, politically and culturally—in the 19th century than Germany: politically highly fragmented, economically agrarian-dominated, culturally bounded to pre-modern ideas at the beginning of the 19th century, around World War I Germany was almost an ideal type of an industrialized economy in the Marxian sense: Germany's industry was dominated by oligopolies and megacompanies and megabanks closely related to each other and to the government.

5.4.1 Ideas Determining the Development of Banking

It may seem that the German cultural order has a lot in common with the British and French situation: liberalism and nationalism was on the rise until liberalism was steadily replaced by interventionism and conservativism at the end of the 19th and the beginning of the 20th century. Liberal classical economics dominated economic theories until protectionism and interventionism was on the rise at the end of the 19th century. However, a closer look shows that the German case was quite different. Elsewhere, nationalism was on the rise; nowhere was the question of the nation more urgent, far-reaching and conflictual than in Germany. Fragmented into dozens smaller and bigger entities, the question of how, if at all, Germany should unite was not just a political issue; the question of unification dominated the cultural, political and economic order.

Like in Britain and France, liberalism was on the rise in Germany. However, German liberalism was much less ideological and carried by different groups than in France and Britain which is why it developed rather different demands and suggestions. While British liberalism increasingly became open for the political left, due to the coalition with conservatives, German liberalism steadily went to the right. Like elsewhere, nationalism became the twin of liberalism. However, unlike in France and Britain, the question of the nation was all but clear in Germany. In Germany, two competing nationalisms emerged: German nationalism demanded the full unification of all German territories and scission nationalism aimed to strengthen national sentiments to the existing segregated national entities. German nationalism was the issue of a small liberal elite prosecuted by the supporters of the much stronger scission nationalism. Before the end of the 19th century German nationalism also reached ordinary people. Nevertheless, German nationalism highly influenced famous economists, advocates of industrialization and money theorists.

The development of economic theory in Germany shares many similarities with France. At the beginning of the 19th century the most famous economists were highly influenced by the rising British classical theory. However, around the 1820s several economists strongly questioned the adequacy of the classical theory for Germany, an economically backward political fragmented entity. Inspired by their French colleagues, industrial fetishism also developed in Germany. Most notable was the economic nationalism of Friedrich List. Like several French colleagues, List was enthusiastic about industrialization and believed that an economically backward country like Germany needs protection to develop its industry. A keen enthusiast of German nationalism, List was convinced that industrialization, and in particular railway building, would foster national sentiments and facilitate Germany's unification. In List's lifetime his economic nationalism failed to overturn the classical economic dominance, but the theory inspired later economists and the nationalist movement. While classical economics dominated economic discussions in Germany around mid-19th century, like in France and Britain, liberal economics were increasingly replaced by more conservative and protectionist views at the end of the century. However, just in Germany a new economic theory emerged which dominated the late 19th and early 20th century: state- or kathedersocialism. In sharp contrast to liberal classical economics, state- or kathedersocialists demanded the heavy intervention of the state, supported the concentration and cartelization of the economy, and suggested a planned industrialization, which was planned and operated within the triangle of the state, big industrial conglomerates and banks.

5.4.1.1 Nationalism and the Unification

No other event changed the economic and political structure of Europe more fundamentally than the unification of Germany. The unification was a highly contested process which lasted for the entire 19th century. At the beginning of the 19th century people arguing for full unification were a clear minority, often prosecuted and facing the hostility of the establishment.

Elsewhere in Europe, nationalism was on the rise. Also, in most countries liberalism and nationalism were closely connected ideas. Nevertheless, the situation in Germany was very special: in France and Britain the nation's boundaries, hence what is part of the nation and what not, were relatively clear. In Germany the question of the nation's territory was highly contested. Two incompatible forms of nationalism existed: German nationalism and scission nationalism; the first demanded the full unification of Germany and the second the strengthening of the existing German entities.

Like in France and Britain, liberals were the main carriers of German nationalism. Not different than in other countries, the rising liberal bourgeoisie faced the rejection of the conservative old aristocracy. However, in Germany the battle between liberal new elites and conservative old elites had a further fundamental dimension: the fight for political influence and over ideas between the new and the old elites was also a contest over the nation itself in Germany; while old elites favored the status quo of segregated German nations cooperating closely in economic and political questions, the new elites mostly favored the full unification of Germany and the liquidation of the old German entities.

Nowhere did nationalism face stronger opposition than in Germany. German nationalism emerged at a time when Germany was still highly divided into dozens smaller and bigger states. Simultaneously with elitist German nationalism, a popular Prussian, Brandenburgian, Bavarian etc. scission nationalism emerged. The two nationalism stood in sharp contrast: the scission nationalism aimed to strengthen the existing national segregation, while German nationalism demanded the full unification of all German territories. Many scission nationalists supported a restrained economic and political unification, but rejected the liquidation of the old entities. German nationalism was usually the case of intellectuals and new elites—professors, students, other intellectuals, parts of the bureaucracy and the rising industrial bourgeoisie; the old elites—high bureaucrats, monarchs, the aristocracy—were usually the main pillars of scission nationalism (c.f. Wehler 1987, p. 396 ff.). Conflicts between German nationalists and scission nationalists were also conflicts between the rising new elites and the establishment: newcomers expected that a full unification would redistribute power and influences while the old elites feared their descent (ibid., p. 396). Attacking the old power elites in particular in the first half of the century, German nationalists were frequently persecuted by the authorities. Hence, before Bismarck's reign, German nationalism was the idea of intellectual, liberal, elites, hardly reaching the popular masses. German nationalism was forwarded by philosophers like Johann Gottfried von Herder, Johann Gottlieb Fichte, the 'Borussen historians' Johann Gustav Droysen, Theodor Mommsen, Heinrich von Sybel, Heinrich von Treitschke, economists around Friedrich List, gymnasts around 'Turnvater' Jahn and the students and professors in the rising 'Burschenschaften'; thus, hardly any common people. Still, at the beginning of Bismarck's reign most common people had national sentiments for their German country, but little affinity to German nationalism.

As maintained, already in the 1830s and 1840s Friedrich List and his followers inspired by the rising German nationalism develop the theory of economic nationalism. For Henderson (1983) List was a "Tragic Patriot": List drew a close connection between economic unification and political unification because he expected that integrated markets and economic national champions, particularly national railways, would strengthen national sentiments. Like many French intellectuals of the time, List believed in the superiority of industrial societies and that industrialization requires a strong, intervening state; regarding his industrialism, List closely followed Saint-Simon. For List, the German industry was still too weak to compete with the British counterparts which is why he demanded protectionist measurements to defend the German industry (ibid.). Supported by a small group of followers, List's economic ideas were widely known, discussed and carried by groups with vested interests in protectionism, like the Rhenish industrialists. However, List's theory was contested by the German classical economics which was also on the rise and attracted many inflectional economists (Brandt 1992, pp. 160–168). From intensive discussion of Adam Smith's work, a group of influential German advocates of free trade emerged: the idea of free trade was predominately carried by Baltic merchants and East Prussian Junkers (Henderson 1983, p. 98 f.); the politically most influential group of the time. Unable to outstrip classical economics in pure economics, List's plans for a German railway system received particular attention.

According to Wehler (1995, pp. 221–251), German nationalism was elitist at the beginning of the century, but steadily spread through the middle class: the Revolution of 1848 was the first rearing up of German nationalism. However, in the early 1860s the opponents of German nationalism were still numerous and strong and a full unification seemed far away. What Wehler (ibid., pp. 251–331) called Bismarck's "Revolutions from above" spread German nationalist sentiments beyond its usual carriers: Bismarck's three hegemony wars strengthened national sentiments and convinced the masses that only a unified Germany is able to meet the challenges of the time. For Wehler (ibid.), Bismarck was the first charismatic German leader: chafed by the conflict between the liberal Parliament and the King and his own claim to pursue and renew the Prussian dominance in a more united Germany, Bismarck was in need of a political success in order to uphold his aura as a charismatic leader. Under strong domestic political pressure, Bismarck was aware that only successes abroad would save his political carrier. According to Wehler, Germany's three hegemony wars were Bismarck's foreign successes which cemented his charismatic leadership, spread German nationalism and opened the door for the relatively stable coalition between Bismarck and the German liberalism, which facilitated the political unification of Germany. Facing the harsh opposition of the liberals, and many other groups by defeating Denmark in the war for Schleswig-Holstein, Bismarck regained momentum. Under political pressure, Bismarck declared war on Austria. Rising German nationalism and the aura of the unbeatable commander hushed opponents and enabled Bismarck to build the North-German alliance. The mostly vocal North-German alliance under the leadership of Prussia further allienated the mainly Catholic South-German alliance of Baden, Bayern, Württemberg and Hessen-Darmstadt. Only the fear of a French attack kept the south alliance from further deviation. Provoking a war with France, Bismarck undertook his most risky, but far-reaching project. Afraid of France, the south alliance joined Bismarck. Defeating the great enemy and annexing Alsace-Lorraine, Bismarck's glory and German nationalism was at its peak; German nationalism widely spread into the south and towards groups which usual rejected nationalism.

Analyzing German social-democrats' view on nationalism, Wehler (1962) found that German social democracy was traditionally divided on the question of nationalism: Bismarck's three wars further divided social democrats, between those considering Schleswig-Holstein a Prussian territory and emphasizing Germany's right to protect itself against the French aggression and those rejecting all kind of war and annexation. However, overall, like the entire society, social democracy became more open to German nationalism in the late 19th century: in particular the group around Ferdinand Lassalle increasingly shifted toward Prussian nationalism. At the time of Wilhelminism, German nationalism further deepened and became more aggressive: in particular the Agitation Associations forwarded an aggressive German nationalism (Wehler 1995, pp. 1071–1081).

Until mid-1870 s German nationalism was connected with social conservativism and economic liberalism. The rather weird combination of nationalism, conservativism and economic liberalism was ideological hardly consistent, but the product of the political balance of power and coalitions; conservative governments relied on the support of the liberal parties. Around 1875 economic nationalism, protectionism and state interventionism replaced economic liberalism as the leading economic policy idea. Blamed for the deep crisis and recession, economic liberalism was strongly criticized. With the rise of state- or kathedersocialism and the wide agreement on the necessity of state interventions and protectionism, Lists' economic nationalism raised after this death: at the end of the 19th and the beginning of the 20th century it was widely agreed that national champions and industrial integration fosters national sentiments. In particular, it was argued that a strong Germany needs a strong industry. Against liberal classical economics it was wide agreed that industrialization needs the governments' heavy intervention and the protection from foreign competition.

5.4.1.2 German Liberalism

According to Eley (1988, p. 260), the history of 19th century German liberalism was often considered a "tragedy", "a chain of defeats"; jammed between socialism and conservativism, interrupted by short periods of liberal heydays, German liberalism was marginalized, pursued and suppressed. Under threat from various sides, degenerated to group interests, liberals became the silent supporters of conservatives anti-liberal policy. Other contributions (see for example Gall 1976; Wehler 1995; Eley 1988; Sheehan 1976, 1978; Henning 1966)—doubt the steady defeat theory and highlight that liberalism was attractive for various social groups and politically more influential than often considered. They showed that even in pre-March Germany liberalism was widespread in many German countries. Wehler (1987, p. 416 ff.) divides the pre-March liberalism into three main groups: the bureaucratic, constitutional and radical liberalism. Bureaucratic liberals aspired to a modern bourgeois society; constitutional liberals favored the establishment of a constitutional monarchy. Bureaucratic and constitutional liberals were usually part of the establishment. Just the radical liberals, a small group of usually left-wing utopists demanded fundamental changes and the full-unification of Germany. While radical liberals usually remained a small persecuted groups of utopists, bureaucratic and constitutional liberals were frequently quite successful; bureaucratic and constitutional liberalism was diluted enough to be open for a wide range of other ideas which made them attractive for diverse groups: aristocrats, farmers, bureaucrats, merchants, craftsman etc.

German liberals were hardly united on central questions of the time like trade, social protection and universal suffrage (Sheehan 1976). Among German liberals, there were diehard protectionists and free traders, social protectionist and advocates of *laissez-faire*, advocates of universal suffrage and its strongest opponents; from the left to the right, democrats and anti-democrats, free traders and protectionist are frequently subsumed under the umbrella of German liberalism. Overall, while British liberalism moved to the left by forming coalitions with the upper working class, German liberalism steadily went towards the right. Two main reasons caused the German liberals to be more open for the political right than for the left: first, the conservative hegemony made conservatives more attractive partners. Second, many liberals feared a socialist revolution which made them open for authoritarian measures against socialists and all kind of political leftism (Muhs 1988, p. 249). Their openness to right-wing ideas caused them to support anti-liberal politics at the end of the century, for which German liberals were harshly criticized.

After the failed Revolution of 1848 in the second half of the 19th century liberals became the notorious coalition partner of conservative governments: active participation enabled liberals to influence governments' policy and to advance unification, at the same time they lost most of their principles and imitated their destruction. The whole second half of the 19th century was characterized by conservatism. In need of support, liberals became the usual coalition partner of conservative governments. After the Second Restoration, liberals were in a strong Parliamentary position when Bismarck came to power. Liberal opposition was Bismarck's most pressing problem. According to Wehler (1995, p. 253 ff.), Bismarck used the hegemonic wars to escape liberal pressure; however, as Bismarck's popularity rose, the liberals had to decide whether to support or fundamentally oppose him. Apart from tactical reasons, in particular the imminent unification caused liberals to became Bismarck's most important and reliable partner. Unification being liberals' most important goal (Winkler 1979, p. 21 ff.), supporting Bismarck enabled liberals to co-design Germany's unification. On the one hand, liberals' intimate relation to power enabled them to actively shape politics and promote their ideas (ibid., p. 301 ff.). On the other hand, due to the close relation with the conservatives they became increasingly undistinguishable. Fearing socialist revolutions and influenced by their conservative coalition partner, liberals steadily shifted toward conservativism and authoritarianism: supporting conservative governments, liberals hoped to get a better initial position for coming post-conservative times, but the price they had to pay was the open support of the anti-liberal and anti-democratic measurements of the conservative governments (Schmidt 1976, p. 237).

Hence, German liberals' influence was bigger than often believed, however, due to their close relation to conservative governments, they became increasingly indistinguishable at the end of the 19th century. However, liberals were the main carriers of the idea of German nationalism and full unification: their most important influence on 19th century Germany was to carry, promote and develop nationalist ideas and unification.

5.4.1.3 Industrialism and State- or Kathedersocialism

In the late 18th and first half of the 19th century, many former mercantilists followed Adam Smith into the liberal camp (Brandt 1992, pp. 160–168). Later Karl Heinrich, Daniel Rau and Johann Heinrich von Thünen became the most prominent German classical economist (Gide and Rist 1923, p. 383). Friedrich List and his followers were the most important opponents of classical economics in Germany during the first half of the 19th century. Also, in the heyday of its influence around mid-19th century, classical economics was heavily criticized by many from various professional backgrounds. However, List was among the few well educated economists—Jean-Charles-Léonard Simonde de Sismondi in Switzerland (Amonn 1949) and Henri de Saint-Simon in France were the other two well-known—with an in-depth knowledge about economic theory, who rejected the classical theory in the first half of the 19th century. List's nationalist, interventionist and protectionist demands (see above and Henderson 1983; Levi-Faur 1997a, b; Helleiner 2002) were fundamental attacks on classical economics.

5.4.1.3.1 Friedrich List's Industrialism

Like many other things, Friedrich List inherited from Saint-Simon the faith in the advantages of industrial society. Unlike classical economics' focus on individuals, List's central unit of investigation was the nation: the ultimate goal of List's economic theory was the development of a national industrial society. For List, economic unification, protectionism and state interventionism are necessary measurements on the way to the liberal industrial society, but are not ultimate goals in themselves. Hence, despite List's nationalist and chauvinist belches, he dreamed the Saint-Simonian dream of an industrial world where all nations life in peace and harmony; "the object of the policy of protection, from List's point of view, was the establishment of an urban industrialized society. This was the promised land" (Henderson 1983, p. 158 f.). Unlike most liberal economists, List and his followers consider that economic and political unification and industrialization are preconditions of liberalism, not the other way around. Only a unified and industrialized Germany would be ready for liberalism. Hence, like Saint-Simonians, List dreamt of a better, liberal, harmonic industrial society, but he considered that the first anti-liberal measurements like protectionism, state interventionism and economic nationalism need to foster Germany's industrialization until a more liberal policy is possible and reasonable.

Failing to convince a political majority of protectionism, the time was not good for industrialism. Farmers, Junkers and craftsmen worried that a fast industrialization would downgrade their social position. Farmers, Junkers and craftsman being liberals and the main followers of conservatives, caused most conservative and liberal politicians to reject or at least not openly support fast industrialization. In addition, liberals also rejected industrialization on more ideological grounds: traditionally, liberals followed the idea of a classless middle-class society (Gall 1976, p. 176; Muhs 1988, p. 224). They feared that industrialization would further divide the society into antagonistic proletarians and capitalists and hence would bring the society further away from the liberal dream of a classless middle-class society (Sheehan 1976, p. 216). Hence, due to the strong anti-industrial coalition, until the Revolution of 1848 openly supporting the industrial society was politically unwise: regional industrial projects were supported by governments and municipality of all political colour, but the idea of a urban, liberal, democratic industrial society was mostly rejected.

In particular, the question of trade tariffs was an ongoing conflict between liberals and anti-liberals: overall, in the first half of the 19th century, the liberal free traders were more successful than protectionists. The demand for free trade was built on a strong coalition between the East-German land aristocracy and merchants (Kindleberger 1978, p. 185 ff; Henderson 1983, p. 98 f.); both expected gains from trade liberalization. The rising industry was still too weak to enforce its favor for protectionism against the free trader coalition.

Supported by many young followers and the rising industry (Henderson 1983), List failed to break up the classical economic predominance in Germany. Pillared by liberal and many conservative politicians, the liberal domination in economics continued until the 1870 s. The liberal dominance manifested in low trade tariffs, several measurements increasing the freedom of movement for workers and other means of production, weakening the protection of guilds and most importantly facilitating joint-stock business.

Anti-industrialism started to crumble with the deepening unification and the economic boom of the 1850s. Voices had been raised that industrialization fosters economic unification and economic, political and military empowers the unifying nation. Considering German the rising central European super power, many German nationalists were convinced that Germany's readiness to compete with Britain and France over European hegemony strongly depends on Germany's ability to economically catch up. In particular, railways were considered pivotal for unification, economic development and military success (Then 1997). In addition, governments became more interested in the economic issue. Principally uninterested in economics, Bismarck and his liberal conservatives turned toward industrialization to support his military ventures, which became pivotal for Bismarck's political survival. Hence, after the Revolution of 1848 industrialization was increasingly considered necessary to politically and militarily foster the uniting country. However, liberal economic policies like free trade and the liberalization of the joint-stock law rather than state interventionism were still considered the best measurements to support the rising industry.

5.4.1.3.2 The Rise of State- or Kathedersocialism

The Gründerkrach and the long-lasting economic slowdown in the late 19th century broke up liberal economists' dominance. Politicians, the general public and even many economists blamed the liberal economic policy which followed the advice of classical economists for deep crisis and the recession. In France and Germany, classical economics and *laissez-faire* were blamed for the deep crisis and recession and were unable to bring steady economic progress (Gide and Rist 1923, p. 413 ff.). In the years following the Gründerkrach, liberal classical economics were replaced by theories suggesting protectionism, active state interventionism and state guidance as the leading economic theory. The rise of anti-classical theories was accompanied by the demand for state-lead industrialization. The spreading conviction that faster industrialization was desirable to foster unification and empower the rising nation was accompanied by the spreading belief that heavy state intervention facilitates and fastens industrialization. Three things were considered necessary for fast industrialization: state interventionism, corporatism and cartelism.

From the 1870s to World War I most agreed on the necessity of heavy state intervention to foster the economic progress, but also to lessen negative consequences of industrialization. For Sombart (1928b, p. 63), the time after 1880 was dominated by neo-mercantilism; according to him, the state again fully supported capitalist interest with all measurements and means available. As maintained, anti-classical economic theories became dominant: in particular rising state- or kathedersocialists' influence was heavy. The name state- or kathedersocialists is misleading because they hardly supported the socialist revolution, on the contrary: the theory was much more about how to avoid the rise of socialism. For Völkerling (1959, p. 10 ff.), state- or kathedersocialism was the conservative, bourgeois, Junkerian reaction to the fear of the 'red ghost'. According to Völkerling, the German industrial bourgeoisie and the landed aristocracy agreed that unequal distribution and the pauperization of the working class seriously threats their dominance. They agreed that only heavy state intervention, redistribution and the extension of the social security system may prevent a socialist revolution and facilitate the steady development of the economy and the country.

State- or kathedersocialists were a quite heterogeneous group of economists, sociologists, politicians and bureaucrats: among them lefty like Karl Rodbertus, Carl August Schramm, liberals like Rudolf von Gneist, Erwin Nasse, Lujo Brentano and conservatives like Gustav von Schmoller, Rudolf Meyer and Adolph Wagner. State- or kathedersocialism integrated liberal, conservative and socialist ideas, but strictly opposed Manchester Liberalism, Marxism and anti-social conservativism (Müller 1991, p. 322). Their focus on production and distribution united most state- or kathedersocialists. State- or kathedersocialists heavily criticized *laissez-faire* for causing growing inequality, the exploitation of workers, social tensions, unstable societies and at the end, due to escalating conflicts, socialist revolutions. For them, the state has the task to cushion the exploitative nature of the individualist bourgeois society in order to overcome the antagonistic relation between the state and the society (Thier 1930, p. 109 f,.). State- or kathedersocialists' main aim was to build a harmonious society which overcomes the class antagonism of the liberal society (Müller 1991, p. 323).

Wagner lined out four principles of state- or kathedersocialist economic policy: (1) Improving the production process to stabilize economic development and ensuring the adequate participation and remuneration of the whole society. (2) Absorption of all rents by the state. (3) Adapting the principle of fair distribution to the fiscal policy. 4) Redistributing tax policy (ibid., p. 354 f.). Unlike the passive policy of classical economics, Wagner proposed the active intervention of the state into production and distribution. Wagner and other state- or kathedersocialists were deeply convinced that unregulated or unguided markets do not lead to a harmonious society, but foster deep crises, long recession, pauperization, social tensions and revolutions. Wehler (1974) considers late 19th century the time of organized capitalism in Germany. The idea of organized capitalism was closely connected with state- or kathedersocialism: principally, all demanded state intervenions and guidance; but they were deeply divided on the favored form and length of state intervenion (Müller 1991, pp. 321–406).

Due to the rise of anti-classical economics, protectionism also became more accepted. Among economists and economic advisers of Bismarck, protectionism became acceptable and was, in particular, advocated by younger economists (Stern 2008, p. 280). Wilhelm von Kardorff was a key figure of the protectionism camp. As an industrialist, nobleman and conservative deputy he was widely respected and heard: the Centralverband Deutscher Industrieller, a lobby group of the heavy industry that he founded in 1876, became the main mouthpiece of protectionism. Kardorff's (1875) book *Gegen den Strom!* was a protectionist manifest: suggesting to investigate the reasons for Germany's unsteady industrialization and deep crises, the entire contribution bears witness to the author's nationalist and Christian feelings, but also to a relatively sound understanding of classical economics. For him, classical trade theory is practically unsound, repeating many of List's ideas, because it ignores that the nation's interests are different from individual interests; it pays too little attention to the importance of inner-country trade; ignores the British economic superiority and the disadvantage of full economic specialization. State- or kathedersocialists took a wise intermediary position between free trade and protectionism: for Schmoller and the Verein für Socialpolitik, free trade or protectionism should not be an ideological question, free trade is the right policy in times of economic prosperity and protectionism of crises and slowdowns (Torp 2014, p. 153 f.). The position of the state- or kathedersocialists opened the possibility to switch relatively freely between free trade and protectionism, dependent on what is considered to be more advantageous at the time. Despite the scientific contributions protectionism was on the rise: protectionism was built on a strong coalition between the rising big industry (Böhme 1967) and the agricultural unions (Aldenhoff-Hübinger 2002, p. 146 ff).

On the question of industrialization, state- or kathedersocialists were, at least at the beginning, divided: among them we find advocates and opponents of industrialization (Barkin 1970). However, state- or kathedersocialists agreed on the necessity of the leadership of the state and strong state interventions that safeguard the social acceptability of industrialization. Rather than any kind of socialism, state- or kathedersocialists argued for a harmonious society that respects private property and individual freedom, but is guided by a heavily intervening state. Conservative state- or kathedersocialists—the most influential group in the Verein für Socialpolitik (Plessen 1975, pp. 19–35), the umbrella organization of state- or kathedersocialists—aspired to a social kingdom or socialist monarchy overcoming exploitation and fostering economic participation of workers and the nationalization of central industries, but politically built on the system of estate. However, unlike left-wing contributors of the time, state- or kathedersocialists were convinced that industrialization and a harmonious society are compatible in principle. State- or kathedersocialists deeply believed that heavy state interventions would enable a fast, steady and planed industrialization without the usual negative consequences like crises, poverty, social polarization and class conflicts.

According to Wehler (1987, pp. 662–680), in the last quarter of the 19th century, from the conservative right to the unionist left, from big business to economists, most agreed that *laissez-faire* causes social, political and economic crises and revolutions, but heavy state interventionism would enable a steady, fast and socially responsible industrialization. Hence, it was widely believed that the intervention and guidance of the state facilitates steady growth, industrialization, political and social peace and the positive development of the nation and the society. Wehler identified four main forms of the late 19th century state interventionism: conservation interventionism that smooths too abrupt changes; adjustment interventionism that mitigates sharp breaks; development interventionism that fosters the development of underdeveloped branches and reform interventionism that implements needed economic reforms.

In addition to state interventions, many demanded the foundation of big monopolies or oligopolistic cartels. From the political right to the left and even liberals, many were convinced that monopolies and cartels better serve the general interest than competitive markets. They expected that big cartels are able to smooth business cycles and sustain a steady economic development and industrialization (Wehler 1995, p. 634). Kleinwächter (1883, p. 43), advocating the cartelization of the German economy, argued that cartels are build to overcome the problem of over-production, are symbols of human cooperativeness and cope with the market anarchy. Illustrating the monopolization of the German industry, Schmoller (1904, p. 58) did not oppose cartelization, but suggested comprehensive regulations and state guidance.

Corporatism between cartels, the industry and banks and between capital and labor was expected to solve the organization mismatch, facilitate financing and overcome the antagonism between capital and labor. Cooperation between the main market players, producers, banks and workers was expected to safeguard all groups with vested interests and ensure that economic development is to everybody's benefit.

5.4.1.4 The Late German Imperialism

Later than Britain and France, the Deutsche Reich also intensified its imperialist pretensions. Until Bismarck's reign and the unification of Germany, neither Lower Prussia nor Austria showed bigger colonialist ambitions. Several private initiatives failed to enthuse German countries for a more active imperialism (Fröhlich 1994, p. 17 ff.). After a century of puny German imperialism, the newly-founded German Empire fast expanded in the 1880s.

As maintained, Baumgart (1975) divided the wide range of imperialism theories into four main groups; economic, social psychological, political historical and political sociological theses. Like in Britain and France, arguments from all four main theses were outlined in favor of German imperialism. Economically, like the rest of Europe, Germany suffered from a deep recession and the over-supply of capital and industrial products at the end of the 19th century. According to Wehler (1976a, pp. 112–142), at the end of the 19th century there was a wide consensus in Germany that over-production and under-consumption caused the lasting economic recession. He argues that from the political extreme right to the extreme left, protagonists agreed that slow growth, rising unemployment and poverty stemmed from the oversupply recession. Agreeing on the problem of over-production and under-consumption, it was considered that only new markets for German goods would remedy the economy. Recognizing the problem of over-production and under-consumption did not automatically mean to support imperialism, but imperialism was considered the one, maybe easiest, way to develop new markets for the excess of German industrial products.

As maintained, the main advocates of economic imperialism consider financial interest the main force behind imperialism: in need of new profitable investment opportunities, big finances convince governments to conquer new markets for investments. Notwithstanding economic imperialism, these Germans banks were, at the beginning, relatively reluctant to Bismarck's colonial policy (Gründer 2012, p. 52). However, many advocates of German imperialism argued that colonialism would open new investment opportunities for excessive German capital and therefore prevent a further fall of interest rates (Wehler 1976a, p. 148).

In accordance with the social-psychological- and political-historical-theses, advocates of imperialism argued that Germany needs colonies to strengthen and legitimize its world power aspiration. In particular, the imperialist policy of Caprivi and Wilhelm II was characterized by the claim of enhancing Germany's glory and pretension to world power. Germany's imperialist 'Sturm und Drang' phase was marked by Wilhelm's mission to cement Germany's world power pretension by augmenting its sphere of influence (Steltzer 1984, p. 175). Due to its late participation, Germany's imperialism was driven by last-minute panic: German feared that if it does not aggressively pursue its colonial claim the rest of the world will also be distributed among European colonial empires (Wehler 1976a, p. 437). Like in Britain and France, German imperialists demanded the conquest of colonies to deport the surplus population (Gründer 2012, p. 27 ff.).

Wehler (1976a, b) developed the concept of social imperialism by analyzing Bismarck's colonialism: according to Wehler, Bismarck's imperialism was a red herring to deflect the public from interior problems. Germany facing a deep persistent recession, elites fearing a socialist revolution and Bismarck losing support and fearing to lose the Parliamentary majority, Bismarck was in need of a success story. As maintained, whenever Bismarck came under strong pressure, he reacted with wars and conquests to strengthen national sentiments and his own glory. In the same vein, Bismarck hoped that extending German territory and manifesting its aspiration of being a first-class nation would save his political career.

5.4.2 The Conservative Backlash

When Napoleon was defeated in 1815, a long period of backward-looking conservativism started in most German countries. For Kindleberger (1978, pp. 185–198), the whole period was dominated by Junker aristocracy interests. Germany was a rarely urbanized, rural, feudalistic society in the first half of the 19th century, with several emerging industrial hubs, but overall the economy was still agriculture-based (Henderson 1967, p. 13 f; Trebilcock 1981, p. 22 ff.), and politics and economics was still largely dominated by landed aristocracy. According to Wehler (1987, pp. 297–322), until the Revolution of 1848, political dominance was built on a relatively stable coalition of the monarchy, the bureaucracy and the landed aristocracy. Comprehensive liberalism and open German nationalism was, in the first half of the 19th century, suppressed and diluted by a general conservative hegemony: liberal bureaucrats were pressurized and silenced by the conservative governments, radical liberals, and German nationalist faced continuous persecution and many constitutional liberals demanded the implementation of a constitutional monarchy, but were conservative on many other issues. For example, many liberals favored state interventionism, were anti-democratic and supported the authoritarian state which they saw as a necessary bulwark against the 'red ghost' (Sheehan 1976). Overall, in the first half of the 19th century German liberalism was on the rise, but often halfheartedly and permeated by much conservatism. German nationalism was prosecuted, suppressed and marginalized. No doubt that liberalism had a certain influence on many German governments, German nationalism became a charismatic idea which elsewhere attracted followers, but in the first half of the 19th century German politics were dominated by conservativism, scission nationalists and a coalition between monarchs, bureaucrats and the landed aristocracy.

5.4.2.1 The Strong Coalition Against Industrialization

Elsewhere in Europe, the 19th century was characterized by the struggle between the overwhelmingly conservative landed aristocracy and the rising liberal and left market classes—the bourgeoisie and workers—over political and economic dominance. A central question of dispute was the aspired economic structure: while the conservative landed aristocracy favored an agricultural, decentralized, rural economy, the industrial bourgeoisie requested an industrial, urban, centralized economy. Conservative, landed interests' predominance created a relatively hostile environment for industrialization and banking. Impressed by Britain's economic, political and military progress, German countries and landed elites did not aim at stopping industrialization, "but to keep it in tutelage," as Mevissen stated (Kindleberger 1978: 200). In addition, even many liberals strongly opposed a British-style industrialization: German liberals feared that an Industrial Revolution would tighten the class conflict, increase political instability (Wehler 1987, p. 423), bring them further away from a classless middle-class society and deteriorate the economic position of many supporters (Sheehan 1976, p. 216). Conservatives and liberals feared the rise of the proletariat leaning toward socialist ideas and of the liberal, urban, cosmopolitan bourgeoisie. Aristocrats, farmers and craftsman opposing the rising market classes, in particular bankers—the epitome of the capitalist bourgeoisie—faced rejection from the leading political groups and the authorities: safeguarding the interests of the Junkers and sharing their conservative views, Prussian governments usually prevented rather than supported banking innovations (Kindleberger 1978, p. 199).

Facing the hostility of wide ranges of the population, at the same time hardly any other group had closer relations with the political power than bankers. As maintained, many private banks were founded by court agents who managed monarchs' financial belongings. In particular, in the first half of the 19th century public debt financing remained the main business of private bankers. Due to their central role in war and government financing, traditional close ties to the court and their role in government foreign policy, private banks' close relation with political power remained (Born 1977, pp. 48–83). Hence, bankers' social position in the first half of the 19th century was quite ambivalent: on the one hand as the Crown's main financers and investors they had quite close ties to the political power. On the other hand, they faced much opposition and hostility from the conservative, landed, often anti-Semitic public.

5.4.2.2 Sedate Industrialization and the Rise of the Bankers

Although political elites hardly supported industrialization, the German industry took off in the first half of the 19th century. Two main reasons are considered to have supported Germany's economic take-off; the Zollverein and the railway boom. There is a long-lasting dispute among economic historians whether the Zollverein or the railway boom was more important for Germany's industrial take-off: advocates (see Lee 1988) of the Zollverein thesis argue that Germany's Zollverein fostered the rise of the industry by withdrawing inner-German trade tariff, which opened much bigger markets for industrial goods; bigger markets facilitate the extension of industries and the use of more capital-intensive methods. Others (Rostow 1962; Fremdling 1975, 1977; Wehler 1987) argued that the railway boom was most important for Germany's industrial take-off, because it necessitated huge capital investments and the development of supplier industry: Spree (1977, p. 232) speaks of a "railway induced industrialization."[4] Usually, it was considered that German governments played a particularly important role in the railway building; Fremdling (1983) shows that states' influence varied among German countries: sometimes states fostered railway construction, and sometimes hindered faster developments.

Recognizing the importance of closer economic ties for Germany's unification, it was discussed whether economic unification caused political unification, or the other way around: Schmoller (1916) and Viner ([1950] 2014, p. 122) argue that in the case of Germany, the economic unification precedes the political unification, Dumke (1978) argued that the Zollverein was considered a political measurement to facilitate state financing rather than built on economic reasons. Mitchell (2000, p. 56) considered that "railway networks was both cause and effect [of unification]."

However, German states agreed in the 1830s on fostering inner-German trade. The commitment to facilitate inner-German trade by reducing trade barriers significantly altered the German money system and banking sector. In the early 19th century, dozens of different coins with unclear value hindered inner-German trade. In the course of the Zollverein, the German coins were steadily standardized: in the late 1830s fixed exchange rates and standards about the metal content were established (Tilly 2003, p. 87 f.). Standardizing coins' metal content and exchange rates were the first important step toward the German currency union. For Friedrich List, the monetary unification is pivotal for further economic and political unification (Eynern 1928, p. 6 f.). However, the standardization of coins did not change much in Germany's underdeveloped money system. Ziegler (1993, p. 485) considered the Prussian monetary system of the 1830s and

[4] „Vom Eisenbahnbau wesentlich induzierten Industrialisierung."

1840s underdeveloped when compared with Britain; the same was true for most other German states. Still, most German countries' money systems were dominated by coins; paper money existed, but played a minor role. People rejecting paper money as unsound doubtlessly contributed to the coin dominance. However, in particular German countries like Prussia lacked the institutional means to distribute bigger amounts of paper money: lacking quasi central banks and big note-issuing banks, no institution was able to distribute bigger amounts of paper money.

Despite of the discussions on whether the Zollverein or the railway boom was more important for Germany's industrialization, financial markets were particularly altered by railway building. Germany's first railway between Fürth and Nürnberg caused a long-lasting railway boom; thousands of kilometers were built and billions of marks invested in the following decades (Fremdling 1975). In hindsight, looking at the kilometers built, the railway mania of the mid-19th century was impressive. However, back then railway building was by no means an easy task. Several issues complicated Germany's railway extension: legal barriers were high; every railway project required a state permission. Three things had to be satisfied for getting a permission (Then 1997, p. 95): (1) Efficiency was desired due to scarce resources. (2) The projects were reviewed by the war ministry on its military implication. (3) Several state departments reviewed the project about its efficiency and its usefulness, hence whether the projects serves the public interest. In addition, Germany's political fragmentation much complicated railway building: as railway routes became longer, state borders were soon reached, but due to the lack of inner-German agreements, crossing borders was difficult.

Each German state following its own railway policy, the political boundaries soon became a serious problem for railway progress (Gall 1999, p. 14 f.): railways were in particular profitable when connecting big cities, trade and production locations, the industrial hubs with the seaports, and for overcoming huge distances. Most German states were too small to fully utilize the benefits of railways, crossing inner German boundaries was necessary to advance railways. Crossing national boundaries was difficult as laws were different and governments were not interested in promoting other states' railway companies and economic hubs: "Anyone could see some possible advantages to be gained through a unified national railway system, but the special interests of the separate states posed a countervailing force of considerable dynamics" (Mitchell 2000, p. 43).

Decelerated by nations' different policies, the military necessity of cross-border railways helped overcome governments' resistances. Facing two potential enemies, France in the West and Russia in the East, railways connecting the North with the South and the East with the West seemed pivotal for military survival in the case of simultaneous attacks of France and Russia. Since the early 19th century, senior militaries of various German states demanded the cross-border connection for fast troop transport. Ambitious railway projects in France, in particular those connecting the German border with the hinterland, further scared German governments (c.f. ibid., p. 43 f.). Fearing enemies' attacks and militaries' stubbornness caused governments to cooperate more closely. After the implementation of the Zollverein, cross-border railway building was a further step toward a closer cooperation between German states and towards unification.

Despite all legal and political problems, railway financing was the most serious challenge: the scarcity of capital was often blamed for slow railway development. Reviewing many contributions and the available data Then (1997, p. 131 ff.) found that capital scarcity was not the problem, but institutional and cultural barriers. The long and difficult legal procedure quenched many potential investors and conservative capital owners often rejected to invest into new technologies. German countries in particular lacked financial institutions able and willing to finance megaprojects like long distance railway building. In addition, metal money inelasticity aggravated the financial problems as more elastic credit granting was necessary (Born 1977, p. 29 f.). Unsatisfied with the slow progress, state railways were discussed, but were practically unrealistic due to Prussia's financial difficulties.

Filling the railway financing vacuum, a group of private bankers, among them those who later revolutionized the German banking sector, became Germany's main railway financers (ibid., p. 88 f.). In particular, the French-influenced Rhineland bankers like Camphausen, Hansemann, Oppenheimer, Schaaffhausen and Rothschild entered the railway business. Heavily investing in a risky but if successful profitable business, bankers who soon entered railway financing had a strong starting advantage when industrialization accelerated: usually they grew faster due to railway profits and in particular gathered much experience in industry financing.

However, railway financing still remained quite difficult: militaries and governments lacking the financial means to finance railways, private bankers also reached their financial limits. The deteriorating problem of railway financing seemed to necessitate a radical legal change: in hindsight, Prussia's new railway law, Preußisches Eisenbahngesetz of 1838, was a legal revolution. The new law permitted railway companies to found joint-stock companies. Prussia's new railway law became the precursor of the general joint-stock company law, the Preußische Aktienrecht of 1843. According to Then (1997, p. 89) the main aim of the new railway law was to balance and safeguard three interests: "Private profit, economic efficiency and regional balance." The Preußische Aktienrecht of 1843 also allowed non-railway companies to found joint-stock conglomerates; however, all joint-stock conglomerates needed state licenses. At the beginning, licenses were strictly bound to companies serving the general interest (Schmoeckel and Maetschke 2008, p. 170), and later issuance guidelines were lightened. However, much beyond accelerating railway building, the general permission for joint-stock companies significantly changed Germany's industrialization. Big joint-stock conglomerates dominated Germany's industrialization and its economy at the end of the 19th century. The Preußisches Eisenbahngesetz of 1838 and the Preußische Aktienrecht of 1843 were early milestones that determined the path of Germany's industrialization.

Passing the Preußisches Eisenbahngesetz of 1838 was no easy task: as in Britain, strong resistance against the planned joint-stock laws was formed. Bureaucrats, politicians, lawyers, Junkers were the main pillars of the resistance against the joint-stock laws. Opponents feared losing political and economic power and argued that managers of joint-stock companies would abuse their power, tolerate too much risk-taking to the disadvantage of small savers and would build megatrusts (Wehler 1987, p. 104). However, despite the heavy criticism from the strong anti-joint-stock coalition, the new laws passed, because railway building was economically, militarily and politically too important. Junkers dominating the Prussian politics had no vested interest in the industrialization of the country (Tilly 1980, p. 56 f.). Following their anti-industrial attitudes, Junker governments were by no means enthusiastic railway supporters, on the contrary, they often prevented further expansion. However, it was in particular the military necessity that convinced governments to stronger support railway building.

The permission for joint-stock companies significantly facilitated railway building. Newly founded railway companies made much use of their right to issue shares. Before joint-stock banks were founded, the rise of railway joint-stock companies significantly changed banking. Facilitating the diffusion of shares and investing in shares became one of the banks' main businesses. Bankers distributed shares, but also became the main investors (Then 1997, p. 135 ff.). According to Tilly (2003, p. 100 ff.), banks used their wide networks to distribute shares and in particular to absorb loanable funds for investments. Wehler (1987, pp. 95–107) considers joint-stock companies a key innovation because they enable companies to attract much more capital. The permission of joint-stock banking also significantly altered private banks as they increasingly became capital intermediaries. Hence, railway company share banking caused German banks to increasingly enter loanable funds intermediation: to absorb much smaller and bigger idle funds to invest it into railway shares.

Industrialists and nationalists were most enthusiastic about railway building. For them, railways were the pivotal technology used to foster industrialization and national sentiments by integrating the politically fragmented country. German nationalists expected that cross-border railways would integrate the German speaking areas by facilitating the exchange of goods and people; "nationalism and liberalism were the two most conspicuous themes of early German writings about railways" (Mitchell 2000, p. 38). List (1838, p. 8 ff.) argued that easier communication may foster the nationalist movement: he expected that railways facilitating the communication between nationalists will cause national associations to rise elsewhere in the country fostering national education, nationalist sentiments and the demand for unification. In addition, List hoped that railways would accelerate industrialization. Fostering unification and industrialization, List was quite enthusiastic about railways, which he considered the most important innovation in the history of mankind, in "the interest of all humanity" (ibid., p. 11) which will "redeem all nations from the plague of war, inflation, hunger, hate between nations, unemployment, ignorance and inefficiency" (ibid., p. 6)[5].

[5]„Völker erlösen wird von der Plage des Kriegs, der Theuerung und Hungersnoth, des nationalhasses und der Arbeitslosigkeit, der Unwissenheit und des Schlendrians."

Most likely, the Zollverein and railway building fostered national sentiments and doubtlessly in particular the latter showed the masses the advantages of industrialization. However, accelerating industrialization and unification fundamentally changed the economic and political balance of power. The railway boom and the Zollverein were victories of the rising industrial bourgeoisie; even if it was a small victory, the foundation of the Zollverein was an important first step toward economic unification and for inner-German free trade. Railway building showed the bourgeoisie's ability to manage and finance capitalist megaprojects. From Zollverein to railway building, industrial take-off and the steady rise of the liberals were small signs of what Wehler (1987, p. 141) considered a general tendency of aristocracy's slow destruction and market classes—bourgeoisie and proletariat—sedate rise.

For Wehler, Germany's pre-industrial societies consisted of three main groups: the landed aristocracy, land proletariat and an urban bourgeoisie; the urban bourgeoisie consisted of small craftsmen, merchants and bureaucrats. Due to the industrial take off, according to Wehler (ibid., pp. 174–241), three new groups emerged: the industrial bourgeoisie, the educated bourgeoisie and the industrial proletariat. The industrial bourgeoisie owned most of the newly formed financial means, the educated bourgeoisie dominated schools, universities and the bureaucracy. In particular, the industrial bourgeoisie heavily opposed the old conservative landed aristocracy and the urban bourgeoisie and became a serious competitor over political influence.

Hence, the industrial take off induced the rise of the industrial bourgeoisie, it also changed the position of bankers. Threatened as the ulcer of society, facing much hostility at the beginning of the 19th century, the bankers' social position much improved due to their heavy involvement in railway building. Sympathetic or not to bankers, it could not have been denied that they played a pivotal role in the organization, implementation and financing of railway building. Thus, overall, the status of the bankers was improved by their new engagement in the financing and organization of industrial megaprojects (ibid., p. 630): private bankers' social position changed from the usurer to the needed partner for politically, militarily and economically necessary capitalist megaprojects. Financially supporting the government railway, the political position of bankers altered. Intensifying the ties with the political elites and their pivotal importance for railway building significantly increased bankers' political influence (Tilly 1966, p. 96 ff.).

5.4.3 The Second Restoration

The Revolution of 1848 was, doubtlessly, the most important political event of the 19th century before full unification. Generally, the revolution was a central event in the general rise of the market classes and the retreat of the old landed aristocracy. Bankers, in particular the rising banking families of the Rhineland, were archetypes of the rising urban, liberal and cosmopolitan bourgeoisie: several of the bankers became important politicians in the revolutionary government (Born 1977, p. 70). Wehler (1987, pp. 780–784) summarizes the effects of the revolution: the land reform fastened the decline of feudalism and landed aristocracy's change into agro-capitalists; the revolution deepened worker and bourgeois class consciousness and the conflict between them; from the failed revolution onwards many liberals agreed that they would be better able to influence politics inside the establishment than by strong opposition; prevailing against the liberal, democratic revolution, the position of the conservatives strengthen for certain time.

The defeat of the revolution was, doubtlessly, a hard blow for liberalism and German nationalism; however, both soon recovered and became stronger. As maintained, since the 1840s German nationalism became a mass phenomenon carried by many quite diverse groups. Liberals became the notorious coalition partners of the conservatives. Two main reasons caused liberals to support the conservative establishment: first, it seemed that conservative forces were still too powerful to be defeated. Second, the infights during the revolution frightened the bourgeoisie from a working class takeover.

According to Wehler (1995, pp. 106–189) after the revolution market classes rise further accelerated: fastening industrialization strengthened the position of the industrial bourgeoisie and sharply increased the number of industrial proletarians. Both market classes being on the rise, the social and political situation could not have been much different: the bourgeoisie became the main pillar of the rising liberal parties. Opposing conservative governments at the beginning, liberal parties soon became their main and most reliable coalition partner, which also increased bourgeoisie's direct political influence. Also, the rising working class increasingly unionized, founded and entered political and organized pressure groups: however, while the bourgeoisie entered the political elites, political working-class organization were persecuted and faced the entire weight of the hostility from the establishment. Despite bourgeoisie's political rise political power in the second half of the 19th century overall remained in the hands of the old aristocracy.

5.4.3.1 Accelerating Industrialization

The Second Restoration –the years after the revolution up to the late 1850s—were politically dominated by conservative governments supported or at least tolerated by liberals. Defeating the liberal revolution momentum was principally on the side of conservatives. However, the general elections of 1849 were a major defeat for conservatives and a great victory for liberals and lefties. The election impressively showed the alarmed elites that the majority leans toward the left or radical democrats. Securing its political dominance, the election result caused the elites to change the suffrage; Prussia's Dreiklassenwahlrecht subdivided voters into three tax classes and weighed the votes by their paid taxes: the higher the tax, the more the vote counted. Highly favoring the landed aristocracy, the Dreiklassenwahlrecht reconstituted the conservatives' dominance. However, Wehler (ibid., pp. 197–221) argued that conducive suffrage and repression would not been enough to consolidate the conservative predominance for almost ten years. According to Wehler, conservative regimes built on an unexpressed coalition with the bureaucracy, the rising industry and much of the liberal bourgeoisie: governments' pseudo constitutionalism satisfied many liberals and bureaucrats, its business- and industry-friendly economic policy attracted parts of the industrial bourgeoisie and fears from socialist revolutions held the coalition together.

Hahn (1998, p. 31) found that post-revolutionary governments promoted industrialization more actively than their pre-revolutionary predecessors. According to him, two main reasons caused governments' new industrialism: first, big German states, like Prussia, were convinced that economic catchup with Britain and France was a key prerequisite for their world power claim. Second, governments hoped that industry and business friendly economic policy would calm and attract the industrial bourgeoisie: several legislative changes facilitated the foundation, operation and financing of industrial companies. Overall, the time of the Second Restoration was characterized by economic *laissez-faire* in most German countries: regulations privileging small groups, like the guilds system, were withdrawn, the foundation of business was facilitated, the freedom of moving increased and overseas trade liberalized (Henderson 1967, p. 31).

5.4.3.2 Paper Money Issuing and the First Joint-Stock Banks

The banking sector changed particularly significantly during the Second Restoration: the foundation of the French Crédit Mobilier's in 1852 and the general joint-stock boom, caused by the Acts of 1838 and 1843, encouraged the Rhenish railway bankers to renew their plan for a German joint-stock bank; in particular Hansemann, Mevissen, Oppenheim and Deichmann were the most active promoters of joint-stock banking. Rhenish bankers were predestinated for bringing banking innovations to Germany: as main railway financers, they were more experiences than most other German bankers in industrial banking; they were prototypes of the liberal, urban, cosmopolitan bourgeoisie with wide ties to the world; and in particular due to their close ties to French colleagues they got in contact with the Saint Simonian banking theory and Saint-Simonian banks.

Convinced by the superiority of joint-stock banks, the Rhenish bankers faced strong opposition from various sides. Arguing that joint-stock banking would dry out agrarian credit (Born 1977, p. 152), what bankers really feared was the competition of joint-stock banks: the banker Heydt in Berlin (Wehler 1995, p. 87) and Rothschild in Frankfurt (Born 1977, p. 152) used all their influence to prevent the foundation of a Crédit Mobilier-style joint-stock bank. Expelled by its powerful opponents from the banking centers, Berlin and Frankfurt joint-stock banking advocates had to swerve to Darmstadt to open Germans first joint-stock bank. Mevissen, Oppenheim, Deichmann and other Rhenish banker, supported by the French Crédit Mobilier, founded in the Hessian province city Darmstadt in 1853 the Darmstädter Bank für Handel und Industrie or just Darmstädter Bank; Germany's first Crédit Mobilier-style bank. Bismarck reported the Prussian government from the foundation of the Darmstädter Bank. He was ambivalent (Seidenzahl 1961): recognizing that the foundation of the Darmstädter Bank was a banking revolution and the advantages of the new-banking-style, he warned of the risks of the new bank, of the opposition of private bankers and the rising French influence due to Crédit Mobilier's heavy involvement.

David Hansemann refused to swerve to the province, but faced the same opposition for his plans to found a joint-stock bank in Prussia: Berlin already had an accidental joint-stock bank since 1848 when the government allowed the Schaaffhausen Bank to issue shares to avoid bankruptcy. Dismissed by the government, Hansemann found a law loophole and opened a joint-stock bank as a Kommanditgesellschaft with silent partners: the Disconto-Gesellschaft (Kindleberger 1978, p. 200). Hansemann's Disconto-Gesellschaft triggered Germany's first joint-stock banking boom because it opened a way to bypass restrictions. Although early joint-stock banks were successful, most governments still refused to give joint-stock permissions to bankers. However, governments hardly tried to plug the loophole that enabled the foundation of joint-stock banks as Kommanditgesellschaft: it seems that Prussian governments were not unhappy that bankers found the loophole to open joint-stock banks, which avoided long political debates on permissions.

The late 1840s and in particular the 1850s were also central years for the development of paper money and central banking. As maintained, during the first European central banking boom in the late 18th century, Germany's oldest public bank, the Prussian Giro- and Lehnbanco was founded. Unlike the Bank of England and the later founded Banque de France, the importance of the Giro- and Lehnbanco, in particular of its note-issuing business, was small. In the first half of the 19th century, due to little demand and its unclear function the Giro- and Lehnbanco faced huge difficulties to distribute its notes (Ziegler 1993, p. 485 ff.). To foster its business, in 1846 the full-public Giro- and Lehnbanco was transferred into the mixed—public- and state-owned—Preußische Bank. One-sixth of Preußische Bank's stocks were held by the state and the rest by private partners; the state's shares decreased as new stocks were distributed. Until 1833, when note issuing became restricted to banks with a governmental license—which meant a quasi-prohibition of issuing—note issuing was not particularly regulated in Prussia, but hardly performed by the three note-issuing Prussian banks (c.f. Smith 1936, p. 49 ff.).

The felt scarcity of money during the industrial takeoff phase of the 1840s caused an intensive discussion on note issuing in Prussia: insisting on its right and ability to (fully) define the amount of money in circulation, the Prussian government was criticized by the rising Rhineland liberal, industrial bourgeoisie suffering from money scarcity, who favored competitive note issuing of private banks (Ziegler 1993, p. 492). According to Vera Smith (1936, p. 51 ff.)—she was by no means a friend of Saint-Simonianism—the Saint-Simonian money-fetish slopped over from France to the German Rhineland and caused Rhineland liberals to demand the lifting of note-issuing restrictions. According to Smith, those demanding changes in the note-issuing regulation may be divided into two main groups: the first group proposed the reduction of state influence on the Preußische Bank, the others, more radical, favored an Adam Smith-style banking system with competitive private note-issuing banks. Submitting dozens of alternative proposals, each failed to convince the Prussian government to change its money policy: the Preußische Bank has the note-issuing monopoly and the state maintaining a strong hand in the bank was the position on which the Prussian government insisted.

Within the strict boundaries of the note-issuing monopoly and the state dominance over the Preußische Bank, in the 1840s Preußische Bank's note-issuing regulations were redesigned by a practical combination of the Currency School and the Banking School principles (Ziegler 1993, p. 491). Following the Banking School, the Real Bill Doctrine was adopted and just one third of the coverage of notes with bullion was required. From the Currency School, note-issuing restrictions and the issuing monopoly were taken over. The new regulation seemed to prevent over-issuing, but at the same time increase money elasticity. That Prussia implemented an issuing regulation closer to the Banking School than to the Currency School seems surprising at first glance: as maintained, in Britain the Currency School was at its peak of power and influence in the 1840s and usually most German economists followed the British leaders closely. However, as outlined, this was not the case for money theory: important German economists like Otto Hübner, Adolf Wagner, Johann Ludwig Tellkampf and Otto Michaels favored combinations of the Currency and Banking Principle over strict monetarism. Overall, the regulation followed Hübner and Tellkampf who suggested convertibility more closely than it followed Wagner who rejected convertibility. However, all of them failed to convince the government to withdraw the note-issuing monopoly.

Around the same time, outside of Prussia public and private banks—dependent on the specific regulation—started or continued to issue notes (Born 1977, p. 29 ff.). New regulations introduced by the Revolutionary government of 1848 facilitated note issuing of private banks; while the Preußische Bank successfully prevent the foundation of many note-issuing competitors within Prussia, the changing regulation and the economic boom of the 1850 s caused a note-issuing boom outside Prussia (Ziegler 1993, p. 493 ff.). Soon the different German policies come into conflict. Guiding and restricting the amount of money remained Prussia's first money policy goal. As maintained, in the 1830s German countries agreed on fixed exchange rates and the free flow of monies. The combination of free flow, Preußische Bank's issuing restriction and Prussia's policy goal to restrict the amount of money got into conflict and challenged Prussia's money policy.

Most non-Prussian note-issuing banks were not limited by any note-issuing restriction why non-Prussian notes flooded the Prussian money market (ibid.). Hence, notes from non-Prussian banks corroded Prussian government's ability to determine the money amount by augmenting Prussia's money stock. Note issuing of the non-Prussian banks thwarted the Prussian government's ability to regulate the money supply and Preußische Bank's competitiveness against its unregulated non-Prussian competitors. In addition because of the restrictive regulation, the Preußische Bank was increasingly unable to meet the rising demand for paper money, why many got convinced that relaxing Preußische Bank issuing boundaries was necessary (Schauer 1912, p. 41). Due to the pressure from note inflows, the Prussian government withdrew the 1856 Preußische Bank's note-issuing limits and prohibited foreign banknotes in 1858. The new laws of 1856 and 1858 gave the Preußische Bank a quasi-issuing monopoly for Prussia and enabled it to pursue a more active issuing policy. Strongly increasing issuing and branching outside Prussia extended Preußische Bank's money power across borders (Born 1977,

p. 32 f.). The regulative changes of 1856 and 1858 paved the way for the Preußische Bank to became Germany's central bank (Ziegler 1993, p. 496): both regulations emphasized and institutionalized Prussia's demand for a note-issuing monopoly system with the Preußische Bank as the state-dependent central bank.

Hence, in the 1850s German industrialization accelerated economically and politically. Politically as a wide range of conservative and liberal parties and governments agreed on the necessity of fast industrialization and state support for industries: "The governments of the various German states […] actively fostered industrial progress in many ways" (Henderson 1967, p. 31). Due to the foundation of joint-stock banks, the spread of paper money and the monopolization of note issuing, the banking sector started to look much like nowadays. Joint-stock banking was a victory of the liberal bourgeoisie over conservatives; the monopolization of note issuing and the state dependent central bank was the victory of conservatives over liberals. However, at the end of the 1850s the main cornerstones of the path on which the German banking sector developed in the following centuries were laid.

The Second Restoration ended with the first global economic crisis of 1857. Between the Second Restoration and the end of the 19th century, German became an industrial, political, military and geographical world power. Economically, the time was characterized by fast industrialization, the emerging of national champions and economic concentration. Politically, the time was dominated by nationalism, liberalism, conservativism, imperialism, the chancellor Bismarck and, of course, in particular the full unification.

5.4.4 Unification, Industrialization and the Rise of Megabanks

When Bismarck came to power in 1862, German nationalism was already a mass phenomenon and on the rise. Also, social democrats, traditionally a bulwark of worker internationalism, became more open to German nationalism (Wehler 1962; Mommsen 1979, p. 83 f.), even if social democrats' nationalism was often rather more tactical than based on conviction (Mommsen 1979, p. 83 f.). As maintained, German nationalism was traditionally closely linked to liberalism: in the late 19th century, German nationalism infiltrated almost all classes and political movements, but liberals remained its main pillar and promoters. Liberals were again on the rise in the first half of Bismarck's chancellorship. After winning the Parliamentary majority, liberals gathered around the Nationalverein, the liberals' umbrella organization; the Nationalverein had two main goals: strengthening liberalism and constitutionalism and advancing the full unification. The new liberalism and the weakness of Austria paved the way for the renewal of the Zollverein; with an even clearer lead of Prussia and the exclusion of Austria (Wehler 1995, p. 227 f.).

Liberals being the strongest political movement of the time, Bismarck's conservative governance faced, at the beginning, the harsh opposition of the powerful liberals. Ruling against the liberal majority, Bismarck escaped the political ruin by what was considered a revolution from above: rising German nationalist sentiments by military conflicts. Unable to overcome the conflict between the liberal Parliament and the king and failing to progress his own claim to pursue and renew the Prussian dominance in a more united Germany, Bismarck was in desperate need of a political success in order to uphold his aura as a charismatic leader. Under strong and increasing political pressure at home, only successes abroad could save Bismarck's political carrier. Henning (1966, p. 59) stated that Bismarck did not even try to find a compromise with the liberals, but preferred to govern by popular foreign policy successes. As maintained, according to Wehler (1995, pp. 251–331), Germany's three hegemony wars were Bismarck's foreign successes which cemented Bismarck's political power, spread nationalist sentiments and paved the way for the coalition with the liberals. The wars against Denmark, Austria and France were all reactions to domestic political crisis. Each war being highly risky, the victories strengthened Bismarck's chancellorship, fostered and spread nationalist sentiments and were important steps towards the full unification of Germany. Politically, the victories in the three hegemonic wars trapped the social democracy into endless debates on war and nationalism and liberals into deep conflicts on how to deal with the conservative and increasingly authoritarian chancellor.

The rapprochement between Bismarck and liberals caused long debates and the division of liberals. Liberals followed two main goals: the unification of Germany and the extension and protection of civil rights. Traditionally, those two goals seemed to be in harmony. However, liberals were strongly divided on the question of how to deal with a conservative ruler who makes progress on unification, but hardly cares about civil rights (Stephan 1966, p. 61 ff.). Bismarck's Bill of Indemnity sharply divided liberals: many right-wing liberals supported the bill, while most from the left-wing camp opposed it (Sheehan 1978, p. 123). Conflicts over the Bill of Indemnity illustrated the much deeper conflict within the liberal camp: liberals were strongly divided on how they should deal with the conservative, authoritarian, but successful policy of Bismarck.

As Bismarck gained momentum after the wars against Denmark and Austria, the unification of Germany seemed near. Continuing their radical opposition against Bismarck seemed dangerous to liberals, because he alone would have reaped the fruits of unification and liberals would not be able to form the process of unification. Supporting him meant pillaring a quite anti-liberal government caring little about parliamentarianism and civil rights. Unable to find a compromise, liberals divided into the Bismarck-supporting Nationalliberale Partei and the Bill of Indemnity-opposing Fortschrittspartei. While the Nationalliberale Partei abandoned most liberal position to became Bismarck's main coalition partner, the Fortschrittspartei was more principled, but lost much of its political influence. However, the liberals' break up was the endpoint of a longer process. Unlike the British counterpart, the German liberal bourgeoisie failed to form a coalition with the, according to its number, fast rising industrial proletariat (Breuilly 1994). The German bourgeoisie which became the main pillar of liberalism feared the industrial proletariat rather than being open for coalitions (Schmidt 1976). As maintained, while British liberalism increasingly looked to the left, German liberalism went to the right. Much less ideological than the British kindred spirits, German liberals increasingly became merely the carriers of bourgeoisie's vested interest (Gall 1976, p. 176). Wehler (1987, p. 203 f.) summarized the position and goals of the German liberals: demanding negative freedoms like the right to free speech, free press and freedom of assembly, the right to found new forms of companies like joint-stock cooperation, the reduction of aristocracy's and urban bourgeoisie's influence and the extension of their own political influence. Concerning free trade, among the liberal bourgeoisie advocates of free trade and protectionism may be found: frequently, the overall position changed from free trade to protectionism and back again. Most importantly, the rising liberal bourgeoisie became the main pillar of constitutional liberalism, but strictly rejected universal suffrage out of fear from proletarian takeover.

Liberals' support for Bismarck was considered a capitulation to conservativism and a betrayal of liberalism (Schmidt 1976, p. 232). There can be little doubt that the Nationalliberale Partei abandoned many liberal principles to sustain the coalition with Bismarck. In particular, the Nationalliberale Partei supported authoritarian laws that clearly cut civil rights. On the other hand, as majority procuring party liberals highly influence the unification and had an almost free hand in governments economic policy. Hardly interested in economic issues, Bismarck followed the liberal *laissez-faire* principle in economic affairs: reducing trade barriers, increasing the freedom of movement and coalition building and the Gewerbeordnung of 1869 had a clear liberal signature. Most important for the development of the German industry, and a central demand of liberals, was the new joint-stock Law of 1870 (Aktienrechtsnovelle): the law withdrew the licensing of joint-stock companies and sharply reduced state supervision.

5.4.4.1 The Gründerkrach and the Anti-liberal Turn in Economics

The Gründerkrach of 1873 was among the deepest crises of the 19th century and caused a long economic slowdown. The general public accused the liberals and their *laissez-faire* policy for the crisis. Following the general trend, saving his head, Bismarck started to follow the rising European protectionism and state interventionism. Apart from protectionist tariffs, several other anti-liberal measures like new tax laws, state monopolies and social insurance laws were implemented (Sheehan 1978, p. 188). Facing the harsh criticism and hostility of the general public, liberals were torn between liberal principles and their love for political power. Maintaining their *laissez-faire* principles, liberals opposed Bismarck's new protectionism: the relation between Bismarck and the liberals was further deteriorated by the socialist laws. Quasi prohibiting all socialist, social democratic and communist parties, activities and books unions and writings was an open and fundamental attack on civil rights. Highly divided on how to react to Bismarck's new policy, the Nationalliberale Partei went to the right as free traders and the remaining left-liberals left the party (ibid., 189-203): from the late 1870s onwards the Nationalliberale Partei and German liberalism was on the retreat. Bismarck's new more authoritarian, protectionist and anti-liberal policy was supported by the remaining loyal parts of the Nationalliberale Partei, the landed aristocracy and parts of the industrial bourgeoisie: many from the industrial bourgeoisie expected that protectionism and state interventionism will ward off annoying competition and Bismarck may get rid of the 'red ghost'. Liberals being divided and in deep crisis, social democrats and all other leftist organizations being forbidden and persecuted, Bismarck was able to turn toward conservativism, state interventionism and authoritarianism.

Bismarck's economic policy can be divided into two main periods: a liberal first and an anti-liberal second half. The economic liberalism of the first half of Bismarck's reign was propelled by his national liberal coalition partner: the period was characterized by free trade, *laissez-faire*, the liberalization of the movement of goods and workers and the withdrawal of many entry barriers. By the crisis of 1873, the hidden tendency against *laissez-faire* and toward more state interventionism and protectionism, which started to dominate economics entered the practical politics. As maintained, the general public and many politicians and economists blamed the *laissez-faire* policy of the government for the crisis and the long-lasting economic slowdown. The Nationalliberale Partei being in deep crisis and internally divided, economic liberalism lost its main political advocate. Farmers, workers, the landed aristocracy, craftsmen and small entrepreneurs under strong economic pressure from the long-lasting economic depression, became increasingly open for anti-liberal economic demands (Kitchen 1978, p. 161). In the environment of rising protectionist and state interventionist demands, the Verein für Socialpolitik became quite influential (Plessen 1975) and the leading economic institute; as maintained, the Verein für Socialpolitik was the umbrella organization of the heterogeneous state- or kathedersocialists. Facing the intensifying rejection of his former liberal policy, Bismarck is supposed to have said that if he would have more time to think about economic problems, he would also be a kathedersocialists. With the rise of the state- or kathedersocialists, the economic policy turned upside down: liberals understood the necessity of state intervenion, but just in cases where it is proven that *laissez-faire* solutions are unfavorable. For state- or kathedersocialists heavy state intervenions were just a usual part of a good economic policy.

From mid-19th century to World War I the German industry and banking sector was characterized by the strong tendency toward concentration and cartelization. Elsewhere in Europe, at the end of the 19th century, economies concentrated; however, nowhere was the trend more pronounced than in Germany. Germany's economic liberalism until the mid-1870 s withdrew many barriers that complicated the formation of heavy industry. However, in particular the new Aktienrecht of 1870 changed the structure of German economy and facilitated concentration: breaking with the German joint-stock tradition, the new Aktienrecht permitted the right to issue stocks independent from companies business and without licenses. Facilitating the foundation and operation of joint-stock companies enabled industrial companies and banks to grow far beyond their original means. Owners' financial means usually built the upper limit of companies' growth: successful joint-stock companies and banks' ability to absorb capital by distributing shares withdrew the growth barrier of owners' limited capital. The new joint-stock law caused a huge founding and economic boom (Horn 1979, p. 135 ff.) which ended in the

Gründerkrach. As maintained, the Gründerkrach and the following recession caused the turnaround in the economic policy; from *laissez-faire* to protectionism and state interventionism. In hindsight, it seems that the chronology of liberalism until the 1870s and then protectionism and state interventionism, was quite fertile for industrialization and in particular economic concentration. Liberal measurements facilitated industries' kickoff and protectionism, state interventionism and the politically supported cartelism protected the rising joint-stock mega-conglomerates from foreign and domestic competition and assured political support.

Economics between the 1870s and World War I were characterized by protectionism, cooperativism, cartelism and state interventionism. In the late 1870s, German entered the phase of protectionism that lasted until World War I. As maintained, the free trade of the mid-19th century was supported by the coalition of landed aristocrats and merchants. Becoming more protectionist, the landed aristocrats formed a new protectionism coalition with the rising heavy industry (Kindleberger 1978, p. 212). At the beginning favoring free trade, Bismarck opportunistically shifted to the protectionist camp: Bismarck hoped that the protectionist turn would attract farmers, craftsmen and industrialist, cause new revenues, enable the implementation of a tobacco monopoly to finance the social programs and would enable the government to eliminate direct taxes (Born 2001, p. 93).

Toughe economic circumstances caused workers, farmers, craftsmen and many other groups to form pressure groups (Kitchen 1978, p. 164). Workers formed unions and increasingly entered the Social Democratic Party; many industrialists united under the umbrella of the Centralverband Deutscher Industrieller; farmers were represented by the Bund der Landwirte. Bundling groups and classes, economic and political power pressure groups increasingly dominated economics and political parties. At the same time, the concentration of the economy reached a new level: industrial cartels were being built and dominated whole sectors. From the political far right to the left and even liberals supported the cartelization of the economy: the main argument in favor of cartels was that they are better able to plan the economy, overcome economic fluctuations and foster economic prosperity than smaller companies in competitive markets (Wehler 1995, pp. 632–637). Strong pressure groups and industrial cartels built the fundament of Germany's interventionism and cooperativism of the late 19th and early 20th century. Considering free capitalism unstable and prone to crises, pressure groups and the cartels demanded a stronger intervention of the state. It was expected that state interventions would balance interests, smooth business cycles into steady growth, enhance wages and stabilize the economy and politics (c.f. ibid., pp. 662–680).

Protectionism, cooperativism, cartelism and state interventionism was the domestic reaction to the crisis and the persistent recession; imperialism was Bismarck's foreign policy tactic to fight the economic slowdown and regain political momentum. Why Bismarck became Germany's first colonial chancellor caused much dispute: at the beginning of his chancellorship, Bismarck was an outspoken opponent of colonialism. Bismarck argued that colonialism is too costly and risky, economically not beneficial and militarily imprudent. However, in 1884 Bismarck started his first colonial project.

Varied theories explain why Bismarck changed his mind: he was always a silent advocate, or there was increasing pressure from various interests groups like merchants and banker for colonialism, there was a public demand for colonies, there was a need to reduce Britain's influence, or to counteract the danger of socialist revolution and the aim to restore the European power equilibrium—all these were considered to have caused Bismarck's imperialist turn (Gründer 2012, pp. 55–65).

As maintained, Wehler (1976a) argued that imperialism enabled Bismarck to detract from inner problems. According to him, colonialism was expected to act as a stimulus program for the weak economy by developing new markets for industrial goods and investable capital and providing cheaper raw materials. In particular, imperialism should have again raised national sentiments, which often saved Bismarck's carrier.

Gründer (2012, pp. 67–83) showed that step by step most German political parties converted to the imperialist camp: the Nationalliberale Partei was traditionally enthusiastic about colonialism; the conservative parties Deutschkonservative Partei and Reichs- und Freikonservative Partei were ambivalent or dismissive at the beginning, but changed their minds at the beginning of Bismarck's colonial adventure; the Catholic Zentrum and the Deutsche Volkspartei opposed it at the beginning, but became more open to colonialism at the end of the 19th century; the political left around the social democrats was the clearest opponent at the beginning, but colonialism steadily gained ground even within the socialist parties.

The time of Wilhelminism, between 1890 and World War I, was characterized by the deepening of what had begun during the second half of Bismarck's rain. Wilhelm II and his chancellors strongly supported fast industrialization. Due to the Kaiser's close ties to the industry (Gall 2017, p. 75), he was quite aware of the demands of Germany's industrialists. Wilhelm and the governments were deeply convinced by the necessity of state intervenion and cooperation between the pressure groups and the cartels. Wehler (1995, p. 1042) considers the Wilhelminian system a "Authoritarian Corporatism"; politics and economics were dominated by a cooperation and a balance of vested interests of the "government, Parliament, political parties and pressure groups" without deepening "Parliamentarization or democratization." Politics of the late 19th and early 20th century Germany was characterized by the organized and institutionalist horse trade. Pressure groups extended their influence inside the Parliament by forming coalitions with political parties and outside by dominating the street: most political parties became the Parliamentary arms of pressure groups' interests (ibid., pp. 1038–1062). In addition, German imperialism also continued and accelerated (Gründer 2012).

Meanwhile, the concentration and cartelization of the economy intensified (Henderson 1975, pp. 178–186). Opposed by the remaining liberals in the 1870s, state interventionism and cartelism was hardly questioned around the turn of the century. State- or kathedersocialism was the unquestioned leading economic idea of the Wilhelminism (Gide and Rist 1923, p. 488 ff.): according to Gide and Rist, state interventions far beyond what state- or kathedersozialists proposed was legitimized by referring to economic theory. Against liberals' warnings that heavy state intervention would stall economic progress, the economic development of the late Bismarck time and the Wilhelmenian era was impressive. In the late 19th century German raised to an industrial superpower (Henderson 1975, p. 234): until World War I Germany had caught up to the industrial leaders (Kindleberger 1978, pp. 211–236). However, despite the fast industrialization, social and political tensions intensified. Radical authoritarian ideologies like radical German nationalism, Marxism and social Darwinism (Wehler 1995, pp. 1066–1085) being on the rise, political conflicts intensified.

5.4.4.2 The Rise of Joint-Stock Megabanks

The time from Bismarck's takeover to World War I was crucial for the development of the German banking sector and monetary policy. The new joint-stock law of 1870 caused a second wave of joint-stock bank foundation. Most of the newly founded banks did not survive the crisis of 1873; however, some of the surviving banks became leading institutions. Joint-stock banks profited from the concentration of the economy and the increasing political support. Opposing industrialization and big finance in the first half of the century, many national liberals became the main defenders and political advocates of the rising German joint-stock banks (Born 1977, pp. 151–172). As maintained, although industrialization was rejected in the first half of the 19th century, in the second half elites got convinced that fast industrialization was political and militarily necessary to be competitive against France and Britain. Still, influential groups opposed industrialization, but they lacked good arguments about how Germany should catch up with France and Britain without a fast industrialization. In particular, banks profited from the new agreement on industrialization; the necessity of the banks' financial support for fast industrialization was widely recognized and the rise of Germany's megabanks was closely related to the state-lead industrialization of the late 19th and early 20th century.

Already in the 1850s and 1860s, private banks were the main financer of the rising industry. However, the facilitation of joint-stock company foundation in 1870, and the rise of the concentrated, cartelized, state interventionist cooperative capitalism initiated a new banking era. Facilitating the foundation of joint-stock companies altered banking in two ways: first, the foundation of new joint-stock banks became much easier. Second, banks' possibilities to directly influence firms' management was fostered: before World War I Germany's megabank were represented in most supervisory boards. The possibility to enter and influence joint-stock companies' management facilitated the concentration of the banking sector; the big banks' ability and power to influence and guide companies or entire sectors was much bigger than of small banks. Even more important for the concentration of the banking sector, was the new agreement on the advantages of cartelization and state interventionism, which stemmed from the destruction of liberalism and the rise of state- or kathedersocialism as the new leading economic theory. It was suggested that industrialization should be planned and operated within the triangle of the active intervening state, industrial cartels and megabanks: megabanks were not just financers, but also, in an almost Saint-Simonian manner, it was suggested that banks should guide and organize industrialization. In the late 19th and early 20th century,

Germany's megabanks became active planners, organizers and leaders of the rising industry: apart from financing, megabanks promoted cartelization, managed joint-stock conglomerates and guided and organized entire economic sectors.

Due to escalating political conflicts and raising criticism, Bismarck needed foreign policy success for his political survival. However, Bismarck was in a dilemma: he needed the wars against Denmark and Austria to regain momentum, but the liberal majority in the Parliament refused to permit him the financial means. Unable to convince the government, Bismarck turned toward private bankers for war financing. The Rothschild representative Bleichröder and Hansemann bailed out Bismarck and organized the financial means for the wars (Stern 2008, p. 134 f.). Thankful for the support, Bismarck provided the public debt monopoly to the newly founded Preußen-Konsortium; the Preußen-Konsortium was an association of big German banks to finance public debt, which included all important private and joint-stock banks under the lead of Bleichröder and the Disconto-Gesellschaft (Wehler 1995, p. 298). For the newly founded joint-stock banks, the Preußen-Konsortium was quite important: it opened the lucrative German public debt market and ensured the political support of the government, which relied heavily on bankers' financial power. Supported by the Preußen-Konsortium, Bismarck's foreign policy was underpinned by Europe's perhaps strongest financial conglomerate. Like in other countries, bankers' financial support for governments' political ventures strongly fostered their political legitimacy. Still, many opposed the rising liberal, urban, often Jewish, bankers; however, political groups shied away from open conflicts because of the government's dependency on the banks' financial support.

Megabanks' political and financial role in Germany's colonialism caused much dispute. According to Hilferding ([1910] 1955), Lenin ([1917] 1999) and Hobson (1902), imperialism was the politicization of big finance and megabanks' vested interest: due to the abundance of capital and falling interest rates banks were in need of new investment markets. Unable to protect investments abroad, banks were dependent on governments' support to enforce their rights. With regard to Germany, the economic imperialism thesis was heavily criticized: according to Gründer (2012, p. 52), German banks were much less enthusiastic than merchants for German colonialism and little interested in colonial investments, as they lacked the experience of overseas banking. Smith (1978, p. 9) found that apart from several banks with were more active oversea like the Bleichröder Bank (Bismarck's house bank), at the beginning, German banks invested little in the newly founded colonies. However, facing an oversupply of capital and falling interests rates, and hence increasingly in need of new investment opportunities German banks started to support imperialism. According to Wehler (1976a, pp. 84–87), the situation was much like described by the advocates of the economic imperialism thesis: profit rates steadily fell as capital accumulated and profitable investment opportunities became scarce why banks increasingly looked abroad for profitable investment opportunities. He found (ibid., p. 165 ff.) that almost all German megabanks were leading members of the Deutscher Kolonialverein—the main promoter of the German imperialism—and argued for colonies to overcome the oversupply of capital.

Feis (1930, pp. 160–186) stressed that in principle in the first two thirds of the 19th century, Germany policy was quite reluctant towards foreign investments: they feared that capital exports may cause capital shortage and harm the domestic economy. However, in the last third of the century, when capital became increasingly abundant and the newly unified nation became much more active abroad, governments increasingly supported foreign investments to foster industrial exports and to underpin their foreign policy. Like in France and Britain, the coincidence of vested interests underpinned the relatively stable imperialist coalition between governments and big finance. Falling domestic interest rates caused financial institutions to increasingly search abroad for more lucrative investment opportunities. To protect the foreign investments megabanks heavily depended on the support of the government. To develop the newly conquered colonies and in particular to form coalitions with other nations the government needed the support of megabanks investing in colonies and their allied countries: governments used foreign investments to reward allies with private investments and punished renegades with the forced withdrawal of capital.

German megabanks invested heavily in foreign public debts. Governments used the foreign public debt investments for their carrot and stick policy to intensify the allies' dependency and sanction renegades. For example, the government used the banks' foreign investment for its Russia and Italy policy: due to the escalating political tensions, Bismarck prohibited banks from holding any kind of Russian assets. Meeting Caprivi's demand to bind Italy closer to the empire, German megabanks built a consortium to invest into Italian public debt (Born 1977, pp. 264 ff.).

Apart from investments in newly conquered colonies and foreign public debt, megabanks' foreign industrial investments strengthened Germany's influence and its reputation as a highly industrialized country and facilitated German industries' foreign investments. Germany was long considered an agrarian country largely underdeveloped. With industrial projects like the Baghdad railway, Germany demonstrated its engineer skills and its industrial potency. Politically, the Baghdad railway strengthened Germany's close ties with the Ottoman empire and broke up the French railway hegemony in Europe. While the Baghdad railway was predominately financed by the Deutsche Bank (Conrad 2012, p. 171), other German megabanks also became quite active abroad. Born (1977, pp. 246–264) and Feis (1930, pp. 62–68) considered that German megabanks became the leaders and organizers of many foreign industrial activities: using their close ties to the domestic big industry and their market overview, megabanks organized foreign industrial projects, takeovers and fundings. For example, the Deutsche Bank took the lead in almost all German economic activities in Turkey.

Apart from the rise of German megabanks, the second half of the 19th century was pivotal for central banking. As outlined, the Acts of 1856 and 1858 substantially changed Prussia's money system. Many influential German economists favored free banking over note-issuing monopolies. However, the governments' persistence caused economists and liberals to abandon their opposition to central banking and concentrate on the deregulation of joint-stock banking and the monetary unification of Germany (Smith 1936,

p. 56 ff.). Recognizing that free note issuing was not realistic due to the government's opposition, liberals and economists instead demanded the money unification of Germany with the Preußische Bank as the only central bank, strong enough to support private banks in the case of crises. German money economic discussions were long characterized by the conflict between advocates of free note issuing and of note-issuing monopolies. In the second half of the 19th century, the main conflict shifted toward disputes between money nationalists and money sectionists. In a long-lasting debate, German nationalists and sectionist nationalists argued over the economic and political necessity of a unique central bank (Eynern 1928, pp. 6–14). In particular money nationalists and money sectionists argued over the implementation of one German currency and the authority of the Preußische Bank: national liberals proposed the centralization of all money authority, sectionists were only willing, in 1870, to agree on the prohibition of the foundation of new central banks. The compromise did not last: gaining Parliamentary majority in 1875, money nationalists were able to enforce the Bankengesetz which permitted the foundation of a unique central bank, the Reichsbank (Born 1977, p. 34). As a concession to sectionists, step by step, the note monopoly was implemented and notes were not yet made legal tender (Smith 1936, p. 59 f.).

In addition to the foundation of the Reichsbank, the note-issuing regulation was modified. Continuing the Banking Principle, the one-third coverage of paper money by bullion was maintained, but the upper issuing limit was relaxed: the bank was allowed to freely issue up to 385 million mark and had to pay a 5% tax for every additional issuing (Born 1977, p. 34 f.). The new regulation was again a combination of Banking School and Currency School ideas: the adopted Real Bill Doctrine remained the main principle restricted by an upper issuing limit. However, the principle became more flexible as the bounding upper limit was replaced by the 5% tax: the new regulation was a step away from the Currency Principle toward the Banking Principle. At the beginning of the 20th century notes became legal tender (ibid., p. 35 f.). However, Bopp (1954) showed that the regulation of 1875 had several major shortcomings: first due to the step by step implementation of the issuing monopoly, the Reichsbank complained about other issuing banks thwarting its policy. Second, and more important, Reichsbank's goals were often mutually exclusive. According to Bopp (ibid., p. 214 ff.), the bank followed four main goals: convertibility of notes, minimizing the discount rate, stabilizing the discount rate and maximizing the portfolio. Occasionally the four goals were in conflict.

5.4.5 The Development of the German Banking System

For Gerschenkron (1962) Germany was economically backward at the beginning of the 19th century and a typical late developer. According to him, late developers like France and Germany are characterized by big banks and strong states: with early developers, like Britain, industrialization was hardly financed by banks and developed without much direct help from and intervention of the government. According to Gerschenkron, industrialization of early developers takeoff in an environment of general *laissez-faire*. In contrast, late developers adopted the capital-intensive production processes of the early developers, but lack developed financial markets able to finance the growing heavy industry: to overcome capital scarcity and support the planed industrialization, late developing governments founded or at least supported the foundation of big industrial banks. Ideologically the industrialization of late developers was underpinned by the great promises of the industrial society (ibid., p. 22 ff.), but harmed by the "existing obstacles to industrial development" (ibid., p. 8).

Dominated by megabanks with close relation to the rising heavy industry, Gerschenkron (ibid., p. 11 ff.) considered Germany an almost ideal-typical example of a second generation developer or late developer. According to him, the German universal banks were the leaders of the economy; dominating the supervisory boards of most big joint-stock companies, universal banks guided the rising industry: "German bank, [...] established the closest possible relations with industrial enterprises. A German bank, [...] accompanied an industrial enterprise from the cradle to the grave" (ibid., p. 14). Banks "controlling competing enterprises" or entire sectors megabanks fostered cartelization and the harmonization of the economy; "banks refused to tolerate fratricidal struggles among their children [the big industry]" (ibid., p. 15). Gerschenkron's theory was considered correct in principle, but overestimated the importance of banks and the intervention of the state. The state strongly intervened and banks took the lead in industrialization in the late 19th and early 20th century. However, in particular in the first half of the 19th century, banks played a minor role for industrialization and governments often opposed rather than supported the rise of the industry.

During the period of absolutism, German banks remained predominately pre-modern and fragmented: in the late 18th century the German banking system was dominated by trading-based banks in the North- and South-German trading hubs and court-based banks focusing on public debt financing. Private lending outside trading hubs was highly underdeveloped and predominately occurred within personal relations: rich merchants, aristocrats etc. lend out their idle hoards to farmers, craftsmen and small entrepreneurs. Several factors hampered the faster development of the German banking sector: at the beginning of the 19th century, the economy was still quite agricultural. The political fragmentation of Germany complicated big banking. In particular, at the beginning of the 19th century bankers faced strong political and public opposition and hostility. However, the unification and industrialization of Germany strongly shaped the German banking system.

At the beginning of the 20th century, according to Kindleberger (1978, pp. 211–236), economically Germany caught up with Britain and became one of Europe's industrial leaders. It is hardly questioned that at the beginning of World War I German was an industrial superpower. In the first half of the 19th century, industrialization in Germany was slow and difficult. As maintained, the landed aristocracy, craftsmen, conservatives and liberals were reluctant or even hostile toward industrialization. Junkers, small entrepreneurs and craftsmen, the main pillars of the most influential political movements of the early 19th century, feared social downgrading through industrialization and the rise of an industrial bourgeoisie. More realistic conservatives like Christian von Rother realized that industrialization was inevitable, but hoped that heavy state interventionism would lead industrialization into bearable, maybe advantageous, trails (Kitchen 1978, p. 88 f.): nationalizing several sectors, however, the states lacked the power and in particular the financial means to guide the economy. Banks, outside the trading hubs still favored public debt over industrial financing, as monarchs seemed better able to repay the loan than private industrial enterprises: occasionally monarchs hindered industrialization to prevent competition for loanable funds (Tilly 1980, p. 31). Apart from banks, favoring public debts over industry financing, wealthy citizens usually refused to lend their idle hoards to the industry.

5.4.5.1 The First Railway Boom and the Rise of the Rhenish Bankers

Regardless of the difficulties, the first industrial centers emerged around 1820 in Sachsen, Berlin, Schlesien, Saar and in particular in the Rhineland (Wehler 1987, p. 64 ff.). The Rhineland, Germany's first industrial hub, also became the center of banking innovation. Tilly (1966) showed that already between 1820 and 1850 the number of banks and banks' capital increased fast in the Rhineland. Mainly originating in wholesale trade, Rhineland bankers initially focused on real estate banking and war financing until they turned toward industry financing; at the beginning of the 19th century banking was a by-business. With the rise of the industry, in particular in the industrial hubs, banking professionalized in the 1830s and 1840s. Lending predominately their own capital at the beginning, Rhineland bankers soon became capital intermediaries.

As maintained, Germany's first railway boom of the 1840s fundamentally changed the economic and in particular the banking landscape. Railway building necessitated and fostered the bundling and concentration of capital. In addition, railway building propelled the development in related sectors like mining and heavy industry. Unlike most other industrial projects, railways achieved broad support; from liberals and nationalists hoping that facilitated transportation would unite the still highly fragmented country; from the military because railways were considered pivotal for the country's defense; and for industry fetishists railway building was an important step toward industrial society.

No other country, except Belgium, extended its railway system faster than Germany in the 1840s (Henderson 1975, p. 49). Fremdling (1975, p. 48) outlined that Germany's railway system increased from 6 km in 1835 to more than 5000 in 1848; he also found that railway net-investments were huge in the 1840s (ibid., 31). As maintained, financing became the main problem of Germany's ambitious railway projects. The railway boom necessitated on of a totally new scale; private banks had neither the capital (Tilly 2003, p. 101) nor the experience to undertake projects of that scale and the state's intention to nationalize railways as soon as possible hung like the sword of Damocles over private financing (Gall 1999, p. 19). It does not seem that Germany suffered from scarcity of capital, investable funds were rather abundant (Then 1997, pp. 131–142), but financial institutions failed to bundle the savings and idle hoards for huge railway projects. Structural, institutional and cultural factors complicated railway financing: structurally, banks' were quite bounded to their region why they preferred to invest into domestic public debt or regional enterprises (Tilly 1966). For huge railway projects, the absorbed regional savings were usually too small. Institutionally, the governments' reticence on joint-stock conglomerates prevented banks and railway companies to form joint-stock companies better suited for big investments. In addition, the unclear and contradictory railway policy of the German countries much complicated profitable railway building. Culturally, ordinary people and bankers were accustomed to investing into short-term trade or public debt and shied away from long-term industrial investment (Tilly 1980, p. 31). In addition, as outlined, the influential landed aristocracy still opposed railways, industry financing and banking: they feared that railways would remove capital from agrarian credit and they feared the rise of the industrial bourgeoisie.

However, despite all difficulties, private bankers, in particular the Rhenish, became the main railway investors (Born 1977, p. 87 ff.). Railway financing significantly changed bankers' business and their political influence: steadily absorbing more capital private bankers increasingly became intermediaries who bundled small savings and tapped foreign financial markets for German railway companies (Tilly 1966). Transforming small savings of short maturity into huge long-term industrial investments, German banks increasingly functioned as size and maturity or risk transformer. In addition, the railway boom caused the first comprehensive banking concentration: just a relatively small group of bankers became quite active in railway financing. Absorbing much capital and investing on a new scale the most active railway financers became the new leaders of the banking sector.

Later banking innovations were predominately pillared, forwarded and implemented by railway bankers. Politically, bankers' influence increased by railway financing: bankers influenced governments' railway plans (Gall 1999, p. 22) and played an active role in the negotiation between railway companies and governments (Tilly 1966, p. 97 ff). Most active private banks entered the management of the newly founded joint-stock railway companies, used their political influence to promote railways and actively intervened into railway planning (ibid., pp. 94–108); hence, already in the 1840s the relation between the rising industry and banks became quite close. More generally, in Germany's railway age private banks steadily shifted from public debt banking toward industrial financing and developed close ties to the industry:

> On the one hand, they [private bankers] provided business enterprises with finance – both short-term and long – on a scale matched by no other contemporary institution. On the other hand, they promoted new corporate enterprises and, by their example, accelerated the flow of savings into industry. In a word, they provided both 'commercial' and 'investment' banking services. Their interest in doing so was shaped by the general requirements of industrialization in the railway Age (ibid., p. 81).

Hence, the railway boom caused the first longer phase of industrialization, which lasted, for most of the 1840 and 1850s. The need for capital on a new scale caused banks to increasingly enter industrial financing and created a railway financing banking aristocracy—like Camphausen, Hansemann, Oppenheimer, Rothschild, Mevissen—with close ties to the industry and the governments.

5.4.5.2 The Foundation and Rise of the First Joint-Stock Banks

Due to the rising demand from the railway boom, the coal, iron, cotton, wool and engineering industry also took off (Henderson 1975, pp. 53–70). However, despite of banking aristocracy's increasing engagement in industrial financing, capital remained scarce for the rising industries: according to Wehler (1987, pp. 95–107) financing became the main problem of the early industries. In contrast to Britain, Germany lacked a developed financial market and the funds of the old capitalist families ready to provide the capital needed for the industry's fast growth. The two joint-stock laws, Preußisches Eisenbahngesetz of 1838 and the Preußische Aktienrecht of 1843, were the government's institutional answers to the problem of financing. In hindsight, the Preußisches Eisenbahngesetz and the Preußische Aktienrecht were pivotal steps for the industrialization of Germany and the concentration of the banking sector. With the Acts of 1838 and 1843 the government followed bankers' demand to facilitate the foundation of joint-stock conglomerates. Alarmed by the huge losses of the railway crisis in 1838 and the continuing problems to cover the financial needs for railway building, bankers also demanded the permission of joint-stock banks (Tilly 2003, p. 101). However, it took another ten years until the banking aristocracy was able to found Germany's first joint-stock banks.

As maintained, opposed by the landed interests and several bankers like Heydt and Rothschild, the early promoters of joint-stock banking faced huge difficulties to found and advance joint-stock banks. However, the foundation of the Darmstädter Bank, Schaaffhausen Bank and Disconto-Gesellschaft caused the first joint-stock banking boom in the 1850s. Despite the foundation enthusiasm, the joint-stock banking development was much more difficult than in France: joint-stock banks were still not allowed to found branches in Prussia or Frankfurt (Born 1977, p. 152 f.). Founded to facilitate industry financing, at the beginning, the share of industrial capital from joint-stock banks remained relatively small (Tilly 1966, p. 111). Nevertheless, the 1850s significantly altered German banking: due to the economic boom of the 1850s, banks increasingly entered industry financing (Born 1977, p. 91). Convinced by the superiority of joint-stock megaconglomerates, which dominated the German industry in the late 19th and early 20th century, banks, the newly founded joint-stock banks, together with important industrialists often founded the first joint-stock conglomerates. The close cooperation between leading industrialists and banks developing and operating joint-stock conglomerates, which started in the 1850s, became the foundation of the German economic model (Wehler 1995, pp. 85–91).

Despite all the hostility and opposition from the old elites and parts of the general public, the 1850s and 1860s were also characterized by the increasing political influence of bankers and the improving political and institutional environment for banks. The rise of the liberal parties was in particular advantageous for banks: first because liberals became bankers' main political supporters in the second half of the 19th century. Second, liberal economic policy, like facilitating the foundation of joint-stock companies, was in the interest of bankers; in particular of the rising joint-stock banks. In addition, Bismarck's problems to finance the patriotic wars strongly increased bankers' political influence and opened the lucrative public debt business. Granting the public debt monopoly to the Preußen-Konsortium had two main effects: first, it facilitated public debt banking to the rising joint-stock banks and second it institutionalized the close ties between Bismarck and the rising bankers and made governments quite dependent on the goodwill of bankers.

Kitchen (1978, pp. 87–101) showed that the 1850s were quite fertile for industrialization and in particular banking: the period between 1850 and 1857 was characterized by fast economic growth and much investment in industry and railways. According to Kitchen, the time was characterized by several important transitions: the economy started to concentrate; for the first time most ordinary people were convinced to invest their idle hoards via new founded joint-stock banks or private banks into the rising industry and railways; inspired by their Keynesian French partners, joint-stock bankers convinced many that high employment, economic prosperity and industrialization needs joint-stock industrial banks able and willing to absorb idle funds and lend at low rates to the economy. Big banks were the main beneficiaries of the changing circumstances. Ordinary peoples' increasing confidence in the banking sector augmented deposits and banks capital base. Bundling the capital of many smaller and bigger investors and depositors increased banks' influence. Joint-stock conglomerates using capital-intensive techniques strongly increased the demand for capital. Bigger and more concentrated companies and sectors were easier to oversee and guide for big banks than a wide range of small enterprises. The spreading Keynesian understanding of the relation between the abundance of credit, interest rates, growth and employment, legitimized banks and put bankers into the center of economic development: even conservatives god convinced that augmenting the supply of credit is the most efficient economic policy.

As maintained, the boom phase of the 1850s ended with the crisis of 1857. Despite frequent deep crises like in 1866, until the Gründerkrach of 1873, the development, which started in the 1850s, continued: industrialization accelerated, the economy further concentrated and banks, in particular joint-stock banks were on the rise.

Until 1870, not more than a handful of joint-stock banks were founded, predominately in the Rhineland. Becoming important to the industry and public debt financers, before 1870 joint-stock banks were still far away from dominating the banking sector. The Aktiennovelle of 1870 fundamentally changed the German economy and banking: permitting the foundation of joint-stock conglomerates without government license facilitated new foundations, and the concentration of the economy. The defeat of France, the unification of Germany and the Aktiennovelle caused one of the most impressive economic bubbles in Germany's history. During the so-called Güderfieber between 1870 and 1873 more than 100 banks were founded (Pohl 1986, p. 35 ff.). While most of the newly founded joint-stock banks were closed again in the Gründerkrach of 1873 and the following recession (Born 1977, p. 157), several of the newly founded banks like the Commerz- und Disconto-Bank, the Dresdner-Bank and the Deutsche Bank became leading institutions of the German banking sector.

5.4.5.3 The Development of Germany's Megabanks

The Gründerkrach of 1873, the most serious crisis of the 19th which ended the Güderfieber and caused a 20-year period of economic slowdown, was one of the most important turning points in the economic history of Germany. As maintained, the Gründerkrach and the persistent recession marked the end of the liberal era and the dominance of the liberal economic policy: economic liberalism was replaced by protectionism, imperialism, cartelism and state interventionism; state- or kathedersocialism replaced classical liberalism as the leading economic Idea. The German economic system of the late 19th and early 20th is usually considered organized capitalism: which meant that economic development was planned, organized and operated in the triangle of industrial cartels, megabanks and the heavy intervening state.

The economic development between the Gründerkrach and World War I was characterized by fast industrialization and in particular by the concentration and cartelization of the economy. As maintained, after the Gründerkrach a relatively wide agreement existed about the advantageousness of cartelization and concentration and the state-led development of the economy. It was argued that cartelized and concentrated economies are easier to lead, are less prone to crises, better suit the interest of the general public and they overcome the worsening class conflict by facilitating cooperation between the different pressure groups.

Several factors fostered cartelized and concentrated: railways and other innovations facilitated communication, the unification provided bigger markets and the Aktiennovelle of 1870 facilitated the foundation and merges of big conglomerates: four fifths of the rising megacompanies were joint-stock conglomerates (Wehler 1995, p. 627). Most importantly, economic and political elites supported and promoted economy's cartelization and concentration. Governments inspired by state- or kathedersocialism, but even liberal politicians, actively promoted the foundation of cartels: governments expected that cartels are easier to direct, less prone to crises, facilitate a fast, but steady industrialization and strengthen national sentiments. Megabanks supported the cartelization because joint-stock megaconglomerates were easier to control and seemed more profitable. Pressure groups expected that they would be better able to enforce their vested interests within megaconglomerates than in a highly fragmented economy. In particular the industry and banking sector strongly concentrated (ibid., pp. 622–661): many of the most notable German industrial megaconglomerates like Siemens, BASF, AEG and Krupp emerged in the late 19th century. The concentration process was accompanied by the fats cartelization of the economy (Henderson 1975, pp. 178–185).

Apart from cartelization and concentration, the German model was characterized by the close interaction and cooperation of the industry, banks and the state. Heavily intervening in most sectors and even companies, the state strongly directed the economy. While industrialists, engineers and other experts operated megacompanies, banks managed the financial issues and codetermined general development directions. Megabanks usually bundled the shareholders' voting right in their hands (Born 1977, p. 161 ff.) why they had much influence on most megacompanies: more than 30% of all 6800 supervisory board position were occupied by joint-stock banks representatives; in particular the biggest banks were present in hundreds of companies (Wehler 1995, p. 629 f.). Tilly (1986) considers that megabanks were the "Development Assistance of the Strong" because they predominately supported megacompanies and showed little interest in small scale investments. Due to their favor for the big industry, Neuberger and Stokes (1974) argued that megabanks misallocated resources because small, innovate enterprises were excluded.

The importance of megabanks for Germany's industrialization and the relation between banks and the heavy industry was heavily discussed. For main contributors of the late 19th and early 20th century, megabanks were the organizer and leader of the economy. The Marxist Rudolf Hilferding ([1910] 1955) describes in his *Das Finanzkapital* how the foundation of joint-stock companies and their close connection and submission to megabanks dismantled competition and caused the concentration of capital and production. He expected that concentration will end up in one megatrust which dominates the entire economy and the concentration of all capital in a few or one megabank. The liberal economist and politician Jacob Riesser came, in his outstanding work on the development and concentration of Germany's Grossbanken (megabanks), to a rather similar result. Riesser (1912, pp. 489–637) draws a close connection between banking and industry concentration; he argues that both concentrations stimulated one another. For Riesser capital increasingly concentrated in the hands of a few megabanks, which sharply increased their market, power and necessitated large-scale investment opportunities. However, for him megabanks became the clear leader of the economy. The main conclusion had not changed much when 50 years later Gerschenkron (1962, p. 14) stated that "the German banks […] established the closest possible relations with industrial enterprises. A German bank, as the saying went, accompanied an industrial enterprise from the cradle to the grave": he left little doubt that in principle he considers banks the leaders of industrial development. Tilly (1998: 16) summarizes the theory of Germany's bank-lead industrialization: banks formed and advanced the railway building in the 1830s and 1840s, the rise of the steel industry in the 1850s and 1860s and the industrialization, concentration and cartelization of the late 19th century. More recently, several contributors doubt banks' leading role in Germany's industrialization (Edwards and Ogilvie 1996, p. 427): Wehler (1995, p. 627 ff.) argues that megabanks were quite important for industrialization, but never had the dominance over the industry. However, there may be little doubt that the German banking sector strongly concentrated in the late 19th and early 20th century, that megabanks and industrial megaconglomerates had quite close ties and in the one or other form megabanks shaped the part of Germany's industrial development.

Many sectors of the German economy strongly concentrated in the late 19th and early 20 century, nowhere was the concentration more pronounced than in the banking sector. Traditionally, Germans hardly deposited money with banks. Steadily, as they became more accustomed to banking, idle hoards were increasingly being deposited. Rising deposits and accumulated profits made investable capital increasingly abundant. While French and British banks increasingly struggled to find domestic investment opportunities, Germany banks could still find domestic investment places. Also, interest rates declined in German (Feis 1930, p. 60 ff.) However, due to the delayed industrialization and unification the scarcity of investment opportunities was less pronounced. Nevertheless, propelled by capital oversupply, falling interest rates and governments' support German megabanks' foreign investment increased fast in the 40 years before World War I. The grant majority of Germany's foreign investments remained in Europe, a lot was also invested in the Middle-East and in North- and Latin-America: according to Feis (ibid., p. 71), the total capital export increased from 5 billion in 1870 to 25 billion in 1914. The biggest amounts were invested in Austria-Hungary, North- and South-America, Russia, the Ottoman Empire and the Balkans. In addition to industrial and foreign investments, the public debt monopoly of the Preußen-Konsortium granted the profitable and safe market of state financing to the rising megabanks.

Hence, several factors fostered the concentration of the German banking sector and the rise of megabanks in the late 19th and early 20th century. According to Tilly (1998), the increasing demand for long-term industrial investments, underdeveloped financial markets and banks "limits of their own resources (and difficulties experienced in building syndicates of bankers) encouraged private bankers to organize joint-stock banks with limited liability" (ibid., p. 13). Germany's model of the organized cooperative capitalism favored megabanks over smaller financial institutions. Better able to control and guide joint-stock conglomerates and entire sectors, to bundle capital for huge investments and to oversee general international economic trends, megabanks became the favored financial institutions of the German cooperative capitalism. Only megabanks had the resources and ability to organize, lead and finance Germany's industrial megaprojects abroad. Expected to plan, coordinate and finance projects in allied countries, megabanks became the governments' favored foreign policy partner. The monopolization of public debt banking for the Preußen-Konsortium privileged the predominately big banks of the consortium. Due to their central role in Germany's fast industrialization, foreign policy and state financing megabanks enjoyed political protection.

Growing much faster than the rest of the economy, megabanks became Germany's biggest companies: by World War I Germany's biggest three companies were banks and 17 out of the 25 biggest companies were also banks (Tilly 1994, 1998). At the beginning of the 20th century, the German banking sector was dominated by just eight megabanks; the big eight. The Deutsche Bank (world's biggest bank at the time) was the biggest with an equity capital of 250 million mark; Dresdner Bank and the Disconto-Gesellschaft had around 200 million and the Darmstädter Bank around 160 million (Born 1977, p. 165 ff.). Tilly (2003, p. 107) estimated that in 1913 Germany's joint-stock banks' active was around 22 billion mark; around the amount of the Sparkassen and much more than any other banking group.

5.5 Central Banking

As maintained, central banking was a core topic among economists and politicians in the 19th century. The debate started in Britain, where the issue of central banking was the longest and most intensively discussed, but soon also reached France and Germany. The 19th century was also the time of the rise of modern central banking.

As outlined above, central banking theories may be, in principle, grouped into monetarist, Keynesian and free banking theories. Monetarists usually suggested binding money rules, convertibility, the restriction of paper money issuing, the monopolization of issuing and the foundation of an independent central bank. Keynesians considered that the amount of money is an endogenous variable which cannot be controlled fully by the state or central banks. They drew a close connection between the amount of money and employment. On the question of convertibility and note-issuing monopolies, Keynesians were not quite clear. However, they rejected inflexible rules and suggested that central banks should be relatively free to act in accordance with economic circumstances; according to them, central banks should take an active part in fostering and sustaining employment, economic growth and industrialization. Free bankers rejected note-issuing monopolies and central banks and instead suggested the free issuing of many smaller competitive banks.

The British discussions between bullionists and anti-bullionists, the Currency School and the Banking School, and the Birmingham School and the Manchester one were, doubtlessly, the most central debates on central banks and central banking theory of the 19th century. The most well-known and outstanding contribution on central banking of the 19th century was Walter Bagehot's *Lombard Street* ([1873] 1962): Bagehot combined much of the Currency and the Banking School theory (Arnon 2011, p. 284 f.), however at the end his work became a monetarist central banking manifesto. Bagehot had sympathy for free banking approaches (Bagehot [1873] 1962, p. 32), but considered the shift from central banking to free banking as unrealistic (Smith 1936, p. 124). Defining the existence of central banks as a hardly changeable historical fact, Bagehot focused on how central banks may stabilize markets in case of financial market disturbances. For Bagehot, being the lender of last resort is the main function of central banks. He argued that central banks should be armed with enough reserves to lend to the weakest banks in case of financial market disturbances. Like maintained Bagehot ([1873] 1962, p. 96 f.) suggested that central banks should lend at rates higher than the market rate in order to safeguard that just banks that are truly in need borrow from central banks: sounder banks borrow elsewhere at lower rates and only those without credit would make use of central bank money. Both Keynesians and free-bankers had a time when they became quite influential—in particular in the first half of the 19th century—but overall, on central banking issues, the 19th century was the time of monetarists in Britain.

As maintained, in France similar issues were discussed: in particular the question of money policy dominated the French controversies. Like in Germany, free bankers were more influential in the first half of the 19th century than in Britain. Inspired by the British discussions, monetarism also spread to France: similar to their British colleagues, French monetarists suggested the note-issuing monopolies, convertibility and the restriction of paper money issuing. While the discussion between free bankers and monetarists about issuing monopolies and issuing restrictions continued throughout the 19th century, the rise of the French Keynesians, in particular its biggest group the Saint-Simonians, fundamentally changed the landscape of the debate. Less interested in questions of central banking and note-issuing monopolies, French Keynesians were highly focused on how flexible money policies may foster economic development and industrialization. French Keynesians in particular demanded a much more permissive money policy and that the Banque de France supports growth, employment and industrialization by low interest rates and easy credit. Hence, in sharp contrast to the British monetarists, French Keynesians demanded an active policy of the central bank which clearly takes side with the industry and commerce; not price stability, but fast industrialization and high employment was considered the main goal of money policy.

Around the same time, money economic issues reached the German countries. Nowhere were free bankers stronger than in Germany. Many of the leading economists were free bankers and even in mid-19th century, when elsewhere they were on the retreat, free bankers remained strong in Germany: fearing that central banks would pool too much power in their hands and that governments would use the bank for their own vested interests, German free bankers suggested to impel private banks' note issuing. Relatively late, monetarism was on the rise and many influential German economists adopted a more monetarist position rather due to governments' rejection of free banking than to sincere conviction. Despite their monetarist, free banking or Keynesian views, most German money economists supported and promoted monetary unification. The Prussian government insisting on the state's determination of the money stock and the monopolization of issuing caused many influential economists to abandon their favor of free banking and focus instead on the monetary unification of Germany. Adjusting to the government's demand, famous German economists of the late 19th century suggested one monetary unit for the newly unified Germany, issued by one central bank.

5.5.1 Bank of England

As maintained, the question of money policy was heavily discussed within parliaments and among the general public: money policy was a hot topic in the 19th century inside and outside parliaments. Nowhere were money issues more intensely discussed than in

Britain. Due to the war against France the Bank of England lent to the government heavily after 1793. Close to the limit due to overstretching government lending, the Bank of England was rescued by suspending the convertibility of its notes in 1797. Released from the boundaries of convertibility, Bank of England notes spread fast. Due to high inflation and recurrent financial crises, advocates of the reintroduction of convertibility gained ground. In 1819 convertibility was reintroduced and the short span of freedom for Bank of England was over for a long to come. However, the time of inconvertibility was pivotal for the British money system and the Bank of England. Fast spreading notes and their function as other banks' main reserve store strengthened Bank of England's position as the bank of banks. According to money theory, inconvertibility caused several leading classical economists to further develop the classical quantity theory or monetarism.

Following Ricardo's Ingot plan in 1819, just two years later the government decided to withdraw the plan and to allow the Bank of England to give out coins: however, the restoration of convertibility remained untouched. The restoration of convertibility was a major victory of the monetarists who argued that metal-based paper money is the sound fundament for a stable financial market. Although convertibility did not meet the promises as deep crises again shook financial markets in the early 1820s and 1830s, it was not suspended again. Rather than changing the monetary principles of convertibility, several of Bank of England's privileges were withdrawn: in 1826 and 1833 the Bank of England lost its joint stock monopoly. As compensation for the lost privileges, the Bank of England was allowed to issue notes smaller than 5£, its notes became legal tender and the interest rate restrictions were de facto withdraw. Again, the Bank of England became more monetarist: monetarists suggested that Bank of England become a purely issuing bank, in the sense that it stops ordinary banking business, makes note legal tender and rejects interest rates restrictions.

After the deep crises of 1836 and 1839 the so-called Bank Charter Act of 1844 was passed in the Parliament. The Act granted the Bank of England a quasi note-issuing monopoly and the bank was divided into a note issuing and a banking department. The Bank of England was allowed to issue 14 million pounds against government securities and every additional note had to be covered with a 100% bullion reserve. The Bank Charter Act was the major monetarist victory of the 19th century. Implementing most of the monetarist Currency Principle, the note-issuing department of the Bank of England became the monetarist central bank blueprint.

Hence, all major British money acts of the 19th century were victories of the monetarists and important steps toward a central banking system following monetarism. The Bank Charter Act was the ultimate victory because it separated the Bank of England, as proposed by monetarists, into a full monetarist central bank and an ordinary joint stock bank (for more details see above and Andreadēs 1966, pp. 187–242; Morgan 2013, pp. 23–48; Smith 1936, p. 11 ff.).

5.5.2 Banque de France

Already in the 1790s, the case of a national bank was heavily discussed in France. Several proposals suggested the foundation of national banks (Essars Des 1896, pp. 49–55). With the takeover of Napoleon Bonaparte, political power shifted toward national bank advocates: already in 1800 Napoleon founded the Banque de France. Napoleon was relatively open to economic innovation, however, his dissatisfaction with the lending behavior of the existing banks caused him to promote a new national bank. It was expected that the Banque de France would lower interest rates and relax government's financial boundaries. Notoriously in financial difficulties, the government hoped to overcome its financial problems by founding a new national bank:

Consul Bonaparte took the initial steps toward founding the Bank of France. He could not get what he wanted from the free banks. On the other hand, he felt that the Treasury needed money, and wanted to have under his hand an establishment which could compel to meet his wishes (Liesse 1909, p. 17).

Because wealthy classes remained cautious about the new state-dependent institute, the Banque de France found it quite difficult to absorb the needed money from private investors (c.f. ibid., p. 15 ff.).

At the time of Banque de France's foundation note issuing was not restricted, which is why several banks issued notes. However, France had a long tradition of note-issuing monopolies so the monopolization of issuing seemed just around the corner. Already in 1803 the Banque de France received an issuing monopoly for Paris and all other issuing banks had to withdraw notes within the short period of six months. Outside Paris, banks needed a governmental concession for issuing, which enabled the government to determine the issuing quantity (ibid., p. 26 f.). Unlike in Britain, after 1819, Banque de France's issuing was not directly restricted: the bank was just required to meet its obligations, which meant to hold enough reserves (Essars Des 1896, p. 56).

Over-issuing and the preparation for the war caused a bank run of the Banque de France and a serious crisis in 1805 (Essars Des 1896, p. 58 f; Liesse 1909, p. 29 f.). Blaming Banque de France's liberty for the crisis (Essars Des 1896, p. 59), Napoleon changed the law in 1806, which strongly increased the influence of the state. In addition, the law of 1806 permitted and demanded Banque de France's branching outside Paris and granted a note-issuing monopoly to the bank for all cities in which it opens branches (Liesse 1909, p. 32 ff.). Bank's branching efforts were of little success; promising at the beginning, the general political slowdown after 1813 and the overstretching public debt financing caused major turbulences (ibid., pp. 32–42)

In 1814 Jacques Laffitte became the governor of the Banque de France: for the first time an outspoken left liberal inspired by Keynesian money theories was leading the bank. Laffitte's reign was a short-lived liberal epoch in the long conservative history of the Banque de France. Unlike former times, Laffitte implemented a much more active central banking policy. In particular, Laffitte ended Banque de France's traditional opposition to issuing institutes outside Paris: under the governance of Laffitte Banque de France welcomed the foundation of provincial note-issuing banks in the portal cities of Rouen (1817), Nantes (1818) and Bordeaux (1818) (Kindleberger 1993, p. 105). When further note-issuing banks were founded in Lyon, Marseille, Lille, Le Havre, Toulouse and Orleans, Banque de France fell back into its traditional conservativism and demanded the note monopoly for the entire country (c.f. Sée 1936, p. 199). During the July Monarchy, the bank started, slowly but steadily, to cover the country with note-issuing branches (Liesse 1909, pp. 47–53).

The political crises of 1847 and 1848 were pivotal events for the development of Banque de France. Suppressing other issuers, since the early 1840s the crises opened the possibility to overcome competitors (Kindleberger 1993, p. 109). Unsettled by the revolution, most private banks stopped doing business. In the general banking shutdown, Banque de France remained the only banking institution that fought the economic turmoil (Liesse 1909, p. 54 ff.). Empowered by their active struggle against the crises, Banque de France demanded the suspension of convertibility, the permission of the issuing of 100 France notes and the making of its notes legal tender (ibid., p. 60). Weakened by the crises and the new regulations, most other issuing banks and departments were absorbed by Banque de France in 1848 (Caron 1979, p. 50). In addition, new regulations increased banks' issuing elasticity, made notes legal tender and granted to the bank a quasi issuing monopoly.

In 1857 further legal changes altered the position of Banque de France: the bank was authorized to give out 50 franc notes and usury restrictions were withdrawn (Liesse 1909, p. 89). Recognizing Banque de France's issuing monopoly, the bank was obliged to open at least one issuing branch in each department: however, Banque de France did not haste to meet the obligation (Mehrens 1911, p. 98 f.). The bank was criticized for rarely using its privilege to issue smaller notes (Kindleberger 1993, p. 107 f.). As maintained, Saint Simonians, in particular the brothers Péreire, became the main critics of Banque de France; they blamed the bank for underusing its privileges to support the economy and industrialization. Quite dissatisfied with Banque de France's policy and criticizing the issuing monopoly, the Péreires tried to use the newly annexed Banque de Savoie for establishing a competing issuing institute. Péreires' plan failed as the government prohibited the branching into a note-issuing institute in Paris (Cameron 1961, p. 191). Péreires' attack was the last serious assault on Banque de France's issuing monopoly. In 1870 and 1871 the bank was authorized to issue notes of 25, 10 and 5 franc (Liesse 1909, p. 144). In 1873 convertibility was reintroduced (Born 1977, p. 27). Despite Banque de France's reluctance towards branching and issuing, notes were on the rise in France, spread throughout the country and were increasingly used in daily life, but paper money was still much less used than in Britain (Kindleberger 1993, p. 110).

5.5.3 Reichsbank

As maintained, in the first half of the 19th century Germany was considered backward in its monetary policy; a wide range of different coins flooded the German trading hubs and paper money was hardly used. Until mid-19th century the monetary policies of the German states were relative autonomous, which is why it seems inappropriate to speak of one German money policy. In 1846 five, private and public, issuing banks existed in politically fragmented Germany (Born 1977, p. 31). According to Tilly (1980, p. 33), the 1835 founded Bayerische Hypotheken- und Wechsel-Bank and the 1838 founded Bank von Leipzig, which later became Bank von Sachsen, are Germany's oldest modern issuing banks. Also, the Prussian Giro- and Lehnbanco (Königliche Bank) issued notes, but on a very small scale. As maintained, the Giro- and Lehnbanco was founded to foster growth and trade by note issuing, but due to lacking support from the government (Born 1977, p. 29) and low demand for notes (Ziegler 1993, p. 486 f.) the amount of notes remained very small. In 1806 the Königliche Bank ceased note issuing and instead issued treasury bills (Born 1977, p. 29). Until 1846 treasury bills counted only for around 10% to 20% of the circulating money (Tilly 1980, p. 42). As maintained, until 1833, when Prussia introduced a quasi note-issuing monopoly, note issuing was not restricted, but nevertheless hardly undertaken.

The new Bank Ordnung in 1846 was the first important step toward central banking in Germany. The new law transferred the fully public Giro- and Lehnbanco into the mixed Preußische Bank with mixed ownership: one sixth of Preußische Bank's stocks were held by the state and the rest by private agents; the state's share decreased as new stocks were distributed. The bank received the right to issue notes of 21 million taler; the upper limit of 21 million was withdrawn in 1856 (Born 1977, p. 30). Unlike the Bank of England, the Preußische Bank was only obligated to cover one third of the issued notes with bullion (Ziegler 1993, p. 491).

Already in 1847, the Preußische Bank issued notes of 19 million taler (Schauer 1912: 39). Due to its upper issuing limit, the bank was unable to cover the rising demand for notes. Preußische Bank's restriction caused many demanders to turn to other issuing banks. The rising demand for money and the lax restriction of note issuing in several German states caused a unique issuing boom in the 1850 s. Between 1847 and 1857 25 private and public issuing banks were founded; most of them outside Prussia (Born 1977: 31). As maintained, the inflow of non-Prussian notes corroded Prussia's money policy. Ziegler (1993: 494) estimated that half of the notes in circulation were non-Prussian notes. As outlined, the Prussian government followed four main goals with its money policy: the implementation of a note-issuing monopoly, the state's control over the Preußische Bank and the money supply and the monetary unification of Germany. The note-issuing boom elsewhere in Germany brought Prussia further away from its money policy goals.

As maintained, the laws of 1856 and 1858 were reactions to Prussia's overflow with foreign notes. Withdrawing Preußische Bank's note-issuing limit in 1856 and prohibiting foreign banknotes in 1858 strengthened the position of the Preußische Bank and were important steps toward a modern central banking system. Prohibiting foreign notes and increasing the issuing elasticity, Preußische Bank's possibility to pursue an active money policy were greatly extended. Strongly augmenting issuing and branching outside Prussia extended Preußische Bank's money power across borders (Born 1977, p. 32 f.). Hence, the regulative changes of 1856 and 1858 paved the way for the Preußische Bank as Germany's central bank (Ziegler 1993, p. 496).

Facilitated by the new regulations and due to the fast rising demand, note issuing greatly extended: Schauer (1912, p. 46) estimated that between 1856 and 1875 notes of the Preußische Bank increased by 688%. According to Tilly (1980, p. 42 f.), bank notes in circulation increased from 6 million Thaler in 1845 to 300 million in 1875. In the 1860 s, the Preußische Bank branched out offensively inside and outside Prussia. Already at the time of the war with Austria, the Preußische Bank became the bank of German banks and its notes dominated the German money market (Born 1977, p. 62 f.).

Prohibiting the foundation of new issuing banks in 1870, the Bankengesetz of 1875 intended the foundation of a unique German central bank; the Reichsbank. Much like the Bank Charter Act 1844 in Britain, the Bankengesetz prescribed the step-by-step introduction of a note-issuing monopoly for entire Germany: however, most other issuing banks voluntarily forwent on issuing (Eynern 1928, p. 15). The upper note-issuing limit was also modified: continuing the requirement of one third coverage, the Reichsbank was allowed to issue 385 million mark freely and had to pay a yearly 5% tax on any further issuing. Taking over the Preußische Bank, the Reichsbank also overtook its legal form as a private and state owned bank with a clear governmental lead (Born 1977, p. 34 f.). Hence, at the beginning of the 19th century the Reichsbank became a modern central bank, with a note-issuing monopoly for the whole of Germany and its notes became legal tender.

Hence, around the turn of the century in France, Germany and Britain central banks were founded looking much like nowadays: central banks issued notes, held note-issuing monopolies and their notes were legal tender.

5.6 Non-profit Banks

As maintained, in the 14th and 15th century in Italian City-States and France Monte di Pietàs were founded to protect the poor from usurers and offer poorer classes an alternative to ordinary banks: later, Monte di Pietàs spread throughout Europe. In contrast to ordinary banks, Monte di Pietàs were not profit oriented and attempted to bring fair banking to poorer classes. Monte di Pietàs were operated by Catholic institutions; predominately the Franciscans. The 19th century was the time of rising private and central banking; it was also the time of non-profit banking. In Britain, France and in particular

Germany, non-profit banks were founded. Although strongly influenced by the Christian social ethics, the newly founded non-profit banks had hardly any direct connection with the Church. Aside from Christian social ethics, liberal and socialists ideas also inspired non-profit banking in the late 18th and 19th century.

Monte di Pietàs were founded to protect the poor from profit-hungry usurers. 19th century non-profit banks focused more on enhancing poorer classes' economic participation and help them help themselves. Despite of the development of banking in the 19th century, many groups and classes were still largely excluded from the banking business. Ordinary banks focusing on public debt financing, mortgages for the old aristocracy, exchange bill discounting and later industry and railway financing, poorer citizens remained excluded. Savings accounts for ordinary people, loans to small farmers, artisans or workers was usually not part of banks' business or, if yes, then only granted at exorbitantly high interest rates. Hence, ordinary people were excluded almost entirely from private banking; not by law, but by business practices (Born 1977, p. 199 f.). Non-profit banking advocates argued that ordinary people, farmers, workers, small craftsman are in need of institutions where they can safely store their small savings, institutions that lend at fair interest rates in order to foster their economic participation and advancement.

5.6.1 Ideas Supporting Non-profit Banks

Monte di Pietàs were based on Catholic social ethics. Non-profit banks founded in the late 18th and through the 19th century were, usually, based on a wired combination of predominately protestant Christian social ethics, conservative morals and liberalism. Christian social ethics was usually the main motive of philanthropic foundations to found and support non-profit orientated banks. However, the mostly puritan, liberal, anti-state favor for help for self-help gave the newly founded non-profit banks their specific drift. The liberal help for self-help was often permeated by the conservative view that the low moral, culture and habits of the poor classes are the main reasons for their poverty. Four main principles became the fundament of help to self-help and most non-profit banks: first, poor and excluded people need help; second, social advancement is possible; third, help should ultimately reduce people's dependency rather than increase it; fourth, the state is unable to sustainably help the poor because state help increases dependency rather than reduce it.

Non-profit banking was part of a bundle of private initiatives to help the poor and overcome the sharpening social conflicts. Wealthy classes' increasing sensitivity and interest in the social issue was caused by reports on the bad living conditions of the poor and their fears from rising criminality and in particular socialist revolutions. Convinced that political measures are insufficient to help the poor, liberals in particular demanded measures for help to self-help (Sommer 1934, p. 666). Mistrusting the state, most non-profit banking advocates were convinced that state donations make the poor even poorer by increasing their dependency. Burdett (1818, p. 1), a Whig parliamentarian and supporter of non-profit banks, stated in his *Annals of Banks for Savings:* "It is from this conviction of the certainty of parish support, that the inferior classes of the English people are habitually far less prudent and thoughtful than those of many other countries." The Hamburg Commission investigating non-profit banks concluded that non-profit banks' main aim is "to make lower classes receptive for the honorable ideal of fend for oneself, stand by oneself […] which makes depositors independent by the feeling of advancing by industriousness and thriftiness"[6] (Sommer 1934, p. 668). Advocating for non-profit banks, Forbes (1815, p. 5) argued in his account on the Edinburgh Savings Bank: "The only effectual method of assisting the poor, is to encourage industry, economy, and sobriety, among them,—to excite and animate their own exertions,— and aid them in securing the full advantages of their success." Further he stated that "Pecuniary aid […] is too often a bribe to the idle and dissolute to indulge in habits which inevitably lead to poverty." Hence, advocates of non-profit banks and other liberal measures against poverty were deeply convinced that governmental subsidies make poverty even worse and only measures changing poor people's habits would help overcome poverty. (Sommer 1934, p. 666). Help to self-help was traditionally part of the liberal conviction on *laissez faire*: as maintained, liberals argued that *laissez faire* enables excluded groups to take their fate in their own hands without being bound by entry restrictions and regulations. Even as liberals became more open for state interventions, the main principle of *laissez faire* and help to self-help was maintained: Mill ([1845] 1967, p. 376) for example stated that "in the matter of their poverty, there is no way in which the rich could have helped them, but by inducing them to help themselves."

In particular, it was expected that non-profit banks would educate the poor to overcome their bad habits, which were considered the main reasons for poverty. Forbes and Burdett agree that the great advantage of saving banks is to change the habits of the poor. According to Forbes (1815, p. 4):

> The poor man is not careful to lay up the small sums which might be easily saved after the supply of his daily wants. […] The want of a place of deposit for the small sums which a poor man has it in his power to lay up, prevents him from thinking of doing so, and from acquiring a habit which is the foundation of so many virtues. Many would gladly adopt the plan, if the facilities were brought within their reach.

[6]„Die untere Klasse unserer Mitbürger für die Idee empfänglich zu machen, daß es ehrenvoll sei, für sich und die Seinigen selbst und allein zu sorgen, und so auf eigenen Füßen zu stehen […] werden die Einleger in dem Gefühle erfüllter Pflichten, in dem Bewußtsein, es durch Arbeitsamkeit und Sparsamkeit zu etwas gebracht zu haben, selbstständig und unabhängig."

In the same manner, Joseph Fletcher Burdett (1818) argued: "This [not to safe] arises from their [the poor] bad habits, which the education of the children and the operation of the Bank would hereafter remove." According to the German cooperate banking theorist Carl August von Malchus (1838), the main advantage of non-profit banks is that they stimulate poor people's thriftiness and industriousness. Analyzing many early German non-profit banking proposals, Sommer (1934, p. 672) frequently found expressions like the diligence of the honest worker, enhancing morality, the problem of rampant luxury and opulence that needs to be overcome. Like many 19th century authors, Pigou (1920, p. 50), the 20th century neoclassical, stated that "a savings bank, if confined to the poor, is an 'engine for teaching thrift." Hence, driven by their puritanical morality, many non-profit banking pioneers were convinced that the squandering of the poor was the main reason for their poverty. It was expected that interest payments on their small savings would teach them the advantageousness of thriftiness.

Fearing fast spreading socialist ideas, help to self-help programs seemed to be the best measure to trap the 'red ghost'. Teaching the poor how to become small thrifty capitalist entrepreneurs and savers was considered the most effective measure against the spread of socialist ideas. Sommer (1934, p. 695) found that since mid-19th century the literature on cooperative banking was full of warnings about the proletarian danger and the strengthening of social democracy: fighting socialism by offering a liberal alternative for economic participation and social advancement became one of the main arguments legitimizing non-profit banks.

In addition to fighting poverty, educating the poor and overcoming the 'red ghost', it was argued that non-profit banks accelerate economic development by absorbing idle savings. As maintained, classical economics assume that capital is scarce by nature and all capital stems from saving. Ordinary banks being unable to absorb the small savings of the poorer classes (Born 1977, p. 199), it was expected that non-profit banks would augment the capital supply by bundling small idle saving and transferring it into capitalist investments: creating capital by absorbing small idle savings, non-profit banks would foster economic development and industrialization. According to Carl August von Malchus (1838), saving banks foster industrialization and economic growth by collecting small savings for investments. In the same vein, Pigou (1920, p. 138) outlined how German Raiffeisen Banks absorbed small savings to lend them out to the economy. The Society for the Suppression of Beggars (1815) summarized the advantages of non-profit banks:

> It [non-profit bank] relieves from want, without checking industry; — it secures independence, without inducing pride; — it removes those painful misgivings which render the approaches of poverty so appalling, and often paralize the exertions which might ward off the blow; — it leads to temperance and the restraint of all the disorderly passions, which a wasteful expenditure of money nourishes;—it produces that sobriety of mind, and steadiness of conduct, which afford the best foundation for the domestic virtues in humble life. The effects of such an institution as this upon the character of the people, were it to become universal, would be almost inappreciable.

5.6.2 The Rise of Non-profit Banks

The umbrella term 'non-profit banks' includes three main groups of non-profit, philanthropic banks: saving banks, mortgage banks and cooperative banks. The explicit goal of saving banks is to store savings and lend at low interest rates to the poorest classes. Usually unable to absorb enough small savings, in particular at the beginning, saving banks depend on the help of rich patrons depositing their wealth or paying interests to the small savers. In Britain, saving banks were founded by private philanthropic initiatives without direct participation of the state; on the Continent, municipalities and governments were usually very involved in saving banks. Mortgage banks were usually founded by governments to support farmers and landlords with mortgages against land collateral. The distinction between cooperative banks and saving banks is not clear-cut. However, saving banks were usually founded and operated by philanthropic initiatives and municipalities, cooperative banks more strictly followed the idea of independency: according to the logic of cooperative banks, depositors and borrowers are of the same class or profession, hence banking activities occur between similar people. For example, small farmers own a cooperative bank where the deposit their small savings that are then lent to other small farmers (Born 1977, pp. 189–231).

Supported by rather different political coalitions, the economic arguments for non-profit banking were quite similar: usually, it was argued that groups like workers, farmers and in general the poor economic development is hampered by their exclusion from ordinary private banking. Despite their growing demand for banking, ordinary people, like workers and smaller farmers, still remained marginalized and excluded from private banks. Centralized megabanks were focused on huge investments and big savings, rather than on small credit. It was expected that non-profit banks facilitate excluded groups' and classes' economic advancement and economic growth in general. In addition, it was hoped that non-profit banks would foster economic progress by absorbing idle hoards and inciting the entrepreneurial spirit of the excluded poor classes.

Non-profit banks were often supported and promoted by strong coalitions and hardly ever opposed. Non-profit banks' success stemmed from their ability to convince supporters from rather different groups and classes: the Christian social ethics on which many banks were built and the idea of educating the poor attracted many conservatives. Help to self-help and the decentralized private organization of many cooperative banks convinced liberals (Sommer 1934, p. 677 ff.). Even many socialists supported or at least did not openly oppose non-profit banks, as banks seemed to help the poor to improve their economic situation. Strongly rejecting the ideas of Schulze-Delitzsch and Huber, the other two main promoters of the cooperative movement in Germany, Lassalle was in principle an enthusiastic supporter of cooperative organizations (Faust 1965, pp. 207–247) and developed the concept of cooperative socialism. Enthusiastically supported by several groups, non-profit banking was ambivalent for socialists: on the one hand non-profit banks supported workers, on the other hand they were founded to steal the socialists' thunder. Like outlined Marx ([1885] 1977, p. 601) was quite cynical and negative about the Monte di Pietàs and their 19th century prosecutors. Against Marx's theoretical position which rejected everything that seemed to prolong the life of capitalism, more practical socialists and left wing politicians supported non-profit banks.

According to Born (1977), the Prussian Landschaften founded in the 1780 s are the oldest European mortgage banks. After the Seven Years War, the Prussian Landschaften were founded elsewhere to support, in particular, big landowners, with credit for the reconstruction of the destroyed estates. Landschaften were organized as solidary credit organizations in which landlords were jointly liable for credits (ibid., p. 63 f.). Max Weber ([1908] 1998) published an article in 1908 about the credit and agro politics of the German Landschaften in which he discussed the foundation and operation of Landschaften from a sociologic perspective. Following Mauer (1907), Weber analyses the impacts of Landschaften on the distribution of land and the structure of farms. Both Weber and Mauer consider Landschaften credit institutions favoring the landed aristocracy and other big landowners. According to Weber, the foundation of the Landschaften was an important push toward the capitalization of agriculture: Landschaften forced farms to further rationalize production. Apart from rationalization, the foundation of the Landschaften caused, though unintentionally, the concentration of farmland. Against the proposers' intentions, the Landschaften quite negatively affected smaller farmers. Weber described two main mechanisms of how the Landschaften are worsening the situation of small farmers: first, equipped with great capital and in need of more land as collateral, the landed aristocracy demanded new land, which sharply increased prices. Excluded from credit markets, for small farmers farmland became unaffordable. Second, because costs for servants decreased aristocrats' creditworthiness, they were forced to keep as few and cheap servants as possible. Overall, Landschaften were quite helpful for the landed aristocracy and big landowners, but unintentionally they became quite disadvantageous to smaller farmers.

In the 1850s the two mortgage banks which still dominate the French mortgaged market were founded: the Crédit Foncier and the Crédit Agricole; while the first was predominately active in housing mortgages, the latter dealt in farming loans. Both were supported by the government (Kindleberger 1993, p. 112) and influenced by the Saint-Simonian spirit of the time. The fact that mortgages were often not available at all or only at horrendous interest rates (Sée 1936, p. 352) caused Napoleon III to permit the foundation of three joint stock mortgages banks, the so-called Crédit Fonciers, in Paris, Marseille and Nevers: soon the three banks merged into one big Crédit Foncier de France. The permission was a concession to farmers and the landed aristocracy who could hardly find credit at tolerable interest rates. Proposed by the French monetarist Louis Wolowski (Clough 1939, p. 174), Saint-Simonian bankers like Émile Péreire took a leading role in the Crédit Fonciers (Born 1977, p. 193 f.). Due to Crédit Foncier's reluctance towards farming mortgages, the Crédit Agricole was founded several years later, focused on farming credit; however, the relation between Crédit Foncier and Crédit Agricole was so close that it can be considered as one bank (ibid., p. 194 f.). Despite frequent difficulties, like in 1876 when it lost a lot of money in Egypt, the Crédit Fonciers became the main financer of several French megaprojects (Clough 1939, p. 173 f.) and one of France's biggest banks (ibid., p. 339 f.). Following the French blueprint, several private joint stock mortgages banks were founded in Germany between the 1850s and 1870s (Born 1997, p. 195). In addition to joint stock mortgage banks, the unavailability of agriculture credit, in particular for smaller farmers, induced the foundation of agricultural cooperative banks, which sustainable altered the German banking sector: the so-called Raiffeisen Banken. The German liberation of the peasants freed small farmers from direct dependency. Freed from direct dependency, they usually lacked any access to money and the credit market (Faust 1965, p. 269 f.). The socially active small-town mayor Friedrich Wilhelm Raiffeisen was hardly the usual banking innovator. Aware of the misery of small farmers thanks to his daily political work, Raiffeisen was convinced that peasants need protection from three main evils: land, cattle and money usurers (ibid., p. 270 ff.). Guided by his Christian faith, Raiffeisen founded several Christian charity organizations to help poor peasants. Soon it turned out that the principle of Christian charity, in which wealthier parts of the society help the poor by donations or credit guarantees, was insufficient to overcome the peasants' poverty: after the founding hype, the charity organizations cooled down as founders and supporters were increasingly less willing to use their wealth for charitable purposes (Born 1977, p. 223). Schulze-Delitzsch, the most notable activist of the German cooperation movement, convinced Raiffeisen that only organizations whose operators have a vested interest in its development are sustainable: promoting his own cooperative organizations, Schulze-Delitzsch argued that only help for self-help in the form of cooperative organizations may sustainably improve the economic situation of the poor (Faust 1965, p. 281 f.).

Convinced by Schulze-Delitzsch's principles, Raiffeisen founded the first cooperative mortgage bank in 1864: the bank lent exclusively to unlimited jointly liable members. Impressed by the North-German cooperative organizations, Raiffeisen joined Schulze-Delitzsch's umbrella organization of Germany's cooperative banks. However, Raiffeisen and Schulze-Delitzsch soon started to argue about the nature and goals of cooperative banking. According to Faust (ibid., p. 291 ff.), three issues built the fundament of the conflict: ideology and the banking and equity principle. Schulze-Delitzsch and his followers were predominately left liberals; for them, cooperative organizations are the social policy most compatible with the liberal principles of help for self-help. In contrast to Lassalle and other socialists, Schulze-Delitzsch was an economic liberal convinced by the positive function of capitalist competition. For him, credit cooperations should not bother capitalism, but make smaller and new entrepreneurs fit for the capitalist competition (Born 1977, p. 217). Unlike the group around Schulze-Delitzsch, Raiffeisen's social engagement was driven by his faith and the principle of Christian charity (Faust 1965, p. 291). For the urban liberal followers of Schulze-Delitzsch, Raiffeisen was part of the retrograde rural population. Apart from the ideological differences between the conservative Christian Raiffeisen and the left liberal

Schulze-Delitzsch, the conflict escalated on more practical issues: for Schulze-Delitzsch the main principle of cooperative banking was that loan maturities should not exceed the maturity of a bank's liabilities (ibid., p. 293 f.). Because most liabilities were of short maturity, Schulze-Delitzsch banks refused to lend for more than three months. Lending only short-term was no problem for Schulze-Delizsch banks that predominately supported small entrepreneurs and craftsmen with liquidity; farming credits are by nature of longer term as farmers usually need the money for at least half a year to pay seed in spring and they do not harvest before autumn. To adequately support farmers, Raiffeisen had no other option than to take maturity risks by borrowing short- and lending long-term: Schulze-Delitzsch heavily criticized Raiffeisen's maturity transformation. In addition to the question of maturity transformation, Schulze-Delitzsch and Raiffeisen were divided on the question of how to guarantee banks safety: for Schulze-Delitzsch, a strong equity base was the fundament of bank safety; only if the equity base was insufficient to save the bank, unlimited jointly liability would hold. Raiffeisen refused to build high equity and used the unlimited joint liability of the members as collateral (Born 1977, p. 225). Regardless of their conflict, the cooperative banks of both Schulze-Delitzsch and Raiffeisen were quite successful and spread fast throughout Germany. Also, abroad in Switzerland, France and Austria Schulze-Delitzsch and Raiffeisen cooperative banks were imitated.

Schulze-Delitzsch and Raiffeisen cooperative banks predominately facilitated banking for the lower middle class. To lend to each other and to be jointly liable meant that participants owned at least some property or money. Hence, the very poor remained excluded from cooperative banking. Unlike cooperative banks founded to facilitate banking of small peasants and craftsman, saving banks had the clear task to support the very poor. Of all non-profit banks, saving banks continued the tradition of the Monte di Pietàs the most. The Hamburgian saving bank founded in 1778 is considered as the oldest saving bank, inspired by the 1629 founded Parisian Bureau d'adresse and the Leyhaus-banks founded in 1717 by Frederick William I in Berlin (ibid.). According to Burdett (1818, p. 51), the Benefit Bank is the oldest British saving bank. Originating in Britain and Germany, saving banks spread throughout Europe.

According to Sommer (1934, pp. 663–676), the early time of the saving bank movement was characterized by the puritanical, liberal ideal of help for self-help. However, saving banks were focused on the poorest parts of the society unable to deposit enough to support themselves with credit. Many early saving banks were dependent on the patronage of rich supporters who deposited their money or even paid interests to the poorer depositors. Saving banks advocates expected that the poor will slowly outgrow the patronage of the rich philanthropists by changing their habits and saving up bigger parts of their small incomes. Hence, early saving banks reflect the puritanical idea of the time that the poor need the guidance of the rich to learn economic prudency and change their disadvantageous habits.

In particular in Britain, saving banks emerged from private initiatives (Born 1977, p. 210 f.). Adopting the idea from private initiatives, Germany's first municipal saving bank opened in 1801 in Göttingen; soon, municipal saving banks dominate the market (Mura 1996, p. 106 f.). According to Sommer (1934, pp. 676–690), the grip of the state on saving banks grew strong between 1830 and 1880. Three main reasons caused the sovereigns to found saving banks: first, pooled savings were attractive for public debt financing (Born 1977, p. 211); second, helping the poor through saving banks was cheaper than by transferring payments (ibid., p. 200); third, help to self-help was expected to prevent socialist revolutions (Sommer 1934, p. 677 ff.). While around the mid-19th century British saving banks were still overwhelmingly private, in France the majority and in Germany almost all were in the hands of the municipalities (Born 1977, pp. 199–216): in particular the Prussian government actively supported the foundation of new saving banks (Sommer 1934, p. 681).

Shaken by recurring crises, the British Parliament attempted to make saving banks more prudent by stricter regulations: all attempts failed due to disagreements over the form of regulation (Born 1977, p. 212). Due to recurrent crises, the liberal parliament activated an old plan: to allow the postal system to accept money deposits. Founded in 1861, the postal saving banks are the world's oldest post banks and Britain's first attempt to form a nationwide system of public saving banks (ibid.). British postal saving banks were considered a "potent philanthropic agency for raising the poor, and as a great national banking office placing large sums at the disposal of the community" (Wolff 1897, p. 278). Outlining how the savings of the postal saving banks were used to support Gladstone's projects, Wolff (ibid., p. 297) concluded that "the interest of the savings banks are, in other words, apt to be subordinated to those of the Exchequer" which brought the exchequer into the difficult situation to "safeguard the interest of the depositors" and "provide cheap money for the nation." France followed the British example and founded the Caisse Dationale D'Epargne in 1881; the French postal saving system (Moster and Vogler 1996, p. 81). In particular, British postal saving banks increasingly replaced private saving banks. Hence, at the end of the 19th century most French, British and German saving banks were operated by the state and municipalities or state-affiliated organizations. However, the government's influence and saving banks' business was not uniform: while German municipal saving banks invested relatively freely, French banks were obliged to invest in securities somehow related to the state and British postal saving banks only invested in public debt (Wolff 1897). In France and Britain, saving banks were defined by law as non-profit organizations (Gosden 1996, p. 137; Moster and Vogler 1996, p. 76) and usually had deposit ceilings. Withdrawing or extending deposit ceilings opened saving banks for the middle class. Once founded as private philanthropic institutions to help the very poor, at the end of the 19th most saving banks were public owned and the favored banking institute of the middle class.

Soon after the kick-off in several German and British cities, saving banks were founded elsewhere in Europe; a detailed description of the rise of saving banks is given for Germany by Malchus (1838) and for Britain by Burdett (1818) and Pratt (1842). In Britain, hundreds of saving banks opened at the beginning of the 19th century; around 1820 more than 300 saving banks were registered (Wadhwani 2011, p. 504). Their number peaked in 1860 at around 600 banks (ibid.); in the late 19th century they were increasingly replaced by post saving banks. At the turn of the century, 1900 private saving banks served around 1.6 million customers who deposited 57 million pounds; in contrast, the post saving banks served over 8 million customers, depositing more than 135 million pounds (Gosden 1996, p. 142). Around 1880, 500 saving banks were registered in France (Wadhwani 2011, p. 504). Afterwards, almost no new saving banks were founded, but the network of branches sharply increased to around 1000 branches in 1900 (Moster and Vogler 1996, p. 78). Wolff (1897, p. 307) estimated that saving banks deposited around 3.4 billion and postal saving banks around 0.8 billion franc in 1895; deposits of postal saving banks rose sharply to around 5 billion in 1933 (Moster and Vogler 1996, p. 81). Most impressive was the development of the German saving banks sector: in 1880, 2000 German saving banks existed (Wadhwani 2011, p. 504). Until 1913 their number increased to 3000, depositing 20 billion mark, which was almost four times the deposit of the eight biggest joint stock banks and almost the amount Germany invested abroad (Born 1977, p. 207). Apart from the saving banks, the Crédit Foncier invested 4.5 billion franc in mortgages between 1876 and 1909 (ibid., p. 195), and thousands of cooperative banks were founded in Germany (ibid., p. 221, 229). Hence, overall, non-profit banking was a huge business in Britain, France and particularly Germany at the end of the 19th century and became the third main pillar, apart from joint stock megabanks and central banks, of the European banking system.

6 Conclusion

In the Introduction it was outlined that usually neither economists nor sociologists doubt the pivotal importance of banks and the banking sector for capitalist economies and societies. Economists and sociologists developed a wide range of rather different arguments about why banks are at the center of capitalist economies. Despite the wide agreement on the importance of banks, for decades banking was widely neglected in economics and sociology. Just relatively recently banks and banking systems receive more attention in economics and sociology. In particular, since the financial and banking crises of 2007 and 2008, financial markets and banks again became core issues of economics and economic sociology.

Several historians, focused on the history of banks, intensively discussed the historical development of different banking sectors (see Born 1977; Tilly 2003; Forsyth and Verdier 2003; Teichova et al. 1997). However, most historical studies describe relatively short time periods and focus on national banking sectors. Historical contributions hardly ever apply general social theories or have the aim to develop general theories and theses on the historical development of the banking sector. At the same time, during the 20th century sociological and economic contributions on the historical development of banking sectors were rare. Back in the 18th and 19th century many economists discussed, at least rudimentarily, the historical developments of the banking sector. Despite several economists focused on banking (for example Thomas Joplin 1827), leading contributors of the classical school of economic thought like Adam Smith (1776), John Stuart Mill ([1848] 1965a, b), Thomas Tooke (1826, 1844), Henry Thornton (1802), at least touched upon banking and pivotal events for the development of the banking sector. In the late 19th and early 20th century members of the historical school of economics contributed on pivotal events for the development of European banking. However, with the neoclassical turn and the mathematization of economics, historical analyses were increasingly upstaged.

F. Brugger, *Ideas, Interests and the Development of the European Banking Systems*, Wirtschaft + Gesellschaft, https://doi.org/10.1007/978-3-658-30597-0_6

Most classical economists, at least implicitly, analyzed historical developments of banking from an economistic, functionalistic perspective. Unlike most neoclassical economists, classical economists frequently took political and social issues, like the distribution of power or the specific political landscape, into consideration: dimensions that lost ground in neoclassical economics. Nevertheless, in most contributions economic reasonability or economic necessity and efficiency are considered the main reasons for banking developments. For example, Smith (1776: IV, III) intensively discussed the foundation and operation of the Bank of Amsterdam. Taken the specific political and economic situation into consideration, economic efficiency is still Smiths' main argument. For him, the reduction of exchange risk and facilitating trade were the main reasons for the foundation of the Bank of Amsterdam; the specific constellation of interests and ideas that fostered and maybe hindered the foundation of public exchange banks were hardly taken into consideration.

In contrast, the rare sociological contributions on the historical development of the banking sector focused on the social, political, economic and institutional context and the intended and unintended consequences of banking innovations. Weber ([1908] 1998) analyzed the foundation of the Landschaften from a sociological perspective and discussed its intended and unintended social and economic consequences. Carruthers (1996) focused on the specific political circumstances and the distribution of power that caused and accompanied the British financial revolution. In addition, he highlighted the state-building effects of the financial revolution and the increasing indebtedness of the state. Focusing on general historical developments, Ingham (2004) interprets the history of money and banking as determined by conflicts between the unequally powerful lenders, debtors and the state. Arrighi (2010) focused on the interaction of falling profits in capital and the political, geographical and economic extension of hegemonic powers. In the same vein, Lenin ([1917] 1999) and Hilferding ([1910] 1955) assume a close connection between the abundance of capital and European imperialism: in need of new profitable investment opportunities, financial interests propelled governments to conquer new investment markets. Arrighi, Lenin and Hilferding highlighted the central importance of banks: for them, banks are pivotal for the concentration of capital and the production and enforcement of specific capital interests.

However, the contributions focused on specific cases and historical periods (Weber; Carruthers), on the ratio between financial interests and imperialism (Lenin; Hilferding) or the historical development of money (Ingham) and capitalism (Arrighi). In contrast, in this book, events and epochs central to the development of Europe's banking and leading banking sectors are understood as path-shaping events that formed the historical path along which the European banking sector developed.

6.1 Ideas, Interests and Institutions or the Three Orders

The main aim of this book is to study how ideas, interests and institutions have determined pivotal events and periods in the historical development of the European banking sector. In the methodological chapter, different views on ideas, interests and institutions and their influence are discussed. The historical empirical part of the book maintains how specific consultations of interests, ideas and institutions caused, fostered and shaped significant changes in the banking sector. Methodologically, it is assumed that ideas, interests and institutions are three dimensions that are principally distinguishable, but also highly interdependent and interconnected: hence, each 'I' influences and shapes the other two 'I's in various ways.

As maintained in the methodological chapter, ideas legitimize, empower, restrict and shape interests. Interests are legitimized by successfully suggesting their consistency with the leading ideas. Ideas empower groups of interests by legitimizing and strengthening their interests. Defining the space of legitimate and illegitimate demands, ideas restrict interests. In addition, ideas shape interests. Ideas concretize interest by transferring general interests into concrete demands. Following Hay (2011), ideas transfer general, abstract natural interests into concrete perceived interests: hence, ideas determine what is considered as own interests.

At the same time, interests influence ideas. Interests determine the content of ideas: producers of ideas are influenced by their own vested interests and groups of interests use their means to determine the content of ideas. Apart from the influence on the content of ideas, ideas need strong carriers to become efficacious. The assertion of ideas is assumed to be a conflictual process. Therefore, ideas need strong carriers to diffuse, be protected against attacks and institutionalize.

Ideas and interests legitimize institutions. Steadily threatened by opponents, institutions need supporters and protectors. Groups carrying ideas and interests that seem supported by the existing institutions, legitimize and protect institutions against recurrent attacks. At the same time, institutions shape ideas and interests. Both ideas and interests are determined and shaped by the institutional environment in which they are created. Institutions frame ideas and interests by specifying the boundaries of legitimate and illegitimate, legal and illegal interests, ideas and demands. However, as ideas and interests institutionalize, they became efficacious, static and binding: static in the sense that institutions usually change more slowly than ideas and interests, and binding means that as ideas and interests institutionalize they also become efficacious and binding for non-carriers.

Developing a macrosociological heuristic to analyze the historical development of the European banking sector, it was assumed that three fundamental types of orders characterize societies: the cultural, economic, and political order. The cultural order comprises different ideas. Bundles of harmonic ideas that are part of the same worldview often dominate cultural order. However, dominant ideas are always challenged by alternative ideas. Two main dimensions dominate the economic order: distribution and production. Who gets what and how much of it (distribution), who makes what, where, how with whom and how much of it (production) are the main questions answered in the economic order. Groups' different positions on the fundamental question of production and distribution are considered natural interests. Production and distribution also determines groups' ability to enforce their interests. In the political order, groups carrying different political interests and ideas compete over institutions, permissions, appointments, organizations and distributions. Groups use their means and form coalitions with other groups to enforce and institutionalize their ideas and interests.

The three orders are highly interwoven and interdependent. In the economic and political order, ideas are constraints which define the space of legitimate actions and demands, function as road maps and concepts about the functioning of the world and transfer abstract natural interests into perceived interests. At the same time, the economic and political orders determine the cultural order. Stronger and weaker economic and political groups of interest shape the content of ideas by influencing the production of ideas and act as carriers that facilitate and prevent the institutionalization of ideas. In addition, the economic and political orders determine the institutional environment in which ideas are produced and distribute resources to different actors of the cultural order. Groups of the economic order carrying different natural interests and ideas, unequally equipped with resources, enter the political order to enforce their interests and ideas. The economic order produces groups' natural interests which they enforce in the political order and unequally distribute the means to enforce the interests among groups. The political order specifies the institutional frame of the economic order. It also shapes the structure of the economic order by defining goals, distributing resources and legitimizing and delegitimizing actions.

6.2 Shifting Ideas, Interests and Institutions

Principally, I distinguished between normal and revolutionary times. Harmonic relations between ideas, interests and institutions characterize normal times. Harmonic means that powerful groups of interests carry dominant ideas and that leading ideas and interests are institutionalized in the most important institutions. Referring to the three order heuristic: during normal times, the main economic and political groups of interests support the leading ideas of the cultural order and both the most powerful interests and the dominant ideas institutionalized in the political order. Hence, normal times means that the three fundamental orders are somehow in a harmonic relation. However, harmonic does not mean that there are no challengers trying to change the status quo. Harmonic means that challengers fail to overturn the dominate constellation of ideas, interests and institutions.

Normal times turn into revolutionary times as the harmonic relation erodes. Principally, each of the three 'I's has a progressive and conservative potential: ideas, interests and institutions may foster and hinder change. The rise and empowerment of new groups of interests, or the changing interest of established groups may break up harmonic relation. The rise and spread of alternative ideas and changing institutions, for example due to international agreements, has the potential to erode harmonic relations and turn normal into revolutionary times. Changes which shift normal into revolutionary times may originate in each of the three orders. Technical change, for example, may break up the harmonic relation by producing and empowering new interests and redistributing resources among groups of interests. The collapse of strong political collations which dominated the political order are occasional examples of the erosion of the harmonic relation which originated in the political order. New ideas, developed in the cultural order or brought in from outside, may also turn normal into revolutionary times.

6.3 Shifting Orders and Banking Revolutions

At the beginning of Italian City-States' rise, the relation between the economic and political order was relatively harmonic. Merchants dominated the economic and a small powerful oligarchy the political order. The political dominance was built on a rather stable coalition between the ruling political oligarchy and merchants. Conquering and protecting profitable overseas trade routes and providing opportunities to invest idle hoards into public debt satisfied the interests of the rising merchants. Protecting their profitable business and economic predominance, merchants supported, with credit and other means, the political rule of the oligarchy. Doubtlessly, scholastic economics, the leading economic idea of the time, rather complicated merchants' business and governments' financing. However, the scholastic restrictions left enough grey areas to maintain and develop trade-related financial business and government financing. Although hampering some and prohibiting other financial business, scholastic economics was nevertheless important for financial markets, as it morally legitimized the tolerated financial services. Hence, at the beginning of the economic rise of Italian City-States the relation between scholastic ideas, the political oligarchy's and the merchants' interests and institutions (such as the institutionalized coalition between merchants and the oligarchy or usury restrictions which left enough room for rudimentary banking services) was overall relatively harmonic or at least not too conflicting.

Escalating inner political conflicts, uprises against the political elites, increasing foreign pressure from neighboring City-States and the extending Ottoman Empire and the exhaustion of trade routes strongly undermined the harmonic relation. Turmoil against the political oligarchy questioned the legitimization of the political domination. Military threats from neighboring City-States and the Ottoman Empire challenged the political domination. In addition, and most challenging for the established political order, merchants became increasingly dissatisfied due to falling trade profits and the scarcity of profitable investment opportunities. To conquer new trade routes, repel foreign assaults and incite City-State patriotism to silence domestic opposition, City-States fought recurrent, increasingly expensive, wars. As winning wars became pivotal for City-States' political stability, war financing became a matter of survival for the political oligarchy. Increasingly, governments faced difficulties in covering rampant war costs. Unable to borrow enough money to finance recurrent wars under the given institutional circumstances, governments had strong vested interests in changing the public debt financing system. Decreasing trade profits, the abundancy of capital and the shortage of investment opportunities equipped wealthy merchants with huge idle hoards searching for profitable investment places. However, the riskiness of public debts kept the wealthy from lending more heavily to the government. In need of investment opportunities, rich merchants and other wealthy groups also had a strong interest in making public debt financing more attractive. State lender associations principally satisfied both governments' and investors' interests: pooling investors' bargaining power made public debt investments more attractive to the wealthy. Facilitating war financing by pooling huge capital was in the interest of the government. Thus the foundation of the state lender associations institutionalized the interest of the wealthy and the government.

However, the deepening of banking and money lending on a new scale collided with the scholastic usury restrictions and general opposition to money lending. Intensive theological discussions, caused by governments' problems to finance wars and Church's own increasing banking involvement, fundamentally shaped the theological position on money lending. Overall, the theological position shifted from 'all money lending against interest payments is prohibited' to 'interest payments under certain circumstances and within certain limits is permitted'. In particular, lending to the government was exempt from many usury restrictions. Broadly speaking, with the foundation of the state lender associations and the changing scholastic position on money lending, a new harmonic relation between ideas, interests and institutions was restored.

Despite the changing scholastic position on lending for interest payments, the Church and the scholastic remained principally reluctant towards money lending. Taking the deepening of banking as a fact, several groups within the Church suggested to found Christian banks in order to protect people from usurers. Founded to save the people from bankers, the Christian Monte di Pietàs themselves deepened banking by spreading banking activities to new groups and further legitimizing banking.

During the time of so-called absolutism, monarchs' dominion was usually built on a, in one or another way, coalition between the Crown, the regional aristocracy, the army and rich merchants. Trade monopolies and a generally trade-friendly policy safeguarded rich merchants' support. Ensuring monarchs' dominion outside the capital in the still highly fragmented countries, regional aristocracies received various privileged and dominated the lucrative public debt financing. Their huge investments in public debt strengthened aristocracies' support to the Crown: satisfied or not with the monarch, overthrowing the King would have jeopardized aristocracies' investments.

With the emerging of the European empires, economic challenges changed and economic discussions secularized. Changing economic circumstances, shifting interests and the secularization of economics underpinned the replacement of the scholastic by the mercantilist economic idea as the leading one. While the scholastic theory was predominately a theological interpretation of economics, mercantilism was constructed as an economic theory of nation building, national economic autarky, economic progress and military force. Despite satisfying merchants', armies', and monarchs' interests, mercantilism should not be interpreted as a theorization of vested interests. However, no doubt, its compatibility with powerful groups' interest fostered mercantilism's fast spread. Regional aristocracies', armies' and merchants' interest, mercantilism and the institutionalization of ideas and interests, for example by trade monopolies to merchants, governments' export and import policy, public debt financing privileges to regional aristocracies and the foundation of huge standing armies, were in a certain harmonic relation.

Accelerating trade and governments' financial needs increased demands for rudimentary banking services like money exchange, short- and increasingly long-term lending, money depositing, public debt intermediation and so on. Emerging early banking was predominately a by-business: rich merchants lent out their idle hoards to colleagues, exchanged and maybe deposited the money of their colleagues during fairs and offered similar banking services. Apart from merchants, other professions like goldsmiths, with close ties to the wealthy population, increasingly developed banking as a by-business. In particular in Britain banking professionalized as by-business bankers gave up their traditional business and fully concentrated on banking. Steadily, British professional banks became more modern as they absorbed capital from a wider range of customers to lend to private businesses, the nobility and in particular to the state. In France, the emerging of banking was more difficult. First by-business banks emerged in the rising fair cities to process trade-based banking services; soon, lending to the sovereign and the nobility became banks' main business. In Britain and France, banks and other financial institutes were aristocracy's main vehicle to lend their idle hoards indirectly to the monarch. However, in Britain and particular in France widespread hostility and opposition to banking hindered banks' development: in France, hostility towards bankers frequently turned violent. In addition to economic backwardness and the general hostility against banking, political fragmentation further hampered Germany's banking development: rich merchants and Hoffaktoren (court agents) or their children founded banks in the 18th century, which later became leading institutes in Germany. However, German banking remain backward even compared with France.

Hence, at the beginning, the time of absolutism was characterized by a relatively harmonic relation between the main interests of monarchs, merchants, rural aristocracies, and armies, and was then underpinned by mercantilism as the leading economic idea. To a certain extent, the main ideas and interests became institutionalized in the banking sector as emerging banks supplied rudimentary banking services to traders and became aristocracies' vehicle to invest idle hoards into public debts. However, the harmonic relation was increasingly threatened by the rise of the bourgeoisie and in particular monarchs' financial difficulties. Governments' inability to provide the same privileges to newcomers as to the old economic elites upset the rising bourgeoisie. In particular, the conflict between the rising bourgeoisie entering central state offices and increasingly dominating the economy, and the privileged aristocracy worsened. In addition, the rise of money-mercantilism further questioned the status quo. Defining the money shortage as the most urgent economic problem, money-mercantilists proposed several banking innovations to augment paper money and facilitate state financing. Promising to foster trade and economic progress by augmenting money, lowering interest rates and facilitating state financing, money-mercantilists' national bank proposals satisfied the interest of the rising bourgeoisie and of monarchs. Supported by merchants and the bourgeoisie, and clandestinely by monarchs, national banks were strongly opposed by bankers and the aristocracy. Dominating the lucrative business of state lending, bankers and the aristocracy feared losing public debt financing to national banks: in addition, the aristocracy feared that national banks would further strengthen the rising bourgeoisie; their main opponents. Despite sound arguments for national banks and their strong supporters, only monarchs' escalating financial problems paved the way for the banking revolution of the late 17th and early 18th century.

Relying on the aristocracy's support, monarchs shied away from antagonizing the aristocracy by permitting the foundation of national banks. It was only the breakdown of the established harmonic relation that opened the door for national banks and therefore for the late 17th and early 18th century banking revolution. In Britain, the Glorious Revolution significantly shifted political power to the Parliament and the bourgeoisie. Granting the veto right over state budgets to the Parliament significantly lowered monarchs' financial abilities. In addition, the Stop of the Exchequer of 1672 escalated monarchs' financial difficulties: after the Stop of the Exchequer, monarchs were mostly unable to borrow at manageable interest rates. Unable to finance the long war with France, William III had only two options: following the aristocratic Tories and scaling back the war, or implement radical changes in the political economy as advised by the bourgeois Whigs. Choosing the second alternative paved the way for the 17th and 18th century British banking revolution. Frightened by the public debt defaults, it seemed that a rebalancing of power between state lenders and the government was needed to prevent a further Stop of the Exchequer. Permitting a national bank, as proposed by money-mercantilists, was a central demand of the Whigs. Inspired by Italian City-States' state lender associations, the Bank of England was founded to bundle state lenders' bargaining power to prevent public debt defaults. Increasing their bargaining power and facilitating the investment of capital into lucrative public debts, the foundation of the Bank of England was in the interest of the rising bourgeoisie. Despite the increasing power of the bourgeoisie, the foundation of the Bank of England was principally in monarchs' interest because it facilitated public debt financing. Able to lend at a new scale in short time, the foundation of the Bank of England, and other public debt investing joint stock conglomerates, shifted the war fortune in favor of Britain. The Bank of England became part of a new harmonic relationship: strengthening the Parliament in the Glorious Revolution and the foundation of the Bank of England institutionalized bourgeoisie's political and financial interests. At the same time, the Bank of England also institutionalized monarchs' interest in easy and cheap public debt financing and strongly increased Britain's military competitiveness. In addition, the Bank of England institutionalized money-mercantilists' central idea of a note-issuing national bank. Abandoning its futile opposition against the bourgeois Bank of England, the nobility instead demanded the permission of competing land-based national banks. Economically ill-founded and not viable, the Land Bank nevertheless marked and symbolized the abundance of conservative landed classes' stark opposition to banking innovations.

French absolutism was built on a relatively stable coalition between the monarch, the rural aristocracy and merchants. To rule the highly fragmented empire, French absolutistic monarchs depended heavily on rural aristocracies' support. Despite all luxury, French absolutistic monarchs were relatively weak and their direct power ended not far from Paris. Unable to enforce their dominion in remote areas of the empire, monarchs heavily depended on local aristocracies' loyalty. To satisfy aristocracies' interests and ensure their loyalty, monarchs handed over the right to collect taxes to the local elites. Collecting taxes and lending the money to the Crown was quite profitable and deepened aristocracies' clandestine dominance over public debt financing. Merchants' interests were satisfied by granting monopolies and other privileges to leading traders.

French monarchs always found it difficult to cover their expenses. However, as long as Britain, France's big enemy, faced the same difficulties, the balance of power hardly changed. With the foundation of the Bank of England, and other public debt financing joint-stock conglomerates, the balance of power shifted in favor of Britain. Fearing British dominance, voices had been raised in France demanding a financial revolution facilitating public debt financing. Though aristocracies' dominance over public debt financing ensured their loyalty to the Crown, fundamentally changing the disadvantageous system of state financing was very risky for the monarch's dominion and the fragmented empire. Only the monarch's near-bankruptcy and the deep crises of the aristocracy paved the way for the 18th century French banking revolution. Lacking alternative to overcome his financial difficulties, the monarch permitted John Law to found history's most money-mercantilist bank, the Banque Royale. Considerably weakened by the Chambre de Justice, the aristocracy was unable to prevent Law's bank. Well-functioning at the beginning, the Banque Royale soon faced huge difficulties. Excessive note issuing caused rampant inflation and Banque Royale's bankruptcy caused one of the deepest banking crises in French history. Law's failure had some long-lasting consequences: it significantly changed the cultural order in France and elsewhere. For centuries, Banque Royale's bankruptcy was used in monetary discussions to demand conservative issuing and money policies. For many money-mercantilists, issuing money was the neatest solution to many economic and political problems. Law's failure heavily questioned the soundness of money-mercantilism and strongly contributed to its slow decline. In France, Law's failure strengthened the widespread opposition to banking and the anti-banking innovation camp and hampered banking innovations and paper money issuing for more than a century.

From the foundation of the Bank of England to the beginning of the 19th century, banking developed in Britain. In London and elsewhere in the country banks were founded. The Parliament's and the bourgeoisie's power was on the rise in the late 17th and early 18th century. However, throughout the 18th century political and economic power remained mostly in the hands of a relatively small old elite. Political and economic privileges were distributed according to the established system of power sharing between landed elites and the traditional predominately merchant bourgeoisie. Old elites' dominance in the banking system was symptomatic for the 18th century situation: Bank of England shareholders and board was a small close group of privileged public debt financers using their power to influence governments' fiscal policy. London banks were in the hands of gentleman capitalists and the old merchant and goldsmith elites. The old regional elites dominated country banks.

Britain's industrialization of the late 18th and early 19th century significantly shaped the structure of the society: the industrialization generated a new industrial bourgeoisie and the fast extending working and middle class. Despite their fast growth, the rising new classes remained particularly politically underrepresented due to the wide-ranging privileges granted to the old elites. From the beginning of the Industrial Revolution onwards, the redistribution of economic and political participation, power and influence and therefore the withdrawal of old elites' privileges was the main demand of the rising classes. The battle of the 'new classes' against old privileges was closely connected with the emerging and rise of liberalism. Opposing all kinds of privileges and suggesting the formulating and institutionalizing of general freedoms and rights for all citizens, liberalism strengthened and empowered rising classes' demands, which is why the new bourgeoisie, the middle class and the working-class aristocracy became the main producers and carriers of liberalism. In the early 19th century, the Whig Party became the main political carrier of rising classes' interest and liberalism.

Due to its pivotal role in capitalist societies and old elites' dominance, the banking sector became the main battleground between the old elites and the rising newcomers. Old elites' dominance over the banking sector ensured its political influence as the main public debt financer and its financial power thanks to the high profits of the sector. Demanding a fundamental restructuring of the banking sector, hence, fiercely attacked old elites' power and resources.

However, the conflict between old elites and newcomers was almost suspended at the beginning of the 19th century. Old Toryism ideologically underpinned the conservative backlash of the time, but the war against France made criticism of the government and the ruling elites almost impossible. Nevertheless, the suspension of convertibility caused intensive discussions on money and banking. During the war, the suspension of convertibility was widely considered as a war time necessity: attempts to reintroduce convertibility failed to find political majorities. However, with the end of the war, the suspension of convertibility lost much of its legitimization. Monetarist classical economists criticized the suspension of convertibility from the money economists' perspective that the facilitation of issuing caused inflation and made financial markets more prone to crises. According to many politicians, critical banking experts and the general public, the suspension of convertibility was a further privilege for the old elite because it facilitated lending and therefore augmented elites' profits to the disadvantages of the general public and the economy, which already suffered from the financial systems' increasing proneness to crises.

Forming a strong coalition between many liberals, monetarists, radicals and the general public, the resumption of convertibility was the first major monetarist success. With the resumption of convertibility, the banking system was institutionalized back to the position it had in the late 18th century. However, the cultural predominance significantly changed. Building on former money theories, monetarism developed in the long discussion of the early 19th century. After the end of the war with France, monetarism became the leading money theory and its hegemony deepened until World War I. Achieving their first main goal, the reintroduction of the metal standard, monetarists focused on their second main demand: the monopolization of note issuing and the restructuring of the Bank of England. The Bank Charter Act of 1844 was the monetarists' most important success in the 19th century: granting the Bank of England a quasi note-issuing monopoly and separating the bank into an ordinary banking department and a non-profit orientated note-issuing department institutionalized the monetarists' main suggestion. In addition, the Bank of England became the monetarists' central bank blueprint inspiring most later formed continental European central banks.

Most prominent classical economists interested in money issues focused on money policy issues, note issuing and central banking. However, several banking experts and liberal economists focused instead on the banking sector and how it should be reformed. According to many liberals, the established banking sector predominantly served the interests of the old elites, slowed growth by hampering lending and was quite prone to crises. In the wave of money discussions, banking experts developed new banking models. In particular joint-stock banking was supported by many liberals, banking experts, industrialists and social reformers: it was suggested that new joint-stock banks would foster growth by facilitating lending, be less prone to crises due to their higher equity base and democratize banking by also issuing smaller shares affordable to poorer people. Strongly opposed by the Bank of England and in particular the country banks, the deep banking crises of the mid-1820s weakened banks' position, raised public anger against banks and paved the way for joint-stock banking permission. Facilitating lending to the private sector and functioning as the main investment vehicle of the wealthy, breaking up Bank of England's joint stock monopoly was in particular a victory of the rising liberals against the old elites. The permission of joint-stock banks paved the way for Britain's banking concentration. Limited to six shareholders, banks' growth was quite restricted. With the permission of joint-stock banking, the growth and size of banks was theoretically endless, because banks always had the possibility to give out additional shares. In addition to the permission of joint-stock banks, the permission of limited liability share issuing fostered the concentration of banking and the rise of joint stock megabanks.

The Bank Charter Act of 1844 and the permission of joint-stock banking were the two main banking revolutions in 19th century Britain. Both fundamentally changed the banking sector and the money system: the Bank Charter Act monopolized note issuing in the hands of the state-dependent note-issuing department and the permission of joint-stock banking paved the way for the fast development and huge concentration of banking. Both the Bank Charter Act of 1844 and the permission of joint-stock banks significantly reduced the power of the old elites and were important successes of the rising classes. Strongly guided by monetarism, most liberals were convinced that the monopolization of issuing and clear issuing rules would make financial markets less prone to crises. Permitting joint-stock banks was expected to facilitate lending to the rising industry and to democratize banking by enabling poorer classes to profit from banks. Hence, the two banking revolutions institutionalized the interest of the rising classes and monetarism as the leading idea.

After the French Revolution and Napoleon's defeat, France was economically, politically and militarily in very bad condition. Collective depression and an inferiority complex further weakened the society. Peoples' weariness of new political experiments and the complex power sharing between the aristocracy and the bourgeoisie underpinned the conservative backlash of the Bourbon Restoration. However, the shift of power towards the aristocracy upset the bourgeoisie. In the 1820 the long lasting discussion on industrialization also started. Parts of the elites were increasingly convinced that Britain's superiority stemmed from France's economic backwardness. It was argued that France needs a fast industrialization in order to catch up with Britain economically, politically and militarily. Inspired by the discussions on industrialization, an industrial fetish spread in France: in particular Saint-Simon and his followers were enthusiastic about industrialization. Others were less euphoric. However, debates on France's economic backwardness questioned conservative governments economic policy.

The escalating conflict between the government and the bourgeoisie caused the July Revolution, the main 19th century victory of the bourgeoisie over the landed aristocracy. Dominated by a small clique from the bourgeoisie, the July monarchy was characterized by half-hearted liberalism, the wide agreement on the necessity of state interventionism into economic affairs, half-hearted industrialism and bourgeoisie's interests. While parts of the elites, in particular engineers and bankers inspired by Saint-Simon, were enthusiastic about industrialization, the monarchs' economic policy remained mostly half-hearted. However, most agreed on the necessity of railway building. Railway building was considered pivotal for France's economic development: to facilitate the transportation of means of production and goods through the country, for political integration, to integrate the still fragmented country, and for the military force, to facilitate transportation of troops over long distances. Despite the wide agreement on the necessity of railways, railway building was practically slow and difficult: the monarch remained unenthusiastic, state intervention often hindered rather than supported progress and in particular the government lacked the financial means to accelerate railway building. Several legal changes were expected to foster railway extension, but with little success. Throughout the first half of the 19th century railway financing remained the main problem. Taking over public debt banking and dominating railway financing, a small banking aristocracy emerged: the Haute Banque.

Financing the government's deficits and ambitious infrastructural projects, the Haute Banque became one of the most influential groups and, due to its close ties to the government and overview of the economy, the spearhead and spokesman of the bourgeoisie. The second pivotal group for railway building were Saint-Simonian engineers: propelled by their enthusiasm for industrialization and railways, Saint-Simonians became the main organizers and planers of railways. At the beginning of the July monarchy, the cooperation between Saint-Simonians and the Haute Banque was relatively intensive and fertile. The loose cooperation between the government, the Haute Banque and Saint-Simonians satisfied bankers' interest in profitable investment opportunities, the government's interest of accelerating railway building and Saint-Simonians' ideal interests of the fast industrialization of France. However, the relation between Haute Banque and Saint-Simonians soon worsened. Unsatisfied with the slow industrialization and railway development, the general public and Saint-Simonians in particular blamed the Haute Banque for being selfish, greedy, egotistic and careless about the homeland's industrialization and railway connections. Convinced that a fundamental change of the banking sector was needed, Saint-Simonians published several industrial bank proposals, suggesting to found banks ready to absorb huge idle hoards to lend to the industry at lowest possible interest rates.

Its main supporter at the beginning, the bourgeoisie increasingly turned away from the government. The bourgeoisie's support for rioting workers caused the Revolution of 1848 that overturned the July Monarchy. Restoring the French hegemony in continental Europe, politically, economically and militarily catching up with Britain and solving the escalating social problems were Napoleon III's main goals. Economic progress and fast industrialization was pivotal for each goal, which is why Napoleon strongly focused on economic issues. Highly impressed by the Saint-Simonian economic theory and their plans for France's industrialization, Saint-Simonians' influence greatly increased during Napoleon's reign. Unlike his predecessors, Napoleon III was enthusiastic about railway building and expected that railways would foster industrialization, integrate the country and enforce military power. However, inspired by Saint-Simonians, Napoleon was convinced that a radical change of banking was needed to overcome the railway financing problem: in particular Saint-Simonian industrial bank proposals impressed Napoleon III. Allowing several Saint-Simonians the foundation of a joint-stock industrial bank caused one of the most pivotal banking revolutions in Europe's history. Against the angry protests of the Haute Banque, the permission of joint-stock banks in France fundamentally changed the French and the entire continental banking sector. Unable to prevent the foundation of the Crédit Mobilier, the Haute Banque changed their reaction and founded their own joint-stock banks: the hostility and race between Saint-Simonians and the Haute Banque for the most lucrative banking places spread joint stock banking throughout France and continental Europe. Soon, joint-stock banks founded either by Saint-Simonians or the Haute Banque dominated most continental European national banking sectors. Joint-stock banks served Napoleon's interests: absorbing capital available for investments and competing for the government's favor, joint-stock banks facilitated the financing of the government's ambitious infrastructural and building projects.

Providing profitable investment opportunities to the wealthy, joint-stock banks also satisfied the interests of the rich. Lowering interest rates and facilitating lending served entrepreneurs' interests. Ideologically, joint-stock banks built on Saint-Simonianism and industrialism. Hence, the foundation of French joint-stock banks restored the harmonic relationship between the main interests of the government, the bourgeoisie and the rich, and leading ideas like Saint-Simonianism and industrialism.

While in France at the beginning of the 19th century the environment for banking was quite difficult, in Germany it was even worse. In Prussia and other German countries, politics was dominated by the landed aristocracy. Traditionally, the landed aristocracy was quite reluctant to banking: first, because they feared the rise of the liberal, cosmopolitan banking bourgeoisie and second, because landlords expected that banks would divert capital from farm mortgages to industrial lending. Also, among others, class reservations on banks were widespread. Hence, the environment for banking was quite unfriendly. In addition, due to economic backwardness, the industrial demand for loans was small and, most importantly, the political fragmentation of Mosaic-Germany hampered the development of big modern banks. At the beginning of the 19th century, banking in the German countries was dominated by merchant banking in the trading hubs and public debt financing elsewhere: modern banking was still quite rare.

Despite all difficulties and hostility, several independent banking centers emerged in the rising industrial hubs: in particular in the Rhineland. However, the German railway boom, which started in the late 1830s and early 1840s, caused the first significant change of the German banking sector. In contrast to the widespread opposition to industrialization, railway building was mostly supported as economically, politically and militarily necessary. However, railway financing was difficult: governments and the wealthy population were unable or unwilling to finance the ambitious railway projects. Like in France, railway building heavily depended on a relatively small group of bankers, predominately from the rising industrial hubs, keen enough to invest heavily in railway companies. Increasingly, railway bankers became the capital intermediaries organizing investments for infrastructural projects: absorbing many smaller and bigger idle hoards and taping foreign financial markets, banks absorbed much of the capital needed for railway financing. In addition, banks were involved in planning and operating railway projects. From the railway-financing bankers, a small, predominately Rhinish, banking aristocracy emerged that became pivotal for the development of the German banking sector.

However, German banking really took off only in the second half of the 19th century. The German banking revolution was caused by several more or less interdependent puzzle pieces: already in the first half of the 19th century several bankers of the Rhinish banking aristocracy proposed to found joint-stock banks to facilitate and reduce the risk of railway financing. After the first plans were rejected, inspired by French Saint-Simonians, joint-stock banking ideas returned in the 1850s. The foundation of the first German joint-stock banks by the Rhinish banking aristocracy and several Berlin colleagues was a significant contribution to the German banking revolution. Developing much slower than in France, joint-stock banks nevertheless became the blueprints and pioneers of big banking. Politically, the liberal era of the 1850s and early 1860s facilitated banking. Liberal parties, dominating the economic policy of the time, deregulation policy and banking friendliness fostered the acceleration of financial market development. Bismarck's inability to finance the hegemony wars contributed to the banking revolution. After being rejected by the Parliament, Bismarck turned to private banks for war financing. Granting the public debt monopoly to the Preußen-Konsortium ensured big banks' dominance over the lucrative business of public debts and intensified banks' ties with the government. In addition, the liberalization of the joint-stock laws in the late 1860s facilitated the foundation of joint-stock banks. Germany's unification was an important push for rising joint-stock banks. Constricted by the small political entities, the unification developed many new markets and investment opportunities for the rising banks.

The rise of state- or kathedersocialism as the new leading German economic idea significantly changed the intended role of banks. State- or kathedersocialism became the linchpin of the German 'Sonderweg'; of the German cooperative capitalism. As German political elites became convinced that Germany needs a fast industrialization to catch up with Britain and France and underpin its aspiration to be a global empire, state- or kathedersocialism suggested a state-led industrialization planned, coordinated and managed within the triangle of the government, banks and industrial companies. It was widely agreed that company and banking cartels are better able to organize a fast industrialization than many small competitive companies. Megabanks and industrial megaconglomerates cooperating with each other and the state were considered as most appropriate for fast industrialization. Due to their good market overview and financial means, German joint-stock megabanks were present in most supervisory boards and coordinated and planned megaconglomerates and entire sectors' development. In the fertile environment of fast growth and state-led industrialization, German megabanks grew to become the world's biggest banks.

Cooperative capitalism mitigated the escalating conflicts between workers and the bourgeoisie and was in the interest of the industry, banks and the government. Cooperative capitalism prevented competition between industrial companies and banks, ensured governments' support, facilitated smooth fast industrialization and fostered fast growth of companies and banks. Governments' interests were satisfied as fast industrialization contributed to Germany's political, economic and military advance and allowed governments to heavily intervene and guide economic progress. The harmonic relation between main interests was built on the fundament of state- or kathedersocialism, the leading idea of the time, which suggested the concentration and cartelization of the economy, the close cooperation between companies, banks and the state and the lead of the state.

References

Abels H (2007) Der Blick auf die Gesellschaft, 3rd edn. VS Verl. für Sozialwissenschaften, Wiesbaden

Abolafia MY (2010) Narrative construction as sensemaking: how a central bank thinks. Organ Stud 31(3):349–367

Abrams L, Miller DJ (1976) Who were the French colonialists? A reassessment of the Parti Colonial, 1890–1914. Hist J 19(3):685–725

Abulafia D (1997) The impact of Italian banking in the late Middle Ages and the Renaissance, 1300–1500. In: Teichova A, Kurgan-van Hentenryk G, Ziegler D (eds) Banking, trade, and industry: Europe, America, and Asia from the thirteenth to the twentieth century. Cambridge University Press, Cambridge, pp 17–33

Abu-Lughod JL (1989) Before European hegemony: the world system A. D. 1250–1350. Oxford University Press, New York

Adorno TW ([1964] 1973) The Jargon of authenticity. Routledge and Kegan Paul, London

Akerlof GA (1970) The market for "lemons": quality uncertainty and the market mechanism. Q J Econ 84(3):488–500

Alborn TL (1998) Conceiving companies: joint-stock politics in Victorian England. Routledge, London

Aldenhoff-Hübinger R (2002) Agrarpolitik und Protektionismus: Deutschland und Frankreich im Vergleich; 1879–1914. Vandenhoeck und Ruprecht, Göttingen

Aldrich R (1996) Greater France: a history of French overseas expansion. Macmillan, London

Allen WR (1970) Modern defenders of mercantilist theory. Hist Polit Econ 2(2):381–397

Amonn A (1949) Simonde de Sismondi: Darstellung seiner Lehren mit einer Einführung und Erläuterungen. Francke, Bern

Andreadēs AM (1966) History of the Bank of England 1640 to 1903, 4th edn. Kelley, New York

Andrew CM, Kanya-Forstner AS (1976) French business and the French colonialists. Hist J 19(4):981–1000

Armstrong L (2004) Usury, conscience and public debt: Angelo Corbinelli's Testament of 1419. In: Marino JA, Kuehn T (eds) A renaissance of conflicts: visions and revisions of law and society in Italy and Spain. Centre for Reformation and Renaissance Studies, Toronto, pp 173–240

Arnon A (1987) Banking between the invisible and visible hands: a reinterpretation of Ricardo's place within the classical school. Oxford Econ Papers 39(2):268–281

Arnon A (2011) Monetary theory and policy from Hume and Smith to Wicksell: money, credit, and the economy. Cambridge University Press, Cambridge

Arrighi G (2010) The long twentieth century: money, power and the origins of our times, 2nd edn. Verso, London

Arrow KJ (1951) Social choice and individual values. Wiley, New York

Asgill J ([1696] 1906) Several assertions proved, in order to create another species of money than gold and silver. John Hopkins Press, Baltimore

Ashcraft R (1972) Marx and Weber on liberalism as bourgeois ideology. Comp Stud Soc Hist 14(2):130–168

F. Brugger, *Ideas, Interests and the Development of the European Banking Systems*, Wirtschaft + Gesellschaft, https://doi.org/10.1007/978-3-658-30597-0

Ashley WJ (1888) An introduction to English economic history and theory. Rivingtons, London

Attwood T (ed) (1816) The remedy, or thoughts on the present distresses: in a letter to a public editor, 2nd edn. Baldwin Cradock and Joy, London

Attwood T (1819) A second letter to the Earl of Liverpool: on the bank reports, as occasioning the national dangers and distresses. R. Wrightson, Birmingham

Axelrod R (2016) The dissemination of culture. J Confl Resolut 41(2):203–226

Bagehot W ([1873] 1962) Lombard street: a description of the money market. Richard D. Irwin, Homewood

Bandelow NC (2015) Advocacy coalition framework. In: Wenzelburger G, Zohlnhöfer R (eds) Handbuch Policy-Forschung. Springer VS, Wiesbaden, pp 305–324

Barbon N (1690) Nicholas Barbon on a discourse of trade. Milboum, London

Baring F (ed) (1797) Observations on the establishment of the Bank of England and on the paper circulation of the country. Minerva Press for Sewell Cornhill and Debrett, London

Barker EJ (1906) The rise and decline of the Netherlands. A political and economic history and a study in practical statesmanship. Smith Elder, London

Barkin KD (1970) The controversy over German industrialization: 1890–1902. University of Chicago Press, Chicago

Barnes V, Newton L (2014) The apple doesn't fall far from the tree: English bank regulation and branching strategies in the nineteenth century. Centre for International Business History Discussion Paper, IBH-2014-01

Battilossi S (2000) Financial innovation and the golden ages of international banking, 1890–1931 and 1958–81. Financ Hist Rev 7(2):141–175

Baumgart W (1975) Der Imperialismus: Idee und Wirklichkeit der englischen und französischen Kolonialexpansion 1880–1914. Steiner, Wiesbaden

Baumgartner FR, Jones BD (2009) Agendas and instability in American politics, 2nd edn. University of Chicago Press, Chicago

Beckert J (2005) Trust and the performative construction of markets. MPIfG Discussion Paper, 2005,8

Beckert J (2009) The social order of markets. Theory Soc 38(3):245–269

Beer WR (1980) The unexpected rebellion: ethnic activism in contemporary France. New York University Press, New York

Béland D (2009) Ideas, institutions, and policy change. J Eur Public Policy 16(5):701–718

Béland D (2016) Kingdon reconsidered: ideas, interests and institutions in comparative policy analysis. J Comp Policy Anal Res Pract 18(3):228–242

Bell DA (2003) The cult of the nation in France: inventing nationalism, 1680–1800. Harvard University Press, Cambridge

Bellet M (2011) Saint-Simonism and utilitarianism: the history of a paradox. Bentham's defence of usury under Saint-Amand Bazard's interpretation. GATE Working paper, 1135

Bellet M (2016) Non-Marxian socialist ideas in France. In: Faccarello G, Kurz HD (eds) Schools of thought in economics, Edward Elgar, Cheltenham, pp 188–205

Benford RD, Snow DA (2000) Framing processes and social movements: an overview and assessment. Ann Rev Sociol 26:611–639

Bentham J (1787) Defence of usury: shewing the impolicy of the present legal restraints on the terms of pecuniary bargains. T. Payne and Son, London

Bentham J (1823) A fragment on government: a comment on the commentaries, 2nd edn. Pickering, London

Bentham J (1894) Theory of legislation. Trübner, London

Bentham J (1907) An introduction to the principles of morals and legislation. Clarendon Press, Oxford

Bentham J (2004) The psychology of economic man. In: Stark W (ed) Jeremy Bentham's economic writings: critical edition based on his printed works and unprinted manuscripts, vol III. Routledge, London

Bentley AF (1908) The process of government: a study of social pressures. University of Chicago Press, Chicago

Béraud A (2016) French classical political economy. In: Faccarello G, Kurz HD (eds) Schools of thought in economics, pp 150–166

Berman S (1998) The social democratic moment: ideas and politics in the making of interwar Europe. Harvard University Press, Cambridge

Berman S (2001) Ideas, norms, and culture in political analysis. Comp Polit 33(2):231–250

Bevir M, Rhodes RAW (2003) Interpreting British governance. Routledge, London

Bisin A, Verdier T (1998) On the cultural transmission of preferences for social status. J Public Econ 1998:75–97

Black D (1958) The theory of committees and elections. Cambridge University Press, Cambridge

Blaug M (1992) Economic theory in retrospect, 4th edn. Cambridge University Press, Cambridge

Blyth M (1997) "Any more bright ideas?" The ideational turn of comparative political economy. Comp Polit 29(2):229–250

Blyth M (2002) Great transformations: economic ideas and institutional change in the twentieth century. Cambridge University Press, Cambridge

Blyth M (2011) Beyond the standard model: the importance of ideas in uncertain and evolving environments. APSA 2011 Annual Meeting Paper

Blyth M, Helgadottir O, Kring W (2016) Ideas and historical institutionalism. In: Fioretos K-O, Falleti TG, Sheingate AD (eds) The Oxford handbook of historical institutionalism. Oxford University Press, Oxford, pp 142–162

Bodin J ([1576] 1955) Six books of the commonwealth. Basil Blackwell, Oxford

Bogaert R, Kurgan-Van Hentenryk G, van der Wee H (1994) A history of European banking. Fonds Mercator Paribas, Antwerp

Böhme H (1967) Big-business pressure groups and Bismarck's turn to protectionism, 1873–79. Hist J 10(2):218–236

Bolingbroke HJ (1749) Letters, on the spirit of patriotism. A. Millar, London

Bonin H (2014) Introduction: issues regarding Asian imperial banking. In: Bonin H, Valério N, Yago K (eds) Asian imperial banking history. Pickering & Chatto Publishers, London, pp 1–20

Böning M (2009) Illusio. In: Fröhlich G, Rehbein B (eds) Bourdieu-Handbuch: Leben, Werk, Wirkung. J.B. Metzler, Stuttgart, pp 129–131

Booth AJ (1871) Saint-Simon and Saint-Simonism: a chapter in the history of socialism in France. Longmans, Green, Reader, and Dyer, London

Bopp KR (1954) Die Tätigkeit der Reichsbank von 1876 bis 1914. Weltwirtschaftliches Arch 72(1):34–59

Bordo MD, White EN British and French finance during the Napoleonic Wars. NBER Working Paper, 3517

Bordo MD, White EN (1991) A tale of two currencies: British and French finance during the Napoleonic Wars. J Econ Hist 50:303–316

Born KE (1977) Geld und Banken im 19. und 20. Jahrhundert. Kröner, Stuttgart

Born KE (2001) Preußen im Deutschen Kaiserreich 1867–1918. In: Neugebauer W (ed) Handbuch der Preußischen Geschichte: Vom Kaiserreich zum 20. Jahrhundert und Große Themen der Geschichte Preußens. de Gruyter, Berlin, pp 15–148

Bourdieu P (1975) The specificity of the scientific field and the social conditions of the progress of reason. Soc Sci Inf 14(6):19–47

Bourdieu P (1986) The forms of capital. In: Richardson JG (ed) Handbook of theory and research for the sociology of education. Greenwood Press, New York, pp 241–258

Bourdieu P (1988) Homo Academicus. Suhrkamp, Frankfurt a. M.

Bourdieu P (1998) Practical reason: on the theory of action. Polity Press, Cambridge

Bourdieu P (2005) The social structures of the economy. Polity, Cambridge

Bourdieu P (2001) Das Politische Feld: Zur Kritik der Politischen Vernunft. UVK-Verl.-Ges, Konstanz

Bowen HV, Cottrell PL (1997) Banking and the evolution of the British economy, 1694–1878. In: Teichova A, Kurgan-van Hentenryk G, Ziegler D (eds) Banking, trade, and industry: Europe, America, and Asia from the thirteenth to the twentieth century. Cambridge University Press, Cambridge, pp 89–112

Boyd W (1801) A letter to the right honourable William Pitt: on the influence of the stoppage of issues in specie at the Bank of England, on the prices of provisions, and other commodities. J. Wright, London

Braggion F, Dwarkasing N, Moore L (2012) From competition to Cartel: bank mergers in the U.K. 1885 to 1925. Available at SSRN

Brandt K (1992) Geschichte der deutschen Volkswirtschaftslehre: Von der Scholastik bis zur klassischen Nationalökonomie. Haufe, Freiburg i. Br.

Braudel F (1981) Civilization and capitalism. 15th–18th century: the structures of everyday life. William Collins Sons & Co Ltd, London

Braudel F (1982) Civilization and capitalism. 15th–18th century: the wheels of commerce. William Collins Sons & Co Ltd, London

Braudel F (1984) Civilization and capitalism 15th–18th century: the perspective of the world. William Collins Sons & Co Ltd, London

Braudel F (1995) The Mediterranean and the Mediterranean world in the age of Philip II. University of California Press, Berkeley

Braun D, Busch A (eds) (2000) Public policy and political ideas. Elgar, Cheltenham

Breuilly J (1994) Labour and liberalism in nineteenth-century Europe: essays in comparative history. Manchester University Press, Manchester

Brinton MC (ed) (1998) The new institutionalism in sociology. Stanford University Press, Stanford

Briscoe J (1694) A discourse on the late funds of the Million-Act, Lottery-Act, and Bank of England. J.D. and sold by R. Baldwin, London

Brugger F (2015) Die ökonomische Geldtheorie und ihre (Finanz-)Krisen: Von David Hume bis zur Gegenwart. In: Kraemer K, Nessel S (eds) Geld und Krise: Die sozialen Grundlagen moderner Geldordnungen. Campus-Verlag, Frankfurt a. M.

Brugger F, Gehrke C (2018) Skilling and deskilling: technological change in classical economic theory and its empirical evidence. Forthcoming

Brugger F, Pantelic N (2018) The production and diffusion of ideas: the case of neoliberalism. Forthcoming

Bryer R (1997) The Mercantile Laws Commission of 1854 and the political economy of limited liability. Econ Hist Rev 50(1):37–56

Burdett F (1818) Annals of banks for savings. J.M. Richardson, London

Burke J (2008) Money for nothing: the sin of usury. AMU Economics Working Paper, 0801

Burt RS (1987) Social contagion and innovation: cohesion versus structural equivalence. Am J Sociol 92(6):1287–1335

Bussière E (1997) Banks, economic development and capitalism in France. In: Teichova A, Kurgan-van Hentenryk G, Ziegler D (eds) Banking, trade, and industry: Europe, America, and Asia from the thirteenth to the twentieth century. Cambridge University Press, Cambridge, pp 113–130

Bussmann W (1958) Zur Geschichte des deutschen Liberalismus im 19. Jahrhundert. Historische Z 186(3):527–557

Cain PJ, Hopkins AG (1986) Gentlemanly capitalism and British expansion overseas I: the old colonial system, 1688–1850. Econ Hist Rev 39(4):501–525

Cain PJ, Hopkins AG (1987) Gentlemanly capitalism and British expansion overseas II: new imperialism, 1850–1945. Econ Hist Rev 40(1):1–26

Cain PJ, Hopkins A (1993) British imperialism: innovation and expansion 1688–1914. Longman, London

Cain PJ, Hopkins AG (2016) British imperialism: 1688–2015, 3rd edn. Routledge, London

Callon M (1998) Introduction: the embeddedness of economic markets in economics. Sociol Rev 46(1_suppl):1–57

Cameron RE (1961) France and the economic development of Europe, 1880–1914: conquests of peace and seeds of war. Princeton University Press, Princeton

Cameron RE (ed) (1967) Banking in the early stages of industrialization: a study in comparative economic history. Oxford University Press, New York

Cameron RE (1967) England, 1750–1844. In: Cameron RE (ed) Banking in the early stages of industrialization: a study in comparative economic history. Oxford University Press, New York, pp 15–59

Cameron RE (1967) France, 1800–1870. In: Cameron RE (ed) Banking in the early stages of industrialization: a study in comparative economic history. Oxford University Press, New York, pp 100–128

Camic C, Gross N (2004) The new sociology of ideas. In: Blau JR (ed) The Blackwell companion to sociology. Blackwell Publishing, Oxford, pp 236–249

Campbell JL (1998) Institutional analysis and the role of ideas in political economy. Theory Soc 27(3):377–409

Campbell JL (2002) Ideas, politics, and public policy: annual review of sociology. Ann Rev Sociol 28:21–38

Capie F, Rodrik-Bali G (1982) Concentration in British banking 1870–1920. Bus Hist 24(3):280–292

Carlson M (1999) Adam Smith's support for money and banking regulation: a case of inconsistency? Hist Econ Rev 29(1):1–15

Caron F (1979) An economic history of modern France. Methuen, London

Carruthers BG (1996) City of capital: politics and markets in the English financial revolution. Princeton University Press, Princeton

Carstensen MB (2011) Ideas are not as stable as political scientists want them to be: a theory of incremental ideational change. Polit Stud 59(3):596–615

Carstensen MB (2015) Conceptualising ideational novelty: a relational approach. Br J Polit Int Relat 17(2):284–297

Caselli PF (2013) Papal finance, 1348–1848. In: Arner DW, Caprio G (eds) Handbook of key global financial markets, institutions, and infrastructure. Academic Press, London, pp 207–220

Castellano C, Fortunato S, Loreto V (2009) Statistical physics of social dynamics. Rev Modern Phys 81(2):591–646

Chadha J, Newby E (2013) 'Midas, transmuting all, into paper': the Bank of England and the Banque de France during the Napoleonic Wars. Cambridge Working Papers in Economics, 1330

Chamberlain ME (1989) Imperialism and social reform. In: Eldridge CC (ed) British imperialism in the nineteenth century. Macmillan, Basingstoke, pp 148–167

Chamberlen H (1700) A few proposals humbly recommending to the serious consideration of his majesty's high commissioner, and the right honourable, the estates of parliament, the establishing a land-credit in this kingdom: together with full answers to all such objections, as have hitherto appeared against it, Edinburgh

Chapman G (1963) The third republic of France. The first phase, 1871–1894. St. Martin's Press, New York

Checkland SG (1948) The Birmingham economists, 1815–1850. Econ Hist Rev 1(1):1–19

Clapham JH (1921) The economic development of France and Germany 1815–1914. Cambridge University Press, Cambridge

Clough SB (1939) France: a history of national economics 1789–1939. Scribner, New York

Coco G, de Meza D (2009) In defense of usury laws. J Money Credit Bank 41(8):1691–1703

Coleman J, Katz E, Menzel H (1957) The diffusion of an innovation among physicians. Sociometry 20(4):253–270

Coleman JS (1990) Foundations of social theory. Belknap Press of Harvard University Press, Cambridge

Coleman JS, Katz E, Menzel H (1966) Medical innovation: a diffusion study. Bobbs-Merrill, Indianapolis

Collins M (2012) Money and banking in the UK: a history. Routledge, London

Committee on the Law of Partnership (1851) Report from the Select Committee on the Law of Partnership: together with the proceedings of the Committee, Minutes of Evidence, Appendix and Index

Connolly WE (1983) The terms of political discourse, 2nd edn. Robertson, Oxford

Conrad S (2012) German colonialism: a short history. Cambridge University Press, Cambridge

Cottrell PL (1980) Industrial finance 1830–1914: the finance and organization of English manufacturing industry. Methuen, London

Cottrell PL (1994) The historical development of modern banking within the United Kingdom. In: Pohl M (ed) Handbook on the history of European Banks. Elgar, Aldershot

Cottrell PL, Newton L (1998) Joint-stock banking in the English Provinces 1826–1857: to branch or not to branch? Bus Econ Hist 1998:115–128

Cottrell PL, Newton L (1999) Banking liberalization in England and Wales, 1826–1844. In: Sylla RE, Tilly RH, Tortella Casares G (eds) The state, the financial system, and economic modernization. Cambridge University Press, Cambridge, pp 75–117

Crick WF, Wadsworth JE (1936) A hundred years of joint stock banking. Hodder & Stoughton, London

Crouch RL (1967) Laissez-Faire in nineteenth century Britain: myth or reality? Manchester Sch 35:199–215

Cunningham W (1892) The growth of English industry and commerce in modern times. Cambridge University Press, Cambridge

Dalton RJ (1994) Communists and democrats: democratic attitudes in the two Germanies. Br J Polit Sci 24(4):469–493

Daugherty MR (1942) The currency-banking controversy: part 1. South Econ J 1942:140–155

Daughton JP (2006) An empire divided: religion, republicanism, and the making of French colonialism, 1880–1914. Oxford University Press, Oxford

Davis GF, Kim S (2015) Financialization of the economy. Ann Rev Sociol 41(1):203–221

Davis GF, Mizruchi MS (1999) The money center cannot hold: commercial banks in the U.S. system of corporate governance. Admin Sci Q 44(2):215–239

Diatkine S, Boyer Jd (2008) British monetary orthodoxy in the 1870s: a victory for the currency principle. Eur J Hist Econ Thought 15(2):181–209

Dicey AV (1905) Lectures on the relation between law & public opinion in England during the nineteenth century. Macmillan, London

Dickson PG (1967) The financial revolution in England: a study in the development of public credit 1688–1756. Macmillan, London

DiMaggio PJ, Powell WW (1983) The iron cage revisited: institutional isomorphism and collective rationality in organizational fields. Am Sociol Rev 48(2):147–160

Djelic M-L (2013) When limited liability was (still) an issue: mobilization and politics of signification in 19th-century England. Organ Stud 34(5/6):595–621

Dobbin F (1997) Forging industrial policy: the United States, Britain and France in the railway age. Cambridge University Press, Cambridge

Doukas KA (1945) The French railroads and the state. Columbia University Press, New York

Duan D (2010) Reconsidering Tocqueville's imperialism. Ethical Perspect 17(3):415–447

Dühring EK (1879) Kritische Geschichte der Nationalökonomie und des Socialismus. Fus's, Leipzig

Dumke RH (1978) The political economy of German economic unification: tariffs, trade and politics of the Zollverein Era. J Econ Hist 1978:277–278

Dunham AL (1955) The industrial revolution in France: 1815–1848. Exposition Press, New York

Durkheim E ([1893] 1984) The division of labour in society. Macmillan, London

de Tarde G ([1890] 1903) The laws of imitation. H. Holt and Company, New York

Durkheim É ([1912] 1995) The elementary forms of religious life. The Free Press, New York

de Vries J, van der Woude AM (1997) The first modern economy: success, failure, and perseverance of the Dutch economy, 1500–1815. Cambridge University Press, Cambridge

de Tocqueville A (1856) The old regime and the revolution. Harper & Brothers, New York

Ebner A (2005) Entrepreneurship and economic development: from classical political economy to economic sociology. J Econ Stud 32(3):256–274

Eckalbar JC (1979) The Saint-Simonians in industry and economic development. Am J Econ Sociol 38(1):83–96

Edgeworth FY (1881) Mathematical Psychics: an essay on the application of mathematics to the moral sciences. Kegan Paul, London

Edwards J, Ogilvie S (1996) Universal banks and German industrialization: a reappraisal. Econ Hist Rev 49(3):427–446

Ehrenberg R ([1896] 1928) Capital & finance in the age of the Renaissance: a study of the fuggers and their connections. Harcourt Brace, New York

Eley G (1988) Liberalismus 1860–1914: Deutschland und Großbritannien im Vergleich. In: Langewiesche D (ed) Liberalismus im 19. Jahrhundert: Deutschland im europäischen Vergleich. Vandenhoeck & Ruprecht, Göttingen, pp 260–276

Elias N (2009) Studien über die Deutschen: Machtkämpfe und Habitusentwicklung im 19. und 20. Jahrhundert. Suhrkamp, Frankfurt a. M.

Elster J (2007) Explaining social behavior: more nuts and bolts for the social sciences. Cambridge University Press, Cambridge

Enfantin P (1905) Die Nationalökonomie des Saint-Simonismus. Hirschfeld, Leipzig

Epstein GA (ed) (2005) Financialization and the world economy. Elgar, Cheltenham

Epstein SR (2001) Freedom and growth: the rise of states and markets in Europe, 1300–1750. Routledge, London

Essars Des P (1896) A history of banking in the Latin nations. In: Summer WG (ed) A history of banking in all the leading nations, vol III. The Journal of Commerce and Commercial Bulletin, London, pp 1–389

Esser H (1996) Soziologie: Allgemeine Grundlagen. Campus-Verl, Frankfurt a. M.

Eynern Gv (1928) Die Reichsbank: Die Probleme des deutschen Zentralnoteninstituts in geschichtlicher Darstellung. Fischer, Jena

Faust H (1965) Geschichte der Genossenschaftsbewegung: Ursprung und Weg der Genossenschaften im deutschen Sprachraum. Knapp, Frankfurt a. M.

Feavearyear AE (1931) The pound sterling: a history of english money. Clarendon Press, Oxford

Feis H (1930) Europe the World's banker 1870–1914: an account of European foreign investment and the connection of world finance with diplomacy before the war. Kelley, New York

Fetter FW (1942) The bullion report Reëxamined. Q J Econ 56(4):655–665

Fetter FW (1959) The politics of the bullion report. Economica 26(102):99–120

Fetter FW (1975) The influence of economists in parliament on British Legislation from Ricardo to John Stuart Mill. J Polit Econ 83(5):1051–1064

Fetter FW (1978) Development of British monetary orthodoxy: 1797–1875. Kelley, Fairfield

Fetter FW (1980) The economist in parliament, 1780–1868. Duke University Press, Durham

Fichte JG ([1800] 1920) Der geschlossne Handelsstaat. Fischer, Jena

Finnemore M (1996) Norms, culture, and world politics: insights from sociology's institutionalism. Int Organ 50(2):325–347

Fisher I (1911) The purchasing power of money. Macmillan, New York

Fligstein N, McAdam D (2015) A theory of fields. Oxford University Press, Oxford

Forbes JH (1815) A short account of the Edinburgh savings bank: directions for establishing similar banks, with the mode of keeping the accounts, and conducting the details of business. Printed for John Anderson and Co, Edinburgh

Force P (2003) Self-interest before Adam Smith: a genealogy of economic science. Cambridge University Press, Cambridge

Forsyth DJ, Verdier D (eds) (2003) The origins of national financial systems: Alexander Gerschenkron reconsidered. Routledge, London

Fremdling R (1975) Eisenbahnen und deutsches Wirtschaftswachstum, 1840–1879: Ein Beitrag zur Entwicklungstheorie und zur Theorie der Infrastruktur. Gesellschaft für westfälische Wirtschaftsgeschichte, Dortmund

Fremdling R (1977) Railroads and German economic growth: a leading sector analysis with a comparison to the United States and Great Britain. J Econ Hist 37(3):583–604

Fremdling R (1983) Germany. In: O'Brien P (ed) Railways and the economic development of Western Europe, 1830–1914. Macmillan, London, pp 121–147

Friedman M (1990) Bimetallism revisited. J Econ Perspect 4(4):5–104

Friemel TN (2010) Diffusionsforschung. In: Stegbauer C, Häussling R (eds) Handbuch Netzwerkforschung. VS Verl. für Sozialwissenschaften, Wiesbaden, pp 825–833

Fröhlich M (1994) Imperialismus: Deutsche Kolonial- und Weltpolitik 1880–1914. Deutscher Taschenbuch Verlag, München

Galam S (2008) Sociophysics: a review of Galam Models. Int J Modern Phys C 19(03):409–440

Gall L (1976) Liberalismus und ‚bürgerliche Gesellschaft': Zu Charakter und Entwicklung der liberalen Bewegung in Deutschland. In: Gall L (ed) Liberalismus. Kiepenheuer & Witsch, Köln, pp 162–186

Gall L (1999) Eisenbahn in Deutschland: Von den Anfängen bis zum Ersten Weltkrieg. In: Gall L, Pohl M (eds) Die Eisenbahn in Deutschland: Von den Anfängen bis zur Gegenwart. Beck, München, pp 13–27

Gall L (2017) Otto von Bismarck und Wilhelm II.: Repräsentanten eines Epochenwechsels? In: Lappenküper U (ed) Otto von Bismarck und das „lange 19. Jahrhundert": Lebendige Vergangenheit im Spiegel der „Friedrichsruher Beiträge" 1996–2016. Ferdinand Schöningh, Paderborn, pp 70–80

Garcia-Parpet M-F (2007) The social construction of a perfect market: the strawberry auction at Fontaines-en-Sologne. In: MacKenzie D, Muniesa F, Siu L (eds) Do economists make markets? On the performativity of economics. Princeton University Press, Princeton, pp 20–53

Gelb J (1989) Feminism and politics: a comparative perspective. University of California Press, Berkeley

Gerschenkron A (1962) Economic backwardness in historical perspective: a book of essays. Belknap Press of Harvard University Press, Cambridge

Gide C, Rist C (1923) Geschichte er volkswirtschaftlichen Lehrmeinungen. Fischer, Jena

Gilbart JW (1837) The history and principles of banking, 3rd edn. Printed for Longman Rees Orme Brown Green and Longman, London

Goffman D (2006) The Ottoman empire and early modern Europe, 5th edn. Cambridge University Press, Cambridge

Goldie M (1994) The reception of hobbes. In: Burns JH, Goldie M (eds) The Cambridge history of political thought, 1450–1700. Cambridge University Press, Cambridge, pp 589–615

Goldstein JS, Keohane RO (eds) (1993) Ideas and foreign policy: beliefs, institutions, and political change. Cornell University Press, Ithaca

Goldthwaite R (2009) The economy of renaissance florence. Johns Hopkins University Press, Baltimore

Gosden P (1996) Great Britain. In: Mura J (ed) History of European savings banks. Dt. Sparkassenverlag, Stuttgart, pp 133–160

Gossen HH (1854) Entwickelung der Gesetze des menschlichen Verkehrs und der daraus fliessenden Regeln für menschliches Handeln. F. Vieweg und Sohn, Braunschweig

Gramsci A (1999) Selections from the Prison Notebooks of Antonio Gramsci. International Publishers, New York

Granovetter M (1978) Threshold models of collective behavior. Am J Sociol 83(6):1420–1443

Greif A (1994) Cultural beliefs and the organization of society: a historical and theoretical reflection on collectivist and individualist societies. J Polit Econ 102(5):912–950

Greif A (2006) Institutions and the path to the modern economy: lessons from medieval trade. Cambridge University Press, Cambridge

Greif A, Tadelis S (2010) A theory of moral persistence: crypto-morality and political legitimacy. J Comp Econ 38(3):229–244

Grice-Hutchinson M (2015) Early economic thought in Spain 1177–1740. Liberty Fund, Indianapolis

Gründer H (2012) Geschichte der Deutschen Kolonien, 6th edn. UTB GmbH, Stuttgart

Guiso L, Sapienza P, Zingales L (2006) Does culture affect economic outcomes? J Econ Perspect 20(2):23–48

Guizot F ([1640] 1854) History of the english revolution: from the accession of Charles I. R. Bently, London

Haas PM (1992) Introduction: epistemic communities and international policy coordination. Int Organ 46(1):1–35

Hahn H-W (1998) Die industrielle Revolution in Deutschland. Oldenbourg, München

Hall PA (1989) The political power of economic ideas: Keynesianism across nations. Princeton University Press, Princeton

Hall PA (1993) Policy paradigms, social learning, and the state: the case of economic policymaking in Britain. Comp Polit 25(3):275–296

Hall PA, Taylor RCR (1996) Political science and the three new institutionalisms. Polit Stud 44(5):936–957

Hamilton EJ (1967) John Law of Lauriston: banker, gamester, merchant, chief? Am Econ Rev 57(2):273–282

Harlen CM (1999) A reappraisal of classical economic nationalism and economic liberalism. Int Stud Q 43(4):733–744

Hasse R, Krücken G (2009) Neo-institutionalistische Theorie. In: Kneer G, Schroer M (eds) Handbuch Soziologische Theorien. Springer VS, Wiesbaden, pp 199–218

Hawtrey RG (1919) Currency and credit. Longmans, Green and Co, London

Hay C (2002) Political analysis: a critical introduction. Palgrave, Basingstoke

Hay C (2008) Constructivist institutionalism. In: Rhodes RAW, Binder SA, Rockman BA (eds) The Oxford handbook of political institutions. Oxford University Press, Oxford, pp 56–74

Hay C (2011) Ideas and the construction of interests. In: Béland D, Cox RH (eds) Ideas and politics in social science research. Oxford University Press, Oxford, pp 65–82

Hayek FA (1944) The road to Serfdom. Routledge, London

Hayek FA (1945) The use of knowledge in society. Am Econ Rev 35(4):519–530

Hayek FA (1949) The intellectuals and socialism. Univ Chicago Law Rev 16(3):417–433

Heckscher EF (1935) Mercantilism, vol 1. Routledge, London

Heckscher EF (1935) Mercantilism, vol 2. Routledge, London

Heckscher EF (1964) The bank of Sweden: in its connection with the bank of Amsterdam. In: van Dillen JG (ed) History of the principal public banks: accompanied by extensive bibliographies of the history of banking and credit in eleven European countries. Cass, London, pp 161–199

Heers J (1974) The »Feudal» economy and capitalism: words, ideas and reality. J Eur Econ Hist 3:609–653

Hegselmann R, Krause U (2002) Opinion dynamics and bounded confidence models, analysis and simulation. J Artif Soc Social Simul 5(3):1–33

Hegselmann R, Krause U (2005) Opinion dynamics driven by various ways of averaging. Comput Econ 25(4):381–405

Heilperin MA (1960) Studies in economic nationalism. Droz, Genève

Helleiner E (2002) Economic nationalism as a challenge to economic liberalism? Lessons from the 19th century. Int Stud Q 46(3):307–329

Henderson WO (1967) The industrial revolution on the continent: Germany, France, Russia; 1800–1914, 2nd edn. Cass, London

Henderson WO (1975) The rise of German industrial power, 1834–1914. University of California Press, Berkeley

Henderson WO (1983) Friedrich list: economist and visionary, 1789–1846. Cass, London

Henning F (1966) Frügeschichte des deutschen Liberalismus. In: Luchtenberg P, Erbe W (eds) Geschichte des deutschen Liberalismus. Westdt. Verl, Köln, pp 27–60

Herrick FH (1944) British liberalism and the idea of social justice. Am J Econ Sociol 4(1):67–79

Hetzel RL (1987) Will recent high growth rates of money revive inflation? Contemp Policy Issues 5(1):41–53

Hickson CR, Turner JD (2003) Shareholder liability regimes in nineteenth-century English banking: the impact upon the market for share. Eur Rev Econ Hist 7(1):99–125

Hilferding R ([1910] 1955) Das Finanzkapital: Eine Studie über die jüngste Entwicklung des Kapitalismus. Dietz Verlag, Berlin

Hirschman AO (1992) Rival views of market society and other recent essays. Harvard University Press, Cambridge

Hobbes T (1651) Leviathan: the matter, forme, & power of a common-wealth ecclesiasticall and civill. Andrew Crooke, London

Hobson JA (1902) Imperialism: a study. James Nisbet & Co, London

Hollander S (1999) Jeremy Bentham and Adam Smith on the usury laws: a "Smithian" reply to Bentham and a new problem. Eur J Hist Econ Thought 6(4):523–551

Holmes DR (2014) Economy of words: communicative imperatives in central banks. University of Chicago Press, Chicago

Holmes S (1990) The secret history of self-interest. In: Mansbridge JJ (ed) Beyond self-interest. University of Chicago Press, Chicago, pp 267–286

Holzapfel H (1903) Die Anfänge der Montes Pietatis: (1462–1515). Verlag der Lentner'schen Buchhandlung, München

Horkheimer M, Adorno TW ([1947] 2002) Dialectic of enlightenment: philosophical fragments. Stanford University Press, Stanford

Horn N (1979) Aktienrechtliche Unternehmensorganisation in der Hochindustrialisierung (1860–1920). In: Kocka J (ed.) Recht und Entwicklung der Großunternehmen im 19. und frühen 20. Jahrhundert: Wirtschafts-, sozial- und rechtshistorische Untersuchungen zur Industrialisierung in Deutschland, Frankreich, England und den USA. Vandenhoeck & Ruprecht, Göttingen, pp 123–189

Horsefield JK (1944) The origins of the Bank Charter Act, 1844. Economica 11(44):180–189

Horsefield JK (1982) The "Stop of the Exchequer" revisited. Econ Hist Rev 35(4):511–528

Hoselitz BF (1955) Entrepreneurship and capital formation in France and Britain since 1700. In: Hoselitz BF (ed) Capital formation and economic growth. Princeton University Press, Princeton, pp 289–336

House of Commons (1856) Law of Partnership and Joint-Stock Companies. HC Deb 01 February 1856, vol 140 cc110-47

Hübner O (1854) Die Banken. Hübner, Leipzig

Hume D (1752) Political discourses, vol 2. Fleming for Kincaid and Donaldson, Edinburgh

Hume D ([1777] 1987) Essays: moral, political, and literary. Liberty Fund, Indianapolis

Humphrey TM (1993) Money, banking and inflation: essays in the history of monetary thought. Elgar, Aldershot

Humphrey TM (1999) Mercantilists and classicals: insights from doctrinal history. FRB Richmond Econ Q 85(2):55–82

Humphrey TM (2004) Alfred Marshall and the quantity theory of money. Federal Reserve Bank of Richmond Working Paper, 04-10

Ingham GK (2004) The nature of money. Polity Press, Cambridge

Inglehart R (1997) Modernization and postmodernization: cultural, economic, and political change in 43 societies. Princeton University Press, Princeton

Ireland PW (1984) The rise of the limited liability company. Int J Sociol Law 1984:239–260

Ito S (2011) The making of institutional credit in England, 1600 to 1688. Eur J Hist Econ Thought 18(4):487–519

Jadlow JM (1977) Adam Smith on usury laws. J Finance 32(4):1195–1200

Johnson R (2003) British imperialism. Palgrave Macmillan, Basingstoke

Jones S, Aiken M (1995) British company legislation and social and political evolution during the nineteenth. Br Account Rev 27(1):61–82

Joplin T (1822) An essay on the general principles and present practice of banking in England and Scotland: with observations upon the justice and policy of an immediate alteration of the charter of the Bank of England, and the measures to be pursued to effect it, 2nd edn. E. Walker, Newcastle

Joplin T (1827) An essay on the general principles and present practice of banking, in England and Scotland: with supplementary observations on the steps proper to form a public bank, and the system on which its accounts ought to be kept, 6th edn. Messrs. Baldwin Cradock & Joy, London

Judt T (2011) Marxism and the French left: studies on labour and politics in France, 1830–1981. New York University Press, New York

Kaiser TE (1991) Money, despotism, and public opinion in early eighteenth-century France: John Law and the debate on royal credit. J Modern Hist 63(1):1–28

Karataşlı ŞS (2016) From communal patriotism to City-State Chauvinism: transformation of collective identities in Northern Italy, 1050–1500. Int J Politics Cult Soc 29(1):73–101

Katzenstein PJ (ed) (1996) The culture of national security: norms and identity in world politics. Columbia University Press, New York

Kawamura T (2015) British exchange banks in the international trade of Asia from 1850 to 1890. In: Bosma U, Webster A (eds) Commodities, ports and Asian maritime trade since 1750. Palgrave Macmillan, Basingstoke, pp 179–197

Keister LA (2002) Financial markets, money, and banking. Ann Rev Sociol 28(1):39–61

Kemp T (1985) Industrialization in nineteenth-century Europe, 2nd edn. Longman, London

Kerr P (2002) Saved from extinction: evolutionary theorising, politics and the state. Br J Polit Int Relat 4(2):330–358

Kerschagl R (1968) John Law: Die Erfindung der modernen Banknote, 2nd edn. Verl. des Notringes der wiss. Verbände Österreichs, Wien

Keynes JM (1921) A treatise on probability. Macmillan, London

Keynes JM (1935) The general theory of employment interest and money. Harcourt Brace & Co, New York

Kimmel MS (1988) Absolutism and its discontents: state and society in seventeenth century France and England. Transaction Books, New Brunswick

Kindleberger CP (1964) Economic growth in France and Britain, 1851–1950. Harvard University Press, Cambridge

Kindleberger CP (1978) Economic response: comparative studies in trade, finance, and growth. Harvard University Press, Cambridge

Kindleberger CP (1984) Was Adam Smith a Monetarist or a Keynesian? Bus Econ 19(1):5–12

Kindleberger CP (1985) Keynesianism vs. Monetarism and other essays in financial history. Allen & Unwin, London

Kindleberger CP (1993) A financial history of Western Europe, 2nd edn. Oxford University Press, New York

Kindleberger CP (2005) Manias, panics, and crashes. Palgrave Macmillan, London

King P (1804) Thoughts on the effects of the bank restrictions, 2nd edn. Cadell, London

Kingdon JW (1984) Agendas, alternatives, and public policies. Little Brown, Boston

Kirshner J (1970) The moral theology of public finance: a study and edition of Nicholas De Anglia's Quaestio Disputata on the Public Debt of Venice. Archivum Fratrum Praedicatorum 40:47–65

Kirshner J (1977) The moral problem of discounting Genoese Paghe, 1450–1550. Archivum Fratrum Praedicatorum 47:109–167

Kitchen M (1978) The political economy of Germany 1815–1914. McGill-Queen's University Press, London

Kleinwächter F (1883) Die Kartelle: Ein Beitrag zur Frage der Organisation der Volkswirthschaft. Wagner, Innsbruck

Knapp GF ([1905] 1973) The state theory of money. Kelley, Cliftin

Knight FH (1921) Risk, uncertainty and profit. Houghton Mifflin, Boston

Knoblauch H (2014) Wissenssoziologie, 3rd edn. UTB GmbH; UVK, Stuttgart

Kohn MG (1999a) Merchant banking in the medieval and early modern economy. Dartmouth College, Department of Economics Working paper, 99-05

Kohn MG (1999b) Early deposit banking. Dartmouth College, Department of Economics Working paper, 99-03

Kornhauser W (1959) The politics of mass society. The Free Press, Glencoe

Kraemer K (2002) Charismatischer Habitus: Zur sozialen Konstruktion symbolischer Macht. Berl J für Soziol 12(2):173–187

Kraemer K (2010) Propheten der Finanzmärkte. Berl J für Soziol 20(2):179–201

Kraemer K (2017) Gibt es eine soziologische Kapitalismusforschung? In: Sachweh P, Münnich S (eds) Kapitalismus als Lebensform?. Springer Fachmedien, Wiesbaden, pp 47–77

Krasner SD (1984) Approaches to the state: alternative conceptions and historical dynamics. Comp Politics 16(2):223–246

Kraus H-C (2006) Englische Verfassung und politisches Denken im Ancien Régime: 1689 bis 1789. Oldenbourg, München

Krippner GR (2005) The financialization of the American economy. Socio Econ Rev 3(2):173–208

Kuhn TS (1970) The structure of scientific revolutions, 2nd edn. The University of Chicago Press, Chicago

Kunisch J (1999) Absolutismus: Europäische Geschichte vom Westfälischen Frieden bis zur Krise des Ancien Régime, 2nd edn. Vandenhoeck & Ruprecht, Göttingen

Kurz HD, Sturn R (2012) Schumpeter für jedermann: Von der Rastlosigkeit des Kapitalismus. Frankfurter Allg. Buch, Frankfurt a. M.

Kurz HD, Sturn R (2013) Adam Smith für jedermann: Pionier der modernen Ökonomie. Frankfurter Allg. Buch, Frankfurt a. M.

Laidler D (1981) Adam Smith as a monetary economist. Can J Econ 14(2):185–200

Laidler DEW (1991) The golden age of the quantity theory: the development of neoclassical monetary economics 1870–1914. Allan, New York

Laidler DEW (2000) Highlights of the bullionist controversy. University of Western Ontario, Dept. of Economics Research Report, 2000-2

Landes DS (1949) French entrepreneurship and industrial growth in the nineteenth century. J Econ Hist 9(1):45–61

Langewiesche D (1988) Deutscher Liberalismus im europäischen Vergleich: Konzeption und Ergebnisse. In: Langewiesche D (ed) Liberalismus im 19. Jahrhundert: Deutschland im europäischen Vergleich. Vandenhoeck & Ruprecht, Göttingen, pp 11–19

Langholm O (1998) The legacy of scholasticism in economic thought: antecedents of choice and power. Cambridge University Press, Cambridge

Langholm O (2008) Scholastic economics. In: Durlauf SN, Blume LE (eds) The new Palgrave dictionary of economics: real balances—stochastic volatility models. Palgrave Macmillan, Basingstoke, pp 305–308

Lasker L (1871) Bankfreiheit oder nicht? Mit besonderer Rücksicht auf Preussen und Deutschland. Julius Springer, Berlin

Lattes E (1869) La Libertà delle Banche a Venezia dal secolo XIII. al XVII. secondo i documenti inediti del R. Archivio dei Frari, con due orazioni contro e per la libertà e pluralità delle banche pronunciate negli anni 1584–1587 dal Senatore Veneziano T. Contarini. Ricerche storiche, etc, Milano

Law & John ([1705] 1750) Money and trade considered: with a proposal for supplying the nation with money. R. & A. Foulis, Glasgow

Lazarsfeld PF, Berelson B, Gaudet H (1944) The people's choice: how the voter makes up his mind in a presidential campaign. Duelle Sloan and Pearce, New York

Leach R (2015) Political ideology in Britain, 3rd edn. Palgrave Macmillan, Basingstoke

Lebaron F, Dogan A (2016) Do central bankers' biographies matter? Sociologica 2

Lee WR (1988) Economic development and the state in nineteenth-century Germany. Econ Hist Rev 41(3):346–367

Leighton WA, López EJ (2014) Madmen, intellectuals, and academic scribblers: the economic engine of political change. Stanford University Press, Stanford

Lemberg E (1950) Geschichte des Nationalismus in Europa. Schwab, Stuttgart

Lenin VI ([1917] 1999) Imperialism, the highest stage of capitalism. Resistance Books, Chippendale

Lepsius MR (2009) Interessen, Ideen und Institutionen, 2nd edn. VS Verl. für Sozialwissenschaften, Wiesbaden

Levi-Faur D (1997) Economic nationalism: from Friedrich list to Robert Reich. Rev Int Stud 23(3):359–370

Levi-Faur D (1997) Friedrich list and the political economy of the nation-state. Rev Int Polit Econ 4(1):154–178

Lieberman RC (2002) Ideas, institutions, and political order: explaining political change. Am Polit Sci Rev 96(4):697–712

Liepmann L (1933) Der Kampf um die Gestaltung der englischen Währungsverfassung: Von der ersten bis zur zweiten Peel's-Act, 1819–1844. Junker u. Dünnhaupt, Berlin

Liesse A (1909) Evolution of credit and banks in France: from the founding of the bank of France to the present time. US Government Printing Office, Washington DC

List F (1838) Das deutsche National-Transport-System in volks- und staatswirthschaftlicher Beziehung beleuchtet. Hammerich, Altona

List, F. ([1841] 1909) The national system of political economy. Longmans, Green and Co, New York

Locke J ([1691] 1824) Some considerations of the consequences of lowering the interest, and raising the value of money. In: Locke J (ed) Economic writings and two treatises of government, vol IV, 12 edn. Rivington, London, pp 1–116

Locke J ([1689] 1824) Two treatises of government. In Locke J (ed) Economic writings and two treatises of government, vol IV, 12th ed. Rivington, London, pp 207–495

Loftus D (2002) Capital and community: limited liability and attempts to democratize the market in mid-nineteenth-century England. Victorian Stud 45(1):93–120

Lopez R (1998) The commercial revolution of the middle ages, 950–1350. Cambridge University Press, Cambridge

Lugard FJD (1893) Uganda: with chapters on administration-past and future, and suggestions for dealing with the country. Blackwood, Edinburgh

Luxemburg R ([1913] 2003) The accumulation of capital. Routledge, London

MacKenzie D, Muniesa F, Siu L (eds) (2007) Do economists make markets? On the performativity of economics. Princeton University Press, Princeton

MacKenzie DA (2006) An engine, not a camera: how financial models shape markets. MIT Press, Cambridge

Maine HS (1886) Popular government: four essays. H. Holt, New York

Majumdar MA (2007) Postcoloniality: the French dimension. Berghahn Books, New York

Malipiero D (1844) Annali veneti dall'anno 1457 al 1500. Archivio Storico Italiano, Firenze

Maloney RP (1973) The teaching of the fathers on usury: an historical study on the development of christian thinking. Vigiliae Christianae 27(4):241–265

Malthus TR (1798) An essay on the principle of population, as it affects the future improvement of society: with remarks on the speculations of Mr. Godwin, M. Condorcet and other writers. J. Johnson, London

Malthus TR (1811) Depreciation of paper currency. Edinb Rev 1811:340–372

Mann M (2012) The sources of social power. Cambridge University Press, Cambridge

Mannheim K (1952) Essays on the sociology of knowledge. Routledge & Kegan Paul, London

Mannheim K ([1925] 1952) The problem of a sociology of knowledge. In: Kecskemeti P (ed) Essays on the sociology of knowledge. Routledge & Kegan Paul, London, pp 134–190

Marcuse H (1964) One-dimensional man: studies in the ideology of advanced industrial society. Beacon Press, Boston

Marengo E, Manfroni C, Pessagno G (1911) Il banco di San Giorgio. Donath, Genova
Marsh D (2009) Keeping ideas in their place: in praise of thin constructivism. Aust J Polit Sci 44(4):679–696
Marsilio C (2013) Genoese finance, 1348–1700. In: Arner DW, Caprio G (eds) Handbook of key global financial markets, institutions, and infrastructure. Academic Press, London, pp 123–132
Martines L (1968) Political conflict in the Italian city states. Govern Opp 3(1):69–91
Martines L (1988) Power and imagination: city-states in Renaissance Italy. Johns Hopkins University Press, Baltimore
Marx K ([1847] 1892) The poverty of philosophy. Foreign Languages Publ. House, Moscow
Marx K ([1867] 1977) Capital: a critique of political economy. The process of production of capital. vol I. Lawrence & Wishart, London
Marx K ([1885] 1977) Capital: a critique of political economy. The process of circulation of capital. vol II. Lawrence and Wishart, London
Marx K (1902) Wage, labor and capital. New York labor news company, New York
Marx K ([1894] 1984) Capital: a critique of political economy. The process of capitalist production as a whole, vol III. Lawrence & Wishart, London
Marx K, Engels F ([1846] 1970) The German ideology. With selections from parts two and three, together with Marx's "Introduction to a critique of political economy." International Publishers, New York
Marx K, Engels F ([1847–1894] 1972) On colonies, industrial monopoly and working class movement: extract from articles and letters 1847–1894. Futura, Copenhagen
Mason ES (1931) Saint-Simonism and the rationalisation of industry. Q J Econ 45(4):640–683
Mattingly G (1955) Renaissance diplomacy. Houghton Mifflin, Boston
Mauer H (1907) Das landschaftliche Kreditwesen Preußens agrargeschichtlich und volkswirtschaftlich betrachtet: Ein Beitrag zur Geschichte der Bodenkreditpolitik des preußischen Staates. Trübner, Straßburg
Mayeur J-M, Rebérioux M (1984) The third republic from its origins to the great war: 1871–1914. Cambridge University Press, Cambridge
McCloskey DN (2016) Bourgeois equality: how ideas, not capital or institutions, enriched the world. University of Chicago Press, Chicago
McMillan JF (1991) Napoleon III. Longman, London
McNamara KR (1999) The currency of ideas: monetary politics in the European Union. Cornell University Press, Ithaca
Mehrens B (1911) Die Entstehung und Entwicklung der grossen französischen Kreditinstitute: Mit Berücksichtigung ihres Einflusses auf die wirtschaftliche Entwicklung Frankreichs. J.G. Cotta, Stuttgart
Mehta J (2011) The varied roles of ideas in politics: from "Whether" to "How". In: Béland D, Cox RH (eds) Ideas and politics in social science research. Oxford University Press, Oxford, pp 23–46
Mehta US (1999) Liberalism and empire: India in British liberal thought. Oxford University Press, New Delhi
Menger C (1900) Geld. Handwörterbuch der Staatswissenschaften 1900:60–106
Menton B (1947) Theories of adjustment of the balance of payments under fixed exchanges. J Stat Soc Inq Soc Ireland 18:25–41
Merton RK (1968) Social theory and social structure. The Free Press, New York
Meserve M (2008) Empires of Islam in Renaissance historical thought. Harvard University Press, Cambridge
Meyer JW (1977) The effects of education as an institution. Am J Sociol 83(1):55–77

Meyer JW, Boli J, Thomas GM (1994) Ontology and rationalization in the western cultural account. In: Scott WR, Meyer JW (eds) Institutional environments and organizations: structural complexity and individualism. Sage, Thousand Oaks, pp 9–28

Meyer JW, Boli J, Thomas GM, Ramirez FO (1997) World society and the nation-state. Am J Sociol 103(1):144–181

Meyer JW, Rowan B (1977) Institutionalized organizations: formal structure as myth and ceremony. Am J Sociol 83(2):340–363

Meyer JW, Scott WR (1985) Organizational environments: ritual and rationality. Sage, Beverly Hills

Mielants E (2000) Perspectives on the origins of merchant capitalism in Europe. Review (Fernand Braudel Center) 23(2):229–292

Mill JS ([1848] 1965a) The principles of political economy: with some of their applications to social philosophy. In: Robson JM (ed) Collected Works of John Stuart Mill, vol III. University of Toronto Press, Toronto

Mill JS ([1848] 1965b) The principles of political economy: with some of their applications to social philosophy. In: Robson JM (ed) Collected works of John Stuart Mill, vol II. University of Toronto Press, Toronto

Mill JS ([1845] 1967) The claims of labour. In: Robson JM (ed) Collected works of John Stuart Mill. Essays on economics and society, vol IV. University of Toronto Press, Toronto, pp 363–389

Mill JS ([1850] 1967) The savings of the middle and working classes. In: Robson JM (ed) Collected works of John Stuart Mill. Essays on economics and society, vol V. University of Toronto Press, Toronto, pp 405–429

Mill JS ([1861] 1977) Considerations on representative government. In: Robson JM (ed) Collected works of John Stuart Mill. Essays on politics and society, vol XIX. University of Toronto Press, Toronto, pp 371–613

Mill JS ([1873] 1981) Autobiography. In: Robson JM (ed) Collected works of John Stuart Mill. Autobiography and literary essays, vol I. J. Stillinger. University of Toronto Press, Toronto, pp 5–290

Mill JS ([1859] 1984) A few words on non-intervention. In: Robson JM (ed) Collected works of John Stuart Mill. Essays on equality, law, and education, vol XXI. University of Toronto Press, Toronto, pp 109–124

Mints LW (1945) A history of banking theory: in Great Britain and the United States. University of Chicago Pr, Chicago

Mintz B, Schwartz M (1981) Interlocking directorates and interest group formation. Am Sociol Rev 46(6):851–869

Miskimin HA (1977) The economy of later Renaissance Europe, 1460–1600. Cambridge University Press, Cambridge

Mitchell A (2000) The great train race: railways and the Franco-German Rivalry, 1815–1914. Berghahn Books, New York

Mokyr J (2017) A culture of growth: the origins of the modern economy. Princeton University Press, Princeton

Molho A (1995) The state and public finance: a hypothesis based on the history of late Medieval Florence. J Modern Hist 67:97–135

Mommsen H (1979) Arbeiterbewegung und nationale Frage: Ausgewählte Aufsätze. Vandenhoeck & Ruprecht, Göttingen

Morgan EV (2013) The theory and practice of central banking, 1797–1913. Cambridge University Press, Cambridge

Mosca G (1939) The ruling class. McGraw-Hill, New York

Moster A, Vogler B (1996) France. In: Mura J (ed) History of European savings banks. Dt. Sparkassenverlag, Stuttgart, pp 75–104

Muckle F (1906) Saint-Simon und die ökonomische Geschichtstheorie: Ein Beitrag zu einer Dogmengeschichte des historischen Materialismus. Fischer, Jena

Muckle F (1908) Henri de Saint-Simon: Die Persönlichkeit und ihr Werk. Fischer, Jena

Mueller RC (1997) Money and banking in Medieval and Renaissance Venice: banks, panics, and the public debt, 1200–1500. John Hopkins University Press, Baltimore

Muhs R (1988) Deutscher und britischer Liberalismus im Vergleich: Trägerschichten, Zielvorstellungen und Rahmenbedingungen (ca. 1830–1870). In: Langewiesche D (ed) Liberalismus im 19. Jahrhundert: Deutschland im europäischen Vergleich. Vandenhoeck & Ruprecht, Göttingen, pp 223–259

Mukand SW, Rodrik D (2015) The political economy of liberal democracy. Centre for economic policy research development Discussion Paper, 10808

Müller J (2016) Bestimmbare Unbestimmtheiten: Skizze einer indeterministischen Soziologie. Wilhelm Fink, Paderborn

Müller V (1991) Staatstätigkeit in den Staatstheorien des 19. Jahrhunderts. Westdt. Verl, Opladen

Mun T ([1664] 1895) England's treasure by forraign trade. Macmillan, New York, London

Münnich S (2010) Interessen und Ideen: Die Entstehung der Arbeitslosenversicherung in Deutschland und den USA. Campus-Verl, Frankfurt a. M.

Munro JH (2003) The medieval origins of the financial revolution: usury, rentes, and negotiability. Int Hist Rev 25(3):505–562

Mura J (1996) Germany. In: Mura J (ed) History of European savings banks. Dt. Sparkassenverlag, Stuttgart, pp 105–132

Murphy, A. (1948) The ideology of French Imperialism 1871–1881. Washington DC, Catholic Univ. of America, Diss., 1948

Murphy AE (1997) Introduction. In: Murphy AE (ed) Monetary theory: 1601–1758. Routledge, London, pp 1–54

Murphy AE (1997) John Law: economic theorist and policy-maker. Clarendon Press, Oxford

Nasse E (1866) Die preußische Bank und die Ausdehnung ihres Geschäftskreises in Deutschland. Marcus, Bonn

Navaretti GB (ed) (1998) Creation and transfer of knowledge: institutions and incentives. Springer-Verlag, Berlin

Neal L (1990) The rise of financial capitalism: international capital markets in the age of reason. Cambridge University Press, Cambridge

Nelson RR, Winter SG (2004) An evolutionary theory of economic change. The Belknap Press of Harvard University Press, Cambridge

Neuberger H, Stokes HH (1974) German banks and German growth, 1883–1913: an empirical view. J Econ Hist 34(3):710–731

Newman FW (1851) Lectures on political economy. John Chapman, London

Newton L (2003) Government, the banks and industry in inter-war Britain. In: Gourvish TR (ed) Business and politics in Europe, 1900–1970: essays in honour of Alice Teichova. Cambridge University Press, Cambridge, pp 145–168

North DC (2005) Understanding the process of economic change. Princeton University Press, Princeton

North DC, Weingast BR (1989) Constitutions and commitment: the evolution of institutions governing public choice in seventeenth-century England. J Econ Hist 49(4):803–832

North M (2013) Hanseatic merchants and credit, 1300–1700. In: Arner DW, Caprio G (eds) Handbook of key global financial markets, institutions, and infrastructure. Academic Press, London, pp 161–167

O'Brien P (ed) (1983) Railways and the economic development of Western Europe, 1830–1914. Macmillan, London

Obst G (1930) Das Bankgeschäft: Bankpolitik. Poeschel, Stuttgart

Oliver PE, Johnston H (2000) What a good idea! Frames and ideologies in social movement research. Mobil Int Q 5(1):37–54

Olson M (1965) The logic of collective action: public goods and the theory of groups. Harvard University Press, Cambridge

O'Rourke KH, La Prados de Escosura L, Daudin G (2010) Trade and empire. In: Broadberry S, ORourke KH (eds) The Cambridge economic history of modern Europe. Cambridge University Press, Cambridge, pp 96–121

Ostrom E (2011) Governing the commons: the evolution of institutions for collective action, 29th edn. Cambridge University Press, Cambridge

Overstone SJL (1837) Reflections suggested by a perusal of Mr. J. Horsley Palmer's Pamphlet: on the causes and consequences of the pressure on the money market. P. Richardson, London

Palloni A (2001) Diffusion in sociological analysis. In: Casterline JB (ed) Diffusion processes and fertility transition: selected perspectives. National Academy Press, Washington, D.C., pp 66–114

Parnell H (1827) Observations on paper money, banking and overtrading which explain the scotch system of banking, 2nd edn. Printed for James R. Piccadilly, London

Parsons T (1949) The structure of social action: a study in social theory with special reference to a group of recent European writers, 2nd edn. The Free Press, Glencoe

Parsons T (1951) The social system. The Free Press, Glencoe

Paterson W (1694) A brief account of the intended bank of England. Randal Taylor, London

Paul EF (1979) Moral revolution and economic science: The demise of Laissez-Faire in nineteenth-century British political economy. Greenwood Press, Westport

Péreire I (2010) Industry: fourth lesson given in the Athenee Hall. In: Jacoud G (ed) Political economy and industrialism: banks in Saint-Simonian economic thought. Routledge, London, pp 134–146

Petermann T (1979) Claude-Henri de Saint-Simon, die Gesellschaft als Werkstatt. Duncker & Humblot, Berlin

Peters BG (1999) Institutional theory in political science: the 'New Institutionalism'. Pinter, London

Petty W ([1676] 1899) Political Arithmetick. In: Hull CH (ed) The economic writings of Sir William Petty, vol I. Cambridge University Press, pp 233–313

Pezzolo L (2007) Government debts and credit markets in Renaissance Italy. University Ca' Foscari of Venice, Department of Economics Research Paper, 05-07

Pezzolo L (2008) Government debts and credit markets in Renaissance Italy. In: Caselli PF (ed) Government debts and financial markets in Europe. Pickering & Chatto, London, pp 17–32

Pierce JJ, Peterson HL, Hicks KC (2017) Policy change: an advocacy coalition framework perspective. Policy Stud J 26(1):73

Pierson P (2004) Politics in time: history, institutions, and social analysis. Princeton University Press, Princeton

Pigou AC (1920) The economics of welfare. Macmillan, London

Pilbeam PM (1990) The middle classes in Europe, 1789–1914: France, Germany, Italy, and Russia. Lyceum Books, Chicago

Pilbeam PM (2014) Saint-Simonians in nineteenth-century France: from free love to Algeria. Palgrave Macmillan, Basingstoke

Pincus SCA (1996) Protestantism and patriotism: ideologies and the making of English Foreign Policy, 1650–1668. Cambridge University Press, Cambridge

Pincus SCA (2009) 1688: the first modern revolution. Yale University Press, New Haven
Pirenne H (1937) Economic and social history of Medieval Europe. Kegan Paul Trench Trubner & Co, London
Pitts J (2000) Empire and democracy: Tocqueville and the Algeria question. J Polit Philos 8(3):295–318
Pitts J (2005) A turn to empire: the rise of imperial liberalism in Britain and France. Princeton University Press, Princeton
Plenge J (1903) Gründung und Geschichte des Crédit Mobilier: Zwei Kapitel aus Anlagebanken; eine Einleitung in die Theorie des Anlagebankgeschäftes. Laupp, Tübingen
Plessis A (1994) The history of banks in France. In: Pohl M (ed) Handbook on the history of European banks. Elgar, Aldershot
Pohl M (1986) Entstehung und Entwicklung des Universalbankensystems: Konzentration und Krise als wichtige Faktoren. F. Knapp, Frankfurt a. M.
Pohl M (ed) (1994) Handbook on the history of European banks. Elgar, Aldershot
Pojani D, Stead D (2014) Ideas, interests, and institutions: explaining Dutch transit-oriented development challenges. Environ Plan A 46(10):2401–2418
Polillo S, Guillén MF (2005) Globalization pressures and the state: the worldwide spread of central bank independence. Am J Sociol 110(6):1764–1802
Pollard S (1964) Fixed capital in the industrial revolution in Britain. J Econ Hist 24(3):299–314
Porter A (1999) Religion, missionary enthusiasm, and empire. In: Porter A, Louis WR (eds) The Oxford history of the British empire, vol III. OUP Oxford, Oxford
Postan MM (1928) Credit in medieval trade. Econ Hist Rev 1(2):234–261
Potter W (1650) The key of wealth: or, a new way for improving of trade. R.A to be sold by Nicolas Bourne, London
Pratt JT (1842) The history of savings banks in England, Wales, Ireland, and Scotland: with the period of the establishment of each institution, the place where it is held, and the number of depositors, classed according to the latest official returns. Printed for the author by Shaw and Sons, London
Pressnell LS (1956) Country banking in the industrial revolution. Clarendon Press, Oxford
Price R (1997) Napoleon III and the second empire. Routledge, London
Ratzenhofer G (1898) Die sociologische Erkenntnis: Positive Philosophie des socialen Lebens. Brockhaus, Leipzig
Redlich F (1948) Jacques Laffitte and the beginnings of investment banking in France. Bull Bus Hist Soc 22(4/6):137–161
Reeves R (2008) John Stuart Mill: Victorian Firebrand. Atlantic Books, London
Ricardo D ([1810] 2005) High price of bullion. A proof of the depreciation of bank notes. In: Sraffa P (ed) The works and correspondence of David Ricardo. Pamphlets and Papers 1809–1811, vol III. Liberty Fund, Indianapolis, pp 47–127
Ricardo D ([1817] 2005) On the principles of political economy and taxation. In: Sraffa P (ed) The works and correspondence of David Ricardo. On the principles of political economy and taxation, vol I. Liberty Fund, Indianapolis
Ricardo D ([1823] 2005a) Plan for the establishment of a national bank. In: Sraffa P (ed) The works and correspondence of David Ricardo. Pamphlets and Papers 1815–1823, vol IV. Liberty Fund, Indianapolis, pp 271–300
Ricardo D ([1823] 2005b) Usury laws Repeal Bill. In: Sraffa P (ed) The works and correspondence of David Ricardo. Speeches and evidence, 1815–1823, vol V. Liberty Fund, Indianapolis, p 323
Richards RD (1965) The early history of banking in England. Kelley, New York
Richter M (1963) Tocqueville on Algeria. Rev Politics 25(3):362–398

Riemersma JC (1952) Usury restrictions in a mercantile economy. Can J Econ Polit Sci 18(1):17–26

Riesser J (1912) Die deutschen Grossbanken und ihre Konzentration im Zusammenhang mit der Entwicklung der Gesamtwirtschaft in Deutschland, 4th edn. Fischer, Jena

Roberds W, Velde FR (2014) Early public banks. Federal Reserve Bank of Chicago Working papers, 2014-03

Robertson TS (1967) The process of innovation and the diffusion of innovation. J Mark 31(1):14–19

Rodrik D (2014) When ideas trump interests: preferences, worldviews, and policy innovations. J Econ Persp 28(1):189–208

Rogers EM (1983) Diffusion of innovations, 3rd edn. The Free Press, New York

Rohrschneider R (1993) Impact of social movements on European party systems. Ann Am Acad Polit Soc Sci 528:157–170

Roll E (1974) A history of economic thought, 4th edn. Faber and Faber, London

Ross EA (1905) Social control: a survey of the foundations of order. Macmillan, New York

Rostow WW (1962) The process of economic growth, 2nd edn. Clarendon Press, Oxford

Roth G (1987) Politische Herrschaft und persönliche Freiheit: Heidelberger Max Weber-Vorlesungen 1983. Suhrkamp, Frankfurt a. M.

Rothbard MN (1995) Classical economics. Edward Elgar, Cheltenham

Rothbard MN (1995) Economic thought before Adam Smith. Edward Elgar, Cheltenham

Rowlands G (2002) The dynastic state and the army under Louis XIV: royal service and private interest 1661–1701. Cambridge University Press, Cambridge

Rubini D (1970) Politics and the battle for the banks, 1688–1697. Eng Hist Rev 85(337):693–714

Rubinstein WD (1983) The end of "Old Corruption" in Britain 1780–1860. Past Present 101:55–86

Saage R (1996) Zur Konvergenz von kontraktualistischem und utopischem Denken in Johann Gottlieb Fichtes Der geschlossene Handelsstaat. In: Neugebauer-Wölk M, Saage R (eds) Die Politisierung des Utopischen im 18. Jahrhundert: Vom utopischen Systementwurf zum Zeitalter der Revolution. Niemeyer, Tübingen, pp 52–68

Sabatier PA (1988) An advocacy coalition framework of policy change and the role of policy-oriented learning therein. Policy Sci 21(2/3):129–168

Sabatier PA (2011) The advocacy coalition framework: revisions and relevance for Europe. J Eur Public Policy 5(1):98–130

Sabatier PA, Weible CM (2009) The advocacy coalition framework: innovations and clarifications. In: Sabatier PA (ed) Theories of the policy process, 2nd edn. Westview Press, Boulder, pp 189–220

Saint-Simon H (1823) Catéchisme des Industriels. Imprimerie de Setier, Paris

De Saint-Simon H ([1821] 1998) Du Système Industriel. Verl. Wirtschaft und Finanzen, Düsseldorf

Salomon-Delatour G ([1919] 2011) Schriften. VS Verl. für Sozialwiss, Wiesbaden

Samuelson PA (1938) A note on the pure theory of consumer's behaviour. Economica 5(17):61–71

Samuelson PA (1948) Consumption theory in terms of revealed preference. Economica 15(60):243–253

Samuelson PA (1948) Economics: an introductory analysis. McGraw-Hill, New York

Sanders E (2008) Historical institutionalism. In: Rhodes RAW, Binder SA, Rockman BA (eds) The Oxford handbook of political institutions. Oxford University Press, Oxford, pp 39–54

Satō Y, Takenaga S (2013) Ricardo on money and finance: a bicentenary Reappraisal. Routledge, Abingdon

Saville J (1956) Sleeping partnership and limited liability, 1850–1856. Econ Hist Rev 8(3):418–433

Schapiro SJ (1976) Was ist Liberalismus? In: Gall L (ed) Liberalismus. Kiepenheuer & Witsch, Köln, pp 20–36
Schauer C (1912) Die Preußische Bank: Unter Benutzung amtlicher Quellen. Münter, Halle a. S
Scheler M ([1926] 1960) Die Wissensformen und die Gesellschaft. In: Scheler M (ed) Gesammelte Werke. Die Wissensformen und die Gesellschaft, vol VIII, 2nd edn. Francke, Bern
Scheler M ([1923] 1963) Moralia. In: Scheler M (ed) Gesammelte Werke. Schriften zur Soziologie und Weltanschauungslehre, vol VI. Francke, Bern, pp 9–114
Schickler E (2001) Disjointed pluralism: institutional innovation and the development of the U.S. Congress. Princeton University Press, Princeton
Schimank U (1996) Theorien gesellschaftlicher Differenzierung. Leske & Budrich, Opladen
Schimank U (2010) Gesellschaftliche Differenzierungsdynamiken – ein Fünf-Fronten-Kampf. In: Greve J (ed) Soziale Differenzierung: Erkenntnisgewinne handlungs- und systemtheoretischer Zugänge. VS Verl. für Sozialwissenschaften, Wiesbaden, pp 261–284
Schmidt G (1976) Politischer Liberalismus,Landed Interests' und Organisierte Arbeiterschaft, 1850–1880. In: Gall L (ed) Liberalismus. Kiepenheuer & Witsch, Köln, pp 232–253
Schmidt VA (2002) Does discourse matter in the politics of welfare state adjustment? Comp Polit Stud 35(2):168–193
Schmidt VA (2008) Discursive institutionalism: the explanatory power of ideas and discourse. Ann Rev Polit Sci 11(1):303–326
Schmidt VA, Radaelli CM (2004) Policy change and discourse in Europe: conceptual and methodological issues. West Eur Polit 27(2):183–210
Schmidt VA, Thatcher M (eds) (2013) Resilient liberalism in Europe's political economy. Cambridge University Press, Cambridge
Schmoeckel M, Maetschke M (2008) Rechtsgeschichte der Wirtschaft: Seit dem 19. Jahrhundert. Mohr Siebeck, Tübingen
Schmoller G (1916) Die Handels- und Zollannäherung Mitteleuropas. Schmollers Jahrbuch für Gesetzgebung, Verwaltung und Volkswirtschaft 40:529–550
Schnabel I, Shin HS (2006) The 'Kipper- und Wipperzeit' and the foundation of public deposit banks. Unpublished
Von Schröder W ([1686] 1737) Fürstliche Schatz- und Rent-Cammer: Nebst seinem Tractat vom Goldmachen, wie auch vom Ministrissimo oder Staats-Bedienten. Eckart, Leipzig und Königsberg
Schubert ES (1988) Innovations, debts, and bubbles: international integration of financial markets in Western Europe, 1688–1720. J Econ Hist 48(2):299–306
Schumpeter JA ([1911] 1934) The theory of economic development: an inquiry into profits, capital, credit, interest, and the business cycle. Harvard University Press, Cambridge
Schumpeter JA ([1939] 1989) Business cycles: a theoretical, historical and statistical analysis of the capitalist process. Porcupine Press, Philadelphia
Scott T (2014) The city-state in Europe, 1000–1600: hinterland, territory region. Oxford University Press, Oxford
Scott WR (2014) Institutions and organizations: ideas, interests and identities, 4th edn. Sage, Thousand Oaks
Scott WR, Meyer JW (eds) (1994) Institutional environments and organizations: structural complexity and individualism. Sage, Thousand Oaks
Screpanti E, Zamagni S (2005) An outline of the history of economic thought, 2nd edn. Oxford University Press, Oxford
Seaman JW (1978) L. T. Hobhouse and the theory of "Social Liberalism". Can J Polit Sci 11(4):777–801
Sée H ([1928] 2004) Modern capitalism: its origin and evolution. Batoche Books, Kitchener

Sée H (1936) Französische Wirtschaftsgeschichte. Fischer, Jena

Seidenzahl F (1961) Bismarck und die Gründung der Darmstädter Bank. Tradition Zeitschrift für Firmengeschichte und Unternehmerbiographie 6(6):252–259

Sen A (1973) Behaviour and the concept of preference. Economica 40(159):241–259

Sen AK (1977) Rational fools: a critique of the behavioral foundations of economic theory. Phil Public Aff 1977:317–344

Sheehan JJ (1976) Liberalismus und Gesellschaft in Deutschland 1815–1848. In: Gall L (ed) Liberalismus. Kiepenheuer & Witsch, Köln, pp 208–231

Sheehan JJ (1978) German liberalism in the nineteenth century. University of Chicago Press, Chicago

Shepsle KA (2008) Rational choice institutionalism. In: Rhodes RAW, Binder SA, Rockman BA (eds) The Oxford handbook of political institutions. Oxford University Press, Oxford, pp 23–38

Sigmund S (2014) Begriffe: Ideen und Interessen. In: Müller H-P, Sigmund S (eds) Max Weber-Handbuch: Leben, Werk, Wirkung. J.B. Metzler, Stuttgart, pp 66–69

Sikkink K (1991) Ideas and institutions: developmentalism in Brazil and Argentina. Cornell University Press, Ithaca

Silberling NJ (1923) British prices and business cycles, 1779–1850. Rev Econ Stat 5:222–261

Silberling NJ (1924) Financial and monetary policy of Great Britain during the Napoleonic Wars. Harvard University Press, Cambridge

Simmel G (1905) Die Probleme der Geschichtsphilosophie: Eine erkenntnistheoretische Studie, 2nd edn. Duncker & Humblot, Leipzig

Simmel G ([1905] 1957) Fashion. Am J Sociol 62(6):541–558

Simmel G ([1908] 2009) Sociology: inquiries into the construction of social forms. Brill, Leiden

Sinclair J (1826) The late prosperity, and the present adversity of the country, explained: the proper remedies considered, and the comparative merits of the English and Scottish systems of banking discussed. J. Ridgeway, London

Small AW (1905) General sociology: an exposition of the main development in sociological theory from Spencer to Ratzenhofer. The University of Chicago Press, Chicago

Smith A ([1759] 1853) The theory of moral sentiments: or, an essay towards an analysis of the principles by which men naturally judge concerning the conduct and character, first of their neighbours, and afterwards of themselves. Bohn, London

Smith A (1776) An inquiry into the nature and causes of the wealth of nations. Reprints of Economic Classics

Smith M (2011) Thomas Tooke and the monetary thought of classical economics. Taylor & Francis, Hoboken

Smith MS (2006) The emergence of modern business enterprise in France, 1800–1930. Harvard University Press, Cambridge

Smith VC (1936) The rationale of central banking. King, London

Smith WD (1978) The German colonial empire. University of North Carolina Press, Chapel Hill

Society for the Suppression of Beggars (1815) Third Report of the Suppression of Beggars. Edinburgh

Sokoloff KL (1984) Investment in fixed and working capital during early industrialization: evidence from U.S. manufacturing firms. J Econ Hist 44(2):545–556

Sombart W (1913) Der Bourgeois: Zur Geistesgeschichte der modernen Wirtschaftsmenschen. Duncker & Humblot, München

Sombart W (1928) Das europäische Wirtschaftsleben im Zeitalter des Frühkapitalismus. Duncker & Humblot, München

Sombart W (1928) Das Wirtschaftsleben im Zeitalter des Hochkapitalismus. Duncker & Humblot, München

Sommer A (1934) Geistesgeschichte der deutschen Sparkassen im Aufriß. Jahrbücher für Nationalökonomie und Statistik 1934:663–698
Sommerville JP (1991) Absolutism and royalism. In: Burns JH, Goldie M (eds) The Cambridge history of political thought: 1450–1700. Cambridge University Press, Cambridge, pp 347–367
Sommerville JP (2012) Early modern absolutism in practice and theory. In: Cuttica C, Burgess G (eds) Monarchism and absolutism in early modern Europe. Pickering & Chatto, London, pp 117–130
Spree R (1977) Die Wachstumszyklen der deutschen Wirtschaft von 1840 bis 1880: Mit einem konjunkturstatistischen Anhang. Duncker & Humblot, Berlin
Stasavage D (2011) States of credit: size, power, and the development of European polities. Princeton University Press, Princeton
Stearns LB, Mizruchi MS (2005) Banking, and financial markets. The handbook of economic sociology, 2nd edn. Princeton University Press, Princeton, pp 284–306
Steele ED (1991) Palmerston and liberalism, 1855–1865. Cambridge University Press, Cambridge
Steinmo S (2010) The evolution of modern states: Sweden, Japan, and the United States. Cambridge University Press, Cambridge
Steltzer HG (1984) Die Deutschen und ihr Kolonialreich. Societäts-Verl, Frankfurt a. M.
Stephan W (1966) 100 Jahre liberale Parteien 1866–1966. In: Luchtenberg P, Erbe W (eds) Geschichte des deutschen Liberalismus. Westdt. Verl, Köln, pp 61–163
Stern FR (2008) Gold und Eisen: Bismarck und sein Bankier Bleichröder. Beck, München
Stiglitz JE (1997) Economics, 2nd edn. Norton, New York
Strang D, Meyer JW (1993) Institutional conditions for diffusion. Theory Soc 22(4):487–511
Streeck W, Höpner M (eds) (2003) Alle Macht dem Markt? Fallstudien zur Abwicklung der Deutschland AG. Campus-Verl, Frankfurt a. M.
Sullivan EP (1983) Liberalism and imperialism: J. S. Mill's defense of the British Empire. J Hist Ideas 44(4):599–617
Sulzbach W (1959) Imperialismus und Nationalbewusstsein. Europ. Verl.-Anstalt, Frankfurt a. M.
Surel Y (2000) The role of cognitive and normative frames in policy-making. J Eur Public Policy 7(4):495–512
Swedberg R (2003) Principles of economic sociology. Princeton University Press, Princeton
Swedberg R (2005) Can there be a sociological concept of interest? Theory Soc 34(4):359–390
Swedberg R (2005) Interest. Open University Press, Maidenhead
Swenson P (2002) Capitalists against markets: the making of labor markets and welfare states in the United States and Sweden. Oxford University Press, Oxford
Sykes A (1997) The rise and fall of British liberalism: 1776–1988. Longman, London
Sznajd-Weron K (2005) Sznajd model and its applications. Acta Phys Pol 36(8):2537–2547
Tabellini G (2008) Presidential address institutions and culture. J Eur Econ Assoc 6(2–3):255–294
Tabellini G (2010) Culture and institutions: economic development in the regions of Europe. J Eur Econ Assoc 8(4):677–716
Tames R (1972) Economy and society in nineteenth-century Britain. Allen & Unwin, London
Tawney RH (1925) Historical introduction to Thomas Wilson's discourse upon usury. In: Tawney RH (ed) discourse upon usury: by way of dialogue and orations, for the better variety and more delight of all those that shall read this treatise. Bell, London, S 1–172
Tawney RH (1948) Religion and the rise of capitalism: a historical study. Penguin Books, West Drayton
Taylor J (2006) Creating capitalism: joint-stock enterprise in British politics and culture 1800–1870. Boydell Press, Suffolk

Teichova A, Kurgan-van Hentenryk G, Ziegler D (eds) (1997) Banking, trade, and industry: Europe, America, and Asia from the thirteenth to the twentieth century. Cambridge University Press, Cambridge

Tellkampf JL (1867) Die Prinzipien des Geld- und Bankwesens. Springer, Berlin

Thelen K, Conran J (2016) Institutional change. In: Fioretos K-O, Falleti TG, Sheingate AD (eds) The Oxford handbook of historical institutionalism. Oxford University Press, Oxford, pp 51–70

Thelen K, Steinmo S (1992) Historical institutionalism in comparative politics. In: Steinmo S, Thelen K, Longstreth F (eds) Structuring politics. Cambridge University Press, Cambridge, pp 1–32

Then V (1997) Eisenbahnen und Eisenbahnunternehmer in der Industriellen Revolution: Ein preußisch/deutsch-englischer Vergleich. Vandenhoeck & Ruprecht, Göttingen

Thier E (1930) Rodbertus, Lassalle, Adolph Wagner: Ein Beitrag zur Theorie und Geschichte des deutschen Staatssozialismus. Fischer, Jena

Thornton H (1802) An enquiry into the nature and effects of the paper credit of Great Britain. J. Hatchard, London

Tilly RH (1966) Financial Institutions and Industrialization in the Rhineland. 1815–1870. University of Wisconsin Press, Madison

Tilly R (1980) Kapital, Staat und sozialer Protest in der deutschen Industrialisierung: Gesammelte Aufsätze. Vandenhoeck & Ruprecht, Göttingen

Tilly R (1994) A short history of the German banking system. In: Pohl M (ed) Handbook on the history of European banks. Elgar, Aldershot, pp 299–312

Tilly R (1998) Universal banking in historical perspective. J Inst Theoret Econ 154(1):7–32

Tilly RH (1986) German banking, 1850–1914: development assistance for the strong. J Eur Econ Hist 1986:113–152

Tilly RH (2003) Geld und Kredit in der Wirtschaftsgeschichte. Steiner, Stuttgart

Timberlake RH (2005) Gold standards and the real bills doctrine in U. S. monetary policy. Econ J Watch 2(2):196–232

Todd D (2015) Free trade and its enemies in France, 1814–1851. Cambridge University Press, Cambridge

Tognato C (2014) Central bank independence: cultural codes and symbolic performance. Palgrave Macmillan, Basingstoke

Tombs R (1999) Inventing politics: from bourbon restoration to republican monarchy. In: Alexander MS (ed) French history since Napoleon. Arnold, London, pp 59–79

Tooke T (1826) Considerations on the state of the currency. J. Murray, London

Tooke T (1840) Report from the select committee on banks of issue: together with the proceedings of the committee, minutes of evidence, and appendix. IV. Committee, London

Tooke T (1844) An Inquiry into the currency principle: the connection of the currency with prices, and the expediency of a separation of issue from banking, 2nd edn. Brown Green and Longmans, London

Torp C (2014) Die Herausforderung der Globalisierung: Wirtschaft und Politik in Deutschland 1860–1914. Vandenhoeck & Ruprecht, Göttingen

Trebilcock C (1981) The industrialization of the continental powers: 1780–1914. Longman, London

Trumann DB (1966) The governmental process: political interests and public opinion, 12th edn. Alfred A. Knopf, New York

Turgot ARJ ([1749] 2011) Letter to L'Abbé de Cicé, since then Bishop of Auxerre, on the Replacing of Money by Paper. In: Gordon D (ed) The Turgot collection: writings, speeches, and letters. Gordon. Ludwig von Mises Institute, Auburn, pp 69–78

Turgot ARJ ([1766] 2011) Reflections on the formation and distribution of wealth. In: Gordon D (ed) The Turgot collection: writings, speeches, and letters. Ludwig von Mises Institute, Auburn, pp 5–65

Turgot ARJ ([1769] 2011) Extracts from "Paper on Lending at Interest". In: Gordon D (ed) The Turgot collection: writings, speeches, and letters. Ludwig von Mises Institute, Auburn, pp 205–221

Turgot ARJ (2011) The Turgot collection: writings, speeches, and letters. Ludwig von Mises Institute, Auburn

Usher AP (1943) The early history of deposit banking in Mediterranean Europe. Harvard University Press, Cambridge

Valente TW (2005) Network models and methods for studying the diffusion of innovations. In: Carrington P, Scott J, Wasserman S (eds) Structural analysis in the social sciences: models and methods in social network analysis. Cambridge University Press, Cambridge, pp 98–116

van der Borght R (1896) Banking in the Netherlands. In: Summer WG (ed) A history of banking in all the leading nations, vol IV. The Journal of Commerce and Commercial Bulletin, London, pp 191–371

Veblen T (1917) The nature of peace and the terms of its perpetuation. Macmillan Co, New York

Velthuis O (2015) Making monetary markets transparent: the European Central Bank's communication policy and its interactions with the media. Econ Soc 44(2):316–340

Viner J (1948) Power versus plenty as objectives of foreign policy in the seventeenth and eighteenth centuries. World Polit 1(1):1–29

Viner J ([1950] 2014) The customs union issue. Oxford University Press, New York

Viner J (1975) Studies in the theory of international trade. Kelley, Clifton

Visser WAM, McIntosh A (1998) A short review of the historical critique of usury. Account Bus Finan Hist 8(2):175–189

Völkerling F (1959) Der deutsche Kathedersozialismus. Die Wirtschaft, Berlin

Vossler O (1937) Der Nationalgedanke: Von Rousseau bis Ranke. R. Oldenbourg, München

von Hayek FA (1932) A note on the development of the doctrine of "Forced Saving". Q J Econ 47(1):123–133

von Kardorff W (1875) Gegen den Strom!: Eine Kritik der Handelspolitik des deutschen Reichs an der Hand der Carey'schen Forschungen, 2nd edn. J Springer, Berlin

von Malchus CA (1838) Die Sparcassen in Europa: Darstellung der statutenmässigen Einrichtungen der grossen Mehrzahl von solchen in Europa, mit einer Nachweise des Betrages der in denselben aufgesammelten Ersparnisse. Heidelberg, Leipzig

von Plessen M-L (1975) Die Wirksamkeit des Vereins für Socialpolitik von 1872–1890: Studien zum Katheder- und Staatssozialismus. Duncker & Humblot, Berlin

Von Schmoller G (1904) Grundriß der allgemeinen Volkswirtschaftslehre. Duncker & Humblot, Leipzig

Von Schmoller G (1944) Das Merkantilsystem in seiner historischen Bedeutung: Städtische, territoriale und staatliche Wirtschaftspolitik. Klostermann, Frankfurt a. M.

Wadhwani RD (2011) The institutional foundations of personal finance: innovation in US savings banks, 1880s–1920s. Bus Hist Rev 85(3):499–528

Wagner A (1857) Beiträge zur Lehre von den Banken. Voss, Leipzig

Wakefield EG (1834) England and America: a comparison of the social and political state of both nations. Harper, New York

Wallerstein IM ([1974] 2011) The modern world-system I: capitalist agriculture and the origins of the European world-economy in the sixteenth century. University of California Press, Berkeley

Webb S, Webb BP ([1894] 1920) The history of trade unionism. Longmans, London

Weber M ([1920] 1930) The protestant ethic and the spirit of capitalism. Charles Scribner's Sons, New York
Weber M ([1922] 1964) The sociology of religion. Beacon Press, Boston
Weber M ([1923] 1927) General economic history. Greenberg, New York
Weber M (1946) The social psychology of the world religions. In: Gerth H, Mills CW (eds) Max Weber: essays in sociology. Oxford University Press, New York, pp 267–301
Weber M ([1956] 1979) Economy and society: an outline of interpretive sociology. University of California Press, Berkeley
Weber M ([1908] 1998) Die Kredit- und Agrarpolitik der preußischen Landschaften. In: Schluchter W (ed) Wirtschaft, Staat und Sozialpolitik: Schriften und Reden 1900–1912. Mohr Siebeck, Tübingen, pp 327–355
Wehler H-U (1962) Sozialdemokratie und Nationalstaat: Die deutsche Sozialdemokratie und die Nationalitätenfragen in Deutschland von Karl Marx bis zum Ausbruch des Ersten Weltkrieges. Holzner, Würzburg
Wehler H-U (1974) Der Aufstieg des Organisierten Kapitalismus in Deutschland. In: Winkler HA (ed) Organisierter Kapitalismus: Voraussetzungen und Anfänge. Vandenhoeck & Ruprecht, Göttingen, pp 36–57
Wehler H-U (1976) Bismarck und der Imperialismus, 4th edn. Dt. Taschenbuch Verl, München
Wehler H-U (1976) Imperialismus, 3rd edn. Kiepenheuer & Witsch, Köln u. a.
Wehler H-U (1987) Deutsche Gesellschaftsgeschichte: Von der Reformära bis zur industriellen und politischen „Deutschen Doppelrevolution" 1815–1845/49. Beck, München
Wehler HU (1989) Deutsche Gesellschaftsgeschichte: Vom Feudalismus des Alten Reiches bis zur defensiven Modernisierung der Reformära 1700–1815, 2nd edn. C. H. Beck, München
Wehler H-U (1995) Deutsche Gesellschaftsgeschichte: Von der „Deutschen Doppelrevolution" bis zum Beginn des Ersten Weltkrieges 1849–1914, 2nd edn. C. H. Beck, München
Weingast BR (2002) Rational choice institutionalism. In: Katznelson I, Milner HV (eds) Political science: the state of the discipline. Norton, New York, pp 660–692
Weir M, Skocpol T (1985) State structures and the possibilities for "Keynesian" responses to the Great Depression in Sweden, Britain, and the United States. In: Evans PB, Rueschemeyer D, Skocpol T (eds) Bringing the state back in. Cambridge University Press, Cambridge, pp 107–164
Welch C (1989) Utilitarianism. In: Eatwell J, Milgate M, Newman P (eds) The invisible hand: the New Palgrave. Norton, New York, pp 257–269
Welch CB (2003) Colonial violence and the rhetoric of evasion: Tocqueville on Algeria. Polit Theory 31(2):235–264
Wennerlind C (2008) An artificial virtue and the oil of commerce: a synthetic view of Hume's theory of money. In: Wennerlind C, Schabas M (eds) David Hume's political economy. Routledge, London, pp 105–126
Wennerlind C (2011) Casualties of credit: the English financial revolution, 1620–1720. Harvard University Press, Cambridge
Werner RA (2016) A lost century in economics: three theories of banking and the conclusive evidence. Int Rev Fin Anal 46:361–379
Westen TA (1967) Usury in the conflict of laws: the doctrine of the lex debitoris. Calif Law Rev 55(1):123–252
Wheatley J (1803) Remarks on currency and commerce. Messrs, Cadell and Davies, London
White LA, Carniero R, Brown BJ, Urish B (2010) Modern capitalist culture. Left Coast Press Inc, Walnut Creek

White O, Daughton JP (2012) Introduction: placing French Missionaries in the modern world. In: White O, Daughton JP (eds) In God's empire: French Missionaries and the modern world. Oxford University Press, Oxford

Wicksell K ([1898] 1936) Interest and prices: a study of the causes regulating the value of money. Macmillan, London

Williamson OE (1985) The economic institutions of capitalism: firms, markets, relational contracting. The Free Press, New York

Wilson CH (1967) Trade, society and the state. In: Rich EE, Wilson C (eds) The Cambridge economic history of Europe: the economy of expanding Europe in the sixteenth and seventeenth centuries, vol IV. Cambridge Univ. Press, Cambridge, pp 487–576

Wilson PH (2000) Absolutism in central Europe. Routledge, London

Wilson T ([1572] 1925) A discourse upon usury: by way of dialogue and orations, for the better variety and more delight of all those that shall read this Treatise. Bell, London

Windolf P (ed) (2005) Finanzmarkt-Kapitalismus: Analysen zum Wandel von Produktionsregimen. VS Verl. für Sozialwiss, Wiesbaden

Windolf P (2005) Was ist Finanzmarkt-Kapitalismus? In: Windolf P (ed) Finanzmarkt-Kapitalismus: Analysen zum Wandel von Produktionsregimen. VS Verl. für Sozialwiss, Wiesbaden, pp 20–57

Winkler HA (1979) Liberalismus und Antiliberalismus: Studien zur politischen Sozialgeschichte des 19. und 20. Jahrhunderts. Vandenhoeck & Ruprecht, Göttingen

Wolff HW (1897) Savings banks at home and abroad. J R Stat Soc 60(2):278–359

Woolf S (ed) (1996) Nationalism in Europe, 1815 to the present: a reader. Routledge, London

Xia H, Wang H, Xuan Z (2011) Opinion dynamics. Int J Knowl Syst Sci 2(4):72–91

Yee AS (1996) The causal effects of ideas on policies. Int Organ 50(1):69–108

Zelizer VAR (2009) Morals and markets: the development of life insurance in the United States, 4th edn. Transaction Books, New Brunswick

Ziegler D (1993) Zentralbankpolitische „Steinzeit"? Preußische Bank und Bank of England im Vergleich. Geschichte und Gesellschaft Zeitschrift für historische Sozialwissenschaft 19(1993):475–505

Zmora H (2001) Monarchy, aristocracy, and the State in Europe 1300–1800. Routledge, London

Zucker LG (1977) The role of institutionalization in cultural persistence. Am Sociol Rev 42(5):726–743

Zugehör R (2003) Die Zukunft des rheinischen Kapitalismus: Unternehmen zwischen Kapitalmarkt und Mitbestimmung. VS Verl. für Sozialwissenschaften, Wiesbaden

Zysman J (1983) Governments, markets, and growth: financial systems and the politics of industrial change. Cornell University Press, Ithaca

GPSR Compliance

The European Union's (EU) General Product Safety Regulation (GPSR) is a set of rules that requires consumer products to be safe and our obligations to ensure this.

If you have any concerns about our products, you can contact us on ProductSafety@springernature.com

In case Publisher is established outside the EU, the EU authorized representative is:

Springer Nature Customer Service Center GmbH
Europaplatz 3
69115 Heidelberg, Germany

Batch number: 07957761

Printed by Printforce, the Netherlands